YOUNG PER...
DRUGLI...

Butterworths Student Statut...
Social Work Law

CW00603010

SOCIAL SERVICES TEAM
uk.

Butterworths Student Statutes

# Social Work Law

**Dr Stephen Hardy** LLB, PhD
Lecturer in Law
University of Salford

**Butterworths**
London, Edinburgh, Dublin
1997

| United Kingdom | Butterworths a Division of Reed Elsevier (UK) Ltd, Halsbury House, 35 Chancery Lane, LONDON WC2A 1EL and 4 Hill Street, EDINBURGH EH2 3JZ |
| Australia | Butterworths, SYDNEY, MELBOURNE, BRISBANE, ADELAIDE, PERTH, CANBERRA and HOBART |
| Canada | Butterworth Canada Ltd, TORONTO and VANCOUVER |
| Ireland | Butterworth (Ireland) Ltd, DUBLIN |
| Malaysia | Malayan Law Journal Sdn Bhd, KUALA LUMPUR |
| New Zealand | Butterworths of New Zealand Ltd, WELLINGTON and AUCKLAND |
| Singapore | Reed Elsevier (Singapore) Pte Ltd, SINGAPORE |
| South Africa | Butterworths Publishers (Pty) Ltd, DURBAN |
| USA | Michie, CHARLOTTESVILLE, Virginia |

All rights reserved. No part of this publication may be reproduced in any material form (including photocopying or storing it in any medium by electronic means and whether or not transiently or incidentally to some other use of this publication) without the written permission of the copyright owner except in accordance with the provisions of the Copyright, Designs and Patents Act 1988 or under the terms of a licence issued by the Copyright Licensing Agency Ltd, 90 Tottenham Court Road, London, England, W1P OLP. Application for the copyright owner's written permission to reproduce any part of this publication should be addressed to the publisher.

Warning: The doing of an unauthorised act in relation to a copyright work may result in both a civil claim for damages and criminal prosecution.

Any Crown copyright material is reproduced with the permission of the Controller of Her Majesty's Stationery Office.

© Reed Elsevier (UK) Ltd 1997

A CIP catalogue record for this book is available from the British Library.

ISBN 0 406 89776 X

Printed and bound in Great Britain by Redwood Books, Trowbridge, Wiltshire

# Preface

In 1988, the Central Council for the Education and Training of Social Workers (CCETSW) published its report into the teaching of law to social work students (see CCETSW Paper 4.1, '*The Law Report*'). It recommended that a greater emphasis be placed on such law teaching and set down minimum standards and content. Thus, since 1990, social workers have been expected to have a greater understanding of their statutory duties.

Consequently, many social work students and practitioners have spent hours of their valuable time in search of the statutory minutiae which govern their duties, or which can assist their client. From now on, however, it is hoped that this task will be easier, whether it be undertaken by the social work student, practitioner or social welfare adviser or lawyer. It is hoped that this collection of relevant statutory materials will not only be a useful examination or course companion, but also a valuable, ready-reference practice counsellor.

I am very grateful to the many social work colleagues, practitioners and students who have suggested that such a selection of statutes be compiled and who have commented on the materials which should be included. In particular, I would like to thank Rhiannon Billingsley, Jeff Edwards, Martin Hannibal, Doug Hearn and various members of the Social Work Law Association. No doubt many Scottish social workers will be aggrieved to note the absence of some of the legislation of paramount importance to their practice, as will other social workers be disappointed with various omissions: for this I can only apologise. Not all of the vast statutory framework which covers social work practice now could have been incoporated into a workable text. In any event, the statutory provisions continue to grow or be amended. To that end, what is enclosed are condsidered by many to be the salient legislative instruments.

Steve Hardy
Salford, August 1997

# Contents

## STATUTORY INSTRUMENTS

## CODE OF PRACTICE (MENTAL HEALTH ACT 1983) . . . . . . . . . . . . . . .477

# PART I
# STATUTES

# CHILDREN AND YOUNG PERSONS ACT 1933

## (C 12)

*An Act to consolidate certain enactments relating to persons under the age of eighteen years*

[13 April 1933]

## PART I
## PREVENTION OF CRUELTY AND EXPOSURE TO MORAL AND PHYSICAL DANGER

*Offences*

### 1 Cruelty to persons under sixteen

(1) If any person who has attained the age of sixteen years and [has responsibility for] any child or young person under that age, wilfully assaults, ill-treats, neglects, abandons, or exposes him, or causes or procures him to be assaulted, ill-treated, neglected, abandoned, or exposed, in a manner likely to cause him unnecessary suffering or injury to health (including injury to or loss of sight, or hearing, or limb, or organ of the body, and any mental derangement), that person shall be guilty of a misdemeanour, and shall be liable—

(a) on conviction on indictment, to a fine . . . , or alternatively, . . . or in addition thereto, to imprisonment for any term not exceeding [ten] years;

(b) on summary conviction, to a fine not exceeding [the prescribed sum] or alternatively, . . . or in addition thereto, to imprisonment for any term not exceeding six months.

(2) For the purposes of this section—

(a) a parent or other person legally liable to maintain a child or young person[, or the legal guardian of a child or young person,] shall be deemed to have neglected him in a manner likely to cause injury to his health if he has failed to provide adequate food, clothing, medical aid or lodging for him, or if, having been unable otherwise to provide such food, clothing, medical aid or lodging, he has failed to take steps to procure it to be provided under [the enactments applicable in that behalf];

(b) where it is proved that the death of an infant under three years of age was caused by suffocation (not being suffocation caused by disease or the presence of any foreign body in the throat or air passages of the infant) while the infant was in bed with some other person who has attained the age of sixteen years, that other person shall, if he was, when he went to bed, under the influence of drink, be deemed to have neglected the infant in a manner likely to cause injury to its health.

(3) A person may be convicted of an offence under this section—

(a) notwithstanding that actual suffering or injury to health, or the likelihood of actual suffering or injury to health, was obviated by the action of another person;

(b) notwithstanding the death of the child or young person in question.

(4)–(6). . .

(7) Nothing in this section shall be construed as affecting the right of any parent, teacher, or other person having the lawful control or charge of a child or young person to administer punishment to him.

NOTES

Sub-s (1): words in first pair of square brackets substituted by the Children Act 1989, s 108(5), Sch 13, para 2; first words omitted repealed by the Children Act 1975, s 108(1)(b), Sch 4, Pt III; second and third words omitted repealed by the Children and Young Persons Act 1963, s 64(1), (3), Sch 3, para 1, Sch 5; word in second pair of square brackets substituted, in relation to the punishment for an offence committed on or after 29 September 1988, by the Criminal Justice Act 1988, s 45; words in third pair of square brackets substituted by virtue of the Magistrates' Courts Act 1980, s 32(2).

Sub-s (2): words in first pair of square brackets inserted by the Children Act 1989, s 108(4), Sch 12, para 2; words in second pair of square brackets substituted by the National Assistance (Adaptation of Enactments) Regulations 1950, SI 1951/174.

Sub-s (4): repealed by the Criminal Law Act 1967, s 10, Sch 2, para 13(1), Sch 3, Pt III.

Sub-ss (5), (6): repealed by the Criminal Justice Act 1988, s 170(2), Sch 16.

*Supplemental*

## [17 Interpretation of Part I

(1) For the purposes of this Part of this Act, the following shall be presumed to have responsibility for a child or young person—
    (a) any person who—
        (i) has parental responsibility for him (within the meaning of the Children Act 1989); or
        (ii) is otherwise legally liable to maintain him; and
    (b) any person who has care of him.

(2) A person who is presumed to be responsible for a child or young person by virtue of subsection (1)(a) shall not be taken to have ceased to be responsible for him by reason only that he does not have care of him.]

NOTES

Substituted by the Children Act 1989, s 108(5), Sch 13, para 5.

# PART III
# PROTECTION OF CHILDREN AND YOUNG PERSONS IN RELATION TO CRIMINAL AND SUMMARY PROCEEDINGS

*General Provisions as to Preliminary Proceedings*

## [34 Attendance at court of parent of child or young person charged with an offence, etc

(1) . . .

[(2) Where a child or young person is in police detention, such steps as are practicable shall be taken to ascertain the identity of a person responsible for his welfare.

(3) If it is practicable to ascertain the identity of a person responsible for the welfare of the child or young person, that person shall be informed, unless it is not practicable to do so—
    (a) that the child or young person has been arrested;
    (b) why he has been arrested; and
    (c) where he is being detained.

(4) Where information falls to be given under subsection (3) above, it shall be given as soon as it is practicable to do so.

(5) For the purposes of this section the persons who may be responsible for the welfare of a child or young person are—
 (a) his parent or guardian; or
 (b) any other person who has for the time being assumed responsibility for his welfare.

(6) If it is practicable to give a person responsible for the welfare of the child or young person the information required by subsection (3) above, that person shall be given it as soon as it is practicable to do so.

(7) If it appears that at the time of his arrest a supervision order, as defined in section 11 of the Children and Young Persons Act 1969 [or Part IV of the Children Act 1989], is in force in respect of him, the person responsible for his supervision shall also be informed as described in subsection (3) above as soon as it is reasonably practicable to do so.

[(7A) If it appears that at the time of his arrest the child or young person is being provided with accommodation by or on behalf of a local authority under section 20 of the Children Act 1989, the local authority shall also be informed as described in subsection (3) above as soon as it is reasonably practicable to do so.]

(8) The reference to a parent or guardian in subsection (5) above is . . . in the case of a child or young person in the care of a local authority, a reference to that authority; . . .

(9) The rights conferred on a child or young person by subsections (2) to (8) above are in addition to his rights under section 56 of the Police and Criminal Evidence Act 1984.

(10) The reference in subsection (2) above to a child or young person who is in police detention includes a reference to a child or young person who has been detained under the terrorism provisions; and in subsection (3) above "arrest" includes such detention.

(11) In subsection (10) above "the terrorism provisions" has the meaning assigned to it by section 65 of the Police and Criminal Evidence Act 1984].]

---

NOTES
 Substituted by the Children and Young Persons Act 1963, s 25(1).
 Sub-s (1): repealed by the Criminal Justice Act 1991, ss 56, 101, Sch 13.
 Sub-ss (2)–(6), (9)–(11): substituted, together with sub-s (7) for sub-s (2) as originally enacted, by the Police and Criminal Evidence Act 1984, s 57.
 Sub-s (7): substituted together with sub-ss (2)–(6), (9)–(11) for sub-s (2) as originally enacted, by the Police and Criminal Evidence Act 1984, s 57; words in square brackets inserted by the Children Act 1989, s 108(5), Sch 13, para 6.
 Sub-s (7A): inserted by the Children Act 1989, s 108(5), Sch 13, para 6.
 Sub-s (8): substituted, together with sub-ss (2)–(7), (9)–(11) for sub-s (2) as originally enacted, by the Police and Criminal Evidence Act 1984, s 57; words omitted repealed by the Children Act 1989, s 108(7), Sch 15.

---

**[34A Attendance at court of parent or guardian**

(1) Where a child or young person is charged with an offence or is for any other reason brought before a court, the court—
 (a) may in any case; and
 (b) shall in the case of a child or a young person who is under the age of sixteen years,

require a person who is a parent or guardian of his to attend at the court during all the stages of the proceedings, unless and to the extent that the court is satisfied that it would be unreasonable to require such attendance, having regard to the circumstances of the case.

(2)    In relation to a child or young person for whom a local authority have parental responsibility and who—

    (a)   is in their care; or

    (b)   is provided with accommodation by them in the exercise of any functions (in particular those under the Children Act 1989) which stand referred to their social services committee under the Local Authority Social Services Act 1970,

the reference in subsection (1) above to a person who is a parent or guardian of his shall be construed as a reference to that authority or, where he is allowed to live with such a person, as including such a reference.

In this subsection "local authority" and "parental responsibility" have the same meanings as in the Children Act 1989.]

### NOTES

Commencement: 1 October 1992.

Inserted by the Criminal Justice Act 1991, s 56.

*Principles to be observed by all Courts in dealing with Children and Young Persons*

## 44    General considerations

(1)    Every court in dealing with a child or young person who is brought before it, either as . . . an offender or otherwise, shall have regard to the welfare of the child or young person and shall in a proper case take steps for removing him from undesirable surroundings, and for securing that proper provision is made for his education and training.

(2)    . . .

### NOTES

Sub-s (1): words omitted repealed by the Children and Young Persons Act 1969, s 72(4), Sch 6.

Sub-s (2): repealed by the Children and Young Persons Act 1969, s 72(4), Sch 6.

*Juvenile Offenders*

## 50    Age of criminal responsibility

It shall be conclusively presumed that no child under the age of [ten] years can be guilty of any offence.

### NOTES

Word in square brackets substituted by the Children and Young Persons Act 1963, s 16(1).

## 53    Punishment of certain grave crimes

[(1)    A person convicted of an offence who appears to the court to have been under the age of eighteen years at the time the offence was committed shall not, if he is convicted of murder, be sentenced to imprisonment for life, nor shall sentence of death be pronounced on or recorded against any such person; but in lieu thereof the court shall (notwithstanding anything in this or any other Act) sentence him to be detained during Her Majesty's pleasure, and if so sentenced he shall be liable to be detained in such place and under such conditions[—

    (a)  as the Secretary of State may direct, or

    (b)  as the Secretary of State may arrange with any person.]]

[(2)  Subsection (3) below applies—

    (a)  where a person of at least 10 but not more than 17 years is convicted on indictment of—

        (i)  any offence punishable in the case of an adult with imprisonment for fourteen years or more, not being an offence the sentence for which is fixed by law, or

        (ii)  an offence under section 14 of the Sexual Offences Act 1956 (indecent assault on a woman);

    (b)  where a young person is convicted of—

        (i)  an offence under section 1 of the Road Traffic Act 1988 (causing death by dangerous driving), or

        (ii)  an offence under section 3A of the Road Traffic Act 1988 (causing death by careless driving while under influence of drink or drugs).

(3)  Where this subsection applies, then, if the court] is of opinion that none of the other methods in which the case may legally be dealt with is suitable, the court may sentence the offender to be detained for such period [not exceeding the maximum term of imprisonment with which the offence is punishable in the case of an adult] as may be specified in the sentence; and where such a sentence has been passed the child or young person shall, during that period, . . . be liable to be detained in such place and on such conditions[—

    (a)  as the Secretary of State may direct, or

    (b)  as the Secretary of State may arrange with any person.

(4)  A person detained pursuant to the directions or arrangements made by the Secretary of State under this section shall, while so detained, be deemed to be in legal custody.]

## NOTES

Commencement: 9 January 1995 (sub-ss (2), (4)); before 1 January 1970 (remainder).

Sub-s (1): substituted by the Murder (Abolition of Death Penalty) Act 1965, ss 1(5), 4; words in square brackets substituted by the Criminal Justice and Public Order Act 1994, s 16(2).

Sub-s (2): (including first words of new sub-s (3)) substituted by the Criminal Justice and Public Order Act 1994, s 16(3); sub-para (a)(ii) substituted by the Crime (Sentences) Act 1997, s 44, as from a day to be appointed, as follows—

      "(ii)  an offence under section 14 (indecent assault on a woman) or section 15 (indecent assault on a man) of the Sexual Offences Act 1956;".

Sub-s (3): words in first pair of square brackets (together with sub-s (2)) substituted by the Criminal Justice and Public Order Act 1994, s 16(3); words in second pair of square brackets substituted by the Criminal Justice Act 1961, ss 2(1), 41(1), (3), Sch 4; words omitted repealed by the Criminal Justice Act 1948, s 83, Sch 10, Pt I; words in third pair of square brackets (which include new sub-s (4)) substituted by the Criminal Justice and Public Order Act 1994, s 16(4).

Sub-s (4): substituted (together with final words in square brackets in sub-s (3)) by the Criminal Justice and Public Order Act 1994, s 16(4).

**[55   Power to order parent or guardian to pay fine, etc**

(1)   Where—

    (a)   a *child or* young person is convicted or found guilty of any offence for the commission of which a fine or costs may be imposed or a compensation order may be made under section 35 of the Powers of Criminal Courts Act 1973; and

    (b)   the court is of opinion that the case would best be met by the imposition of a fine or costs or the making of such an order, whether with or without any other punishment,

it shall be the duty of the court to order that the fine, compensation or costs awarded be paid by the parent or guardian of the *child or* young person instead of by the *child or* young person himself, unless the court is satisfied—

    (i)   that the parent or guardian cannot be found; or

    (ii)   that it would be unreasonable to make an order for payment, having regard to the circumstances of the case.

[(1A) Where but for this subsection—

    (a)   a court would order a child or young person to pay a fine under section 15(2A) of the Children and Young Persons Act 1969 (failure to comply with requirement included in supervision order); or

    (b)   a court would impose a fine on a young person under section 16(3) of the Powers of Criminal Courts Act 1973 (breach of requirements of community service order),

    [(c)   a court would impose a fine on a child or young person under section 4(3) of the Criminal Justice and Public Order Act 1994 (breach of requirements of supervision under secure training order),]

it shall be the duty of the court to order that the fine be paid by the parent or guardian of the child or young person instead of by the child or young person himself, unless the court is satisfied—

    (i)   that the parent or guardian cannot be found; or

    (ii)   that it would be unreasonable to make an order for payment, having regard to the circumstances of the case.]

[(1B) In the case of a young person who has attained the age of sixteen years, subsections (1) and (1A) above shall have effect as if, instead of imposing a duty, they conferred a power to make such an order as is mentioned in those subsections.]

(2)   An order under this section may be made against a parent or guardian who, having been required to attend, has failed to do so, but, save as aforesaid, no such order shall be made without giving the parent or guardian an opportunity of being heard.

(3)   A parent or guardian may appeal to the Crown Court against an order under this section made by a magistrates' court.

(4)   A parent or guardian may appeal to the Court of Appeal against an order made under this section by the Crown Court, as if he had been convicted on indictment and the order were a sentence passed on his conviction.]

[(5)   In relation to a child or young person for whom a local authority have parental responsibility and who—

    (a)   is in their care; or

(b)   is provided with accommodation by them in the exercise of any functions (in particular those under the Children Act 1989) which stand referred to their social services committee under the Local Authority Social Services Act 1970,

references in this section to his parent or guardian shall be construed as references to that authority.

In this subsection 'local authority' and 'parental responsibility' have the same meanings as in the Children Act 1989.]

### NOTES

Substituted by the Criminal Justice Act 1982, s 26.

Sub-s (1): words in italics repealed by the Children and Young Persons Act 1969, ss 69(4)(c), (5), 72(4), as from a day to be appointed.

Sub-s (1A): inserted by the Criminal Justice Act 1988, s 127; para (c) inserted by the Criminal Justice and Public Order Act 1994, s 168(2), Sch 10, para 4, as from a day to be appointed.

Sub-ss (1B), (5): inserted by the Criminal Justice Act 1991, s 57(1), (2).

## 56   Power of other courts to remit juvenile offenders to [youth courts]

(1)   Any court by or before which a *child or* young person is found guilty of an offence other than homicide, may [and, if it is not a [youth court], shall unless satisfied that it would be undesirable to do so], remit the case to a [youth court] acting for the place where the offender was committed for trial, or, if he was not committed for trial, to a [youth court] acting either for the same place as the remitting court or for the place where the offender [habitually resides]; and, where any such case is so remitted, the offender shall be brought before a [youth court] accordingly, and that court may deal with him in any way in which it might have dealt with him if he had been tried and found guilty by that court.

[(2)   Where any case is so remitted—

(a)   the offender shall have the same right of appeal against any order of the court to which the case is remitted as if he had been found guilty by that court, but shall have no right of appeal against the order of remission; and

(b)   . . .]

(3)   A court by which an order remitting a case to a [youth court] is made under this section may[, subject to section 25 of the Criminal Justice and Public Order Act 1994,] give such directions as appear to be necessary with respect to the custody of the offender or for his release on bail until he can be brought before the [youth court], and shall cause to be transmitted to the clerk of the [youth court] a certificate setting out the nature of the offence and stating that the offender has been found guilty thereof, and that the case has been remitted for the purpose of being dealt with under this section.

### NOTES

Section heading: words in square brackets substituted by the Criminal Justice Act 1991, s 100, Sch 11, para 40.

Sub-s (1): words in italics repealed by the Children and Young Persons Act 1969, s 72(4), Sch 6, as from a day to be appointed; words in first (outer) pair of square brackets substituted by the Children and Young Persons Act 1963, s 64(1), Sch 3, para 14, words in second (inner) pair of square brackets substituted by the Criminal Justice Act 1991, s 100, Sch 11, para 40(1), (2)(a); words in third and fifth pairs of square brackets substituted by the Criminal Justice Act 1991, s 100, Sch 11, para 40(1), (2)(a); words in fourth pair of square brackets substituted by the Children and Young Persons Act 1969, s 72(3), Sch 5, para 6.

Sub-s (2): substituted by the Children and Young Persons Act 1963, s 64(1), Sch 3, para 14; para (b) repealed by the Courts Act 1971, s 56, Sch 11, Pt IV.

Sub-s (3): words in first, third and fourth pairs of square brackets substituted by the Criminal Justice Act 1991, s 100, Sch 11, para 40; second words in square brackets inserted by the Criminal Justice and Public Order Act 1994, s 168(2), Sch 10, para 5.

## PART VI
## SUPPLEMENTAL

### General

**109   Short title, commencement, extent and repeals**

(1)   This Act may be cited as the Children and Young Persons Act 1933.

(2)   . . .

(3)   Save as therein otherwise expressly provided, this Act shall not extend to Scotland or Northern Ireland.

(4)   . . .

NOTES

Sub-ss (2), (4): repealed by the Statute Law Revision Act 1950.

# EDUCATION ACT 1944

## (C 31)

*An Act to reform the law relating to education in England and Wales*

[3 August 1944]

## PART II
## THE STATUTORY SYSTEM OF EDUCATION

## SUPPLEMENTARY PROVISIONS AS TO PRIMARY, SECONDARY AND FURTHER EDUCATION

### Miscellaneous Provisions

**68   Power of [Secretary of State] to prevent unreasonable exercise of functions**

If [the Secretary of State] is satisfied, either on complaint by any person or otherwise, that any local education authority or the . . . governors of any county or voluntary school have acted or are proposing to act unreasonably with respect to the exercise of any power conferred or the performance of any duty imposed by or under this Act, he may, notwithstanding any enactment rendering the exercise of the power or the performance of the duty contingent upon the opinion of the authority or of the . . . governors, give such directions as to the exercise of the power or the performance of the duty as appear to him to be expedient. [In this section, references to a local education authority shall be construed as including references to any body of persons authorised, in accordance with the First Schedule to this Act . . . to exercise functions of such an authority.]

NOTES

Section-heading: words in square brackets substituted by the Secretary of State for Education and Science Order 1964, SI 1964/490, art 3(2)(a).

First and second words omitted repealed by the Education Act 1980, s 1(3), Sch 1, para 1; words in the second pair of square brackets added by the Education Act 1946, s 14(1), Sch 2, Pt I; third words omitted repealed by the Local Government Act 1972, s 272(1), Sch 30.

## 99 Powers of [Secretary of State] in default of local education authorities or . . . governors

(1) If [the Secretary of State] is satisfied, either upon complaint by any person interested or otherwise, that any local education authority, or the . . . governors of any county school or voluntary school, have failed to discharge any duty imposed upon them by or for the purposes of this Act, [the Secretary of State] may make an order declaring the authority, or the . . . governors, as the case may be, to be in default in respect of that duty, and giving such directions for the purpose of enforcing the execution thereof as appear to [the Secretary of State] to be expedient; and any such directions shall be enforceable, on an application made on behalf of [the Secretary of State], by mandamus.

(2) Where it appears to [the Secretary of State] that by reason of the default of any person there is no properly constituted body of . . . governors of any county school or voluntary school, [the Secretary of State] may make such appointments and give such directions as he thinks desirable for the purpose of securing that there is a properly constituted body of . . . governors thereof, and may give directions rendering valid any acts or proceedings which in his opinion are invalid or otherwise defective by reason of the default.

(3) Where it appears to [the Secretary of State] that a local education authority have made default in the discharge of their duties relating to the maintenance of a voluntary school, [the Secretary of State] may direct that any act done by or on behalf of the . . . governors of the school for the purpose of securing the proper maintenance thereof shall be deemed to have been done by or on behalf of the authority, and may reimburse to the . . . governors any sums which in his opinion they have properly expended for that purpose; and the amount of any sum so reimbursed shall be a debt due to the Crown from the authority, and, without prejudice to any other method of recovery, the whole or any part of such a sum may be deducted from any sums payable to the authority by [the Secretary of State] in pursuance of any regulations relating to the payments of grants.

---

NOTES

Words in square brackets substituted by the Secretary of State for Education and Science Order 1964, SI 1964/490, art 3(2)(a); words omitted repealed by the Education Act 1980, s 1(3), Sch 1, para 1.

---

# PART V
# SUPPLEMENTAL

## 122 Short title and extent

(1) This Act may be cited as the Education Act 1944.

(2) This Act shall not extend to Scotland or to Northern Ireland.

# NATIONAL ASSISTANCE ACT 1948

## (C 29)

*An Act to terminate the existing poor law and to provide in lieu thereof for the assistance of persons in need by the National Assistance Board and by local authorities; to make further provision for the welfare of disabled, sick, aged and other persons and for regulating homes for disabled and aged persons and charities for disabled persons; to amend the law relating to non-contributory old age pensions; to make provision as to the burial or cremation of deceased persons; and for purposes connected with the matters aforesaid*

[13 May 1948]

## PART III
## LOCAL AUTHORITY SERVICES

*Provision of Accommodation*

### 21    Duty of local authorities to provide accommodation

(1)    [Subject to and in accordance with the provisions of this Part of this Act, a local authority may with the approval of the Secretary of State, and to such extent as he may direct shall, make arrangements for providing]—

    (a)    residential accommodation for persons [aged eighteen or over] who by reason of age, [illness, disability] or any other circumstances are in need of care and attention which is not otherwise available to them; [and

    (aa)    residential accommodation for expectant and nursing mothers who are in need of care and attention which is not otherwise available to them.]

    (b)    . . .

(2)    In [making any such arrangements] a local authority shall have regard to the welfare of all persons for whom accommodation is provided, and in particular to the need for providing accommodation of different descriptions suited to different descriptions of such persons as are mentioned in the last foregoing subsection.

(3)    . . .

(4)    [Subject to the provisions of section 26 of this Act] accommodation provided by a local authority in the exercise of their [functions under this section] shall be provided in premises managed by the authority or, to such extent as may be [determined in accordance with the arrangements] under this section, in such premises managed by another local authority as may be agreed between the two authorities and on such terms, including terms as to the reimbursement of expenditure incurred by the said other authority, as may be so agreed.

(5)    References in this Act to accommodation provided under this Part thereof shall be construed as references to accommodation provided in accordance with this and the five next following sections, and as including references to board and other services, amenities and requisites provided in connection with the accommodation except where in the opinion of the authority managing the premises their provision is unnecessary.

(6)    References in this Act to a local authority providing accommodation shall be construed, in any case where a local authority agree with another local authority for the provision of accommodation in premises managed by the said other authority, as references to the first-mentioned local authority.

(7)    Without prejudice to the generality of the foregoing provisions of this section, a local authority may—

    (a)   provide, in such cases as they may consider appropriate, for the conveyance of persons to and from premises in which accommodation is provided for them under this Part of the Act;

    [(b)  make arrangements for the provision on the premises in which accommodation is being provided of such other services as appear to the authority to be required.]

    . . .

(8)    . . . nothing in this section shall authorise or require a local authority to make any provision authorised or required to be made (whether by that or by any other authority) by or under any enactment not contained in this Part of this Act [or authorised or required to be provided under the National Health Service Act 1977].

---

NOTES

    Sub-s (1): words in first pair of square brackets substituted by the Local Government Act 1972, s 195, Sch 23, para 2; words in second pair of square brackets inserted by the Children Act 1989, s 108(5), Sch 13, para 11(1); words in third pair of square brackets substituted, and words in fourth pair of square brackets inserted, by the National Health Service and Community Care Act 1990, s 42(1); para (b) repealed by the Housing (Homeless Persons) Act 1977, s 20(4), Schedule.

    Sub-s (2): words in square brackets substituted by the Local Government Act 1972, s 195, Sch 23, para 2.

    Sub-s (3): repealed by the Local Government Act 1972, ss 195, 272, Sch 23, para 2, Sch 30.

    Sub-s (4): words in first pair of square brackets inserted by the National Health Service and Community Care Act 1990, s 66(1), Sch 9, para 5(1); words in second and third pairs of square brackets substituted by the Local Government Act 1972, s 195, Sch 23, para 2.

    Sub-s (7): para (b) substituted, for paras (b), (c) as originally enacted, by the National Health Service and Community Care Act 1990, s 66(1), Sch 9, para 5(2); words omitted repealed by the National Health Service Reorganisation Act 1973, s 58, Sch 5.

    Sub-s (8): words omitted repealed, and words in square brackets added, by the National Health Service and Community Care Act 1990, s 66(1), (2), Sch 9, para 5(3), Sch 10.

---

## 22   Charges to be made for accommodation

(1)    [Subject to section 26 of this Act, where a person is provided with accommodation under this Part of this Act the local authority providing the accommodation shall recover from him the amount of the payment which he is liable to make] in accordance with the following provisions of this section.

(2)    Subject to the following provisions of this section, the payment [which a person is liable to make] for any such accommodation shall be in accordance with a standard rate fixed for that accommodation by the authority managing the premises in which it is provided [and that standard rate shall represent the full cost to the authority of providing that accommodation].

(3)    Where a person for whom accommodation in premises managed by any local authority is provided, or proposed to be provided, under this Part of this Act satisfies the local authority that he is unable to pay therefor at the standard rate, the authority shall assess his ability to pay . . ., and accordingly determine at what lower rate he shall be liable to pay for the accommodation:

    . . .

(4)    In assessing for the purposes of the last foregoing subsection a person's ability to pay, a local authority shall assume that he will need for his personal requirements such sum per week as may be prescribed by the Minister, or such other sum as in special circumstances the authority may consider appropriate.

[(4A) Regulations made for the purposes of subsection (4) of this section may prescribe different sums for different circumstances.]

(5)    In assessing as aforesaid a person's ability to pay, a local authority shall give effect to [regulations made by the Secretary of State for the purposes of this subsection] [except that, until the first such regulations come into force, a local authority shall give effect to Part III of Schedule 1 to the Supplementary Benefits Act 1976, as it had effect immediately before the amendments made by Schedule 2 to the Social Security Act 1980].

[(5A) If they think fit, an authority managing premises in which accommodation is provided for a person shall have power on each occasion when they provide accommodation for him, irrespective of his means, to limit to [such amount as appears to them reasonable for him to pay] the payments required from him for his accommodation during a period commencing when they begin to provide the accommodation for him and ending not more than eight weeks after that.]

(6), (7). . .

(8)    Where accommodation is provided by a local authority in premises managed by another local authority, the payment therefor under this section shall be made to the authority managing the premises and not to the authority providing accommodation, but the authority managing the premises shall account for the payment to the authority providing the accommodation.

(9)    . . .

NOTES

Commencement: 1 April 1993 (sub-s (4A)); 15 August 1983 (sub-s (5A)); before 1 January 1970 (remainder).

Sub-s (1): words in square brackets substituted by the National Health Service and Community Care Act 1990, s 44(2); repealed in relation to Scotland by the Social Work (Scotland) Act 1968, s 95(2), Sch 9, Pt I.

Sub-s (2): words in first pair of square brackets inserted, and words in second pair of square brackets added, by the National Health Service and Community Care Act 1990, s 44(3).

Sub-s (3): words omitted repealed by the National Health Service and Community Care Act 1990, s   44(4).

Sub-s (4A): inserted by the National Health Service and Community Care Act 1990, s 44(5).

Sub-s (5): words in first pair of square brackets substituted by the Social Security Act 1980, s 20, Sch 4, para 2(1); words in second pair of square brackets added by the Social Security Act 1986, s 86(1), Sch 10, Pt II, para 32(2) (although cease to have effect on the repeal of that amending provision by the National Health Service and Community Care Act 1990, s 66(2), Sch 10).

Sub-s (5A): inserted by the Health and Social Services and Social Security Adjudications Act 1983, s   20(1); words in square brackets substituted by the National Health Service and Community Care Act 1990, s 44(6).

Sub-s (6): repealed by the Housing (Homeless Persons) Act 1977, s 20(4), Schedule.

Sub-s (7): repealed by the National Health Service and Community Care Act 1990, s 66(2), Sch 10.

Sub-s (9): repealed by the Social Security Act 1980, s 21, Sch 5, Pt II.

## 23    Management of premises in which accommodation provided

(1)    Subject to the provisions of this Part of this Act, a local authority may make rules as to the conduct of premises under their management in which accommodation is provided under this Part of this Act and as to the preservation of order in the premises.

(2)    Rules under this section may provide that where by reason of any change in a person's circumstances he is no longer qualified to receive accommodation under this Part of this Act or where a person has otherwise become unsuitable therefor, he may be required by the local authority managing the premises to leave the premises in which the accommodation is provided.

(3)  Rules under this section may provide for the waiving of part of the payments due under the last foregoing section where in compliance with the rules persons for whom accommodation is provided assist in the running of the premises.

---

NOTES

Repealed in relation to Scotland by the Social Work (Scotland) Act 1968, s 95(2), Sch 9, Pt I.

---

### 24  Authority liable for provision of accommodation

(1)  The local authority [empowered] under this Part of this Act to provide residential accommodation for any person shall subject to the following provisions of this Part of this Act be the authority in whose area the person is ordinarily resident.

(2)  . . .

(3)  Where a person in the area of a local authority—

(a) is a person with no settled residence, or

(b) not being ordinarily resident in the area of the local authority, is in urgent need of residential accommodation under this Part of this Act,

the authority shall have the like [power] to provide residential accommodation for him as if he were ordinarily resident in their area.

(4)  Subject to and in accordance with the [arrangements] under section twenty-one of this Act, a local authority shall have power, as respects a person ordinarily resident in the area of another local authority, with the consent of that other authority to provide residential accommodation for him in any case where the authority would have a duty to provide such accommodation if he were ordinarily resident in their area.

(5)  Where a person is provided with residential accommodation under this Part of this Act, he shall be deemed for the purposes of this Act to continue to be ordinarily resident in the area in which he was ordinarily resident immediately before the residential accommodation was provided for him.

[(6)  For the purposes of the provision of residential accommodation under this Part of this Act, a [patient in a hospital vested in the Secretary of State or an NHS trust shall] be deemed to be ordinarily resident in the area, if any, in which he was ordinarily resident immediately before he was admitted as a patient to the hospital, whether or not he in fact continues to be ordinarily resident in that area.]

[(7)  In subsection (6) above "NHS trust" means a National Health Service trust established under Part I of the National Health Service and Community Care Act 1990 or under the National Health Service (Scotland) Act 1978.]

---

NOTES

Repealed in relation to Scotland by the Social Work (Scotland) Act 1968, s 95(2), Sch 9, Pt I.

Sub-ss (1), (3), (4): words in square brackets substituted by the Local Government Act 1972, s 195, Sch 23, para 2.

Sub-s (2): repealed by the Housing (Homeless Persons) Act 1977, s 20(4), Schedule.

Sub-s (6): added, with retrospective effect, by the National Assistance (Amendment) Act 1959, s 1(1); words in square brackets substituted by the National Health Service and Community Care Act 1990, s 66(1), Sch 9, para 5(4)(a).

Sub-s (7): added by the National Health Service and Community Care Act 1990, s 66(1), Sch 9, para 5(4)(b).

---

## 26 Provision of accommodation in premises maintained by voluntary organisations

[(1) Subject to subsections (1A) and (1B) below, arrangements under section 21 of this Act may include arrangements made with a voluntary organisation or with any other person who is not a local authority where—

> (a) that organisation or person manages premises which provide for reward accommodation falling within subsection (1)(a) or (aa) of that section, and
>
> (b) the arrangements are for the provision of such accommodation in those premises.

(1A) Subject to subsection (1B) below, arrangements made with any voluntary organisation or other person by virtue of this section must, if they are for the provision of residential accommodation with both board and personal care for such persons as are mentioned in section 1(1) of the Registered Homes Act 1984 (requirement of registration), be arrangements for the provision of such accommodation in a residential care home which is managed by the organisation or person in question, being such a home in respect of which that organisation or person—

> (a) is registered under Part I of that Act, or
>
> (b) is not required to be so registered by virtue of section 1(4)(a) or (b) of that Act (certain small homes) or by virtue of the home being managed or provided by an exempt body;

and for this purpose "personal care" and "residential care home" have the same meaning as in that Part of that Act.

(1B) Arrangements made with any voluntary organisation or other person by virtue of this section must, if they are for the provision of residential accommodation where nursing care is provided, be arrangements for the provision of such accommodation in premises which are managed by the organisation or person in question, being premises—

> (a) in respect of which that organisation or person is registered under Part II of the Registered Homes Act 1984, or
>
> (b) which, by reason only of being maintained or controlled by an exempt body, do not fall within the definition of a nursing home in section 21 of that Act.

(1C) Subject to subsection (1D) below, no such arrangements as are mentioned in subsection (1B) above may be made by an authority for the accommodation of any person without the consent of such [Health Authority] as may be determined in accordance with regulations.

(1D) Subsection (1C) above does not apply to the making by an authority of temporary arrangements for the accommodation of any person as a matter of urgency; but, as soon as practicable after any such temporary arrangements have been made, the authority shall seek the consent required by subsection (1C) above to the making of appropriate arrangements for the accommodation of the person concerned.

(1E) No arrangements may be made by virtue of this section with a person who has been convicted of an offence under any provision of—

> (a) the Registered Homes Act 1984 (or any enactment replaced by that Act); or
>
> (b) regulations made under section 16 or section 26 of that Act (or under any corresponding provisions of any such enactment).]

(2)    Any [arrangements made by virtue of . . . this section] shall provide for the making by the local authority to [the other party thereto] of payments in respect of the accommodation provided at such rates as may be determined by or under the arrangements [and subject to subsection (3A) below the local authority shall recover from each person for whom accommodation is provided under the arrangements the amount of the refund which he is liable to make in accordance with the following provisions of this section].

(3)    [Subject to subsection (3A) below] a person for whom accommodation is provided under any such arrangements shall, in lieu of being liable to make payment therefor in accordance with section twenty-two of this Act, refund to the local authority any payments made in respect of him under the last foregoing subsection:

Provided that where a person for whom accommodation is provided, or proposed to be provided, under any such arrangements satisfies the local authority that he is unable to make a refund at the full rate determined under that subsection, subsections (3) to (5) of section twenty-two of this Act shall, with the necessary modifications, apply as they apply where a person satisfies the local authority of his inability to pay at the standard rate as mentioned in the said subsection (3).

[(3A) Where accommodation in any premises is provided for any person under arrangements made by virtue of this section and the local authority, the person concerned and the voluntary organisation or other person managing the premises (in this subsection referred to as "the provider") agree that this subsection shall apply—

   (a)    so long as the person concerned makes the payments for which he is liable under paragraph (b) below, he shall not be liable to make any refund under subsection (3) above and the local authority shall not be liable to make any payment under subsection (2) above in respect of the accommodation provided for him;

   (b)    the person concerned shall be liable to pay to the provider such sums as he would otherwise (under subsection (3) above) be liable to pay by way of refund to the local authority; and

   (c)    the local authority shall be liable to pay to the provider the difference between the sums paid by virtue of paragraph (b) above and the payments which, but for paragraph (a) above, the authority would be liable to pay under subsection (2) above.]

(4)    Subsections [(5A)] . . . (7) and (9) of the said section twenty-two shall, with the necessary modifications, apply for the purposes of the last foregoing subsection as they apply for the purposes of the said section twenty-two.

[(4A) Section 21(5) of this Act shall have effect as respects accommodation provided under arrangements made by virtue of this section with the substitution for the reference to the authority managing the premises of a reference to the authority making the arrangements.]

(5)    Where in any premises accommodation is being provided under . . . this section in accordance with arrangements made by any local authority, any person authorised in that behalf by the authority may at all reasonable times enter and inspect the premises.

(6)    . . .

(7)    In this section the expression "voluntary organisation" includes any association which is a housing association for the purposes of the Housing Act 1936 . . . [. . . and "exempt body" means an authority or body constituted by an Act of Parliament or incorporated by Royal Charter].

NOTES

Commencement: 1 April 1993 (sub-ss (1)–(1E), (3A), (4A)); before 1 January 1970 (remainder).

Sub-ss (1)–(1B), (1D), (1E): substituted, together with sub-s (1C) for existing sub-ss (1), (1A) (as substituted for original sub-s (1) by the Health Services and Public Health Act 1968, s 44(1), (2)), by the Community Care (Residential Accommodation) Act 1992, s 1(1).

Sub-s (1C): substituted as noted to sub-ss (1)–(1B), (1D), (1E) above; words in square brackets substituted by the Health Authorities Act 1995, s 2(1), Sch 1, para 87(2).

Sub-s (2): words in first pair of square brackets substituted by the Local Government Act 1972, s 195, Sch 23, para 2; words in second pair of square brackets substituted by the Health Services and Public Health Act 1968, s 44(2); words omitted repealed, and words in third pair of square brackets added, by the National Health Service and Community Care Act 1990, ss 42(3), 66, Sch 9, para 5(5)(a), Sch 10.

Sub-s (3): words in square brackets inserted by the National Health Service and Community Care Act 1990, s 42(4).

Sub-s (3A): inserted by the National Health Service and Community Care Act 1990, s 42(4).

Sub-s (4): figure in square brackets inserted by the Health and Social Services and Social Security Adjudications Act 1983, s 20(1); words omitted repealed by the Housing (Homeless Persons) Act 1977, s 20(4), Schedule.

Sub-s (4A): inserted by the National Health Service and Community Care Act 1990, s 66(1), Sch 9, para 5(5)(b).

Sub-s (5): words omitted repealed by the National Health Service and Community Care Act 1990, s 66, Sch 9, para 5(5)(c), Sch 10; repealed in relation to Scotland by the Social Work (Scotland) Act 1968, s 95(2), Sch 9, Pt I.

Sub-s (6): repealed by the Health Services and Public Health Act 1968, s 78(2), Sch 4.

Sub-s (7): first words omitted repealed by the Social Work (Scotland) Act 1968, s 95(2), Sch 9, Pt I; words in square brackets added by the National Health Service and Community Care Act 1990, s 42(5), second words omitted repealed by the Registered Homes (Amendment) Act 1991, s 2(5).

## [26A Exclusion of powers to provide accommodation under this Part in certain cases

(1) Subject to subsection (3) of this section, no accommodation may be provided under section 21 or 26 of this Act for any person who immediately before the date on which this section comes into force was ordinarily resident in relevant premises.

(2) In subsection (1) "relevant premises" means—

(a) premises in respect of which any person is registered under the Registered Homes Act 1984;

(b) premises in respect of which such registration is not required by virtue of their being managed or provided by an exempt body;

(c) premises which do not fall within the definition of a nursing home in section 21 of that Act by reason only of their being maintained or controlled by an exempt body; and

(d) such other premises as the Secretary of State may by regulations prescribe;

and in this subsection "exempt body" has the same meaning as in section 26 of this Act.

(3) The Secretary of State may by regulations provide that, in such cases and subject to such conditions as may be prescribed, subsection (1) of this section shall not apply in relation to such classes of persons as may be prescribed in the regulations.

(4) The Secretary of State shall by regulations prescribe the circumstances in which persons are to be treated as being ordinarily resident in any premises for the purposes of subsection (1) of this section.

(5) This section does not affect the validity of any contract made before the date on which this section comes into force for the provision of accommodation on or after that date or anything done in pursuance of such a contract.]

NOTES

Commencement: 1 April 1993.

Inserted by the National Health Service and Community Care Act 1990, s 43.

*Welfare Services*

## 30 Voluntary organisations for disabled persons' welfare

(1)    A local authority may, [in accordance with arrangements made under section 29 of this Act], employ as their agent for the purposes of that section [any voluntary organisation or any person carrying on, professionally or by way of trade or business, activities which consist of or include the provision of services for any of the persons to whom section 29 above applies, being an organisation or person appearing to the authority to be capable of providing the service to which the arrangements apply].

(2), (3). . .

### NOTES

Repealed in relation to Scotland by the Social Work (Scotland) Act 1968, s 95(2), Sch 9, Pt I.

Sub-s (1): words in first pair of square brackets substituted by the Local Government Act 1972, s 195, Sch 23, para 2; words in second pair of square brackets substituted by the National Health Service and Community Care Act 1990, s 42(6).

Sub-s (2): repealed by the Health Services and Public Health Act 1968, s 78(2), Sch 4.

Sub-s (3): repealed by the Statute Law Revision Act 1953.

## PART IV
## GENERAL AND SUPPLEMENTARY

*Supplementary*

## 68    Short title and commencement

(1)    This Act may be cited as the National Assistance Act 1948.

(2)    This Act shall come into operation on such day as the Minister of Health, or as respects Scotland the Secretary of State, may be order appoint, and differenct days may be appointed in relation to different provisions of this Act.


# PRISON ACT 1952

## (C 52)

*An Act to consolidate certain enactments relating to prisons and other institutions for offenders and related matters with corrections and improvements made under the Consolidation of Enactments (Procedure) Act 1949*

[1 August 1952]

*Central administration*

## 1    General control over prisons

All powers and jurisdiction in relation to prisons and prisoners which before the commencement of the Prison Act 1877 were exercisable by any other authority shall, subject to the provisions of this Act, be exercisable by the Secretary of State.

## 4    General duties of [the Secretary of State]

(1)    [The Secretary of State] shall have the general superintendence of prisons and shall make the contracts and do the other acts necessary for the maintenance of prisons and the maintenance of prisoners.

(2)  [Officers of the Secretary of State duly authorised in that behalf] shall visit all prisons and examine the state of buildings, the conduct of officers, the treatment and conduct of prisoners and all other matters concerning the management of prisons and shall ensure that the provisions of this Act and of any rules made under this Act are duly complied with.

(3)  [The Secretary of State and his officers] may exercise all powers and jurisdiction exercisable at common law, by Act of Parliament, or by charter by visiting justices of a prison.

NOTES

Section heading: words in square brackets substituted by the Prison Commissioners Dissolution Order 1963, SI 1963/597, art 3(2), Sch 1.

Sub-ss (1)–(3): words in square brackets substituted by SI 1963/597, art 3(2), Sch 1.

## 5  Annual report of [the Secretary of State]

[(1)  The Secretary of State shall issue an annual report on every prison and shall lay every such report before Parliament.]

(2)  The report shall contain—

    (a)  a statement of the accommodation of each prison and the daily average and highest number of prisoners confined therein;

    (b)  such particulars of the work done by prisoners in each prison, including the kind and quantities of articles produced and the number of prisoners employed, as may in the opinion of the Secretary of State give the best information to Parliament;

    (c)  a statement of the punishments inflicted in each prison and of the offences for which they were inflicted . . .

NOTES

Section heading: words in square brackets substituted by the Prison Commissioners Dissolution Order 1963, SI 1963/597, art 3(2), Sch 1.

Sub-s (1): substituted by SI 1963/597, art 3(2), Sch 1.

Sub-s (2): words omitted repealed by the Criminal Justice Act 1967, s 103(2), Sch 7, Pt I.

## [5A  Appointment and functions of Her Majesty's Chief Inspector of Prisons

(1)  Her Majesty may appoint a person to be Chief Inspector of Prisons.

(2)  It shall be the duty of the Chief Inspector to inspect or arrange for the inspection of prisons in England and Wales and to report to the Secretary of State on them.

(3)  The Chief Inspector shall in particular report to the Secretary of State on the treatment of prisoners and conditions in prisons.

(4)  The Secretary of State may refer specific matters connected with prisons in England and Wales and prisoners in them to the Chief Inspector and direct him to report on them.

(5)  The Chief Inspector shall in each year submit to the Secretary of State a report in such form as the Secretary of State may direct, and the Secretary of State shall lay a copy of that report before Parliament.

(6)  The Chief Inspector shall be paid such salary and allowances as the Secretary of State may with the consent of the Treasury determine.]

NOTES

Inserted by the Criminal Justice Act 1982, s 57.

*Visiting committees and boards of visitors*

## 6 Visiting committees and boards of visitors

(1) . . .

(2) The Secretary of State shall appoint for every prison . . . a board of visitors of whom not less than two shall be justices of the peace.

(3) Rules made as aforesaid shall prescribe the functions of . . . boards of visitors and shall among other things require members to pay frequent visits to the prison and hear any complaints which may be made by the prisoners and report to the Secretary of State any matter which they consider it expedient to report; and any member of a . . . board of visitors may at any time enter the prison and shall have free access to every part of it and to every prisoner.

(4) . . .

**NOTES**

Words omitted repealed by, or by virtue of, the Courts Act 1971, ss 53 (3), 56(4), Sch 7, Pt II, para 4, Sch 11, Pt IV.

*Prison officers*

## 7 Prison officers

(1) Every prison shall have a governor, a chaplain and a medical officer and such other officers as may be necessary.

(2) Every prison in which women are received shall have a sufficient number of women officers; . . .

(3) A prison which in the opinion of the Secretary of State is large enough to require it may have a deputy governor or an assistant chaplain or both.

(4) The chaplain and any assistant chaplain shall be a clergyman of the Church of England and the medical officer shall be duly registered under the Medical Acts.

(5) . . .

**NOTES**

Sub-s (2): words omitted repealed by the Sex Discriminiation Act 1975, s 18(2).

Sub-s (5): repealed by the Prison Commissioners Dissolution Order 1963, SI 1963/597, art 3(2), Sch 1.

## 8 Powers of prison officers

Every prison officer while acting as such shall have all the powers, authority, protection and privileges of a constable.

## [8A Powers of search by authorised employees

(1) An authorised employee at a prison shall have the power to search any prisoner for the purpose of ascertaining whether he has any unauthorised property on his person.

(2) An authorised employee searching a prisoner by virtue of this section—

    (a) shall not be entitled to require a prisoner to remove any of his clothing other than an outer coat, jacket, headgear, gloves and footwear;

(b)  may use reasonable force where necessary; and

(c)  may seize and detain any unauthorised property found on the prisoner in the course of the search.

(3)    In this section "authorised employee" means an employee of a description for the time being authorised by the governor to exercise the powers conferred by this section.

(4)    The governor of a prison shall take such steps as he considers appropriate to notify to prisoners the descriptions of persons who are for the time being authorised to exercise the powers conferred by this section.

(5)    In this section "unauthorised property", in relation to a prisoner, means property which the prisoner is not authorised by prison rules or by the governor to have in his possession or, as the case may be, in his possession in a particular part of the prison.]

---

NOTES

Commencement: 3 February 1995.
Inserted by the Criminal Justice and Public Order Act 1994, s 152(1).

---

## 9    Exercise of office of chaplain

(1)    A person shall not officiate as chaplain of two prisons unless the prisons are within convenient distance of each other and are together designed to receive not more than one hundred prisoners.

(2)    Notice of the nomination of a chaplain or assistant chaplain to a prison shall, within one month after it is made, be given to the bishop of the diocese in which the prison is situate; and the chaplain or assistant chaplain shall not officiate in the prison except under the authority of a licence from the bishop.

## 10    Appointment of prison ministers

(1)    Where in any prison the number of prisoners who belong to a religious denomination other than the Church of England is such as in the opinion of the Secretary of State to require the appointment of a minister of that denomination, the Secretary of State may appoint such a minister to that prison.

(2)    The Secretary of State may pay a minister appointed under the preceding subsection such remuneration as he thinks reasonable.

(3)    [The Secretary of State] may allow a minister of any denomination other than the Church of England to visit prisoners of his denomination in a prison to which no minister of that denomination has been appointed under this section.

(4)    No prisoner shall be visited against his will by such a minister as is mentioned in the last preceding subsection; but every prisoner not belonging to the Church of England shall be allowed, in accordance with the arrangements in force in the prison in which he is confined, to attend chapel or to be visited by the chaplain.

(5)    The governor of a prison shall on the reception of each prisoner record the religious denomination to which the prisoner declares himself to belong, and shall give to any minister who under this section is appointed to the prison or permitted to visit prisoners therein a list of the prisoners who have declared themselves to belong to his denomination; and the minister shall not be permitted to visit any other prisoners.

NOTES
Sub-s (3): words in square brackets substituted by the Prison Commissioners Dissolution Order 1963, SI 1963/597, art 3(2), Sch 1.

## 11    Ejectment of prison officers and their families refusing to quit

(1)    Where any living accommodation is provided for a prison officer or his family by virtue of his office, then, if he ceases to be a prison officer or is suspended from office or dies, he, or, as the case may be, his family, shall quit the accommodation when required to do so by notice of [the Secretary of State].

(2)    Where a prison officer or the family of a prison officer refuses or neglects to quit the accommodation forty-eight hours after the giving of such a notice as aforesaid, any two justices of the peace, on proof made to them of the facts authorising the giving of the notice and of the service of the notice and of the neglect or refusal to comply therewith, may, by warrant under their hands and seals, direct any constable, within a period specified in the warrant, to enter by force, if necessary, into the accommodation and deliver possession of it to [a person acting on behalf of the Secretary of State].

NOTES
Sub-ss (1), (2): words in square brackets substituted by the Prison Commissioners Dissolution Order 1963, SI 1963/597, art 3(2), Sch 1.

*Confinement and treatment of prisoners*

## 12    Place of confinement of prisoners

(1)    A prisoner, whether sentenced to imprisonment or committed to prison on remand or pending trial or otherwise, may be lawfully confined in any prison.

(2)    Prisoners shall be committed to such prisons as the Secretary of State may from time to time direct; and may by direction of the Secretary of State be removed during the term of their imprisonment from the prison in which they are confined to any other prison.

(3)    A writ, warrant or other legal instrument addressed to the governor of a prison and identifying that prison by its situation or by any other sufficient description shall not be invalidated by reason only that the prison is usually known by a different description.

## 13    Legal custody of prisoner

(1)    Every prisoner shall be deemed to be in the legal custody of the governor of the prison.

(2)    A prisoner shall be deemed to be in legal custody while he is confined in, or is being taken to or from, any prison and while he is working, or is for any other reason, outside the prison in the custody or under the control of an officer of the prison [and while he is being taken to any place to which he is required or authorised by or under this Act [or the Criminal Justice Act 1982] to be taken, or is kept in custody in pursuance of any such requirement or authorisation].

NOTES
Sub-s (2): words in outer pair of square brackets inserted by the Criminal Justice Act 1961, s 41(1), Sch    4, words in inner pair of square brackets inserted by the Criminal Justice Act 1982, s 77, Sch 14, para 4.

## 14   Cells

(1)   The Secretary of State shall satisfy himself from time to time that in every prison sufficient accommodation is provided for all prisoners.

(2)   No cell shall be used for the confinement of a prisoner unless it is certified by an inspector that its size, lighting, heating, ventilation and fittings are adequate for health and that it allows the prisoner to communicate at any time with a prison officer.

(3)   A certificate given under this section in respect of any cell may limit the period for which a prisoner may be separately confined in the cell and the number of hours a day during which a prisoner may be employed therein.

(4)   The certificate shall identify the cell to which it relates by a number or mark and the cell shall be marked by that number or mark placed in a conspicuous position; and if the number or mark is changed without the consent of an inspector the certificate shall cease to have effect.

(5)   An inspector may withdraw a certificate given under this section in respect of any cell if in his opinion the conditions of the cell are no longer as stated in the certificate.

(6)   In every prison special cells shall be provided for the temporary confinement of refractory or violent prisoners.

---

NOTES

Modification: references to an inspector to be construed as references to an officer (not being an officer of the prison) acting on behalf of the Secretary of State, by virtue of the Prison Commissioners Dissolution Order 1963, SI 1963/597, art 3(2), Sch 1.

---

## 16   Photographing and measuring of prisoners

The Secretary of State may make regulations as to the measuring and photographing of prisoners and such regulations may prescribe the time or times at which and the manner and dress in which prisoners shall be measured and photographed and the number of copies of the measurements and photographs of each prisoner which shall be made and the persons to whom they shall be sent.

## [16A   Testing prisoners for drugs

(1)   If an authorisation is in force for the prison, any prison officer may, at the prison, in accordance with prison rules, require any prisoner who is confined in the prison to provide a sample of urine for the purpose of ascertaining whether he has any drug in his body.

(2)   If the authorisation so provides, the power conferred by subsection (1) above shall include power to require a prisoner to provide a sample of any other description specified in the authorisation, not being an intimate sample, whether instead of or in addition to a sample of urine.

(3)   In this section—
   "authorisation" means an authorisation by the governor;
   "drug" means any drug which is a controlled drug for the purposes of the Misuse of Drugs Act 1971;
   "intimate sample" has the same meaning as in Part V of the Police and Criminal Evidence Act 1984;

"prison officer" includes a prisoner custody officer within the meaning of Part IV of the Criminal Justice Act 1991; and

"prison rules" means rules under section 47 of this Act.]

**NOTES**
Commencement: 9 January 1995.
Inserted by the Criminal Justice and Public Order Act 1994, s 151(1).

## [16B    Power to test prisoners for alcohol

(1)    If an authorisation is in force for the prison, any prison officer may, at the prison, in accordance with prison rules, require any prisoner who is confined in the prison to provide a sample of breath for the purpose of ascertaining whether he has alcohol in his body.

(2)    If the authorisation so provides, the power conferred by subsection (1) above shall include power—
(a)    to require a prisoner to provide a sample of urine, whether instead of or in addition to a sample of breath, and
(b)    to require a prisoner to provide a sample of any other description specified in the authorisation, not being an intimate sample, whether instead of or in addition to a sample of breath, a sample of urine or both.

(3)    In this section—
"authorisation" means an authorisation by the governor;
"intimate sample" has the same meaning as in Part V of the Police and Criminal Evidence Act 1984;
"prison officer" includes a prisoner custody officer within the meaning of Part IV of the Criminal Justice Act 1991;
"prison rules" means rules under section 47 of this Act.]

**NOTES**
Commencement: 21 May 1997.
Inserted by the Prisons (Alcohol Testing) Act 1997, s 1.

*Discharged prisoners*

## [30    Payments for discharged prisoners

The Secretary of State may make such payments to or in respect of persons released or about to be released from prison as he may with the consent of the Treasury determine.]

**NOTES**
Substituted for ss 30–32 by the Criminal Justice Act 1967, s 66(3).

*Provision, maintenance and closing of prisons*

## 33    Power to provide prisons, etc

(1)    The Secretary of State may with the approval of the Treasury alter, enlarge or rebuild any prison and build new prisons.

[(2)    The Secretary of State may provide new prisons by declaring to be a prison—
(a)    any building or part of a building built for the purpose or vested in him or under his control; or

(b) any floating structure or part of such a structure constructed for the purpose or vested in him or under his control.]

(3)   A declaration under this section may with respect to the building or part of a building declared to be a prison make the same provisions as an order under the next following section may make with respect to an existing prison.

(4)   A declaration under this section may at any time be revoked by the Secretary of State.

(5)   A declaration under this section shall not be sufficient to vest the legal estate of any building in the [Secretary of State].

NOTES
Commencement: 3 November 1994 (sub-s (2)); before 1 January 1970 (remainder).
Sub-s (2): substituted by the Criminal Justice and Public Order Act 1994, s 100(1).
Sub-s (5): words in square brackets substituted by the Prison Commissioners Dissolution Order 1963, SI 1963/597, art 3(2), Sch 1.
Modification: sub-s (2) modified, in relation to contracted out prisons, by the Criminal Justice and Public Order Act 1994, s 100(2), (3).

## [35   Prison property

(1)   Every prison and all real and personal property belonging to a prison shall be vested in the Secretary of State and may be disposed of in such manner as the Secretary of State, with the consent of the Treasury, may determine.

(2)   For the purposes of this section the Secretary of State shall be deemed to be a corporation sole.

(3)   Any instrument in connection with the acquisition, management or disposal of any property to which this section applies may be executed on behalf of the Secretary of State by an Under-Secretary of State or any other person authorised by the Secretary of State in that behalf; and any instrument purporting to have been so executed on behalf of the Secretary of State shall be deemed, until the contrary is proved, to have been so executed on his behalf.

(4)   The last foregoing subsection shall be without prejudice to the execution of any such instrument as aforesaid, or of any other instrument, on behalf of the Secretary of State in any other manner authorised by law.]

NOTES
Substituted by the Prison Commissioners Dissolution Order 1963, SI 1963/597, art 3(2), Sch 1.

*Offences*

## 39   Assisting prisoner to escape

Any person who aids any prisoner in escaping or attempting to escape from a prison or who, with intent to facilitate the escape of any prisoner, conveys any thing into a prison or to a prisoner [sends any thing (by post or otherwise) into a prison or to a prisoner] or places any thing anywhere outside a prison with a view to its coming into the possession of a prisoner, shall be guilty of felony and liable to imprisonment for a term not exceeding [ten years].

NOTES
Words in first pair of square brackets inserted, and words in second pair of square brackets substituted, by the Prison Security Act 1992, s 2(1), (4).

*Remand centres [and young offender institutions]*

## [43 Remand centres [and young offender institutions]

(1) The Secretary of State may provide—
- (a) remand centres, that is to say places for the detention of persons not less than fourteen but under 21 years of age who are remanded or committed in custody for trial or sentence;
- [(aa) young offender institutions, that is to say places for the detention of offenders sentenced to detention in a young offender institution [or to custody for life];]
- (b), (c) . . .; [and
- (d) secure training centres, that is to say places in which offenders not less than 12 but under 17 years of age in respect of whom secure training orders have been made under section 1 of the Criminal Justice and Public Order Act 1994 may be detained and given training and education and prepared for their release].

(2) The Secretary of State may from time to time direct—
- (a) that a woman aged 21 years or over who is serving a sentence of imprisonment or who has been committed to prison for default shall be detained in a remand centre or a [young offender institution] instead of a prison;
- (b) that a woman aged 21 years or over who is remanded in custody or committed in custody for trial or sentence shall be detained in a remand centre instead of a prison;
- (c) that a person under 21 but not less than 17 years of age who is remanded in custody or committed in custody for trial or sentence shall be detained in a prison instead of a remand centre or a remand centre instead of a prison, notwithstanding anything in section 27 of the Criminal Justice Act 1948 or section 23(3) of the Children and Young Persons Act 1969.

(3) Notwithstanding subsection (1) above, any person required to be detained in an institution to which this Act applies may be detained in a remand centre for any temporary purpose [and a person [aged 18 years] or over may be detained in such a centre] for the purpose of providing maintenance and domestic services for that centre.

(4) Sections 5A, 6(2) and (3), 16, 22, 25 and 36 of this Act shall apply to remand centres [and young offender institutions] and to persons detained in them as they apply to prisons and prisoners.

[(4A) Sections 16, 22 and 36 of this Act shall apply to secure training centres and to persons detained in them as they apply to prisons and prisoners.]

(5) The other provisions of this Act preceding this section, except sections 28 and 37(2) above, shall apply to [centres of the descriptions specified in subsection (4) above] and to persons detained in them as they apply to prisons and prisoners, but subject to such adaptations and modifications as may be specified in rules made by the Secretary of State.

[(5A) The other provisions of this Act preceding this section, except sections 5, 5A, 6(2) and (3), 12, 14, 19, 25, 28 and 37(2) and (3) above, shall apply to secure training centres and to persons detained in them as they apply to prisons and prisoners, but subject to such adaptations and modifications as may be specified in rules made by the Secretary of State.]

(6) References in the preceding provisions of this Act to imprisonment shall, so far as those provisions apply to institutions provided under this section, be construed as including references to detention in those institutions.

(7) Nothing in this section shall be taken to prejudice the operation of section 12 of the Criminal Justice Act 1982.]

NOTES
Commencement: 3 November 1994 (sub-ss (4A), (5A)); 24 May 1983 (remainder).
Substituted by the Criminal Justice Act 1982, s 11.
Cross-heading: words in square brackets substituted by the Criminal Justice Act 1988, s 123(6), Sch 8, para 1.
Section heading: words in square brackets substituted by the Criminal Justice Act 1988, s 123(6), Sch 8, para 1.
Sub-s (1): para (aa) inserted by the Criminal Justice Act 1988, s 170, Sch 15, para 11, words in inner pair of square brackets inserted by the Criminal Justice and Public Order Act 1994, s 18(3); paras (b), (c) repealed by the Criminal Justice Act 1988, s 170, Sch 16; para (d) and word preceding it added by the Criminal Justice and Public Order Act 1994, s 5(2).
Sub-s (2): words in square brackets in para (a) substituted by virtue of the Criminal Justice Act 1988, s 123(6), Sch 8, para 1.
Sub-s (3): words in outer pair of square brackets substituted by the Criminal Justice Act 1988, s 170(1), Sch 15, para 12, words in inner pair of square brackets substituted by the Criminal Justice Act 1991, s 68, Sch 8, para 2.
Sub-s (4): words in square brackets substituted by the Criminal Justice Act 1988, s 123(6), Sch 8, para 1.
Sub-ss (4A), (5A): inserted by the Criminal Justice and Public Order Act 1994, s 5(3), (5).
Sub-s (5): words in square brackets substituted by the Criminal Justice and Public Order Act 1994, s 5(4).

*Rules for the management of prisons and other institutions*

## 47 Rules for the management of prisons, remand centres [and young offender institutions]

(1) The Secretary of State may make rules for the regulation and management of prisons, remand centres[, young offender institutions or secure training centres] respectively, and for the classification, treatment, employment, discipline and control of persons required to be detained therein.

(2) Rules made under this section shall make provision for ensuring that a person who is charged with any offence under the rules shall be given a proper opportunity of presenting his case.

(3) Rules made under this section may provide for the training of particular classes of persons and their allocation for that purpose to any prison or other institution in which they may lawfully be detained.

(4) Rules made under this section shall provide for the special treatment of the following persons whilst required to be detained in a prison, that is to say—
    (a)–(c) . . .
    (d) any . . . person detained in a prison, not being a person serving a sentence or a person imprisoned in default of payment of a sum adjudged to be paid by him on his conviction [or a person committed to custody on his conviction].

[(4A) Rules made under this section shall provide for the inspection of secure training centres and the appointment of independent persons to visit secure training centres and to whom representations may be made by offenders detained in secure training centres.]

(5)    Rules made under this section may provide for the temporary release of persons [detained in a prison, [remand centre][, young offender institution or secure training centre] not being persons committed in custody for trial [before the Crown Court] or committed to be sentenced or otherwise dealt with by [the Crown Court] or remanded in custody by any court].

NOTES

Commencement: 3 November 1994 (sub-s (4A)); before 1 January 1970 (remainder).

Section heading: words in square brackets substituted by the Criminal Justice Act 1988, s 123(6), Sch 8, paras 1, 3(2).

Sub-s (1): words in square brackets substituted by the Criminal Justice and Public Order Act 1994, s 6(2).

Sub-s (4): paras (a)–(c) repealed, and words in square brackets added, by the Criminal Justice Act 1967, ss 66(5), 103(2), Sch 7, Pt I.

Sub-s (4A): inserted by the Criminal Justice and Public Order Act 1994, s 6(3).

Sub-s (5): words in outer pair of square brackets substituted by the Criminal Justice Act 1961, s 41(1), (3), Sch 4, words in first (inner) pair of square brackets substituted by the Criminal Justice Act 1982, s 77, Sch 14, para 7, words in second (inner) pair of square brackets substituted by the Criminal Justice and Public Order Act 1994, s 6(4), words in third and fourth (inner) pairs of square brackets substituted by the Courts Act 1971, s 56(1), Sch 8, Pt II, para 33.

## 55    Short title, commencement and extent

(1)    This Act may be cited as the Prison Act 1952.

(2)    This Act shall come into operation on the first day of October, nineteen hundred and fifty-two.

(3)    . . .

(4)    Except as provided in  . . . [the Criminal Justice Act 1961], this Act shall not extend to Scotland.

(5)    This Act shall not extend to Northern Ireland.

NOTES

Sub-s (3): repealed by the Statute Law (Repeals) Act 1993, s 1(1), Sch 1, Pt I.

Sub-s (4): words omitted repealed by the Statute Law (Repeals) Act 1993, s 1(1), Sch 1, Pt I; words in square brackets substituted by the Criminal Justice Act 1961, s 41, Sch 4.

# SEXUAL OFFENCES ACT 1956

## (C 69)

*An Act to consolidate (with corrections and improvements made under the Consolidation of Enactments (Procedure) Act 1949) the statute law of England and Wales relating to sexual crimes, to the abduction, procuration and prostitution of women and to kindred offences, and to make such adaptations of statutes extending beyond England and Wales as are needed in consequence of that consolidation*

[2 August 1956]

## PART I
## OFFENCES, AND THE PROSECUTION AND PUNISHMENT OF OFFENCES

*Intercourse by force, intimidation, etc*

## [1    Rape of women and men

(1)    It is an offence for a man to rape a woman or another man.

(2)     A man commits rape if—

    (a)    he has sexual intercourse with a person (whether vaginal or anal) who at the time of the intercourse does not consent to it; and

    (b)    at the time he knows that the person does not consent to the intercourse or is reckless as to whether that person consents to it.

(3)     A man also commits rape if he induces a married woman to have sexual intercourse with him by impersonating her husband.

(4)     Subsection (2) applies for the purpose of any enactment.]

**NOTES**

Commencement: 3 November 1994.

Substituted by the Criminal Justice and Public Order Act 1994, s 142.

*Unnatural Offences*

## 12    Buggery

(1)     It is felony for a person to commit buggery with another person [otherwise than in circumstances described in subsection (1A) below] or with an animal.

[(1A) The circumstances referred to in subsection (1) are that the act of buggery takes place in private and both parties have attained the age of eighteen.

(1B)  An act of buggery by one man with another shall not be treated as taking place in private if it takes place—

    (a)    when more than two persons take part or are present; or

    (b)    in a lavatory to which the public have or are permitted to have access, whether on payment or otherwise.

(1C)  In any proceedings against a person for buggery with another person it shall be for the prosecutor to prove that the act of buggery took place otherwise than in private or that one of the parties to it had not attained the age of eighteen.]

(2), (3). . .

**NOTES**

Sub-s (1): words in square brackets inserted by the Criminal Justice and Public Order Act 1994, s 143(2).

Sub-ss (1A)–(1C): inserted by the Criminal Justice and Public Order Act 1994, s 143(3).

Sub-ss (2), (3): repealed by the Police and Criminal Evidence Act 1984, s 119(2), Sch 7, Pt V.

*Powers and procedure for dealing with offenders*

## 37    Prosecution and punishment of offences

(1)     The Second Schedule to this Act shall have effect, subject to and in accordance with the following provisions of this section, with respect to the prosecution and punishment of the offences listed in the first column of the Schedule, being the offences under this Act and attempts to commit certain of those offences.

(2)     The second column in the Schedule shows, for any offence, if it may be prosecuted on indictment or summarily, or either . . . and what special restrictions (if any) there are on the commencement of a prosecution.

(3)     The third column in the Schedule shows, for any offence, the punishments which may be imposed on conviction on indictment or on summary conviction, a reference to a period giving the maximum term of imprisonment and a reference to a sum of money the maximum fine.

(4)   The fourth column in the Schedule contains provisions which are either supplementary to those in the second or third column or enable a person charged on indictment with the offence specified in the first column to be found guilty of another offence if the jury are not satisfied that he is guilty of the offence charged or of an attempt to commit it, but are satisfied that he is guilty of the other offence.

(5)   A provision in the fourth column of the Schedule enabling the jury to find the accused guilty of an offence specified in that provision authorises them, if not satisfied that he is guilty of the offence so specified, to find him guilty of any other offence of which they could find him guilty if he had been indicted for the offence so specified.

(6)   Where in the Schedule there is used a phrase descriptive of an offence or group of offences followed by a reference to a section by its number only, the reference is to a section of this Act, and the phrase shall be taken as referring to any offence under the section mentioned.

(7)   Nothing in this section or in the Second Schedule to this Act shall exclude the application to any of the offences referred to in the first column of the Schedule—

(a)   of [section 24 of the Magistrates' Courts Act 1980 (which relates)] to the summary trial of young offenders for indictable offences); or

(b)   of [subsection (5) of section 121 of the Magistrates' Courts Act 1980] (which limits the punishment which may be imposed by a magistrates' court sitting in an occasional courthouse); or

(c)   of any enactment or rule of law restricting a court's power to imprison; or

(d)   of any enactment or rule of law authorising an offender to be dealt with in a way not authorised by the enactments specially relating to his offence; or

(e)   of any enactment or rule of law authorising a jury to find a person guilty of an offence other than that with which he is charged.

NOTES

Sub-s (2): words omitted repealed by the Courts Act 1971, s 56(4), Sch 11, Pt IV.

Sub-s (7): words in square brackets in paras (a), (b) substituted by the Magistrates' Courts Act 1980, s 154(1), Sch 7, para 17.

# PART II
# SUPPLEMENTARY

*Consequential amendments*

## 55   Short title

This Act may be cited as the Sexual Offences Act 1956.

# SECOND SCHEDULE
## TABLE OF OFFENCES, WITH MODE OF PROSECUTION, PUNISHMENTS, ETC

Section 37

## PART I

*Felonies and attempts at felonies*

| Offence | Mode of prosecution | Punishment | Provisions as to alternative verdicts etc. |
|---|---|---|---|
| 1. (a) Rape (section one) | On indictment | Life | The jury may find the accused guilty—<br>(i) of procurement of a woman by threats (section two); or<br>(ii) of procurement of a woman by false pretences (section three); or<br>(iii) of administering drugs to obtain or facilitate intercourse (section four);<br>. . .<br>(iv)–(ix). . . |
| (b) An attempt to commit this offence. | On indictment | [Life] | — |
| 2. (a) Intercourse with girl under thirteen (section five). | On indictment | Life | . . . |
| (b) An attempt to commit this offence. | On indictment | [Seven years] | — |
| 3. (a) Buggery (section twelve). | On indictment | [If with a person under the age of sixteen or with an animal, life; if the accused is of or over the age of twenty-one and the other person is under the age of eighteen, five years, but otherwise two years.] | — |

| Offence | Mode of prosecution | Punishment | Provisions as to alternative verdicts etc. |
|---|---|---|---|
| (b) An attempt to commit this offence. | On indictment | [If with a person under the age of sixteen or with an animal, life; if the accused is of or over the age of twenty-one and the other person is under the age of eighteen, five years, but otherwise two years.] | — |
| 4. Abduction of woman by force or for the sake of her property (section seventeen). | On indictment | Fourteen years | — |
| 5. ... | | | — |
| 6. Permitting girl under thirteen to use premises for intercourse (section twenty-five). | On indictment | Life | |

## PART II
## OFFENCES OTHER THAN FELONIES AND ATTEMPTS AT FELONIES

| Offence | Mode of prosecution | Punishment | Provisions as to alternative verdicts etc. |
|---|---|---|---|
| 7. (a) Procurement of woman by threats (section two). | On indictment | Two years | — |
| (b) An attempt to commit this offence. | On indictment | Two years | — |
| 8. Procurement of woman by false pretences (section three). | On indictment | Two years | — |
| 9. Administering drugs to obtain or facilitate intercourse (section four). | On indictment | Two years | — |
| 10. (a) Intercourse with girl [under sixteen] (section six). | On indictment ... ; a prosecution may not be commenced more than twelve months after the offence charged. | Two years | — |

| Offence | Mode of prosecution | Punishment | Provisions as to alternative verdicts etc. |
|---|---|---|---|
| (b) An attempt to commit this offence. | On indictment . . . ; a prosecution may not be commenced more than twelve months after the offence charged | Two years | — |
| 11.(a) Intercourse with [defective] (section seven). | On indictment | Two years | — |
| (b) An attempt to commit this offence. | On indictment | Two years | — |
| 12. . . . | | | |
| 13.(a) Procurement of defective (section nine). | On indictment | Two years | — |
| (b) An attempt to commit this offence. | On indictment | Two years | — |
| 14.(a) Incest by a man (section ten). | On indictment . . . ; a prosecution may not be commenced [except by or with the consent] of the Director of Public Prosecutions . . . | If with a girl under thirteen, and so charged in the indictment, life; otherwise seven years. | The jury may find the accused guilty— (i) of intercourse with a girl under thirteen (section five); or (ii) of intercourse with a girl between thirteen and sixteen (section six); . . . . . . |
| (b) An attempt to commit this offence. | On indictment . . . ; a prosecution may not be commenced [except by or with the consent] of the Director of Public Prosecutions . . . | [If with a girl under thirteen who is stated to have been so in the indictment, seven years; otherwise two years.] | — |
| 15.(a) Incest by a woman (section eleven). | On indictment . . . ; a prosecution may not be commenced [except by or with the consent] of the Director of Public Prosecutions . . . | Seven years | — |
| (b) An attempt to commit this offence. | On indictment . . . ; a prosecution may not be commenced [except by or with the consent] of the Director of Public Prosecutions . . . | Two years | — |

| Offence | Mode of prosecution | Punishment | Provisions as to alternative verdicts etc. |
|---|---|---|---|
| 16.(a) Indecency between men (section thirteen). | On indictment | [If by a man of or over the age of twenty-one with a man under the age of eighteen, five years; otherwise two years.] | — |
| (b) An attempt to procure the commission by a man of an act of gross indecency with another man. | On indictment | [If the attempt is by a man of or over the age of twenty-one to procure a man under the age of eighteen to commit an act of gross indecency with another man, five years; otherwise two years.] | — |
| 17. Indecent assault on a woman (section fourteen). | (i) On indictment | [Ten years] | — |
|  | [(ii) Summarily (by virtue of section 17(1) of the Magistrates' Courts Act 1980).] | [As provided by [section 32(1) of that Act] (that is to say, six months or the prescribed sum within the meaning of that section, or both).] | — |
| 18. Indecent assault on a man (section fifteen). | (i) On indictment | Ten years | — |
|  | [(ii) Summarily (by virtue of [section 17(1) of the Magistrates' Courts Act 1980]).] | [As provided by [section 32(1) of that Act] (that is to say, six months or the prescribed sum within the meaning of that section, or both).] | — |
| 19. Assault with intent to commit buggery (section sixteen). | On indictment | Ten years | — |
| 20. Abduction of girl under eighteen from parent or guardian (section nineteen). | On indictment | Two years | — |
| 21. Abduction of girl under sixteen from parent or guardian (section twenty). | On indictment | Two years | — |
| 22. Abduction of defective from parent of guardian (section twenty-one). | On indictment | Two years | — |

| Offence | Mode of prosecution | Punishment | Provisions as to alternative verdicts etc. |
|---|---|---|---|
| 23.(a) Causing prostitution of a woman (section twenty-two). | On indictment | Two years | — |
| (b) An attempt to commit this offence. | On indictment | Two years | — |
| 24.(a) Procuration of girl under twenty-one (section twenty-three). | On indictment | Two years | — |
| (b) An attempt to commit this offence. | On indictment | Two years | — |
| 25. Detention of woman in brothel (section twenty-four). | On indictment | Two years | — |
| 26. Permitting girl [under sixteen] to use premises for intercourse (section twenty-six). | On indictment | Two years | . . . |
| 27. Permitting defective to use premises for intercourse (section twenty-seven). | On indictment | Two years | — |
| 28. Causing or encouraging prostitution, etc, of girl under sixteen (section twenty-eight). | On indictment | Two years | — |
| 29. Causing or encouraging prostitution of defective (section twenty-nine). | On indictment | Two years | — |
| 30. Living on earnings of prostitution (section thirty). | (i)  On indictment | [Seven years] | — |
|  | (ii)  Summarily | Six months | . . . |
| 31. Controlling a prostitute (section thirty-one). | (i)  On indictment | [Seven years] | — |
|  | (ii)  Summarily | Six months | . . . |
| 32. Solicitation by a man (section thirty-two). | (i)  On indictment | Two years | — |
|  | (ii)  Summarily | Six months | . . . |

| Offence | Mode of prosecution | Punishment | Provisions as to alternative verdicts etc. |
|---|---|---|---|
| 33. Keeping a brothel (section thirty-three). | Summarily | For an offence committed after a previous conviction, six months, or [level 4 on the standard scale] or both; otherwise, three months, or [level 3 on the standard scale] or both. | A conviction of an offence punishable under section thirty-four, thirty-five or thirty-six of this Act, or under section thirteen of the Criminal Law Amendment Act 1885 (the section replaced for England and Wales by sections thirty-three to thirty-six of this Act), shall be taken into account as a previous conviction in the same way as a conviction of an offence punishable under section thirty-three of this Act. |
| 34. Letting premises for use as brothel (section thirty-four). | Summarily | For an offence committed after a previous conviction, six months, or [level 4 on the standard scale] or both; otherwise, three months, or [level 3 on the standard scale] or both. | A conviction of an offence punishable under section thirty-three, thirty-five or thirty-six of this Act, or under section thirteen of the Criminal Law Amendment Act 1885 (the section replaced for England and Wales by sections thirty-three to thirty-six of this Act), shall be taken into account as a previous conviction in the same way as a conviction of an offence punishable under section thirty-four of this Act. |

| Offence | Mode of prosecution | Punishment | Provisions as to alternative verdicts etc. |
|---|---|---|---|
| 35. Tenant permitting premises to be used as brothel (section thirty-five). | Summarily | For an offence committed after a previous conviction, six months, or [level 4 on the standard scale] or both; otherwise, three months, or [level 3 on the standard scale] or both. | A conviction of an offence punishable under section thirty-three, thirty-four or thirty-six of this Act, or under section thirteen of the Criminal Law Amendment Act 1885 (the section replaced for England and Wales by sections thirty-three to thirty-six of this Act), shall be taken into account as a previous conviction in the same way as a conviction of an offence punishable under section thirty-five of this Act. |
| 36. Tenant permitting premises to be used for prostitution (section thirty-six). | Summarily | For an offence committed after a previous conviction, six months, or [level 4 on the standard scale] or both; otherwise, three months, or [level 3 on the standard scale] or both. | A conviction of an offence punishable under section thirty-three, thirty-four or thirty-five of this Act, or under section thirteen of the Criminal Law Amendment Act 1885 (the section replaced for England and Wales by sections thirty-three to thirty-six of this Act), shall be taken into account as a previous conviction in the same way as a conviction of an offence punishable under section thirty-six of this Act. |

NOTES

This Schedule is set out as amended by, or as amended by virtue of, or as repealed in part by, the following enactments—

Street Offences Act 1959, s 4; Mental Health Act 1959, s 149(1), (2), Sch 7, Pt I, Sch 8, Pt I; Indecency with Children Act 1960, s 2(3); Criminal Law Act 1967, s 10, Sch 2, paras 13, 14, Sch 3, Pt III; Sexual Offences Act 1967, ss 3(1), (2), (4), 9; Family Law Reform Act 1969, s 11(c); Courts Act 1971, s 56(4), Sch 11, Pt IV; Criminal Jurisdiction Act 1975, ss 13(3), 14(5), Sch 6, Pt I; Criminal Law Act 1977, s 65(4), (5), Schs 12, 13; Magistrates' Courts Act 1980, s 154(1), Sch 7, para 18; Criminal Justice Act 1982, ss 38, 42; Sexual Offences Act 1985, s 3; Criminal Justice and Public Order Act 1994, s 144.

# SEXUAL OFFENCES ACT 1967

## (C 60)

*An Act to amend the law of England and Wales relating to homosexual acts*

[27 July 1967]

### 1 Amendment of law relating to homosexual acts in private

(1) Notwithstanding any statutory or common law provision, . . . a homosexual act in private shall not be an offence provided that the parties consent thereto and have attained the age of [eighteen] years.

(2) An act which would otherwise be treated for the purposes of this Act as being done in private shall not be so treated if done—
  (a) when more than two persons take part or are present; or
  (b) in a lavatory to which the public have or are permitted to have access, whether on payment or otherwise.

(3) A man who is suffering from [severe mental handicap] . . . cannot in law give any consent which, by virtue of subsection (1) of this section, would prevent a homosexual act from being an offence, but a person shall not be convicted, on account of the incapacity of such a man to consent, of an offence consisting of such an act if he proves that he did not know and had no reason to suspect that man to be suffering from [severe mental handicap].

[(3A) In subsection (3) of this section "severe mental handicap" means a state of arrested or incomplete development of mind which includes severe impairment of intelligence and social functioning.]

(4) Section 128 of the Mental Health Act 1959 (prohibition on men on the staff of a hospital, or otherwise having responsibility for mental patients, having sexual intercourse with women patients) shall have effect as if any reference therein to having unlawful sexual intercourse with a woman included a reference to committing buggery or an act of gross indecency with another man.

(5) . . .

(6) It is hereby declared that where in any proceedings it is charged that a homosexual act is an offence the prosecutor shall have the burden of proving that the act was done otherwise than in private or otherwise than with the consent of the parties or that any of the parties had not attained the age of [eighteen] years.

(7) For the purposes of this section a man shall be treated as doing a homosexual act if, and only if, he commits buggery with another man or commits an act of gross indecency with another man or is a party to the commission by a man of such an act.

---

NOTES

Sub-s (1): words omitted repealed, and number in square brackets substituted, by the Criminal Justice and Public Order Act 1994, ss 145(1), 146(1), 168(3), Sch 11.

Sub-s (3): words in square brackets substituted, and words omitted repealed, by the Mental Health (Amendment) Act 1982, s 65(1), (2), Sch 3, Pt I, para 34(a), Sch 4, Pt I.

Sub-s (3A): inserted by the Mental Health (Amendment) Act 1982, s 65(1), Sch 3, Pt I, para 34(b).

Sub-s (5): repealed by the Criminal Justice and Public Order Act 1994, ss 146(1), 168(3), Sch 11.

Sub-s (6): number in square brackets substituted by the Criminal Justice and Public Order Act 1994, s 145(1).

---

**11 Short title, citation, interpretation, saving and extent**

(1)    This Act may be cited as the Sexual Offences Act 1967 and the Act of 1956 and this Act may be cited as the Sexual Offences Acts 1956 and 1967.

(2)    In this Act "the Act of 1952" means the Magistrates' Courts Act 1952 and "the Act of 1956" means the Sexual Offences Act 1956.

(3)    . . .

(4)    References in this Act to any enactment shall, except in so far as the context otherwise requires, be construed as references to that enactment as amended or applied by or under any subsequent enactment including this Act.

(5)    This Act shall not extend to Scotland or Northern Ireland.

---

NOTES

Sub-s (3): outside the scope of this work.

---

# CRIMINAL APPEAL ACT 1968

## (C 19)

*An Act to consolidate certain enactments relating to appeals in criminal cases to the criminal division of the Court of Appeal, and thence to the House of Lords*

[8 May 1968]

## PART I
## APPEAL TO COURT OF APPEAL IN CRIMINAL CASES

*Appeal against conviction on indictment*

**1 Right of appeal**

(1)    [Subject to subsection (3) below] a person convicted of an offence on indictment may appeal to the Court of Appeal against his conviction.

[(2)    An appeal under this section lies only—
    (a)    with the leave of the Court of Appeal; or
    (b)    if the judge of the court of trial grants a certificate that the case is fit for appeal.]

[(3)    Where a person is convicted before the Crown Court of a scheduled offence it shall not be open to him to appeal to the Court of Appeal against the conviction on the ground that the decision of the court which committed him for trial as to the value involved was mistaken.

(4)    . . .]

---

NOTES

Sub-s (1): words in square brackets substituted by the Magistrates' Courts Act 1980, s 154, Sch 7, para    71.

Sub-s (2): substituted by the Criminal Appeal Act 1995, s 1(1).

Sub-s (3): added by the Magistrates' Courts Act 1980, s 154, Sch 7, para 71.

Sub-s (4): outside the scope of this work.

---

## 2 Grounds for allowing an appeal under s 1

[(1) Subject to the provisions of this Act, the Court of Appeal—

    (a) shall allow an appeal against conviction if they think that the conviction is unsafe; and

    (b) shall dismiss such an appeal in any other case.]

(2) In the case of an appeal against conviction the Court shall, if they allow the appeal, quash the conviction.

(3) An order of the Court of Appeal quashing a conviction shall, except when under section 7 below the appellant is ordered to be retried, operate as a direction to the court of trial to enter, instead of the record of conviction, a judgment and verdict of acquittal.

NOTES

    Sub-s (1): substituted by the Criminal Appeal Act 1995, s 2(1).

*Supplementary*

## [31A Powers of Court under Part I which are exercisable by registrar

(1) The powers of the Court of Appeal under this Part of this Act which are specified in subsection (2) below may be exercised by the registrar.

(2) The powers mentioned in subsection (1) above are the following—

    (a) to extend the time within which notice of appeal or of application for leave to appeal may be given;

    (b) to order a witness to attend for examination; and

    (c) to vary the conditions of bail granted to an appellant by the Court of Appeal or the Crown Court.

(3) No variation of the conditions of bail granted to an appellant may be made by the registrar unless he is satisfied that the respondent does not object to the variation; but, subject to that, the powers specified in that subsection are to be exercised by the registrar in the same manner as by the Court of Appeal and subject to the same provisions.

(4) If the registrar refuses an application on the part of an appellant to exercise in his favour any of the powers specified in subsection (2) above, the appellant shall be entitled to have the application determined by a single judge.]

NOTES

    Commencement: 1 January 1996.

    Inserted by the Criminal Appeal Act 1995, s 6.

# PART III
# MISCELLANEOUS AND GENERAL

## [44A Appeals in cases of death

(1) Where a person has died—

    (a) any relevant appeal which might have been begun by him had he remained alive may be begun by a person approved by the Court of Appeal; and

    (b) where any relevant appeal was begun by him while he was alive or is begun in relation to his case by virtue of paragraph (a) above or by a reference by the Criminal Cases Review Commission, any further step which might have been taken by him in connection with the appeal if he were alive may be taken by a person so approved.

(2)    In this section "relevant appeal" means—

(a)    an appeal under section 1, 9, 12 or 15 of this Act; or

(b)    an appeal under section 33 of this Act from any decision of the Court of Appeal on an appeal under any of those sections.

(3)    Approval for the purposes of this section may only be given to—

(a)    the widow or widower of the dead person;

(b)    a person who is the personal representative (within the meaning of section 55(1)(xi) of the Administration of Estates Act 1925) of the dead person; or

(c)    any other person appearing to the Court of Appeal to have, by reason of a family or similar relationship with the dead person, a substantial financial or other interest in the determination of a relevant appeal relating to him.

(4)    Except in the case of an appeal begun by a reference by the Criminal Cases Review Commission, an application for such approval may not be made after the end of the period of one year beginning with the date of death.

(5)    Where this section applies, any reference in this Act to the appellant shall, where appropriate, be construed as being or including a reference to the person approved under this section.

(6)    The power of the Court of Appeal to approve a person under this section may be exercised by a single judge in the same manner as by the Court of Appeal and subject to the same provisions; but if the single judge refuses the application, the applicant shall be entitled to have the application determined by the Court of Appeal.]

NOTES

Commencement: 31 March 1997 (certain purposes); 1 January 1996 (otherwise).

Inserted by the Criminal Appeal Act 1995, s 7(1).

# PART III
## MISCELLANEOUS AND GENERAL

### 55    Short title, commencement and extent

(1)    This Act may be cited as the Criminal Appeal Act 1968.

(2)    This Act shall come into force on the day appointed under section 106(5) of the Criminal Justice Act 1967 for the coming into force of section 98 of that Act.

(3)    So much of Schedule 5 to this Act as amends the Geneva Conventions Act 1957 shall extend to Scotland and Northern Ireland and the repeal by this Act of section 2(2) of the Administration of Justice Act 1960 shall extend to Northern Ireland; but except as aforesaid this Act shall not extend to Scotland or Northern Ireland.

# CHILDREN AND YOUNG PERSONS ACT 1969

## (C 54)

*An Act to amend the law relating to children and young persons; and for purposes connected therewith*

[22 October 1969]

# PART I
## CARE AND OTHER TREATMENT OF JUVENILES
## THROUGH COURT PROCEEDINGS

*Consequential changes in criminal proceedings etc*

## 7 Alterations in treatment of young offenders etc

(1)–(4) . . .

(5)   An order sending a person to an approved school shall not be made after such day as the Secretary of State may by order specify for the purposes of this subsection.

(6)   Sections 54 and 57 of the Act of 1933 (which among other things enable a child or young person found guilty of an offence to be sent to a remand home or committed to the care of a fit person) shall cease to have effect.

(7)   Subject [. . .] to the enactments requiring cases to be remitted to [youth courts] and to section 53 (1) of the Act of 1933 (which provides for detention for certain grave crimes), where a child . . . or a young person is found guilty of any offence by or before any court, that court or the court to which his case is remitted shall have power—

    (a)   . . .
    (b)   to make a supervision order in respect of him; or
    (c)   . . .

and, if it makes such an order as is mentioned in this subsection while another such order made by any court is in force in respect of the child or young person, shall also have power to discharge the earlier order; . . .

[(7A)–(7C) . . . ]

(8)   Without prejudice to the power to remit any case to a [youth court] which is conferred on a magistrates' court other than a [youth court] by section 56 (1) of the Act of 1933, in a case where such a magistrates' court finds a person guilty of an offence and either he is a young person or was a young person when the proceedings in question were begun it shall be the duty of the court to exercise that power unless the court [is of the opinion that the case is one which can properly be dealt with by means of—

    (a)   an order discharging him absolutely or conditionally, or
    (b)   an order for the payment of a fine, or
    (c)   an order requiring his parent or guardian to enter into a recognisance to take proper care of him and exercise proper control over him,

with or without any other order that the court has power to make when absolutely or conditionally discharging an offender.]

---

NOTES

    Sub-ss (1), (3), (4): repealed by the Criminal Justice Act 1982, s 78, Sch 16.

    Sub-s (2): repealed by the Powers of Criminal Courts Act 1973, ss 56(2), 60(2), Sch 6.

    Sub-s (7): words in first pair of square brackets inserted by the Criminal Justice Act 1982, s 23, repealed by the Children Act 1989, s 108(7), Sch 15; words in second pair of square brackets substituted, second words omitted, and para (c) repealed, by the Criminal Justice Act 1991, ss 100, 101(2), Sch 11, para 40, Sch 13; para (a) repealed by the Children Act 1989, s 108(7), Sch 15.

    Sub-s (7A): inserted by the Criminal Justice Act 1982, s 23, repealed by the Children Act 1989, s 108(7), Sch 15.

    Sub-ss (7B), (7C): inserted by the Children Act 1989, s 108(5), Sch 12, para 21, repealed by the Criminal Justice Act 1991, s 101, Sch 12, para 14, Sch 13.

    Sub-s (8): words in first and second pairs of square brackets substituted by the Criminal Justice Act 1991, s 100, Sch 11, para 40; words in third pair of square brackets substituted by the Criminal Justice Act 1972, ss 23, 64(1), Sch 5.

    Act of 1933: Children and Young Persons Act 1933.

*Supervision*

## 11   Supervision orders

Any provision of this Act authorising a court to make a supervision order in respect of any person shall be construed as authorising the court to make an order placing him under the supervision of a local authority designated by the order or of a probation officer; and in this Act "supervision order" shall be construed accordingly and "supervised person" and "supervisor", in relation to a supervision order, mean respectively the person placed or to be placed under supervision by the order and the person under whose supervision he is placed or to be placed by the order.

## [12   Power to include requirements in supervision orders

(1)   A supervision order may require the supervised person to reside with an individual named in the order who agrees to the requirement, but a requirement imposed by a supervision order in pursuance of this subsection shall be subject to any such requirement of the order as is authorised by the following provisions of this section or by section 12A, 12B or 12C below.

(2)   Subject to section 19(12) of this Act, a supervision order may require the supervised person to comply with any directions given from time to time by the supervisor and requiring him to do all or any of the following things—

    (a)   to live at a place or places specified in the directions for a period or periods so specified;

    (b)   to present himself to a person or persons specified in the directions at a place or places and on a day or days so specified;

    (c)   to participate in activities specified in the directions on a day or days so specified;

but it shall be for the supervisor to decide whether and to what extent he exercises any power to give directions conferred on him by virtue of this subsection and to decide the form of any directions; and a requirement imposed by a supervision order in pursuance of this subsection shall be subject to any such requirement of the order as is authorised by subsection 12B(1) of this Act.

(3)   The total number of days in respect of which a supervised person may be required to comply with directions given by virtue of paragraph (a), (b) or (c) of subsection (2) above in pursuance of a supervision order shall not exceed 90 or such lesser number, if any, as the order may specify for the purposes of this subsection; and for the purpose of calculating the total number of days in respect of which such directions may be given the supervisor shall be entitled to disregard any day in respect of which directions were previously given in pursuance of the order and on which the directions were not complied with.]

---

NOTES

    Substituted, together with ss 12A–12D, for s 12 as originally enacted, by the Criminal Justice Act 1988, s 128(1), Sch 10, Pt I.

---

## [12A   Young offenders

[(1)   This subsection applies to any supervision order made under section 7(7) of this Act unless it requires the supervised person to comply with directions given by the supervisor under section 12(2) of this Act.]

(3)    Subject to the following provisions of this section and to section 19(13) of this Act, a supervision order to which subsection (1) of this section applies may require a supervised person—

(a)  to do anything that by virtue of section 12(2) of this Act a supervisor has power, or would but for section 19(12) of this Act have power, to direct a supervised person to do;

(b)  to remain for specified periods between 6 pm and 6 am—
   (i)   at a place specified in the order; or
   (ii)  at one of several places so specified;

(c)  to refrain from participating in activities specified in the order—
   (i)   on a specified day or days during the period for which the supervision order is in force; or
   (ii)  during the whole of that period or a specified portion of it.

(4)    Any power to include a requirement in a supervision order which is exercisable in relation to a person by virtue of this section or the following provisions of this Act may be exercised in relation to him whether or not any other such power is exercised.

(5)    The total number of days in respect of which a supervised person may be subject to requirements imposed by virtue of subsection (3)(a) or (b) above shall not exceed 90.

(6)    The court may not include requirements under subsection (3) above in a supervision order unless—

(a)  it has first consulted the supervisor as to—
   (i)   the offender's circumstances; and
   (ii)  the feasibility of securing compliance with the requirements,
   and is satisfied, having regard to the supervisor's report, that it is feasible to secure compliance with them;

(b)  having regard to the circumstances of the case, it considers the requirements necessary for securing the good conduct of the supervised person or for preventing a repetition by him of the same offence or the commission of other offences; and

(c)  the supervised person or, if he is a child, his parent or guardian, consents to their inclusion.

(7)    The court shall not include in such an order by virtue of subsection (3) above—

(a)  any requirement that would involve the co-operation of a person other than the supervisor and the supervised person unless that other person consents to its inclusion; or

(b)  any requirement requiring the supervised person to reside with a specified individual; or

(c)  any such requirement as is mentioned in section 12B(1) of this Act.

(8)    The place, or one of the places, specified in a requirement under subsection (3)(b) above ("a night restriction") shall be the place where the supervised person lives.

(9)    A night restriction shall not require the supervised person to remain at a place for longer than 10 hours on any one night.

(10)   A night restriction shall not be imposed in respect of any day which falls outside the period of three months beginning with the date when the supervision order is made.

(11)   A night restriction shall not be imposed in respect of more than 30 days in all.

(12) A supervised person who is required by a night restriction to remain at a place may leave it if he is accompanied—

    (a) by his parent or guardian;

    (b) by his supervisor; or

    (c) by some other person specified in the supervision order.

(13) A night restriction imposed in respect of a period of time beginning in the evening and ending in the morning shall be treated as imposed only in respect of the day upon which the period begins.]

---

NOTES

    Substituted as noted to s 12.

    Sub-s (1): substituted, for sub-ss (1), (2) as originally enacted, by the Children Act 1989, s 108(4), Sch 12, para 22.

    Sub-s (6): para (c) substituted by the Crime (Sentences) Act 1997, s 38(1), as from a day to be appointed, as follows—

        "(c) if the supervised person is under the age of sixteen, it has obtained and considered information about his family circumstances and the likely effect of the requirements on those circumstances.".

---

## [12AA  Requirement for young offender to live in local authority accommodation

(1)  Where the conditions mentioned in subsection (6) of this section are satisfied, a supervision order may impose a requirement ("a residence requirement") that a child or young person shall live for a specified period in local authority accommodation.

(2)  A residence requirement shall designate the local authority who are to receive the child or young person and that authority shall be the authority in whose area the child or young person resides.

(3)  The court shall not impose a residence requirement without first consulting the designated authority.

(4)  A residence requirement may stipulate that the child or young person shall not live with a named person.

(5)  The maximum period which may be specified in a residence requirement is six months.

(6)  The conditions are that—

    (a) a supervision order has previously been made in respect of the child or young person;

    (b) that order imposed—

        (i) a requirement under section 12A(3) of this Act, or

        (ii) a residence requirement;

    (c) he is found guilty of an offence which—

        (i) was committed while that order was in force;

        (ii) if it had been committed by a person over the age of twenty-one, would have been punishable with imprisonment; and

        (iii) in the opinion of the court is serious; and

    (d) the court is satisfied that the behaviour which constituted the offence was due, to a significant extent, to the circumstances in which he was living,

except that the condition in paragraph (d) of this subsection does not apply where the condition in paragraph (b)(ii) is satisfied.

(7), (8) . . .

(9)   A court shall not include a residence requirement in respect of a child or young person who is not legally represented at the relevant time in that court unless—

  (a)  he has applied for legal aid for the purposes of the proceedings and the application was refused on the ground that it did not appear that his resources were such that he required assistance; or

  (b)  he has been informed of his right to apply for legal aid for the purposes of the proceedings and has had the opportunity to do so, but nevertheless refused or failed to apply.

(10)  In subsection (9) of this section—

  (a)  "the relevant time" means the time when the court is considering whether or not to impose the requirement; and

  (b)  "the proceedings" means—

    (i)  the whole proceedings; or

    (ii)  the part of the proceedings relating to the imposition of the requirement.

(11)  A supervision order imposing a residence requirement may also impose any of the requirements mentioned in sections 12, 12A, 12B or 12C of this Act.

(12)  . . . ]

---

NOTES

  Inserted by the Children Act 1989, s 108(4), Sch 12, para 23.

  Sub-ss (7), (8), (12): repealed by the Criminal Justice Act 1991, s 101(2), Sch 13.

---

## [12B   Requirements as to mental treatment

(1)   Where a court which proposes to make a supervision order is satisfied, on the evidence of a medical practitioner approved for the purposes of section 12 of the Mental Health Act 1983, that the mental condition of a supervised person is such as requires and may be susceptible to treatment but is not such as to warrant his detention in pursuance of a hospital order under Part III of that Act, the court may include in the supervision order a requirement that the supervised person shall, for a period specified in the order, submit to treatment of one of the following descriptions so specified, that is to say—

  (a)  treatment by or under the direction of a fully registered medical practitioner specified in the order;

  (b)  treatment as a non-resident patient at a place specified in the order; or

  (c)  treatment as a resident patient in a hospital or mental nursing home within the meaning of the said Act of 1983, but not a special hospital within the meaning of that Act.

(2)   A requirement shall not be included in a supervision order in pursuance of subsection (1) above—

  (a)  in any case, unless the court is satisfied that arrangements have been or can be made for the treatment in question and, in the case of treatment as a resident patient, for the reception of the patient;

  (b)  in the case of an order made or to be made in respect of a person who has attained the age of 14, unless he consents to its inclusion;

and a requirement so included shall not in any case continue in force after the supervised person becomes 18.]

---

NOTES

  Substituted as noted to s 12.

---

## [12C    Requirements as to education

(1)    Subject to subsection (3) below, a supervision order to which section 12A(1) of this Act applies may require a supervised person, if he is of compulsory school age, to comply, for as long as he is of that age and the order remains in force, with such arrangements for his education as may from time to time be made by his parent, being arrangements for the time being approved by the local education authority.

(2)    The court shall not include such a requirement in a supervision order unless it has consulted the local education authority with regard to its proposal to include the requirement and is satisfied that in the view of the local education authority arrangements exist for the child or young person to whom the supervision order will relate to receive efficient full-time education suitable to his age, ability and aptitude and to any special educational need he may have.

(3)    Expressions used in subsection (1) above and in [the Education Act 1996] have the same meaning there as in that Act.

(4)    The court may not include a requirement under subsection (1) above unless it has first consulted the supervisor as to the offender's circumstances and, having regard to the circumstances of the case, it considers the requirement necessary for securing the good conduct of the supervised person or for preventing a repetition by him of the same offence or the commission of other offences.]

NOTES

Substituted as noted to s 12.

Sub-s (3): words in square brackets substituted by the Education Act 1996, s 582(1), Sch 37, Pt I, para   15.

## [12D    Duty of court to state in certain cases that requirement in place of custodial sentence

(1)    Where—
   (a)   in pursuance of section 12A(3)(a) of this Act a court includes a requirement in a supervision order directing the supervised person to participate in specified activities; and
   (b)   it would have imposed a custodial sentence if it had not made a supervision order including such a requirement,

it shall state in open court—
   (i)    that it is making the order instead of a custodial sentence;
   (ii)   that it is satisfied that—
      [(a)   the offence of which he has been convicted, or the combination of that offence and one [or more offences] associated with it, was so serious that only a supervision order containing such a requirement or a custodial sentence can be justified for that offence; or
      (b)   that offence was a violent or sexual offence and only a supervision order containing such a requirement or such a sentence would be adequate to protect the public from serious harm from him;]
   (iii)  why it is so satisfied.

[(1A) Sub-paragraphs (a) and (b) of subsection (1)(ii) above shall be construed as if they were contained in Part I of the Criminal Justice Act 1991.]

(2)    Where the Crown Court makes such a statement, it shall certify in the supervision order that it has made such a statement.

(3)   Where a magistrates' court makes such a statement, it shall certify in the supervision order that it has made such a statement and shall cause the statement to be entered in the register.]

NOTES

Commencement: 1 October 1992 (sub-s (1A)); 1 October 1988 (remainder).

Substituted as noted to s 12.

Sub-s (1): words in outer pair of square brackets substituted by the Criminal Justice Act 1991, s 100, Sch 11, para 6; words in inner pair of square brackets substituted by the Criminal Justice Act 1993, s 66(7), (9).

Sub-s (1A): inserted by the Criminal Justice Act 1991, s 100, Sch 11, para 6.

## 13   Selection of supervisor

(1)   A court shall not designate a local authority as the supervisor by a provision of a supervision order unless the authority agree or it appears to the court that the supervised person resides or will reside in the area of the authority.

(2)   A court shall not insert in a supervision order a provision placing a child under the supervision of a probation officer unless the local authority of which the area is named or to be named in the order in pursuance of section 18(2)(a) of this Act so request and a probation officer is already exercising or has exercised, in relation to another member of the household to which the child belongs, duties imposed [on probation officers by section 14, or by rules under section 25(1)(c), of the Probation Service Act 1993].

(3)   Where a provision of a supervision order places a person under the supervision of a probation officer, the supervisor shall be a probation officer appointed for or assigned to the petty sessions area named in the order in pursuance of section 18(2)(a) of this Act and selected under arrangements [made under section 4(1)(d) of the Probation Service Act 1993 (arrangements made by probation committee)].

NOTES

Sub-ss (2), (3): words in square brackets substituted by the Probation Service Act 1993, s 32(2), Sch 3, para 3(1), (2).

## 14   Duty of supervisor

While a supervision order is in force it shall be the duty of the supervisor to advise, assist and befriend the supervised person.

## [15   Variation and discharge of supervision orders

(1)   If while a supervision order is in force in respect of a supervised person it appears to a relevant court, on the application of the supervisor or the supervised person, that it is appropriate to make an order under this subsection, the court may make an order discharging the supervision order or varying it—

    (a)   by cancelling any requirement included in it in pursuance of section 12, 12A, 12AA, 12B, 12C or 18(2)(b) of this Act; or

    (b)   by inserting in it (either in addition to or in substitution for any of its provisions) any provision which could have been included in the order if the court had then had power to make it and were exercising the power.

(2)   The powers of variation conferred by subsection (1) above do not include power—

(a) to insert in the supervision order, after the expiration of three months beginning with the date when the order was originally made, a requirement in pursuance of section 12B(1) of this Act, unless it is in substitution for such a requirement already included in the order; or

(b) to insert in the supervision order a requirement in pursuance of section 12A(3)(b) of this Act in respect of any day which falls outside the period of three months beginning with the date when the order was originally made.

(3) If while a supervision order made under section 7(7) of this Act is in force in respect of a person it is proved to the satisfaction of a relevant court, on the application of the supervisor, that the supervised person has failed to comply with any requirement included in the supervision order in pursuance of section 12, 12A, 12AA, 12C or 18(2)(b) of this Act, the court—

(a) whether or not it also makes an order under subsection (1) above, may order him to pay a fine of an amount not exceeding £1,000 or, subject to section 16A(1) of this Act, may make an attendance centre order in respect of him; or

(b) in the case of a person who has attained the age of eighteen, may (if it also discharges the supervision order) make an order imposing on him any punishment, other than a sentence of detention in a young offender institution, which it could have imposed on him if it—

(i) had then had power to try him for the offence in consequence of which the supervision order was made; and

(ii) had convicted him in the exercise of that power.

(4) If while a supervision order is in force in respect of a person it is proved to the court under subsection (3) above that the supervised person has failed to comply with any requirement included in the supervision order in pursuance of section 12A(3)(a) of this Act directing the supervised person to participate in specified activities, the court may, if it also discharges the supervision order, make an order imposing on him any sentence which it could have imposed on him if it—

(a) had then had power to try him for the offence in consequence of which the supervision order was made; and

(b) had convicted him in the exercise of that power.

(5) In a case falling within subsection (3)(b) or (4) above where the offence in question is of a kind which the court has no power to try, or has no power to try without appropriate consents, the sentence imposed by virtue of that provision—

(a) shall not exceed that which any court having power to try such an offence could have imposed in respect of it; and

(b) where the case falls within subsection (3)(b) above and the sentence is a fine, shall not in any event exceed £5,000; and

(c) where the case falls within subsection (4) above, shall not in any event exceed a custodial sentence for a term of six months and a fine of £5,000.

(6) A court may not make an order by virtue of subsection (4) above unless the court which made the supervision order made a statement under subsection (1) of section 12D of this Act; and for the purposes of this subsection a certificate under that section shall be evidence of the making of the statement to which it relates.

[(7) A fine imposed under subsection (3) or (4) above shall be deemed, for the purposes of any enactment, to be a sum adjudged to be paid by a conviction.]

(8)   In dealing with a supervised person under subsection (3) or (4) above, the court shall take into account the extent to which that person has complied with the requirements of the supervision order.

(9)   If a medical practitioner by whom or under whose direction a supervised person is being treated for his mental condition in pursuance of a requirement included in a supervision order by virtue of section 12B(1) of this Act is unwilling to continue to treat or direct the treatment of the supervised person or is of opinion—

(a)   that the treatment should be continued beyond the period specified in that behalf in the order; or

(b)   that the supervised person needs different treatment; or

(c)   that he is not susceptible to treatment; or

(d)   that he does not require further treatment,

the practitioner shall make a report in writing to that effect to the supervisor.

(10)   On receiving a report under subsection (9) above, the supervisor shall refer it to a relevant court; and on such a reference, the court may make an order cancelling or varying the requirement.

(11)   In this section 'relevant court' means—

(a)   in the case of a supervised person who has not attained the age of eighteen, a youth court;

(b)   in the case of a supervised person who has attained that age, a magistrates' court other than a youth court.

(12)   The provisions of this section shall have effect subject to the provisions of section 16 of this Act.]

NOTES

Commencement: 20 September 1993 (para (7)); 1 October 1992 (remainder).

Substituted by the Criminal Justice Act 1991, s 66, Sch 7.

Sub-s (7): substituted by the Criminal Justice Act 1993, s 65(3), (4), Sch 3, para 6(1).

## 16   Provisions supplementary to s 15

(1)   Where the supervisor makes an application or reference under the preceding section to a court he may bring the supervised person before the court, and subject to subsection (5) of this section a court shall not make an order under that section unless the supervised person is present before the court.

(2)   Without prejudice to any power to issue a summons or warrant apart from this subsection, a justice may issue a summons or warrant for the purpose of securing the attendance of a supervised person before the court to which any application or reference in respect of him is made under the preceding section; but [subsections (3) and (4) of section 55 of the Magistrates' Courts Act 1980] (which among other things restrict the circumstances in which a warrant may be issued) shall apply with the necessary modifications to a warrant under this subsection as they apply to a warrant under that section and as if in subsection (3) after the word "summons" there were inserted the words "cannot be served or".

(3)   Where the supervised person is arrested in pursuance of a warrant issued by virtue of the preceding subsection and cannot be brought immediately before the court referred to in that subsection, the person in whose custody he is—

(a)   may make arrangements for his detention in a place of safety for a period of not more than seventy-two hours from the time of the arrest (and it shall be lawful for him to be detained in pursuance of the arrangements); and

(b) shall within that period, unless within it the [supervised person] is brought before the court aforesaid, bring him before a justice;

. . .

[(3A) Where a supervised person is brought before a justice under subsection (3) of this section, the justice may—

(a) direct that he be released forthwith; or

(b) subject to subsection (3C) of this section, remand him to local authority accommodation.

(3B) A justice who remands a person to local authority accommodation shall designate, as the authority who are to receive him, the authority named in the supervision order in respect of which the application or reference is being made.

(3C) Where the supervised person has attained the age of eighteen at the time when he is brought before the justice, he shall not be remanded to local authority accommodation but may instead be remanded—

(a) to a remand centre, if the justice has been notified that such a centre is available for the reception of persons under this subsection; or

(b) to a prison, if he has not been so notified.]

[(4) Where an application is made to [a youth court] under section 15(1) of this Act, the court may remand (or further remand) the supervised person to local authority accommodation if—

(a) a warrant has been issued under subsection (2) of this section for the purpose of securing the attendance of the supervised person before the court; or

(b) the court considers that remanding (or further remanding) him will enable information to be obtained which is likely to assist the court in deciding whether and, if so, how to exercise its powers under section 15(1).]

(5)    A court may make an order under the preceding section in the absence of the supervised person if the effect of the order is one or more of the following, that is to say—

(a) discharging the supervision order;

(b) cancelling a provision included in the supervision order in pursuance of section 12[, 12A, [12AA] 12B or 12C] or section 18(2)(b) of this Act;

(c) reducing the duration of the supervision order or any provision included in it in pursuance of the said section 12[, 12A, [12AA] 12B or 12C];

(d) altering in the supervision order the name of any area;

(e) changing the supervisor.

(6)    A [youth court] shall not—

(a) exercise its powers under subsection (1) of the preceding section to make  . . . an order discharging a supervision order or inserting in it a requirement authorised by section 12[, 12A, [12AA] 12B or 12C] of this Act or varying or cancelling such a requirement except in a case where the court is satisfied that the supervised person either is unlikely to receive the care or control he needs unless the court makes the order or is likely to receive it notwithstanding the order;

(b) exercise its powers to make an order under [subsection (10)] of the preceding section except in such a case as is mentioned in paragraph (a) of this subsection;

    (c)  exercise its powers under the said subsection (1) to make an order inserting a requirement authorised by section [12B(1)] of this Act in a supervision order which does not already contain such a requirement unless the court is satisfied as mentioned in the said section [12B(1)] on such evidence as is there mentioned.

(7)    Where the supervised person has attained the age of fourteen, then except with his consent a court shall not make an order under the preceding section containing provisions which insert in the supervision order a requirement authorised by section [12B(1)] of this Act or which alter such a requirement already included in the supervision order otherwise than by removing it or reducing its duration.

(8)    The supervised person [ . . . ] may appeal to [the Crown Court] against—

    (a)  any order made under the preceding section, except an order made or which could have been made in the absence of the supervised person and an order containing only provisions to which he consented in pursuance of the preceding subsection;

    (b)  the dismissal of an application under that section to discharge a supervision order.

(9)    Where an application under the preceding section for the discharge of a supervision order is dismissed, no further application for its discharge shall be made under that section by any person during the period of three months beginning with the date of the dismissal except with the consent of a court having jurisdiction to entertain such an application.

(10)  In [paragraph (a) of subsection (3)] of the preceding section "attendance centre order" means such an order to attend an attendance centre as is mentioned in subsection (1) of section [17 of the Criminal Justice Act 1982]; . . .

(11)  In this and the preceding section references to a [youth court] or any other magistrates' court, in relation to a supervision order, are references to such a court acting for the petty sessions area for the time being named in the order in pursuance of section 18(2)(a) of this Act; and if while an application to a [youth court] in pursuance of the preceding section is pending the supervised person to whom it relates attains the age of seventeen or eighteen, the court shall deal with the application as if he had not attained the age in question.

---

NOTES

Sub-s (2): words in square brackets substituted by the Magistrates' Courts Act 1980, s 154, Sch 7, para 81.

Sub-s (3): words in square brackets substituted, and words omitted repealed, by the Courts and Legal Services Act 1990, ss 116, 125(7), Sch 16, para 4, Sch 20.

Sub-ss (3A)–(3C): inserted by the Courts and Legal Services Act 1990, s 116, Sch 16, para 4.

Sub-s (4): substituted by the Courts and Legal Services Act 1990, s 116, Sch 16, para 4; words in square brackets substituted by the Criminal Justice Act 1991, s 100, Sch 11, para 7.

Sub-s (5): references to section "12AA" inserted by the Courts and Legal Services Act 1990, s 116, Sch 16, para 4; words in other pairs of square brackets inserted by the Criminal Justice Act 1988, s 128(2), Sch 10, Pt II, paras (b), (c).

Sub-s (6): words omitted repealed by the Children Act 1989, s 108(7), Sch 15; reference to section "12AA" inserted by the Courts and Legal Services Act 1990, s 116, Sch 16, para 4; words in first and third pairs of square brackets substituted by the Criminal Justice Act 1991, s 100, Sch 11, paras 7, 40; words in other pairs of square brackets inserted or substituted by the Criminal Justice Act 1988, s 128(2), Sch 10, Pt II, paras (b), (c).

Sub-s (7): words in square brackets substituted by the Criminal Justice Act 1988, s 128(2), Sch 10, Pt II, paras (b), (c).

Sub-s (8): words omitted, inserted by the Children and Young Persons (Amendment) Act 1986, s 2(2), repealed by the Children Act 1989, s 108(7), Sch 15; words in square brackets substituted by the Courts Act 1971, s 56(2), Sch 9, Pt I.

Sub-s (10): words in first pair of square brackets substituted by the Criminal Justice Act 1991, s 100, Sch 11, para 7; words in second pair of square brackets substituted by the Criminal Justice Act 1982, s 77, Sch 14, para 26; words omitted repealed by the Criminal Justice Act 1988, s 170(2), Sch 16.

Sub-s (11): words in square brackets substituted by the Criminal Justice Act 1991, s 100, Sch 11, para 40.

## [16A    Application of sections 17 to 19 of Criminal Justice Act 1982

(1)    The provisions of section 17 of the Criminal Justice Act 1982 (attendance centre orders) shall apply for the purposes of [section 15(3)(a)] of this Act but as if—

(a)    in subsection (1), for the words from "has power" to "probation order" there were substituted the words "considers it appropriate to make an attendance centre order in respect of any person in pursuance of section 15(2A) or (4) of the Children and Young Persons Act 1969";

(b)    for references to an offender there were substituted references to a supervised person; and

(c)    subsection (13) were omitted.

(2)    Sections 18 and 19 of the Criminal Justice Act 1982 (discharge and variation of attendance centre order and breach of attendance centre orders or attendance centre rules) shall also apply for the purposes of [section 15(3)(a) of this Act] but as if—

(a)    for the references to an offender there were substituted references to the person in respect of whom the attendance centre order has been made; and

(b)    there were omitted—

(i)    from subsections (3) and (5) of section 19, the words ", for the offence in respect of which the order was made," and "for that offence"; and

(ii)    from subsection (6), the words "for an offence".]

NOTES

Inserted by the Criminal Justice Act 1988, s 128(4), Sch 10, Pt IV.

Sub-ss (1), (2): words in square brackets substituted by the Criminal Justice Act 1991, s 100, Sch 11, para 8.

## 17    Termination of supervision

A supervision order shall, unless it has previously been discharged, cease to have effect—

(a)    in any case, on the expiration of the period of three years, or such shorter period as may be specified in the order, beginning with the date on which the order was originally made;

(b), [(c)] . . .

NOTES

Para (b) repealed by the Children Act 1989, s 108(6), (7), Sch 14, paras 1, 27, 36, Sch 15; para (c) added by the Child Abduction and Custody Act 1985, s 25(3), repealed by the Children Act 1989, s 108(7), Sch 15.

## [19    Facilities for the carrying out of supervisor's directions and and requirements included in supervision orders by virtue of section [12A(3)]

(1)    It shall be the duty of a local authority, acting either individually or in association with other local authorities, to make arrangements with such persons as appear to them to be appropriate, for the provision by those persons of facilities for enabling—

(a)    directions given by virtue of section 12(2) of this Act to persons resident in their area; and

(b) requirements that may only be included in a supervision order by virtue of section [12A(3)] of this Act if they are for the time being specified in a scheme,

to be carried out effectively.

(2) The authority or authorities making any arrangements in accordance with subsection (1) of this section shall consult each relevant probation committee as to the arrangements.

(3) Any such arrangements shall be specified in a scheme made by the authority or authorities making them.

(4) A scheme shall come into force on a date to be specified in it.

(5) The authority or authorities making a scheme shall send copies of it to the clerk to the justices for each petty sessions area of which any part is included in the area to which the scheme relates.

(6) A copy of the scheme shall be kept available at the principal office of every authority who are a party to it for inspection by members of the public at all reasonable hours, and any such authority shall on demand by any person furnish him with a copy of the scheme free of charge.

(7) The authority or authorities who made a scheme may at any time make a further scheme altering the arrangements or specifying arrangements to be substituted for those previously specified.

(8) A scheme which specifies arrangements to be substituted for those specified in a previous scheme shall revoke the previous scheme.

(9) The powers conferred by subsection (7) of this section shall not be exercisable by an authority or authorities unless they have first consulted each relevant probation committee.

(10) The authority or authorities who made a scheme shall send to the clerk to the justices for each petty sessions area of which any part is included in the area for which arrangements under this section have been specified in the scheme notice of any exercise of a power conferred by subsection (7) of this section, specifying the date for the coming into force, and giving details of the effect, of the new or altered arrangements, and the new or altered arrangements shall come into force on that date.

(11) Arrangements shall not be made under this section for the provision of any facilities unless the facilities are approved or are of a kind approved by the Secretary of State for the purposes of this section.

(12) A supervision order shall not require compliance with directions given by virtue of section 12(2) of this Act unless the court making it is satisfied that a scheme under this section is in force for the area where the supervised person resides or will reside; and no such directions may involve the use of facilities which are not for the time being specified in a scheme in force under this section for that area.

(13) Subject to subsection (14) of this section, a supervision order may not include by virtue of subsection [12A(3)] of this Act—

(a) any requirement that would involve the supervised person in absence from home—
   (i) for more than 2 consecutive nights; or
   (ii) for more than 2 nights in any one week; or

(b)  if the supervised person is of compulsory school age, any requirement to participate in activities during normal school hours,

unless the court making the order is satisfied that the facilities whose use would be involved are for the time being specified in a scheme in force under this section for the area in which the suspervised person resides or will reside.

(14)  Subsection (13)(b) of this section does not apply to activities carried out in accordance with arrangements made or approved by the local education authority in whose area the supervised person resides or will reside.

(15)  It shall be the duty of every local authority to ensure that a scheme made by them in accordance with this section, either individually or in association with any other local authority, comes into force for their area not later than 30th April 1983 or such later date as the Secretary of State may allow.

(16)  In this section "relevant probation committee" means a probation committee for an area of which any part is included in the area to which a scheme under this section relates.

(17)  Expressions used in this section and in [the Education Act 1996] have the same meanings in this section as in that Act.]

NOTES
   Substituted by the Criminal Justice Act 1982, s 21(1).
   Section-heading: reference in square brackets substituted by the Criminal Justice Act 1988, s 128(2), Sch 10, Pt II, para (a).
   Sub-ss (1), (13): references in square brackets substituted by the Criminal Justice Act 1988, s 128(2), Sch 10, Pt II, para (a).
   Sub-s (17): words in square brackets substituted by the Education Act 1996, s 582(1), Sch 37, Pt I, para   16.

*Committal to care of local authorities*

## [23   Remand to local authority accommodation, committal of young persons of unruly character, etc

(1)   Where—
   (a)   a court remands a child or young person charged with or convicted of one or more offences or commits him for trial or sentence; and
   (b)   he is not released on bail,

the remand or committal shall be to local authority accommodation; and in the following provisions of this section, any reference (however expressed) to a remand shall be construed as including a reference to a committal.

(2)   A court remanding a person to local authority accommodation shall designate the local authority who are to receive him; and that authority shall be—
   (a)   in the case of a person who is being looked after by a local authority, that authority; and
   (b)   in any other case, the local authority in whose area it appears to the court that he resides or the offence or one of the offences was committed.

(3)   Where a person is remanded to local authority accommodation, it shall be lawful for any person acting on behalf of the designated authority to detain him.

(4)   Subject to subsection (5) below, a court remanding a person to local authority accommodation may, after consultation with the designated authority, require that authority to comply with a security requirement, that is to say, a requirement that the person in question be placed and kept in secure accommodation.

(5)    A court shall not impose a security requirement except in respect of a *young person who has attained the age of fifteen*, and then only if—

    (a)   he is charged with or has been convicted of a violent or sexual offence, or an offence punishable in the case of an adult with imprisonment for a term of fourteen years or more; or

    (b)   he has a recent history of absconding while remanded to local authority accommodation, and is charged with or has been convicted of an imprisonable offence alleged or found to have been committed while he was so remanded,

and (in either case) the court is of opinion that only such a requirement would be adequate to protect the public from serious harm from him.

(6)    Where a court imposes a security requirement in respect of a person, it shall be its duty—

    (a)   to state in open court that it is of such opinion as is mentioned in subsection (5) above; and

    (b)   to explain to him in open court and in ordinary language why it is of that opinion;

and a magistrates' court shall cause a reason stated by it under paragraph (b) above to be specified in the warrant of commitment and to be entered in the register.

(7)    A court remanding a person to local authority accommodation without imposing a security requirement may, after consultation with the designated authority, require that person to comply with any such conditions as could be imposed under section 3(6) of the Bail Act 1976 if he were then being granted bail.

(8)    Where a court imposes on a person any such conditions as are mentioned in subsection (7) above, it shall be its duty to explain to him in open court and in ordinary language why it is imposing those conditions; and a magistrates' court shall cause a reason stated by it under this subsection to be specified in the warrant of commitment and to be entered in the register.

(9)    A court remanding a person to local authority accommodation without imposing a security requirement may, after consultation with the designated authority, impose on that authority requirements—

    (a)   for securing compliance with any conditions imposed on that person under subsection (7) above; or

    (b)   stipulating that he shall not be placed with a named person.

(10)   Where a person is remanded to local authority accommodation, a relevant court—

    (a)   may, on the application of the designated authority, impose on that person any such conditions as could be imposed under subsection (7) above if the court were then remanding him to such accommodation; and

    (b)   where it does so, may impose on that authority any requirements for securing compliance with the conditions so imposed.

(11)   Where a person is remanded to local authority accommodation, a relevant court may, on the application of the designated authority or that person, vary or revoke any conditions or requirements imposed under subsection (7), (9) or (10) above.

(12)   In this section—

    "court" and "magistrates' court" include a justice;

"imprisonable offence" means an offence punishable in the case of an adult with imprisonment;

"relevant court", in relation to a person remanded to local authority accommodation, means the court by which he was so remanded, or any magistrates' court having jurisdiction in the place where he is for the time being;

"secure accommodation" means accommodation which is provided in a community home[, a voluntary home or a registered children's home] for the purpose of restricting liberty, and is approved for that purpose by the Secretary of State;

"sexual offence" and "violent offence" have the same meanings as in Part I of the Criminal Justice Act 1991;

"young person" means a person who has attained the age of fourteen years and is under the age of seventeen years;

[but, for the purposes of the definition of "secure accommodation", "local authority accommodation" includes any accommodation falling within section 61(2) of the Criminal Justice Act 1991.]

(13) In this section—

(a) any reference to a person who is being looked after by a local authority shall be construed in accordance with section 22 of the Children Act 1989;

(b) any reference to consultation shall be construed as a reference to such consultation (if any) as is reasonably practicable in all the circumstances of the case; and

(c) any reference, in relation to a person charged with or convicted of a violent or sexual offence, to protecting the public from serious harm from him shall be construed as a reference to protecting members of the public from death or serious personal injury, whether physical or psychological, occasioned by further such offences committed by him.

(14) This section has effect subject to—

(a) section 37 of the Magistrates' Courts Act 1980 (committal to the Crown Court with a view to a sentence of detention in a young offender institution); and

(b) section 128(7) of that Act (remands to the custody of a constable for periods of not more than three days),

but section 128(7) shall have effect in relation to a child or young person as if for the reference to three clear days there were substituted a reference to twenty-four hours.]

---

NOTES

Commencement: 1 October 1992.

Substituted by the Criminal Justice Act 1991, s 60.

Sub-s (5): words in italics substituted by the Criminal Justice and Public Order Act 1994, s 20, as from a day to be appointed (but no substitution may be brought into force on more than one occasion), as follows—

(a) "person who has attained the age of fourteen";

(b) "person who has attained the age of thirteen"; or

(c) "person who has attained the age of twelve".

Sub-s (12): words in square brackets added by the Criminal Justice and Public Order Act 1994, s 19(1).

---

## PART III
## MISCELLANEOUS AND GENERAL

*Supplemental*

### 73  Citation, commencement and extent

(1)  This Act may be cited as the Children and Young Persons Act 1969, and this Act and the Children and Young Persons Acts 1933 to 1963 may be cited together as the Children and Young Persons Acts 1933 to 1969.

(2)–(7). . .

NOTES

Sub-ss (2)–(7): outside the scope of this work.

# CHRONICALLY SICK AND DISABLED PERSONS ACT 1970

### (C 44)

*An Act to make further provision with respect to the welfare of chronically sick and disabled persons; and for connected purposes*

[29 May 1970]

*Welfare and housing*

### 1  Information as to need for and existence of welfare services

(1)  It shall be the duty of every local authority having functions under section 29 of the National Assistance Act 1948 to inform themselves of the number of persons to whom that section applies within their area and of the need for the making by the authority of arrangements under that section for such persons.

(2)  Every such local authority—

    (a)  shall cause to be published from time to time at such times and in such manner as they consider appropriate general information as to the services provided under arrangements made by the authority under the said section 29 which are for the time being available in their area; and

    (b)  shall ensure that any such person as aforesaid who uses any of those services is informed of [any other service provided by the authority (whether under any such arrangements or not)] which in the opinion of the authority is relevant to his needs [and of any service provided by any other authority or organisation which in the opinion of the authority is so relevant and of which particulars are in the authority's possession.]

(3)  This section shall come into operation on such date as the Secretary of State may by order made by statutory instrument appoint.

NOTES

Sub-s (2): words in first pair of square brackets in para (b) substituted, and second words in square brackets added, by the Disabled Persons (Services, Consultation and Representation) Act 1986, s 9.

## 2 Provision of welfare services

(1) Where a local authority having functions under section 29 of the National Assistance Act 1948 are satisfied in the case of any person to whom that section applies who is ordinarily resident in their area that it is necessary in order to meet the needs of that person for that authority to make arrangements for all or any of the following matters, namely—

    (a) the provision of practical assistance for that person in his home;

    (b) the provision for that person of, or assistance to that person in obtaining, wireless, television, library or similar recreational facilities;

    (c) the provision for that person of lectures, games, outings or other recreational facilities outside his home or assistance to that person in taking advantage of educational facilities available to him;

    (d) the provision for that person of facilities for, or assistance in, travelling to and from his home for the purpose of participating in any services provided under arrangements made by the authority under the said section 29 or, with the approval of the authority, in any services provided otherwise than as aforesaid which are similar to services which could be provided under such arrangements;

    (e) the provision of assistance for that person in arranging for the carrying out of any works of adaptation in his home or the provision of any additional facilities designed to secure his greater safety, comfort or convenience;

    (f) facilitating the taking of holidays by that person, whether at holiday homes or otherwise and whether provided under arrangements made by the authority or otherwise;

    (g) the provision of meals for that person whether in his home or elsewhere;

    (h) the provision for that person of, or assistance to that person in obtaining, a telephone and any special equipment necessary to enable him to use a telephone,

then, . . . subject . . . [. . . to the provisions of section 7(1) of the Local Authority Social Services Act 1970 (which requires local authorities in the exercise of certain functions, including functions under the said section 29, to act under the general guidance of the Secretary of State)] [and to the provisions of section 7A of that Act (which requires local authorities to exercise their social services functions in accordance with directions given by the Secretary of State)], it shall be the duty of that authority to make those arrangements in exercise of their functions under the said section 29.

(2) . . .

---

NOTES

    Sub-s (1): first words omitted repealed by the Local Government Act 1972, s 272(1), Sch 30; words in first pair of square brackets inserted by the Local Authority Social Services Act 1970, s 14(1), Sch 2, para 12; words in second pair of square brackets inserted, and second and third words omitted repealed, by the National Health Service and Community Care Act 1990, s 66, Sch 9, para 12, Sch 10.

    Sub-s (2): repealed by the Local Government Act 1972, s 272(1), Sch 30.

---

*Miscellaneous provisions*

## 29 Short title, extent and commencement

(1) This Act may be cited as the Chronically Sick and Disabled Persons Act 1970.

(2) . . .

(3)    Save as otherwise expressly provided by sections 9, 14 and 23, this Act does not extend to Northern Ireland.

(4)    This Act shall come into force as follows—
 (a)   sections 1 and 21 shall come into force on the day appointed thereunder;
 (b)   sections 4, 5, 6, 7 and 8 shall come into force at the expiration of six months beginning with the date this Act is passed;
 (c)   the remainder shall come into force at the expiration of three months beginning with that date.

**NOTES**
Sub-s (2): outside the scope of this work.

# LOCAL AUTHORITY SOCIAL SERVICES ACT 1970

## (C 42)

*An Act to make further provision with respect to the organisation, management and administration of local authority social services; to amend the Health Visiting and Social Work (Training) Act 1962; and for connected purposes*

[29 May 1970]

## 1   Local Authorities

The local authorities for the purposes of this Act shall be the councils of [non-metropolitan counties, metropolitan districts] and London boroughs and the Common Council of the City of London [but, in relation to Wales, shall be the councils of counties and county boroughs].

**NOTES**
Words in first pair of square brackets substituted by the Local Government Act 1972, s 195(1), (3); words in second pair of square brackets added by the Local Government (Wales) Act 1994, s 22(4), Sch 10, para 7.

## 6   The director of social services

(1)    A local authority shall appoint an officer, to be known as the director of social services, for the purposes of their social services functions.

(2)    Two or more local authorities may, if they consider that the same person can efficiently discharge, for both or all of them, the functions of director of social services, concur in the appointment of a person as director of social services for both or all of those authorities.

(3), (4). . .

(5)    The director of social services of a local authority shall not, without the approval of the Secretary of State (which may be given either generally or in relation to a particular authority), be employed by that authority in connection with the discharge of any of the authority's functions other than their social services functions.

(6)    A local authority which have appointed, or concurred in the appointment of, a director of social services, shall secure the provision of adequate staff for assisting him in the exercise of his functions.

(7), (8). . .

NOTES

Sub-ss (3), (4): repealed by the Local Government, Planning and Land Act 1980, ss 183(3), 194, Sch 34, Pt XVI.

Sub-s (7): repealed by the Local Government Act 1972, s 272(1), Sch 30.

Sub-s (8): outside the scope of this work.

## 7 Local authorities to exercise social services functions under guidance of Secretary of State

(1) Local authorities shall, in the exercise of their social services functions, including the exercise of any discretion conferred by any relevant enactment, act under the general guidance of the Secretary of State.

(2), (3). . .

NOTES

Sub-ss (2), (3): repealed by the Local Government Act 1972, s 272(1), Sch 30.

## 15 Citation, interpretation, commencement and extent

(1) This Act may be cited as the Local Authority Social Services Act 1970.

(2) In this Act "functions" includes powers and duties and "social services functions" has the meaning given by section 3 . . . of this Act.

(3) Any reference in this Act to an enactment shall be construed as including a reference to that enactment as amended, applied or extended by or under any other enactment, including this Act.

(4) This Act shall come into force on a day appointed by the Secretary of State by order; and different days may be so appointed for different provisions of this Act.

(5) If it appears to the Secretary of State desirable in the interest of the efficient discharge of the functions of a particular local authority to postpone the coming into force of any provision of this Act in the area of that authority, the Secretary of State may by an order under subsection (4) above relating to that provision either appoint a different day later in date for the coming into force of that provision in the area of that authority or except that area from the operation of the order and make a subsequent order under that subsection appointing a day for the coming into force of that provision in that area.

(6) This Act, . . ., shall not extend to Scotland.

(7) This Act, except . . . this subsection, shall not extend to Northern Ireland; . . .

NOTES

Sub-s (2): words omitted repealed by the Local Government, Planning and Land Act 1980, s 194, Sch 34, Part XVI.

Sub-s (6): words omitted repealed by the Health and Social Services and Social Security Adjudications Act 1983, s 30, Sch 10, Pt I.

Sub-s (7): first words omitted repealed by the Health and Social Services and Social Security Adjudications Act 1983, s 30, Sch 10, Pt I; second words omitted repealed by the Northern Ireland Constitution Act 1973, s 41(1), Sch 6, Pt I.

# MATRIMONIAL CAUSES ACT 1973

## (C 18)

*An Act to consolidate certain enactments relating to matrimonial proceedings, maintenance agreements, and declarations of legitimacy, validity of marriage and British nationality, with amendments to give effect to recommendations of the Law Commission*

[23 May 1973]

## PART I
## DIVORCE, NULLITY AND OTHER MATRIMONIAL SUITS

*Divorce*

### 1 Divorce on breakdown of marriage

*(1) Subject to section 3 below, a petition for divorce may be presented to the court by either party to a marriage on the ground that the marriage has broken down irretrievably.*

*(2) The court hearing a petition for divorce shall not hold the marriage to have broken down irretrievably unless the petitioner satisfies the court of one or more of the following facts, that is to say—*

   (a) *that the respondent has committed adultery and the petitioner finds it intolerable to live with the respondent;*
   (b) *that the respondent has behaved in such a way that the petitioner cannot reasonably be expected to live with the respondent;*
   (c) *that the respondent has deserted the petitioner for a continuous period of at least two years immediately preceding the presentation of the petition;*
   (d) *that the parties of the marriage have lived apart for a continuous period of at least two years immediately preceding the presentation of the petition (hereafter in this Act referred to as "two years' separation") and the respondent consents to a decree being granted;*
   (e) *that the parties to the marriage have lived apart for a continuous period of at least five years immediately preceding the presentation of the petition (hereafter in this Act referred to as "five years' separation").*

*(3) On a petition for divorce it shall be the duty of the court to inquire, so far as it reasonably can, into the facts alleged by the petitioner and into any facts alleged by the respondent.*

*(4) If the court is satisfied on the evidence of any such fact as is mentioned in subsection (2) above, then, unless it is satisfied on all the evidence that the marriage has not broken down irretrievably, it shall, subject to [section 5] below, grant a decree of divorce.*

*(5) Every decree of divorce shall in the first instance be a decree nisi and shall not be made absolute before the expiration of six months from its grant unless the High Court by general order from time to time fixes a shorter period, or unless in any particular case the court in which the proceedings are for the time being pending from time to time by special order fixes a shorter period than the period otherwise applicable for the time being by virtue of this subsection.*

NOTES

Sub-s (4): words in square brackets substituted by the Matrimonial and Family Proceedings Act 1984, s 46(1), Sch 1, para 10.

Repealed, together with ss 2–7, 9, 10, 17, 18, 20, 22 of this Act, by the Family Law Act 1996, s 66(3), Sch 10, subject to savings in s 66(2) of, and Sch 9, para 5 to, the 1996 Act, as from a day to be appointed.

## 2   *Supplemental provisions as to facts raising presumption of breakdown*

*(1)   One party to a marriage shall not be entitled to rely for the purposes of section 1(2)(a) above on adultery committed by the other if, after it became known to him that the other had committed that adultery, the parties have lived with each other for a period exceeding, or periods together exceeding, six months.*

*(2)   Where the parties to a marriage have lived with each other after it became known to one party that the other had committed adultery, but subsection (1) above does not apply, in any proceedings for divorce in which the petitioner relies on that adultery the fact that the parties have lived with each other after that time shall be disregarded in determining for the purposes of section 1(2)(a) above whether the petitioner finds it intolerable to live with the respondent.*

*(3)   Where in any proceedings for divorce the petitioner alleges that the respondent has behaved in such a way that the petitioner cannot reasonably be expected to live with him, but the parties to the marriage have lived with each other for a period or periods after the date of the occurrence of the final incident relied on by the petitioner and held by the court to support his allegation, that fact shall be disregarded in determining for the purposes of section 1(2)(b) above whether the petitioner cannot reasonably be expected to live with the respondent if the length of that period or of those periods together was six months or less.*

*(4)   For the purposes of section 1(2)(c) above the court may treat a period of desertion as having continued at a time when the deserting party was incapable of continuing the necessary intention if the evidence before the court is such that, had that party not been so incapable, the court would have inferred that his desertion continued at that time.*

*(5)   In considering for the purposes of section 1(2) above whether the period for which the respondent has deserted the petitioner or the period for which the parties to a marriage have lived apart has been continuous, no account shall be taken of any one period (not exceeding six months) or of any two or more periods (not exceeding six months in all) during which the parties resumed living with each other, but no period during which the parties lived with each other shall count as part of the period of desertion or of the period for which the parties to the marriage lived apart, as the case may be.*

*(6)   For the purposes of section 1(2)(d) and (e) above and this section a husband and wife shall be treated as living apart unless they are living with each other in the same household, and references in this section to the parties to a marriage living with each other shall be construed as references to their living with each other in the same household.*

*(7)   Provision shall be made by rules of court for the purpose of ensuring that where in pursuance of section 1(2)(d) above the petitioner alleges that the respondent consents to a decree being granted the respondent has been given such information as will enable him to understand the consequences to him of his consenting to a decree being granted and the steps which he must take to indicate that he consents to the grant of a decree.*

NOTES

Repealed as noted to s 1.

*Nullity*

## 11 Grounds on which a marriage is void

A marriage celebrated after 31st July 1971 shall be void on the following grounds only, that is to say—

(a) that it is not a valid marriage under the provisions of [the [Marriage Acts 1949 to 1986]] (that is to say where—

   (i) the parties are within the prohibited degrees of relationship;

   (ii) either party is under the age of sixteen; or

   (iii) the parties have intermarried in disregard of certain requirements as to the formation of marriage);

(b) that at the time of the marriage either party was already lawfully married;

(c) that the parties are not respectively male and female;

(d) in the case of a polygamous marriage entered into outside England and Wales, that either party was at the time of the marriage domiciled in England and Wales.

For the purposes of paragraph (d) of this subsection a marriage [is not polygamous if] at its inception neither party has any spouse additional to the other.

NOTES

Words in first (outer) pair of square brackets in para (a) substituted by the Marriage Act 1983, s 2(4); words in second (inner) pair of square brackets substituted by the Marriage (Prohibited Degrees of Relationship) Act 1986, s 6(4); words in third pair of square brackets substituted by the Private International Law (Miscellaneous Provisions) Act 1995, s 8(2), Sch, para 2(2).

## 12 Grounds on which a marriage is voidable

A marriage celebrated after 31st July 1971 shall be voidable on the following grounds only, that is to say—

(a) that the marriage has not been consummated owing to the incapacity of either party to consummate it;

(b) that the marriage has not been consummated owing to the wilful refusal of the respondent to consummate it;

(c) that either party to the marriage did not validly consent to it, whether in consequence of duress, mistake, unsoundness of mind or otherwise;

(d) that at the time of the marriage either party, though capable of giving a valid consent, was suffering (whether continuously or intermittently) from mental disorder within the meaning of [the Mental Health Act 1983] of such a kind or to such an extent as to be unfitted for marriage;

(e) that at the time of the marriage the respondent was suffering from venereal disease in a communicable form;

(f) that at the time of the marriage the respondent was pregnant by some person other than the petitioner.

NOTES

Words in square brackets in para (d) substituted by the Mental Health Act 1983, s 148, Sch 4, para 34.

## 13 Bars to relief where marriage is voidable

(1)   The court shall not, in proceedings instituted after 31st July 1971, grant a decree of nullity on the ground that a marriage is voidable if the respondent satisfies the court—

(a)   that the petitioner, with knowledge that it was open to him to have the marriage avoided, so conducted himself in relation to the respondent as to lead the respondent reasonably to believe that he would not seek to do so; and

(b)   that it would be unjust to the respondent to grant the decree.

[(2)   Without prejudice to subsection (1) above, the court shall not grant a decree of nullity by virtue of section 12 above on the grounds mentioned in paragraph (c), (d), (e) or (f) of that section unless—

(a)   it is satisfied that proceedings were instituted within the period of three years from the date of the marriage, or

(b)   leave for the institution of proceedings after the expiration of that period has been granted under subsection (4) below.]

(3)   Without prejudice to subsections (1) and (2) above, the court shall not grant a decree of nullity by virtue of section 12 above on the grounds mentioned in paragraph (e) or (f) of that section unless it is satisfied that the petitioner was at the time of the marriage ignorant of the facts alleged.

[(4)   In the case of proceedings for the grant of a decree of nullity by virtue of section 12 above on the grounds mentioned in paragraph (c), (d), (e) or (f) of that section, a judge of the court may, on an application made to him, grant leave for the institution of proceedings after the expiration of the period of three years from the date of the marriage if—

(a)   he is satisfied that the petitioner has at some time during that period suffered from mental disorder within the meaning of the Mental Health Act 1983, and

(b)   he considers that in all the circumstances of the case it would be just to grant leave for the institution of proceedings.

(5)   An application for leave under subsection (4) above may be made after the expiration of the period of three years from the date of the marriage.]

### NOTES

Sub-s (2): substituted by the Matrimonial and Family Proceedings Act 1984, s 2.

Sub-ss (4), (5): added by the Matrimonial and Family Proceedings Act 1984, s 2.

## 14 Marriages governed by foreign law or celebrated abroad under English law

(1)   Where, apart from this Act, any matter affecting the validity of a marriage would fall to be determined (in accordance with the rules of private international law) by reference to the law of a country outside England and Wales, nothing in section 11, 12 or 13(1) above shall—

(a)   preclude the determination of that matter as aforesaid; or

(b)   require the application to the marriage of the grounds or bar there mentioned except so far as applicable in accordance with those rules.

(2)  In the case of a marriage which purports to have been celebrated under the Foreign Marriage Acts 1892 to 1947 or has taken place outside England and Wales and purports to be a marriage under common law, section 11 above is without prejudice to any ground on which the marriage may be void under those Acts or, as the case may be, by virtue of the rules governing the celebration of marriages outside England and Wales under common law.

## 15   Application of ss 1(5), 8 and 9 to nullity proceedings

Sections 1(5), 8 and 9 above shall apply in relation to proceedings for nullity of marriage as if for any reference in those provisions to divorce there were substituted a reference to nullity of marriage.

---

NOTES

Substituted, together with new ss 15A, 15B, for s 15 as originally enacted, by the Family Law Act 1996, s 66(1), Sch 8, Pt I, paras 4, 6, subject to savings in s 66(2) of, and Sch 9, para 5 to, the 1996 Act, as from a day to be appointed, as follows—

**"15   Decrees of nullity to be decrees nisi**
Every decree of nullity of marriage shall in the first instance be a decree nisi and shall not be made absolute before the end of six weeks from its grant unless—

  (a)   the High Court by general order from time to time fixes a shorter period; or

  (b)   in any particular case, the court in which the proceedings are for the time being pending from time to time by special order fixes a shorter period than the period otherwise applicable for the time being by virtue of this section.

**15A   Intervention of Queen's Proctor**
(1)   In the case of a petition for nullity of marriage—

  (a)   the court may, if it thinks fit, direct all necessary papers in the matter to be sent to the Queen's Proctor, who shall under the directions of the Attorney-General instruct counsel to argue before the court any question in relation to the matter which the court considers it necessary or expedient to have fully argued;

  (b)   any person may at any time during the progress of the proceedings or before the decree nisi is made absolute give information to the Queen's Proctor on any matter material to the due decision of the case, and the Queen's Proctor may thereupon take such steps as the Attorney-General considers necessary or expedient.

(2)   If the Queen's Proctor intervenes or shows cause against a decree nisi in any proceedings for nullity of marriage, the court may make such order as may be just as to the payment by other parties to the proceedings of the costs incurred by him in so doing or as to the payment by him of any costs incurred by any of those parties by reason of his so doing.

(3)   Subsection (3) of section 8 above applies in relation to this section as it applies in relation to that section.

**15B   Proceedings after decree nisi: general powers of court**
(1)   Where a decree of nullity of marriage has been granted under this Act but not made absolute, then, without prejudice to section 15A above, any person (excluding a party to the proceedings other than the Queen's Proctor) may show cause why the decree should not be made absolute by reason of material facts not having been brought before the court; and in such a case the court may—

  (a)   notwithstanding anything in section 15 above (but subject to section 41 below) make the decree absolute; or

  (b)   rescind the decree; or

  (c)   require further inquiry; or

  (d)   otherwise deal with the case as it thinks fit.

(2)   Where a decree of nullity of marriage has been granted under this Act and no application for it to be made absolute has been made by the party to whom it was granted, then, at any time after the expiration of three months from the earliest date on which that party could have made such an application, the party against whom it was granted may make an application to the court, and on that application the court may exercise any of the powers mentioned in paragraphs (a) to (d) of subsection (1) above.".

---

# PART II
# FINANCIAL RELIEF FOR PARTIES TO MARRIAGE AND CHILDREN OF FAMILY

*Financial provision and property adjustment orders*

### 24 *Property adjustment orders in connection with divorce proceedings, etc*

*(1)   On granting a decree of divorce, a decree of nullity of marriage or a decree of judicial separation or at any time thereafter (whether, in the case of a decree of divorce or of nullity of marriage, before or after the decree is made absolute), the court may make any one or more of the following orders, that is to say—*

(a)   *an order that a party to the marriage shall transfer to the other party, to any child of the family or to such person as may be specified in the order for the benefit of such a child such property as may be so specified, being property to which the first-mentioned party is entitled, either in possession or reversion;*

(b)   *an order that a settlement of such property as may be so specified, being property to which a party to the marriage is so entitled, be made to the satisfaction of the court for the benefit of the other party to the marriage and of the children of the family or either or any of them;*

(c)   *an order varying for the benefit of the parties to the marriage and of the children of the family or either or any of them any ante-nuptial or post-nuptial settlement (including such a settlement made by will or codicil) made on the parties to the marriage;*

(d)   *an order extinguishing or reducing the interest of either of the parties to the marriage under any such settlement;*

*subject, however, in the case of an order under paragraph (a) above, to the restrictions imposed by section 29(1) and (3) below on the making of orders for a transfer of property in favour of children who have attained the age of eighteen.*

*(2)   The court may make an order under subsection (1)(c) above notwithstanding that there are no children of the family.*

*(3)   Without prejudice to the power to give a direction under section 30 below for the settlement of an instrument by conveyancing counsel, where an order is made under this section on or after granting a decree of divorce or nullity of marriage, neither the order nor any settlement made in pursuance of the order shall take effect unless the decree has been made absolute.*

---

NOTES

  Substituted by the Family Law Act 1996, s 15(1), (3), Sch 2, paras 1, 6, subject to savings in s 66(2) of, and Sch 9, para 5 to, the 1996 Act, as from a day to be appointed.

---

## [24A   Orders for sale of property

(1)   Where the court makes under *section 23 or 24 of this Act* a secured periodical payments order, an order for the payment of a lump sum or a property adjustment order, then, on making that order or at any time thereafter, the court may make a further order for the sale of such property as may be specified in the order, being property in which or in the proceeds of sale of which either or both of the parties to the marriage has or have a beneficial interest, either in possession or reversion.

(2)    Any order made under subsection (1) above may contain such consequential or supplementary provisions as the court thinks fit and, without prejudice to the generality of the foregoing provision, may include—

    (a)  provision requiring the making of a payment out of the proceeds of sale of the property to which the order relates, and

    (b)  provision requiring any such property to be offered for sale to a person, or class of persons, specified in the order.

(3)    Where an order is made under subsection (1) above on or after the grant of a decree of *divorce or* nullity of marriage, the order shall not take effect unless the decree has been made absolute.

(4)    Where an order is made under subsection (1) above, the court may direct that the order, or such provision thereof as the court may specify, shall not take effect until the occurrence of an event specified by the court or the expiration of a period so specified.

(5)    Where an order under subsection (1) above contains a provision requiring the proceeds of sale of the property to which the order relates to be used to secure periodical payments to a party to the marriage, the order shall cease to have effect on the death or re-marriage of that person.

[(6)    Where a party to a marriage has a beneficial interest in any property, or in the proceeds of sale thereof, and some other person who is not a party to the marriage also has a beneficial interest in that property or in the proceeds of sale thereof, then, before deciding whether to make an order under this section in relation to that property, it shall be the duty of the court to give that other person an opportunity to make representations with respect to the order; and any representations made by that other person shall be included among the circumstances to which the court is required to have regard under section 25(1) below.]]

---

NOTES

Inserted by the Matrimonial Homes and Property Act 1981, s 7.

Sub-s (1): words in italics substituted by the words "any of sections 22A to 24 above" by the Family Law Act 1996, s 66(1), Sch 8, Pt I, paras 4, 8, subject to savings in s 66(2) of, and Sch 9, para 5 to, the 1996 Act, as from a day to be appointed.

Sub-s (3): words in italics repealed by the Family Law Act 1996, s 66(3), Sch 10, subject to savings in s 66(2) of, and Sch 9, para 5 to, the 1996 Act, as from a day to be appointed.

Sub-s (6): added by the Matrimonial and Family Proceedings Act 1984, s 46(1), Sch 1.

---

## [25    Matters to which court is to have regard in deciding how to exercise its powers under ss 23, 24 and 24A

(1)    It shall be the duty of the court in deciding whether to exercise its powers under *section 23, 24 or 24A* above and, if so, in what manner, to have regard to all the circumstances of the case, first consideration being given to the welfare while a minor of any child of the family who has not attained the age of eighteen.

(2)    As regards the exercise of the powers of the court under *section 23(1)(a), (b) or (c),* 24 or 24A above in relation to a party to the marriage, the court shall in particular have regard to the following matters—

    (a)  the income, earning capacity, property and other financial resources which each of the parties to the marriage has or is likely to have in the foreseeable future, including in the case of earning capacity any increase in that capacity which it would in the opinion of the court be reasonable to expect a party to the marriage to take steps to acquire;

    (b)  the financial needs, obligations and responsibilities which each of the parties to the marriage has or is likely to have in the foreseeable future;

    (c)  the standard of living enjoyed by the family before the breakdown of the marriage;

    (d)  the age of each party to the marriage and the duration of the marriage;

    (e)  any physical or mental disability of either of the parties to the marriage;

    (f)  the contributions which each of the parties has made or is likely in the foreseeable future to make to the welfare of the family, including any contribution by looking after the home or caring for the family;

    (g)  the conduct of each of the parties[, whatever the nature of the conduct and whether it occurred during the marriage or after the separation of the parties or (as the case may be) dissolution or annulment of the marriage,], if that conduct is such that it would in the opinion of the court be inequitable to disregard it;

    (h)  *in the case of proceedings for divorce or nullity of marriage,* the value to each of the parties to the marriage of any benefit *(for example, a pension)* which, by reason of the dissolution or annulment of the marriage, that party will lose the chance of acquiring.

(3)    As regards the exercise of the powers of the court under *section 23(1)(d), (e) or (f), (2) or (4)* 24 or 24A above in relation to a child of the family, the court shall in particular have regard to the following matters—

    (a)  the financial needs of the child;

    (b)  the income, earning capacity (if any), property and other financial resources of the child;

    (c)  any physical or mental disability of the child;

    (d)  the manner in which he was being and in which the parties to the marriage expected him to be educated or trained;

    (e)  the considerations mentioned in relation to the parties to the marriage in paragraphs (a), (b), (c) and (e) of subsection (2) above.

(4)    As regards the exercise of the powers of the court under *section 23(1)(d), (e) or (f), (2) or (4), 24 or 24A* above against a party to a marriage in favour of a child of the family who is not the child of that party, the court shall also have regard—

    (a)  to whether that party assumed any responsibility for the child's maintenance, and, if so, to the extent to which, and the basis upon which, that party assumed such responsibility and to the length of time for which that party discharged such responsibility;

    (b)  to whether in assuming and discharging such responsibility that party did so knowing that the child was not his or her own;

    (c)  to the liability of any other person to maintain the child.

[(5)    In relation to any power of the court to make an interim periodical payments order or an interim order for the payment of a lump sum, the preceding provisions of this section, in imposing any obligation on the court with respect to the matters to which it is to have regard, shall not require the court to do anything which would cause such a delay as would, in the opinion of the court, be inappropriate having regard—

    (a)  to any immediate need for an interim order;

    (b)  to the matters in relation to which it is practicable for the court to inquire before making an interim order; and

    (c)  to the ability of the court to have regard to any matter and to make appropriate adjustments when subsequently making a financial provision order which is not interim.]]

NOTES

Commencement: to be appointed (sub-s (5)); 12 October 1984 (sub-ss (1)–(4)).

Substituted by the Matrimonial and Family Proceedings Act 1984, s 3.

Sub-s (1): words in italics substituted by the words "any of sections 22A to 24A" by the Family Law Act 1996, s 66(1), Sch 8, Pt I, paras 4, 9(1), (2), subject to savings in s 66(2) of, and Sch 9, para 5 to, the 1996 Act, as from a day to be appointed.

Sub-s (2): first words in italics substituted by the words "section 22A or 23 above to make a financial provision order in favour of a party to a marriage or the exercise of its powers under section 23A,", words in square brackets in para (g) inserted, and first words in italics in para (h) repealed, by the Family Law Act 1996, s 66(1), (3), Sch 8, Pt I, paras 4, 9(1), (3), Sch 10, subject to savings in s 66(2) of, and Sch 9, para 5 to, the 1996 Act, as from a day to be appointed; second words in italics in para (h) repealed by the Pensions Act 1995, s 166(2), subject to savings in the Pensions Act (Commencement) (No 5) Order 1996, SI 1996/1675, arts 4, 5.

Sub-s (3): words in italics substituted by the words "section 22A or 23 above to make a financial provision order in favour of a child of the family or the exercise of its powers under section 23A," by the Family Law Act 1996, s 66(1), Sch 8, Pt I, paras 4, 9(1), (4), subject to savings in s 66(2) of, and Sch 9, para 5 to, the 1996 Act, as from a day to be appointed.

Sub-s (4): words in italics substituted by the words "any of sections 22A to 24A" by the Family Law Act 1996, s 66(1), Sch 8, Pt I, paras 4, 9(1), (5), subject to savings in s 66(2) of, and Sch 9, para 5 to, the 1996 Act, as from a day to be appointed.

Sub-s (5): added by the Family Law Act 1996, s 66(1), Sch 8, Pt I, paras 4, 9(1), (6), subject to savings in s 66(2) of, and Sch 9, para 5 to, the 1996 Act, as from a day to be appointed.

## PART IV
## MISCELLANEOUS AND SUPPLEMENTAL

**55  Citation, commencement and extent**

(1)  This Act may be cited as the Matrimonial Causes Act 1973.

(2)  This Act shall come into force on such day as the Lord Chancellor may appoint by order made by statutory instrument.

(3)  Subject to the provisions of paragraphs 3(2) . . . of Schedule 2 below, this Act does not extend to Scotland or Northern Ireland.

NOTES

Sub-s (3): words omitted repealed by the Statute Law (Repeals) Act 1977.

# REHABILITATION OF OFFENDERS ACT 1974

## (C 53)

*An Act to rehabilitate offenders who have not been reconvicted of any serious offence for periods of years, to penalise the unauthorised disclosure of their previous convictions, to amend the law of defamation, and for purposes connected therewith*

[31 July 1974]

**4  Effect of rehabilitation**

(1)  Subject to sections 7 and 8 below, a person who has become a rehabilitated person for the purposes of this Act in respect of a conviction shall be treated for all purposes in law as a person who has not committed or been charged with or prosecuted for or convicted of or sentenced for the offence or offences which were the subject of that conviction; and, notwithstanding the provisions of any other enactment or rule of law to the contrary, but subject as aforesaid—

(a)  no evidence shall be admissible in any proceedings before a judicial authority exercising its jurisdiction or functions in Great Britain to prove that any such person has committed or been charged with or prosecuted for or convicted of or sentenced for any offence which was the subject of a spent conviction; and

(b)  a person shall not, in any such proceedings, be asked, and, if asked, shall not be required to answer, any question relating to his past which cannot be answered without acknowledging or referring to a spent conviction or spent convictions or any circumstances ancillary thereto.

(2)  Subject to the provisions of any order made under subsection (4) below, where a question seeking information with respect to a person's previous convictions, offences, conduct or circumstances is put to him or to any other person otherwise than in proceedings before a judicial authority—

(a)  the question shall be treated as not relating to spent convictions or to any circumstances ancillary to spent convictions, and the answer thereto may be framed accordingly; and

(b)  the person questioned shall not be subjected to any liability or otherwise prejudiced in law by reason of any failure to acknowledge or disclose a spent conviction or any circumstances ancillary to a spent conviction in his answer to the question.

(3)  Subject to the provisions of any order made under subsection (4) below,—

(a)  any obligation imposed on any person by any rule of law or by the provisions of any agreement or arrangement to disclose any matters to any other person shall not extend to requiring him to disclose a spent conviction or any circumstances ancillary to a spent conviction (whether the conviction is his own or another's); and

(b)  a conviction which has become spent or any circumstances ancillary thereto, or any failure to disclose a spent conviction or any such circumstances, shall not be a proper ground for dismissing or excluding a person from any office, profession, occupation or employment, or for prejudicing him in any way in any occupation or employment.

(4)  The Secretary of State may by order—

(a)  make such provision as seems to him appropriate for excluding or modifying the application of either or both of paragraphs (a) and (b) of subsection (2) above in relation to questions put in such circumstances as may be specified in the order;

(b)  provide for such exceptions from the provisions of subsection (3) above as seem to him appropriate, in such cases or classes of case, and in relation to convictions of such a description, as may be specified in the order.

(5)  For the purposes of this section and section 7 below any of the following are circumstances ancillary to a conviction, that is to say—

(a)  the offence or offences which were the subject of that conviction;

(b)  the conduct constituting that offence or those offences; and

(c)  any process or proceedings preliminary to that conviction, any sentence imposed in respect of that conviction, any proceedings (whether by way of appeal or otherwise) for reviewing that conviction or any such sentence, and anything done in pursuance of or undergone in compliance with any such sentence.

(6)    For the purposes of this section and section 7 below "proceedings before a judicial authority" includes, in addition to proceedings before any of the ordinary courts of law, proceedings before any tribunal, body or person having power—

(a)   by virtue of any enactment, law, custom or practice;

(b)   under the rules governing any association, institution, profession, occupation or employment; or

(c)   under any provision of an agreement providing for arbitration with respect to questions arising thereunder;

to determine any question affecting the rights, privileges, obligations or liabilities of any person, or to receive evidence affecting the determination of any such question.

## 5    Rehabilitation periods for particular sentences

(1)    The sentences excluded from rehabilitation under this Act are—

(a)   a sentence of imprisonment for life;

(b)   a sentence of imprisonment[, youth custody] [detention in a young offender institution] or corrective training for a term exceeding thirty months;

(c)   a sentence of preventive detention; . . .

(d)   a sentence of detention during Her Majesty's pleasure or for life, [or under section 205(2) or (3) of the Criminal Procedure (Scotland) Act 1975,] or for a term exceeding thirty months, passed under section 53 of the Children and Young Persons Act 1933 [(young offenders convicted of grave crimes) or under section 206 of the said Act of 1975 (detention of children convicted on indictment)] [or a corresponding court-martial punishment];

[(e)   a sentence of custody for life]

and any other sentence is a sentence subject to rehabilitation under this Act.

[(1A) In subsection (1)(d) above "corresponding court-martial punishment" means a punishment awarded under section 71A(3) or (4) of the Army Act 1955, section 71A(3) or (4) of the Air Force Act 1955 or section 43A(3) or (4) of the Naval Discipline Act 1957.]

(2)    For the purposes of this Act—

(a)   the rehabilitation period applicable to a sentence specified in the first column of Table A below is the period specified in the second column of that Table in relation to that sentence, or, where the sentence was imposed on a person who was under [eighteen years of age] at the date of his conviction, half that period; and

(b)   the rehabilitation period applicable to a sentence specified in the first column of Table B below is the period specified in the second column of that Table in relation to that sentence;

reckoned in either case from the date of the conviction in respect of which the sentence was imposed.

# TABLE A

Rehabilitation periods subject to reduction by half for persons [under 18]

| Sentence | Rehabilitation period |
| --- | --- |
| A sentence of imprisonment [detention in a young offender institution] [or youth custody] or corrective training for a term exceeding six months but not exceeding thirty months. | Ten years |
| A sentence of cashiering, discharge with ignominy or dismissal with disgrace from Her Majesty's service. | Ten years |
| A sentence of imprisonment [detention in a young offender institution] [or youth custody] for a term not exceeding six months. | Seven years |
| A sentence of dismissal from Her Majesty's service. | Seven years |
| Any sentence of detention in respect of a conviction in service disciplinary proceedings. | Five years |
| A fine or any other sentence subject to rehabilitation under this Act, not being a sentence to which Table B below or any of subsections (3)[, 4A] to (8) below applies. | Five years |

# TABLE B

Rehabilitation periods for certain sentences confined to young offenders

| Sentence | Rehabilitation period |
| --- | --- |
| A sentence of Borstal training. | Seven years |
| [A custodial order under Schedule 5A to the Army Act 1955 or the Air Force Act 1955, or under Schedule 4A to the Naval Discipline Act 1957, where the maximum period of detention specified in the order is more than six months. | Seven years] |
| [A custodial order under section 71AA of the Army Act 1955 or the Air Force Act 1955, or under section 43AA of the Naval Discipline Act 1957, where the maximum period of detention specified in the order is more than six months. | Seven years] |
| A sentence of detention for a term exceeding six months but not exceeding thirty months passed under section 53 of the said Act of 1933 or under section [206 of the Criminal Procedure (Scotland) Act 1975.] | Five years |
| A sentence of detention for a term not exceeding six months passed under either of those provisions. | Three years |

| | |
|---|---|
| An order for detention in a detention centre made under [section 4 of the Criminal Justice Act 1982,] section 4 of the Criminal Justice Act 1961 . . . | Three years |
| [A custodial order under any of the Schedules to the said Acts of 1955 and 1957 mentioned above, where the maximum period of detention specified in the order is six months or less. | Three years] |
| [A custodial order under section 71AA of the said Acts of 1955, or section 43AA of the said Act of 1957, where the maximum period of detention specified in the order is six months or less. | Three years] |

(3) The rehabilitation period applicable—
    (a) to an order discharging a person absolutely for an offence; and
    (b) to the discharge by a children's hearing under section *43(2) of the Social Work (Scotland) Act 1968* of the referral of a child's case;

shall be six months from the date of conviction.

(4) Where in respect of a conviction a person was conditionally discharged, bound over to keep the peace or be of good behaviour, . . . the rehabilitation period applicable to the sentence shall be one year from the date of conviction or a period beginning with that date and ending when the order for conditional discharge or probation order or (as the case may be) the recognisance or bond of caution to keep the peace or be of good behaviour ceases or ceased to have effect, whichever is the longer.

[(4A) Where in respect of a conviction a person was placed on probation, the rehabilitation period applicable to the sentence shall be—
    (a) in the case of a person aged eighteen years or over at the date of his conviction, five years from the date of conviction;
    (b) in the case of a person aged under the age of eighteen years at the date of his conviction, two and a half years from the date of conviction or a period beginning with the date of conviction and ending when the probation order ceases or ceased to have effect, whichever is the longer.]

(5)–(8) . . .

(9) For the purposes of this section—
    (a) "sentence of imprisonment" includes a sentence of detention [under section 207 or 415 of the Criminal Procedure (Scotland) Act 1975] and a sentence of penal servitude, and "term of imprisonment" shall be construed accordingly;
    (b) consecutive terms of imprisonment or of detention under section 53 of the said Act of 1933 or [section 206 of the said Act of 1975] and terms which are wholly or partly concurrent (being terms of imprisonment or detention imposed in respect of offences of which a person was convicted in the same proceedings) shall be treated as a single term;
    (c) no account shall be taken of any subsequent variation, made by a court in dealing with a person in respect of a suspended sentence of imprisonment, of the term originally imposed; and
    (d) a sentence imposed by a court outside Great Britain shall be treated as a sentence of that one of the descriptions mentioned in this section which most nearly corresponds to the sentence imposed.

(10), (10A) . . .

(11) The Secretary of State may by order—

    (a) substitute different periods or terms for any of the periods or terms mentioned in subsections (1) to (8) above; and

    (b) substitute a different age for the age mentioned in subsection (2)(a) above.

---

NOTES

Sub-s (1): in para (b), words in first pair of square brackets inserted by the Criminal Justice Act 1982, ss 77, 78, Sch 14, para 36, words in second pair of square brackets inserted by the Criminal Justice Act 1988, s 123(6), Sch 8, para 9(a); in para (c) words omitted repealed and para (e) inserted by the Criminal Justice Act 1982, ss 77, 78, Sch 14, para 36, Sch 16; in para (d), words in first pair of square brackets inserted and words in second pair of square brackets substituted by the Criminal Justice (Scotland) Act 1980, s 83(2), Sch 7, para 24, words in final pair of square brackets inserted by the Armed Forces Act 1976, s 22, Sch 9, para 20(4).

Sub-s (1A): inserted by the Armed Forces Act 1976, s 22, Sch 9, paras 20(5), 21(3).

Sub-s (2): in para (a) and heading to Table A, words in square brackets substituted (with additional effect in relation to any sentence imposed on any person who was convicted before 1 October 1992 and was aged 17 at the date of his conviction) by the Criminal Justice Act 1991, ss 68, 101(1), Sch 8, para 5, Sch 12, para 22; in Table A first and third words in square brackets inserted by the Criminal Justice Act 1988, s 123(6), Sch 8, para 9(b), second and fourth words in square brackets inserted by the Criminal Justice Act 1982, s 77, Sch 14, para 37; word in fifth pair of square brackets inserted by the Criminal Justice and Public Order Act 1994, s 168(1), (3), Sch 9, para 11; in Table B, words omitted repealed and third words in square brackets substituted by the Criminal Justice (Scotland) Act 1980, s 83(2), Sch 7, para 24, first and fifth words in square brackets added by the Armed Forces Act 1976, s 22, Sch 9, para 21(1), second and final words in square brackets added by the Armed Forces Act 1981, s 28, Sch 4, para 2, fourth words in square brackets inserted by the Criminal Justice Act 1982, s 77, Sch 14, para 37.

Sub-s (3): for the words in italics in para (b) there are substituted the words "69(1)(b) and (12) of the Children (Scotland) Act 1995" by the Children (Scotland) Act 1995, s 105(4), (5), Sch 4, para 23(1), (3), as from a day to be appointed.

Sub-ss (4), (4A): words omitted from sub-s (4) repealed, and sub-s (4A) inserted, by the Criminal Justice and Public Order Act 1994, s 168(1), (3), Sch 9, para 11, Sch 11. These amendments, which extend the rehabilitation period for a sentence involving probation, apply only in relation to persons placed on probation after the date of commencement of Sch 9, para 11: ibid para 11(2). This was 3 February 1995 (see the Criminal Justice and Public Order Act 1994 (Commencement No 5 and Transitional Provisions) Order 1995, SI 1995/127).

Sub-s (9): words in square brackets substituted by the Criminal Justice (Scotland) Act 1980, s 83(2), Sch 7, para 24.

Sub-ss (5)–(8), (10), (10A): outside the scope of this work.

---

## 7 Limitations on rehabilitation under this Act, etc

(1) Nothing in section 4(1) above shall affect—

    (a) any right of Her Majesty, by virtue of Her Royal prerogative or otherwise, to grant a free pardon, to quash any conviction or sentence, or to commute any sentence;

    (b) the enforcement by any process or proceedings of any fine or other sum adjudged to be paid by or imposed on a spent conviction;

    (c) the issue of any process for the purpose of proceedings in respect of any breach of a condition or requirement applicable to a sentence imposed in respect of a spent conviction; or

    (d) the operation of any enactment by virtue of which, in consequence of any conviction, a person is subject, otherwise than by way of sentence, to any disqualification, disability, prohibition or other penalty the period of which extends beyond the rehabilitation period applicable in accordance with section 6 above to the conviction.

(2) . . .

(3)    If at any stage in any proceedings before a judicial authority in Great Britain (not being proceedings to which, by virtue of any of paragraphs (a) to (e) of subsection (2) above or of any order for the time being in force under subsection (4) below, section 4(1) above has no application, or proceedings to which section 8 below applies) the authority is satisfied, in the light of any considerations which appear to it to be relevant (including any evidence which has been or may thereafter be put before it), that justice cannot be done in the case except by admitting or requiring evidence relating to a person's spent convictions or to circumstances ancillary thereto, that authority may admit or, as the case may be, require the evidence in question notwithstanding the provisions of subsection (1) of section 4 above, and may determine any issue to which the evidence relates in disregard, so far as necessary, of those provisions.

(4)    The Secretary of State may by order exclude the application of section 4(1) above in relation to any proceedings specified in the order (other than proceedings to which section 8 below applies) to such extent and for such purposes as may be so specified.

(5)    No order made by a court with respect to any person otherwise than on a conviction shall be included in any list or statement of that person's previous convictions given or made to any court which is considering how to deal with him in respect of any offence.

---

NOTES

Sub-s (2): outside the scope of this work.

---

## 10    Orders

(1)    Any power of the Secretary of State to make an order under any provision of this Act shall be exercisable by statutory instrument, and an order made under any provision of this Act except section 11 below may be varied or revoked by a subsequent order made under that provision.

(2)    No order shall be made by the Secretary of State under any provision of this Act other than section 11 below unless a draft of it has been laid before, and approved by resolution of, each House of Parliament.

## 11    Citation, commencement and extent

(1)    This Act may be cited as the Rehabilitation of Offenders Act 1974.

(2)    This Act shall come into force on 1st July 1975 or such earlier day as the Secretary of State may by order appoint.

(3)    This Act shall not apply to Northern Ireland.

# SEX DISCRIMINATION ACT 1975

## (C 65)

*An Act to render unlawful certain kinds of sex discrimination and discrimination on the ground of marriage, and establish a Commission with the function of working towards the elimination of such discrimination and promoting equality of opportunity between men and women generally; and for related purposes*

[12 November 1975]

# PART I
# DISCRIMINATION TO WHICH ACT APPLIES

## 1   Sex discrimination against women

(1)   A person discriminates against a woman in any circumstances relevant for the purposes of any provision of this Act if—

    (a)   on the ground of her sex he treats her less favourably than he treats or would treat a man, or

    (b)   he applies to her a requirement or condition which he applies or would apply equally to a man but—

        (i)   which is such that the proportion of women who can comply with it is considerably smaller than the proportion of men who can comply with it, and

        (ii)   which he cannot show to be justifiable irrespective of the sex of the person to whom it is applied, and

        (iii)   which is to her detriment because she cannot comply with it.

(2)   If a person treats or would treat a man differently according to the man's marital status, his treatment of a woman is for the purposes of subsection (1)(a) to be compared to his treatment of a man having the like marital status.

## 2   Sex discrimination against men

(1)   Section 1, and the provisions of Parts II and III relating to sex discrimination against women, are to be read as applying equally to the treatment of men, and for that purpose shall have effect with such modifications as are requisite.

(2)   In the application of subsection (1) no account shall be taken of special treatment afforded to women in connection with pregnancy or childbirth.

## 3   Discrimination against married persons in employment field

(1)   A person discriminates against a married person of either sex in any circumstances relevant for the purposes of any provision of Part II if—

    (a)   on the ground of his or her marital status he treats that person less favourably than he treats or would treat an unmarried person of the same sex, or

    (b)   he applies to that person a requirement or condition which he applies or would apply equally to an unmarried person but—

        (i)   which is such that the proportion of married persons who can comply with it is considerably smaller than the proportion of unmarried persons of the same sex who can comply with it, and

        (ii)   which he cannot show to be justifiable irrespective of the marital status of the person to whom it is applied, and

        (iii)   which is to that person's detriment because he cannot comply with it.

(2)   For the purposes of subsection (1), a provision of Part II framed with reference to discrimination against women shall be treated as applying equally to the treatment of men, and for that purpose shall have effect with such modifications as are requisite.

## 4   Discrimination by way of victimisation

(1)   A person ("the discriminator") discriminates against another person ("the person victimised") in any circumstances relevant for the purposes of any provision of this Act if he treats the person victimised less favourably than in those circumstances he treats or would treat other persons, and does so by reason that the person victimised has—

(a) brought proceedings against the discriminator or any other person under this Act or the Equal Pay Act 1970 [or sections 62 to 65 of the Pensions Act 1995], or

(b) given evidence or information in connection with proceedings brought by any person against the discriminator or any other person under this Act or the Equal Pay Act 1970 [or sections 62 to 65 of the Pensions Act 1995], or

(c) otherwise done anything under or by reference to this Act or the Equal Pay Act 1970 [or sections 62 to 65 of the Pensions Act 1995] in relation to the discriminator or any other person, or

(d) alleged that the discriminator or any other person has committed an act which (whether or not the allegation so states) would amount to a contravention of this Act or give rise to a claim under the Equal Pay Act 1970 [or under sections 62 to 65 of the Pensions Act 1995],

or by reason that the discriminator knows the person victimised intends to do any of those things, or suspects the person victimised has done, or intends to do, any of them.

(2)　Subsection (1) does not apply to treatment of a person by reason of any allegation made by him if the allegation was false and not made in good faith.

(3)　For the purposes of subsection (1), a provision of Part II or III framed with reference to discrimination against women shall be treated as applying equally to the treatment of men and for that purpose shall have effect with such modifications as are requisite.

---

NOTES

Sub-s (1): words in square brackets in paras (a)–(d) inserted by the Pensions Act 1995, s 66(2).

---

# PART II
# DISCRIMINATION IN THE EMPLOYMENT FIELD

*Discrimination by employers*

## 6　Discrimination against applicants and employees

(1)　It is unlawful for a person, in relation to employment by him at an establishment in Great Britain, to discriminate against a woman—

(a) in the arrangements he makes for the purpose of determining who should be offered that employment, or

(b) in the terms on which he offers her that employment, or

(c) by refusing or deliberately omitting to offer her that employment.

(2)　It is unlawful for a person, in the case of a woman employed by him at an establishment in Great Britain, to discriminate against her—

(a) in the way he affords her access to opportunities for promotion, transfer or training, or to any other benefits, facilities or services, or by refusing or deliberately omitting to afford her access to them, or

(b) by dismissing her, or subjecting her to any other detriment.

(3)　. . .

[(4)　Subsections (1)(b) and (2) do not render it unlawful for a person to discriminate against a woman in relation to her membership of, or rights under, an occupational pension scheme in such a way that, were any term of the scheme to provide for discrimination in that way, then, by reason only of any provision made by or under sections 62 to 64 of the Pensions Act 1995 (equal treatment), an equal treatment rule would not operate in relation to that term.

(4A) In subsection (4), "occupational pension scheme" has the same meaning as in the Pension Schemes Act 1993 and "equal treatment rule" has the meaning given by section 62 of the Pensions Act 1995].

(5)   Subject to section 8(3), subsection (1)(b) does not apply to any provision for the payment of money which, if the woman in question were given the employment, would be included (directly . . . or otherwise) in the contract under which she was employed.

(6)   Subsection (2) does not apply to benefits consisting of the payment of money when the provision of those benefits is regulated by the woman's contract of employment.

(7)   Subsection (2) does not apply to benefits, facilities or services of any description if the employer is concerned with the provision (for payment or not) of benefits, facilities or services of that description to the public, or to a section of the public comprising the woman in question, unless—

(a)   that provision differs in a material respect from the provision of the benefits, facilities or services by the employer to his employees, or

(b)   the provision of the benefits, facilities or services to the woman in question is regulated by her contract of employment, or

(c)   the benefits, facilities or services relate to training.

NOTES

Sub-s (3): repealed by the Sex Discrimination Act 1986, ss 1(1), 9(2), Schedule, Pt II.

Sub-ss (4), (4A): substituted for original sub-s (4) by the Pensions Act 1995, s 66(3).

Sub-s (5): words omitted repealed by the Sex Discrimination Act 1986, s 9, Schedule, Pt II.

Modified, in relation to governing bodies with delegated budgets, by the Education (Modification of Enactments Relating to Employment) Order 1989, SI 1989/901, art 3, Schedule.

## 7   Exception where sex is a genuine occupational qualification

(1)   In relation to sex discrimination—

(a)   section 6(1)(a) or (c) does not apply to any employment where being a man is a genuine occupational qualification for the job, and

(b)   section 6(2)(a) does not apply to opportunities for promotion or transfer to, or training for, such employment.

(2)   Being a man is a genuine occupational qualification for a job only where—

(a)   the essential nature of the job calls for a man for reasons of physiology (excluding physical strength or stamina) or, in dramatic performances or other entertainment, for reasons of authenticity, so that the essential nature of the job would be materially different if carried out by a woman; or

(b)   the job needs to be held by a man to preserve decency or privacy because—

(i)   it is likely to involve physical contact with men in circumstances where they might reasonably object to its being carried out by a woman, or

(ii)   the holder of the job is likely to do his work in circumstances where men might reasonably object to the presence of a woman because they are in a state of undress or are using sanitary facilities; or

[(ba)   the job is likely to involve the holder of the job doing his work, or living, in a private home and needs to be held by a man because objection might reasonably be taken to allowing to a woman—

(i)   the degree of physical or social contact with a person living in the home, or

       (ii)  the knowledge of intimate details of such a person's life,

which is likely, because of the nature or circumstances of the job or of the home, to be allowed to, or available to, the holder of the job; or]

(c)  the nature or location of the establishment makes it impracticable for the holder of the job to live elsewhere than in premises provided by the employer, and—

    (i)  the only such premises which are available for persons holding that kind of job are lived in, or normally lived in, by men and are not equipped with separate sleeping accommodation for women and sanitary facilities which could be used by women in privacy from men, and

   (ii)  it is not reasonable to expect the employer either to equip those premises with such accommodation and facilities or to provide other premises for women; or

(d)  the nature of the establishment, or of the part of it within which the work is done, requires the job to be held by a man because—

    (i)  it is, or is part of, a hospital, prison or other establishment for persons requiring special care, supervision or attention, and

   (ii)  those persons are all men (disregarding any woman whose presence is exceptional), and

  (iii)  it is reasonable, having regard to the essential character of the establishment or that part, that the job should not be held by a woman; or

(e)  the holder of the job provides individuals with personal services promoting their welfare or education, or similar personal services, and those services can most effectively be provided by a man, or

(f)  . . .

(g)  the job needs to be held by a man because it is likely to involve the performance of duties outside the United Kingdom in a country whose laws or customs are such that the duties could not, or could not effectively, be performed by a woman, or

(h)  the job is one of two to be held by a married couple.

(3)    Subsection (2) applies where some only of the duties of the job fall within paragraphs (a) to (g) as well as where all of them do.

(4)    Paragraph (a), (b), (c), (d), (e) . . . or (g) of subsection (2) does not apply in relation to the filling of a vacancy at a time when the employer already has male employees—

(a)  who are capable of carrying out the duties falling within that paragraph, and

(b)  whom it would be reasonable to employ on those duties, and

(c)  whose numbers are sufficient to meet the employer's likely requirements in respect of those duties without undue inconvenience.

---

NOTES

    Sub-s (2): para (ba) inserted by the Sex Discrimination Act 1986, s 1(2); para (f) repealed with savings by the Employment Act 1989, ss 3(1), (2), 29(4), (6), 53(2), Sch 7, Pt II, Sch 9, para 1.

    Sub-s (4): omitted letter repealed by the Employment Act 1989, s 29(4), Sch 7, Pt II, Sch 9.

    Modified, in relation to governing bodies with delegated budgets, by the Education (Modification of Enactments Relating to Employment) Order 1989, SI 1989/901, art 3, Schedule.

---

## 8    Equal Pay Act 1970

(1)    . . .

(2)    Section 1(1) of the Equal Pay Act 1970 (as set out in subsection (1) above) does not apply in determining for the purposes of section 6(1)(b) of this Act the terms on which employment is offered.

(3)    Where a person offers a woman employment on certain terms, and if she accepted the offer then, by virtue of an equality clause, any of those terms would fall to be modified, or any additional term would fall to be included, the offer shall be taken to contravene section 6(1)(b).

(4)    Where a person offers a woman employment on certain terms, and subsection (3) would apply but for the fact that, on her acceptance of the offer, section 1(3) of the Equal Pay Act 1970 (as set out in subsection (1) above) would prevent the equality clause from operating, the offer shall be taken not to contravene section 6(1)(b).

(5)    An act does not contravene section 6(2) if—
    (a)    it contravenes a term modified or included by virtue of an equality clause, or
    (b)    it would contravene such a term but for the fact that the equality clause is prevented from operating by section 1(3) of the Equal Pay Act 1970.

(6)    . . .

---

**NOTES**
Sub-ss (1), (6): amend the Equal Pay Act 1970, ss 1–3.

---

## 9    Discrimination against contract workers

(1)    This section applies to any work for a person ("the principal") which is available for doing by individuals ("contract workers") who are employed not by the principal himself but by another person, who supplies them under a contract made with the principal.

(2)    It is unlawful for the principal, in relation to work to which this section applies, to discriminate against a woman who is a contract worker—
    (a)    in the terms on which he allows her to do that work, or
    (b)    by not allowing her to do it or continue to do it, or
    (c)    in the way he affords her access to any benefits, facilities or services or by refusing or deliberately omitting to afford her access to them, or
    (d)    by subjecting her to any other detriment.

(3)    The principal does not contravene subsection (2)(b) by doing any act in relation to a woman at a time when if the work were to be done by a person taken into his employment being a man would be a genuine occupational qualification for the job.

(4)    Subsection (2)(c) does not apply to benefits, facilities or services of any description if the principal is concerned with the provision (for payment or not) of benefits, facilities or services of that description to the public, or to a section of the public to which the woman belongs, unless that provision differs in a material respect from the provision of the benefits, facilities or services by the principal to his contract workers.

---

**NOTES**
Modified, in relation to governing bodies with delegated budgets, by the Education (Modification of Enactments Relating to Employment) Order 1989, SI 1989/901, art 3, Schedule.

---

# PART IV
# OTHER UNLAWFUL ACTS

## 37  Discriminatory practices

(1)   In this section "discriminatory practice" means the application of a requirement or condition which results in an act of discrimination which is unlawful by virtue of any provision of Part II or III taken with section 1(1)(b) or 3(1)(b) or which would be likely to result in such an act of discrimination if the persons to whom it is applied were not all of one sex.

(2)   A person acts in contravention of this section if and so long as—
    (a)  he applies a discriminatory practice, or
    (b)  he operates practices or other arrangements which in any circumstances would call for the application by him of a discriminatory practice.

(3)   Proceedings in respect of a contravention of this section shall be brought only by the Commission in accordance with sections 67 to 71 of this Act.

## 38  Discriminatory advertisements

(1)   It is unlawful to publish or cause to be published an advertisement which indicates, or might reasonably be understood as indicating, an intention by a person to do any act which is or might be unlawful by virtue of Part II or III.

(2)   Subsection (1) does not apply to an advertisement if the intended act would not in fact be unlawful.

(3)   For the purposes of subsection (1), use of a job description with a sexual connotation (such as "waiter", "salesgirl", "postman" or "stewardess") shall be taken to indicate an intention to discriminate, unless the advertisement contains an indication to the contrary.

(4)   The publisher of an advertisement made unlawful by subsection (1) shall not be subject to any liability under that subsection in respect of the publication of the advertisement if he proves—
    (a)  that the advertisement was published in reliance on a statement made to him by the person who caused it to be published to the effect that, by reason of the operation of subsection (2), the publication would not be unlawful, and
    (b)  that it was reasonable for him to rely on the statement.

(5)   A person who knowingly or recklessly makes a statement such as is referred to in subsection (4) which in a material respect is false or misleading commits an offence, and shall be liable on summary conviction to a fine not exceeding [level 5 on the standard scale].

---

NOTES

  Sub-s (5): maximum fine increased and converted to a level on the standard scale by the Criminal Justice Act 1982, ss 37, 38, 46.

---

## 39  Instructions to discriminate

It is unlawful for a person—
    (a)  who has authority over another person, or
    (b)  in accordance with whose wishes that other person is accustomed to act,

to instruct him to do any act which is unlawful by virtue of Part II or III, or procure or attempt to procure the doing by him of any such act.

## 40   Pressure to discriminate

(1)   It is unlawful to induce, or attempt to induce, a person to do any act which contravenes Part II or III by—

    (a)   providing or offering to provide him with any benefit, or

    (b)   subjecting or threatening to subject him to any detriment.

(2)   An offer or threat is not prevented from falling within subsection (1) because it is not made directly to the person in question, if it is made in such a way that he is likely to hear of it.

## 41   Liability of employers and principals

(1)   Anything done by a person in the course of his employment shall be treated for the purposes of this Act as done by his employer as well as by him, whether or not it was done with the employer's knowledge or approval.

(2)   Anything done by a person as agent for another person with the authority (whether express or implied, and whether precedent or subsequent) of that other person shall be treated for the purposes of this Act as done by that other person as well as by him.

(3)   In proceedings brought under this Act against any person in respect of an act alleged to have been done by an employee of his it shall be a defence for that person to prove that he took such steps as were reasonably practicable to prevent the employee from doing that act, or from doing in the course of his employment acts of that description.

NOTES

    Modified, in relation to governing bodies with delegated budgets, by the Education (Modification of Enactments Relating to Employment) Order 1989, SI 1989/901, art 3, Schedule.

# PART VI
# EQUAL OPPORTUNITIES COMMISSION

## 54   Research and education

(1)   The Commission may undertake or assist (financially or otherwise) the undertaking by other persons of any research, and any educational activities, which appear to the Commission necessary or expedient for the purposes of section 53(1).

(2)   The Commission may make charges for educational or other facilities or services made available by them.

## 55   Review of discriminatory provisions in health and safety legislation

(1)   Without prejudice to the generality of section 53(1), the Commission, in pursuance of the duties imposed by paragraphs (a) and (b) of that subsection—

    (a)   shall keep under review the relevant statutory provisions in so far as they require men and women to be treated differently, and

    (b)   if so required by the Secretary of State, make to him a report on any matter specified by him which is connected with those duties and concerns the relevant statutory provisions.

    Any such report shall be made within the time specified by the Secretary of State, and the Secretary of State shall cause the report to be published.

(2)　Whenever the Commission think it necessary, they shall draw up and submit to the Secretary of State proposals for amending the relevant statutory provisions.

(3)　The Commission shall carry out their duties in relation to the relevant statutory provisions in consultation with the Health and Safety Commission.

(4)　In this section "the relevant statutory provisions" has the meaning given by section 53 of the Health and Safety at Work etc Act 1974.

## 56　Annual reports

(1)　As soon as practicable after the end of each calendar year the Commission shall make to the Secretary of State a report on their activities during the year (an "annual report").

(2)　Each annual report shall include a general survey of developments, during the period to which it relates, in respect of matters falling within the scope of the Commission's duties.

(3)　The Secretary of State shall lay a copy of every annual report before each House of Parliament, and shall cause the report to be published.

*[Codes of Practice]*

## [56A　Codes of practice

(1)　The Commission may issue codes of practice containing such practical guidance as the Commission think fit for either or both of the following purposes, namely—

    (a)　the elimination of discrimination in the field of employment;

    (b)　the promotion of equality of opportunity in that field between men and women.

(2)　When the Commission propose to issue a code of practice, they shall prepare and publish a draft of that code, shall consider any representations made to them about the draft and may modify the draft accordingly.

(3)　In the course of preparing any draft code of practice for eventual publication under subsection (2) the Commission shall consult with—

    (a)　such organisations or associations of organisations representative of employers or of workers; and

    (b)　such other organisations, or bodies,

as appear to the Commission to be appropriate.

(4)　If the Commission determine to proceed with the draft, they shall transmit the draft to the Secretary of State who shall—

    (a)　if he approves of it, lay it before the Houses of Parliament; and

    (b)　if he does not approve of it, publish details of his reasons for withholding approval.

(5)　If, within the period of forty days beginning with the day on which a copy of a draft code of practice is laid before each House of Parliament, or, if such copies are laid on different days, with the later of the two days, either House so resolves, no further proceedings shall be taken thereon, but without prejudice to the laying before Parliament of a new draft.

(6)　In reckoning the period of forty days referred to in subsection (5), no account shall be taken of any period during which Parliament is dissolved or prorogued or during which both Houses are adjourned for more than four days.

(7)    If no such resolution is passed as is referred to in subsection (5), the Commission shall issue the code in the form of the draft and the code shall come into effect on such days as the Secretary of State may by order appoint.

(8)    Without prejudice to section 81(4), an order under subsection (7) may contain such transitional provisions or savings as appear to the Secretary of State to be necessary or expedient in connection with the code of practice thereby brought into operation.

(9)    The Commission may from time to time revise the whole or any part of a code of practice issued under this section and issue that revised code, and subsection (2) to (8) shall apply (with appropriate modifications) to such a revised code as they apply to the first issue of a code.

(10)    A failure on the part of any person to observe any provision of a code of practice shall not of itself render him liable to any proceedings; but in any proceedings under this Act [or the Equal Pay Act 1970] before an industrial tribunal any code of practice issued under this section shall be admissible in evidence, and if any provision of such a code appears to the tribunal to be relevant to any question arising in the proceedings it shall be taken into account in determining that question.

(11)    Without prejudice to subection (1), a code of practice issued under this section may include such practical guidance as the Commission think fit as to what steps it is reasonably practicable for employers to take for the purpose of preventing their employees from doing in the course of their employment acts made unlawful by this Act.]

NOTES

Inserted, together with cross-heading, by the Race Relations Act 1976, s 76, Sch 4, para 1.

Sub-s (10): words in square brackets inserted by the Trade Union Reform and Employment Rights Act 1993, s 49(1), Sch 7, para 15.

*Investigations*

## 57    Power to conduct formal investigations

(1)    Without prejudice to their general power to do anything requisite for the performance of their duties under section 53(1), the Commission may if they think fit, and shall if required by the Secretary of State, conduct a formal investigation for any purpose connected with the carrying out of those duties.

(2)    The Commission may, with the approval of the Secretary of State, appoint, on a full-time or part-time basis, one or more individuals as additional Commissioners for the purposes of a formal investigation.

(3)    The Commission may nominate one or more Commissioners, with or without one or more additional Commissioners, to conduct a formal investigation on their behalf, and may delegate any of their functions in relation to the investigation to the persons so nominated.

## 58    Terms of reference

(1)    The Commission shall not embark on a formal investigation unless the requirements of this section have been complied with.

(2)    Terms of reference for the investigation shall be drawn up by the Commission or, if the Commission were required by the Secretary of State to conduct the investigation, by the Secretary of State after consulting the Commission.

(3)    It shall be the duty of the Commission to give general notice of the holding of the investigation unless the terms of reference confine it to activities of persons named in them, but in such case the Commission shall in the prescribed manner give those persons notice of the holding of the investigation.

[(3A) Where the terms of reference of the investigation confine it to activities of persons named in them and the Commission in the course of it propose to investigate any act made unlawful by this Act which they believe that a person so named may have done, the Commission shall—

(a)    inform that person of their belief and of their proposal to investigate the act in question; and

(b)    offer him an opportunity of making oral or written representations with regard to it (or both oral and written representations if he thinks fit);

and a person so named who avails himself of an opportunity under this subsection of making oral representations may be represented—

(i)    by counsel or a solicitor; or

(ii)    by some other person of his choice, not being a person to whom the Commission object on the ground that he is unsuitable.]

(4)    The Commission or, if the Commission were required by the Secretary of State to conduct the investigation, the Secretary of State after consulting the Commission may from time to time revise the terms of reference; and subsections (1) [(3) and (3A)] shall apply to the revised investigation and terms of reference as they applied to the original.

---

NOTES

Sub-ss (3A), (4): words in square brackets inserted by the Race Relations Act 1976, s 79(4), Sch 4, para 2.

---

## 59    Power to obtain information

(1)    For the purposes of a formal investigation the Commission, by a notice in the prescribed form served on him in the prescribed manner,—

(a)    may require any person to furnish such written information as may be described in the notice, and may specify the time at which, and the manner and form in which, the information is to be furnished;

(b)    may require any person to attend at such time and place as is specified in the notice and give oral information about, and produce all documents in his possession or control relating to, any matter specified in the notice.

(2)    Except as provided by section 69, a notice shall be served under subsection (1) only where—

(a)    service of the notice was authorised by an order made by or on behalf of the Secretary of State, or

(b)    the terms of reference of the investigation state that the Commission believe that a person named in them may have done or may be doing acts of all or any of the following descriptions—

(i)    unlawful discriminatory acts,

(ii)    contraventions of section 37,

(iii)    contraventions of sections 38, 39 or 40, and

(iv)    acts in breach of a term modified or included by virtue of an equality clause,

and confine the investigation to those acts.

(3)    A notice under subsection (1) shall not require a person—

(a)    to give information, or produce any documents, which he could not be compelled to give in evidence, or produce, in civil proceedings before the High Court or the Court of Session, or

(b)    to attend at any place unless the necessary expenses of his journey to and from that place are paid or tendered to him.

(4)    If a person fails to comply with a notice served on him under subsection (1) or the Commission has reasonable cause to believe that he intends not to comply with it, the Commission may apply to a county court for an order requiring him to comply with it or with such directions for the like purpose as may be contained in the order; and [section 55 (penalty for neglecting or refusing to give evidence) of the County Courts Act 1984] shall apply to failure without reasonable excuse to comply with any such order as it applies in the cases there provided.

(5)    In the application of subsection (4) to Scotland—

(a)    for the reference to a county court there shall be substituted a reference to a sheriff court, and

(b)    for the words after "order; and" to the end of the subsection there shall be substituted the words "paragraph 73 of the First Schedule to the Sheriff Courts (Scotland) Act 1907 (power of sheriff to grant second diligence for compelling the attendances of witnesses or havers) shall apply to any such order as it applies in proceedings in the sheriff court".

(6)    A person commits an offence if he—

(a)    wilfully alters, suppresses, conceals or destroys a document which he has been required by a notice or order under this section to produce, or

(b)    in complying with such a notice or order, knowingly or recklessly makes any statement which is false in a material particular,

and shall be liable on summary conviction to a fine not exceeding [level 5 on the standard scale].

(7)    Proceedings for an offence under subsection (6) may (without prejudice to any jurisdiction exercisable apart from this subsection) be instituted—

(a)    against any person at any place at which he has an office or other place of business;

(b)    against an individual at any place where he resides, or at which he is for the time being.

NOTES

Sub-s (4): words in square brackets substituted by the County Courts Act 1984, s 148(1), Sch 2, Pt V, para 54.

Sub-s (6): maximum fine increased and converted to a level on the standard scale by the Criminal Justice Act 1982, ss 37, 38, 46.

## 60    Recommendations and reports on formal investigations

(1)    If in the light of any of their findings in a formal investigation it appears to the Commission necessary or expedient, whether during the course of the investigation or after its conclusion,—

(a)    to make to any persons, with a view to promoting equality of opportunity between men and women who are affected by any of their activities, recommendations for changes in their policies or procedures, or as to any other matters, or

(b) to make to the Secretary of State any recommendations, whether for changes in the law or otherwise,

the Commission shall make those recommendations accordingly.

(2) The Commission shall prepare a report of their findings in any formal investigation conducted by them.

(3) If the formal investigation is one required by the Secretary of State—

(a) the Commission shall deliver the report to the Secretary of State, and

(b) the Secretary of State shall cause the report to be published,

and unless required by the Secretary of State the Commission shall not publish the report.

(4) If the formal investigation is not one required by the Secretary of State, the Commission shall either publish the report, or make it available for inspection in accordance with subsection (5).

(5) Where under subsection (4) a report is to be made available for inspection, any person shall be entitled, on payment of such fee (if any) as may be determined by the Commission—

(a) to inspect the report during ordinary office hours and take copies of all or any part of the report, or

(b) to obtain from the Commission a copy, certified by the Commission to be correct, of the report.

(6) The Commission may if they think fit determine that the right conferred by subsection (5)(a) shall be exercisable in relation to a copy of the report instead of, or in addition to, the original.

(7) The Commission shall give general notice of the place or places where, and the times when, reports may be inspected under subsection (5).

## 61   Restriction on disclosure of information

(1) No information given to the Commission by any person ("the informant") in connection with a formal investigation shall be disclosed by the Commission, or by any person who is or has been a Commissioner, additional Commissioner or employee of the Commission, except—

(a) on the order of any court, or

(b) with the informant's consent, or

(c) in the form of a summary or other general statement published by the Commission which does not identify the informant or any other person to whom the information relates, or

(d) in a report of the investigation published by the Commission or made available for inspection under section 60(5), or

(e) to the Commissioners, additional Commissioners or employees of the Commission or, so far as may be necessary for the proper performance of the functions of the Commission, to other persons, or

(f) for the purpose of any civil proceedings under this Act to which the Commission are a party, or any criminal proceedings.

(2) Any person who discloses information in contravention of subsection (1) commits an offence and shall be liable on summary conviction to a fine not exceeding [level 5 on the standard scale].

(3)   In preparing any report for publication or for inspection the Commission shall exclude, so far as is consistent with their duties and the object of the report, any matter which relates to the private affairs of any individual or business interests of any person where the publication of that matter might, in the opinion of the Commission, prejudicially affect that individual or person.

NOTES

Sub-s (2): words in square brackets substituted by the Criminal Justice Act 1982, ss 38, 46.

# PART VII
# ENFORCEMENT

*General*

## [62   Restriction of proceedings for breach of Act

(1)   Except as provided by this Act no proceedings, whether civil or criminal, shall lie against any person in respect of an act by reason that the act is unlawful by virtue of a provision of this Act.

(2)   Subsection (1) does not preclude the making of an order of certiorari, mandamus or prohibition.

(3)   . . .]

NOTES

Substituted by the Race Relations Act 1976, s 79(4), Sch 4, para 3.
Sub-s (3): outside the scope of this work.

*Enforcement in employment field*

## 63   Jurisdiction of industrial tribunals

(1)   A complaint by any person ("the complainant") that another person ("the respondent")—

    (a)   has committed an act of discrimination against the complainant which is unlawful by virtue of Part II, or

    (b)   is by virtue of section 41 or 42 to be treated as having committed such an act of discrimination against the complainant,

may be presented to an industrial tribunal.

(2)   Subsection (1) does not apply to a complaint under section 13(1) of an act in respect of which an appeal, or proceedings in the nature of an appeal, may be brought under any enactment.

## 64   Conciliation in employment cases

(1)   Where a complaint has been presented to an industrial tribunal under section 63, or under section 2(1) of the Equal Pay Act 1970, and a copy of the complaint has been sent to a conciliation officer, it shall be the duty of the conciliation officer—

    (a)   if he is requested to do so both by the complainant and the respondent, or

    (b)   if, in the absence of requests by the complainant and the respondent, he considers that he could act under this subsection with a reasonable prospect of success,

to endeavour to promote a settlement of the complaint without its being determined by an industrial tribunal.

(2)    Where, before a complaint such as is mentioned in subsection (1) has been presented to an industrial tribunal, a request so made to a conciliation officer to make his services available in the matter by a person who, if the complaint were so presented, would be the complainant or respondent, subsection (1) shall apply as if the complaint had been so presented and a copy of it had been sent to the conciliation officer.

(3)    In proceeding under subsection (1) or (2), a conciliation officer shall where appropriate have regard to the desirablility of encouraging the use of other procedures available for the settlement of grievances.

(4)    Anything communicated to a conciliation officer in connection with the performance of his functions under this section shall not be admissible in evidence in any proceedings before an industrial tribunal except with the consent of the person who communicated it to that officer.

## 65    Remedies on complaint under section 63

(1)    Where an industrial tribunal finds that a complaint presented to it under section 63 is well-founded the tribunal shall make such of the following as it considers just and equitable—

(a)   an order declaring the rights of the complainant and the respondent in relation to the act to which the complaint relates;

(b)   an order requiring the respondent to pay to the complainant compensation of an amount corresponding to any damages he could have been ordered by a county court or by a sheriff court to pay to the complainant if the complaint had fallen to be dealt with under section 66;

(c)   a recommendation that the respondent take within a specified period action appearing to the tribunal to be practicable for the purpose of obviating or reducing the adverse effect on the complainant of any act of discrimination to which the complaint relates.

[(1A) In applying section 66 for the purposes of subsection (1)(b), no account shall be taken of subsection (3) of that section.

(1B) As respects an unlawful act of discrimination falling within section 1(1)(b) or section 3(1)(b), if the respondent proves that the requirement or condition in question was not applied with the intention of treating the complainant unfavourably on the ground of his sex or marital status as the case may be, an order may be made under subsection (1)(b) only if the industrial tribunal—

(a)   makes such order under subsection (1)(a) and such recommendation under subsection (1)(c) (if any) as it would have made if it had no power to make an order under subsection (1)(b); and

(b)   (where it makes an order under subsection (1)(a) or a recommendation under subsection (1)(c) or both) considers that it is just and equitable to make an order under subsection (1)(b) as well.]

(2)    . . .

(3)    If without reasonable justification the respondent to a complaint fails to comply with a recommendation made by an industrial tribunal under subsection (1)(c), then, if they think it just and equitable to do so—

   (a)   the tribunal may [. . . ] increase the amount of compensation required to be paid to the complainant in respect of the complaint by an order made under subsection (1)(b), or

   (b)   if an order under subsection (1)(b) [was not made], the tribunal may make such an order.

NOTES

   Sub-ss (1A), (1B): inserted by the Sex Discrimination and Equal Pay (Miscellaneous Amendments) Regulations 1996, SI 1996/438, reg 2(2).

   Sub-s (2) repealed by the Sex Discrimination and Equal Pay (Remedies) Regulations 1993, SI   1993/2798, regs 1(3), 2.

   Sub-s (3): words omitted from para (a) repealed by the Sex Discrimination and Equal Pay (Remedies) Regulations 1993, SI 1993/2798, reg 1(3), Schedule, para 1; words in square brackets in para (b) substituted by the Sex Discrimination and Equal Pay (Miscellaneous Amendments) Regulations 1996, SI   1996/438, reg 2(3).

# PART VIII
# SUPPLEMENTAL

## 87   Short title and extent

(1)    This Act may be cited as the Sex Discrimination Act 1975.

(2)    This Act (except paragraph 16 of Schedule 3) does not extend to Northern Ireland.

# ADOPTION ACT 1976

## (C 36)

*An Act to consolidate the enactments having effect in England and Wales in relation to adoption*
[22 July 1976]

## PART I
## THE ADOPTION SERVICE

*Welfare of children*

### 6  Duty to promote welfare of children

In reaching any decision relating to the adoption of a child a court or adoption agency shall have regard to all the circumstances, first consideration being given to the need to safeguard and promote, the welfare of the child throughout his childhood; and shall so far as practicable ascertain the wishes and feelings of the child regarding the decision and give due consideration to them, having regard to his age and understanding.

## PART II
## ADOPTION ORDERS

*The making of adoption orders*

### 12  Adoption orders

(1)   An adoption order is an order [giving parental responsibility for a child to] the adopters, made on their application by an authorised court.

(2)   The order does not affect [parental responsibility so far as it relates] to any period before the making of the order.

(3)   The making of an adoption order operates to extinguish—
  [(a)  the parental responsibility which any person has for the child immediately before the making of the order;
  (aa) any order under the Children Act 1989]; and
  (b)  any duty arising by virtue of an agreement or the order of a court to make payments, so far as the payments are in respect of the child's maintenance [or upbringing for any period after the making of the order.]

(4)   Subsection (3)(b) does not apply to a duty arising by virtue of an agreement—
  (a)  which constitutes a trust, or
  (b)  which expressly provides that the duty is not to be extinguished by the making of an adoption order.

(5)   An adoption order may not be made in relation to a child who is or has been married.

(6)   An adoption order may contain such terms and conditions as the court thinks fit.

(7)   An adoption order may be made notwithstanding that the child is already an adopted child.

NOTES
  Sub-ss (1)–(3): words in square brackets substituted by the Children Act 1989, s 88, Sch 10, para 3.

### 13 Child to live with adopters before order is made

(1) Where—

(a) the applicant, or one of the applicants, is a parent, step-parent or relative of the child, or

(b) the child was placed with the applicants by an adoption agency or in pursuance of an order of the High Court,

an adoption order shall not be made unless the child is at least 19 weeks old and at all times during the preceding 13 weeks had his home with the applicants or one of them.

(2) Where subsection (1) does not apply, an adoption order shall not be made unless the child is at least 12 months old and at all times during the preceding 12 months had his home with the applicants or one of them.

(3) An adoption order shall not be made unless the court is satisfied that sufficient opportunities to see the child with the applicant or, in the case of an application by a married couple, both applicants together in the home environment have been afforded—

(a) where the child was placed with the applicant by an adoption agency, to that agency, or

(b) in any other case, to the local authority within whose area the home is.

## PART III
## CARE AND PROTECTION OF CHILDREN AWAITING ADOPTION

*Protected children*

### 37 Miscellaneous provisions relating to protected children

(1) . . .

(2) A person who maintains a protected child shall be deemed for the purposes of the Life Assurance Act 1774 to have no interest in the life of the child.

(3), (4) . . .

---

NOTES

Sub-ss (1), (3), (4): repealed by the Children Act 1989, s 108(7), Sch 15.

## PART V
## REGISTRATION AND REVOCATION OF ADOPTION ORDERS AND CONVENTION ADOPTIONS

### 50 Adopted Children Register

(1) The Registrar General shall maintain at the General Register Office a register, to be called the Adopted Children Register, in which shall be made such entries as may be directed to be made therein by adoption orders, but no other entries.

(2) A certified copy of an entry in the Adopted Children Register, if purporting to be sealed or stamped with the seal of the General Register Office, shall, without any further or other proof of that entry, be received as evidence of the adoption to which it relates and, where the entry contains a record of the date of the birth or the country or the district and sub-district of the birth of the adopted person, shall also be received as aforesaid as evidence of that date or country or district and sub-district in all respects as if the copy were a certified copy of an entry in the Registers of Births.

(3)　The Registrar General shall cause an index of the Adopted Children Register to be made and kept in the General Register Office; and every person shall be entitled to search that index and to have a certified copy of any entry in the Adopted Children Register in all respects upon and subject to the same terms, conditions and regulations as to payment of fees and otherwise as are applicable under the Births and Deaths Registration Act 1953, and the Registration Service Act 1953, in respect of searches in other indexes kept in the General Register Office and in respect of the supply from that office or certified copies of entries in the certified copies of the Registers of Births and Deaths.

(4)　The Registrar General shall, in addition to the Adopted Children Register and the index thereof, keep such other registers and books, and make such entries therein, as may be necessary to record and make traceable the connection between any entry in the Registers of Births which has been marked "Adopted" and any corresponding entry in the Adopted Children Register.

(5)　The registers and books kept under subsection (4) shall not be, nor shall any index thereof be, open to public inspection or search, and the Registrar General shall not furnish any person with any information contained in or with any copy or extract from any such registers or books except in accordance with section 51 or under an order of any of the following courts, that is to say—

(a)　the High Court;

(b)　the Westminster County Court or such other county court as may be prescribed; and

(c)　the court by which an adoption order was made in respect of the person to whom the information, copy or extract relates.

(6)　In relation to an adoption order made by a magistrates' court, the reference in paragraph (c) of subsection (5) to the court by which the order was made includes a reference to a court acting for the same petty sessions area.

(7)　Schedule 1 to this Act, which, among other things, provides for the registration of adoptions and the amendment of adoption orders, shall have effect.

## 51　Disclosure of birth records of adopted children

(1)　Subject to [what follows], the Registrar General shall on an application made in the prescribed manner by an adopted person a record of whose birth is kept by the Registrar General and who has attained the age of 18 years supply to that person on payment of the prescribed fee (if any) such information as is necessary to enable that person to obtain a certified copy of the record of his birth.

(2)　On an application made in the prescribed manner by an adopted person under the age of 18 years, a record of whose birth is kept by the Registrar General and who is intending to be married in England or Wales, and on payment of the prescribed fee (if any), the Registrar General shall inform the applicant whether or not it appears from information contained in the registers of live births or other records that the applicant and the person whom he intends to marry may be within the prohibited degrees of relationship for the purposes of the Marriage Act 1949.

[(3)　Before supplying any information to an applicant under subsection (1), the Registrar General shall inform the applicant that counselling services are available to him—

(a)　if he is in England and Wales—

(i)　at the General Register Office;

(ii) from the local authority in whose area he is living;

(iii) where the adoption order relating to him was made in England and Wales, from the local authority in whose area the court which made the order sat; or

(iv) from any other local authority;

(b) if he is in Scotland—

(i) from the regional or islands council in whose area he is living;

(ii) where the adoption order relating to him was made in Scotland, from the council in whose area the court which made the order sat; or

(iii) from any other regional or islands council;

(c) if he is in Northern Ireland—

(i) from the Board in whose area he is living;

(ii) where the adoption order relating to him was made in Northern Ireland, from the Board in whose area the court which made the order sat; or

(iii) from any other Board;

(d) if he is in the United Kingdom and his adoption was arranged by an adoption society—

(i) approved under section 3,

(ii) approved under section 3 of the Adoption (Scotland) Act 1978,

(iii) registered under Article 4 of the Adoption (Northern Ireland) Order 1987,

from that society.

(4) Where an adopted person who is in England and Wales—

(a) applies for information under—

(i) subsection (1), or

(ii) Article 54 of the Adoption (Northern Ireland) Order 1987, or

(b) is supplied with information under section 45 of the Adoption (Scotland) Act 1978,

it shall be the duty of the persons and bodies mentioned in subsection (5) to provide counselling for him if asked by him to do so.

(5) The persons and bodies are—

(a) the Registrar General;

(b) any local authority falling within subsection (3)(a)(ii) to (iv);

(c) any adoption society falling within subsection (3)(d) in so far as it is acting as an adoption society in England and Wales.

(6) If the applicant chooses to receive counselling from a person or body falling within subsection (3), the Registrar General shall send to the person or body the information to which the applicant is entitled under subsection (1).

(7) Where a person—

(a) was adopted before 12th November 1975, and

(b) applies for information under subsection (1),

the Registrar General shall not supply the information to him unless he has attended an interview with a counsellor arranged by a person or body from whom counselling services are available as mentioned in subsection (3).

(8) Where the Registrar General is prevented by subsection (7) from supplying information to a person who is not living in the United Kingdom, he may supply the information to any body which—

(a) the Registrar General is satisfied is suitable to provide counselling to that person, and

(b) has notified the Registrar General that it is prepared to provide such counselling.

(9) In this section—

"a Board" means a Health and Social Services Board established under Article 16 of the Health and Personal Social Services (Northern Ireland) Order 1972; and

"prescribed" means prescribed by regulations made by the Registrar General.]

**NOTES**

Sub-s (1): words in square brackets substituted by the Children Act 1989, s 88, Sch 10, para 20.

Sub-ss (3)–(9): substituted, for sub-ss (3)–(7) as originally enacted, by the Children Act 1989, s 88, Sch 10, para 20.

## PART VI
## MISCELLANEOUS AND SUPPLEMENTAL

### 74 Short title, commencement and extent

(1) This Act may be cited as the Adoption Act 1976.

(2) This Act shall come into force on such date as the Secretary of State may be order appoint and different dates may be appointed for different provisions.

[(3) This Act extends to England and Wales only.]

**NOTES**

Sub-s (3): substituted, for sub-ss (3), (4) as originally enacted, by the Children Act 1989, s 88, Sch 10, para 31.

# BAIL ACT 1976

## (C 63)

*An Act to make provision in relation to bail in or in connection with criminal proceedings in England and Wales, to make it an offence to agree to indemnify sureties in criminal proceedings, to make provision for legal aid limited to questions of bail in certain cases and for legal aid for persons kept in custody for inquiries or reports, to extend the powers of coroners to grant bail and for connected purposes*

[15 November 1976]

*Preliminary*

### 1 Meaning of "bail in criminal proceedings"

(1) In this Act "bail in criminal proceedings" means—

(a) bail grantable in or in connection with proceedings for an offence to a person who is accused or convicted of the offence, or

(b) bail grantable in connection with an offence to a person who is under arrest for the offence or for whose arrest for the offence a warrant (endorsed for bail) is being issued.

(2)　In this Act "bail" means bail grantable under the law (including common law) for the time being in force.

(3)　Except as provided by section 13(3) of this Act, this section does not apply to bail in or in connection with proceedings outside England and Wales.

(4)　. . .

(5)　This section applies—

    (a)　whether the offence was committed in England or Wales or elsewhere, and

    (b)　whether it is an offence under the law of England and Wales, or of any other country or territory.

(6)　Bail in criminal proceedings shall be granted (and in particular shall be granted unconditionally or conditionally) in accordance with this Act.

NOTES

    Sub-s (4): repealed by the Criminal Justice and Public Order Act 1994, s 168(3), Sch 11.

## 2　Other definitions

(1)　In this Act, unless the context otherwise requires, "conviction" includes—

    (a)　a finding of guilt,

    (b)　a finding that a person is not guilty by reason of insanity,

    (c)　a finding under [section 30(1) of the Magistrates' Courts Act 1980] (remand for medical examination) that the person in question did the act or made the omission charged, and

    (d)　a conviction of an offence for which an order is made placing the offender on probation or discharging him absolutely or conditionally,

and "convicted" shall be construed accordingly.

(2)　In this Act, unless the context otherwise requires—

    ["bail hostel" and "probation hostel" have the same meanings as in the Powers of Criminal Courts Act 1973,]

    "child" means a person under the age of fourteen,

    . . .

    "court" includes a judge of a court [or a justice of the peace] and, in the case of a specified court, includes a judge or (as the case may be) justice having powers to act in connection with proceedings before that court,

    "Courts-Martial Appeal rules" means rules made under section 49 of the Courts-Martial (Appeals) Act 1968,

    "Crown Court rules" means rules made under section 15 of the Courts Act 1971,

    "magistrates' courts rules" means rules made under section 15 of the Justices of the Peace Act 1949,

    "offence" includes an alleged offence,

    "proceedings against a fugitive offender" means proceedings under [the Extradition Act 1989] or section 2(1) or 4(3) of the Backing of Warrants (Republic of Ireland) Act 1965,

    "Supreme Court rules" means rules made under section 99 of the Supreme Court of Judicature (Consolidation) Act 1925,

    "surrender to custody" means, in relation to a person released on bail, surrendering himself into the custody of the court or of the constable (according to the requirements of the grant of bail) at the time and place for the time being appointed for him to do so, "vary", in relation to bail, means imposing further conditions after bail is granted, or varying or rescinding conditions,

"young person" means a person who has attained the age of fourteen and is under the age of seventeen.

(3) Where an enactment (whenever passed) which relates to bail in criminal proceedings refers to the person bailed appearing before a court it is to be construed unless the context otherwise requires as referring to his surrendering himself into the custody of the court.

(4) Any reference in this Act to any other enactment is a reference thereto as amended, and includes a reference thereto as extended or applied, by or under any other enactment, including this Act.

NOTES

Sub-s (1): words in square brackets in para (c) substituted by the Magistrates' Courts Act 1980, s 154(1), Sch 7, para 143.

Sub-s (2): definitions "bail hostel" and "probation hostel" inserted by the Criminal Justice Act 1988, s 170(1), Sch 15, para 52; definition omitted repealed, and words in square brackets in definition "court" substituted, by the Criminal Law Act 1977, s 65(4), (5), Schs 12, 13; words in square brackets in definition "proceedings against a fugitive offender" substituted by the Extradition Act 1989, s 36(3).

*Incidents of bail in criminal proceedings*

## 3 General provisions

(1) A person granted bail in criminal proceedings shall be under a duty to surrender to custody, and that duty is enforceable in accordance with section 6 of this Act.

(2) No recognizance for his surrender to custody shall be taken from him.

(3) Except as provided by this section—

(a) no security for his surrender to custody shall be taken from him,
(b) he shall not be required to provide a surety or sureties for his surrender to custody, and
(c) no other requirement shall be imposed on him as a condition of bail.

(4) He may be required, before release on bail, to provide a surety or sureties to secure his surrender to custody.

(5) If it appears that he is unlikely to remain in Great Britain until the time appointed for him to surrender to custody, he may be required, before release on bail, to give security for his surrender to custody.

The security may be given by him or on his behalf.

(6) He may be required . . . to comply, before release on bail or later, with such requirements as appear to the court to be necessary to secure that—

(a) he surrenders to custody,
(b) he does not commit an offence while on bail,
(c) he does not interfere with witnesses or otherwise obstruct the course of justice whether in relation to himself or any other person,
(d) he makes himself available for the purpose of enabling inquiries or a report to be made to assist the court in dealing with him for the offence

[and, in any Act, "the normal powers to impose conditions of bail" means the powers to impose conditions under paragraph (a), (b) or (c) above].

[(6ZA)Where he is required under subsection (6) above to reside in a bail hostel or probation hostel, he may also be required to comply with the rules of the hostel.]

[(6A) In the case of a person accused of murder the court granting bail shall, unless it considers that satisfactory reports on his mental condition have already been obtained, impose as conditions of bail—

    (a)  a requirement that the accused shall undergo examination by two medical practitioners for the purpose of enabling such reports to be prepared; and

    (b)  a requirement that he shall for that purpose attend such an institution or place as the court directs and comply with any other directions which may be given to him for that purpose by either of those practitioners.

(6B) Of the medical practitioners referred to in subsection (6A) above at least one shall be a practitioner approved for the purposes of [section 12 of the Mental Health Act 1983].]

(7)    If a parent or guardian of a child or young person consents to be surety for the child or young person for the purposes of this subsection, the parent or guardian may be required to secure that the child or young person complies with any requirement imposed on him by virtue of [subsection (6) or (6A) above] but—

    (a)  no requirement shall be imposed on the parent or the guardian of a young person by virtue of this subsection where it appears that the young person will attain the age of seventeen before the time to be appointed for him to surrender to custody; and

    (b)  the parent or guardian shall not be required to secure compliance with any requirement to which his consent does not extend and shall not, in respect of those requirements to which his consent does extend, be bound in a sum greater than £50.

(8)    Where a court has granted bail in criminal proceedings [that court or, where that court has committed a person on bail to the Crown Court for trial or to be sentenced or otherwise dealt with, that court or the Crown Court may] on application—

    (a)  by or on behalf of the person to whom [bail was] granted, or

    (b)  by the prosecutor or a constable,

vary the conditions of bail or impose conditions in respect of bail which [has been] granted unconditionally.

[(8A) Where a notice of transfer is given under [a relevant transfer provision], subsection (8) above shall have effect in relation to a person in relation to whose case the notice is given as if he had been committed on bail.]

(9)    This section is subject to [sub-section (2) of section 30 of the Magistrates' Courts Act 1980] (conditions of bail on remand for medical examination).

[(10) This section is subject, in its application to bail granted by a constable, to section 3A of this Act.]

[(10) In subsection (8A) above "relevant transfer provision" means—

    (a)  section 4 of the Criminal Justice Act 1987, or

    (b)  section 53 of the Criminal Justice Act 1991.]

---

NOTES

    Commencment: 10 April 1995 (first sub-s (10)); 3 February 1995 (second sub-s (10)); 31 October 1988 (sub-s (8A)); 12 October 1988 (sub-s (6ZA)); 30 September 1983 (sub-ss (6A), (6B)); 17 April 1978 (remainder).

Sub-s (6): words omitted repealed, and words in square brackets added, by the Criminal Justice and Public Order Act 1994, ss 27(2)(a), (b), 168(1), (3), Sch 11.

Sub-s (6ZA): inserted by the Criminal Justice Act 1988, s 131(1).

Sub-s (6A): inserted by the Mental Health (Amendment) Act 1982, s 34(2).

Sub-s (6B): inserted by the Mental Health (Amendment) Act 1982, s 34(2); words in square brackets substituted by the Mental Health Act 1983, s 148, Sch 4, para 46.

Sub-s (7): words in square brackets substituted by the Mental Health (Amendment) Act 1982, s 34(3).

Sub-s (8): words in square brackets substituted by the Criminal Law Act 1977, s 65(4), Sch 12.

Sub-s (8A): inserted by the Criminal Justice Act 1987, s 15, Sch 2, para 9; words in square brackets substituted by the Criminal Justice and Public Order Act 1994, 168(1), Sch 9, para 12(a).

Sub-s (9): words in square brackets substituted by the Magistrates' Courts Act 1980, s 154, Sch 7, para 144.

First sub-s (10): added by the Criminal Justice and Public Order Act 1994, s 27(2)(c).

Second sub-s (10): added by the Criminal Justice and Public Order Act 1994, s 168(1), Sch 9, para 12(b).

*Bail for accused persons and others*

## 4   General right to bail of accused persons and others

(1)   A person to whom this section applies shall be granted bail except as provided in Schedule 1 to this Act.

(2)   This section applies to a person who is accused of an offence when—

(a)   he appears or is brought before a magistrates' court or the Crown Court in the course of or in connection with proceedings for the offence, or

(b)   he applies to a court for bail [or for a variation of the conditions of bail] in connection with the proceedings.

This subsection does not apply as respects proceedings on or after a person's conviction of the offence or proceedings against a fugitive offender for the offence.

(3)   This section also applies to a person who, having been convicted of an offence, appears or is brought before a magistrates' court to be dealt with under [Part II of Schedule 2 to the Criminal Justice Act 1991 (breach of requirement of probation, community service, combination or curfew order)].

(4)   This section also applies to a person who has been convicted of an offence and whose case is adjourned by the court for the purpose of enabling inquiries or a report to be made to assist the court in dealing with him for the offence.

(5)   Schedule 1 to this Act also has effect as respects conditions of bail for a person to whom this section applies.

(6)   In Schedule 1 to this Act "the defendant" means a person to whom this section applies and any reference to a defendant whose case is adjourned for inquiries or a report is a reference to a person to whom this section applies by virtue of subsection   (4) above.

(7)   This section is subject to [section 41 of the Magistrates' Courts Act 1980] (restriction of bail by magistrates court in cases of treason).

[(8)   This section is subject to section 25 of the Criminal Justice and Public Order Act 1994 (exclusion of bail in cases of homicide and rape).]

NOTES

Commencement: 10 April 1995 (sub-s (8)); 17 April 1978 (remainder).

Sub-s (2): words in square brackets in para (b) inserted by the Criminal Justice and Public Order Act 1994, s 168(2), Sch 10, para 33.

Sub-s (3): words in square brackets substituted by the Criminal Justice Act 1991, s 100, Sch 11, para 21.

Sub-s (7): words in square brackets substituted by the Magistrates' Courts Act 1980, s 154(1), Sch 7, para 145.

Sub-s (8): added by the Criminal Justice and Public Order Act 1994, s 168(2), Sch 10, para 32.

*Supplementary*

## [5B Reconsideration of decisions granting bail

(1) Where a magistrates' court has granted bail in criminal proceedings in connection with an offence, or proceedings for an offence, to which this section applies or a constable has granted bail in criminal proceedings in connection with proceedings for such an offence, that court or the appropriate court in relation to the constable may, on application by the prosecutor for the decision to be reconsidered,—

    (a) vary the conditions of bail,

    (b) impose conditions in respect of bail which has been granted unconditionally, or

    (c) withhold bail.

(2) The offences to which this section applies are offences triable on indictment and offences triable either way.

(3) No application for the reconsideration of a decision under this section shall be made unless it is based on information which was not available to the court or constable when the decision was taken.

(4) Whether or not the person to whom the application relates appears before it, the magistrates' court shall take the decision in accordance with section 4(1) (and Schedule 1) of this Act.

(5) Where the decision of the court on a reconsideration under this section is to withhold bail from the person to whom it was originally granted the court shall—

    (a) if that person is before the court, remand him in custody, and

    (b) if that person is not before the court, order him to surrender himself forthwith into the custody of the court.

(6) Where a person surrenders himself into the custody of the court in compliance with an order under subsection (5) above, the court shall remand him in custody.

(7) A person who has been ordered to surrender to custody under subsection (5) above may be arrested without warrant by a constable if he fails without reasonable cause to surrender to custody in accordance with the order.

(8) A person arrested in pursuance of subsection (7) above shall be brought as soon as practicable, and in any event within 24 hours after his arrest, before a justice of the peace for the petty sessions area in which he was arrested and the justice shall remand him in custody.

In reckoning for the purposes of this subsection any period of 24 hours, no account shall be taken of Christmas Day, Good Friday or any Sunday.

(9) Magistrates' court rules shall include provision—

    (a) requiring notice of an application under this section and of the grounds for it to be given to the person affected, including notice of the powers available to the court under it;

    (b) for securing that any representations made by the person affected (whether in writing or orally) are considered by the court before making its decision; and

    (c) designating the court which is the appropriate court in relation to the decision of any constable to grant bail.]

NOTES

Commencement: 10 April 1995.

Inserted by the Criminal Justice and Public Order Act 1994, s 30.

## 8   Bail with sureties

(1)   This section applies where a person is granted bail in criminal proceedings on condition that he provides one or more surety or sureties for the purpose of securing that he surrenders to custody.

(2)   In considering the suitability for that purpose of a proposed surety, regard may be had (amongst other things) to—

(a)   the surety's financial resources;

(b)   his character and any previous convictions of his; and

(c)   his proximity (whether in point of kinship, place of residence or otherwise) to the person for whom he is to be surety.

(3)   Where a court grants a person bail in criminal proceedings on such a condition but is unable to release him because no surety or no suitable surety is available, the court shall fix the amount in which the surety is to be bound and subsections (4) and (5) below, or in a case where the proposed surety resides in Scotland subsection (6) below, shall apply for the purpose of enabling the recognizance of the surety to be entered into subsequently.

(4)   Where this subsection applies the recognizance of the surety may be entered into before such of the following persons or descriptions of persons as the court may by order specify or, if it makes no such order, before any of the following persons, that is to say—

(a)   where the decision is taken by a magistrates' court, before a justice of the peace, a justices' clerk or a police officer who either is of the rank of inspector or above or is in charge of a police station or, if magistrates' courts rules so provide, by a person of such other description as is specified in the rules;

(b)   where the decision is taken by the Crown Court, before any of the persons specified in paragraph (a) above or, if Crown Court rules so provide, by a person of such other description as is specified in the rules;

(c)   where the decision is taken by the High Court or the Court of Appeal, before any of the persons specified in paragraph (a) above or, if Supreme Court rules so provide, by a person of such other description as is specified in the rules;

(d)   where the decision is taken by the Courts-Martial Appeal Court, before any of the persons specified in paragraph (a) above or, if Courts-Martial Appeal rules so provide, by a person of such other description as is specified in the rules;

and Supreme Court rules, Crown Court rules, Courts-Martial Appeal rules or magistrates' courts rules may also prescribe the manner in which a recognizance which is to be entered into before such a person is to be entered into and the persons by whom and the manner in which the recognizance may be enforced.

(5)   Where a surety seeks to enter into his recognizance before any person in accordance with subsection (4) above but that person declines to take his recognizance because he is not satisfied of the surety's suitability, the surety may apply to—

(a)   the court which fixed the amount of the recognizance in which the surety was to be bound, or

(b)   a magistrates' court for the petty sessions area in which he resides,

for that court to take his recognizance and that court shall, if satisfied of his suitability, take his recognizance.

(6)    Where this subsection applies, the court, if satisfied of the suitability of the proposed surety, may direct that arrangements be made for the recognizance of the surety to be entered into in Scotland before any constable, within the meaning of the Police (Scotland) Act 1967, having charge at any police office or station in like manner as the recognizance would be entered into in England or Wales.

(7)    Where, in pursuance of subsection (4) or (6) above, a recognizance is entered into otherwise than before the court that fixed the amount of the recognizance, the same consequences shall follow as if it had been entered into before that court.

*Miscellaneous*

**13    Short title, commencement, application and extent**

(1)    This Act may be cited as the Bail Act 1976.

(2)    This Act (except this section) shall come into force on such day as the Secretary of State may by order in a statutory instrument appoint.

(3)    Section 1 of this Act applies to bail grantable by the Courts-Martial Appeal Court when sitting outside England and Wales and accordingly section 6 of this Act applies to a failure outside England and Wales by a person granted bail by that Court to surrender to custody.

(4)    Except as provided by subsection (3) above and with the exception of so much of section 8 as relates to entering into recognizances in Scotland and paragraphs 31 and 46 of Schedule 2 to this Act, this Act does not extend beyond England and Wales.

# SCHEDULE 1
# PERSONS ENTITLED TO BAIL: SUPPLEMENTARY PROVISIONS

Section 4

## PART I
### DEFENDANTS ACCUSED OR CONVICTED OF IMPRISONABLE OFFENCES

*Defendants to whom Part I applies*

1.    Where the offence or one of the offences of which the defendant is accused or convicted in the proceedings is punishable with imprisonment the following provisions of this Part of this Schedule apply.

*Exceptions to right to bail*

2.    The defendant need not be granted bail if the court is satisfied that there are substantial grounds for believing that the defendant, if released on bail (whether subject to conditions or not) would—
   (a)    fail to surrender to custody, or
   (b)    commit an offence while on bail, or
   (c)    interfere with witnesses or otherwise obstruct the course of justice, whether in relation to himself or any other person.

[2A. The defendant need not be granted bail if—
   (a)    the offence is an indictable offence or an offence triable either way; and
   (b)    it appears to the court that he was on bail in criminal proceedings on the date of the offence.]

3.    The defendant need not be granted bail if the court is satisfied that the defendant should be kept in custody for his own protection or, if he is a child or young person, for his own welfare.

4.    The defendant need not be granted bail if he is in custody in pursuance of the sentence of a court or of any authority acting under any of the Services Acts.

5.    The defendant need not be granted bail where the court is satisfied that it has not been practicable to obtain sufficient information for the purpose of taking the decisions required by this Part of this Schedule for want of time since the institution of the proceedings against him.

6.    The defendant need not be granted bail if, having been released on bail in or in connection with the proceedings for the offence, he has been arrested in pursuance of section 7 of this Act.

*Exception applicable only to defendant whose case is adjourned for inquiries or a report*

7.    Where his case is adjourned for inquiries or a report, the defendant need not be granted bail if it appears to the court that it would be impracticable to complete the inquiries or make the report without keeping the defendant in custody.

*Restriction of conditions of bail*

8.—(1)Subject to sub-paragraph (3) below, where the defendant is granted bail, no conditions shall be imposed under subsections (4) to (7) [(except subsection (6)(d))] of section 3 of this Act unless it appears to the court that it is necessary to do so for the purpose of preventing the occurrence of any of the events mentioned in paragraph 2 of this Part of this Schedule . . .

[(1A)No condition shall be imposed under section 3(6)(d) of this Act unless it appears to be necessary to do so for the purpose of enabling inquiries or a report to be made.]

(2)  [Sub-paragraphs (1) and (1A) above also apply] on any application to the court to vary the conditions of bail or to impose conditions in respect of bail which has been granted unconditionally.

(3)  The restriction imposed by [sub-paragraph (1A)] above shall not [apply to the conditions required to be imposed under section 3(6A) of this Act or] operate to override the direction in [section 30(2) of the Magistrates' Courts Act 1980] to a magistrates' court to impose conditions of bail under section 3(6)(d) of this Act of the description specified in [the said section 30(2)] in the circumstances so specified.

*Decisions under paragraph 2*

9.    In taking the decisions required by paragraph 2 [or 2A] of this Part of this Schedule, the court shall have regard to such of the following considerations as appear to it to be relevant, that is to say—

  (a)   the nature and seriousness of the offence or default (and the probable method of dealing with the defendant for it),

  (b)   the character, antecedents, associations and community ties of the defendant,

  (c)   the defendant's record as respects the fulfilment of his obligations under previous grants of bail in criminal proceedings,

  (d)   except in the case of a defendant whose case is adjourned for inquiries or a report, the strength of the evidence of his having committed the offence or having defaulted,

as well as to any others which appear to be relevant.

[9A.—(1)If—

  (a)   the defendant is charged with an offence to which this paragraph applies; and

  (b)   representations are made as to any of the matters mentioned in paragraph 2 of this Part of this Schedule; and

  (c)   the court decides to grant him bail,

the court shall state the reasons for its decision and shall cause those reasons to be included in the record of the proceedings.

(2) The offences to which this paragraph applies are—
  (a) murder;
  (b) manslaughter;
  (c) rape;
  (d) attempted murder; and
  (e) attempted rape.]

[*Cases under section 128A of Magistrates' Courts Act 1980*

9B. Where the court is considering exercising the power conferred by section 128A of the Magistrates' Courts Act 1980 (power to remand in custody for more than 8 clear days), it shall have regard to the total length of time which the accused would spend in custody if it were to exercise the power.]

NOTES

Commencement: 10 April 1995 (para 2A); 5 January 1989 (para 9A); 12 October 1988 (para 9B); 17 April 1978 (remainder).

Para 2A: inserted by the Criminal Justice and Public Order Act 1994, s 26(a).

Para 8: words in square brackets in sub-para (1) inserted, and words omitted repealed, sub-para (1A) inserted, and words in square brackets in sub-para (2) substituted, by the Criminal Justice Act 1991, ss 100, 101(2), Sch 11, para 22, Sch 13; words in first pair of square brackets in sub-para (3) substituted by the Criminal Justice Act 1991, s 100, Sch 11, para 22, words in second pair of square brackets inserted by the Mental Health (Amendment) Act 1982, s 34(4), third and fourth words in square brackets substituted by the Magistrates' Courts Act 1980, s 154, Sch 7, para 146.

Para 9: words in square brackets inserted by the Criminal Justice and Public Order Act 1994, s 26(b).

Para 9A: added by the Criminal Justice Act 1988, s 153.

Para 9B: added, together with cross-heading, by the Criminal Justice Act 1988, s 155(2).

Services Acts: Army Act 1955, Air Force Act 1955, Naval Discipline Act 1957.

# PART II
## DEFENDANTS ACCUSED OR CONVICTED OF NON-IMPRISONABLE OFFENCES

*Defendants to whom Part II applies*

1.  Where the offence or every offence of which the defendant is accused or convicted in the proceedings is one which is not punishable with imprisonment the following provisions of this Part of this Schedule apply.

*Exceptions to right to bail*

2.  The defendant need not be granted bail if—
  (a) it appears to the court that, having been previously granted bail in criminal proceedings, he has failed to surrender to custody in accordance with his obligations under the grant of bail; and
  (b) the court believes, in view of that failure, that the defendant, if released on bail (whether subject to conditions or not) would fail to surrender to custody.

3.  The defendant need not be granted bail if the court is satisfied that the defendant should be kept in custody for his own protection or, if he is a child or young person, for his own welfare.

4.  The defendant need not be granted bail if he is in custody in pursuance of the sentence of a court or of any authority acting under any of the Services Acts.

5.  The defendant need not be granted bail if, having been released on bail in or in connection with the proceedings for the offence, he has been arrested in pursuance of section 7 of this Act.

NOTES

Services Acts: Army Act 1955, Air Force Act 1955, Naval Discipline Act 1957.

## [PART IIA
### DECISIONS WHERE BAIL REFUSED ON PREVIOUS HEARING

1.   If the court decides not to grant the defendant bail, it is the court's duty to consider, at each subsequent hearing while the defendant is a person to whom section 4 above applies and remains in custody, whether he ought to be granted bail.

2.   At the first hearing after that at which the court decided not to grant the defendant bail he may support an application for bail with any argument as to fact or law that he desires (whether or not he has advanced that argument previously).

3.   At subsequent hearings the court need not hear arguments as to fact or law which it has heard previously.]

**NOTES**
Inserted by the Criminal Justice Act 1988, s 154.

## PART III
### INTERPRETATION

1.   For the purposes of this Schedule the question whether an offence is one which is punishable with imprisonment shall be determined without regard to any enactment prohibiting or restricting the imprisonment of young offenders or first offenders.

2.   References in this Schedule to previous grants of bail in criminal proceedings include references to bail granted before the coming into force of this Act; [and so as respects the reference to an offence committed by a person on bail in relation to any period before the coming into force of paragraph 2A of Part I of this Schedule].

3.   References in this Schedule to a defendant's being kept in custody or being in custody include (where the defendant is a child or young person) references to his being kept or being in the care of a local authority in pursuance of a warrant of commitment under section 23(1) of the Children and Young Persons Act 1969.

4.   In this Schedule—
     "court", in the expression "sentence of a court" includes a service court as defined in section 12(1) of the Visiting Forces Act 1952 and "sentence", in that expression, shall be construed in accordance with that definition;
     "default", in relation to the defendant, means the default for which he is to be dealt with under section 6 or section 16 of the Powers of Criminal Courts Act 1973;
     "the Services Acts" means the Army Act 1955, the Air Force Act 1955 and the Naval Discipline Act 1957.

**NOTES**
Para 2: words in square brackets added by the Criminal Justice and Public Order Act 1994, s 168(2), Sch 10, para 34.

# DOMESTIC VIOLENCE AND MATRIMONIAL PROCEEDINGS ACT 1976

## (C 50)

*An Act to amend the law relating to matrimonial injunction; to provide the police with powers of arrest for the breach of injunction in cases of domestic violence; to amend section 1(2) of the Matrimonial Homes Act 1967; to make provision for varying rights of occupation where both spouses have the same rights in the matrimonial home; and for purposes connected therewith*
[26 October 1976]

**1   Matrimonial injunctions in the county court**

*(1)    Without prejudice to the jurisdiction of the High Court, on an application by a party to a marriage a county court shall have jurisdiction to grant an injunction containing one or more of the following provisions, namely,—*

  *(a)   a provision restraining the other party to the marriage from molesting the applicant;*

  *(b)   a provision restraining the other party from molesting a child living with the applicant;*

  *(c)   a provision excluding the other party from the matrimonial home or a part of the matrimonial home or from a specified area in which the matrimonial home is included;*

  *(d)   a provision requiring the other party to permit the applicant to enter and remain in the matrimonial home or a part of the matrimonial home;*

*whether or not any other relief is sought in the proceedings.*

*(2)    Subsection (1) above shall apply to a man and a woman who are living with each other in the same household as husband and wife as it applies to the parties to a marriage and any reference to the matrimonial home shall be construed accordingly.*

NOTES

Repealed, together with s 5 of this Act, by the Family Law Act 1996, s 66(3), Sch 10, subject to savings in s 66(2) of, and Sch 9, paras 5, 8, 10 to, the 1996 Act, as from 1 October 1997.

**5   Short title, commencement and extent**

*(1)    This Act may be cited as the Domestic Violence and Matrimonial Proceedings Act 1976.*

*(2)    This Act shall come into force on such day as the Lord Chancellor may appoint by order made by statutory instrument, and different days may be appointed for different provisions of this Act:*

*Provided that if any provisions of this Act are not in force on 1st April 1977, the Lord Chancellor shall then make an order by statutory instrument bringing such provisions into force.*

*(3)    This Act shall not extend to Northern Ireland or Scotland.*

NOTES

Repealed as noted to s 1.

# RACE RELATIONS ACT 1976

## (C 74)

*An Act to make fresh provision with respect to discrimination on racial grounds and relations between people of different racial groups; and to make in the Sex Discrimination Act 1975 amendments for bringing provisions in that Act relating to its administration and enforcement into conformity with the corresponding provisions in this Act*

[22 November 1976]

# PART I
# DISCRIMINATION TO WHICH ACT APPLIES

## 1 Racial discrimination

(1)   A person discriminates against another in any circumstances relevant for the purposes of any provision of this Act if—

    (a)  on racial grounds he treats that other less favourably than he treats or would treat other persons; or

    (b)  he applies to that other a requirement or condition which he applies or would apply equally to persons not of the same racial group as that other but—

        (i)  which is such that the proportion of persons of the same racial group as that other who can comply with it is considerably smaller than the proportion of persons not of that racial group who can comply with it; and

        (ii)  which he cannot show to be justifiable irrespective of the colour, race, nationality or ethnic or national origins of the person to whom it is applied; and

        (iii)  which is to the detriment of that other because he cannot comply with it.

(2)   It is hereby declared that, for the purposes of this Act, segregating a person from other persons on racial grounds is treating him less favourably than they are treated.

## 2 Discrimination by way of victimisation

(1)   A person ("the discriminator") discriminates against another person ("the person victimised") in any circumstances relevant for the purposes of any provision of this Act if he treats the person victimised less favourably than in those circumstances he treats or would treat other persons, and does so by reason that the person victimised has—

    (a)  brought proceedings against the discriminator or any other person under this Act; or

    (b)  given evidence or information in connection with proceedings brought by any person against the discriminator or any other person under this Act; or

    (c)  otherwise done anything under or by reference to this Act in relation to the discriminator or any other person; or

    (d)  alleged that the discriminator or any other person has committed an act which (whether or not the allegation so states) would amount to a contravention of this Act,

or by reason that the discriminator knows that the person victimised intends to do any of those things, or suspects that the person victimised has done, or intends to do, any of them.

(2)   Subsection (1) does not apply to treatment of a person by reason of any allegation made by him if the allegation was false and not made in good faith.

## 3 Meaning of "racial grounds", "racial group" etc

(1)   In this Act, unless the context otherwise requires—

    "racial grounds" means any of the following grounds, namely colour, race nationality or ethnic or national origins;

    "racial group" means a group of persons defined by reference to colour, race, nationality or ethnic or national origins, and references to a person's racial group refer to any racial group into which he falls.

(2)–(4). . .

NOTES

Sub-ss (2)–(4): outside the scope of this work.

# PART II
# DISCRIMINATION IN THE EMPLOYMENT FIELD

*Discrimination by employers*

## 4 Discrimination against applicants and employees

(1)    It is unlawful for a person, in relation to employment by him at an establishment in Great Britain, to discriminate against another—

    (a)   in the arrangements he makes for the purpose of determining who should be offered that employment; or

    (b)   in the terms on which he offers him that employment; or

    (c)   by refusing or deliberately omitting to offer him that employment.

(2)    It is unlawful for a person, in the case of a person employed by him at an establishment in Great Britain, to discriminate against that employee—

    (a)   in the terms of employment which he affords him; or

    (b)   in the way he affords him access to opportunities for promotion, transfer or training, or to any other benefits, facilities or services, or by refusing or deliberately omitting to afford him access to them; or

    (c)   by dismissing him, or subjecting him to any other detriment.

(3)    Except in relation to discrimination falling within section 2, subsections (1) and    (2) do not apply to employment for the purposes of a private household.

(4)    Subsection (2) does not apply to benefits, facilities or services of any description if the employer is concerned with the provision (for payment or not) of benefits, facilities or services of that description to the public, or to a section of the public comprising the employee in question, unless—

    (a)   that provision differs in a material respect from the provision of the benefits, facilities or services by the employer to his employees; or

    (b)   the provision of the benefits, facilities or services to the employee in question is regulated by his contract of employment; or

    (c)   the benefits, facilities or services relate to training.

NOTES

Modified, in relation to governing bodies with delegated budgets, by the Education (Modification of Enactments Relating to Employment) Order 1989, SI 1989/901, art 3, Schedule.

## 5 Exceptions for genuine occupational qualifications

(1)    In relation to racial discrimination—

    (a)   section 4(1)(a) or (c) does not apply to any employment where being of a particular racial group is a genuine occupational qualification for the job; and

    (b)   section 4(2)(b) does not apply to opportunities for promotion or transfer to, or training for, such employment.

(2)    Being of a particular racial group is a genuine occupational qualification for a job only where—

(a) the job involves participation in a dramatic performance or other entertainment in a capacity for which a person of that racial group is required for reasons of authenticity; or

(b) the job involves participation as an artist's or photographic model in the production of a work of art, visual image or sequence of visual images for which a person of that racial group is required for reasons of authenticity; or

(c) the job involves working in a place where food or drink is (for payment or not) provided to and consumed by members of the public or a section of the public in a particular setting for which, in that job, a person of that racial group is required for reasons of authenticity; or

(d) the holder of the job provides persons of that racial group with personal services promoting their welfare, and those services can most effectively be provided by a person of that racial group.

(3) Subsection (2) applies where some only of the duties of the job fall within paragraph (a), (b), (c) or (d) as well as where all of them do.

(4) Paragraph (a), (b), (c) or (d) of subsection (2) does not apply in relation to the filling of a vacancy at a time when the employer already has employees of the racial group in question—

(a) who are capable of carrying out the duties falling within that paragraph; and

(b) whom it would be reasonable to employ on those duties; and

(c) whose numbers are sufficient to meet the employer's likely requirements in respect of those duties without undue inconvenience.

NOTES

Modified, in relation to governing bodies with delegated budgets, by the Education (Modification of Enactments Relating to Employment) Order 1989, SI 1989/901, art 3, Schedule.

# PART IV
# OTHER UNLAWFUL ACTS

## 28 Discriminatory practices

(1) In this section "discriminatory practice" means the application of a requirement or condition which results in an act of discrimination which is unlawful by virtue of any provision of Part II or III taken with section 1(1)(b), or which would be likely to result in such an act of discrimination if the persons to whom it is applied included persons of any particular racial group as regards which there has been no occasion for applying it.

(2) A person acts in contravention of this section if and so long as—

(a) he applies a discriminatory practice; or

(b) he operates practices or other arrangements which in any circumstances would call for the application by him of a discriminatory practice.

(3) Proceedings in respect of a contravention of this section shall be brought only by the Commission in accordance with sections 58 to 62.

## 29 Discriminatory advertisements

(1) It is unlawful to publish or to cause to be published an advertisement which indicates, or might reasonably be understood as indicating, an intention by a person to do an act of discrimination, whether the doing of that act by him would be lawful or, by virtue of Part II or III, unlawful.

(2)    Subsection (1) does not apply to an advertisement—

    (a)   if the intended act would be lawful by virtue of any of sections 5, 6, 7(3) and (4), 10(3), 26, 34(2)(b), 35 to 39 and 41; or

    (b)   if the advertisement relates to the services of an employment agency (within the meaning of section 14(1)) and the intended act only concerns employment which the employer could by virtue of section 5, 6 or 7(3) or (4) lawfully refuse to offer to persons against whom the advertisement indicates an intention to discriminate.

(3)    Subsection (1) does not apply to an advertisement which indicates that persons of any class defined otherwise than by reference to colour, race or ethnic or national origins are required for employment outside Great Britain.

(4)    The publisher of an advertisement made unlawful by subsection (1) shall not be subject to any liability under that subsection in respect of the publication of the advertisement if he proves—

    (a)   that the advertisement was published in reliance on a statement made to him by the person who caused it to be published to the effect that, by reason of the operation of subsection (2) or (3), the publication would not be unlawful; and

    (b)   that it was reasonable for him to rely on the statement.

(5)    A person who knowingly or recklessly makes a statement such as is mentioned in subsection (4)(a) which in a material respect is false or misleading commits an offence, and shall be liable on summary conviction to a fine not exceeding [level 5 on the standard scale].

---

NOTES

Sub-s (5): maximum fine increased and converted to a level on the standard scale by the Criminal Justice Act 1982, ss 37, 38, 46.

---

### 30    Instructions to discriminate

It is unlawful for a person—

    (a)   who has authority over another person; or

    (b)   in accordance with whose wishes that other person is accustomed to act,

to instruct him to do any act which is unlawful by virtue of Part II or III, or procure or attempt to procure the doing by him of any such act.

### 31    Pressure to discriminate

(1)    It is unlawful to induce, or attempt to induce, a person to do any act which contravenes Part II or III.

(2)    An attempted inducement is not prevented from falling within subsection (1) because it is not made directly to the person in question, if it is made in such a way that he is likely to hear of it.

### 32    Liability of employers and principals

(1)    Anything done by a person in the course of his employment shall be treated for the purposes of this Act (except as regards offences thereunder) as done by his employer as well as by him, whether or not it was done with the employer's knowledge or approval.

(2) ...

(3) In proceedings brought under this Act against any person in respect of an act alleged to have been done by an employee of his it shall be a defence for that person to prove that he took such steps as were reasonably practicable to prevent the employee from doing that act, or from doing in the course of his employment acts of that description.

NOTES

Modified, in relation to governing bodies with delegated budgets, by the Education (Modification of Enactments Relating to Employment) Order 1989, SI 1989/901, art 3, Schedule.

Sub-s (2): outside the scope of this work.

# PART VII
# THE COMMISSION FOR RACIAL EQUALITY

*General*

## 43 Establishment and duties of Commission

(1) There shall be a body of Commissioners named the Commission for Racial Equality consisting of at least eight but not more than fifteen individuals each appointed by the Secretary of State on a full-time or part-time basis, which shall have the following duties—

   (a) to work towards the elimination of discrimination;
   (b) to promote equality of opportunity, and good relations, between persons of different racial groups generally; and
   (c) to keep under review the working of this Act and, when they are so required by the Secretary of State or otherwise think it necessary, draw up and submit to the Secretary of State proposals for amending it.

(2) The Secretary of State shall appoint—

   (a) one of the Commissioners to be chairman of the Commission; and
   (b) either one or more of the Commissioners (as the Secretary of State thinks fit) to be deputy chairman or deputy chairmen of the Commission.

(3) The Secretary of State may by order amend subsection (1) so far as it regulates the number of Commissioners.

(4) Schedule 1 shall have effect with respect to the Commission.

(5) The Race Relations Board and the Community Relations Commission are hereby abolished.

## 44 Assistance to organisations

(1) The Commission may give financial or other assistance to any organisation appearing to the Commission to be concerned with the promotion of equality of opportunity, and good relations, between persons of different racial groups, but shall not give any such financial assistance out of money provided (through the Secretary of State) by Parliament except with the approval of the Secretary of State given with the consent of the Treasury.

(2) Except in so far as other arrangements for their discharge are made and approved under paragraph 13 of Schedule 1—

   (a) the Commission's functions under subsection (1); and

(b)   other functions of the Commission in relation to matters connected with the giving of such financial or other assistance as is mentioned in that subsection,

shall be discharged under the general direction of the Commission by a committee of the Commission consisting of at least three but not more than five Commissioners, of whom one shall be the deputy chairman or one of the deputy chairmen of the Commission.

## 45   Research and education

(1)   The Commission may undertake or assist (financially or otherwise) the undertaking by other persons of any research, and any educational activities, which appear to the Commission necessary or expedient for the purposes of section 43(1).

(2)   The Commission may make charges for educational or other facilities or services made available by them.

## 46   Annual reports

(1)   As soon as practicable after the end of each calendar year the Commission shall make to the Secretary of State a report on their activities during the year (an "annual report").

(2)   Each annual report shall include a general survey of developments, during the period to which it relates, in respect of matters falling within the scope of the Commission's functions.

(3)   The Secretary of State shall lay a copy of every annual report before each House of Parliament, and shall cause the report to be published.

*Codes of practice*

## 47   Codes of practice

(1)   The Commission may issue codes of practice containing such practical guidance as the Commission think fit for [all or any] of the following purposes, namely—

    (a)   the elimination of discrimination in the field of employment;
    (b)   the promotion of equality of opportunity in that field between persons of different racial groups;
    [(c)   the elimination of discrimination in the field of housing . . . ;
    (d)   the promotion of equality of opportunity in the field of . . . housing between persons of different racial groups].

(2)   When the Commission propose to issue a code of practice, they shall prepare and publish a draft of that code, shall consider any representations made to them about the draft and may modify the draft accordingly.

(3)   In the course of preparing any draft code of practice [relating to the field of employment] for eventual publication under subsection (2) the Commission shall consult with—

    (a)   such organisations or associations of organisations representative of employers or of workers; and
    (b)   such other organisations, or bodies,

as appear to the Commission to be appropriate.

[(3A) In the course of preparing any draft code of practice relating to the field of . . . housing for eventual publication under subsection (2) the Commission shall consult with such organisations or bodies as appear to the Commission to be appropriate having regard to the content of the draft code.]

(4)   If the Commission determine to proceed with [a draft code of practice], they shall transmit the draft to the Secretary of State who shall—

(a)   if he approves of it, lay it before both Houses of Parliament; and

(b)   if he does not approve of it, publish details of his reasons for withholding approval.

(5)   If, within the period of forty days beginning with the day on which a copy of a draft code of practice is laid before each House of Parliament, or, if such copies are laid on different days, with the later of the two days, either House so resolves, no further proceedings shall be taken thereon, but without prejudice to the laying before Parliament of a new draft.

(6)   In reckoning the period of forty days referred to in subsection (5), no account shall be taken of any period during which Parliament is dissolved or prorogued or during which both Houses are adjourned for more than four days.

(7)   If no such resolution is passed as is referred to in subsection (5), the Commission shall issue the code in the form of the draft and the code shall come into effect on such day as the Secretary of State may by order appoint.

(8)   Without prejudice to section 74(3), an order under subsection (7) may contain such transitional provisions or savings as appear to the Secretary of State to be necessary or expedient in connection with the code of practice thereby brought into operation.

(9)   The Commission may from time to time revise the whole or any part of a code of practice issued under this section and issue that revised code, and subsections (2) to (8) shall apply (with appropriate modifications) to such a revised code as they apply to the first issue of a code.

(10)   A failure on the part of any person to observe any provision of a code of practice shall not of itself render him liable to any proceedings; but in any proceedings under this Act before an industrial tribunal [a county court or, in Scotland, a sheriff court] any code of practice issued under this section shall be admissible in evidence, and if any provision of such a code appears to the tribunal [or the court] to be relevant to any question arising in the proceedings it shall be taken into account in determining that question.

(11)   Without prejudice to subsection (1), a code of practice issued under this section may include such practical guidance as the Commission think fit as to what steps it is reasonably practicable for employers to take for the purpose of preventing their employees from doing in the course of their employment acts made unlawful by this Act.

---

NOTES

Sub-s (1): words in first pair of square brackets substituted, and sub-paras (c), (d) added, by the Housing Act 1988, s 137(2); words omitted repealed by the Local Government and Housing Act 1989, ss 180, 194(4), Sch 12, Pt II.

Sub-ss (3), (10): words in square brackets inserted by the Housing Act 1988, s 137(3), (5).

Sub-s (3A): inserted by the Housing Act 1988, s 137(3); word omitted repealed by the Local Government and Housing Act 1989, ss 180, 194(4), Sch 12, Pt II.

Sub-s (4): words in square brackets substituted by the Housing Act 1988, s 137(4).

The only relevant code made under this section is the Code of Practice for the Elimination of Racial Discrimination and the Promotion of Equality of Opportunity in Employment 1983. Other Codes of Practice relate to rented and non-rented housing.

---

*Investigations*

## 48 Power to conduct formal investigations

(1) Without prejudice to their general power to do anything requisite for the performance of their duties under section 43(1) the Commission may if they think fit, and shall if required by the Secretary of State, conduct a formal investigation for any purpose connected with the carrying out of those duties.

(2) The Commission may, with the approval of the Secretary of State, appoint, on a full-time or part-time basis, one or more individuals as additional Commissioners for the purposes of a formal investigation.

(3) The Commission may nominate one or more Commissioners, with or without one or more additional Commissioners, to conduct a formal investigation on their behalf, and may delegate any of their functions in relation to the investigation to the persons so nominated.

## 49 Terms of reference

(1) The Commission shall not embark on a formal investigation unless the requirements of this section have been complied with.

(2) Terms of reference for the investigation shall be drawn up by the Commission or, if the Commission were required by the Secretary of State to conduct the investigation, by the Secretary of State after consulting the Commission.

(3) It shall be the duty of the Commission to give general notice of the holding of the investigation unless the terms of reference confine it to activities of persons named in them, but in such a case the Commission shall in the prescribed manner give those persons notice of the holding of the investigation.

(4) Where the terms of reference of the investigation confine it to activities of persons named in them and the Commission in the course of it propose to investigate any act made unlawful by this Act which they believe that a person so named may have done, the Commission shall—

    (a) inform that person of their belief and of their proposal to investigate the act in question; and

    (b) offer him an opportunity of making oral or written representations with regard to it (or both oral and written representations if he thinks fit);

and a person so named who avails himself of an opportunity under this subsection of making oral representations may be represented—

    (i) by counsel or a solicitor; or

    (ii) by some other person of his choice, not being a person to whom the Commission object on the ground that he is unsuitable.

(5) The Commission or, if the Commission were required by the Secretary of State to conduct the investigation, the Secretary of State after consulting the Commission may from time to time revise the terms of reference; and subsections (1), (3) and (4) shall apply to the revised investigation and terms of reference as they applied to the original.

## PART VIII
## ENFORCEMENT

*Help for persons suffering discrimination*

### 66 Assistance by Commission

(1)   Where, in relation to proceedings or prospective proceedings under this Act, an individual who is an actual or prospective complainant or claimant applies to the Commission for assistance under this section, the Commission shall consider the application and may grant it if they think fit to do so—

(a)   on the ground that the case raises a question of principle; or

(b)   on the ground that it is unreasonable, having regard to the complexity of the case, or to the applicant's position in relation to the respondent or another person involved, or to any other matter, to expect the applicant to deal with the case unaided; or

(c)   by reason of any other special consideration.

(2)   Assistance by the Commission under this section may include—

(a)   giving advice;

(b)   procuring or attempting to procure the settlement of any matter in dispute;

(c)   arranging for the giving of advice or assistance by a solicitor or counsel;

(d)   arranging for representation by any person, including all such assistance as is usually given by a solicitor or counsel in the steps preliminary or incidental to any proceedings, or in arriving at or giving effect to a compromise to avoid or bring to an end any proceedings;

(e)   any other form of assistance which the Commission may consider appropriate,

but paragraph (d) shall not affect the law and practice regulating the descriptions of persons who may appear in, conduct, defend, and address the court in, any proceedings.

(3)   Where under subsection (1) an application for assistance under this section is made in writing, the Commission shall, within the period of two months beginning when the application is received—

(a)   consider the application after making such enquiries as they think fit; and

(b)   decide whether or not to grant it; and

(c)   inform the applicant of their decision, stating whether or not assistance under this section is to be provided by the Commission and, if so, what form it will take.

(4)   If, in a case where subsection (3) applies, the Commission within the period of two months there mentioned give notice to the applicant that, in relation to his application—

(a)   the period of two months allowed them by that subsection is by virtue of the notice extended to three months; and

(b)   the reference to two months in section 68(3) is by virtue of the notice to be read as a reference to three months,

subsection (3) and section 68(3) shall have effect accordingly.

(5)   In so far as expenses are incurred by the Commission in providing the applicant with assistance under this section, the recovery of those expenses (as taxed or assessed in such manner as may be prescribed by rules or regulations) shall constitute a first charge for the benefit of the Commission—

   (a)   on any costs or expenses which (whether by virtue of a judgment or order of a court or tribunal or an agreement or otherwise) are payable to the applicant by any other person in respect of the matter in connection with which the assistance is given; and

   (b)   so far as relates to any costs or expenses, on his rights under any compromise or settlement arrived at in connection with that matter to avoid or bring to an end any proceedings.

(6)   The charge conferred by subsection (5) is subject to any charge under the [Legal Aid Act 1988], or any charge or obligation for payment in priority to other debts under [the Legal Aid (Scotland) Act 1986], and is subject to any provision in [either of those Acts for payment of any sum to the Legal Aid Board or into the Scottish Legal Aid Fund].

(7)   In this section "respondent" includes a prospective respondent and "rules or regulations"—

   (a)   in relation to county court proceedings, means county court rules;

   (b)   in relation to sheriff court proceedings, means sheriff court rules;

   (c)   in relation to industrial tribunal proceedings, means regulations made under [industrial tribunal procedure regulations under Part I of the Industrial Tribunals Act 1996].

NOTES

Sub-s (6): words in first and third pairs of square brackets substituted by the Legal Aid Act 1988, s 45(1), (3), Sch 5, para 7; words in second pair of square brackets substituted by the Legal Aid (Scotland) Act 1986, s 45(1), Sch 3, para 6.

Sub-s (7): words in square brackets substituted by the Industrial Tribunals Act 1996, s 43, Sch 1, para 4.

# NATIONAL HEALTH SERVICE ACT 1977

## (C 49)

*An Act to consolidate certain provisions relating to the health service for England and Wales; and to repeal certain enactments relating to the health service which have ceased to have any effect*

[29 July 1977]

## PART I
## SERVICES AND ADMINISTRATION

*Functions of the Secretary of State*

### 1   Secretary of State's duty as to health service

(1)   It is the Secretary of State's duty to continue the promotion in England and Wales of a comprehensive health service designed to secure improvement—

   (a)   in the physical and mental health of the people of those countries, and

   (b)   in the prevention, diagnosis and treatment of illness,

and for that purpose to provide or secure the effective provision of services in accordance with this Act.

(2)   The services so provided shall be free of charge except in so far as the making and recovery of charges is expressly provided for by or under any enactment, whenever passed.

## 2   Secretary of State's general power as to services

Without prejudice to the Secretary of State's powers apart from this section, he has power—

(a) to provide such services as he considers appropriate for the purpose of discharging any duty imposed on him by this Act; and

(b) to do any other thing whatsoever which is calculated to facilitate, or is conducive or incidental to, the discharge of such a duty.

This section is subject to section 3(3) below.

## 3   Services generally

(1)   It is the Secretary of State's duty to provide throughout England and Wales, to such extent as he considers necessary to meet all reasonable requirements—

(a) hospital accommodation;

(b) other accommodation for the purpose of any service provided under this Act;

(c) medical, dental, nursing and ambulance services;

(d) such other facilities for the care of expectant and nursing mothers and young children as he considers are appropriate as part of the health service;

(e) such facilities for the prevention of illness, the care of persons suffering from illness and the after-care of persons who have suffered from illness as he considers are appropriate as part of the health service;

(f) such other services as are required for the diagnosis and treatment of illness.

(2)   Where any hospital provided by the Secretary of State in accordance with this Act was a voluntary hospital transferred by virtue of the National Health Service Act 1946, and—

(a) the character and associations of that hospital before its transfer were such as to link it with a particular religious denomination, then

(b) regard shall be had in the general administration of the hospital to the preservation of that character and those associations.

(3)   Nothing in section 2 above or in this section affects the provisions of Part II of this Act (which relates to arrangements with practitioners for the provision of medical, dental, ophthalmic and pharmaceutical services).

*Local administration*

## [17   Directions as to exercise of functions

(1)   The Secretary of State may give directions with respect to the exercise—

(a) by Health Authorities of any functions exercisable by them under or by virtue of this or any other Act; and

(b) by Special Health Authorities of any functions exercisable by them by virtue of section 11 or 13 above or under the National Health Service and Community Care Act 1990.

(2)   It shall be the duty of a Health Authority or Special Health Authority to whom directions are given under subsection (1) above to comply with the directions.]

NOTES

Commencement: 1 April 1996 (certain purposes), 28 June 1995 (remaining purposes).
Substituted by the Health Authorities Act 1995, ss 2(1), 8, Sch 1, para 8.

*Co-operation and assistance*

## 21 Local social services authorities

(1) Subject to paragraphs (d) and (e) of section 3(1) above, the services described in Schedule 8 to this Act in relation to—

    (a) care of mothers . . .,

    (b) prevention, care and after-care,

    (c) home help and laundry facilities,

are functions exercisable by local social services authorities, and that Schedule has effect accordingly.

(2) A local social services authority who provide premises, furniture or equipment for any of the purposes of this Act may permit the use of the premises, furniture or equipment—

    (a) by any other local social services authority, or

    (b) by any of the bodies constituted under this Act, or

    (c) by a local education authority.

This permission may be on such terms (including terms with respect to the services of any staff employed by the authority giving permission) as may be agreed.

(3) A local social services authority may provide (or improve or furnish) residential accommodation—

    (a) for officers employed by them for the purposes of any of their functions as a local social services authority, or

    (b) for officers employed by a voluntary organisation for the purposes of any services provided under this section and Schedule 8.

**NOTES**

Sub-s (1): words omitted from para (a) repealed by the Children Act 1989, s 108(7), Sch 15.

# PART VI
# MISCELLANEOUS AND SUPPLEMENTARY

*Supplementary*

## 130 Short title, extent and commencement

(1) This Act may be cited as the National Health Service Act 1977.

(2)–(4) . . .

(5) This Act shall come into force on the expiry of the period of one month beginning on the date of its passing.

**NOTES**

Sub-ss (2)–(4): outside the scope of this work.

Sub-s (3): para (c) repealed by the Health Service Commissioners Act 1993, s 20, Sch 3.

# DOMESTIC PROCEEDINGS AND MAGISTRATES' COURTS ACT 1978

## (C 22)

*An Act to make fresh provision for matrimonial proceedings in magistrates' courts; to amend enactments relating to other proceedings so as to eliminate certain differences between the law relating to those proceedings and the law relating to matrimonial proceedings in magistrates' courts; to extend section 15 of the Justices of the Peace Act 1949; to amend Part II of the Magistrates' Courts Act 1952; to amend section 2 of the Administration of Justice Act 1964; to amend the Maintenance Orders (Reciprocal Enforcement) Act 1972; to amend certain enactments relating to adoption; and for purposes connected with those matters*

[30 June 1978]

## PART I
## MATRIMONIAL PROCEEDINGS IN MAGISTRATES' COURTS

*Powers of court to make orders for financial provision for parties to a marriage and children of the family*

### 1 Grounds of application for financial provision

Either party to a marriage may apply to a magistrates' court for an order under section 2 of this Act on the ground that the other party to the marriage . . . —

(a) has failed to provide reasonable maintenance for the applicant; or
(b) has failed to provide, or to make a proper contribution towards, reasonable maintenance for any child of the family; *or*
(c) *has behaved in such a way that the applicant cannot reasonably be expected to live with the respondent; or*
(d) *has deserted the applicant.*

---

NOTES

First words omitted repealed by the Matrimonial and Family Proceedings Act 1984, s 46(1), Sch 1; paras (c), (d) repealed by the Family Law Act 1996, ss 18(1), 66(3), Sch 10, subject to savings in s 66(2) of, and Sch 9, para 5 to, the 1996 Act, as from a day to be appointed.

---

### 2 Powers of court to make orders for financial provision

(1) Where on an application for an order under this section the applicant satisfies the court of any ground mentioned in section 1 of this Act, the court may, subject to the provisions of this Part of this Act, make any one or more of the following orders, that is to say—

(a) an order that the respondent shall make to the applicant such periodical payments, and for such term, as may be specified in the order;
(b) an order that the respondent shall pay to the applicant such lump sum as may be so specified;
(c) an order that the respondent shall make to the applicant for the benefit of a child of the family to whom the application relates, or to such a child, such periodical payments, and for such term, as may be so specified;
(d) an order that the respondent shall pay to the applicant for the benefit of a child of the family to whom the application relates, or to such a child, such lump sum as may be so specified.

(2)    Without prejudice to the generality of subsection (1)(b) or (d) above, an order under this section for the payment of a lump sum may be made for the purpose of enabling any liability or expenses reasonably incurred in maintaining the applicant, or any child of the family to whom the application relates, before the making of the order to be met.

(3)    The amount of any lump sum required to be paid by an order under this section shall not exceed £500 or such larger amount as the [Lord Chancellor] may from time to time by order fix for the purposes of this subsection.

Any order made by the [Lord Chancellor] under this subsection shall be made by statutory instrument and shall be subject to annulment in pursuance of a resolution of either House of Parliament.

NOTES
Sub-s (3): words in square brackets substituted by the Transfer of Functions (Magistrates' Courts and Family Law) Order 1992, SI 1992/709, art 3(2), Sch 2.

## 6    Orders for payments which have been agreed by the parties

(1)    Either party to a marriage may apply to a magistrates' court for an order under this section on the ground that either the party making the application or the other party to the marriage has agreed to make such financial provision as may be specified in the application and, subject to subsection (3) below, the court on such an application may, if—

(a)   it is satisfied that the applicant or the respondent, as the case may be, has agreed to make that provision, and

(b)   it has no reason to think that it would be contrary to the interests of justice to exercise its powers hereunder,

order that the applicant or the respondent, as the case may be, shall make the financial provision specified in the application.

(2)    In this section "financial provision" means the provision mentioned in any one or more of the following paragraphs, that is to say—

(a)   the making of periodical payments by one party to the other,

(b)   the payment of a lump sum by one party to the other,

(c)   the making of periodical payments by one party to a child of the family or to the other party for the benefit of such a child,

(d)   the payment by one party of a lump sum to a child of the family or to the other party for the benefit of such a child,

and any reference in this section to the financial provision specified in an application made under subsection (1) above or specified by the court under subsection (5) below is a reference to the type of provision specified in the application or by the court, as the case may be, to the amount so specified as the amount of any payment to be made thereunder and, in the case of periodical payments, to the term so specified as the term for which the payments are to be made.

(3)    Where the financial provision specified in an application under subsection (1) above includes or consists of provision in respect of a child of the family, the court shall not make an order under that subsection unless it considers that the provision which the applicant or the respondent, as the case may be, has agreed to make in respect of that child provides for, or makes a proper contribution towards, the financial needs of the child.

(4)   A party to a marriage who has applied for an order under section 2 of this Act shall not be precluded at any time before the determination of that application from applying for an order under this section; but if an order is made under this section on the application of either party and either of them has also made an application for an order under section 2 of this Act, the application made for the order under section 2 shall be treated as if it had been withdrawn.

(5)   Where on an application under subsection (1) above the court decides—

(a)   that it would be contrary to the interests of justice to make an order for the making of the financial provision specified in the application, or

(b)   that any financial provision which the applicant or the respondent, as the case may be, has agreed to make in respect of a child of the family does not provide for, or make a proper contribution towards, the financial needs of that child,

but is of the opinion—

(i)   that it would not be contrary to the interests of justice to make an order for the making of some other financial provision specified by the court, and

(ii)   that, in so far as that other financial provision contains any provision for a child of the family, it provides for, or makes a proper contribution towards, the financial needs of that child,

then if both the parties agree, the court may order that the applicant or the respondent, as the case may be, shall make that other financial provision.

(6)   Subject to subsection (8) below, the provisions of section 4 of this Act shall apply in relation to an order under this section which requires periodical payments to be made to a party to a marriage for his own benefit as they apply in relation to an order under section 2(1)(a) of this Act.

(7)   Subject to subsection (8) below, the provisions of section 5 of this Act shall apply in relation to an order under this section for the making of financial provision in respect of a child of the family as they apply in relation to an order under section 2(1)(c) or (d) of this Act.

(8)   Where the court makes an order under this section which contains provision for the making of periodical payments and, by virtue of subsection (4) above, an application for an order under section 2 of this Act is treated as if it had been withdrawn, then the term which may be specified as the term for which the payments are to be made may begin with the date of the making of the application for the order under section 2 or any later date.

(9)   Where the respondent is not present or represented by counsel or solicitor at the hearing of an application for an order under subsection (1) above, the court shall not make an order under this section unless there is produced to the court such evidence as may be prescribed by rules of—

(a)   the consent of the respondent to the making of the order,

(b)   the financial resources of the respondent, and

(c)   in a case where the financial provision specified in the application includes or consists of provision in respect of a child of the family to be made by the applicant to the respondent for the benefit of the child or to the child, the financial resources of the child.]

NOTES

Substituted by the Matrimonial and Family Proceedings Act 1984, s 10.

## 7 Powers of court where parties are living apart by agreement

(1)   Where the parties to a marriage have been living apart for a continuous period exceeding three months, *neither party having deserted the other*, and one of the parties has been making periodical payments for the benefit of the other party or of a child of the family, that other party may apply to a magistrates' court for an order under this section, and any application made under this subsection shall specify the aggregate amount of the payments so made during the period of three months immediately preceding the date of the making of the application.

(2)   Where on an application for an order under this section the court is satisfied that the respondent has made the payments specified in the application, the court may, subject to the provisions of this Part of this Act, make one or both of the following orders, that is to say—

(a)   an order that the respondent shall make to the applicant such periodical payments, and for such term, as may be specified in the order;

(b)   an order that the respondent shall make to the applicant for the benefit of a child of the family to whom the application relates, or to such a child, such periodical payments, and for such term, as may be so specified.

(3)   The court in the exercise of its powers under this section—

(a)   shall not require the respondent to make payments which exceed in aggregate during any period of three months the aggregate amount paid by him for the benefit of the applicant or a child of the family during the period of three months immediately preceding the date of the making of the application;

(b)   shall not require the respondent to make payments to or for the benefit of any person which exceed in amount the payments which the court considers that it would have required the respondent to make to or for the benefit of that person on an application under section 1 of this Act;

(c)   shall not require payments to be made to or for the benefit of a child of the family who is not a child of the respondent unless the court considers that it would have made an order in favour of that child on an application under section 1 of this Act.

(4)   Where on an application under this section the court considers that the orders which it has the power to make under this section—

(a)   would not provide reasonable maintenance for the applicant, or

(b)   if the application relates to a child of the family, would not provide, or make a proper contribution towards reasonable maintenance for that child,

the court shall refuse to make an order under this section, but the court may treat the application as if it were an application for an order under section 2 of this Act.

(5)   The provisions of section 3 of this Act shall apply in relation to an application for an order under this section as they apply in relation to an application for an order under section 2 of this Act subject to the modification that for the reference in [subsection (2)(c)] of the said section 3 to the occurrence of the conduct which is alleged as the ground of the application there shall be substituted a reference to the living apart of the parties to the marriage.

(6)   The provisions of section 4 of this Act shall apply in relation to an order under this section which requires periodical payments to be made to the applicant for his own benefit as they apply in relation to an order under section 2(1)(a) of this Act.

(7)   The provisions of section 5 of this Act shall apply in relation to an order under this section for the making of periodical payments in respect of a child of the family as they apply in relation to an order under section 2(1)(c) of this Act.

NOTES

Sub-s (1): words in italics repealed by the Family Law Act 1996, ss 18(2), 66(3), Sch 10, subject to savings in s 66(2) of, and para 5 of Sch 9 to, the 1996 Act, as from a day to be appointed.

Sub-s (5): words in square brackets substituted by the Matrimonial and Family Proceedings Act 1984, s 46(1), Sch 1, para 22.

*Powers of the court to make orders for the protection of a party to a marriage or a child of the family*

## 16 Powers of court to make orders for the protection of a party to a marriage or a child of the family

(1)  Either party to a marriage may, whether or not an application is made by that party for an order under section 2 of this Act, apply to a magistrates' court for an order under this section.

(2)  Where on an application for an order under this section the court is satisfied that the respondent has used, or threatened to use, violence against the person of the applicant or a child of the family and that it is necessary for the protection of the applicant or a child of the family that an order should be made under this subsection, the court may make one or both of the following orders, that is to say—

(a)  an order that the respondent shall not use, or threaten to use, violence against the person of the applicant;

(b)  an order that the respondent shall not use, or threaten to use, violence against the person of a child of the family.

(3)  Where on an application for an order under this section the court is satisfied—

(a)  that the respondent has used violence against the person of the applicant or a child of the family, or

(b)  that the respondent has threatened to use violence against the person of the applicant or a child of the family and has used violence against some other person, or

(c)  that the respondent has in contravention of an order made under subsection (2) above threatened to use violence against the person of the applicant or a child of the family,

and that the applicant or a child of the family is in danger of being physically injured by the respondent (or would be in such danger if the applicant or child were to enter the matrimonial home) the court may make one or both of the following orders, that is to say—

(i)  an order requiring the respondent to leave the matrimonial home;

(ii)  an order prohibiting the respondent from entering the matrimonial home.

(4)  Where the court makes an order under subsection (3) above, the court may, if it thinks fit, make a further order requiring the respondent to permit the applicant to enter and remain in the matrimonial home.

(5)  Where on an application for an order under this section the court considers that it is essential that the application should be heard without delay, the court may hear the application notwithstanding—

(a)  that the court does not include both a man and a woman,

(b)  that any member of the court is not a member of a [family panel], or

(c)  that the proceedings on the application are not separated from the hearing and determination of proceedings which are not [family proceedings].

*(6)   Where on an application for an order under this section the court is satisfied that there is imminent danger of physical injury to the applicant or a child of the family, the court may make an order under subsection (2) above notwithstanding [that the respondent has not been given such notice of the proceedings as may be prescribed by rules] and any order made by virtue of this subsection is in this section and in section 17 of this Act referred to as an "expedited order".*

*(7)   . . .*

*(8)   An expedited order shall not take effect until the date on which notice of the making of the order is served on the respondent in such manner as may be prescribed or, if the court specifies a later date as the date on which the order is to take effect, that later date, and an expedited order shall cease to have effect on whichever of the following dates occurs first, that is to say—*

> *(a)   the date of the expiration of the period of 28 days beginning with the date of the making of the order; or*
>
> *(b)   the date of the commencement of the hearing, in accordance with the provisions of [Part II of the Magistrates' Courts Act 1980], of the application for an order under this section.*

*(9)   An order under this section may be made subject to such exceptions or conditions as may be specified in the order and, subject in the case of an expedited order to subsection (8) above, may be made for such term as may be so specified.*

*(10)   The court in making an order under subsection (2)(a) or (b) above may include provision that the respondent shall not incite or assist any other person to use, or threaten to use, violence against the person of the applicant or, as the case may be, the child of the family.*

---

NOTES

Sub-s (5): words in square brackets substituted by the Children Act 1989, s 92, Sch 11, para 6.

Sub-s (6): words in square brackets substituted by the Courts and Legal Services Act 1990, s 125(3), Sch 18, para 21.

Sub-s (7): repealed by the Courts and Legal Services Act 1990, s 125(7), Sch 20.

Sub-s (8): words in square brackets substituted by the Magistrates' Courts Act 1980, s 154, Sch 7, para   159.

Repealed, together with ss 17, 18, by the Family Law Act 1996, s 66(3), Sch 10, subject to savings in s   66(2) of, and Sch 9, paras 5, 8–10 to, the 1996 Act, as from 1 October 1997.

---

### 17   Supplementary provisions with respect to orders under s 16

*(1)   A magistrates' court shall, on an application made by either party to the marriage in question, have power by order to vary or revoke any order made under section 16 of this Act.*

*(2)   . . .*

*(3)   The expiry by virtue of subsection (8) of section 16 of this Act of an expedited order shall not prejudice the making of a further expedited order under that section.*

*(4)   Except so far as the exercise by the respondent of a right to occupy the matrimonial home is suspended or restricted by virtue of an order made under subsection (3) of section 16 of this Act, an order made under that section shall not affect any estate or interest in the matrimonial home of the respondent or any other person.*

---

NOTES

Sub-s (2): repealed by the Courts and Legal Services Act 1990, s 125(7), Sch 20.

Repealed as noted to s 16.

---

### 18   Powers of arrest for breach of s 16 order

*(1)   Where a magistrates' court makes an order under section 16 of this Act which provides that the respondent—*

*(a)   shall not use violence against the person of the applicant, or*

*(b)   shall not use violence against a child of the family, or*

*(c)   shall not enter the matrimonial home,*

*the court may, if it is satisfied that the respondent has physically injured the applicant or a child of the family and considers that he is likely to do so again, attach a power of arrest to the order.*

*(2)   Where by virtue of subsection (1) above a power of arrest is attached to an order, a constable may arrest without warrant a person whom he has reasonable cause for suspecting of being in breach of any such provision of the order as is mentioned in paragraph (a), (b) or (c) of subsection (1) above by reason of that person's use of violence or, as the case may be, his entry into the matrimonial home.*

*(3)   Where a power of arrest is attached to an order under subsection (1) above and the respondent is arrested under subsection (2) above—*

*(a)   he shall be brought before a justice of the peace within a period of 24 hours beginning at the time of his arrest, and*

*(b)   the justice of the peace before whom he is brought may remand him.*

*In reckoning for the purposes of this subsection any period of 24 hours, no account shall be taken of Christmas Day, Good Friday, or any Sunday.*

*(4)   Where a court has made an order under section 16 of this Act but has not attached to the order a power of arrest under subsection (1) above, then, if at any time the applicant for that order considers that the other party to the marriage in question has disobeyed the order, he may apply for the issue of a warrant for the arrest of that other party to a justice of the peace for the commission area in which either party to the marriage ordinarily resides; but a justice of the peace shall not issue a warrant on such an application unless—*

*(a)   the application is substantiated on oath, and*

*(b)   the justice has reasonable grounds for believing that the other party to the marriage has disobeyed that order.*

*(5)   The magistrates' court before whom any person is brought by virtue of a warrant issued under subsection (4) above may remand him.*

NOTES

Repealed as noted to s 16.

# PART V
# SUPPLEMENTARY PROVISIONS

### 90   Short title and extent

(1)   This Act may be cited as the Domestic Proceedings and Magistrates' Courts Act 1978.

(2)   . . .

(3)   Except for the following provisions, that is to say—

(a)   sections 54, 59, 74(5), 88(5), 89(2), (3) and (4) and this section, and

(b)   [paragraphs 12, 13, 14 and 33] of Schedule 2 and Schedule 3, this Act does not extend to Northern Ireland, and in section 88(5) of this Act any reference to an enactment includes a reference to an enactment contained in an Act of the Parliament of Northern Ireland or a Measure of the Northern Ireland Assembly.

**NOTES**
Sub-s (2): outside the scope of this work.
Sub-s (3): words in square brackets substituted by the Maintenance Orders (Reciprocal Enforcement) Act 1992, s 2(1), Sch 2, para 1.

# MAGISTRATES' COURTS ACT 1980

## (C 43)

*An Act to consolidate certain enactments relating to the jurisdiction of, and the practice and procedure before, magistrates' courts and the functions of justices' clerks, and to matters connected therewith, with amendments to give effect to recommendations of the Law Commission*

[1 August 1980]

## PART I
## CRIMINAL JURISDICTION AND PROCEDURE

*Offences triable on indictment or summarily*

### 22  Certain offences triable either way to be tried summarily if value involved is small

(1)   If the offence charged by the information is one of those mentioned in the first column of Schedule 2 to this Act (in this section referred to as "scheduled offences") then, . . ., the court shall, before proceeding in accordance with section 19 above, consider whether, having regard to any representations made by the prosecutor or the accused, the value involved (as defined in subsection (10) below) appears to the court to exceed the relevant sum.

For the purposes of this section the relevant sum is [£5,000].

(2)   If, where subsection (1) above applies, it appears to the court clear that, for the offence charged, the value involved does not exceed the relevant sum, the court shall proceed as if the offence were triable only summarily, and sections 19 to 21 above shall not apply.

(3)   If, where subsection (1) above applies, it appears to the court clear that, for the offence charged, the value involved exceeds the relevant sum, the court shall thereupon proceed in accordance with section 19 above in the ordinary way without further regard to the provisions of this section.

(4)   If, where subsection (1) above applies, it appears to the court for any reason not clear whether, for the offence charged, the value involved does or does not exceed the relevant sum, the provisions of subsections (5) and (6) below shall apply.

(5)   The court shall cause the charge to be written down, if this has not already been done, and read to the accused, and shall explain to him in ordinary language—

(a) that he can, if he wishes, consent to be tried summarily for the offence and that if he consents to be so tried, he will definitely be tried in that way; and

(b) that if he is tried summarily and is convicted by the court, his liability to imprisonment or a fine will be limited as provided in section 33 below.

(6)    After explaining to the accused as provided by subsection (5) above the court shall ask him whether he consents to be tried summarily and—

(a)   if he so consents, shall proceed in accordance with subsection (2) above as if that subsection applied;

(b)   if he does not so consent, shall proceed in accordance with subsection (3) above as if that subsection applied.

(7)    . . .

(8)    Where a person is convicted by a magistrates' court of a scheduled offence, it shall not be open to him to appeal to the Crown Court against the conviction on the ground that the convicting court's decision as to the value involved was mistaken.

(9)    If, where subsection (1) above applies, the offence charged is one with which the accused is charged jointly with a person who has not attained [the age of 18 years], the reference in that subsection to any representations made by the accused shall be read as including any representations made by the person [under 18].

(10)   In this section "the value involved", in relation to any scheduled offence, means the value indicated in the second column of Schedule 2 to this Act, measured as indicated in the third column of that Schedule; and in that Schedule "the material time" means the time of the alleged offence.

[(11) Where—

(a)   the accused is charged on the same occasion with two or more scheduled offences and it appears to the court that they constitute or form part of a series of two or more offences of the same or a similar character; or

(b)   the offence charged consists in incitement to commit two or more scheduled offences,

this section shall have effect as if any reference in it to the value involved were a reference to the aggregate of the values involved.]

[(12) Subsection (8) of section 12A of the Theft Act 1968 (which determines when a vehicle is recovered) shall apply for the purposes of paragraph 3 of Schedule 2 to this Act as it applies for the purposes of that section.]

NOTES

   Commencement: 1 April 1992 (sub-s (12)); 12 October 1988 (sub-s (11)); 6 July 1981 (remainder).
   Sub-s (1): words omitted repealed, and sum in square brackets substituted, by the Criminal Justice and Public Order Act 1994, ss 46, 168(3), Sch 11.
   Sub-s (7): repealed by the Criminal Justice Act 1988, s 170(2), Sch 16.
   Sub-s (9): words in square brackets substituted by the Criminal Justice Act 1991, s 68, Sch 8, para 6.
   Sub-s (11): added by the Criminal Justice Act 1988, s 38(3), (4).
   Sub-s (12): added by the Aggravated Vehicle-Taking Act 1992, s 2(2).

# PART II
# CIVIL JURISDICTION AND PROCEDURE

*Orders other than for payment of money*

## 63   Orders other than for payment of money

(1)    Where under any Act passed after 31st December 1879 a magistrates' court has power to require the doing of anything other than the payment of money, or to prohibit the doing of anything, any order of the court for the purpose of exercising that power may contain such provisions for the manner in which anything is to be done, for the time within which anything is to be done, or during which anything is not to be done, and generally for giving effect to the order, as the court thinks fit.

(2)　The court may by order made on complaint suspend or rescind any such order as aforesaid.

(3)　Where any person disobeys an order of a magistrates' court made under an Act passed after 31st December 1879 to do anything other than the payment of money or to abstain from doing anything the court may—

    (a)　order him to pay a sum not exceeding £50 for every day during which he is in default or a sum not exceeding [£5,000]; or

    (b)　commit him to custody until he has remedied his default or for a period not exceeding 2 months;

but a person who is ordered to pay a sum for every day during which he is in default or who is committed to custody until he has remedied his default shall not by virtue of this section be ordered to pay more than £1,000 or be committed for more than 2 months in all for doing or abstaining from doing the same thing contrary to the order (without prejudice to the operation of this section in relation to any subsequent default).

(4)　Any sum ordered to be paid under subsection (3) above shall for the purposes of this Act be treated as adjudged to be paid by a conviction of a magistrates' court.

(5)　The preceding provisions of this section shall not apply to any order for the enforcement of which provision is made by any other enactment.

---

NOTES

    Sub-s (3): sum in square brackets in para (a) substituted by the Criminal Justice Act 1991, s 17(3), Sch 4, Pt I.

---

# PART III
# SATISFACTION AND ENFORCEMENT

*General provisions*

## 76　Enforcement of sums adjudged to be paid

(1)　Subject to the following provisions of this Part of this Act, and to section 132 below . . ., where default is made in paying a sum adjudged to be paid by a conviction or order of a magistrates' court, the court may issue a warrant of distress for the purpose of levying the sum or issue a warrant committing the defaulter to prison.

(2)　A warrant of commitment may be issued as aforesaid either—

    (a)　where it appears on the return to a warrant of distress that the money and goods of the defaulter are insufficient to satisfy the sum with the costs and charges of levying the sum; or

    (b)　instead of a warrant of distress.

(3)　The period for which a person may be committed to prison under such a warrant as aforesaid shall not, subject to the provisions of any enactment passed after 31st December 1879, exceed the period applicable to the case under Schedule 4 to this Act.

[(4)　Where proceedings are brought for the enforcement of a magistrates' court maintenance order under this section, the court may vary the order by exercising one of its powers under paragraphs (a) to (d) of section 59(3) above.

(5)    Subsections (4), (5) and (7) of section 59 above shall apply for the purposes of subsection (4) above as they apply for the purposes of that section.

(6)    Subsections (4) and (5) above shall not have effect in relation to a maintenance order which is not a qualifying maintenance order (within the meaning of section 59 above).]

NOTES

Commencement: 1 April 1992 (sub-ss (4)–(6)); 6 July 1981 (remainder).
Sub-s (1): words omitted repealed by the Criminal Justice Act 1982, s 78, Sch 16.
Sub-ss (4)–(6): added by the Maintenance Enforcement Act 1991, s 7.

*Sums adjudged to be paid by a conviction*

## 82    Restriction on power to impose imprisonment for default

(1)    A magistrates' court shall not on the occasion of convicting an offender of an offence issue a warrant of commitment for a default in paying any sum adjudged to be paid by the conviction unless—

(a)    in the case of an offence punishable with imprisonment, he appears to the court to have sufficient means to pay the sum forthwith;

(b)    it appears to the court that he is unlikely to remain long enough at a place of abode in the United Kingdom to enable payment of the sum to be enforced by other methods; or

(c)    on the occasion of that conviction the court sentences him to immediate imprisonment or [detention in a young offender institution] for that or another offence or he is already serving [a sentence of custody for life, or a term of imprisonment, . . ., detention under section 9 of the Criminal Justice Act 1982] or detention in a [young offender institution].

(2)    A magistrates' court shall not in advance of the issue of a warrant of commitment fix a term of imprisonment which is to be served by an offender in the event of a default in paying a sum adjudged to be paid by a conviction, except where it has power to issue a warrant of commitment forthwith, but postpones issuing the warrant under section 77(2) above.

(3)    Where on the occasion of the offender's conviction a magistrates' court does not issue a warrant of commitment for a default in paying any such sum as aforesaid or fix a term of imprisonment under the said section 77(2) which is to be served by him in the event of any such default, it shall not thereafter issue a warrant of commitment for any such default or for want of sufficient distress to satisfy such a sum unless—

(a)    he is already serving [a sentence of custody for life, or a term of imprisonment, . . ., detention under section 9 of the Criminal Justice Act 1982] or detention in a [young offender institution]; or

(b)    the court has since the conviction inquired into his means in his presence on at least one occasion.

(4)    Where a magistrates' court is required by subsection (3) above to inquire into a person's means, the court may not on the occasion of the inquiry or at any time thereafter issue a warrant of commitment for a default in paying any such sum unless—

(a)    in the case of an offence punishable with imprisonment, the offender appears to the court to have sufficient means to pay the sum forthwith; or

   (b)  the court—
      (i)  is satisfied that the default is due to the offender's wilful refusal or culpable neglect; and
     (ii)  has considered or tried all other methods of enforcing payment of the sum and it appears to the court that they are inappropriate or unsuccessful.

[(4A) The methods of enforcing payment mentioned in subsection (4)(b)(ii) above are—

   (a)  a warrant of distress under section 76 above;
   (b)  an application to the High Court or county court for enforcement under section 87 below;
   (c)  an order under section 88 below;
   (d)  an attachment of earnings order; and
   (e)  if the offender is under the *age of 21*, an order under section 17 of the Criminal Justice Act 1982 (attendance centre orders).]

(5)   After the occasion of an offender's conviction by a magistrates' court, the court shall not, unless—

   (a)  the court has previously fixed a term of imprisonment under section 77(2) above which is to be served by the offender in the event of a default in paying a sum adjudged to be paid by the conviction; or
   (b)  the offender is serving [a sentence of custody for life, or a term of imprisonment, . . ., detention under section 9 of the Criminal Justice Act 1982] or detention in a [young offender institution],

issue a warrant of commitment for a default in paying the sum or fix such a term except at a hearing at which the offender is present.

[(5A) A magistrates' court may not issue a warrant of commitment under subsection (5) above at a hearing at which the offender is not present unless the clerk of the court has first served on the offender a notice in writing stating that the court intends to hold a hearing to consider whether to issue such a warrant and giving the reason why the court so intends.

(5B)  Where after the occasion of an offender's conviction by a magistrates' court the court holds a hearing for the purpose of considering whether to issue a warrant of commitment for default in paying a sum adjudged to be paid by the conviction, it shall consider such information about the offender's means as is available to it unless it has previously—

   (a)  inquired into the offender's means; and
   (b)  postponed the issue of the warrant of commitment under section 77(2) above.

(5C)  A notice under subsection (5A) above—

   (a)  shall state the time and place appointed for the hearing; and
   (b)  shall inform the offender that, if he considers that there are grounds why the warrant should not be issued, he may make representations to the court in person or in writing,

but the court may exercise its powers in relation to the issue of a warrant whether or not he makes representations.

(5D) Except as mentioned in subsection (5E) below, the time stated in a notice under subsection (5A) above shall not be earlier than 21 days after the issue of the notice.

(5E) Where a magistrates' court exercises in relation to an offender the power conferred by section 77(2) above and at the same hearing issues a notice under subsection (5A) above in relation to him, the time stated in the notice may be a time on any day following the end of the period for which the issue of the warrant of commitment has been postponed.

(5F) A notice under subsection (5A) above to be served on any person shall be deemed to be served on that person if it is sent by registered post or the recorded delivery service addressed to him at his last known address, notwithstanding that the notice is returned as undelivered or is for any other reason not received by that person.]

(6)    Where a magistrates' court issues a warrant of commitment on the ground that one of the conditions mentioned in subsection (1) or (4) above is satisfied, it shall state that fact, specifying the ground, in the warrant.

NOTES

References to "young offender institution" and "detention in a young offender institution" substituted by virtue of, and words omitted from sub-ss (1), (3), (5) in pursuance of, the Criminal Justice Act 1988, s 123(6), Sch 8, paras 1, 2.

Sub-ss (1), (3), (5): words in square brackets substituted or inserted by the Criminal Justice Act 1982, s 77, Sch 14, para 52.

Sub-s (4A): inserted by the Criminal Justice Act 1988, s 61(1); words in italics substituted by the words "under the age of 25" by the Crime (Sentences) Act 1997, s 55, Sch 4, para 10(1), as from a day to be appointed.

Sub-ss (5A)–(5F): inserted by the Criminal Justice Act 1988, s 61(3), (4).

# PART VI
# RECOGNIZANCES

*Other provisions*

## 117    Warrant endorsed for bail

(1)    A justice of the peace on issuing a warrant for the arrest of any person may grant him bail by endorsing the warrant for bail, that is to say, by endorsing the warrant with a direction in accordance with subsection (2) below.

(2)    A direction for bail endorsed on a warrant under subsection (1) above shall—

(a)   in the case of bail in criminal proceedings, state that the person arrested is to be released on bail subject to a duty to appear before such magistrates' court and at such time as may be specified in the endorsement;

(b)   in the case of bail otherwise than in criminal proceedings, state that the person arrested is to be released on bail on his entering into such a recognizance (with or without sureties) conditioned for his appearance before a magistrates' court as may be specified in the endorsement;

and the endorsement shall fix the amounts in which any sureties and, in a case falling within paragraph (b) above, that person is or are to be bound.

[(3)   Where a warrant has been endorsed for bail under subsection (1) above—

(a)   where the person arrested is to be released on bail on his entering into a recognizance without sureties, it shall not be necessary to take him to a police station, but if he is so taken, he shall be released from custody on his entering into the recognizance; and

(b)  where he is to be released on his entering into a recognizance with sureties, he shall be taken to a police station on his arrest, and the custody officer there shall (subject to his approving any surety tendered in compliance with the endorsement) release him from custody as directed in the endorsement.]

NOTES

Sub-s (3): substituted by the Police and Criminal Evidence Act 1984, s 47.

# PART VII
# MISCELLANEOUS AND SUPPLEMENTARY

*Process*

## 125  Warrants

(1)  A warrant of arrest issued by a justice of the peace shall remain in force until it is executed or withdrawn.

(2)  A warrant of arrest, warrant of commitment, warrant of distress or search warrant issued by a justice of the peace may be executed anywhere in England and Wales by any person to whom it is directed or by any constable acting within his police area.

[A warrant of arrest, warrant of commitment or warrant of distress which is issued by a justice of the peace for the enforcement of [any sum adjudged to be paid] may also be executed by a person who—

(a)  is employed by an authority of a prescribed class;

(b)  is authorised in the prescribed manner to execute such warrants; and

(c)  is acting within the area for which the authority that employs him performs its functions.]

This subsection does not apply to a warrant of commitment or a warrant of distress issued under Part VI of the General Rate Act 1967.

(3)  A warrant to [which this subsection applies] may be executed by a constable notwithstanding that it is not in his possession at the time; but the warrant shall, on the demand of the person arrested, be shown to him as soon as practicable.

[(4)  The warrants to which subsection (3) above applies are—

(a)  a warrant to arrest a person in connection with an offence;

(b)  without prejudice to paragraph (a) above, a warrant under section 186(3) of the Army Act 1955, section 186(3) of the Air Force Act 1955, section 105(3) of the Naval Discipline Act 1957 or [Schedule 2 to the Reserve Forces Act 1996] (desertion etc);

(c)  a warrant under—

  (i)  section 102 or 104 of the General Rate Act 1967 (insufficiency of distress);

  (ii)  section 18(4) of the Domestic Proceedings and Magistrates' Courts Act 1978 (protection of parties to marriage and children of family); and

  (iii)  section 55, 76, 93 or 97 above.]

NOTES

Sub-s (2): words in outer pair of square brackets inserted by the Criminal Justice Act 1988, s 65(1); words in inner pair of square brackets substituted by the Courts and Legal Services Act 1990, s 125(2), Sch 17, para 11.

Sub-s (3): words in square brackets substituted by the Police and Criminal Evidence Act 1984, s 33.

Sub-s (4): added by the Police and Criminal Evidence Act 1984, s 33; words in square brackets in para (b) substituted by the Reserve Forces Act 1996, s 131(1), Sch 10, para 18.

## 126  Execution of certain warrants outside England and Wales

Sections 12 to 14 of the Indictable Offences Act 1848 (which relate, among other things, to the execution in Scotland, Northern Ireland, the Isle of Man and the Channel Islands of warrants of arrest for the offences referred to in those sections) shall, so far as applicable, apply to—

    (a)  warrants of arrest issued under section 1 above for offences other than those referred to in the said sections 12 to 14;

    (b)  warrants of arrest issued under section 13 above;

    (c)  warrants of arrest issued under section 97 above other than warrants issued in bastardy proceedings to arrest a witness; and

    (d)  warrants of commitment issued under this Act.

*Limitation of time*

## 127  Limitation of time

(1)  Except as otherwise expressly provided by any enactment and subject to subsection (2) below, a magistrates' court shall not try an information or hear a complaint unless the information was laid, or the complaint made, within 6 months from the time when the offence was committed, or the matter of complaint arose.

(2)  Nothing in—

    (a)  subsection (1) above; or

    (b)  subject to subsection (4) below, any other enactment (however framed or worded) which, as regards any offence to which it applies, would but for this section impose a time-limit on the power of a magistrates' court to try an information summarily or impose a limitation on the time for taking summary proceedings,

shall apply in relation to any indictable offence.

(3)  Without prejudice to the generality of paragraph (b) of subsection (2) above, that paragraph includes enactments which impose a time-limit that applies only in certain circumstances (for example, where the proceedings are not instituted by or with the consent of the Director of Public Prosecutions or some other specified authority).

(4)  Where, as regards any indictable offence, there is imposed by any enactment (however framed or worded, and whether falling within subsection (2)(b) above or not) a limitation on the time for taking proceedings on indictment for that offence no summary proceedings for that offence shall be taken after the latest time for taking proceedings on indictment.

*Remand*

## 128  Remand in custody or on bail

(1)  Where a magistrates' court has power to remand any person, then, subject to section 4 of the Bail Act 1976 and to any other enactment modifying that power, the court may—

(a) remand him in custody, that is to say, commit him to custody to be brought before the court[, subject to subsection (3A) below,] at the end of the period of remand or at such earlier time as the court may require; or

(b) where it is inquiring into or trying an offence alleged to have been committed by that person or has convicted him of an offence, remand him on bail in accordance with the Bail Act 1976, that is to say, by directing him to appear as provided in subsection (4) below; or

(c) except in a case falling within paragraph (b) above, remand him on bail by taking from him a recognizance (with or without sureties) conditioned as provided in that subsection;

and may, in a case falling within paragraph (c) above, instead of taking recognizances in accordance with that paragraph, fix the amount of the recognizances with a view to their being taken subsequently in accordance with section 119 above.

[(1A) Where—

(a) on adjourning a case under section 5, 10(1)[, 17C] or 18(4) above the court proposes to remand or further remand a person in custody; and

(b) he is before the court; and

(c) . . .

(d) he is legally represented in that court,

it shall be the duty of the court—

(i) to explain the effect of subsections (3A) and (3B) below to him in ordinary language; and

(ii) to inform him in ordinary language that, notwithstanding the procedure for a remand without his being brought before a court, he would be brought before a court for the hearing and determination of at least every fourth application for his remand, and of every application for his remand heard at a time when it appeared to the court that he had no [legal representative] acting for him in the case.

(1B) For the purposes of subsection (1A) above a person is to be treated as legally represented in a court if, but only if, he has the assistance of [a legal representative] to represent him in the proceedings in that court.

(1C) After explaining to an accused as provided by subsection (1A) above the court shall ask him whether he consents to the hearing and determination of such applications in his absence.]

(2) Where the court fixes the amount of a recognizance under subsection (1) above or section 8(3) of the Bail Act 1976 with a view to its being taken subsequently the court shall in the meantime commit the person so remanded to custody in accordance with paragraph (a) of the said subsection (1).

(3) Where a person is brought before the court after remand, the court may further remand him.

[(3A) Subject to subsection (3B) below, where a person has been remanded in custody, [and the remand was not a remand under section 128A below for a period exceeding 8 clear days,] the court may further remand him [(otherwise than in the exercise of the power conferred by that section)] on an adjournment under section 5, 10(1)[, 17C] or 18(4) above without his being brought before it if it is satisfied—

(a) that he gave his consent, either in response to a question under subsection (1C) above or otherwise, to the hearing and determination in his absence of any application for his remand on an adjournment of the case under any of those provisions; and

    (b)   that he has not by virtue of this subsection been remanded without being brought before the court on more than two such applications immediately preceding the application which the court is hearing; and

    (c)   . . .

    (d)   that he has not withdrawn his consent to their being so heard and determined.

(3B)  The court may not exercise the power conferred by subsection (3A) above if it appears to the court, on an application for a further remand being made to it, that the person to whom the application relates has no [legal representative] acting for him in the case (whether present in court or not).

(3C)  Where—

    (a)   a person has been remanded in custody on an adjournment of a case under section 5, 10(1)[, 17C] or 18(4) above; and

    (b)   an application is subsequently made for his further remand on such an adjournment; and

    (c)   he is not brought before the court which hears and determines the application; and

    (d)   that court is not satisfied as mentioned in subsection (3A) above,

the court shall adjourn the case and remand him in custody for the period for which it stands adjourned.

(3D)  An adjournment under subsection (3C) above shall be for the shortest period that appears to the court to make it possible for the accused to be brought before it.

(3E)  Where—

    (a)   on an adjournment of a case under [section 4(4)], 10(1)[, 17C] or 18(4) above a person has been remanded in custody without being brought before the court; and

    (b)   it subsequently appears—

        (i)   to the court which remanded him in custody; or

        (ii)  to an alternate magistrates' court to which he is remanded under section 130 below,

that he ought not to have been remanded in custody in his absence, the court shall require him to be brought before it at the earliest time that appears to the court to be possible.]

(4)    Where a person is remanded on bail under subsection (1) above the court may, where it remands him on bail in accordance with the Bail Act 1976 direct him to appear or, in any other case, direct that his recognizance be conditioned for his appearance—

    (a)   before that court at the end of the period of remand; or

    (b)   at every time and place to which during the course of the proceedings the hearing may be from time to time adjourned;

and, where it remands him on bail conditionally on his providing a surety during an inquiry into an offence alleged to have been committed by him, may direct that the recognizance of the surety be conditioned to secure that the person so bailed appears—

    (c)   at every time and place to which during the course of the proceedings the hearing may be from time to time adjourned and also before the Crown Court in the event of the person so bailed being committed for trial there.

(5)    Where a person is directed to appear or a recognizance is conditioned for a person's appearance in accordance with paragraph (b) or (c) of subsection (4) above, the fixing at any time of the time for him next to appear shall be deemed to be a remand; but nothing in this subsection or subsection (4) above shall deprive the court of power at any subsequent hearing to remand him afresh.

(6)    Subject to the provisions of [sections 128A and] 129 below, a magistrates' court shall not remand a person for a period exceeding 8 clear days, except that—

    (a)    if the court remands him on bail, it may remand him for a longer period if he and the other party consent;

    (b)    where the court adjourns a trial under section 10(3) or 30 above, the court may remand him for the period of the adjournment;

    (c)    where a person is charged with an offence triable either way, then, if it falls to the court to try the case summarily but the court is not at the time so constituted, and sitting in such a place, as will enable it to proceed with the trial, the court may remand him until the next occasion on which it will be practicable for the court to be so constituted, and to sit in such a place, as aforesaid, notwithstanding that the remand is for a period exceeding 8 clear days.

(7)    A magistrates' court having power to remand a person in custody may, if the remand is for a period not exceeding 3 clear days, commit him to [detention at a police station].

[(8)    Where a person is committed to detention at a police station under subsection (7) above—

    (a)    he shall not be kept in such detention unless there is a need for him to be so detained for the purposes of inquiries into other offences;

    (b)    if kept in such detention, he shall be brought back before the magistrates' court which committed him as soon as that need ceases;

    (c)    he shall be treated as a person in police detention to whom the duties under section 39 of the Police and Criminal Evidence Act 1984 (responsibilities in relation to persons detained) relate;

    (d)    his detention shall be subject to periodic review at the times set out in section 40 of that Act (review of police detention).]

NOTES

    Sub-s (1): words in square brackets in para (a) inserted by the Criminal Justice Act 1982, s 59, Sch 9, para 2.

    Sub-s (1A): inserted by the Criminal Justice Act 1982, s 59, Sch 9, paras 3, 4; number in square brackets in para (a) inserted, in relation to appearances before a magistrates' court on or after a day to be appointed, and para (c) revoked, in relation to offences committed on or after 1 February 1997, by the Criminal Procedure and Investigations Act 1996, ss 49(1), (5)(a), (6), 52(1), (3), 80, Sch 5(4); final words in square brackets substituted by the Courts and Legal Services Act 1990, s 125(3), Sch 18, para 25.

    Sub-ss (1B), (3B): inserted by the Criminal Justice Act 1982, s 59, Sch 9, paras 3, 4; words in square brackets substituted by the Courts and Legal Services Act 1990, s 125(3), Sch 18, para 25.

    Sub-ss (1C), (3D): inserted by the Criminal Justice Act 1982, s 59, Sch 9, paras 3, 4.

    Sub-s (3A): inserted by the Criminal Justice Act 1982, s 59, Sch 9, para 4; words in first and second pairs of square brackets inserted by the Criminal Justice Act 1988, s 170(1), Sch 15, paras 65, 69(1); number in square brackets inserted, in relation to appearances before a magistrates' court on or after a day to be appointed, and para (c) revoked, in relation to offences committed on or after 1 February 1997, by the Criminal Procedure and Investigations Act 1996, ss 49(1), (5)(a), (6), 52(1), (3), 80, Sch 5(4).

    Sub-ss (3C), (3E): inserted by the Criminal Justice Act 1982, s 59, Sch 9, paras 3, 4; final numbers in square brackets inserted, in relation to appearances before a magistrates' court on or after a day to be appointed, by the Criminal Procedure and Investigations Act 1996, s 49(5)(a), (6).

    Sub-s (6): words in square brackets substituted by the Criminal Justice Act 1988, s 170(1), Sch 15, paras 65, 69(2).

    Sub-s (7): words in square brackets substituted by the Police and Criminal Evidence Act 1984, s 48.

    Sub-s (8): added by the Police and Criminal Evidence Act 1984, s 48.

*Power to rectify mistakes, etc*

## 142 Power of magistrates' court to re-open cases to rectify mistakes etc

(1) [A magistrates' court may vary or rescind a sentence or other order imposed or made by it when dealing with an offender if it appears to the court to be in the interests of justice to do so;] and it is hereby declared that this power extends to replacing a sentence or order which for any reason appears to be invalid by another which the court has power to impose or make.

[(1A) The power conferred on a magistrates' court by subsection (1) above shall not be exercisable in relation to any sentence or order imposed or made by it when dealing with an offender if—
  (a) the Crown Court has determined an appeal against—
    (i) that sentence or order;
    (ii) the conviction in respect of which that sentence or order was imposed or made; or
    (iii) any other sentence or order imposed or made by the magistrates' court when dealing with the offender in respect of that conviction (including a sentence or order replaced by that sentence or order); or
  (b) the High Court has determined a case stated for the opinion of that court on any question arising in any proceeding leading to or resulting from the imposition or making of the sentence or order.]

(2) Where a person is [convicted by a magistrates' court] and it subsequently appears to the court that it would be in the interests of justice that the case should be heard again by different justices, the court may . . . so direct.

[(2A) The power conferred on a magistrates' court by subsection (2) above shall not be exercisable in relation to a conviction if—
  (a) the Crown Court has determined an appeal against—
    (i) the conviction; or
    (ii) any sentence or order imposed or made by the magistrates' court when dealing with the offender in respect of the conviction; or
  (b) the High Court has determined a case stated for the opinion of that court on any question arising in any proceeding leading to or resulting from the conviction.]

(3) Where a court gives a direction under subsection (2) above—
  (a) the [conviction] and any sentence or other order imposed or made in consequence thereof shall be of no effect; and
  (b) section 10(4) above shall apply as if the trial of the person in question had been adjourned.

(4) . . .

(5) Where a sentence or order is varied under subsection (1) above, the sentence or other order, as so varied, shall take effect from the beginning of the day on which it was originally imposed or made, unless the court otherwise directs.

---

NOTES

  Commencement: 1 January 1996 (sub-ss (1A), (2A)); 6 July 1981 (remainder).
  Sub-ss (1), (3): words in square brackets substituted by the Criminal Appeal Act 1995, s 26(2), (6).
  Sub-ss (1A), (2A): inserted by the Criminal Appeal Act 1995, s 26(3), (5).
  Sub-s (2): words in square brackets substituted, and words omitted repealed, by the Criminal Appeal Act 1995, ss 26(4), 29, Sch 3.
  Sub-s (4): repealed by the Criminal Appeal Act 1995, ss 26(7), 29, Sch 3.

---

*Repeals, short title, etc*

**155   Short title, extent and commencement**

(1)   This Act may be cited as the Magistrates' Courts Act 1980.

(2)   The following provisions of this Act extend to Scotland—

    (a)   sections 8 (except subsection (9)), [12(13)], 83(3), 90 and 91 and this section; and

    (b)   section 154 and Schedules 7, 8 and 9 so far as they relate to any enactment extending to Scotland.

(3)   The following provisions of this Act extend to Northern Ireland—

    (a)   sections 83(3), 90 and 91 and this section; and

    (b)   section 154 and Schedules 7, 8 and 9 so far as they relate to any enactment extending to Northern Ireland.

(4)   The provisions of section 126 above have the same extent as the sections of the Indictable Offences Act 1848 to which they refer.

(5)   . . .

(6)   Except as stated in subsections (2) to (5) above, and except so far as relates to the interpretation or commencement of the provisions mentioned in those subsections, this Act extends to England and Wales only.

(7)   This Act shall come into force on such date as the Secretary of State may appoint by order made by statutory instrument.

---

NOTES

    Sub-s (2): number in square brackets in para (a) substituted by the Criminal Justice and Public Order Act 1994, s 45, Sch 5, para 3(1), (4).

    Sub-s (5): repealed by the Statute Law (Repeals) Act 1993, s 1(1), Sch 1, Pt XIV.

---

# MENTAL HEALTH ACT 1983

## (C 20)

*An Act to consolidate the law relating to mentally disordered persons.*

[9 May 1983]

## PART I
## APPLICATION OF ACT

**1   Application of Act: "mental disorder"**

(1)   The provisions of this Act shall have effect with respect to the reception, care and treatment of mentally disordered patients, the management of their property and other related matters.

(2)   In this Act—

    "mental disorder" means mental illness, arrested or incomplete development of mind, psychopathic disorder and any other disorder or disability of mind and "mentally disordered" shall be construed accordingly;

"severe mental impairment" means a state of arrested or incomplete development of mind which includes severe impairment of intelligence and social functioning and is associated with abnormally aggressive or seriously irresponsible conduct on the part of the person concerned and "severely mentally impaired" shall be construed accordingly;

"mental impairment" means a state of arrested or incomplete development of mind (not amounting to severe mental impairment) which includes significant impairment of intelligence and social functioning and is associated with abnormally aggressive or seriously irresponsible conduct on the part of the person concerned and "mentally impaired" shall be construed accordingly;

"psychopathic disorder" means a persistent disorder or disability of mind (whether or not including significant impairment of intelligence) which results in abnormally aggressive or seriously irresponsible conduct on the part of the person concerned;

and other expressions shall have the meanings assigned to them in section 145 below.

(3)   Nothing in subsection (2) above shall be construed as implying that a person may be dealt with under this Act as suffering from mental disorder, or from any form of mental disorder described in this section, by reason only of promiscuity or other immoral conduct, sexual deviancy or dependence on alcohol or drugs.

# PART II
# COMPULSORY ADMISSION TO HOSPITAL AND GUARDIANSHIP

*Procedure for hospital admission*

## 2   Admission for assessment

(1)   A patient may be admitted to a hospital and detained there for the period allowed by subsection (4) below in pursuance of an application (in this Act referred to as "an application for admission for assessment") made in accordance with subsections   (2) and (3) below.

(2)   An application for admission for assessment may be made in respect of a patient on the grounds that—

(a)   he is suffering from mental disorder of a nature or degree which warrants the detention of the patient in a hospital for assessment (or for assessment followed by medical treatment) for at least a limited period; and

(b)   he ought to be so detained in the interests of his own health or safety or with a view to the protection of other persons.

(3)   An application for admission for assessment shall be founded on the written recommendations in the prescribed form of two registered medical practitioners, including in each case a statement that in the opinion of the practitioner the conditions set out in subsection (2) above are complied with.

(4)   Subject to the provisions of section 29(4) below, a patient admitted to hospital in pursuance of an application for admission for assessment may be detained for a period not exceeding 28 days beginning with the day on which he is admitted, but shall not be detained after the expiration of that period unless before it has expired he has become liable to be detained by virtue of a subsequent application, order or direction under the following provisions of this Act.

### 3 Admission for treatment

(1)  A patient may be admitted to a hospital and detained there for the period allowed by the following provisions of this Act in pursuance of an application (in this Act referred to as "an application for admission for treatment") made in accordance with this section.

(2)  An application for admission for treatment may be made in respect of a patient on the grounds that—

(a)  he is suffering from mental illness, severe mental impairment, psychopathic disorder or mental impairment and his mental disorder is of a nature or degree which makes it appropriate for him to receive medical treatment in a hospital; and

(b)  in the case of psychopathic disorder or mental impairment, such treatment is likely to alleviate or prevent a deterioration of his condition; and

(c)  it is necessary for the health or safety of the patient or for the protection of other persons that he should receive such treatment and it cannot be provided unless he is detained under this section.

(3)  An application for admission for treatment shall be founded on the written recommendations in the prescribed form of two registered medical practitioners, including in each case a statement that in the opinion of the practitioner the conditions set out in subsection (2) above are complied with; and each such recommendation shall include—

(a)  such particulars as may be prescribed of the grounds for that opinion so far as it relates to the conditions set out in paragraphs (a) and (b) of that subsection; and

(b)  a statement of the reasons for that opinion so far as it relates to the conditions set out in paragraph (c) of that subsection, specifying whether other methods of dealing with the patient are available and, if so, why they are not appropriate.

*Guardianship*

### 7 Application for guardianship

(1)  A patient who has attained the age of 16 years may be received into guardianship, for the period allowed by the following provisions of this Act, in pursuance of an application (in this Act referred to as "a guardianship application") made in accordance with this section.

(2)  A guardianship application may be made in respect of a patient on the grounds that—

(a)  he is suffering from mental disorder, being mental illness, severe mental impairment, psychopathic disorder or mental impairment and his mental disorder is of a nature or degree which warrants his reception into guardianship under this section; and

(b)  it is necessary in the interests of the welfare of the patient or for the protection of other persons that the patient should be so received.

(3)  A guardianship application shall be founded on the written recommendations in the prescribed form of two registered medical practitioners, including in each case a statement that in the opinion of the practitioner the conditions set out in subsection (2) above are complied with; and each such recommendation shall include—

(a)  such particulars as may be prescribed of the grounds for that opinion so far as it relates to the conditions set out in paragraph (a) of that subsection; and

(b) a statement of the reasons for that opinion so far as it relates to the conditions set out in paragraph (b) of that subsection.

(4) A guardianship application shall state the age of the patient or, if his exact age is not known to the applicant, shall state (if it be the fact) that the patient is believed to have attained the age of 16 years.

(5) The person named as guardian in a guardianship application may be either a local social services authority or any other person (including the applicant himself); but a guardianship application in which a person other than a local social services authority is named as guardian shall be of no effect unless it is accepted on behalf of that person by the local social services authority for the area in which he resides, and shall be accompanied by a statement in writing by that person that he is willing to act as guardian.

*Supplemental*

## 32 Regulations for purposes of Part II

(1) The Secretary of State may make regulations for prescribing anything which, under this Part of this Act, is required or authorised to be prescribed, and otherwise for carrying this Part of this Act into full effect.

(2) Regulations under this section may in particular make provision—

(a) for prescribing the form of any application, recommendation, report, order, notice or other document to be made or given under this Part of this Act;

(b) for prescribing the manner in which any such application, recommendation, report, order, notice or other document may be proved, and for regulating the service of any such application, report, order or notice;

(c) for requiring [such bodies as may be prescribed by the regulations] to keep such registers or other records as may be [so prescribed] in respect of patients liable to be detained or subject to guardianship [or to after-care under supervision] under this Part of this Act, and to furnish or make available to those patients, and their relatives, such written statements of their rights and powers under this Act as may be so prescribed;

(d) for the determination in accordance with the regulations of the age of any person whose exact age cannot be ascertained by reference to the registers kept under the Births and Deaths Registration Act 1953; and

(e) for enabling the functions under this Part of this Act of the nearest relative of a patient to be performed, in such circumstances and subject to such conditions (if any) as may be prescribed by the regulations, by any person authorised in that behalf by that relative;

and for the purposes of this Part of this Act any application, report or notice the service of which is regulated under paragraph (b) above shall be deemed to have been received by or furnished to the authority or person to whom it is authorised or required to be furnished, addressed or given if it is duly served in accordance with the regulations.

(3) Without prejudice to subsections (1) and (2) above, but subject to section 23(4) above, regulations under this section may determine the manner in which functions under this Part of this Act of the managers of hospitals, local social services authorities, [Health Authorities, Special Health Authorities or National Health Service trusts] are to be exercised, and such regulations may in particular specify the circumstances in which, and the conditions subject to which, any such functions may be performed by officers of or other persons acting on behalf of those managers [authorities and trusts].

## NOTES

Sub-s (2): words in first and second pairs of square brackets in para (c) substituted, and words in third pair of square brackets inserted, by the Mental Health (Patients in the Community) Act 1995, s 1(2), Sch 1, para 2.

Sub-s (3): words in first pair of square brackets substituted by the Health Authorities Act 1995, s 2(1), Sch 1, para 107(4); words in second pair of square brackets substituted by the National Health Service and Community Care Act 1990, s 66(1), Sch 9, para 24(5).

# PART III
# PATIENTS CONCERNED IN CRIMINAL PROCEEDINGS OR UNDER SENTENCE

*Remands to hospital*

*Hospital and guardianship orders*

## 37  Powers of courts to order hospital admission or guardianship

(1)   Where a person is convicted before the Crown Court of an offence punishable with imprisonment other than an offence the sentence for which is fixed by law [or falls to be imposed under section 2(2) of the Crime (Sentences) Act 1997], or is convicted by a magistrates' court of an offence punishable on summary conviction with imprisonment, and the conditions mentioned in subsection (2) below are satisfied, the court may by order authorise his admission to and detention in such hospital as may be specified in the order or, as the case may be, place him under the guardianship of a local social services authority or of such other person approved by a local social services authority as may be so specified.

[(1A) In the case of an offence the sentence for which would otherwise fall to be imposed under subsection (2) of section 3 or 4 of the Crime (Sentences) Act 1997, nothing in that subsection shall prevent a court from making an order under subsection (1) above for the admission of the offender to a hospital.]

(2)   The conditions referred to in subsection (1) above are that—

    (a)   the court is satisfied, on the written or oral evidence of two registered medical practitioners, that the offender is suffering from mental illness, psychopathic disorder, severe mental impairment or mental impairment and that either—

        (i)   the mental disorder from which the offender is suffering is of a nature or degree which makes it appropriate for him to be detained in a hospital for medical treatment and, in the case of psychopathic disorder or mental impairment, that such treatment is likely to alleviate or prevent a deterioration of his condition; or

        (ii)   in the case of an offender who has attained the age of 16 years, the mental disorder is of a nature or degree which warrants his reception into guardianship under this Act; and

    (b)   the court is of the opinion, having regard to all the circumstances including the nature of the offence and the character and antecedents of the offender, and to the other available methods of dealing with him, that the most suitable method of disposing of the case is by means of an order under this section.

(3)   Where a person is charged before a magistrates' court with any act or omission as an offence and the court would have power, on convicting him of that offence, to make an order under subsection (1) above in his case as being a person suffering from mental illness or severe mental impairment, then, if the court is satisfied that the accused did the act or made the omission charged, the court may, if it thinks fit, make such an order without convicting him.

(4)   An order for the admission of an offender to a hospital (in this Act referred to as "a hospital order") shall not be made under this section unless the court is satisfied on the written or oral evidence of the registered medical practitioner who would be in charge of his treatment or of some other person representing the managers of the hospital that arrangements have been made for his admission to that hospital *in the event of such an order being made by the court*, and for his admission to it within the period of 28 days beginning with the date of the making of such an order; and the court may, pending his admission within that period, give such directions as it thinks fit for his conveyance to and detention in a place of safety.

(5)   If within the said period of 28 days it appears to the Secretary of State that by reason of an emergency or other special circumstances it is not practicable for the patient to be received into the hospital specified in the order, he may give directions for the admission of the patient to such other hospital as appears to be appropriate instead of the hospital so specified; and where such directions are given—
  (a)   the Secretary of State shall cause the person having the custody of the patient to be informed, and
  (b)   the hospital order shall have effect as if the hospital specified in the directions were substituted for the hospital specified in the order.

(6)   An order placing an offender under the guardianship of a local social services authority or of any other person (in this Act referred to as "a guardianship order") shall not be made under this section unless the court is satisfied that that authority or person is willing to receive the offender into guardianship.

(7)   A hospital order or guardianship order shall specify the form or forms of mental disorder referred to in subsection (2)(a) above from which, upon the evidence taken into account under that subsection, the offender is found by the court to be suffering; and no such order shall be made unless the offender is described by each of the practitioners whose evidence is taken into account under that subsection as suffering from the same one of those forms of mental disorder, whether or not he is also described by either of them as suffering from another of them.

(8)   Where an order is made under this section, the court shall not pass sentence of imprisonment or impose a fine or make a probation order in respect of the offence or make any such order as is mentioned in paragraph (b) or (c) of section 7(7) of the Children and Young Persons Act 1969 in respect of the offender, but may make any other order which the court has power to make apart from this section; and for the purposes of this subsection "sentence of imprisonment" includes any sentence or order for detention.

---

NOTES
  Commencement: 30 September 1983 (sub-ss (1), (2)–(8)); to be appointed (remainder).
  Sub-s (1): words in square brackets inserted by the Crime (Sentences) Act 1997, s 55, Sch 4, para 12(1), as from a day to be appointed.
  Sub-s (1A): inserted by the Crime (Sentences) Act 1997, s 55, Sch 4, para 12(2), as from a day to be appointed.
  Sub-s (4): words in italics repealed by the Crime (Sentences) Act 1997, s 55, Sch 4, para 12(3), as from a day to be appointed.

---

## 38 Interim hospital orders

(1)   Where a person is convicted before the Crown Court of an offence punishable with imprisonment (other than an offence the sentence for which is fixed by law) or is convicted by a magistrates' court of an offence punishable on summary conviction with imprisonment and the court before or by which he is convicted is satisfied, on the written or oral evidence of two registered medical practitioners—

(a)   that the offender is suffering from mental illness, psychopathic disorder, severe mental impairment or mental impairment; and

(b)   that there is reason to suppose that the mental disorder from which the offender is suffering is such that it may be appropriate for a hospital order to be made in his case,

the court may, before making a hospital order or dealing with him in some other way, make an order (in this Act referred to as "an interim hospital order") authorising his admission to such hospital as may be specified in the order and his detention there in accordance with this section.

(2)   In the case of an offender who is subject to an interim hospital order the court may make a hospital order without his being brought before the court if he is represented by counsel or a solicitor and his counsel or solicitor is given an opportunity of being heard.

(3)   At least one of the registered medical practitioners whose evidence is taken into account under subsection (1) above shall be employed at the hospital which is to be specified in the order.

(4)   An interim hospital order shall not be made for the admission of an offender to a hospital unless the court is satisfied, on the written or oral evidence of the registered medical practitioner who would be in charge of his treatment or of some other person representing the managers of the hospital, that arrangements have been made for his admission to that hospital and for his admission to it within the period of 28 days beginning with the date of the order; and if the court is so satisfied the court may, pending his admission, give directions for his conveyance to and detention in a place of safety.

(5)   An interim hospital order—

(a)   shall be in force for such period, not exceeding 12 weeks, as the court may specify when making the order; but

(b)   may be renewed for further periods of not more than 28 days at a time if it appears to the court, on the written or oral evidence of the responsible medical officer, that the continuation of the order is warranted;

but no such order shall continue in force for more than *six months* in all and the court shall terminate the order if it makes a hospital order in respect of the offender or decides after considering the written or oral evidence of the responsible medical officer to deal with the offender in some other way.

(6)   The power of renewing an interim hospital order may be exercised without the offender being brought before the court if he is represented by counsel or a solicitor and his counsel or solicitor is given an opportunity of being heard.

(7)   If an offender absconds from a hospital in which he is detained in pursuance of an interim hospital order, or while being conveyed to or from such a hospital, he may be arrested without warrant by a constable and shall, after being arrested, be brought as soon as practicable before the court that made the order; and the court may thereupon terminate the order and deal with him in any way in which it could have dealt with him if no such order had been made.

NOTES
Sub-s (5): words in italics substituted by the words "twelve months" by the Crime (Sentences) Act 1997, s 49(1), as from a day to be appointed.

## 39 Information as to hospitals

(1)  Where a court is minded to make a hospital order or interim hospital order in respect of any person it may request—

(a)  the [Health Authority] for [the area] in which that person resides or last resided; or

(b)  any other [Health Authority] that appears to the court to be appropriate,

to furnish the court with such information as [that Health Authority have] or can reasonably obtain with respect to the hospital or hospitals (if any) in [their area] or elsewhere at which arrangements could be made for the admission of that person in pursuance of the order, and [that Health Authority shall] comply with any such request.

(2)  . . .

NOTES
Sub-s (1): words in square brackets substituted by the Health Authorities Act 1995, s 2(1), Sch 1, para 107(5).
Sub-s (2): repealed by the Health Authorities Act 1995, ss 2(1), 5(1), Sch 1, para 107(5), Sch 3.

*Hospital and guardianship*

## [39A  Information to facilitate guardianship orders

Where a court is minded to make a guardianship order in respect of any offender, it may request the local social services authority for the area in which the offender resides or last resided, or any other local social services authority that appears to the court to be appropriate—

(a)  to inform the court whether it or any other person approved by it is willing to receive the offender into guardianship; and

(b)  if so, to give such information as it reasonably can about how it or the other person could be expected to exercise in relation to the offender the powers conferred by section 40(2) below;

and that authority shall comply with any such request.]

NOTES
Commencement: 1 October 1992.
Inserted by the Criminal Justice Act 1991, s 27(1).

*Hospital and guardianship orders*

## 40  Effect of hospital orders, guardianship orders and interim hospital orders

(1)  A hospital order shall be sufficient authority—

(a)  for a constable, an approved social worker or any other person directed to do so by the court to convey the patient to the hospital specified in the order within a period of 28 days; and

(b)  for the managers of the hospital to admit him at any time within that period and thereafter detain him in accordance with the provisions of this Act.

(2)    A guardianship order shall confer on the authority or person named in the order as guardian the same powers as a guardianship application made and accepted under Part II of this Act.

(3)    Where an interim hospital order is made in respect of an offender—

(a)   a constable or any other person directed to do so by the court shall convey the offender to the hospital specified in the order within the period mentioned in section 38(4) above; and

(b)   the managers of the hospital shall admit him within that period and thereafter detain him in accordance with the provisions of section 38 above.

(4)    A patient who is admitted to a hospital in pursuance of a hospital order, or placed under guardianship by a guardianship order, shall, subject to the provisions of this subsection, be treated for the purposes of the provisions of this Act mentioned in Part I of Schedule 1 to this Act as if he had been so admitted or placed on the date of the order in pursuance of an application for admission for treatment or a guardianship application, as the case may be, duly made under Part II of this Act, but subject to any modifications of those provisions specified in that Part of that Schedule.

(5)    Where a patient is admitted to a hospital in pursuance of a hospital order, or placed under guardianship by a guardianship order, any previous application, hospital order or guardianship order by virtue of which he was liable to be detained in a hospital or subject to guardianship shall cease to have effect; but if the first-mentioned order, or the conviction on which it was made, is quashed on appeal, this subsection shall not apply and section 22 above shall have effect as if during any period for which the patient was liable to be detained or subject to guardianship under the order, he had been detained in custody as mentioned in that section.

[(6)    Where—

(a)   a patient admitted to a hospital in pursuance of a hospital order is absent without leave;

(b)   a warrant to arrest him has been issued under section 72 of the Criminal Justice Act 1967; and

(c)   he is held pursuant to the warrant in any country or territory other than the United Kingdom, any of the Channel Islands and the Isle of Man,

he shall be treated as having been taken into custody under section 18 above on first being so held.]

NOTES

Commencement: 1 April 1996 (sub-s (6)); 1 October 1984 (sub-s (3)); 30 September 1983 (remainder).

Sub-s (6): added by the Mental Health (Patients in the Community) Act 1995, s 2(4).

*Restriction orders*

## 41   Power of higher courts to restrict discharge from hospital

(1)    Where a hospital order is made in respect of an offender by the Crown Court, and it appears to the court, having regard to the nature of the offence, the antecedents of the offender and the risk of his committing further offences if set at large, that it is necessary for the protection of the public from serious harm so to do, the court may, subject to the provisions of this section, further order that the offender shall be subject to the special restrictions set out in this section, either without limit of time or during such period as may be specified in the order; and an order under this section shall be known as "a restriction order".

(2)    A restriction order shall not be made in the case of any person unless at least one of the registered medical practitioners whose evidence is taken into account by the court under section 37(2)(a) above has given evidence orally before the court.

(3)    The special restrictions applicable to a patient in respect of whom a restriction order is in force are as follows—

(a)    none of the provisions of Part II of this Act relating to the duration, renewal and expiration of authority for the detention of patients shall apply, and the patient shall continue to be liable to be detained by virtue of the relevant hospital order until he is duly discharged under the said Part II or absolutely discharged under section 42, 73, 74 or 75 below;

[(aa) none of the provisions of Part II of this Act relating to after-care under supervision shall apply;]

(b)    no application shall be made to a Mental Health Review Tribunal in respect of a patient under section 66 or 69(1) below;

(c)    the following powers shall be exercisable only with the consent of the Secretary of State, namely—

(i)    power to grant leave of absence to the patient under section 17 above;

(ii)    power to transfer the patient in pursuance of regulations under section 19 above [or in pursuance of subsection (3) of that section]; and

(iii)    power to order the discharge of the patient under section 23 above;

and if leave of absence is granted under the said section 17 power to recall the patient under that section shall vest in the Secretary of State as well as the responsible medical officer; and

(d)    the power of the Secretary of State to recall the patient under the said section 17 and power to take the patient into custody and return him under section 18 above may be exercised at any time;

and in relation to any such patient section 40(4) above shall have effect as if it referred to Part II of Schedule 1 to this Act instead of Part I of that Schedule.

(4)    A hospital order shall not cease to have effect under section 40(5) above if a restriction order in respect of the patient is in force at the material time.

(5)    Where a restriction order in respect of a patient ceases to have effect while the relevant hospital order continues in force, the provisions of section 40 above and Part I of Schedule 1 to this Act shall apply to the patient as if he had been admitted to the hospital in pursuance of a hospital order (without a restriction order) made on the date on which the restriction order ceased to have effect.

(6)    While a person is subject to a restriction order the responsible medical officer shall at such intervals (not exceeding one year) as the Secretary of State may direct examine and report to the Secretary of State on that person; and every report shall contain such particulars as the Secretary of State may require.

---

NOTES

Sub-s (3): para (aa) inserted by the Mental Health (Patients in the Community) Act 1995, s 1(2), Sch 1, para 5; words in square brackets in para (c)(ii) inserted by the Crime (Sentences) Act 1997, s 49(2), as from a day to be appointed.

---

*Transfer to hospital of prisoners, etc*

## 47 Removal to hospital of persons serving sentences of imprisonment, etc

(1)   If in the case of a person serving a sentence of imprisonment the Secretary of State is satisfied, by reports from at least two registered medical practitioners—

    (a)   that the said person is suffering from mental illness, psychopathic disorder, severe mental impairment or mental impairment; and

    (b)   that the mental disorder from which that person is suffering is of a nature or degree which makes it appropriate for him to be detained in a hospital for medical treatment and, in the case of psychopathic disorder or mental impairment, that such treatment is likely to alleviate or prevent a deterioration of his condition;

the Secretary of State may, if he is of the opinion having regard to the public interest and all the circumstances that it is expedient so to do, by warrant direct that that person be removed to and detained in such hospital *(not being a mental nursing home)* as may be specified in the direction; and a direction under this section shall be known as "a transfer direction".

(2)   A transfer direction shall cease to have effect at the expiration of the period of 14 days beginning with the date on which it is given unless within that period the person with respect to whom it was given has been received into the hospital specified in the direction.

(3)   A transfer direction with respect to any person shall have the same effect as a hospital order made in his case.

(4)   A transfer direction shall specify the form or forms of mental disorder referred to in paragraph (a) of subsection (1) above from which, upon the reports taken into account under that subsection, the patient is found by the Secretary of State to be suffering; and no such direction shall be given unless the patient is described in each of those reports as suffering from the same form of disorder, whether or not he is also described in either of them as suffering from another form.

(5)   References in this Part of this Act to a person serving a sentence of imprisonment include references—

    (a)   to a person detained in pursuance of any sentence or order for detention made by a court in criminal proceedings (other than an order under any enactment to which section 46 above applies);

    (b)   to a person committed to custody under section 115(3) of the Magistrates' Courts Act 1980 (which relates to persons who fail to comply with an order to enter into recognisances to keep the peace or be of good behaviour); and

    (c)   to a person committed by a court to a prison or other institution to which the Prison Act 1952 applies in default of payment of any sum adjudged to be paid on his conviction.

---

NOTES

    Sub-s (1): words in italics repealed by the Crime (Sentences) Act 1997, ss 49(3), 56(2), Sch 6, as from a day to be appointed.

---

## 48 Removal to hospital of other prisoners

(1)  If in the case of a person to whom this section applies the Secretary of State is satisfied by the same reports as are required for the purposes of section 47 above that that person is suffering from mental illness or severe mental impairment of a nature or degree which makes it appropriate for him to be detained in a hospital for medical treatment and that he is in urgent need of such treatment, the Secretary of State shall have the same power of giving a transfer direction in respect of him under that section as if he were serving a sentence of imprisonment.

(2)  This section applies to the following persons, that is to say—
   (a) persons detained in a prison or remand centre, not being persons serving a sentence of imprisonment or persons falling within the following paragraphs of this subsection;
   (b) persons remanded in custody by a magistrates' court;
   (c) civil prisoners, that is to say, persons committed by a court to prison for a limited term (including persons committed to prison in pursuance of a writ of attachment), who are not persons falling to be dealt with under section 47 above;
   (d) persons detained under the Immigration Act 1971.

(3)  Subsections (2) to (4) of section 47 above shall apply for the purposes of this section and of any transfer direction given by virtue of this section as they apply for the purposes of that section and of any transfer direction under that section.

## 49 Restriction on discharge of prisoners removed to hospital

(1)  Where a transfer direction is given in respect of any person, the Secretary of State, if he thinks fit, may by warrant further direct that that person shall be subject to the special restrictions set out in section 41 above; and where the Secretary of State gives a transfer direction in respect of any such person as is described in paragraph (a) or (b) of section 48(2) above, he shall also give a direction under this section applying those restrictions to him.

(2)  A direction under this section shall have the same effect as a restriction order made under section 41 above and shall be known as "a restriction direction".

(3)  While a person is subject to a restriction direction the responsible medical officer shall at such intervals (not exceeding one year) as the Secretary of State may direct examine and report to the Secretary of State on that person; and every report shall contain such particulars as the Secretary of State may require.

# PART VIII
# MISCELLANEOUS FUNCTIONS OF LOCAL AUTHORITIES AND THE SECRETARY OF STATE

*After-care*

## 117 After-care

(1)  This section applies to persons who are detained under section 3 above, or admitted to a hospital in pursuance of a hospital order made under section 37 above, or transferred to a hospital in pursuance of [a hospital direction made under section 45A above or] a transfer direction made under section 47 or 48 above, and then cease to be detained and [(whether or not immediately after so ceasing)] leave hospital.

(2)    It shall be the duty of the [Health Authority] and of the local social services authority to provide, in co-operation with relevant voluntary agencies, after-care services for any person to whom this section applies until such time as the [Health Authority] and the local social services authority are satisfied that the person concerned is no longer in need of such services[; but they shall not be so satisfied in the case of a patient who is subject to after-care under supervision at any time while he remains so subject.]

[(2A) It shall be the duty of the Health Authority to secure that at all times while a patient is subject to after-care under supervision—

(a)    a person who is a registered medical practitioner approved for the purposes of section 12 above by the Secretary of State as having special experience in the diagnosis or treatment of mental disorder is in charge of the medical treatment provided for the patient as part of the after-care services provided for him under this section; and

(b)    a person professionally concerned with any of the after-care services so provided is supervising him with a view to securing that he receives the after-care services so provided.

(2B)    Section 32 above shall apply for the purposes of this section as it applies for the purposes of Part II of this Act.]

(3)    In this [section "the Health Authority" means the Health Authority, and "the local social services authority" means the local social services authority, for the area] in which the person concerned is resident or to which he is sent on discharge by the hospital in which he was detained.

NOTES
Commencement: 1 April 1996 (sub-ss (2A), (2B)); 30 September 1983 (remainder).
Sub-s (1): words in first pair of square brackets inserted by the Crime (Sentences) Act 1997, s 55, Sch 4, para 12(17), as from a day to be appointed; words in second pair of square brackets inserted by the Mental Health (Patients in the Community) Act 1995, s 1(2), Sch 1, para 15(2).
Sub-s (2): words in first and second pairs of square brackets substituted by the Health Authorities Act 1995, s 2(1), Sch 1, para 107(8); words in third pair of square brackets added by the Mental Health (Patients in the Community) Act 1995, s 1(2), Sch 1, para 15(3).
Sub-ss (2A), (2B): inserted by the Mental Health (Patients in the Community) Act 1995, s 1(2), Sch 1, para 15(4).
Sub-s (3): words in square brackets substituted by the Health Authorities Act 1995, s 2(1), Sch 1, para 107(8).

# PART X
# MISCELLANEOUS AND SUPPLEMENTARY
## *Supplemental*

### 149    Short title, commencement and application to Scilly Isles

(1)    This Act may be cited as the Mental Health Act 1983.

(2)    Subject to subsection (3) below and Schedule 5 to this Act, this Act shall come into force on 30th September 1983.

(3)    Sections 35, 36, 38 and 40(3) above shall come into force on such day (not being earlier than the said 30th September) as may be appointed by the Secretary of State and a different day may be appointed for each of those sections or for different purposes of any of those sections.

(4)    . . .

NOTES
Sub-s (4): outside the scope of this work.

# POLICE AND CRIMINAL EVIDENCE ACT 1984

## (C 60)

*An Act to make further provision in relation to the powers and duties of the police, persons in police detention, criminal evidence, police discipline and complaints against the police; to provide for arrangements for obtaining the views of the community on policing and for a rank of deputy chief constable; to amend the law relating to the Police Federations and Police Forces and Police Cadets in Scotland; and for connected purposes*

[31 October 1984]

## PART I
## POWERS TO STOP AND SEARCH

### 1 Power of constable to stop and search persons, vehicles etc

(1) A constable may exercise any power conferred by this section—
  (a) in any place to which at the time when he proposes to exercise the power the public or any section of the public has access, on payment or otherwise, as of right or by virtue of express or implied permission; or
  (b) in any other place to which people have ready access at the time when he proposes to exercise the power but which is not a dwelling.

(2) Subject to subsection (3) to (5) below, a constable—
  (a) may search—
    (i) any person or vehicle;
    (ii) anything which is in or on a vehicle,
    for stolen or prohibited articles [or any article to which subsection (8A) below applies]; and
  (b) may detain a person or vehicle for the purpose of such a search.

(3) This section does not give a constable power to search a person or vehicle or anything in or on a vehicle unless he has reasonable grounds for suspecting that he will find stolen or prohibited articles [or any article to which subsection (8A) below applies].

(4) If a person is in a garden or yard occupied with and used for the purposes of a dwelling or on other land so occupied and used, a constable may not search him in the exercise of the power conferred by this section unless the constable has reasonable grounds for believing—
  (a) that he does not reside in the dwelling; and
  (b) that he is not in the place in question with the express or implied permission of a person who resides in the dwelling.

(5) If a vehicle is in a garden or yard occupied with and used for the purposes of a dwelling or on other land so occupied and used, a constable may not search the vehicle or anything in or on it in the exercise of the power conferred by this section unless he has reasonable grounds for believing—
  (a) that the person in charge of the vehicle does not reside in the dwelling; and
  (b) that the vehicle is not in the place in question with the express or implied permission of a person who resides in the dwelling.

(6) If in the course of such a search a constable discovers an article which he has reasonable grounds for suspecting to be a stolen or prohibited article [or an article to which subsection (8A) below applies], he may seize it.

(7)  An article is prohibited for the purposes of this Part of this Act if it is—
  (a)  an offensive weapon; or
  (b)  an article—
      (i)  made or adapted for use in the course of or in connection with an offence to which this sub-paragraph applies; or
      (ii)  intended by the person having it with him for such use by him or by some other person.

(8)  The offences to which subsection (7)(b)(i) above applies are—
  (a)  burglary;
  (b)  theft;
  (c)  offences under section 12 of the Theft Act 1968 (taking motor vehicle or other conveyance without authority); and
  (d)  offences under section 15 of that Act (obtaining property by deception).

[(8A) This subsection applies to any article in relation to which a person has committed, or is committing or is going to commit an offence under section 139 of the Criminal Justice Act 1988.]

(9)  In this Part of this Act "offensive weapon" means any article—
  (a)  made or adapted for use for causing injury to persons; or
  (b)  intended by the person having it with him for such use by him or by some other person.

---

NOTES

Sub-ss (2), (3), (6): words in square brackets inserted by the Criminal Justice Act 1988, s 140(1).
Sub-s (8A): inserted by the Criminal Justice Act 1988, s 140(1).

---

## 2  Provisions relating to search under section 1 and other powers

(1)  A constable who detains a person or vehicle in the exercise—
  (a)  of the power conferred by section 1 above; or
  (b)  of any other power—
      (i)  to search a person without first arresting him; or
      (ii)  to search a vehicle without making an arrest,

need not conduct a search if it appears to him subsequently—
      (i)  that no search is required; or
      (ii)  that a search is impracticable.

(2)  If a constable contemplates a search, other than a search of an unattended vehicle, in the exercise—
  (a)  of the power conferred by section 1 above; or
  (b)  of any other power, except the power conferred by section 6 below and the power conferred by section 27(2) of the Aviation Security Act 1982—
      (i)  to search a person without first arresting him; or
      (ii)  to search a vehicle without making an arrest,

it shall be his duty, subject to subsection (4) below, to take reasonable steps before he commences the search to bring to the attention of the appropriate person—
      (i)  if the constable is not in uniform, documentary evidence that he is a constable; and
      (ii)  whether he is in uniform or not, the matters specified in subsection (3) below;

and the constable shall not commence the search until he has performed that duty.

(3)   The matters referred to in subsection (2)(ii) above are—
(a)   the constable's name and the name of the police station to which he is attached;
(b)   the object of the proposed search;
(c)   the constable's grounds for proposing to make it; and
(d)   the effect of section 3(7) or (8) below, as may be appropriate.

(4)   A constable need not bring the effect of section 3(7) or (8) below to the attention of the appropriate person if it appears to the constable that it will not be practicable to make the record in section 3(1) below.

(5)   In this section "the appropriate person" means—
(a)   if the constable proposes to search a person, that person; and
(b)   if he proposes to search a vehicle, or anything in or on a vehicle, the person in charge of the vehicle.

(6)   On completing a search of an unattended vehicle or anything in or on such a vehicle in the exercise of any such power as is mentioned in subsection (2) above a constable shall leave a notice—
(a)   stating that he has searched it;
(b)   giving the name of the police station to which he is attached;
(c)   stating that an application for compensation for any damage caused by the search may be made to that police station; and
(d)   stating the effect of section 3(8) below.

(7)   The constable shall leave the notice inside the vehicle unless it is not reasonably practicable to do so without damaging the vehicle.

(8)   The time for which a person or vehicle may be detained for the purposes of such a search is such time as is reasonably required to permit a search to be carried out either at the place where the person or vehicle was first detained or nearby.

(9)   Neither the power conferred by section 1 above nor any other power to detain and search a person without first arresting him or to detain and search a vehicle without making an arrest is to be construed—
(a)   as authorising a constable to require a person to remove any of his clothing in public other than an outer coat, jacket or gloves; or
(b)   as authorising a constable not in uniform to stop a vehicle.

(10)   This section and section 1 above apply to vessels, aircraft and hovercraft as they apply to vehicles.

## 3   Duty to make records concerning searches

(1)   Where a constable has carried out a search in the exercise of any such power as is mentioned in section 2(1) above, other than a search—
(a)   under section 6 below; or
(b)   under section 27(2) of the Aviation Security Act 1982,

he shall make a record of it in writing unless it is not practicable to do so.

(2)   If—
(a)   a constable is required by subsection (1) above to make a record of a search; but
(b)   it is not practicable to make the record on the spot,

he shall make it as soon as practicable after the completion of the search.

(3)   The record of a search of a person shall include a note of his name, if the constable knows it, but a constable may not detain a person to find out his name.

(4)   If a constable does not know the name of the person whom he has searched, the record of the search shall include a note otherwise describing that person.

(5)   The record of a search of a vehicle shall include a note describing the vehicle.

(6)   The record of a search of a person or a vehicle—
   (a)   shall state—
      (i)   the object of the search;
      (ii)   the grounds for making it;
      (iii)   the date and time when it was made;
      (iv)   the place where it was made;
      (v)   whether anything, and if so what, was found;
      (vi)   whether any, and if so what, injury to a person or damage to property appears to the constable to have resulted from the search; and
   (b)   shall identify the constable making it.

(7)   If a constable who conducted a search of a person made a record of it, the person who was searched shall be entitled to a copy of the record if he asks for one before the end of the period specified in subsection (9) below.

(8)   If—
   (a)   the owner of a vehicle which has been searched or the person who was in charge of the vehicle at the time when it was searched asks for a copy of the record of the search before the end of the period specified in subsection (9) below; and
   (b)   the constable who conducted the search made a record of it,

the person who made the request shall be entitled to a copy.

(9)   The period mentioned in subsections (7) and (8) above is the period of 12 months beginning with the date on which the search was made.

(10)   The requirements imposed by this section with regard to records of searches of vehicles shall apply also to records of searches of vessels, aircraft and hovercraft.

## 4   Road checks

(1)   This section shall have effect in relation to the conduct of road checks by police officers for the purpose of ascertaining whether a vehicle is carrying—
   (a)   a person who has committed an offence other than a road traffic offence or a [vehicle] excise offence;
   (b)   a person who is a witness to such an offence;
   (c)   a person intending to commit such an offence; or
   (d)   a person who is unlawfully at large.

(2)   For the purposes of this section a road check consists of the exercise in a locality of the power conferred by [section 163 of the Road Traffic Act 1988] in such a way as to stop during the period for which its exercise in that way in that locality continues all vehicles or vehicles selected by any criterion.

(3)   Subject to subsection (5) below, there may only be such a road check if a police officer of the rank of superintendent or above authorises it in writing.

(4)   An officer may only authorise a road check under subsection (3) above—
   (a)   for the purpose specified in subsection (1)(a) above, if he has reasonable grounds—

      (i)  for believing that the offence is a serious arrestable offence; and

      (ii)  for suspecting that the person is, or is about to be, in the locality in which vehicles would be stopped if the road check were authorised;

  (b)  for the purpose specified in subsection (1)(b) above, if he has reasonable grounds for believing that the offence is a serious arrestable offence;

  (c)  for the purpose specified in subsection (1)(c) above, if he has reasonable grounds—

      (i)  for believing that the offence would be a serious arrestable offence; and

      (ii)  for suspecting that the person is, or is about to be, in the locality in which vehicles would be stopped if the road check were authorised;

  (d)  for the purpose specified in subsection (1)(d) above, if he has reasonable grounds for suspecting that the person is, or is about to be, in that locality.

(5)    An officer below the rank of superintendent may authorise such a road check if it appears to him that it is required as a matter of urgency for one of the purposes specified in subsection (1) above.

(6)    If an authorisation is given under subsection (5) above, it shall be the duty of the officer who gives it—

  (a)  to make a written record of the time at which he gives it; and

  (b)  to cause an officer of the rank of superintendent or above to be informed that it has been given.

(7)    The duties imposed by subsection (6) above shall be performed as soon as it is practicable to do so.

(8)    An officer to whom a report is made under subsection (6) above may, in writing, authorise the road check to continue.

(9)    If such an officer considers that the road check should not continue, he shall record in writing—

  (a)  the fact that it took place; and

  (b)  the purpose for which it took place.

(10)  An officer giving an authorisation under this section shall specify the locality in which vehicles are to be stopped.

(11)  An officer giving an authorisation under this section, other than an authorisation under subsection (5) above—

  (a)  shall specify a period, not exceeding seven days, during which the road check may continue; and

  (b)  may direct that the road check—

      (i)  shall be continuous; or

      (ii)  shall be conducted at specified times,

    during that period.

(12)  If it appears to an officer of the rank of superintendent or above that a road check ought to continue beyond the period for which it has been authorised he may, from time to time, in writing specify a further period, not exceeding seven days, during which it may continue.

(13)  Every written authorisation shall specify—

  (a)  the name of the officer giving it;

  (b)  the purpose of the road check; and

  (c)  the locality in which vehicles are to be stopped.

(14)   The duties to specify the purposes of a road check imposed by subsections (9) and (13) above include duties to specify any relevant serious arrestable offence.

(15)   Where a vehicle is stopped in a road check, the person in charge of the vehicle at the time when it is stopped shall be entitled to obtain a written statement of the purpose of the road check if he applies for such a statement not later than the end of the period of twelve months from the day on which the vehicle was stopped.

(16)   Nothing in this section affects the exercise by police officers of any power to stop vehicles for purposes other than those specified in subsection (1) above.

---

**NOTES**

Sub-s (1): word in square brackets substituted by the Vehicle Excise and Registration Act 1994, s 63, Sch 3, para 19.

Sub-s (2): words in square brackets substituted by the Road Traffic (Consequential Provisions) Act 1988, s 4, Sch 3, para 27(1).

---

# PART II
## POWERS OF ENTRY, SEARCH AND SEIZURE

### 9   Special provisions as to access

(1)   A constable may obtain access to excluded material or special procedure material for the purposes of a criminal investigation by making an application under Schedule 1 below and in accordance with that Schedule.

(2)   Any Act (including a local Act) passed before this Act under which a search of premises for the purposes of a criminal investigation could be authorised by the issue of a warrant to a constable shall cease to have effect so far as it relates to the authorisation of searches—

  (a)   for items subject to legal privilege; or
  (b)   for excluded material; or
  (c)   for special procedure material consisting of documents or records other than documents.

### 10   Meaning of "items subject to legal privilege"

(1)   Subject to subsection (2) below, in this Act "items subject to legal privilege" means—

  (a)   communications between a professional legal adviser and his client or any person representing his client made in connection with the giving of legal advice to the client;
  (b)   communications between a professional legal adviser and his client or any person representing his client or between such an adviser or his client or any such representative and any other person made in connection with or in contemplation of legal proceedings and for the purposes of such proceedings; and
  (c)   items enclosed with or referred to in such communications and made—
    (i)   in connection with the giving of legal advice; or
    (ii)   in connection with or in contemplation of legal proceedings and for the purposes of such proceedings,

when they are in the possession of a person who is entitled to possession of them.

(2)   Items held with the intention of furthering a criminal purpose are not items subject to legal privilege.

**11    Meaning of "excluded material"**

(1)    Subject to the following provisions of this section, in this Act "excluded material" means—

    (a)    personal records which a person has acquired or created in the course of any trade, business, profession or other occupation or for the purposes of any paid or unpaid office and which he holds in confidence;

    (b)    human tissue or tissue fluid which has been taken for the purposes of diagnosis or medical treatment and which a person holds in confidence;

    (c)    journalistic material which a person holds in confidence and which consists—

        (i)    of documents; or

        (ii)    of records other than documents.

(2)    A person holds material other than journalistic material in confidence for the purposes of this section if he holds it subject—

    (a)    to an express or implied undertaking to hold it in confidence; or

    (b)    to a restriction on disclosure or an obligation of secrecy contained in any enactment, including an enactment contained in an Act passed after this Act.

(3)    A person holds journalistic material in confidence for the purposes of this section if—

    (a)    he holds it subject to such an undertaking, restriction or obligation; and

    (b)    it has been continuously held (by one or more persons) subject to such an undertaking, restriction or obligation since it was first acquired or created for the purposes of journalism.

# PART III
# ARREST

**24    Arrest without warrant for arrestable offences**

(1)    The powers of summary arrest conferred by the following subsections shall apply—

    (a)    to offences for which the sentence is fixed by law;

    (b)    to offences for which a person of 21 years of age or over (not previously convicted) may be sentenced to imprisonment for a term of five years (or might be so sentenced but for the restrictions imposed by section 33 of the Magistrates' Courts Act 1980); and

    (c)    to the offences to which subsection (2) below applies,

and in this Act "arrestable offence" means any such offence.

(2)    The offences to which this subsection applies are—

    (a)    offences for which a person may be arrested under the customs and excise Acts, as defined in section 1(1) of the Customs and Excise Management Act 1979;

    (b)    offences under [the Official Secrets Act 1920] that are not arrestable offences by virtue of the term of imprisonment for which a person may be sentenced in respect of them;

    [(bb)offences under any provision of the Official Secrets Act 1989 except section 8(1), (4) or (5);]

    (c)    offences under section . . . , 22 (causing prostitution of women) or 23 (procuration of girl under 21) of the Sexual Offences Act 1956;

(d) offences under section 12(1) (taking motor vehicle or other conveyance without authority etc) or 25(1) (going equipped for stealing, etc) of the Theft Act 1968; and

[(e) any offence under the Football (Offences) Act 1991.]

[(f) an offence under section 2 of the Obscene Publications Act 1959 (publication of obscene matter);

(g) an offence under section 1 of the Protection of Children Act 1978 (indecent photographs and pseudo-photographs of children);

(h) an offence under section 166 of the Criminal Justice and Public Order Act 1994 (sale of tickets by unauthorised persons);

(i) an offence under section 19 of the Public Order Act 1986 (publishing, etc material intended or likely to stir up racial hatred);

(j) an offence under section 167 of the Criminal Justice and Public Order Act 1994 (touting for hire car services).]

[(k) an offence under section 1(1) of the Prevention of Crime Act 1953 (prohibition of the carrying of offensive weapons without lawful authority or reasonable excuse);

(l) an offence under section 139(1) of the Criminal Justice Act 1988 (offence of having article with blade or point in public place);

(m) an offence under section 139A(1) or (2) of the Criminal Justice Act 1988 (offence of having article with blade or point (or offensive weapon) on school premises).]

[(n) an offence under section 2 of the Protection from Harassment Act 1997 (harassment).]

(3) Without prejudice to section 2 of the Criminal Attempts Act 1981, the powers of summary arrest conferred by the following subsections shall also apply to the offences of—

(a) conspiring to commit any of the offences mentioned in subsection (2) above;

(b) attempting to commit any such offence [other than an offence under section 12(1) of the Theft Act 1968];

(c) inciting, aiding, abetting, counselling or procuring the commission of any such offence;

and such offences are also arrestable offences for the purposes of this Act.

(4) Any person may arrest without a warrant—

(a) anyone who is in the act of committing an arrestable offence;

(b) anyone whom he has reasonable grounds for suspecting to be committing such an offence.

(5) Where an arrestable offence has been committed, any person may arrest without a warrant—

(a) anyone who is guilty of the offence;

(b) anyone whom he has reasonable grounds for suspecting to be guilty of it.

(6) Where a constable has reasonable grounds for suspecting that an arrestable offence has been committed, he may arrest without a warrant anyone whom he has reasonable grounds for suspecting to be guilty of the offence.

(7) A constable may arrest without a warrant—

(a) anyone who is about to commit an arrestable offence;

(b) anyone whom he has reasonable grounds for suspecting to be about to commit an arrestable offence.

NOTES

Sub-s (2): words in square brackets in sub-para (b) substituted, and sub-para (bb) inserted, by the Official Secrets Act 1989, s 11(1); in para (c) words omitted repealed by the Sexual Offences Act 1985, s 5(3), Schedule; original para (e) repealed by the Criminal Justice Act 1988, s 170(2), Sch 16, new para (e) added by the Football (Offences) Act 1991, s 5(1); paras (f)–(j) inserted by the Criminal Justice and Public Order Act 1994, ss 85(1), (2), 155, 166(4), 167(7); paras (k)–(m) added by the Offensive Weapons Act 1996, s 1(1); para (n) added by the Protection from Harassment Act 1997, s 2(3).

Sub-s (3): in para (b) words in square brackets added by the Criminal Justice Act 1988, s 170(11), Sch 15, paras 97, 98.

Modified in relation to offences relating to the breaching of UN sanctions, by the Serbia and Montenegro (United Nations Sanctions) Order 1992, SI 1992/1302, art 17(13).

## 25    General arrest conditions

(1)    Where a constable has reasonable grounds for suspecting that any offence which is not an arrestable offence has been committed or attempted, or is being committed or attempted, he may arrest the relevant person if it appears to him that service of a summons is impracticable or inappropriate because any of the general arrest conditions is satisfied.

(2)    In this section "the relevant person" means any person whom the constable has reasonable grounds to suspect of having committed or having attempted to commit the offence or of being in the course of committing or attempting to commit it.

(3)    The general arrest conditions are—
  (a)  that the name of the relevant person is unknown to, and cannot be readily ascertained by, the constable;
  (b)  that the constable has reasonable grounds for doubting whether a name furnished by the relevant person as his name is his real name;
  (c)  that—
    (i)  the relevant person has failed to furnish a satisfactory address for service; or
    (ii) the constable has reasonable grounds for doubting whether an address furnished by the relevant person is a satisfactory address for service;
  (d)  that the constable has reasonable grounds for believing that arrest is necessary to prevent the relevant person—
    (i)   causing physical injury to himself or any other person;
    (ii)  suffering physical injury;
    (iii) causing loss of or damage to property;
    (iv)  committing an offence against public decency; or
    (v)   causing an unlawful obstruction of the highway;
  (e)  that the constable has reasonable grounds for believing that arrest is necessary to protect a child or other vulnerable person from the relevant person.

(4)    For the purposes of subsection (3) above an address is a satisfactory address for service if it appears to the constable—
  (a)  that the relevant person will be at it for a sufficiently long period for it to be possible to serve him with a summons; or
  (b)  that some other person specified by the relevant person will accept service of a summons for the relevant person at it.

(5)    Nothing in subsection (3)(d) above authorises the arrest of a person under sub-paragraph (iv) of that paragraph except where members of the public going about their normal business cannot reasonably be expected to avoid the person to be arrested.

(6)    This section shall not prejudice any power of arrest conferred apart from this section.

## 28    Information to be given on arrest

(1)    Subject to subsection (5) below, where a person is arrested, otherwise than by being informed that he is under arrest, the arrest is not lawful unless the person arrested is informed that he is under arrest as soon as is practicable after his arrest.

(2)    Where a person is arrested by a constable, subsection (1) above applies regardless of whether the fact of the arrest is obvious.

(3)    Subject to subsection (5) below, no arrest is lawful unless the person arrested is informed of the ground for the arrest at the time of, or as soon as is practicable after, the arrest.

(4)    Where a person is arrested by a constable, subsection (3) above applies regardless of whether the ground for the arrest is obvious.

(5)    Nothing in this section is to be taken to require a person to be informed—
    (a)    that he is under arrest; or
    (b)    of the ground for the arrest,

if it was not reasonably practicable for him to be so informed by reason of his having escaped from arrest before the information could be given.

# PART IV
# DETENTION

*Detention—conditions and duration*

## 35    Designated police stations

(1)    The chief officer of police for each police area shall designate the police stations in his area which, subject to section 30(3) and (5) above, are to be the stations in that area to be used for the purpose of detaining arrested persons.

(2)    A chief officer's duty under subsection (1) above is to designate police stations appearing to him to provide enough accommodation for that purpose.

(3)    Without prejudice to section 12 of the Interpretation Act 1978 (continuity of duties) a chief officer—
    (a)    may designate a station which was not previously designated; and
    (b)    may direct that a designation of a station previously made shall cease to operate.

(4)    In this Act "designated police station" means a police station designated under this section.

## 36    Custody officers at police stations

(1)    One or more custody officers shall be appointed for each designated police station.

(2)    A custody officer for a designated police station shall be appointed—
    (a)    by the chief officer of police for the area in which the designated police station is situated; or
    (b)    by such other police officer as the chief officer of police for that area may direct.

(3)   No officer may be appointed a custody officer unless he is of at least the rank of sergeant.

(4)   An officer of any rank may perform the functions of a custody officer at a designated police station if a custody officer is not readily available to perform them.

(5)   Subject to the following provisions of this section and to section 39(2) below, none of the functions of a custody officer in relation to a person shall be performed by an officer who at the time when the function falls to be performed is involved in the investigation of an offence for which that person is in police detention at that time.

(6)   Nothing in subsection (5) above is to be taken to prevent a custody officer—
    (a)   performing any function assigned to custody officers—
        (i)   by this Act; or
        (ii)   by a code of practice issued under this Act;
    (b)   carrying out the duty imposed on custody officers by section 39 below;
    (c)   doing anything in connection with the identification of a suspect; or
    (d)   doing anything under [sections 7 and 8 of the Road Traffic Act 1988].

(7)   Where an arrested person is taken to a police station which is not a designated police station, the functions in relation to him which at a designated police station would be the functions of a custody officer shall be performed—
    (a)   by an officer who is not involved in the investigation of an offence for which he is in police detention, if such an officer is readily available; and
    (b)   if no such officer is readily available, by the officer who took him to the station or any other officer.

(8)   References to a custody officer in the following provisions of this Act include references to an officer other than a custody officer who is performing the functions of a custody officer by virtue of subsection (4) or (7) above.

(9)   Where by virtue of subsection (7) above an officer of a force maintained by a police authority who took an arrested person to a police station is to perform the functions of a custody officer in relation to him, the officer shall inform an officer who—
    (a)   is attached to a designated police station; and
    (b)   is of at least the rank of inspector,
that he is to do so.

(10)   The duty imposed by subsection (9) above shall be performed as soon as it is practicable to perform it.

NOTES
    Sub-s (6): in para (d) words in square brackets substituted by the Road Traffic (Consequential Provisions) Act 1988, s 4, Sch 3, para 27(3).

## 37   Duties of custody officer before charge

(1)   Where—
    (a)   a person is arrested for an offence—
        (i)   without a warrant; or
        (ii)   under a warrant not endorsed for bail, . . .
    (b)   . . .

the custody officer at each police station where he is detained after his arrest shall determine whether he has before him sufficient evidence to charge that person with the offence for which he was arrested and may detain him at the police station for such period as is necessary to enable him to do so.

(2)   If the custody officer determines that he does not have such evidence before him, the person arrested shall be released either on bail or without bail, unless the custody officer has reasonable grounds for believing that his detention without being charged is necessary to secure or preserve evidence relating to an offence for which he is under arrest or to obtain such evidence by questioning him.

(3)   If the custody officer has reasonable grounds for so believing, he may authorise the person arrested to be kept in police detention.

(4)   Where a custody officer authorises a person who has not been charged to be kept in police detention, he shall, as soon as is practicable, make a written record of the grounds for the detention.

(5)   Subject to subsection (6) below, the written record shall be made in the presence of the person arrested who shall at that time be informed by the custody officer of the grounds for his detention.

(6)   Subsection (5) above shall not apply where the person arrested is, at the time when the written record is made—
  (a)   incapable of understanding what is said to him;
  (b)   violent or likely to become violent; or
  (c)   in urgent need of medical attention.

(7)   Subject to section 41(7) below, if the custody officer determines that he has before him sufficient evidence to charge the person arrested with the offence for which he was arrested, the person arrested—
  (a)   shall be charged; or
  (b)   shall be released without charge, either on bail or without bail.

(8)   Where—
  (a)   a person is released under subsection (7)(b) above; and
  (b)   at the time of his release a decision whether he should be prosecuted for the offence for which he was arrested has not been taken,
it shall be the duty of the custody officer so to inform him.

(9)   If the person arrested is not in a fit state to be dealt with under subsection (7) above, he may be kept in police detention until he is.

(10)   The duty imposed on the custody officer under subsection (1) above shall be carried out by him as soon as practicable after the person arrested arrives at the police station or, in the case of a person arrested at the police station, as soon as practicable after the arrest.

(11)–(14). . .

(15)   In this Part of this Act—
    "arrested juvenile" means a person arrested with or without a warrant who appears to be under the age of 17 . . .;
    "endorsed for bail" means endorsed with a direction for bail in accordance with section 117(2) of the Magistrates' Courts Act 1980.

---

NOTES

Sub-s (1): words omitted repealed by the Criminal Justice and Public Order Act 1994, ss 29(1), (4)(a), 168(3), Sch 11.

Sub-ss (11)–(14): repealed by the Criminal Justice Act 1991, ss 72, 101(2), Sch 13.

Sub-s (15): words omitted repealed by the Children Act 1989, s 108(7), Sch 15.

---

## 40  Review of police detention

(1)    Reviews of the detention of each person in police detention in connection with the investigation of an offence shall be carried out periodically in accordance with the following provisions of this section—
  (a)  in the case of a person who has been arrested and charged, by the custody officer; and
  (b)  in the case of a person who has been arrested but not charged, by an officer of at least the rank of inspector who has not been directly involved in the investigation.

(2)    The officer to whom it falls to carry out a review is referred to in this section as a "review officer".

(3)    Subject to subsection (4) below—
  (a)  the first review shall be not later than six hours after the detention was first authorised;
  (b)  the second review shall be not later than nine hours after the first;
  (c)  subsequent reviews shall be at intervals of not more than nine hours.

(4)    A review may be postponed—
  (a)  if, having regard to all the circumstances prevailing at the latest time for it specified in subsection (3) above, it is not practicable to carry out the review at that time;
  (b)  without prejudice to the generality of paragraph (a) above—
      (i)  if at that time the person in detention is being questioned by a police officer and the review officer is satisfied that an interruption of the questioning for the purpose of carrying out the review would prejudice the investigation in connection with which he is being questioned; or
      (ii)  if at that time no review officer is readily available.

(5)    If a review is postponed under subsection (4) above it shall be carried out as soon as practicable after the latest time specified for it in subsection (3) above.

(6)    If a review is carried out after postponement under subsection (4) above, the fact that it was so carried out shall not affect any requirement of this section as to the time at which any subsequent review is to be carried out.

(7)    The review officer shall record the reasons for any postponement of a review in the custody record.

(8)    Subject to subsection (9) below, where the person whose detention is under review has not been charged before the time of the review, section 37(1) to (6) above shall have effect in relation to him, but with the substitution—
  (a)  of references to the person whose detention is under review for references to the person arrested; and
  (b)  of references to the review officer for references to the custody officer

(9)    Where a person has been kept in police detention by virtue of section 37(9) above, section 37(1) to (6) shall not have effect in relation to him but it shall be the duty of the review officer to determine whether he is yet in a fit state.

(10)  Where the person whose detention is under review has been charged before the time of the review, section 38(1) to (6) above shall have effect in relation to him, with the substitution of references to the person whose detention is under review for references to the person arrested.

(11) Where—
  (a) an officer of higher rank than the review officer gives directions relating to a person in police detention; and
  (b) the directions are at variance—
      (i) with any decision made or action taken by the review officer in the performance of a duty imposed on him under this Part of this Act; or
      (ii) with any decision or action which would but for the directions have been made or taken by him in the performance of such a duty,

the review officer shall refer the matter at once to an officer of the rank of superintendent or above who is responsible for the police station for which the review officer is acting as review officer in connection with the detention.

(12) Before determining whether to authorise a person's continued detention the review officer shall give—
  (a) that person (unless he is asleep); or
  (b) any solicitor representing him who is available at the time of the review,

an opportunity to make representations to him about the detention.

(13) Subject to subsection (14) below, the person whose detention is under review or his solicitor may make representations under subsection (12) above either orally or in writing.

(14) The review officer may refuse to hear oral representations from the person whose detention is under review if he considers that he is unfit to make such representations by reason of his condition or behaviour.

NOTES
  Modification: any reference to solicitor(s) etc modified to include references to bodies recognised under the Administration of Justice Act 1985, s 9, by the Solicitors' Incorporated Practices Order 1991, SI 1991/2684, arts 4, 5, Sch 1.

## 41  Limits on period of detention without charge

(1)  Subject to the following provisions of this section and to sections 42 and 43 below, a person shall not be kept in police detention for more than 24 hours without being charged.

(2)  The time from which the period of detention of a person is to be calculated (in this Act referred to as "the relevant time")—
  (a) in the case of a person to whom this paragraph applies, shall be—
      (i) the time at which that person arrives at the relevant police station; or
      (ii) the time 24 hours after the time of that person's arrest,
      whichever is the earlier;
  (b) in the case of a person arrested outside England and Wales, shall be—
      (i) the time at which that person arrives at the first police station to which he is taken in the police area in England or Wales in which the offence for which he was arrested is being investigated; or
      (ii) the time 24 hours after the time of that person's entry into England and Wales,
      whichever is the earlier;
  (c) in the case of a person who—
      (i) attends voluntarily at a police station; or
      (ii) accompanies a constable to a police station without having been arrested,
      and is arrested at the police station, the time of his arrest;

(d) in any other case, except where subsection (5) below applies, shall be the time at which the person arrested arrives at the first police station to which he is taken after his arrest.

(3) Subsection (2)(a) above applies to a person if—

(a) his arrest is sought in one police area in England and Wales;

(b) he is arrested in another police area; and

(c) he is not questioned in the area in which he is arrested in order to obtain evidence in relation to an offence for which he is arrested;

and in sub-paragraph (i) of that paragraph "the relevant police station" means the first police station to which he is taken in the police area in which his arrest was sought.

(4) Subsection (2) above shall have effect in relation to a person arrested under section 31 above as if every reference in it to his arrest or his being arrested were a reference to his arrest or his being arrested for the offence for which he was originally arrested.

(5) If—

(a) a person is in police detention in a police area in England and Wales ("the first area"); and

(b) his arrest for an offence is sought in some other police area in England and Wales ("the second area"); and

(c) he is taken to the second area for the purposes of investigating that offence, without being questioned in the first area in order to obtain evidence in relation to it,

the relevant time shall be—

(i) the time 24 hours after he leaves the place where he is detained in the first area; or

(ii) the time at which he arrives at the first police station to which he is taken in the second area,

whichever is the earlier.

(6) When a person who is in police detention is removed to hospital because he is in need of medical treatment, any time during which he is being questioned in hospital or on the way there or back by a police officer for the purpose of obtaining evidence relating to an offence shall be included in any period which falls to be calculated for the purposes of this Part of this Act, but any other time while he is in hospital or on his way there or back shall not be so included.

(7) Subject to subsection (8) below, a person who at the expiry of 24 hours after the relevant time is in police detention and has not been charged shall be released at that time either on bail or without bail.

(8) Subsection (7) above does not apply to a person whose detention for more than 24 hours after the relevant time has been authorised or is otherwise permitted in accordance with section 42 or 43 below.

(9) A person released under subsection (7) above shall not be re-arrested without a warrant for the offence for which he was previously arrested unless new evidence justifying a further arrest has come to light since his release[; but this subsection does not prevent an arrest under section 46A below.]

NOTES

Sub-s (9): words in square brackets inserted by the Criminal Justice and Public Order Act 1994, s 29(1), (4)(b).

## 42 Authorisation of continued detention

(1)    Where a police officer of the rank of superintendent or above who is responsible for the police station at which a person is detained has reasonable grounds for believing that—

(a)    the detention of that person without charge is necessary to secure or preserve evidence relating to an offence for which he is under arrest or to obtain such evidence by questioning him;

(b)    an offence for which he is under arrest is a serious arrestable offence; and

(c)    the investigation is being conducted diligently and expeditiously,

he may authorise the keeping of that person in police detention for a period expiring at or before 36 hours after the relevant time.

(2)    Where an officer such as is mentioned in subsection (1) above has authorised the keeping of a person in police detention for a period expiring less than 36 hours after the relevant time, such an officer may authorise the keeping of that person in police detention for a further period expiring not more than 36 hours after that time if the conditions specified in subsection (1) above are still satisfied when he gives the authorisation.

(3)    If it is proposed to transfer a person in police detention to another police area, the officer determining whether or not to authorise keeping him in detention under subsection (1) above shall have regard to the distance and the time the journey would take.

(4)    No authorisation under subsection (1) above shall be given in respect of any person—

(a)    more than 24 hours after the relevant time; or

(b)    before the second review of his detention under section 40 above has been carried out.

(5)    Where an officer authorises the keeping of a person in police detention under subsection (1) above, it shall be his duty—

(a)    to inform that person of the grounds for his continued detention; and

(b)    to record the grounds in that person's custody record.

(6)    Before determining whether to authorise the keeping of a person in detention under subsection (1) or (2) above, an officer shall give—

(a)    that person; or

(b)    any solicitor representing him who is available at the time when it falls to the officer to determine whether to give the authorisation,

an opportunity to make representations to him about the detention.

(7)    Subject to subsection (8) below, the person in detention or his solicitor may make representations under subsection (6) above either orally or in writing.

(8)    The officer to whom it falls to determine whether to give the authorisation may refuse to hear oral representations from the person in detention if he considers that he is unfit to make such representations by reason of his condition or behaviour.

(9)   Where—
  (a)  an officer authorises the keeping of a person in detention under subsection
       (1) above; and
  (b)  at the time of the authorisation he has not yet exercised a right conferred
       on him by section 56 or 58 below,

the officer—
  (i)    shall inform him of that right;
  (ii)   shall decide whether he should be permitted to exercise it;
  (iii)  shall record the decision in his custody record; and
  (iv)   if the decision is to refuse to permit the exercise of the right, shall also
         record the grounds for the decision in that record.

(10)  Where an officer has authorised the keeping of a person who has not been
charged in detention under subsection (1) or (2) above, he shall be released from
detention, either on bail or without bail, not later than 36 hours after the relevant
time, unless—
  (a)  he has been charged with an offence; or
  (b)  his continued detention is authorised or otherwise permitted in
       accordance with section 43 below.

(11)  A person released under subsection (10) above shall not be re-arrested without a
warrant for the offence for which he was previously arrested unless new evidence
justifying a further arrest has come to light since his release[; but this subsection does
not prevent an arrest under section 46A below.]

---

NOTES
  Sub-s (11): words in square brackets inserted by the Criminal Justice and Public Order Act 1994, s
29(1), (4)(b).
  Modification: any reference to solicitor(s) etc modified to include references to bodies recognised
under the Administration of Justice Act 1985, s 9, by the Solicitors' Incorporated Practices Order 1991, SI
1991/2684, arts 4, 5, Sch 1.

---

## 43   Warrants of further detention

(1)   Where, on an application on oath made by a constable and supported by an
information, a magistrates' court is satisfied that there are reasonable grounds for
believing that the further detention of the person to whom the application relates is
justified, it may issue a warrant of further detention authorising the keeping of that
person in police detention.

(2)   A court may not hear an application for a warrant of further detention unless
the person to whom the application relates—
  (a)  has been furnished with a copy of the information; and
  (b)  has been brought before the court for the hearing.

(3)   The person to whom the application relates shall be entitled to be legally
represented at the hearing and, if he is not so represented but wishes to be so
represented—
  (a)  the court shall adjourn the hearing to enable him to obtain representation;
       and
  (b)  he may be kept in police detention during the adjournment.

(4)   A person's further detention is only justified for the purposes of this section or
section 44 below if—
  (a)  his detention without charge is necessary to secure or preserve evidence
       relating to an offence for which he is under arrest or to obtain such
       evidence by questioning him;

    (b)  an offence for which he is under arrest is a serious arrestable offence; and

    (c)  the investigation is being conducted diligently and expeditiously.

(5)   Subject to subsection (7) below, an application for a warrant of further detention may be made—

    (a)  at any time before the expiry of 36 hours after the relevant time; or

    (b)  in a case where—

        (i)  it is not practicable for the magistrates' court to which the application will be made to sit at the expiry of 36 hours after the relevant time; but

       (ii)  the court will sit during the 6 hours following the end of that period, at any time before the expiry of the said 6 hours.

(6)   In a case to which subsection (5)(b) above applies—

    (a)  the person to whom the application relates may be kept in police detention until the application is heard; and

    (b)  the custody officer shall make a note in that person's custody record—

        (i)  of the fact that he was kept in police detention for more than 36 hours after the relevant time; and

       (ii)  of the reason why he was so kept.

(7)   If—

    (a)  an application for a warrant of further detention is made after the expiry of 36 hours after the relevant time; and

    (b)  it appears to the magistrates' court that it would have been reasonable for the police to make it before the expiry of that period,

the court shall dismiss the application.

(8)   Where on an application such as is mentioned in subsection (1) above a magistrates' court is not satisfied that there are reasonable grounds for believing that the further detention of the person to whom the application relates is justified, it shall be its duty—

    (a)  to refuse the application; or

    (b)  to adjourn the hearing of it until a time not later than 36 hours after the relevant time.

(9)   The person to whom the application relates may be kept in police detention during the adjournment.

(10)  A warrant of further detention shall—

    (a)  state the time at which it is issued;

    (b)  authorise the keeping in police detention of the person to whom it relates for the period stated in it.

(11)  Subject to subsection (12) below, the period stated in a warrant of further detention shall be such period as the magistrates' court thinks fit, having regard to the evidence before it.

(12)  The period shall not be longer than 36 hours.

(13)  If it is proposed to transfer a person in police detention to a police area other than that in which he is detained when the application for a warrant of further detention is made, the court hearing the application shall have regard to the distance and the time the journey would take.

(14)  Any information submitted in support of an application under this section shall state—

(a)  the nature of the offence for which the person to whom the application relates has been arrested;

(b)  the general nature of the evidence on which that person was arrested;

(c)  what inquiries relating to the offence have been made by the police and what further inquiries are proposed by them;

(d)  the reasons for believing the continued detention of that person to be necessary for the purposes of such further inquiries.

(15)  Where an application under this section is refused, the person to whom the application relates shall forthwith be charged or, subject to subsection (16) below, released, either on bail or without bail.

(16)  A person need not be released under subsection (15) above—

(a)  before the expiry of 24 hours after the relevant time; or

(b)  before the expiry of any longer period for which his continued detention is or has been authorised under section 42 above.

(17)  Where an application under this section is refused, no further application shall be made under this section in respect of the person to whom the refusal relates, unless supported by evidence which has come to light since the refusal.

(18)  Where a warrant of further detention is issued, the person to whom it relates shall be released from police detention, either on bail or without bail, upon or before the expiry of the warrant unless he is charged.

(19)  A person released under subsection (18) above shall not be re-arrested without a warrant for the offence for which he was previously arrested unless new evidence justifying a further arrest has come to light since his release[; but this subsection does not prevent an arrest under section 46A below.]

---

NOTES

Sub-s (19): words in square brackets inserted by the Criminal Justice and Public Order Act 1994, s 29(1), (4)(b).

---

## 44  Extension of warrants of further detention

(1)  On an application on oath made by a constable and supported by an information a magistrates' court may extend a warrant of further detention issued under section 43 above if it is satisfied that there are reasonable grounds for believing that the further detention of the person to whom the application relates is justified.

(2)  Subject to subsection (3) below, the period for which a warrant of further detention may be extended shall be such period as the court thinks fit, having regard to the evidence before it.

(3)  The period shall not—

(a)  be longer than 36 hours; or

(b)  end later than 96 hours after the relevant time.

(4)  Where a warrant of further detention has been extended under subsection (1) above, or further extended under this subsection, for a period ending before 96 hours after the relevant time, on an application such as is mentioned in that subsection a magistrates' court may further extend the warrant if it is satisfied as there mentioned; and subsections (2) and (3) above apply to such further extensions as they apply to extensions under subsection (1) above.

(5)  A warrant of further detention shall, if extended or further extended under this section, be endorsed with a note of the period of the extension.

(6)    Subsections (2), (3), and (14) of section 43 above shall apply to an application made under this section as they apply to an application made under that section.

(7)    Where an application under this section is refused, the person to whom the application relates shall forthwith be charged or, subject to subsection (8) below, released, either on bail or without bail.

(8)    A person need not be released under subsection (7) above before the expiry of any period for which a warrant of further detention issued in relation to him has been extended or further extended on an earlier application made under this section.

# PART V
# QUESTIONING AND TREATMENT OF PERSONS BY POLICE

### 55    Intimate searches

(1)    Subject to the following provisions of this section, if an officer of at least the rank of superintendent has reasonable grounds for believing—
    (a)   that a person who has been arrested and is in police detention may have concealed on him anything which—
       (i)   he could use to cause physical injury to himself or others; and
       (ii)  he might so use while he is in police detention or in the custody of a court; or
    (b)   that such a person—
       (i)   may have a Class A drug concealed on him; and
       (ii)  was in possession of it with the appropriate criminal intent before his arrest,

he may authorise [an intimate search] of that person.

(2)    An officer may not authorise an intimate search of a person for anything unless he has reasonable grounds for believing that it cannot be found without his being intimately searched.

(3)    An officer may give an authorisation under subsection (1) above orally or in writing but, if he gives it orally, he shall confirm it in writing as soon as is practicable.

(4)    An intimate search which is only a drug offence search shall be by way of examination by a suitably qualified person.

(5)    Except as provided by subsection (4) above, an intimate search shall be by way of examination by a suitably qualified person unless an officer of at least the rank of superintendent considers that this is not practicable.

(6)    An intimate search which is not carried out as mentioned in subsection (5) above shall be carried out by a constable.

(7)    A constable may not carry out an intimate search of a person of the opposite sex.

(8)    No intimate search may be carried out except—
    (a)   at a police station;
    (b)   at a hospital;
    (c)   at a registered medical practitioner's surgery; or
    (d)   at some other place used for medical purposes.

(9)    An intimate search which is only a drug offence search may not be carried out at a police station.

(10) If an intimate search of a person is carried out, the custody record relating to him shall state—

(a) which parts of his body were searched; and

(b) why they were searched.

(11) The information required to be recorded by subsection (10) above shall be recorded as soon as practicable after the completion of the search.

(12) The custody officer at a police station may seize and retain anything which is found on an intimate search of a person, or cause any such thing to be seized and retained—

(a) if he believes that the person from whom it is seized may use it—

(i) to cause physical injury to himself or any other person;

(ii) to damage property;

(iii) to interfere with evidence; or

(iv) to assist him to escape; or

(b) if he has reasonable grounds for believing that it may be evidence relating to an offence.

(13) Where anything is seized under this section, the person from whom it is seized shall be told the reason for the seizure unless he is—

(a) violent or likely to become violent; or

(b) incapable of understanding what is said to him.

(14) Every annual report—

[(a) under section 22 of the Police Act 1996; or]

(b) made by the Commissioner of Police of the Metropolis,

shall contain information about searches under this section which have been carried out in the area to which the report relates during the period to which it relates.

[(14A) Every annual report under section 57 of the Police Act 1997 (reports by Director General of the National Crime Squad) shall contain information about searches authorised under this section by members of the National Crime Squad during the period to which the report relates.]

(15) The information about such searches shall include—

(a) the total number of searches;

(b) the number of searches conducted by way of examination by a suitably qualified person;

(c) the number of searches not so conducted but conducted in the presence of such a person; and

(d) the result of the searches carried out.

(16) The information shall also include, as separate items—

(a) the total number of drug offence searches; and

(b) the result of those searches.

(17) In this section—

"the appropriate criminal intent" means an intent to commit an offence under—

(a) section 5(3) of the Misuse of Drugs Act 1971 (possession of controlled drug with intent to supply to another); or

(b) section 68(2) of the Customs and Excise Management Act 1979 (exportation etc with intent to evade a prohibition or restriction);

"Class A drug" has the meaning assigned to it by section 2(1)(b) of the Misuse of Drugs Act 1971;

"drug offence search" means an intimate search for a Class A drug which an officer has authorised by virtue of subsection (1)(b) above; and

"suitably qualified person" means—

(a) a registered medical practitioner; or

(b) a registered nurse.

NOTES

Sub-s (1): words in square brackets substituted by the Criminal Justice Act 1988, s 170(1), Sch 15, paras 97, 99.

Sub-s (14): para (a) substituted by the Police Act 1996, s 103(1), Sch 7, Pt II, para 36.

Sub-s (14A): inserted by the Police Act 1997, s 134(1), Sch 9, para 47, as from a day to be appointed.

Modified by the Police and Criminal Evidence Act (Application to Customs and Excise) Order 1985, SI 1985/1800.

## 56   Right to have someone informed when arrested

(1)   Where a person has been arrested and is being held in custody in a police station or other premises, he shall be entitled, if he so requests, to have one friend or relative or other person who is known to him or who is likely to take an interest in his welfare told, as soon as is practicable except to the extent that delay is permitted by this section, that he has been arrested and is being detained there.

(2)   Delay is only permitted—

(a) in the case of a person who is in police detention for a serious arrestable offence; and

(b) if an officer of at least the rank of superintendent authorises it.

(3)   In any case the person in custody must be permitted to exercise the right conferred by subsection (1) above within 36 hours from the relevant time, as defined in section 41(2) above.

(4)   An officer may give an authorisation under subsection (2) above orally or in writing but, if he gives it orally, he shall confirm it in writing as soon as is practicable.

(5)   [Subject to sub-section (5A) below] an officer may only authorise delay where he has reasonable grounds for believing that telling the named person of the arrest—

(a) will lead to interference with or harm to evidence connected with a serious arrestable offence or interference with or physical injury to other persons; or

(b) will lead to the alerting of other persons suspected of having committed such an offence but not yet arrested for it; or

(c) will hinder the recovery of any property obtained as a result of such offence.

[(5A) An officer may also authorise delay where the serious arrestable offence is a drug trafficking offence [or an offence to which Part VI of the Criminal Justice Act 1988 applies (offences in respect of which confiscation orders under that Part may be made)] and the officer has reasonable grounds for believing—

[(a) where the offence is a drug trafficking offence, that the detained person has benefited from drug trafficking and that the recovery of the value of that person's proceeds of drug trafficking will be hindered by the exercise of the right conferred by subsection (1) above; and

(b) where the offence is one to which Part VI of the Criminal Justice Act 1988 applies, that the detained person has benefited from the offence and that the recovery of the value of the property obtained by that person from or in connection with the offence or of the pecuniary advantage derived by him from or in connection with it will be hindered by the exercise of the right conferred by subsection (1) above].]

(6)   If a delay is authorised—
  (a)   the detained person shall be told the reason for it; and
  (b)   the reason shall be noted on his custody record.

(7)   The duties imposed by subsection (6) above shall be performed as soon as is practicable.

(8)   The rights conferred by this section on a person detained at a police station or other premises are exercisable whenever he is transferred from one place to another; and this section applies to each subsequent occasion on which they are exercisable as it applies to the first such occasion.

(9)   There may be no further delay in permitting the exercise of the right conferred by subsection (1) above once the reason for authorising delay ceases to subsist.

(10)   In the foregoing provisions of this section references to a person who has been arrested include references to a person who has been detained under the terrorism provisions and "arrest" includes detention under those provisions.

(11)   In its application to a person who has been arrested or detained under the terrorism provisions—
  (a)   subsection (2)(a) above shall have effect as if for the words "for a serious arrestable offence" there were substituted the words "under the terrorism provisions";
  (b)   subsection (3) above shall have effect as if for the words from "within" onwards there were substituted the words "before the end of the period beyond which he may no longer be detained without the authority of the Secretary of State"; and
  (c)   subsection (5) above shall have effect as if at the end there were added "or
  (d)   will lead to interference with the gathering of information about the commission, preparation or instigation of acts of terrorism; or
  (e)   by alerting any person, will make it more difficult—
    (i)   to prevent an act of terrorism; or
    (ii)   to secure the apprehension, prosecution or conviction of any person in connection with the commission, preparation or instigation of an act of terrorism.".

---

NOTES
   Sub-s (5): words in square brackets inserted by the Drug Trafficking Offences Act 1986, s 32(1).
   Sub-s (5A): inserted by the Drug Trafficking Offences Act 1986, s 32(1); words in first pair of square brackets inserted, and paras (a), (b) substituted, by the Criminal Justice Act 1988, s 99(1), (2).

## 60   Tape-recording of interviews

(1)   It shall be the duty of the Secretary of State—
  (a)   to issue a code of practice in connection with the tape-recording of interviews of persons suspected of the commission of criminal offences which are held by police officers at police stations; and
  (b)   to make an order requiring the tape-recording of interviews of persons suspected of the commission of criminal offences, or of such descriptions of criminal offences as may be specified in the order, which are so held, in accordance with the code as it has effect for the time being.

(2)   An order under subsection (1) above shall be made by statutory instrument and shall be subject to annulment in pursuance of a resolution of either House of Parliament.

NOTES

Commencement: 1 January 1986 (sub-s (1), in part); 29 November 1991 (sub-s (1) in part, sub-s (2)); 9 November 1992 (sub-s (1), remainder).

## 61   Fingerprinting

(1)   Except as provided by this section no person's fingerprints may be taken without the appropriate consent.

(2)   Consent to the taking of a person's fingerprints must be in writing if it is given at a time when he is at a police station.

(3)   The fingerprints of a person detained at a police station may be taken without the appropriate consent—

    (a)   if an officer of at least the rank of superintendent authorises them to be taken; or

    (b)   if—

       (i)   he has been charged with a recordable offence or informed that he will be reported for such an offence; and

      (ii)   he has not had his fingerprints taken in the course of the investigation of the offence by the police.

(4)   An officer may only give an authorisation under subsection (3)(a) above if he has reasonable grounds—

    (a)   for suspecting the involvement of the person whose fingerprints are to be taken in a criminal offence; and

    (b)   for believing that his fingerprints will tend to confirm or disprove his involvement.

(5)   An officer may give an authorisation under subsection (3)(a) above orally or in writing but, if he gives it orally, he shall confirm it in writing as soon as is practicable.

(6)   Any person's fingerprints may be taken without the appropriate consent if he has been convicted of a recordable offence.

(7)   In a case where by virtue of subsection (3) or (6) above a person's fingerprints are taken without the appropriate consent—

    (a)   he shall be told the reason before his fingerprints are taken; and

    (b)   the reason shall be recorded as soon as is practicable after the fingerprints are taken.

[(7A) If a person's fingerprints are taken at a police station, whether with or without the appropriate consent—

    (a)   before the fingerprints are taken, an officer shall inform him that they may be the subject of a speculative search; and

    (b)   the fact that the person has been informed of this possibility shall be recorded as soon as is practicable after the fingerprints have been taken.]

(8)   If he is detained at a police station when the fingerprints are taken, the reason for taking them [and, in the case falling within subsection (7A) above, the fact referred to in paragraph (b) of that subsection] shall be recorded on his custody record.

(9)   Nothing in this section—

    (a)   affects any power conferred by paragraph 18(2) of Schedule 2 to the Immigration Act 1971; or

(b) [except as provided in section 15(10) of, and paragraph 7(6) of Schedule 5 to, the Prevention of Terrorism (Temporary Provisions) Act 1989,] applies to a person arrested or detained under the terrorism provisions.

NOTES

Commencement: 1 January 1986 (sub-ss (1)–(7), (8), (9)); 10 April 1995 (sub-s (7A)).

Sub-s (7A): inserted by the Criminal Justice and Public Order Act 1994, s 168(2), Sch 10, para 56(a).

Sub-s (8): words in square brackets inserted by the Criminal Justice and Public Order Act 1994, s 168(2), Sch 10, para 56(b).

Sub-s (9): words in square brackets in sub-para (b) inserted by the Prevention of Terrorism (Temporary Provisions) Act 1989, s 25(1), Sch 8, para 6(1), (5).

Modified by the Police and Criminal Evidence Act 1984 (Application to Armed Forces) Order 1985, SI 1985/1882, art 6.

# PART VIII
# EVIDENCE IN CRIMINAL PROCEEDINGS—GENERAL

*Confessions*

## 76 Confessions

(1) In any proceedings a confession made by an accused person may be given in evidence against him in so far as it is relevant to any matter in issue in the proceedings and is not excluded by the court in pursuance of this section.

(2) If, in any proceedings where the prosecution proposes to give in evidence a confession made by an accused person, it is represented to the court that the confession was or may have been obtained—

(a) by oppression of the person who made it; or

(b) in consequence of anything said or done which was likely, in the circumstances existing at the time, to render unreliable any confession which might be made by him in consequence thereof,

the court shall not allow the confession to be given in evidence against him except in so far as the prosecution proves to the court beyond reasonable doubt that the confession (notwithstanding that it may be true) was not obtained as aforesaid.

(3) In any proceedings where the prosecution proposes to give in evidence a confession made by an accused person, the court may of its own motion require the prosecution, as a condition of allowing it to do so, to prove that the confession was not obtained as mentioned in subsection (2) above.

(4) The fact that a confession is wholly or partly excluded in pursuance of this section shall not affect the admissibility in evidence—

(a) of any facts discovered as a result of the confession; or

(b) where the confession is relevant as showing that the accused speaks, writes or expresses himself in a particular way, of so much of the confession as is necessary to show that he does so.

(5) Evidence that a fact to which this subsection applies was discovered as a result of a statement made by an accused person shall not be admissible unless evidence of how it was discovered is given by him or on his behalf.

(6) Subsection (5) above applies—

(a) to any fact discovered as a result of a confession which is wholly excluded in pursuance of this section; and

    (b)  to any fact discovered as a result of a confession which is partly so excluded, if the fact is discovered as a result of the excluded part of the confession.

(7)    Nothing in Part VII of this Act shall prejudice the admissibility of a confession made by an accused person.

(8)    In this section "oppression" includes torture, inhuman or degrading treatment, and the use or threat of violence (whether or not amounting to torture).

[(9)  Where the proceedings mentioned in subsection (1) above are proceedings before a magistrates' court inquiring into an offence as examining justices this section shall have effect with the omission of—

    (a)  in subsection (1) the words "and is not excluded by the court in pursuance of this section", and

    (b)  subsections (2) to (6) and (8).]

**NOTES**

    Sub-s (9): added by the Criminal Procedure and Investigations Act 1996, s 47, Sch 1, Pt II, para 25, with effect in accordance with provision made by order under Sch 1, Pt III, para 39 to the 1996 Act.

## 77   Confessions by mentally handicapped persons

(1)    Without prejudice to the general duty of the court at a trial on indictment to direct the jury on any matter on which it appears to the court appropriate to do so, where at such a trial—

    (a)  the case against the accused depends wholly or substantially on a confession by him; and

    (b)  the court is satisfied—

        (i)  that he is mentally handicapped; and

        (ii)  that the confession was not made in the presence of an independent person,

the court shall warn the jury that there is special need for caution before convicting the accused in reliance on the confession, and shall explain that the need arises because of the circumstances mentioned in paragraphs (a) and (b) above.

(2)    In any case where at the summary trial of a person for an offence it appears to the court that a warning under subsection (1) above would be required if the trial were on indictment, the court shall treat the case as one in which there is a special need for caution before convicting the accused on his confession.

(3)    In this section—

    "independent person" does not include a police officer or a person employed for, or engaged on, police purposes;

    "mentally handicapped", in relation to a person, means that he is in a state of arrested or incomplete development of mind which includes significant impairment of intelligence and social functioning; and

    "police purposes" has the meaning assigned to it by [section 101(2) of the Police Act 1996].

**NOTES**

    Sub-s (3): in definition "police purposes" words in square brackets substituted by the Police Act 1996, s 103(1), Sch 7, Pt II, para 38.

*Miscellaneous*

## 78  Exclusion of unfair evidence

(1)   In any proceedings the court may refuse to allow evidence on which the prosecution proposes to rely to be given if it appears to the court that, having regard to all the circumstances, including the circumstances in which the evidence was obtained, the admission of the evidence would have such an adverse effect on the fairness of the proceedings that the court ought not to admit it.

(2)   Nothing in this section shall prejudice any rule of law requiring a court to exclude evidence.

[(3)   This section shall not apply in the case of proceedings before a magistrates' court inquiring into an offence as examining justices.]

### NOTES

Sub-s (3): added by the Criminal Procedure and Investigations Act 1996, s 47, Sch 1, Pt II, para 26, with effect in accordance with provision made by order under Sch 1, Pt III, para 39, to the 1996 Act.

# PART IX
# POLICE COMPLAINTS AND DISCIPLINE

*Handling of complaints etc*

## 90  Steps to be taken after investigation—general

(1)   It shall be the duty of the appropriate authority, on receiving—
  (a)   a report concerning the conduct of a senior officer which is submitted to them under section 86(6) above; or
  (b)   a copy of a report concerning the conduct of a senior officer which is sent to them under section 89(6) above

to send a copy of the report to the Director of Public Prosecutions unless the report satisfies them that no criminal offence has been committed.

(2)   Nothing in the following provisions of this section or in sections 91 to 94 below has effect in relation to senior officers.

(3)   On receiving—
  (a)   a report concerning the conduct of an officer who is not a senior officer which is submitted to him under section 85(9) above; or
  (b)   a copy of a report concerning the conduct of such an officer which is sent to him under section 89(6) above

it shall be the duty of a chief officer of police—
  (i)    to determine whether the report indicates that a criminal offence may have been committed by a member of the police force for his area; and
  (ii)   if he determines that it does, to consider whether the offence indicated is such that the officer ought to be charged with it.

(4)   If the chief officer—
  (a)   determines that the report does indicate that a criminal offence may have been committed by a member of the police force for his area; and
  (b)   considers that the offence indicated is such that the officer ought to be charged with it,

he shall send a copy of the report to the Director of Public Prosecutions.

(5)  Subject to section 91(1) below [In such cases as may be prescribed by regulations made by the Secretary of State], after the Director has dealt with the question of criminal proceedings, the chief officer shall send the Authority a memorandum, signed by him and stating whether he has preferred disciplinary charges in respect of the conduct which was the subject of the investigation and, if not, his reasons for not doing so [brought (or purposes to bring) disciplinary proceedings in respect of the conduct which was the subject of the investigation and, if not, giving his reasons].

(6)  If the chief officer—
  (a)  determines that the report does indicate that a criminal offence may have been committed by a member of the police force for his area; and
  (b)  considers that the offence indicated is not such that the officer ought to be charged with it,

he shall send the Authority a memorandum to that effect, signed by him and stating whether he proposes to prefer disciplinary charges in respect of the conduct which was the subject of the investigation and, if not, his reasons for not proposing to do so.

(7)  Subject to section 91(1) below [In such cases as may be prescribed by regulations made by the Secretary of State], if the chief officer considers that the report does not indicate that a criminal offence may have been committed by a member of the police force for his area, he shall send the Authority a memorandum to that effect, signed by him and stating whether he has preferred disciplinary charges in respect of the conduct which was the subject of the investigation and, if not, his reasons for not doing so [brought (or purposes to bring) disciplinary proceedings in respect of the conduct which was the subject of the investigation and, if not, giving his reasons].

(8)  A memorandum under this section—
  (a)  shall give particulars—
    (i)  of any disciplinary charges which a chief officer has preferred or proposes to prefer in respect of the conduct which was the subject of the investigation; and
    (ii)  of any exceptional circumstances affecting the case by reason of which he considers that section 94 below should apply to the hearing; and
  (b)  shall state his opinion of the complaint or other matter to which it relates.

(9)  Where the investigation—
  (a)  related to conduct which was the subject of a complaint; and
  (b)  was not supervised by the Authority,

the chief officer shall send the Authority—
  (i)  a copy of the complaint or of the record of the complaint; and
  (ii)  a copy of the report of the investigation

at the same time as he sends them the memorandum [then, if the chief officer is required by virtue of regulations under subsection (5) or (7) above to send the Authority a memorandum, he shall at the same time send them a copy of the complaint, of the record of the complaint, and a copy of the report of the investigation].

(10)  Subject to section 93(6) below—
  (a)  if a chief officer's memorandum states that he proposes to prefer disciplinary charges, it shall be his duty to prefer and proceed with them; and [bring disciplinary proceedings, it shall be his duty to bring and proceed with them; and]

(b) if such a memorandum states that he has preferred such charges [brought such proceedings], it shall be his duty to proceed with them.

**NOTES**

Repealed by the Police Act 1996, s 103, Sch 9, Pt II, as from a day to be appointed.

Sub-s (3): para (ii) and preceding word "and" repealed by the Police and Magistrates' Courts Act 1994, ss 35(2), 93, Sch 9, Pt I, subject to savings in s 38 of the 1994 Act, as from a day to be appointed.

Sub-s (4): para (b) and preceding word "and" repealed by the Police and Magistrates' Courts Act 1994, ss 35(3), 93, Sch 9, Pt I, subject to savings in s 38 of the 1994 Act, as from a day to be appointed.

Sub-ss (5), (7): words "Subject to section 91(1) below", and words from "preferred disciplinary charges" to "not doing so" repealed, and subsequent words in square brackets substituted, by the Police and Magistrates' Courts Act 1994, s 35(4), (6), subject to savings in s 38 of the 1994 Act, as from a day to be appointed.

Sub-ss (6), (8): repealed by the Police and Magistrates' Courts Act 1994, ss 35(5), (7), 93, Sch 9, Pt I, subject to savings in s 38 of the 1994 Act, as from a day to be appointed.

Sub-s (9): words from "the chief officer" to "the memorandum" repealed, and subsequent words in square brackets substituted, by the Police and Magistrates' Courts Act 1994, s 35(8), subject to savings in s 38 of the 1994 Act, as from a day to be appointed.

Sub-s (10): words from "prefer disciplinary charges" to "proceed with them; and" in para (a), and words "preferred such charges" in para (b) repealed, and subsequent words in square brackets substituted, by the Police and Magistrates' Courts Act 1994, s 35(9), subject to savings in s 38 of the 1994 Act, as from a day to be appointed.

## 91 Steps to be taken where accused has admitted charges

(1) No memorandum need be sent to the Authority under section 90 above if disciplinary charges have been preferred in respect of the conduct which was the subject of the investigation and the accused has admitted the charges and has not withdrawn his admission.

(2) In any such case the chief officer shall send to the Authority, after the conclusion of the disciplinary proceedings (including any appeal to the Secretary of State), particulars of the disciplinary charges preferred and of any punishment imposed.

(3) If—

(a) the charges related to conduct which was the subject of a complaint; and

(b) the investigation of the complaint was not supervised by the Authority,

the chief officer shall also send the Authority—

(i) a copy of the complaint or of the record of the complaint; and

(ii) a copy of the report of the investigation.

**NOTES**

Repealed by the Police Act 1996, s 103, Sch 9, Pt II, as from a day to be appointed.

Repealed by the Police and Magistrates' Courts Act 1994, ss 44, 93, Sch 5, Pt II, para 28, Sch 9, Pt I, subject to savings in s 38 of the 1994 Act, as from a day to be appointed.

## 92 Powers of Authority to direct reference of reports etc to Director of Public Prosecutions

(1) When a chief officer of police has performed all duties imposed on him by sections 90 and 91 above in relation to the report of an investigation concerning the conduct of an officer who is not a senior officer, it shall be the duty of the Authority—

(a) to determine whether the report indicates that a criminal offence may have been committed by that officer; and

(b) if so, to consider whether the offence is such that the officer ought to be charged with it.

(2)   If the Authority consider that the officer ought to be charged, it shall be their duty to direct the chief officer to send the Director of Public Prosecutions a copy of the report.

(3)   When the Authority give a direction under subsection (2) above, they may also direct the chief officer to send the Director the information contained in the memorandum under section 90 above.

(4)   If the investigation was an investigation of a complaint, the Authority shall direct the chief officer to send the Director a copy of the complaint or of the record of the complaint.

(5)   It shall be the duty of a chief officer to comply with any direction under this section.

(6)   Sections 90 and 91 above shall apply where a copy of a report is sent to the Director under this section as they apply where a copy is sent to him under section 90(4) above.

NOTES
Repealed by the Police Act 1996, s 103, Sch 9, Pt II, as from a day to be appointed.
Repealed by the Police and Magistrates' Courts Act 1994, ss 37(b), 93, Sch 9, Pt I, subject to savings in s 38 of the 1994 Act, as from a day to be appointed.

## 93   Powers of Authority as to disciplinary charges

(1)   Where a memorandum under section 90 above states that a chief officer of police has not preferred disciplinary charges or does not propose to do so, the Authority may recommend him to prefer such disciplinary charges as they may specify.

(2)   Subject to subsection (6) below, a chief officer may not withdraw charges which he has preferred in accordance with a recommendation under subsection (1) above.

(3)   If after the Authority have made a recommendation under this section and consulted the chief officer he is still unwilling to prefer such charges as the Authority consider appropriate, they may direct him to prefer such charges as they may specify.

(4)   Where the Authority give a chief officer a direction under this section, they shall furnish him with a written statement of their reasons for doing so.

(5)   Subject to subsection (6) below, it shall be the duty of a chief officer to prefer and proceed with charges specified in such a direction.

(6)   The Authority may give a chief officer leave—
   (a)   not to prefer charges which section 90(10) above or subsection (5) above would otherwise oblige him to prefer; or
   (b)   not to proceed with charges with which section 90(10) above or subsection (2) or (5) above would otherwise oblige him to proceed.

(7)   The Authority may request a chief officer of police to furnish them with such information as they may reasonably require for the purpose of discharging their functions under this section.

(8)   It shall be the duty of a chief officer to comply with any such request.

NOTES
Repealed by the Police Act 1996, s 103, Sch 9, Pt II, as from a day to be appointed.

Sub-s (1): words from "preferred disciplinary charges" to "as they may specify" substituted by the words "brought disciplinary proceedings or does not propose to do so, the Authority may recommend him to bring such proceedings" by the Police and Magistrates' Courts Act 1994, s 36(2), subject to savings in s 38 of the 1994 Act, as from a day to be appointed.

Sub-s (2): words "withdraw charges which he has preferred" substituted by the words "discontinue disciplinary proceedings that he has brought" by the Police and Magistrates' Courts Act 1994, s 36(3), subject to savings in s 38 of the 1994 Act, as from a day to be appointed.

Sub-s (3): words from "prefer such charges" to "as they may specify" substituted by the words "bring disciplinary proceedings, they may direct him to do so" by the Police and Magistrates' Courts Act 1994, s 36(4), subject to savings in s 38 of the 1994 Act, as from a day to be appointed.

Sub-s (5): words "prefer and proceed with charges specified in" substituted by the words "comply with" by the Police and Magistrates' Courts Act 1994, s 36(5), subject to savings in s 38 of the 1994 Act, as from a day to be appointed.

Sub-s (6): substituted by the Police and Magistrates' Courts Act 1994, s 36(6), subject to savings in s 38 of the 1994 Act, as from a day to be appointed, as follows—

"(6) The Authority may withdraw a direction given under this section.".

Sub-ss (7), (8): substituted by the Police and Magistrates' Courts Act 1994, s 36(7), subject to savings in s 38 of the 1994 Act, as from a day to be appointed, as follows—

"(7) A chief officer shall—

(a) advise the Authority of what action he has taken in response to a recommendation or direction under this section, and

(b) furnish the Authority with such other information as they may reasonably require for the purpose of discharging their functions under this section.".

## 94 Disciplinary tribunals

(1)   Where a chief officer of police prefers a disciplinary charge in respect of a matter to which a memorandum under section 90 above relates, this section applies—

(a) to the hearing of any charge in pursuance of a direction under section 93 above; and

(b) to the hearing of any other charge to which the Authority direct that it shall apply.

(2)   The Authority may direct that this section shall apply to the hearing of a charge if they consider that to be desirable by reason of any exceptional circumstances affecting the case.

(3)   Where this section applies to the hearing of a disciplinary charge—

(a) the function of determining whether the accused is guilty of the charge shall be discharged by a tribunal consisting of—

  (i) a chairman who shall, subject to subsection (4) below, be the chief officer of police by whom that function would fall to be discharged apart from this section; and

  (ii) two members of the Authority nominated by the Authority, being members who have not been concerned with the case; and

(b) the function of determining any punishment to be imposed shall, subject to subsection (7) below, be discharged by the chairman after consulting the other members of the tribunal.

(4)   Where—

(a) the accused is a member of the metropolitan police force; and

(b) the function of determining whether he is guilty of the charge would, apart from this section, fall to be discharged by a person or persons other than a chief officer of police (whether the Commissioner of Police of the Metropolis or the chief officer of another police force),

the chairman of the tribunal shall be—

> (i)  a person nominated by the Commissioner, being either an Assistant Commissioner of Police of the Metropolis or an officer of the metropolitan police force of such rank as may be prescribed by regulations made by the Secretary of State; or
>
> (ii)  in default of any such nomination, the Commissioner.

(5)   The Secretary of State may by regulations provide for the procedure to be followed by tribunals constituted under this section.

(6)   The decision of the tribunal as to whether the accused is guilty of the charge may be a majority decision.

(7)   Where—

> (a)  the chairman of the tribunal is not the chief officer of police of the police force to which the accused belongs; and
>
> (b)  that chief officer is neither interested in the case otherwise than in his capacity as such nor a material witness,

the function of determining any punishment to be imposed shall be discharged by that chief officer after considering any recommendation as to punishment made by the chairman.

(8)   Before making any recommendation the chairman shall consult the other members of the tribunal.

(9)   Where—

> (a)  this section applies to the hearing of a disciplinary charge; and
>
> (b)  there is another disciplinary charge against the accused which, in the opinion of the chief officer of police of the police force to which he belongs, can conveniently and fairly be determined at the same time,

the chief officer may direct that this section shall apply also to the hearing of the other charge.

NOTES

Repealed by the Police Act 1996, s 103, Sch 9, Pt II, as from a day to be appointed.

Repealed by the Police and Magistrates' Courts Act 1994, ss 37(c), 93, Sch 9, Pt I, subject to savings in s 38 of the 1994 Act, as from a day to be appointed.

## 95   Information as to the manner of dealing with complaints etc

Every police authority in carrying out their duty with respect to the maintenance of an [efficient and effective] police force, and inspectors of constabulary in carrying out their duties with respect to the efficiency [and effectiveness] of any police force, shall keep themselves informed as to the working of sections 84 to 93 above in relation to the force.

NOTES

Repealed by the Police Act 1996, s 103, Sch 9, Pt II, as from a day to be appointed.

Words in first pair of square brackets substituted, and words in second pair of square brackets inserted, by the Police and Magistrates' Courts Act 1994, s 44, Sch 5, Pt II, para 29.

## 96   Constabularies maintained by authorities other than police authorities

(1)   An agreement for the establishment in relation to any body of constables maintained by an authority other than a police authority of procedures corresponding [or similar] to any of those established by or by virtue of this Part of this Act may, with the approval of the Secretary of State, be made between the Authority and the authority maintaining the body of constables.

(2)   Where no such procedures are in force in relation to any body of constables, the Secretary of State may by order establish such procedures.

(3)    An agreement under this section may at any time be varied or terminated with the approval of the Secretary of State.

(4)    Before making an order under this section the Secretary of State shall consult—
   (a)  the Authority; and
   (b)  the authority maintaining the body of constables to whom the order would relate.

(5)    The power to make orders under this section shall be exercisable by statutory instrument; and any statutory instrument containing such an order shall be subject to annulment in pursuance of a resolution of either House of Parliament.

(6)    Nothing in any other enactment shall prevent an authority who maintain a body of constables from carrying into effect procedures established by virtue of this section.

(7)    No such procedures shall have effect in relation to anything done by a constable outside England and Wales.

NOTES
   Repealed by the Police Act 1996, s 103, Sch 9, Pt II, as from a day to be appointed.
   Sub-s (1): words in square brackets inserted by the Police and Magistrates' Courts Act 1994, s 44, Sch 5, Pt II, para 30.

## 97    Reports

(1)    The Authority shall, at the request of the Secretary of State, report to him on such matters relating generally to their functions as the Secretary of State may specify, and the Authority may for that purpose carry out research into any such matters.

(2)    The Authority may make a report to the Secretary of State on any matters coming to their notice under this Part of this Act to which they consider that his attention should be drawn by reason of their gravity or of other exceptional circumstances; and the Authority shall send a copy of any such report to the police authority and to the chief officer of police of any police force which appears to the Authority to be concerned or, if the report concerns any such body of constables as is mentioned in section 96 above, to the authority maintaining it and the officer having the direction and the control of it.

(3)    As soon as practicable after the end of each calendar year the Authority shall make to the Secretary of State a report on the discharge of their functions during that year.

(4)    The Authority shall keep under review the working of sections 84 to 96 above and shall make to the Secretary of State a report on it at least once in every three years after the coming into force of this section.

(5)    The Secretary of State shall lay before Parliament a copy of every report received by him under this section and shall cause every such report to be published.

(6)    The Authority shall send to every police authority—
   (a)  a copy of every report made by the Authority under subsection (3) above; and
   (b)  any statistical or other general information which relates to the year dealt with by the report and to the area of that authority and which the Authority consider should be brought to the police authority's attention in connection with their functions under section 95 above.

NOTES
   Repealed by the Police Act 1996, s 103, Sch 9, Pt II, as from a day to be appointed.
   Sub-s (4): repealed by the Police and Magistrates' Courts Act 1994, ss 37(d), 93, Sch 9, Pt I, subject to savings in s 38 of the 1994 Act, as from a day to be appointed.

**98    Restriction on disclosure of information**

(1)    No information received by the Authority in connection with any of their functions under sections 84 to 97 above or regulations made by virtue of section 99 below shall be disclosed by any person who is or has been a member, officer or servant of the Authority except—

- (a) to the Secretary of State or to a member, officer or servant of the Authority or, so far as may be necessary for the proper discharge of the functions of the Authority, to other persons;
- (b) for the purposes of any criminal, civil or disciplinary proceedings; or
- (c) in the form of a summary or other general statement made by the Authority which does not identify the person from whom the information was received or any person to whom it relates.

(2)    Any person who discloses information in contravention of this section shall be guilty of an offence and liable on summary conviction to a fine of an amount not exceeding level 5 on the standard scale . . .

NOTES

Repealed by the Police Act 1996, s 103, Sch 9, Pt II, as from a day to be appointed.

Sub-s (2): words omitted repealed by the Statute Law (Repeals) Act 1993.

## PART XI
## MISCELLANEOUS AND SUPPLEMENTARY

**122    Short title**

This Act may be cited as the Police and Criminal Evidence Act 1984.

# REGISTERED HOMES ACT 1984

## (C 23)

*An Act to consolidate certain enactments relating to residential care homes and nursing homes and Registered Homes Tribunals, with amendments to give effect to recommendations of the Law Commission*

[26 June 1984]

## PART I
## RESIDENTIAL CARE HOMES

*Registration and conduct of residential care homes*

**1    Requirement of registration**

(1)    Subject to the following provisions of this section, registration under this Part of this Act is required in respect of any establishment which provides or is intended to provide, whether for reward or not, residential accommodation with both board and personal care for persons in need of personal care by reason of old age, disablement, past or present dependence on alcohol or drugs, or past or present mental disorder.

(2)     Such an establishment is referred to in this Part of this Act as a "residential care home".

(3)     Registration under this Part of this Act does not affect any requirement to register under Part II of this Act.

[(4)     Registration under this Part of this Act is not required in respect of a small home—

    (a)     if the only persons for whom it provides or is intended to provide residential accommodation with both board and personal care are persons carrying on or intending to carry on the home or employed or intended to be employed there or their relatives, or

    (b)     in such other cases as may be prescribed by the Secretary of State.

(4A)     In this Part a "small home" means an establishment which provides or is intended to provide residential accommodation with both board and personal care for fewer than 4 persons, excluding persons carrying on or intending to carry on the home or employed or intended to be employed there and their relatives.

(4B)     The references in subsections (4) and (4A) to the persons for whom residential accommodation is or is intended to be provided relate only to persons who are in need of personal care by reason of old age, disablement, past or present dependence on alcohol or drugs, or past or present mental disorder.]

(5)     Registration under this Part of this Act is not required in respect of any of the following—

    (a)     any establishment which is used, or is intended to be used, solely as a nursing home or mental nursing home;

    (b)     any hospital as defined in section 128 of the National Health Service Act 1977 which is maintained in pursuance of an Act of Parliament;

    (c)     any hospital as defined in section 145(1) of the Mental Health Act 1983;

    [(d)     any community home, voluntary home or children's home within the meaning of the Children Act 1989;]

    (f)     subject to subsection (6) below, any school, as defined in [section 4 of the Education Act 1996];

    (g)     subject to subsection (7) below, any establishment to which the Secretary of State has made a payment of maintenance grant under regulations made by virtue of [section 485 of the Education Act 1996];

    (h)     any university or university college or college, school or hall of a university;

    (j)     any establishment managed or provided by a government department or local authority or by any authority or body constituted by an Act of Parliament or incorporated by Royal Charter.

(6)     An independent school within the meaning of [the Education Act 1996] is not excluded by subsection (5) above if the school provides accommodation for 50 or less children under the age of 18 years and is not for the time being approved by the Secretary of State under [section 347 of the Education Act 1996].

(7)     An establishment to which the Secretary of State has made a payment of maintenance grant under regulations made by virtue of [section 485 of the Education Act 1996] is only excluded by subsection (5) above until the end of the period of 12 months from the date on which the Secretary of State made the payment.

NOTES

Commencement: 1 April 1993 (sub-ss (4)–(4B)); 1 January 1986 (sub-ss (1)–(3), certain purposes); 1 January 1985 (sub-ss (5)–(7), remaining purposes).

Sub-ss (4)–(4B): substituted, for sub-s (4) as originally enacted, by the Registered Homes (Amendment) Act 1991, s 1(1), (2).

Sub-s (5): para (d) substituted, for paras (d), (e) as originally enacted, by the Children Act 1989, s 108(5), Sch 13, para 49(1); words in square brackets in paras (f), (g) substituted by the Education Act 1996, s 582(1), Sch 37, Pt I, para 58(2).

Sub-ss (6), (7): words in square brackets substituted by the Education Act 1996, s 582(1), Sch 37, Pt I, para 58(3), (4).

### 3 Registration of managers etc and persons in control

Where the manager or intended manager of a residential care home is not in control of it (whether as owner or otherwise) both the manager or intended manager and the person in control are to be treated as carrying on or intending to carry on the home and accordingly as requiring to be registered under this Part of this Act.

### [4 Registration in respect of small home registered under Part II

(1)    A person who—

(a)   is required to be registered under this Part in respect of a small home, and

(b)   is registered under Part II of this Act in respect of the same premises,

may apply to be registered under this Part as if the home were not a small home.

(2)    If he does so the provisions of this Part have effect as in relation to a home which is not a small home.]

NOTES

Commencement: 1 April 1993.

Substituted by the Registered Homes (Amendment) Act 1991, s 1(1), (3).

### [8A Annual return in respect of small home

(1)    The Secretary of State may by regulations require a person registered under this Part in respect of a small home to make an annual return to the registration authority.

(2)    Provision may be made by the regulations as to the contents of the return and the period in respect of which and date by which it is to be made.]

NOTES

Commencement: 1 April 1993.

Inserted by the Registered Homes (Amendment) Act 1991, s 1(1), (6).

### 9 Refusal of registration

[(1)] The registration authority may refuse to register an application for registration in respect of a residential care home [(other than a small home)] if they are satisfied—

(a)   that he or any other person concerned or intended to be concerned in carrying on the home is not a fit person to be concerned in carrying on a residential care home;

(b)   that for reasons connected with their situation, construction, state of repair, accommodation, staffing, or equipment, the premises used or intended to be used for the purposes of the home, or any other premises used or intended to be used in connection with it, are not fit to be so used; or

(c)   that the way in which it is intended to carry on the home is such as not to provide services or facilities reasonably required.

[(2)   The registration authority may refuse to register an applicant for registration in respect of a small home only if they are satisfied that he or any other person concerned or intended to be concerned in carrying on the home is not a fit person to be concerned in carrying on a residential care home.]

NOTES

Commencement: 1 April 1993 (sub-s (2)); 1 January 1985 (remainder).

Sub-s (1): numbered as such, and words in square brackets inserted, by the Registered Homes (Amendment) Act 1991, s 1(1), (7).

Sub-s (2): added by the Registered Homes (Amendment) Act 1991, s 1(1), (7).

## 17   Inspection of homes

(1)   Any person authorised in that behalf by the Secretary of State may at all times enter and inspect any premises which are used, or which that person has reasonable cause to believe to be used, for the purposes of a residential care home.

(2)   Any person authorised in that behalf by a registration authority may at all times enter and inspect any premises in the area of the authority which are used, or which that person has reasonable cause to believe to be used, for those purposes.

(3)   The powers of inspection conferred by subsections (1) and (2) above shall include power to inspect any records required to be kept in accordance with regulations under this Part of this Act.

(4)   The Secretary of State may by regulations require that residential care homes shall be inspected on such occasions or at such intervals as the regulations may prescribe.

(5)   A person who proposes to exercise any power of entry or inspection conferred by this section shall if so required produce some duly authenticated document showing his authority to exercise the power.

(6)   Any person who obstructs the exercise of any such power shall be guilty of an offence.

*Provisions supplementary to Part I*

## 20   General interpretation

(1)   In this Part of this Act—

"disablement", in relation to persons, means that they are blind, deaf or dumb or substantially and permanently handicapped by illness, injury or congenital deformity or any other disability prescribed by the Secretary of State;

"personal care" means care which includes assistance with bodily functions where such assistance is required;

"prescribed" means prescribed by regulations under this Part of this Act;

"registration authority", in relation to a residential care home, means, subject to subsection (2) below, the local social services authority for the area in which the home is situated;

["small home" has the meaning given by section 1(4A) above].

(2)   The Council of the Isles of Scilly is the registration authority in relation to a residential care home in the Isles.

NOTES

Sub-s (1): definition "small home" added by the Registered Homes (Amendment) Act 1991, s 1(1), (9).

# PART II
# NURSING HOMES AND MENTAL NURSING HOMES

*Interpretation*

## 21  Meaning of "nursing home"

(1)  In this Act "nursing home" means, subject to subsection (3) below—

    (a)  any premises used, or intended to be used, for the reception of, and the provision of nursing for, persons suffering from any sickness, injury or infirmity;

    (b)  any premises used, or intended to be used, for the reception of pregnant women, or of women immediately after childbirth (in this Act referred to as a "maternity home"); and

    (c)  any premises not falling within either of the preceding paragraphs which are used, or intended to be used, for the provision of all or any of the following services, namely—

       (i)  the carrying out of surgical procedures under anaesthesia;

      (ii)  the termination of pregnancies;

     (iii)  endoscopy;

     (iv)  haemodialysis or peritoneal dialysis;

      (v)  treatment by specially controlled techniques.

(2)  In subsection (1) above "specially controlled techniques" means techniques specified under subsection (4) below as subject to control for the purposes of this Part of this Act.

(3)  The definition in subsection (1) above does not include—

    (a)  any [health service hospital, within the meaning of the National Health Service Act 1977, or any] other premises maintained or controlled by a government department or local authority or any other authority or body instituted by special Act of Parliament or incorporated by Royal Charter;

    (b)  any mental nursing home;

    (c)  any sanatorium provided at a school or educational establishment and used, or intended to be used, solely by persons in attendance at, or members of the staff of, that school or establishment or members of their families;

    (d)  any first aid or treatment room provided at factory premises, at premises to which the Offices, Shops and Railway Premises Act 1963 applies or at a sports ground, show ground or place of public entertainment;

    (e)  any premises used, or intended to be used, wholly or mainly—

       (i)  by a medical practitioner for the purpose of consultations with his patients;

      (ii)  by a dental practitioner or chiropodist for the purpose of treating his patients; or

     (iii)  for the provision of occupational health facilities,

    unless they are used, or intended to be used, for the provision of treatment by specially controlled techniques and are not excepted by regulations under paragraph (g) below;

    (f)  any premises used, or intended to be used, wholly or mainly as a private dwelling; or

    (g)  any other premises excepted from that definition by regulations made by the Secretary of State.

(4)    The Secretary of State may by regulations specify as subject to control for the purposes of this Part of this Act any technique of medicine or surgery (including cosmetic surgery) as to which he is satisfied that its use may create a hazard for persons treated by means of it or for the staff of any premises where the technique is used.

(5)    Without prejudice to the generality of section 56 below, regulations under subsection (4) above may define a technique by reference to any criteria which the Secretary of State considers appropriate.

(6)    In this section "treatment" includes diagnosis and "treated" shall be construed accordingly.

NOTES

Sub-s (3): words in square brackets in para (a) substituted by the National Health Service and Community Care Act 1990, s 66(1), Sch 9, para 27.

## 22    Meaning of "mental nursing home"

(1)    In this Act "mental nursing home" means, subject to subsection (2) below, any premises used, or intended to be used, for the reception of, and the provision of nursing or other medical treatment (including care, habilitation and rehabilitation under medical supervision) for, one or more mentally disordered patients (meaning persons suffering, or appearing to be suffering, from mental disorder), whether exclusively or in common with other persons.

(2)    In this Act "mental nursing home" does not include any hospital as defined in subsection (3) below, or any other premises managed by a government department or provided by a local authority.

(3)    In subsection (2) above, "hospital" means—
    (a)    any health service hospital within the meaning of the National Health Service Act 1977; and
    (b)    any accommodation provided by a local authority and used as a hospital by or on behalf of the Secretary of State under that Act.

*Registration and conduct of nursing homes and mental nursing homes*

## 23    Registration of nursing homes and mental nursing homes

(1)    Any person who carries on a nursing home or a mental nursing home without being registered under this Part of this Act in respect of that home shall be guilty of an offence.

(2)    Registration under this Part of this Act does not affect any requirement to register under Part I of this Act.

(3)    An application for registration under this Part of this Act—
    (a)    shall be made to the Secretary of State;
    (b)    shall be accompanied by a fee of such amount as the Secretary of State may by regulations prescribe;
    (c)    in the case of a mental nursing home, shall specify whether or not it is proposed to receive in the home patients who are liable to be detained under the provisions of the Mental Health Act 1983.

(4)    Subject to section 25 below, the Secretary of State shall, on receiving an application under subsection (3) above, register the applicant in respect of the home named in the application, and shall issue to the applicant a certificate of registration.

(5)    Where a person is registered in pursuance of an application stating that it is proposed to receive in the home such patients as are described in subsection (3)(c) above—

(a)    that fact shall be specified in the certificate of registration; and

(b)    the particulars of the registration shall be entered by the Secretary of State in a separate part of the register.

(6)    The certificate of registration issued under this Part of this Act in respect of any nursing home or mental nursing home shall be kept affixed in a conspicuous place in the home, and if default is made in complying with this subsection, the person carrying on the home shall be guilty of an offence.

## 25    Refusal of registration

(1)    The Secretary of State may refuse to register an applicant in respect of a nursing home or a mental nursing home if he is satisfied—

(a)    that the applicant, or any person employed or proposed to be employed by the applicant at the home, is not a fit person (whether by reason of age or otherwise) to carry on or be employed at a home of such a description as that named in the application; or

(b)    that, for reasons connected with situation, construction, state of repair, accommodation, staffing or equipment, the home is not, or any premises used in connection with the home are not, fit to be used for such a home; or

(c)    that the home is, or any premises used in connection with the home are, used, or proposed to be used, for purposes which are in any way improper or undesirable, in the case of such a home; or

(d), (e). . .; or

(f)    that the home is not, or will not be, in the charge of a person who is either a registered medical practitioner or a qualified nurse or, in the case of a maternity home, a registered midwife; or

(g)    that the condition mentioned in subsection (3) below is not, or will not be, fulfilled in relation to the home.

(2)    In subsection (1) above "qualified nurse", in relation to a home, means a nurse possessing such qualifications as may be specified in a notice served by the Secretary of State on the person carrying on or proposing to carry on the home.

(3)    The condition referred to in subsection (1) above is that such number of nurses possessing such qualifications and, in the case of a maternity home, such number of registered midwives as may be specified in a notice served by the Secretary of State on the person carrying on or proposing to carry on the home are on duty in the home at such times as may be so specified.

(4)    In preparing any notice under subsection (2) or (3) above, the Secretary of State shall have regard to the class and, in the case of a notice under subsection (3) above, the number of patients for whom nursing care is or is to be provided in the home.

NOTES

    Sub-s (1): paras (d), (e) repealed by the National Health Service and Community Care Act 1990, s 66(2), Sch 10.

## PART V
## SUPPLEMENTARY

### 59  Short title and commencement

(1)   This Act may be cited as the Registered Homes Act 1984.

(2)   This Act shall come into force on such day as the Secretary of State may by order appoint and different days may be so appointed for different provisions and for different purposes.

# CHILD ABDUCTION AND CUSTODY ACT 1985

### (C 60)

*An Act to enable the United Kingdom to ratify two international Conventions relating respectively to the civil aspects of international child abduction and to the recognition of custody decisions*
[25 July 1985]

## PART I
## INTERNATIONAL CHILD ABDUCTION

### 1  The Hague Convention

(1)   In this Part of this Act "the Convention" means the Convention on the Civil Aspects of International Child Abduction which was signed at The Hague on 25th October 1980.

(2)   Subject to the provisions of this Part of this Act, the provisions of that Convention set out in Schedule 1 to this Act shall have the force of law in the United Kingdom.

## PART II
## RECOGNITION AND ENFORCEMENT OF CUSTODY DECISIONS

### 12  The European Convention

(1)   In this Part of this Act "the Convention" means the European Convention on Recognition and Enforcement of Decisions concerning Custody of Children and on the Restoration of Custody of Children which was signed in Luxembourg on 20th May 1980.

(2)   Subject to the provisions of this Part of this Act, the provisions of that Convention set out in Schedule 2 to this Act (which includes Articles 9 and 10 as they have effect in consequence of a reservation made by the United Kingdom under Article 17) shall have the force of law in the United Kingdom.

## PART III
## SUPPLEMENTARY

**29  Short title, commencement and extent**

(1)   This Act may be cited as the Child Abduction and Custody Act 1985.

(2)   This Act shall come into force on such day as may be appointed by an order made by statutory instrument by the Lord Chancellor and the Lord Advocate; and different days may be so appointed for different provisions.

(3)   This Act extends to Northern Ireland.

## SCHEDULE 1
## CONVENTION ON THE CIVIL ASPECTS OF INTERNATIONAL CHILD ABDUCTION

Section 1(2)

## CHAPTER I
## SCOPE OF THE CONVENTION

*Article 3*

The removal or the retention of a child is to be considered wrongful where—
- (a)   it is in breach of rights of custody attributed to a person, an institution or any other body, either jointly or alone, under the law of the State in which the child was habitually resident immediately before the removal or retention; and
- (b)   at the time of removal or retention those rights were actually exercised, either jointly or alone, or would have been so exercised but for the removal or retention.

The rights of custody mentioned in sub-paragraph (a) above may arise in particular by operation of law or by reason of a judicial or administrative decision, or by reason of an agreement having legal effect under the law of that State.

*Article 4*

The Convention shall apply to any child who was habitually resident in a Contracting State immediately before any breach of custody or access rights. The Convention shall cease to apply when the child attains the age of sixteen years.

*Article 5*

For the purposes of this Convention—
- (a)   "rights of custody" shall include rights relating to the care of the person of the child and, in particular, the right to determine the child's place of residence;
- (b)   "rights of access" shall include the right to take a child for a limited period of time to a place other than the child's habitual residence.

## CHAPTER II
## CENTRAL AUTHORITIES

*Article 7*

Central Authorities shall co-operate with each other and promote co-operation amongst the competent authorities in their respective States to secure the prompt return of children and to achieve the other objects of this Convention.

In particular, either directly or through any intermediary, they shall take all appropriate measures—
- (a)   to discover the whereabouts of a child who has been wrongfully removed or retained;

(b)  to prevent further harm to the child or prejudice to interested parties by taking or causing to be taken provisional measures;

(c)  to secure the voluntary return of the child or to bring about an amicable resolution of the issues;

(d)  to exchange, where desirable, information relating to the social background of the child;

(e)  to provide information of a general character as to the law of their State in connection with the application of the Convention;

(f)  to initiate or facilitate the institution of judicial or administrative proceedings with a view to obtaining the return of the child and, in a proper case, to make arrangements for organizing or securing the effective exercise of rights of access;

(g)  where the circumstances so require, to provide or facilitate the provision of legal aid and advice, including the participation of legal counsel and advisers;

(h)  to provide such administrative arrangements as may be necessary and appropriate to secure the safe return of the child;

(i)  to keep each other informed with respect to the operation of this Convention and, as far as possible, to eliminate any obstacles to its application.

# CHAPTER III
# RETURN OF CHILDREN

*Article 8*

Any person, institution or other body claiming that a child has been removed or retained in breach of custody rights may apply either to the Central Authority of the child's habitual residence or to the Central Authority of any other Contracting State for assistance in securing the return of the child.

The application shall contain—

(a)  information concerning the identity of the applicant, of the child and of the person alleged to have removed or retained the child;

(b)  where available, the date of birth of the child;

(c)  the grounds on which the applicant's claim for return of the child is based;

(d)  all available information relating to the whereabouts of the child and the identity of the person with whom the child is presumed to be.

The application may be accompanied or supplemented by—

(e)  an authenticated copy of any relevant decision or agreement;

(f)  a certificate or an affidavit emanating from a Central Authority, or other competent authority of the State of the child's habitual residence, or from a qualified person, concerning the relevant law of that State;

(g)  any other relevant document.

*Article 9*

If the Central Authority which receives an application referred to in Article 8 has reason to believe that the child is in another Contracting State, it shall directly and without delay transmit the application to the Central Authority of that Contracting State and inform the requesting Central Authority, or the applicant, as the case may be.

*Article 10*

The Central Authority of the State where the child is shall take or cause to be taken all appropriate measures in order to obtain the voluntary return of the child.

*Article 11*

The judicial or administrative authorities of Contracting States shall act expeditiously in proceedings for the return of children.

If the judicial or administrative authority concerned has not reached a decision within six weeks from the date of commencement of the proceedings, the applicant or the Central Authority of the requested State, on its own initiative or if asked by the Central Authority of the requesting State, shall have the right to request a statement of the reasons for the delay. If a reply is received by the Central Authority of the requested State, that Authority shall transmit the reply to the Central Authority of the requesting State, or to the applicant, as the case may be.

*Article 12*

Where a child has been wrongfully removed or retained in terms of Article 3 and, at the date of the commencement of the proceedings before the judicial or administrative authority of the Contracting State where the child is, a period of less than one year has elapsed from the date of the wrongful removal or retention, the authority concerned shall order the return of the child forthwith.

The judicial or administrative authority, even where the proceedings have been commenced after the expiration of the period of one year referred to in the preceding paragraph, shall also order the return of the child, unless it is demonstrated that the child is now settled in its new environment.

Where the judicial or administrative authority in the requested state has reason to believe that the child has been taken to another State, it may stay the proceedings or dismiss the application for the return of the child.

*Article 13*

Notwithstanding the provisions of the preceding Article, the judicial or administrative authority of the requested State is not bound to order the return of the child if the person, institution or other body which opposes its return establishes that—

(a)   the person, institution or other body having the care of the person of the child was not actually exercising the custody rights at the time of removal or retention, or had consented to or subsequently acquiesced in the removal or retention; or

(b)   there is a grave risk that his or her return would expose the child to physical or psychological harm or otherwise place the child in an intolerable situation.

The judicial or administrative authority may also refuse to order the return of the child if it finds that the child objects to being returned and has attained an age and degree of maturity at which it is appropriate to take account of its views.

In considering the circumstances referred to in this Article, the judicial and administrative authorities shall take into account the information relating to the social background of the child provided by the Central Authority or other competent authority of the child's habitual residence.

*Article 14*

In ascertaining whether there has been a wrongful removal or retention within the meaning of Article 3, the judicial or administrative authorities of the requested State may take notice directly of the law of, and of judicial or administrative decisions, formally recognised or not in the State of the habitual residence of the child, without recourse to the specific procedures for the proof of that law or for the recognition of foreign decisions which would otherwise be applicable.

*Article 15*

The judicial or administrative authorities of a Contracting State may, prior to the making of an order for the return of the child, request that the applicant obtain from the authorities of the State of the habitual residence of the child a decision or other determination that the removal or retention was wrongful within the meaning of Article 3 of the Convention, where such a decision or determination may be obtained in that State. The Central Authorities of the Contracting States shall so far as practicable assist applicants to obtain such a decision or determination.

*Article 16*

After receiving notice of a wrongful removal or retention of a child in the sense of Article 3, the judicial or administrative authorities of the Contracting State to which the child has been removed or in which it has been retained shall not decide on the merits of rights of custody until it has been determined that the child is not to be returned under this Convention or unless an application under this Convention is not lodged within a reasonable time following receipt of the notice.

*Article 17*

The sole fact that a decision relating to custody has been given in or is entitled to recognition in the requested State shall not be a ground for refusing to return a child under this Convention, but the judicial or administrative authorities of the requested State may take account of the reasons for that decision in applying this Convention.

*Article 18*

The provisions of this Chapter do not limit the power of a judicial or administrative authority to order the return of the child at any time.

*Article 19*

A decision under this Convention concerning the return of the child shall not be taken to be a determination on the merits of any custody issue.

# CHAPTER IV
# RIGHTS OF ACCESS

*Article 21*

An application to make arrangements for organising or securing the effective exercise of rights of access may be presented to the Central Authorities of the Contracting States in the same way as an application for the return of a child.

The Central Authorities are bound by the obligations of co-operation which are set forth in Article 7 to promote the peaceful enjoyment of access rights and the fulfilment of any conditions to which the exercise of those rights may be subject. The Central Authorities shall take steps to remove, as far as possible, all obstacles to the exercise of such rights. The Central Authorities, either directly or through intermediaries, may initiate or assist in the institution of proceedings with a view to organising or protecting these rights and securing respect for the conditions to which the exercise of these rights may be subject.

# CHAPTER V
# GENERAL PROVISIONS

*Article 22*

No security , bond or deposit, however described, shall be required to guarantee the payment of costs and expenses in the judicial or administrative proceedings falling within the scope of this Convention.

*Article 24*

Any application, communication or other document sent to the Central Authority of the requested State shall be in the original language, and shall be accompanied by a translation into the official language or one of the official languages of the requested State or, where that is not feasible, a translation into French or English.

### Article 26

Each Central Authority shall bear its own costs in applying this Convention.

Central Authorities and other public services of Contracting States shall not impose any charges in relation to applications submitted under this Convention. In particular, they may not require any payment from the applicant towards the costs and expenses of the proceedings or, where applicable, those arising from the participation of legal counsel or advisers. However, they may require the payment of the expenses incurred or to be incurred in implementing the return of the child.

However, a Contracting State may, by making a reservation in accordance with Article 42, declare that it shall not be bound to assume any costs referred to in the preceding paragraph resulting from the participation of legal counsel or advisers or from court proceedings, except insofar as those costs may be covered by its system of legal aid and advice.

Upon ordering the return of a child or issuing an order concerning rights of access under this Convention, the judicial or administrative authorities may, where appropriate, direct the person who removed or retained the child, or who prevented the exercise of rights of access, to pay necessary expenses incurred by or on behalf of the applicant, including travel expenses, any costs incurred or payments made for locating the child, the costs of legal representation of the applicant, and those of returning the child.

### Article 27

When it is manifest that the requirements of this Convention are not fulfilled or that the application is otherwise not well founded, a Central Authority is not bound to accept the application. In that case, the Central Authority shall forthwith inform the applicant or the Central Authority through which the application was submitted, as the case may be, of its reasons.

### Article 28

A Central Authority may require that the application be accompanied by a written authorisation empowering it to act on behalf of the applicant, or to designate a representative so to act.

### Article 29

This Convention shall not preclude any person, institution or body who claims that there has been a breach of custody or access rights within the meaning of Article 3 or 21 from applying directly to the judicial or administrative authorities of a Contracting State, whether or not under the provisions of this Convention.

### Article 30

Any application submitted to the Central Authorities or directly to the judicial or administrative authorities of a Contracting State in accordance with the terms of this Convention, together with documents and any other information appended thereto or provided by a Central Authority, shall be admissible in the courts or administrative authorities of the Contracting States.

### Article 31

In relation to a State which in matters of custody of children has two or more systems of law applicable in different territorial units—

    (a)   any reference to habitual residence in that State shall be construed as referring to habitual residence in a territorial unit of that State;

    (b)   any reference to the law of the State of habitual residence shall be construed as referring to the law of the territorial unit in that State where the child habitually resides.

*Article 32*

In relation to a State which in matters of custody of children has two or more systems of law applicable to different categories of persons, any reference to the law of that State shall be construed as referring to the legal system specified by the law of that State.

# SCHEDULE 2
## EUROPEAN CONVENTION ON RECOGNITION AND ENFORCEMENT OF DECISIONS CONCERNING CUSTODY OF CHILDREN

Section 12(2)

*Article 1*

For the purposes of this Convention:

    (a)  "child" means a person of any nationality, so long as he is under 16 years of age and has not the right to decide on his own place of residence under the law of his habitual residence, the law of his nationality or the internal law of the State addressed;

    (b)  "authority" means a judicial or administrative authority;

    (c)  "decision relating to custody" means a decision of an authority in so far as it relates to the care of the person of the child, including the right to decide on the place of his residence, or to the right of access to him;

    (d)  "improper removal" means the removal of a child across an international frontier in breach of a decision relating to his custody which has been given in a Contracting State and which is enforceable in such a State; "improper removal" also includes:

        (i)  the failure to return a child across an international frontier at the end of a period of the exercise of the right of access to this child or at the end of any other temporary stay in a territory other than that where the custody is exercised;

        (ii)  a removal which is subsequently declared unlawful within the meaning of Article 12.

*Article 4*

(1)  Any person who has obtained in a Contracting State a decision relating to the custody of a child and who wishes to have that decision recognised or enforced in another Contracting State may submit an application for this purpose to the central authority in any Contracting State.

(2)  The application shall be accompanied by the documents mentioned in Article 13.

(3)  The central authority receiving the application, if it is not the central authority in the State addressed, shall send the documents directly and without delay to that central authority.

(4)  The central authority receiving the application may refuse to intervene where it is manifestly clear that the conditions laid down by this Convention are not satisfied.

(5)  The central authority receiving the application shall keep the applicant informed without delay of the progress of his application.

*Article 5*

(1)  The central authority in the State addressed shall take or cause to be taken without delay all steps which it considers to be appropriate, if necessary by instituting proceedings before its competent authorities, in order:

    (a)  to discover the whereabouts of the child;

    (b)  to avoid, in particular by any necessary provisional measures, prejudice to the interests of the child or of the applicant;

    (c)  to secure the recognition or enforcement of the decision;

    (d)  to secure the delivery of the child to the applicant where enforcement is granted;

    (e)  to inform the requesting authority of the measures taken and their results.

(2)   Where the central authority in the State addressed has reason to believe that the child is in the territory of another Contracting State it shall send the documents directly and without delay to the central authority of that State.

(3)   With the exception of the cost of repatriation, each Contracting State undertakes not to claim any payment from an applicant in respect of any measures taken under paragraph (1) of this Article by the central authority of that State on the applicant's behalf, including the costs of proceedings and, where applicable, the costs incurred by the assistance of a lawyer.

(4)   If recognition or enforcement is refused, and if the central authority of the State addressed considers that it should comply with a request by the applicant to bring in that State proceedings concerning the substance of the case, that authority shall use its best endeavours to secure the representation of the applicant in the proceedings under conditions no less favourable than those available to a person who is resident in and a national of that State and for this purpose it may, in particular, institute proceedings before its competent authorities.

*Article 7*

A decision relating to custody given in a Contracting State shall be recognised and, where it is enforceable in the State of origin, made enforceable in every other Contracting State.

*Article 9*

(1)   (*Recognition and enforcement may be refused*) if:
- (a)   in the case of a decision given in the absence of the defendant or his legal representative, the defendant was not duly served with the document which instituted the proceedings or an equivalent document in sufficient time to enable him to arrange his defence; but such a failure to effect service cannot constitute a ground for refusing recognition or enforcement where service was not effected because the defendant had concealed his whereabouts from the person who instituted the proceedings in the State of origin;
- (b)   in the case of a decision given in the absence of the defendant or his legal representative, the competence of the authority giving the decision was not founded:
  - (i)   on the habitual residence of the defendant; or
  - (ii)   on the last common habitual residence of the child's parents, at least one parent being still habitually resident there, or
  - (iii)   on the habitual residence of the child;
- (c)   the decision is incompatible with a decision relating to custody which became enforceable in the State addressed before the removal of the child, unless the child has had his habitual residence in the territory of the requesting State for one year before his removal.

(3)   In no circumstances may the foreign decision be reviewed as to its substance.

*Article 10*

(1)   (*Recognition and enforcement may also be refused*) on any of the following grounds:
- (a)   if it is found that the effects of the decision are manifestly incompatible with the fundamental principles of the law relating to the family and children in the State addressed;
- (b)   if it is found that by reason of a change in the circumstances including the passage of time but not including a mere change in the residence of the child after an improper removal, the effects of the original decision are manifestly no longer in accordance with the welfare of the child;
- (c)   if at the time when the proceedings were instituted in the State of origin:
  - (i)   the child was a national of the State addressed or was habitually resident there and no such connection existed with the State of origin;
  - (ii)   the child was a national both of the State of origin and of the State addressed and was habitually resident in the State addressed;

(d) if the decision is incompatible with a decision given in the State addressed or enforceable in that State after being given in a third State, pursuant to proceedings begun before the submission of the request for recognition or enforcement, and if the refusal is in accordance with the welfare of the child.

(2) Proceedings for recognition or enforcement may be adjourned on any of the following grounds:

(a) if an ordinary form of review of the original decision has been commenced;

(b) if proceedings relating to the custody of the child, commenced before the proceedings in the State of origin were instituted, are pending in the State addressed;

(c) if another decision concerning the custody of the child is the subject of proceedings for enforcement or of any other proceedings concerning the recognition of the decision.

## Article 11

(1) Decisions on rights of access and provisions of decisions relating to custody which deal with the rights of access shall be recognised and enforced subject to the same conditions as other decisions relating to custody.

(2) However, the competent authority of the State addressed may fix the conditions for the implementation and exercise of the right of access taking into account, in particular, undertakings given by the parties on this matter.

(3) Where no decision on the right of access has been taken or where recognition or enforcement of the decision relating to custody is refused, the central authority of the State addressed may apply to its competent authorities for a decision on the right of access if the person claiming a right of access so requests.

## Article 12

Where, at the time of the removal of a child across an international frontier, there is no enforceable decision given in a Contracting State relating to his custody, the provisions of this Convention shall apply to any subsequent decision, relating to the custody of that child and declaring the removal to be unlawful, given in a Contracting State at the request of any interested person.

## Article 13

(1) A request for recognition or enforcement in another Contracting State of a decision relating to custody shall be accompanied by:

(a) a document authorising the central authority of the State addressed to act on behalf of the applicant or to designate another representative for that purpose;

(b) a copy of the decision which satisfies the necessary conditions of authenticity;

(c) in the case of a decision given in the absence of the defendant or his legal representative, a document which establishes that the defendant was duly served with the document which instituted the proceedings or an equivalent document;

(d) if applicable, any document which establishes that, in accordance with the law of the State of origin, the decision is enforceable;

(e) if possible, a statement indicating the whereabouts or likely whereabouts of the child in the State addressed;

(f) proposals as to how the custody of the child should be restored.

## Article 15

(1) Before reaching a decision under paragraph (1)(b) of Article 10, the authority concerned in the State addressed:

(a) shall ascertain the child's views unless this is impracticable having regard in particular to his age and understanding; and

(b) may request that any appropriate enquiries be carried out.

(2) The cost of enquiries in any Contracting State shall be met by the authorities of the State where they are carried out.

Requests for enquiries and the results of enquiries may be sent to the authority concerned through the central authorities.

*Article 26*

(1) In relation to a State which has in matters of custody two or more systems of law of territorial application:

    (a) reference to the law of a person's habitual residence or to the law of a person's nationality shall be construed as referring to the system of law determined by the rules in force in that State or, if there are no such rules, to the system of law with which the person concerned is most closely connected;

    (b) reference to the State of origin or to the State addressed shall be construed as referring, as the case may be, to the territorial unit where the decision was given or to the territorial unit where recognition or enforcement of the decision or restoration of custody is requested.

(2) Paragraph (1)(a) of this Article also applies *mutatis mutandis* to States which have in matters of custody two or more systems of law of personal application.

# HOUSING ACT 1985

## (C 68)

*An Act to consolidate the Housing Acts (except those provisions consolidated in the Housing Associations Act 1985 and the Landlord and Tenant Act 1985), and certain related provisions, with amendments to give effect to recommendations of the Law Commission*

[30 October 1985]

*Main definitions*

### 59 Priority need for accommodation

(1) The following have a priority need for accommodation—

    (a) a pregnant woman or a person with whom a pregnant woman resides or might reasonably be expected to reside;

    (b) a person with whom dependent children reside or might reasonably be expected to reside;

    (c) a person who is vulnerable as a result of old age, mental illness or handicap or physical disability or other special reason, or with whom such a person resides or might reasonably be expected to reside;

    (d) a person who is homeless or threatened with homelessness as a result of an emergency such as flood, fire or other disaster.

(2) The Secretary of State may by order made by statutory instrument—

    (a) specify further descriptions of persons as having a priority need for accommodation, and

    (b) amend or repeal any part of subsection (1).

(3) Before making such an order the Secretary of State shall consult such associations representing relevant authorities, and such other persons, as he considers appropriate.

(4) No order shall be made unless a draft of it has been approved by resolution of each House of Parliament.

NOTES

Repealed, together with ss 60, 61, 69, 72 of this Act, by the Housing Act 1996, s 227, Sch 19, Pt VIII, except in relation to an applicant whose application for accommodation or assistance in obtaining accommodation was made before 20 January 1997; see the Housing Act 1996 (Commencement No 5 and Transitional Provisions) Order 1996, SI 1996/2959.

## 60 Becoming homeless intentionally

(1)   A person becomes homeless intentionally if he deliberately does or fails to do anything in consequence of which he ceases to occupy accommodation which is available for his occupation and which it would have been reasonable for him to continue to occupy.

(2)   A person becomes threatened with homelessness intentionally if he deliberately does or fails to do anything the likely result of which is that he will be forced to leave accommodation which is available for his occupation and which it would have been reasonable for him to continue to occupy.

(3)   For the purposes of subsection (1) or (2) an act or omission in good faith on the part of a person who was unaware of any relevant fact shall not be treated as deliberate.

(4)   Regard may be had, in determining whether it would have been reasonable for a person to continue to occupy accommodation, to the general circumstances prevailing in relation to housing in the district of the local housing authority to whom he applied for accommodation or for assistance in obtaining accommodation.

NOTES

Repealed as noted to s 59.

## 61 Local connection

(1)   References in this Part to a person having a local connection with the district of a local housing authority are to his having a connection with that district—
  (a)   because he is, or in the past was, normally resident in that district, and that residence is or was of his own choice, or
  (b)   because he is employed in that district, or
  (c)   because of family associations, or
  (d)   because of special circumstances.

(2)   For the purposes of this section—
  (a)   a person is not employed in a district if he is serving in the regular armed forces of the Crown;
  (b)   residence in a district is not of a person's own choice if he becomes resident in it because he, or a person who might reasonably be expected to reside with him, is serving in the regular armed forces of the Crown.

(3)   Residence in a district is not of a person's own choice for the purpose of this section if he, or a person who might reasonably be expected to reside with him, became resident in it because he was detained under the authority of an Act of Parliament.

(4)   The Secretary of State may by order specify other circumstances in which—
  (a)   a person is not to be treated for the purposes of this section as employed in a district, or
  (b)   residence in a district is not to be treated for those purposes as of a person's own choice.

(5)    An order shall be made by statutory instrument which shall be subject to annulment in pursuance of a resolution of either House of Parliament.

NOTES
Repealed as noted to s 59.

*Duties of local housing authorities with respect to homelessness and threatened homelessness*

## 69    Provisions supplementary to ss 63, 65 and 68

[(1)    A local housing authority may perform any duty under section 65 or 68 (duties to persons found to be homeless) to secure that accommodation becomes available for the occupation of a person—

(a)    by making available suitable accommodation held by them under Part II (provision of housing) or any enactment, or

(b)    by securing that he obtains suitable accommodation from some other person, or

(c)    by giving him such advice and assistance as will secure that he obtains suitable accommodation from some other person,

and in determining whether accommodation is suitable they shall have regard to Part IX (slum clearance), X (overcrowding) and XI (houses in multiple occupation) of this Act.]

(2)    A local housing authority may require a person to whom they were subject to a duty under section 63, 65 or 68 (interim duty to accommodate pending inquiries and duties to persons found to be homeless)—

(a)    to pay such reasonable charges as they may determine in respect of accommodation which they secure for his occupation (either by making it available themselves or otherwise), or

(b)    to pay such reasonable amount as they may determine in respect of sums payable by them for accommodation made available by another person.

NOTES
Repealed as noted to s 59.

## 72    Co-operation between authorities

Where a local housing authority—

(a)    request another local housing authority in England, Wales or Scotland, a new town corporation, a [registered social landlord] [a housing action trust] or [Scottish Homes] to assist them in the discharge of their functions under sections 62, 63, 65 to 67 and 68(1) and (2) (which relate to homelessness and threatened homelessness as such),

(b)    request a social services authority in England, Wales or Scotland to exercise any of their functions in relation to a case which the local housing authority are dealing with under those provisions, or

(c)    request another local housing authority in England, Wales or Scotland to assist them in the discharge of their functions under section 70 (protection of property of homeless persons and persons threatened with homelessness),

the authority [or other body] to whom the request is made shall co-operate in rendering such assistance in the discharge of the functions to which the request relates as is reasonable in the circumstances.

NOTES

Repealed as noted to s 59.

Words in first pair of square brackets in para (a) substituted by the Housing Act 1996 (Consequential Provisions) Order 1996, SI 1996/2325, art 5, Sch 2, para 14(1), (6); words in second and fourth pairs of square brackets inserted by the Housing Act 1988, s 70; words in third pair of square brackets substituted by the Housing (Scotland) Act 1988, ss 1, 3(3), Sch 2, para 1.

# PART IV
# SECURE TENANCIES AND RIGHTS OF SECURE TENANTS

*Security of tenure*

## 79 Secure tenancies

(1)    A tenancy under which a dwelling-house is let as a separate dwelling is a secure tenancy at any time when the conditions described in sections 80 and 81 as the landlord condition and the tenant condition are satisfied.

(2)    Subsection (1) has effect subject to—

    (a)   the exceptions in Schedule 1 (tenancies which are not secure tenancies),

    (b)   sections 89(3) and (4) and 90(3) and (4) (tenancies ceasing to be secure after death of tenant), and

    (c)   sections 91(2) and 93(2) (tenancies ceasing to be secure in consequence of assignment or subletting).

(3)    The provisions of this Part apply in relation to a licence to occupy a dwelling-house (whether or not granted for a consideration) as they apply in relation to a tenancy.

(4)    Subsection (3) does not apply to a licence granted as a temporary expedient to a person who entered the dwelling-house or any other land as a trespasser (whether or not, before the grant of that licence, another licence to occupy that or another dwelling-house had been granted to him).

## 80 The landlord condition

(1)    The landlord condition is that the interest of the landlord belongs to one of the following authorities or bodies—

    a local authority,

    a new town corporation,

    [a housing action trust]

    an urban development corporation,

    the Development Board for Rural Wales,

    . . . . .

    a housing trust which is a charity, or

    a housing co-operative to which this section applies.

(2)    *This section applies to—*

    *(a)   a [registered social landlord] other than a co-operative housing association, and*

    *[(b)   a co-operative housing association which is not a registered social landlord].*

(3)    If a co-operative housing association ceases to be [a registered social landlord], it shall, within the period of 21 days beginning with the date on which it ceases to be [a registered social landlord], notify each of its tenants who thereby becomes a secure tenant, in writing, that he has become a secure tenant.

[(4) This section applies to a housing co-operative within the meaning of section 27B (agreements under certain superseded provisions) where the dwelling-house is comprised in a housing co-operative agreement within the meaning of that section.]

NOTES

Sub-s (1): words in square brackets inserted by the Housing Act 1988, s 83(1), (2); words omitted repealed with savings, by the Housing Act 1988, ss 35, 140(2), Sch 18.

Sub-s (2): repealed with savings by the Housing Act 1988, ss 35, 140, Sch 18; word in square brackets in para (a) and para (b) substituted by the Housing Act 1996 (Consequential Provisions) Order 1996, SI 1996/2325, art 5, Sch 2, para 14(1), (8).

Sub-s (3): words in square brackets substituted by SI 1996/2325, art 5, Sch 2, para 14(1), (8).

Sub-s (4): substituted by the Housing and Planning Act 1986, s 24(2), Sch 5, Pt II, para 26.

**81   The tenant condition**

The tenant condition is that the tenant is an individual and occupies the dwelling-house as his only or principal home; or, where the tenancy is a joint tenancy, that each of the joint tenants is an individual and at least one of them occupies the dwelling-house as his only or principal home.

## PART XVIII
## MISCELLANEOUS AND GENERAL PROVISIONS

*Final provisions*

**625   Short title, commencement and extent**

(1)   This Act may be cited as the Housing Act 1985.

(2)   This Act comes into force on 1st April 1986.

(3)   This Act extends to England and Wales only.

# DISABLED PERSONS (SERVICES, CONSULTATION AND REPRESENTATION) ACT 1986

## (C 33)

*An Act to provide for the improvement of the effectiveness of, and the co-ordination of resources in, the provision of services for people with mental or physical handicap and for people with mental illness; to make further provision for the assessment of the needs of such people; to establish further consultative processes and representational rights for such people; and for connected purposes*

[8 July 1986]

## PART I
## REPRESENTATION AND ASSESSMENT

**1   Appointment of authorised representatives of disabled persons**

(1)   In this Act "authorised representative", in relation to a disabled person, means a person for the time being appointed by or on behalf of that disabled person (in accordance with regulations made under this section) to act as his authorised representative for the purposes of this Act.

(2)   The Secretary of State may by regulations make provision with respect to the appointment of persons to act as the authorised representatives of disabled persons, including provision—

(a)   for the manner in which the appointment of a person as an authorised representative is to be made; and

(b)   for any such appointment to be notified to the relevant local authority (as defined in the regulations) if made otherwise than by that authority.

(3)   Any such regulations—

(a)   may provide for

[(i)   the parent of a disabled person under the age of sixteen, or

(ii)   any other person who is not a parent of his but who has parental responsibility for him]

to appoint himself or some other person as the authorised representative of the disabled person (but shall not permit a person under that age himself to appoint a person as his authorised representative);

(b)   may provide for the appointment of a person as the authorised representative of a disabled person who is a child [looked after by] a local authority to be made by that authority in such circumstances as may be specified in the regulations;

(c)   may, in accordance with subsection (4), provide for the appointment of a person as the authorised representative of a disabled person to be made by, or under arrangements made by, a local authority in a case where the disabled person appears to the authority to be unable to appoint a person as his authorised representative by reason of any mental or physical incapacity;

(d)   may contain such incidental or supplementary provisions as the Secretary of State thinks fit.

(4)   Regulations under paragraph (c) of subsection (3) may make provision—

(a)   for requiring a local authority, for the purpose of enabling them to determine whether a disabled person is unable to appoint a person as his authorised representative as mentioned in that paragraph, to obtain the opinion of a registered medical practitioner;

(b)   for authorising a local authority, where they determine that a disabled person is so unable, either—

(i)   themselves to appoint a person as the disabled person's authorised representative, or

(ii)   to make with any voluntary organisation, person or persons approved by them for the purpose such arrangements as they think fit for such an appointment to be made by the organisation, person or persons concerned;

(c)   for requiring or authorising a local authority, before determining the question specified in paragraph (a), or (as the case may be) before making any appointment of an authorised representative, or any arrangements, in pursuance of paragraph (b), to consult any of the following, namely—

(i)   a person or persons appointed by them for the purpose, or

(ii)   a person or persons falling within any class or description specified in the regulations;

(d) for requiring a local authority, in such circumstances as may be specified in the regulations, to review the case of a disabled person whose authorised representative has been appointed in pursuance of paragraph (b) (whether by the local authority or under any arrangements made by them) for the purpose of determining whether he is still unable to appoint a person as his authorised representative as mentioned in subsection (3)(c).

(5)   Subsections (2) to (4) shall apply, with any necessary modifications, in relation to the termination of the appointment of a person as an authorised representative as they apply in relation to the making of such an appointment.

(6)   It is hereby declared that any person exercising under Part II of the 1983 Act or Part V of the 1984 Act—

(a) the functions of the nearest relative of a disabled person, or

(b) the functions of the guardian of a disabled person received into guardianship under that Part of that Act,

may, if appointed as such in accordance with this section, also act as that person's authorised representative.

### NOTES

Commencement: to be appointed.
Sub-s (3): words in square brackets substituted by the Children Act 1989, s 108(5), Sch 13, para 58.
1983 Act: Mental Health Act 1983.
1984 Act: Mental Health (Scotland) Act 1984.

## 2   Rights of authorised representatives of disabled persons

(1)   A local authority shall permit the authorised representative of a disabled person, if so requested by the disabled person—

(a) to act as the representative of the disabled person in connection with the provision by the authority of any services for him in the exercise of any of their functions under the welfare enactments, or

(b) to accompany the disabled person (otherwise than as his representative) to any meeting or interview held by or on behalf of the authority in connection with the provision by them of any such services.

(2)   For the purpose of assisting the authorised representative of a disabled person to do any of the things mentioned in subsection (1)(a) and (b) a local authority shall, if so requested by the disabled person—

(a) supply to the authorised representative any information, and

(b) make available for his inspection any documents,

that the disabled person would be entitled to require the authority to supply to him or (as the case may be) to make available for his inspection.

(3)   In relation to a disabled person whose authorised representative has been appointed by virtue of subsection (3) of section 1, subsections (1) and (2) above shall each have effect as follows—

(a) if the appointment was made by virtue of subsection (3)(a) of that section, [for the words "if so requested by the disabled person" there shall be substituted "if so requested by any person mentioned in section 1(3)(a)(i) or (ii)"]; and

(b) if the appointment was made by virtue of subsection (3)(b) or (c) of that section, the words "if so requested by the disabled person" shall be omitted.

(4)   A local authority shall not be required by virtue of subsection (1) or (2)—

(a)   to permit an authorised representative to be present at any meeting or interview or part of a meeting or interview, or

(b)   to supply any information to an authorised representative or to make any documents available for the inspection of an authorised representative,

if the authority are satisfied that to do so would be likely to be harmful to the interests of the disabled person by whom or on whose behalf the representative has been appointed; and in determining that matter the authority shall have regard to any wishes expressed by the disabled person.

(5)   Where a disabled person is residing—

(a)   in hospital accommodation provided by the Secretary of State under section 3(1)(a) of the 1977 Act [or by a National Health Service trust established under the provisions of the National Health Service and Community Care Act 1990] or, in Scotland, in hospital accommodation (other than accommodation at a State hospital) provided by the Secretary of State under section 36(1)(a) of the 1978 Act [or by a National Health Service trust established under that Act], or

(b)   in accommodation provided by a local authority under Part III of the 1948 Act *or Schedule 8 to the 1977 Act* or, in Scotland, under Part IV of the 1968 Act or section 7 of the 1984 Act, or

[(bb)in accommodation provided by or on behalf of a local authority under Part III of the Children Act 1989, or]

(c)   in accommodation provided by a voluntary organisation [or other person] in accordance with arrangements made by a local authority under section 26 of the 1948 Act or, in Scotland, provided by a voluntary organisation or other persons in accordance with arrangements made by a local authority under section 59(2)(c) of the 1968 Act, or

[(cc)in accommodation provided by a voluntary organisation [or other person] in accordance with arrangements made by a local authority under section 17 of the Children Act 1989, or]

(d)   in a residential care home within the meaning of Part I of the Registered Homes Act 1984 or, in Scotland, in an establishment (other than accommodation falling within paragraph (c) above) registered under section 61 of the 1968 Act, or

[(dd)in accommodation provided by any educational establishment,]

(e)   at any place specified by a person having the guardianship of the disabled person under Part II of the 1983 Act or Part V of the 1984 Act,

the disabled person's authorised representative may at any reasonable time visit him there and interview him in private.

(6)   In paragraph (c) of subsection (5) "voluntary organisation" in relation to England and Wales includes a housing association within the meaning of the Housing Associations Act 1985.

(7)   The Secretary of State may, after consulting such bodies representing health authorities or local authorities as appear to him to be appropriate and such other bodies as appear to him to be concerned, provide by order for any of the preceding provisions of this section to have effect (with such modifications as may be prescribed by the order) in relation to—

(a)   the provision of services by health authorities in the exercise of such of their functions under the 1977 Act or the 1978 Act as may be prescribed by the order, or

    (b) the provisions of services by local authorities in the exercise of such of their functions as may be so prescribed.

(8) An order under subsection (7) may provide for any provision of regulations made under section 1 to have effect for the purposes of the order with such modifications as may be prescribed by the order, and in that event the reference in subsection (1) of that section to regulations made under that section shall be read as a reference to any such regulations as they have effect in accordance with the order.

(9) In subsection (7)—

"health authority"—

    (a) in relation to England and Wales, [means a Health Authority or a Special Health Authority], and

    (b) in relation to Scotland, means a Health Board; and

"local authority"—

    (a) in relation to England and Wales, has the meaning given by section 270(1) of the Local Government Act 1972; and

    (b) in relation to Scotland, means a [council constituted under section 2 of the Local Government etc (Scotland) Act 1994].

---

NOTES

Commencement: to be appointed.

Sub-s (3): words in square brackets substituted by the Children Act 1989, s 108(5), Sch 13, para 59(2).

Sub-s (5): words in square brackets in para (a) inserted by the National Health Service and Community Care Act 1990, s 66(1), Sch 9, para 30(1)(a); paras (bb), (cc), (dd) inserted by the Children Act 1989, s 108(4), (5), Sch 12, para 44, Sch 13, para 59; words in italics in para (b) repealed, and words in square brackets in paras (c), (cc) inserted, by the National Health Service and Community Care Act 1990, s 66, Sch 9, para 30(1)(b), (c), Sch 10, as from a day to be appointed.

Sub-s (9): in definition "health authority" words in square brackets substituted by the Health Authorities Act 1995, s 2(1), Sch 1, para 111(2); in definition "local authority" words in square brackets substituted by the Local Government etc (Scotland) Act 1994, s 180(1), Sch 13, para 148(2).

1948 Act: National Assistance Act 1948.

1968 Act: Social Work (Scotland) Act 1968.

1977 Act: National Health Service Act 1977.

1978 Act: National Health Service (Scotland) Act 1978.

1983 Act: Mental Health Act 1983.

1984 Act: Mental Health (Scotland) Act 1984.

---

## 3   Assessment by local authorities of needs of disabled persons

(1) Where—

    (a) on any assessment carried out by them in pursuance of any provision of this Act, or

    (b) on any other occasion,

it falls to a local authority to decide whether the needs of a disabled person call for the provision by the authority (in accordance with any of the welfare enactments) of any statutory services for that person, the authority shall afford an opportunity to the disabled person or his authorised representative to make, within such reasonable period as the authority may allow for the purpose, representations to an officer of the authority as to any needs of the disabled person calling for the provision by the authority (in accordance with any of those enactments) of any statutory services for him.

(2) Where any such representations have been made to a local authority in accordance with subsection (1) or the period mentioned in that subsection has expired without any such representations being made, and the authority have reached

a decision on the question referred to in that subsection (having taken into account any representations made as mentioned above), the authority shall, if so requested by the disabled person or his authorised representative, supply the person making the request with a written statement—

    (a)  either specifying—

        (i)  any needs of the disabled person which in the opinion of the authority call for the provision by them of any statutory services, and

        (ii)  in the case of each such need, the statutory services that they propose to provide to meet that need,

        or stating that, in their opinion, the disabled person has no needs calling for the provision by them of any such services; and

    (b)  giving an explanation of their decision; and

    (c)  containing particulars of the right of the disabled person or his authorised representative to make representations with respect to the statement under subsection (4).

(3)   Where the local authority do not propose to provide any statutory services to meet a particular need identified in any representations under subsection (1), any statement supplied under subsection (2) must state that fact together with the reasons why the authority do not propose to provide any such services.

(4)   If the disabled person or his authorised representative is dissatisfied with any matter included in the statement supplied under subsection (2), that person may, within such reasonable period as the authority may allow for the purpose, make representations to an officer of the authority with respect to that matter.

(5)   Where any such representations have been made to the authority in accordance with subsection (4), the authority shall—

    (a)  consider (or, as the case may be, reconsider) whether any, and (if so) what, statutory services should be provided by them for the disabled person to meet any need identified in the representations; and

    (b)  inform the disabled person or his authorised representative in writing of their decision on that question and their reasons for that decision.

(6)   Where—

    (a)  the disabled person or his authorised representative is unable to communicate, or (as the case may be) be communicated with, orally or in writing (or in each of those ways) by reason of any mental or physical incapacity, or

    (b)  both of those persons are in that position (whether by reason of the same incapacity or not),

the local authority shall provide such services as, in their opinion, are necessary to ensure that any such incapacity does not—

    (i)  prevent the authority from discharging their functions under this section in relation to the disabled person, or

    (ii)  prevent the making of representations under this section by or on behalf of that person.

(7)   In determining whether they are required to provide any services under subsection (6) to meet any need of the disabled person or his authorised representative, and (if so) what those services should be, the local authority shall have regard to any views expressed by either of those persons as to the necessity for any such services or (as appropriate) to any views so expressed as to the services which should be so provided.

(8)  In this section "representations" means representations made orally or in writing (or both).

NOTES
Commencement: to be appointed.

### 4  Services under s 2 of the 1970 Act: duty to consider needs of disabled persons

When requested to do so by—
  (a)  a disabled person,
  (b)  his authorised representative, or
  (c)  any person who provides care for him in the circumstances mentioned in section 8,

a local authority shall decide whether the needs of the disabled person call for the provision by the authority of any services in accordance with section 2(1) of the 1970 Act (provision of welfare services).

NOTES
Commencement: 1 April 1987 (in part, England and Wales); 1 October 1987 (in part, Scotland); to be appointed (remainder).
1970 Act: Chronically Sick and Disabled Persons Act 1970.

### 5  Disabled persons leaving special education

(1)  Where—
  (a)  a local education authority have made a statement under section 7 of the Education Act 1981 [section 168 of the Education Act 1993 or section 324 of the Education Act 1996] (statement of child's educational needs) in respect of a child under the age of 14, and
  (b)  the statement is still maintained by the authority at whichever is the earlier of the following times, namely—
    (i)  the time when they institute the first annual review of the statement following the child's fourteenth birthday, and
    (ii)  any time falling after that birthday when they institute a re-assessment of his educational needs,

the authority shall at that time require the appropriate officer to give to the authority his opinion as to whether the child is or is not a disabled person.

(2)  Where—
  (a)  a local education authority make any such statement in respect of a child after he has attained the age of 14, or
  (b)  a local education authority maintain any such statement in respect of a child in whose case the appropriate officer has, in pursuance of subsection (1), given his opinion that the child is not a disabled person, but the authority have become aware of a significant change in the mental or physical condition of the child giving them reason to believe that he may now be a disabled person,

the authority shall, at the time of making the statement or (as the case may be) of becoming aware of that change, require the appropriate officer to give to the authority his opinion as to whether the child is or is not a disabled person.

[(3)   In the following provisions of this section and in section 6 a person in respect of whom the appropriate officer has given his opinion that he is a disabled person is referred to as a "disabled student".

(3A) The responsible authority shall give to the appropriate officer written notification for the purposes of subsection (5) of the date on which any disabled student will cease to be of compulsory school age, and the notification shall state—

(a)   his name and address; and

(b)   whether or not he intends to remain in full-time education and, if he does, the name of the school or other institution at which the education will be received;

and shall be given not earlier than twelve months, nor later than eight months, before that date.

(3B) Where, in the case of a disabled student over compulsory school age who is receiving relevant full-time education, that is—

(a)   full-time education at a school; or

(b)   full-time further or higher education at an institution other than a school;

it appears to the responsible authority that the student will cease to receive relevant full-time education on a date ("the leaving date") on which he will be under the age of nineteen years and eight months, the responsible authority shall give written notification for the purposes of subsection (5) to the appropriate officer.

(3C) That notification shall state—

(a)   his name and address; and

(b)   the leaving date;

and shall be given not earlier than twelve months, nor later than eight months, before the leaving date.

(4)   If at any time it appears to the responsible authority—

(a)   that a disabled student has ceased to receive relevant full-time education or will cease to do so on a date less than 8 months after that time, and

(b)   that no notification has been given under subsection (3B), but

(c)   that, had the responsible authority for the time being been aware of his intentions 8 months or more before that date, they would have been required to give notification under that subsection with respect to him,

that authority shall, as soon as is reasonably practicable, give written notification for the purposes of subsection (5) to the appropriate officer of his name and address and of the date on which he ceased to receive, or will cease to receive, that education.]

(5)   When the appropriate officer receives a notification given with respect to [a student under subsection (3A) that he does not intend to remain in full-time education or under subsection (3B)] or (4), he shall (subject to subsections (6) and   (7)) make arrangements for the local authority of which he is an officer to carry out an assessment of the needs of that person with respect to the provision by that authority of any statutory services for that person in accordance with any of the welfare enactments, and any such assessment shall be carried out—

(a)   in the case of a [notification under subsection (3A) or (3B)], not later than the end of the period of 5 months beginning with the date of receipt of the notification, or

(b)   in the case of a notification under subsection (4), before the date specified in the notification, if reasonably practicable, and in any event not later than the end of the period referred to in paragraph (a) above.

(6)    If—

    (a)    a notification has been given to the appropriate officer with respect to any person under subsection [(3A) that he does not intend to remain in full-time education or under subsection (3B)] or (4), but

    (b)    it subsequently appears to [the responsible authority that the person will be receiving relevant full-time education] at a time later than the date specified in the notification,

the authority shall give written notification of the relevant facts to that officer as soon as is reasonably practicable; and on receiving any such notification that officer shall cease to be required under subsection (5) to make arrangements for the assessment of the needs of the person in question (but without prejudice to the operation of that subsection in relation to any further notification given with respect to that person under subsection [(3A) that he does not intend to remain in full-time education or under subsection (3B)] or (4)).

(7)    Nothing in subsection (5) shall require the appropriate officer to make arrangements for the assessment of the needs of a person—

    (a)    if, having attained the age of 16, he has requested that such arrangements should not be made under that subsection, or

    (b)    if, being under that age, his parent or [other person who is not a parent of his but who has parental responsibility for him] has made such a request.

(8)    Regulations under [paragraph 7 of Schedule 27 to the Education Act 1996] (assessments and statements of special educational needs) may, in relation to the transfer of statements [maintained under section 324] of that Act, make such provision as appears to the Secretary of State to be necessary or expedient in connection with the preceding provisions of this section.

(9)    In this section—

    "the appropriate officer", in relation to the child or person referred to in the provision of this section in question, means such officer as may be appointed for the purposes of this section by the local authority for the area in which that child or person is for the time being ordinarily resident;

    "child" means a person of compulsory school age or a person who has attained that age but not the age of 19 and is registered as a pupil at a school or [as a student at] [an establishment of higher or further education]; and

    ["establishment of higher or further education" means an institution which provides higher education or further education (or both);]

    "the responsible authority"—

        (a)    in relation to a child at school, means the local education authority who are responsible for the child for the purposes of [Part IV of the Education Act 1996];

        [(b)    in relation to a person receiving full-time further education or higher education at an institution within the further education sector or the higher education sector, means the governing body of the institution; and

        (c)    in relation to a person for whom a further education funding council has secured full-time further education at an institution (other than a school) outside the further education sector or the higher education sector, the council]

    in each case whether any such opinion as is mentioned in subsection (3) was given to that authority or not;

and other expressions used in this section and in [the Education Act 1996] [or the Further and Higher Education Act 1992] (and not defined in this Act) have the same meaning in this section as in [those Acts].

(10) This section applies to England and Wales only.

NOTES
Commencement: 1 April 1993 (sub-ss (3), (3A)–(3C), (4)); 1 February 1988 (remainder).
Sub-s (1): words in square brackets inserted by the Education Act 1993, s 307(1), Sch 19, para 87(a), substituted by the Education Act 1996, s 582(1), Sch 37, para 64(2).
Sub-ss (3), (3A)–(3C), (4): substituted for sub-ss (3), (4), as originally enacted, by the Further and Higher Education Act 1992, s 93, Sch 8, Pt II, para 91(2).
Sub-ss (5), (6): words in square brackets substituted by the Further and Higher Education Act 1992, s 93, Sch 8, Pt II, para 91(3), (4).
Sub-s (7): words in square brackets substituted by the Children Act 1989, s 108(5), Sch 13, para 60.
Sub-s (8): words in square brackets substituted by the Education Act 1996, s 582(1), Sch 37, Pt I, para 64(3).
Sub-s (9): in definition "child", words in first pair of square brackets inserted by the Further and Higher Education Act 1992, s 93, Sch 8, Pt II, para 91(5), words in second pair of square brackets inserted by the Education Reform Act 1988, s 237, Sch 12, Pt III, para 97; definition "establishment of higher or further education" inserted by the Education Reform Act 1988, s 237, Sch 12, Pt III, para 97; in definition "the responsible authority", words in square brackets in para (a) substituted by the Education Act 1996, s 582(1), Sch 37, para 64(4)(a), paras (b), (c) substituted, for para (b) as originally enacted, by the Further and Higher Education Act 1992, s 93, Sch 8, Pt II, para 91(5); words "the Education Act 1996" substituted by the Education Act 1996, s 582(1), Sch 37, para 64(4)(b); words "or the Further and Higher Education Act 1992" inserted, and final words in square brackets substituted, by the Further and Higher Education Act 1992, s 93, Sch 8, Pt II, para 91(5).

## 6 Review of expected leaving dates from full-time education of disabled persons

[(1) The responsible authority shall for the purposes of section 5 above keep under review the date when any disabled student is expected to cease to receive relevant full-time education.]

(2) Subsection (9) of section 5 shall have effect for the purposes of this section as it has effect for the purposes of that section.

NOTES
Commencement: 1 April 1993 (sub-s (1)); 1 February 1988 (remainder).
Sub-s (1): substituted by the Further and Higher Education Act 1992, s 93, Sch 8, Pt II, para 92.

## 8 Duty of local authority to take into account abilities of carer

(1) Where—
   (a) a disabled person is living at home and receiving a substantial amount of care on a regular basis from another person (who is not a person employed to provide such care by any body in the exercise of its functions under any enactment), and
   (b) it falls to a local authority to decide whether the disabled person's needs call for the provision by them of any services for him under any of the welfare enactments,

the local authority shall, in deciding that question, have regard to the ability of that other person to continue to provide such care on a regular basis.

(2) Where that other person is unable to communicate, or (as the case may be) be communicated with, orally or in writing (or in each of those ways) by reason of any mental or physical incapacity, the local authority shall provide such services as, in their opinion, are necessary to ensure that any such incapacity does not prevent the authority from being properly informed as to the ability of that person to continue to provide care as mentioned in subsection (1).

(3)   Section 3(7) shall apply for the purposes of subsection (2) above as it applies for the purposes of section 3(6), but as if any reference to the disabled person or his authorised representative were a reference to the person mentioned in subsection (2).

NOTES

Commencement: 1 April 1987 (sub-s (1), England and Wales); 1 October 1987 (sub-s (1), Scotland); to be appointed (remainder).

## PART IV
## SUPPLEMENTAL

**18   Short title, commencement, regulations, orders and extent**

(1)   This Act may be cited as the Disabled Persons (Services, Consultation and Representation) Act 1986.

(2)   This Act shall come into force on such date as the Secretary of State may by order appoint and different dates may be appointed for different provisions or different purposes, and different provision may be made under this subsection for England and Wales and for Scotland.

(3)   Any regulations or order made under this Act shall be made by statutory instrument and (except in the case of an order under subsection (2)) shall be subject to annulment in pursuance of a resolution of either House of Parliament.

(4)   This Act does not extend to Northern Ireland.

# MARRIAGE (PROHIBITED DEGREES OF RELATIONSHIP) ACT 1986

## (C 16)

*An Act to make further provision with regard to the marriage of persons related by affinity*
[20 May 1986]

**1   Marriage between certain persons related by affinity not to be void**

(1)   A marriage solemnized after the commencement of this Act between a man and a woman who is the daughter or grand-daughter of a former spouse of his (whether the former spouse is living or not) or who is the former spouse of his father or grand-father (whether his father or grandfather is living or not) shall not be void by reason only of that relationship if both the parties have attained the age of twenty-one at the time of the marriage and the younger party has not at any time before attaining the age of eighteen been a child of the family in relation to the other party.

(2)   A marriage solemnized after the commencement of this Act between a man and a woman who is the grandmother of a former spouse of his (whether the former spouse is living or not) or is a former spouse of his grandson (whether his grandson is living or not) shall not be void by reason only of that relationship.

(3)   A marriage solemnized after the commencement of this Act between a man and a woman who is the mother of a former spouse of his shall not be void by reason only of that relationship if the marriage is solemnized after the death of both that spouse and the father of that spouse and after both the parties to the marriage have attained the age of twenty-one.

(4)    A marriage solemnized after the commencement of this Act between a man and a woman who is a former spouse of his son shall not be void by reason only of that relationship if the marriage is solemnized after the death of both his son and the mother of his son and after both the parties to the marriage have attained the age of twenty-one.

(5)    In this section "child of the family" in relation to any person, means a child who has lived in the same household as that person and been treated by that person as a child of his family.

(6)    The Marriage Act 1949 shall have effect subject to the amendments specified in the Schedule to this Act, being amendments consequential on the preceding provisions of this section.

(7)    Where, apart from this Act, any matter affecting the validity of a marriage would fall to be determined (in accordance with the rules of private international law) by reference to the law of a country outside England and Wales nothing in this Act shall preclude the determination of that matter in accordance with that law.

(8)    Nothing in this section shall affect any marriage solemnized before the commencement of this Act.

**6    Short title, citation, commencement and extent**

(1)    This Act may be cited as the Marriage (Prohibited Degrees of Relationship) Act 1986.

(2)    This Act so far as it extends to England and Wales may be cited with the Marriage Acts 1949 to 1983 and the Marriage (Wales) Act 1986 as the Marriage Acts 1949 to 1986.

(3)    This Act so far as it relates to the Marriage (Scotland) Act 1977 may be cited with that Act as the Marriage (Scotland) Acts 1977 and 1986.

(4)    . . .

(5)    This Act shall come into force on such day as the Secretary of State may by order made by statutory instrument appoint and different days may be so appointed for different provisions.

(6)    Section 2 and Schedule 2 shall extend to Scotland only, but save as aforesaid this Act shall not extend to Scotland or to Northern Ireland.

NOTES

Sub-s (4): amends the Matrimonial Causes Act 1973, s 11(a).

# PUBLIC ORDER ACT 1986
## (C 64)

*An Act to abolish the common law offences of riot, rout, unlawful assembly and affray and certain statutory offences relating to public order; to create new offences relating to public order; to control public processions and assemblies; to control the stirring up of racial hatred; to provide for the exclusion of certain offenders from sporting events; to create a new offence relating to the contamination of or interference with goods; to confer power to direct certain trespassers to leave land; to amend section 7 of the Conspiracy and Protection of Property Act 1875, section 1 of the Prevention of Crime Act 1953, Part V of the Criminal Justice (Scotland) Act 1980 and the Sporting Events (Control of Alcohol etc) Act 1985; to repeal certain obsolete or unnecessary enactments; and for connected purposes*

[7 November 1986]

NOTES

The provisions reproduced apply only to England and Wales.

# PART I
# NEW OFFENCES

## 1 Riot

(1)   Where 12 or more persons who are present together use or threaten unlawful violence for a common purpose and the conduct of them (taken together) is such as would cause a person of reasonable firmness present at the scene to fear for his personal safety, each of the persons using unlawful violence for the common purpose is guilty of riot.

(2)   It is immaterial whether or not the 12 or more use or threaten unlawful violence simultaneously.

(3)   The common purpose may be inferred from conduct.

(4)   No person of reasonable firmness need actually be, or be likely to be, present at the scene.

(5)   Riot may be committed in private as well as in public places.

(6)   A person guilty of riot is liable on conviction on indictment to imprisonment for a term not exceeding ten years or a fine or both.

## 2 Violent disorder

(1)   Where 3 or more persons who are present together use or threaten unlawful violence and the conduct of them (taken together) is such as would cause a person of reasonable firmness present at the scene to fear for personal safety, each of the persons using or threatening unlawful violence is guilty of violent disorder.

(2)   It is immaterial whether or not the 3 or more use or threaten unlawful violence simultaneously.

(3)   No person of reasonable firmness need actually be, or be likely to be, present at the scene.

(4)   Violent disorder may be committed in private as well as in public places.

(5)   A person guilty of violent disorder is liable on conviction on indictment to imprisonment for a term not exceeding 5 years or a fine or both, or on summary conviction to imprisonment for a term not exceeding 6 months or a fine not exceeding the statutory maximum or both.

## 3 Affray

(1)   A person is guilty of affray if he uses or threatens unlawful violence towards another and his conduct is such as would cause a person of reasonable firmness present at the scene to fear for his personal safety.

(2)   Where 2 or more persons use or threaten the unlawful violence, it is the conduct of them taken together that must be considered for the purposes of subsection (1).

(3)   For the purposes of this section a threat cannot be made by the use of words alone.

(4)   No person of reasonable firmness need actually be, or be likely to be, present at the scene.

(5)    Affray may be committed in private as well as in public places.

(6)    A constable may arrest without warrant anyone he reasonably suspects is committing affray.

(7)    A person guilty of affray is liable on conviction on indictment to imprisonment for a term not exceeding 3 years or a fine or both, or on summary conviction to imprisonment for a term not exceeding 6 months or a fine not exceeding the statutory maximum or both.

## 4    Fear or provocation of violence

(1)    A person is guilty of an offence if he—
   (a)  uses towards another person threatening, abusive or insulting words or behaviour, or
   (b)  distributes or displays to another person any writing, sign or other visible representation which is threatening, abusive or insulting,

with intent to cause that person to believe that immediate unlawful violence will be used against him or another by any person, or to provoke the immediate use of unlawful violence by that person or another, or whereby that person is likely to believe that such violence will be used or it is likely that such violence will be provoked.

(2)    An offence under this section may be committed in a public or a private place, except that no offence is committed where the words or behaviour are used, or the writing, sign or other visible representation is distributed or displayed, by a person inside a dwelling and the other person is also inside that or another dwelling.

(3)    A constable may arrest without warrant anyone he reasonably suspects is committing an offence under this section.

(4)    A person guilty of an offence under this section is liable on summary conviction to imprisonment for a term not exceeding 6 months or a fine not exceeding level 5 on the standard scale or both.

## [4A    Intentional harassment, alarm or distress

(1)    A person is guilty of an offence if, with intent to cause a person harassment, alarm or distress, he—
   (a)  uses threatening, abusive or insulting words or behaviour, or disorderly behaviour, or
   (b)  displays any writing, sign or other visible representation which is threatening, abusive or insulting,

thereby causing that or another person harassment, alarm or distress.

(2)    An offence under this section may be committed in a public or a private place, except that no offence is committed where the words or behaviour are used, or the writing, sign or other visible representation is displayed, by a person inside a dwelling and the person who is harassed, alarmed or distressed is also inside that or another dwelling.

(3)    It is a defence for the accused to prove—
   (a)  that he was inside a dwelling and had no reason to believe that the words or behaviour used, or the writing, sign or other visible representation displayed, would be heard or seen by a person outside that or any other dwelling, or
   (b)  that his conduct was reasonable.

(4)    A constable may arrest without a warrant anyone he reasonably suspects is committing an offence under this section.

(5)    A person guilty of an offence under this section is liable on summary conviction to imprisonment for a term not exceeding 6 months or a fine not exceeding level 5 on the standard scale or both.]

NOTES

Commencement: 3 February 1995.

Inserted by the Criminal Justice and Public Order Act 1994, s 154.

## 5    Harassment, alarm or distress

(1)    A person is guilty of an offence if he—
   (a)  uses threatening, abusive or insulting words or behaviour, or disorderly behaviour, or
   (b)  displays any writing, sign or other visible representation which is threatening, abusive or insulting,

within the hearing or sight of a person likely to be caused harassment, alarm or distress thereby.

(2)    An offence under this section may be committed in a public or a private place, except that no offence is committed where the words or behaviour are used, or the writing, sign or other visible representation is displayed, by a person inside a dwelling and the other person is also inside that or another dwelling.

(3)    It is a defence for the accused to prove—
   (a)  that he had no reason to believe that there was any person within hearing or sight who was likely to be caused harassment, alarm or distress, or
   (b)  that he was inside a dwelling and had no reason to believe that the words or behaviour used, or the writing, sign or other visible representation displayed, would be heard or seen by a person outside that or any other dwelling, or
   (c)  that his conduct was reasonable.

(4)    A constable may arrest a person without warrant if—
   (a)  he engages in offensive conduct which the constable warns him to stop, and
   (b)  he engages in further offensive conduct immediately or shortly after the warning.

(5)    In subsection (4) "offensive conduct" means conduct the constable reasonably suspects to constitute an offence under this section, and the conduct mentioned in paragraph (a) and the further conduct need not be of the same nature.

(6)    A person guilty of an offence under this section is liable on summary conviction to a fine not exceeding level 3 on the standard scale.

# PART II
# PROCESSIONS AND ASSEMBLIES

## 11    Advance notice of public processions

(1)    Written notice shall be given in accordance with this section of any proposal to hold a public procession intended—

(a) to demonstrate support for or opposition to the views or actions of any person or body of persons,

(b) to publicise a cause or campaign, or

(c) to mark or commemorate an event,

unless it is not reasonaly practicable to give any advance notice of the procession.

(2) Subsection (1) does not apply where the procession is one commonly or customarily held in the police area (or areas) in which it is proposed to be held or is a funeral procession organised by a funeral director acting in the normal course of his business.

(3) The notice must specify the date when it is intended to hold the procession, the time when it is intended to start it, its proposed route, and the name and address of the person (or of one of the persons) proposing to organise it.

(4) Notice must be delivered to a police station—

(a) in the police area in which it is proposed the procession will start, or

(b) where it is proposed the procession will start in Scotland and cross into England, in the first police area in England on the proposed route.

(5) If delivered not less than 6 clear days before the date when the procession is intended to be held, the notice may be delivered by post by the recorded delivery service; but section 7 of the Interpretation Act 1978 (under which a document sent by post is deemed to have been served when posted and to have been delivered in the ordinary course of post) does not apply.

(6) If not delivered in accordance with subsection (5), the notice must be delivered by hand not less than 6 clear days before the date when the procession is intended to be held or, if that is not reasonably practicable, as soon as delivery is reasonably practicable.

(7) Where a public procession is held, each of the persons organising it is guilty of an offence if—

(a) the requirements of this section as to notice have not been satisfied, or

(b) the date when it is held, the time when it starts, or its route, differs from the date, time or route specified in the notice.

(8) It is a defence for the accused to prove that he did not know of, and neither suspected nor had reason to suspect, the failure to satisfy the requirements or (as the case may be) the difference of date, time or route.

(9) To the extent that an alleged offence turns on a difference of date, time or route, it is a defence for the accused to prove that the difference arose from circumstances beyond his control or from something done with the agreement of a police officer or by his direction.

(10) A person guilty of an offence under subsection (7) is liable on summary conviction to a fine not exceeding level 3 on the standard scale.

## 12 Imposing conditions on public processions

(1) If the senior police officer, having regard to the time or place at which and the circumstances in which any public procession is being held or is intended to be held and to its route or proposed route, reasonably believes that—

(a) it may result in serious public disorder, serious damage to property or serious disruption to the life of the community, or

(b)  the purpose of the persons organising it is the intimidation of others with a view to compelling them not to do an act they have a right to do, or to do an act they have a right not to do,

he may give directions imposing on the persons organising or taking part in the procession such conditions as appear to him necessary to prevent such disorder, damage, disruption or intimidation, including conditions as to the route of the procession or prohibiting it from entering any public place specified in the directions.

(2)  In subsection (1) "the senior police officer" means—

(a)  in relation to a procession being held, or to a procession intended to be held in a case where persons are assembling with a view to taking part in it, the most senior in rank of the police officers present at the scene, and

(b)  in relation to a procession intended to be held in a case where paragraph (a) does not apply, the chief officer of police.

(3)  A direction given by a chief officer of police by virtue of subsection (2)(b) shall be given in writing.

(4)  A person who organises a public procession and knowingly fails to comply with a condition imposed under this section is guilty of an offence, but it is a defence for him to prove that the failure arose from circumstances beyond his control.

(5)  A person who takes part in a public procession and knowingly fails to comply with a condition imposed under this section is guilty of an offence, but it is a defence for him to prove that the failure arose from circumstances beyond his control.

(6)  A person who incites another to commit an offence under subsection (5) is guilty of an offence.

(7)  A constable in uniform may arrest without warrant anyone he reasonably suspects is committing an offence under subsection (4), (5) or (6).

(8)  A person guilty of an offence under subsection (4) is liable on summary conviction to imprisonment for a term not exceeding 3 months or a fine not exceeding level 4 on the standard scale or both.

(9)  A person guilty of an offence under subsection (5) is liable on summary conviction to a fine not exceeding level 3 on the standard scale.

(10)  A person guilty of an offence under subsection (6) is liable on summary conviction to imprisonment for a term not exceeding 3 months or a fine not exceeding level 4 on the standard scale or both, notwithstanding section 45(3) of the Magistrates' Courts Act 1980 (inciter liable to same penalty as incited).

(11)  In Scotland this section applies only in relation to a procession being held, and to a procession intended to be held in a case where persons are assembling with a view to taking part in it.

## 13  Prohibiting public processions

(1)  If at any time the chief officer of police reasonably believes that, because pf particular circumstances existing in any district or part of a district, the powers under section 12 will not be sufficient to prevent the holding of public processions in that district or part from resulting in serious public disorder, he shall apply to the council of the district for an order prohibiting for such period not exceeding 3 months as may be specified in the application the holding of all public processions (or of any class of public procession so specified) in the district or part concerned.

(2)   On receiving such an application, a council may with the consent of the Secretary of State make an order either in the terms of the application or with such modifications as may be approved by the Secretary of State.

(3)   Subsection (1) does not apply in the City of London or the metropolitan police district.

(4)   If at any time the Commissioner of Police for the City of London or the Commissioner of Police of the Metropolis reasonably believes that, because of particular circumstances existing in his police area or part of it, the powers under section 12 will not be sufficient to prevent the holding of public processions in that area or part from resulting in serious public disorder, he may with the consent of the Secretary of State make an order prohibiting for such period not exceeding 3 months as may be specified in the order the holding of all public processions (or of any class of public procession so specified) in the area or part concerned.

(5)   An order made under this section may be revoked or varied by a subsequent order made in the same way, that is, in accordance with subsections (1) and (2) or subsection (4), as the case may be.

(6)   Any order under this section shall, if not made in writing, be recorded in writing as soon as practicable after being made.

(7)   A person who organises a public procession the holding of which he knows is prohibited by virtue of an order under this section is guilty of an offence.

(8)   A person who takes part in a public procession the holding of which he knows is prohibited by virtue of an order under this section is guilty of an offence.

(9)   A person who incites another to commit an offence under subsection (8) is guilty of an offence.

(10)   A constable in uniform may arrest without warrant anyone he reasonably suspects is committing an offence under subsection (7), (8) or (9).

(11)   A person guilty of an offence under subsection (7) is liable on summary conviction to imprisonment for a term not exceeding 3 months or a fine not exceeding level 4 on the standard scale or both.

(12)   A person guilty of an offence under subsection (8) is liable on summary conviction to a fine not exceeding level 3 on the standard scale.

(13)   A person guilty of an offence under subsection (9) is liable on summary conviction to imprisonment for a term not exceeding 3 months or a fine not exceeding level 4 on the standard scale or both, notwithstanding section 45(3) of the Magistrates' Courts Act 1980.

## 14   Imposing conditions on public assemblies

(1)   If the senior police officer, having regard to the time or place at which and the circumstances in which any public assembly is being held or is intended to be held, reasonably believes that—

   (a)   it may result in serious public disorder, serious damage to property or serious disruption to the life of the community, or
   (b)   the purpose of the persons organising it is the intimdation of others with a view to compelling them not to do an act they have a right to do, or to do an act they have a right not to do,

he may give directions imposing on the persons organising or taking part in the assembly such conditions as to the place at which the assembly may be (or continue to be) held, its maximum duration, or the maximum number of persons who may constitute it, as appear to him necessary to prevent such disorder, damage, disruption or intimidation.

(2)    In subsection (1) "the senior police officer" means—
    (a)    in relation to an assembly being held, the most senior in rank of the police officers present at the scene, and
    (b)    in relation to an assembly intended to be held, the chief officer of police.

(3)    A direction given by a chief officer of police by virtue of subsection (2)(b) shall be given in writing.

(4)    A person who organises a public assembly and knowingly fails to comply with a condition imposed under this section is guilty of an offence, but it is a defence for him to prove that the failure arose from circumstances beyond his control.

(5)    A person who takes part in a public assembly and knowingly fails to comply with a condition imposed under this section is guilty of an offence, but it is a defence for him to prove that the failure arose from circumstances beyond his control.

(6)    A person who incites another to commit an offence under subsection (5) is guilty of an offence.

(7)    A constable in uniform may arrest without warrant anyone he reasonably suspects is committing an offence under subsection (4), (5) or (6).

(8)    A person guilty of an offence under subsection (4) is liable on summary conviction to imprisonment for a term not exceeding 3 months or a fine not exceeding level 4 on the standard scale or both.

(9)    A person guilty of an offence under subsection (5) is liable on summary conviction to a fine not exceeding level 3 on the standard scale.

(10)    A person guilty of an offence under subsection (6) is liable on summary conviction to imprisonment for a term not exceeding 3 months or a fine not exceeding level 4 on the standard scale or both, notwithstanding section 45(3) of the Magistrates' Courts Act 1980.

## PART V
## MISCELLANEOUS AND GENERAL

### 43    Short title

This Act may be cited as the Public Order Act 1986.

# CHILDREN ACT 1989

## (C 41)

*An Act to reform the law relating to children; to provide for local authority services for children in need and others; to amend the law with respect to children's homes, community homes, voluntary homes and voluntary organisations; to make provision with respect to fostering, child minding and day care for young children and adoption; and for connected purposes*

[16 November 1989]

# PART I
# INTRODUCTORY

## 1  Welfare of the child

(1)   When a court determines any question with respect to—
  (a)  the upbringing of a child; or
  (b)  the administration of a child's property or the application of any income arising from it,

the child's welfare shall be the court's paramount consideration.

(2)   In any proceedings in which any question with respect to the upbringing of a child arises, the court shall have regard to the general principle that any delay in determining the question is likely to prejudice the welfare of the child.

(3)   In the circumstances mentioned in subsection (4), a court shall have regard in particular to—
  (a)  the ascertainable wishes and feelings of the child concerned (considered in the light of his age and understanding);
  (b)  his physical, emotional and educational needs;
  (c)  the likely effect on him of any change in his circumstances;
  (d)  his age, sex, background and any characteristics of his which the court considers relevant;
  (e)  any harm which he has suffered or is at risk of suffering;
  (f)  how capable each of his parents, and any other person in relation to whom the court considers the question to be relevant, is of meeting his needs;
  (g)  the range of powers available to the court under this Act in the proceedings in question.

(4)   The circumstances are that—
  (a)  the court is considering whether to make, vary or discharge a section 8 order, and the making, variation or discharge of the order is opposed by any party to the proceedings; or
  (b)  the court is considering whether to make, vary or discharge an order under Part IV.

(5)   Where a court is considering whether or not to make one or more orders under this Act with respect to a child, it shall not make the order or any of the orders unless it considers that doing so would be better for the child than making no order at all.

## 2  Parental responsibility for children

(1)   Where a child's father and mother were married to each other at the time of his birth, they shall each have parental responsibility for the child.

(2)   Where a child's father and mother were not married to each other at the time of his birth—
  (a)  the mother shall have parental responsibility for the child;
  (b)  the father shall not have parental responsibility for the child, unless he acquires it in accordance with the provisions of this Act.

(3)   References in this Act to a child whose father and mother were, or (as the case may be) were not, married to each other at the time of his birth must be read with section 1 of the Family Law Reform Act 1987 (which extends their meaning).

(4)   The rule of law that a father is the natural guardian of his legitimate child is abolished.

(5)   More than one person may have parental responsibility for the same child at the same time.

(6)   A person who has parental responsibility for a child at any time shall not cease to have that responsibility solely because some other person subsequently acquires parental responsibility for the child.

(7)   Where more than one person has parental responsibility for a child, each of them may act alone and without the other (or others) in meeting that responsibility; but nothing in this Part shall be taken to affect the operation of any enactment which requires the consent of more than one person in a matter affecting the child.

(8)   The fact that a person has parental responsibility for a child shall not entitle him to act in any way which would be incompatible with any order made with respect to the child under this Act.

(9)   A person who has parental responsibility for a child may not surrender or transfer any part of that responsibility to another but may arrange for some or all of it to be met by one or more persons acting on his behalf.

(10)   The person with whom any such arrangement is made may himself be a person who already has parental responsibility for the child concerned.

(11)   The making of any such arrangement shall not affect any liability of the person making it which may arise from any failure to meet any part of his parental responsibility for the child concerned.

### 3   Meaning of "parental responsibility"

(1)   In this Act "parental responsibility" means all the rights, duties, powers, responsibilities and authority which by law a parent of a child has in relation to the child and his property.

(2)   It also includes the rights, powers and duties which a guardian of the child's estate (appointed, before the commencement of section 5, to act generally) would have had in relation to the child and his property.

(3)   The rights referred to in subsection (2) include, in particular, the right of the guardian to receive or recover in his own name, for the benefit of the child, property of whatever description and wherever situated which the child is entitled to receive or recover.

(4)   The fact that a person has, or does not have, parental responsibility for a child shall not affect—

(a)   any obligation which he may have in relation to the child (such as a statutory duty to maintain the child); or

(b)   any rights which, in the event of the child's death, he (or any other person) may have in relation to the child's property.

(5)   A person who—

(a)   does not have parental responsibility for a particular child; but

(b)   has care of the child,

may (subject to the provisions of this Act) do what is reasonable in all the circumstances of the case for the purpose of safeguarding or promoting the child's welfare.

## 4 Acquisition of parental responsibility by father

(1)  Where a child's father and mother were not married to each other at the time of his birth—

    (a)  the court may, on the application of the father, order that he shall have parental responsibility for the child; or

    (b)  the father and mother may by agreement ("a parental responsibility agreement") provide for the father to have parental responsibility for the child.

(2)  No parental responsibility agreement shall have effect for the purposes of this Act unless—

    (a)  it is made in the form prescribed by regulations made by the Lord Chancellor; and

    (b)  where regulations are made by the Lord Chancellor prescribing the manner in which such agreements must be recorded, it is recorded in the prescribed manner.

(3)  Subject to section 12(4), an order under subsection (1)(*a*), or a parental responsibility agreement, may only be brought to an end by an order of the court made on the application—

    (a)  of any person who has parental responsibility for the child; or

    (b)  with leave of the court, of the child himself.

(4)  The court may only grant leave under subsection (3)(*b*) if it is satisfied that the child has sufficient understanding to make the proposed application.

## 5 Appointment of guardians

(1)  Where an application with respect to a child is made to the court by any individual, the court may by order appoint that individual to be the child's guardian if—

    (a)  the child has no parent with parental responsibility for him; or

    (b)  a residence order has been made with respect to the child in favour of a parent or guardian of his who has died while the order was in force.

(2)  The power conferred by subsection (1) may also be exercised in any family proceedings if the court considers that the order should be made even though no application has been made for it.

(3)  A parent who has parental responsibility for his child may appoint another individual to be the child's guardian in the event of his death.

(4)  A guardian of a child may appoint another individual to take his place as the child's guardian in the event of his death.

(5)  An appointment under subsection (3) or (4) shall not have effect unless it is made in writing, is dated and is signed by the person making the appointment or—

    (a)  in the case of an appointment made by a will which is not signed by the testator, is signed at the direction of the testator in accordance with the requirements of section 9 of the Wills Act 1837; or

    (b)  in any other case, is signed at the direction of the person making the appointment, in his presence and in the presence of two witnesses who each attest the signature.

(6)  A person appointed as a child's guardian under this section shall have parental responsibility for the child concerned.

(7)   Where—

    (a)   on the death of any person making an appointment under subsection (3) or (4), the child concerned has no parent with parental responsibility for him; or

    (b)   immediately before the death of any person making such an appointment, a residence order in his favour was in force with respect to the child,

the appointment shall take effect on the death of that person.

(8)   Where, on the death of any person making an appointment under subsection (3) or (4)—

    (a)   the child concerned has a parent with parental responsibility for him; and

    (b)   subsection (7)(b) does not apply,

the appointment shall take effect when the child no longer has a parent who has parental responsibility for him.

(9)   Subsections (1) and (7) do not apply if the residence order referred to in paragraph (b) of those subsections was also made in favour of a surviving parent of the child.

(10)   Nothing in this section shall be taken to prevent an appointment under subsection (3) or (4) being made by two or more persons acting jointly.

(11)   Subject to any provision made by rules of court, no court shall exercise the High Court's inherent jurisdiction to appoint a guardian of the estate of any child.

(12)   Where rules of court are made under subsection (11) they may prescribe the circumstances in which, and conditions subject to which, an appointment of such a guardian may be made.

(13)   A guardian of a child may only be appointed in accordance with the provisions of this section.

## 7   Welfare reports

(1)   A court considering any question with respect to a child under this Act may—

    (a)   ask a probation officer; or

    (b)   ask a local authority to arrange for—

        (i)   an officer of the authority; or

        (ii)   such other person (other than a probation officer) as the authority considers appropriate,

to report to the court on such matters relating to the welfare of that child as are required to be dealt with in the report.

(2)   The Lord Chancellor may make regulations specifying matters which, unless the court orders otherwise, must be dealt with in any report under this section.

(3)   The report may be made in writing, or orally, as the court requires.

(4)   Regardless of any enactment or rule of law which would otherwise prevent it from doing so, the court may take account of—

    (a)   any statement contained in the report; and

    (b)   any evidence given in respect of the matters referred to in the report,

in so far as the statement or evidence is, in the opinion of the court, relevant to the question which it is considering.

(5)   It shall be the duty of the authority or probation officer to comply with any request for a report under this section.

# PART II
# ORDERS WITH RESPECT TO CHILDREN IN FAMILY PROCEEDINGS

*General*

## 8 Residence, contact and other orders with respect to children

(1)  In this Act—

"a contact order" means an order requiring the person with whom a child lives, or is to live, to allow the child to visit or stay with the person named in the order, or for that person and the child otherwise to have contact with each other;

"a prohibited steps order" means an order that no step which could be taken by a parent in meeting his parental responsibility for a child, and which is of a kind specified in the order, shall be taken by any person without the consent of the court;

"a residence order" means an order settling the arrangements to be made as to the person with whom a child is to live; and

"a specific issue order" means an order giving directions for the purpose of determining a specific question which has arisen, or which may arise, in connection with any aspect of parental responsibility for a child.

(2)  In this Act "a section 8 order" means any of the orders mentioned in subsection (1) and any order varying or discharging such an order.

(3)  For the purposes of this Act "family proceedings" means [(subject to subsection (5))] any proceedings—

(a)  under the inherent jurisdiction of the High Court in relation to children; and

(b)  under the enactments mentioned in subsection (4),

but does not include proceedings on an application for leave under section 100(3).

(4)  The enactments are—

(a)  Parts I, II and IV of this Act;

(b)  the Matrimonial Causes Act 1973;

(c)  the Domestic Violence and Matrimonial Proceedings Act 1976;

(d)  the Adoption Act 1976;

(e)  the Domestic Proceedings and Magistrates' Courts Act 1978;

(f)  sections 1 and 9 of the Matrimonial Homes Act 1983;

(g)  Part III of the Matrimonial and Family Proceedings Act 1984.

[(h) the Family Law Act 1996.]

[(5)  For the purposes of any reference in this Act to family proceedings powers which under this Act are exercisable in family proceedings shall also be exercisable in relation to a child, without any such proceedings having been commenced or any application having been made to the court under this Act, if—

(a)  a statement of marital breakdown under section 5 of the Family Law Act 1996 with respect to the marriage in relation to which that child is a child of the family has been received by the court; and

(b)  it may, in due course, become possible for an application for a divorce order or for a separation order to be made by reference to that statement.]

NOTES

Commencement: 14 October 1991 (sub-ss (1)–(4)); to be appointed (remainder).

Sub-s (3): words in square brackets inserted by the Family Law Act 1996, s 66(1), Sch 8, para 41(1), (3), subject to savings in s 66(2) of, and Sch 9, para 5 to, the 1996 Act, as from a day to be appointed.

Sub-s (4): paras (c) and (f) repealed, and para (h) added, by the Family Law Act 1996, s 66(1), (3), Sch 8, para 60(1), Sch 10, subject to savings in s 66(2) of, and Sch 9, paras 5, 8–10 to, the 1996 Act, as from a day to be appointed.

Sub-s (5): added by the Family Law Act 1996, s 66(1), Sch 8, para 41(4), subject to savings in s 66(2) of, and Sch 9, paras 5, 8–10 to, the 1996 Act, as from a day to be appointed.

## 10  Power of court to make section 8 orders

(1)  In any family proceedings in which a question arises with respect to the welfare of any child, the court may make a section 8 order with respect to the child if—

(a)  an application for the order has been made by a person who—

(i)  is entitled to apply for a section 8 order with respect to the child; or

(ii)  has obtained the leave of the court to make the application; or

(b)  the court considers that the order should be made even though no such application has been made.

(2)  The court may also make a section 8 order with respect to any child on the application of a person who—

(a)  is entitled to apply for a section 8 order with respect to the child; or

(b)  has obtained the leave of the court to make the application.

(3)  This section is subject to the restrictions imposed by section 9.

(4)  The following persons are entitled to apply to the court for any section 8 order with respect to a child—

(a)  any parent or guardian of the child;

(b)  any person in whose favour a residence order is in force with respect to the child.

(5)  The following persons are entitled to apply for a residence or contact order with respect to a child—

(a)  any party to a marriage (whether or not subsisting) in relation to whom the child is a child of the family;

(b)  any person with whom the child has lived for a period of at least three years;

(c)  any person—

(i)  in any case where a residence order is in force with respect to the child, has the consent of each of the persons in whose favour the order was made;

(ii)  in any case where the child is in the care of a local authority, has the consent of that authority; or

(iii)  in any other case, has the consent of each of those (if any) who have parental responsibility for the child.

(6)  A person who would not otherwise be entitled (under the previous provisions of this section) to apply for the variation or discharge of a section 8 order shall be entitled to do so if—

(a)  the order was made on his application; or

(b)  in the case of a contact order, he is named in the order.

(7)  Any person who falls within a category of person prescribed by rules of court is entitled to apply for any such section 8 order as may be prescribed in relation to that category of person.

(8)   Where the person applying for leave to make an application for a section 8 order is the child concerned, the court may only grant leave if it is satisfied that he has sufficient understanding to make the proposed application for the section 8 order.

(9)   Where the person applying for leave to make an application for a section 8 order is not the child concerned, the court shall, in deciding whether or not to grant leave, have particular regard to—

(a)   the nature of the proposed application for the section 8 order;

(b)   the applicant's connection with the child;

(c)   any risk there might be of that proposed application disrupting the child's life to such an extent that he would be harmed by it; and

(d)   where the child is being looked after by a local authority—

(i)   the authority's plans for the child's future; and

(ii)   the wishes and feelings of the child's parents.

(10)   The period of three years mentioned in subsection (5)(b) need not be continuous but must not have begun more than five years before, or ended more than three months before, the making of the application.

## 11   General principles and supplementary provisions

(1)   In proceedings in which any question of making a section 8 order, or any other question with respect to such an order, arises, the court shall (in the light of any rules made by virtue of subsection (2))—

(a)   draw up a timetable with a view to determining the question without delay; and

(b)   give such directions as it considers appropriate for the purpose of ensuring, so far as is reasonably practicable, that that timetable is adhered to.

(2)   Rules of court may—

(a)   specify periods within which specified steps must be taken in relation to proceedings in which such questions arise; and

(b)   make other provision with respect to such proceedings for the purpose of ensuring, so far as is reasonably practicable, that such questions are determined without delay.

(3)   Where a court has power to make a section 8 order, it may do so at any time during the course of the proceedings in question even though it is not in a position to dispose finally of those proceedings.

(4)   Where a residence order is made in favour of two or more persons who do not themselves all live together, the order may specify the periods during which the child is to live in the different households concerned.

(5)   Where—

(a)   a residence order has been made with respect to a child; and

(b)   as a result of the order the child lives, or is to live, with one of two parents who each have parental responsibility for him,

the residence order shall cease to have effect if the parents live together for a continuous period of more than six months.

(6)   A contact order which requires the parent with whom a child lives to allow the child to visit, or otherwise have contact with, his other parent shall cease to have effect if the parents live together for a continuous period of more than six months.

(7)   A section 8 order may—

(a)   contain directions about how it is to be carried into effect;

(b)   impose conditions which must be complied with by any person—

      (i)  in whose favour the order is made;

      (ii)  who is a parent of the child concerned;

      (iii)  who is not a parent of his but who has parental responsibility for him; or

      (iv)  with whom the child is living,

      and to whom the conditions are expressed to apply;

(c)  be made to have effect for a specified period, or contain provisions which are to have effect for a specified period;

(d)  make such incidental, supplemental or consequential provision as the court thinks fit.

*Financial relief*

## 15 Orders for financial relief with respect to children

(1)    Schedule 1 (which consists primarily of the re-enactment, with consequential amendments and minor modifications, of provisions of [section 6 of the Family Law Reform Act 1969] the Guardianship of Minors Acts 1971 and 1973, the Children Act 1975 and of sections 15 and 16 of the Family Law Reform Act 1987) makes provision in relation to financial relief for children.

(2)    The powers of a magistrates' court under section 60 of the Magistrates' Courts Act 1980 to revoke, revive or vary an order for the periodical payment of money [and the power of the clerk of a magistrates' court to vary such an order] shall not apply in relation to an order made under Schedule 1.

NOTES

    Sub-s (1): words in square brackets inserted by the Courts and Legal Services Act 1990, s 116, Sch 16, para 10.

    Sub-s (2): words in square brackets inserted by the Maintenance Enforcement Act 1991, s 11(1), Sch 2, para 10.

*Family assistance orders*

## 16 Family assistance orders

(1)    Where, in any family proceedings, the court has power to make an order under this Part with respect to any child, it may (whether or not it makes such an order) make an order requiring—

(a)  a probation officer to be made available; or

(b)  a local authority to make an officer of the authority available,

to advise, assist and (where appropriate) befriend any person named in the order.

(2)    The persons who may be named in an order under this section ("a family assistance order") are—

(a)  any parent or guardian of the child;

(b)  any person with whom the child is living or in whose favour a contact order is in force with respect to the child;

(c)  the child himself.

(3)    No court may make a family assistance order unless—

(a)  it is satisfied that the circumstances of the case are exceptional; and

(b)  it has obtained the consent of every person to be named in the order other than the child.

(4)    A family assistance order may direct—
  (a)  the person named in the order; or
  (b)  such of the persons named in the order as may be specified in the order,

to take such steps as may be so specified with a view to enabling the officer concerned to be kept informed of the address of any person named in the order and to be allowed to visit any such person.

(5)    Unless it specifies a shorter period, a family assistance order shall have effect for a period of six months beginning with the day on which it is made.

(6)    Where—
  (a)  a family assistance order is in force with respect to a child; and
  (b)  a section 8 order is also in force with respect to the child,

the officer concerned may refer to the court the question whether the section 8 order should be varied or discharged.

(7)    A family assistance order shall not be made so as to require a local authority to make an officer of theirs available unless—
  (a)  the authority agree; or
  (b)  the child concerned lives or will live within their area.

(8)    Where a family assistance order requires a probation officer to be made available, the officer shall be selected in accordance with arrangements made by the probation committee for the area in which the child lives or will live.

(9)    If the selected probation officer is unable to carry out his duties, or dies, another probation officer shall be selected in the same manner.

# PART III
# LOCAL AUTHORITY SUPPORT FOR CHILDREN AND FAMILIES

*Provision of services for children and their families*

## 17    Provision of services for children in need, their families and others

(1)    It shall be the general duty of every local authority (in addition to the other duties imposed on them by this Part)—
  (a)  to safeguard and promote the welfare of children within their area who are in need; and
  (b)  so far as is consistent with that duty, to promote the upbringing of such children by their families,

by providing a range and level of services appropriate to those children's needs.

(2)    For the purpose principally of facilitating the discharge of their general duty under this section, every local authority shall have the specific duties and powers set out in Part I of Schedule 2.

(3)    Any service provided by an authority in the exercise of functions conferred on them by this section may be provided for the family of a particular child in need or for any member of his family, if it is provided with a view to safeguarding or promoting the child's welfare.

(4)    The Secretary of State may by order amend any provision of Part I of Schedule 2 or add any further duty or power to those for the time being mentioned there.

(5)     Every local authority—

    (a)    shall facilitate the provision by others (including in particular voluntary organisations) of services which the authority have power to provide by virtue of this section, or section 18, 20, 23 or 24; and

    (b)    may make such arrangements as they see fit for any person to act on their behalf in the provision of any such service.

(6)     The services provided by a local authority in the exercise of functions conferred on them by this section may include giving assistance in kind or, in exceptional circumstances, in cash.

(7)     Assistance may be unconditional or subject to conditions as to the repayment of the assistance or of its value (in whole or in part).

(8)     Before giving any assistance or imposing any conditions, a local authority shall have regard to the means of the child concerned and of each of his parents.

(9)     No person shall be liable to make any repayment of assistance or of its value at any time when he is in receipt of income support[, family credit or disability working allowance] under the [Part VII of the Social Security Contributions and Benefits Act 1992] [or of an income-based jobseeker's allowance].

(10)   For the purposes of this Part a child shall be taken to be in need if—

    (a)    he is unlikely to achieve or maintain, or to have the opportunity of achieving or maintaining, a reasonable standard of health or development without the provision for him of services by a local authority under this Part;

    (b)    his health or development is likely to be significantly impaired, or further impaired, without the provision for him of such services; or

    (c)    he is disabled,

and "family", in relation to such a child, includes any person who has parental responsibility for the child and any other person with whom he has been living.

(11)   For the purposes of this Part, a child is disabled if he is blind, deaf or dumb or suffers from mental disorder of any kind or is substantially and permanently handicapped by illness, injury or congenital deformity or such other disability as may be prescribed; and in this Part—

    "development" means physical, intellectual, emotional, social or behavioural development; and

    "health" means physical or mental health.

---

NOTES

    Sub-s (9): words in first pair of square brackets substituted by the Disability Living Allowance and Disability Working Allowance Act 1991, s 7, Sch 3, Pt II, para 13; words in second pair of square brackets substituted by the Social Security (Consequential Provisions) Act 1992, s 4, Sch 2, para 108(a); words in third pair of square brackets added by the Jobseekers Act 1995, s 41(4), Sch 2, para 19(2).

---

## 18    Day care for pre-school and other children

(1)     Every local authority shall provide such day care for children in need within their area who are—

    (a)    aged five or under; and

    (b)    not yet attending schools,

as is appropriate.

(2)    A local authority may provide day care for children within their area who satisfy the conditions mentioned in subsection (1)(*a*) and (*b*) even though they are not in need.

(3)    A local authority may provide facilities (including training, advice, guidance and counselling) for those—
(a)   caring for children in day care; or
(b)   who at any time accompany such children while they are in day care.

(4)    In this section "day care" means any form of care or supervised activity provided for children during the day (whether or not it is provided on a regular basis).

(5)    Every local authority shall provide for children in need within their area who are attending any school such care or supervised activities as is appropriate—
(a)   outside school hours; or
(b)   during school holidays.

(6)    A local authority may provide such care or supervised activities for children within their area who are attending any school even though those children are not in need.

(7)    In this section "supervised activity" means an activity supervised by a responsible person.

*Provision of accommodation for children*

## 20    Provision of accommodation for children: general

(1)    Every local authority shall provide accommodation for any child in need within their area who appears to them to require accommodation as a result of—
(a)   there being no person who has parental responsibility for him;
(b)   his being lost or having been abandoned; or
(c)   the person who has been caring for him being prevented (whether or not permanently, and for whatever reason) from providing him with suitable accommodation or care.

(2)    Where a local authority provide accommodation under subsection (1) for a child who is ordinarily resident in the area of another local authority, that other local authority may take over the provision of accommodation for the child within—
(a)   three months of being notified in writing that the child is being provided with accommodation; or
(b)   such other longer period as may be prescribed.

(3)    Every local authority shall provide accommodation for any child in need within their area who has reached the age of sixteen and whose welfare the authority consider is likely to be seriously prejudiced if they do not provide him with accommodation.

(4)    A local authority may provide accommodation for any child within their area (even though a person who has parental responsibility for him is able to provide him with accommodation) if they consider that to do so would safeguard or promote the child's welfare.

(5)    A local authority may provide accommodation for any person who has reached the age of sixteen but is under twenty-one in any community home which takes children who have reached the age of sixteen if they consider that to do so would safeguard or promote his welfare.

(6)    Before providing accommodation under this section, a local authority shall, so far as is reasonably practicable and consistent with the child's welfare—

  (a)   ascertain the child's wishes regarding the provision of accommodation; and

  (b)   give due consideration (having regard to his age and understanding) to such wishes of the child as they have been able to ascertain.

(7)    A local authority may not provide accommodation under this section for any child if any person who—

  (a)   has parental responsibility for him; and

  (b)   is willing and able to—

    (i)   provide accommodation for him; or

    (ii)  arrange for accommodation to be provided for him,

    objects.

(8)    Any person who has parental responsibility for a child may at any time remove the child from accommodation provided by or on behalf of the local authority under this section.

(9)    Subsections (7) and (8) do not apply while any person—

  (a)   in whose favour a residence order is in force with respect to the child; or

  (b)   who has care of the child by virtue of an order made in the exercise of the High Court's inherent jurisdiction with respect to children,

agrees to the child being looked after in accommodation provided by or on behalf of the local authority.

(10)   Where there is more than one such person as is mentioned in subsection (9), all of them must agree.

(11)   Subsections (7) and (8) do not apply where a child who has reached the age of sixteen agrees to being provided with accommodation under this section.

## 21    Provision for accommodation for children in police protection or detention or on remand, etc

(1)    Every local authority shall make provision for the reception and accommodation of children who are removed or kept away from home under Part V.

(2)    Every local authority shall receive, and provide accommodation for, children—

  (a)   in police protection whom they are requested to receive under section 46(3)(f);

  (b)   whom they are requested to receive under section 38(6) of the Police and Criminal Evidence Act 1984;

  (c)   who are—

    (i)   on remand [(within the meaning of the section)] under section [16(3A) or] 23(1) of the Children and Young Persons Act 1969; or

    (ii)  the subject of a supervision order imposing a residence requirement under section 12AA of that Act,

    and with respect to whom they are the designated authority.

(3)    Where a child has been—

  (a)   removed under Part V; or

  (b)   detained under section 38 of the Police and Criminal Evidence Act 1984,

and he is not being provided with accommodation by a local authority or in a hospital vested in the Secretary of State [or otherwise made available pursuant to arrangements made by a [Health Authority]], any reasonable expenses of acccommodating him shall be recoverable from the local authority in whose area he is ordinarily resident.

NOTES

Sub-s (2): words in first pair of square brackets in para (c) inserted by the Criminal Justice and Public Order Act 1994, s 168(1), Sch 9, para 38, as from a day to be appointed, words in second pair of square brackets inserted by the Courts and Legal Services Act 1990, s 116, Sch 16, para 11.

Sub-s (3): words in outer pair of square brackets inserted by the National Health Service and Community Care Act 1990, s 66(1), Sch 9, para 36(1), words in inner pair of square brackets substituted by the Health Authorities Act 1995, s 2(1), Sch 1, para 118(3).

*Duties of local authorities in relation to children looked after by them*

## 22 General duty of local authority in relation to children looked after by them

(1) In this Act, any reference to a child who is looked after by a local authority is a reference to a child who is—

(a) in their care; or

(b) provided with accommodation by the authority in the exercise of any functions (in particular those under this Act) which stand referred to their social services committee under the Local Authority Social Services Act 1970.

(2) In subsection (1) "accommodation" means accommodation which is provided for a continuous period of more than 24 hours.

(3) It shall be the duty of a local authority looking after any child—

(a) to safeguard and promote his welfare; and

(b) to make such use of services available for children cared for by their own parents as appears to the authority reasonable in his case.

(4) Before making any decision with respect to a child whom they are looking after, or proposing to look after, a local authority shall, so far as is reasonably practicable, ascertain the wishes and feelings of—

(a) the child;

(b) his parents;

(c) any person who is not a parent of his but who has parental responsibility for him; and

(d) any other person whose wishes and feelings the authority consider to be relevant,

regarding the matter to be decided.

(5) In making any such decision a local authority shall give due consideration—

(a) having regard to his age and understanding, to such wishes and feelings of the child as they have been able to ascertain;

(b) to such wishes and feelings of any person mentioned in subsection (4)(*b*) to (*d*) as they have been able to ascertain; and

(c) to the child's religious persuasion, racial origin and cultural and linguistic background.

(6) If it appears to a local authority that it is necessary, for the purpose of protecting members of the public from serious injury, to exercise their powers with respect to a child whom they are looking after in a manner which may not be consistent with their duties under this section, they may do so.

(7) If the Secretary of State considers it necessary, for the purpose of protecting members of the public from serious injury, to give directions to a local authority with respect to the exercise of their powers with respect to a child whom they are looking after, he may give such directions to the authority.

(8)    Where any such directions are given to an authority they shall comply with them even though doing so is inconsistent with their duties under this section.

### 23    Provision of accommodation and maintenance by local authority for children whom they are looking after

(1)    It shall be the duty of any local authority looking after a child—
   (a)   when he is in their care, to provide accommodation for him; and
   (b)   to maintain him in other respects apart from providing accommodation for him.

(2)    A local authority shall provide accommodation and maintenance for any child whom they are looking after by—
   (a)   placing him (subject to subsection (5) and any regulations made by the Secretary of State) with—
      (i)    a family;
      (ii)   a relative of his; or
      (iii)  any other suitable person,
      on such terms as to payment by the authority and otherwise as the authority may determine;
   (b)   maintaining him in a community home;
   (c)   maintaining him in a voluntary home;
   (d)   maintaining him in a registered children's home;
   (e)   maintaining him in a home provided [in accordance with arrangements made] by the Secretary of State under section 82(5) on such terms as the Secretary of State may from time to time determine; or
   (f)   making such other arrangements as—
      (i)    seem appropriate to them; and
      (ii)   comply with any regulations made by the Secretary of State.

(3)    Any person with whom a child has been placed under subsection (2)(*a*) is referred to in this Act as a local authority foster parent unless he falls within subsection (4).

(4)    A person falls within this subsection if he is—
   (a)   a parent of the child;
   (b)   a person who is not a parent of the child but who has parental responsibility for him; or
   (c)   where the child is in care and there was a residence order in force with respect to him immediately before the care order was made, a person in whose favour the residence order was made.

(5)    Where a child is in the care of a local authority, the authority may only allow him to live with a person who falls within subsection (4) in accordance with regulations made by the Secretary of State.

[(5A) For the purposes of subsection (5) a child shall be regarded as living with a person if he stays with that person for a continuous period of more than 24 hours].

(6)    Subject to any regulations made by the Secretary of State for the purposes of this subsection, any local authority looking after a child shall make arrangements to enable him to live with—
   (a)   a person falling within subsection (4); or
   (b)   a relative, friend or other person connected with him,

unless that would not be reasonably practicable or consistent with his welfare.

(7)   Where a local authority provide accommodation for a child whom they are looking after, they shall, subject to the provisions of this Part and so far as is reasonably practicable and consistent with his welfare, secure that—

(a)   the accommodation is near his home; and

(b)   where the authority are also providing accommodation for a sibling of his, they are accommodated together.

(8)   Where a local authority provide accommodation for a child whom they are looking after and who is disabled, they shall, so far as is reasonably practicable, secure that the accommodation is not unsuitable to his particular needs.

(9)   Part II of Schedule 2 shall have effect for the purposes of making further provision as to children looked after by local authorities and in particular as to the regulations that may be made under subsections (2)(*a*) and (*f*) and (5).

---

NOTES

Sub-s (2): words in square brackets in para (e) inserted by the Courts and Legal Services Act 1990, s   116, Sch 16, para 12.

Sub-s (5A): inserted by the Courts and Legal Services Act 1990, s 116, Sch 16, para 12.

---

*Advice and assistance for certain children*

## 24   Advice and assistance for certain children

(1)   Where a child is being looked after by a local authority, it shall be the duty of the authority to advise, assist and befriend him with a view to promoting his welfare when he ceases to be looked after by them.

(2)   In this Part "a person qualifying for advice and assistance" means a person within the area of the authority who is under twenty-one and who was, at any time after reaching the age of sixteen but while still a child—

(a)   looked after by a local authority;

(b)   accommodated by or on behalf of a voluntary organisation;

(c)   accommodated in a registered children's home;

(d)   accommodated—

(i)   by any [Health Authority, Special Health Authority] or local education authority; or

(ii)   in any residential care home, nursing home or mental nursing home [or in any accommodation provided by a National Health Service trust],

for a consecutive period of at least three months; or

(e)   privately fostered,

but who is no longer so looked after, accommodated or fostered.

(3)   Subsection (2)(d) applies even if the period of three months mentioned there began before the child reached the age of sixteen.

(4)   Where—

(a)   a local authority know that there is within their area a person qualifying for advice and assistance;

(b)   the conditions in subsection (5) are satisfied; and

(c)   that person has asked them for help of a kind which they can give under this section,

they shall (if he was being looked after by a local authority or was accommodated by or on behalf of a voluntary organisation) and may (in any other case) advise and befriend him.

(5)    The conditions are that—

(a)    it appears to the authority that the person concerned is in need of advice and being befriended;

(b)    where that person was not being looked after by the authority, they are satisfied that the person by whom he was being looked after does not have the necessary facilities for advising or befriending him.

(6)    Where as a result of this section a local authority are under a duty, or are empowered, to advise and befriend a person, they may also give him assistance.

(7)    Assistance given under subsections (1) to (6) may be in kind or, in exceptional circumstances, in cash.

(8)    A local authority may give assistance to any person who qualifies for advice and assistance by virtue of subsection (2)(a) by—

(a)    contributing to expenses incurred by him in living near the place where he is, or will be—

(i)   employed or seeking employment; or

(ii)  receiving education or training; or

(b)    making a grant to enable him to meet expenses connected with his education or training.

(9)    Where a local authority are assisting the person under subsection (8) by making a contribution or grant with respect to a course of education or training, they may—

(a)    continue to do so even though he reaches the age of twenty-one before completing the course; and

(b)    disregard any interruption in his attendance on the course if he resumes it as soon as is reasonably practicable.

(10)  Subsections (7) to (9) of section 17 shall apply in relation to assistance given under this section (otherwise than under subsection (8)) as they apply in relation to assistance given under that section.

(11)  Where it appears to a local authority that a person whom they have been advising and befriending under this section, as a person qualifying for advice and assistance, proposes to live, or is living, in the area of another local authority, they shall inform that other local authority.

(12)  Where a child who is accommodated—

(a)    by a voluntary organisation or in a registered children's home;

(b)    by any [Health Authority, Special Health Authority] or local education authority; or

(c)    in any residential care home, nursing home or mental nursing home [or any accommodation provided by a National Health Service trust],

ceases to be so accommodated, after reaching the age of sixteen, the organisation, authority or (as the case may be) person carrying on the home shall inform the local authority within whose area the child proposes to live.

(13)  Subsection (12) only applies, by virtue of paragraph (b) or (c), if the accommodation has been provided for a consecutive period of at least three months.

[(14) Every local authority shall establish a procedure for considering any representations (including any complaint) made to them by a person qualifying for advice and assistance about the discharge of their functions under this Part in relation to him.

(15) In carrying out any consideration of representations under subsection (14), a local authority shall comply with any regulations made by the Secretary of State for the purposes of this subsection.]

NOTES

Sub-ss (2), (12): words in first pairs of square brackets substituted by the Health Authorities Act 1995, s 2(1), Sch 1, para 118(4); words in second pairs of square brackets inserted by the National Health Service and Community Care Act 1990, s 66(1), Sch 9, para 36(2).

Sub-ss (14), (15): added by the Courts and Legal Services Act 1990, s 116, Sch 16, para 13.

*Secure accommodation*

## 25 Use of accommodation for restricting liberty

(1) Subject to the following provisions of this section, a child who is being looked after by a local authority may not bÂ placed, and, if placed, may not be kept, in accommodation provided for the purpose of restricting liberty ("secure accommodation") unless it appears—

    (a) that—

        (i) he has a history of absconding and is likely to abscond from any other description of accommodation; and

        (ii) if he absconds, he is likely to suffer significant harm; or

    (b) that if he is kept in any other description of accommodation he is likely to injure himself or other persons.

(2) The Secretary of State may by regulations—

    (a) specify a maximum period—

        (i) beyond which a child may not be kept in secure accommodation without the authority of the court; and

        (ii) for which the court may authorise a child to be kept in secure accommodation;

    (b) empower the court from time to time to authorise a child to be kept in secure accommodation for such further period as the regulations may specify; and

    (c) provide that applications to the court under this section shall be made only by local authorities.

(3) It shall be the duty of a court hearing an application under this section to determine whether any relevant criteria for keeping a child in secure accommodation are satisfied in his case.

(4) If a court determines that any such criteria are satisfied, it shall make an order authorising the child to be kept in secure accommodation and specifying the maximum period for which he may be so kept.

(5) On any adjournment of the hearing of an application under this section, a court may make an interim order permitting the child to be kept during the period of the adjournment in secure accommodation.

(6) No court shall exercise the powers conferred by this section in respect of a child who is not legally represented in that court unless, having been informed of his right to apply for legal aid and having had the opportunity to do so, he refused or failed to apply.

(7) The Secretary of State may by regulations provide that—

    (a) this section shall or shall not apply to any description of children specified in the regulations;

(b) this section shall have effect in relation to children of a description specified in the regulations subject to such modifications as may be so specified;

(c) such other provisions as may be so specified shall have effect for the purpose of determining whether a child of a description specified in the regulations may be placed or kept in secure accommodation.

(8) The giving of an authorisation under this section shall not prejudice any power of any court in England and Wales or Scotland to give directions relating to the child to whom the authorisation relates.

(9) This section is subject to section 20(8).

*Supplemental*

## 26 Review of cases and inquiries into representations

(1) The Secretary of State may make regulations requiring the case of each child who is being looked after by a local authority to be reviewed in accordance with the provisions of the regulations.

(2) The regulations may, in particular, make provision—

(a) as to the manner in which each case is to be reviewed;

(b) as to the considerations to which the local authority are to have regard in reviewing each case;

(c) as to the time when each case is first to be reviewed and the frequency of subsequent reviews;

(d) requiring the authority, before conducting any review, to seek the views of—

(i) the child;

(ii) his parents;

(iii) any person who is not a parent of his but who has parental responsibility for him; and

(iv) any other person whose views the authority consider to be relevant,

including, in particular, the views of those persons in relation to any particular matter which is to be considered in the course of the review;

(e) requiring the authority to consider, in the case of a child who is in their care, whether an application should be made to discharge the care order;

(f) requiring the authority to consider, in the case of a child in accommodation provided by the authority, whether the accommodation accords with the requirements of this Part;

(g) requiring the authority to inform the child, so far as is reasonably practicable, of any steps he may take under this Act;

(h) requiring the authority to make arrangements, including arrangements with such other bodies providing services as it considers appropriate, to implement any decision which they propose to make in the course, or as a result, of the review;

(i) requiring the authority to notify details of the result of the review and of any decision taken by them in consequence of the review to—

(i) the child;

(ii) his parents;

(iii) any person who is not a parent of his but who has parental responsibility for him; and

(iv) any other person whom they consider ought to be notified;

(j) requiring the authority to monitor the arrangements which they have made with a view to ensuring that they comply with the regulations.

(3)   Every local authority shall establish a procedure for considering any representations (including any complaint) made to them by—

(a)   any child who is being looked after by them or who is not being looked after by them but is in need;

(b)   a parent of his;

(c)   any person who is not a parent of his but who has parental responsibility for him;

(d)   any local authority foster parent;

(e)   such other person as the authority consider has a sufficient interest in the child's welfare to warrant his representations being considered by them,

about the discharge by the authority of any of their functions under this Part in relation to the child.

(4)   The procedure shall ensure that at least one person who is not a member or officer of the authority takes part in—

(a)   the consideration; and

(b)   any discussions which are held by the authority about the action (if any) to be taken in relation to the child in the light of the consideration.

(5)   In carrying out any consideration of representations under this section a local authority shall comply with any regulations made by the Secretary of State for the purpose of regulating the procedure to be followed.

(6)   The Secretary of State may make regulations requiring local authorities to monitor the arrangements that they have made with a view to ensuring that they comply with any regulations made for the purposes of subsection (5).

(7)   Where any representation has been considered under the procedure established by a local authority under this section, the authority shall—

(a)   have due regard to the findings of those considering the representation; and

(b)   take such steps as are reasonably practicable to notify (in writing)—

(i)   the person making the representation;

(ii)   the child (if the authority consider that he has sufficient understanding); and

(iii)   such other persons (if any) as appear to the authority to be likely to be affected,

of the authority's decision in the matter and their reasons for taking that decision and of any action which they have taken, or propose to take.

(8)   Every local authority shall give such publicity to their procedure for considering representations under this section as they consider appropriate.

## 27   Co-operation between authorities

(1)   Where it appears to a local authority that any authority . . . mentioned in subsection (3) could, by taking any specified action, help in the exercise of any of their functions under this Part, they may request the help of that other authority . . ., specifying the action in question.

(2)   An authority whose help is so requested shall comply with the request if it is compatible with their own statutory or other duties and obligations and does not unduly prejudice the discharge of any of their functions.

(3)   The [authorities] are—

    (a)   any local authority;

    (b)   any local education authority;

    (c)   any local housing authority;

    (d)   any [Health Authority, Special Health Authority] [or National Health Service trust]; and

    (e)   any person authorised by the Secretary of State for the purposes of this section.

(4)   . . .

---

**NOTES**

Sub-s (1): words omitted repealed by the Courts and Legal Services Act 1990, ss 116, 125(7), Sch 16, para 14, Sch 20.

Sub-s (3): word in first pair of square brackets substituted, and words in third pair of square brackets inserted, by the Courts and Legal Services Act 1990, s 116, Sch 16, para 14; words in second pair of square brackets substituted by the Health Authorities Act 1995, s 2(1), Sch 1, para 118(5).

Sub-s (4): repealed by the Education Act 1993, s 307(1), (3), Sch 19, para 147, Sch 21, Pt II.

---

# PART IV
# CARE AND SUPERVISION

*General*

### 31   Care and supervision orders

(1)   On the application of any local authority or authorised person, the court may make an order—

    (a)   placing the child with respect to whom the application is made in the care of a designated local authority; or

    (b)   putting him under the supervision of a designated local authority or of a probation officer.

(2)   A court may only make a care order or supervision order if it is satisfied—

    (a)   that the child concerned is suffering, or is likely to suffer, significant harm; and

    (b)   that the harm, or likelihood of harm, is attributable to—

        (i)   the care given to the child, or likely to be given to him if the order were not made, not being what it would be reasonable to expect a parent to give to him; or

        (ii)   the child's being beyond parental control.

(3)   No care order or supervision order may be made with respect to a child who has reached the age of seventeen (or sixteen, in the case of a child who is married).

(4)   An application under this section may be made on its own or in any other family proceedings.

(5)   The court may—

    (a)   on an application for a care order, make a supervision order;

    (b)   on an application for a supervision order, make a care order.

(6)   Where an authorised person proposes to make an application under this section he shall—

    (a)   if it is reasonably practicable to do so; and

    (b)   before making the application,

consult the local authority appearing to him to be the authority in whose area the child concerned is ordinarily resident.

(7) An application made by an authorised person shall not be entertained by the court if, at the time when it is made, the child concerned is—
  (a) the subject of an earlier application for a care order, or supervision order, which has not been disposed of; or
  (b) subject to—
      (i) a care order or supervision order;
      (ii) an order under section 7(7)(b) of the Children and Young Persons Act 1969; or
      (iii) a supervision requirement within the meaning of [Part II of the Children (Scotland) Act 1995].

(8) The local authority designated in a care order must be—
  (a) the authority within whose area the child is ordinarily resident; or
  (b) where the child does not reside in the area of a local authority, the authority within whose area any circumstances arose in consequence of which the order is being made.

(9) In this section—
  "authorised person" means—
      (a) the National Society for the Prevention of Cruelty to Children and any of its officers; and
      (b) any person authorised by order of the Secretary of State to bring proceedings under this section and any officer of a body which is so authorised;
  "harm" means ill-treatment or the impairment of health or development;
  "development" means physical, intellectual, emotional, social or behavioural development;
  "health" means physical or mental health; and
  "ill-treatment" includes sexual abuse and forms of ill-treatment which are not physical.

(10) Where the question of whether harm suffered by a child is significant turns on the child's health or development, his health or development shall be compared with that which could reasonably be expected of a similar child.

(11) In this Act—
  "a care order" means (subject to section 105(1)) an order under subsection (1)(a) and (except where express provision to the contrary is made) includes an interim care order made under section 38; and
  "a supervision order" means an order under subsection (1)(b) and (except where express provision to the contrary is made) includes an interim supervision order made under section 38.

---

NOTES
  Sub-s (7): words in square brackets in para (b) substituted by the Children (Scotland) Act 1995, s 105(4), Sch 4, para 48(1), (2).

---

## 32 Period within which application for order under this Part must be disposed of

(1) A court hearing an application for an order under this Part shall (in the light of any rules made by virtue of subsection (2))—
  (a) draw up a timetable with a view to disposing of the application without delay; and

    (b)  give such directions as it considers appropriate for the purpose of ensuring, so far as is reasonably practicable, that that timetable is adhered to.

(2)    Rules of court may—

    (a)  specify periods within which specified steps must be taken in relation to such proceedings; and

    (b)  make other provisions with respect to such proceedings for the purpose of ensuring, so far as is reasonably practicable, that they are disposed of without delay.

*Care orders*

### 33   Effect of care order

(1)    Where a care order is made with respect to a child it shall be the duty of the local authority designated by the order to receive the child into their care and to keep him in their care while the order remains in force.

(2)    Where—

    (a)  a care order has been made with respect to a child on the application of an authorised person; but

    (b)  the local authority designated by the order was not informed that that person proposed to make the application,

the child may be kept in the care of that person until received into the care of the authority.

(3)    While a care order is in force with respect to a child, the local authority designated by the order shall—

    (a)  have parental responsibility for the child; and

    (b)  have the power (subject to the following provisions of this section) to determine the extent to which a parent or guardian of the child may meet his parental responsibility for him.

(4)    The authority may not exercise the power in subsection (3)(b) unless they are satisfied that it is necessary to do so in order to safeguard or promote the child's welfare.

(5)    Nothing in subsection (3)(b) shall prevent a parent or guardian of the child who has care of him from doing what is reasonable in all the circumstances of the case for the purpose of safeguarding or promoting his welfare.

(6)    While a care order is in force with respect to a child, the local authority designated by the order shall not—

    (a)  cause the child to be brought up in any religious persuasion other than that in which he would have been brought up if the order had not been made; or

    (b)  have the right—

      (i)  to consent or refuse to consent to the making of an application with respect to the child under section 18 of the Adoption Act 1976;

      (ii)  to agree or refuse to agree to the making of an adoption order, or an order under section 55 of the Act of 1976, with respect to the child; or

      (iii)  to appoint a guardian for the child.

(7)    While a care order is in force with respect to a child, no person may—

    (a)  cause the child to be known by a new surname; or

    (b)  remove him from the United Kingdom,

without either the written consent of every person who has parental responsibility for the child or the leave of the court.

(8)    Subsection (7)(b) does not—
    (a)  prevent the removal of such a child, for a period of less than one month, by the authority in whose care he is; or
    (b)  apply to arrangements for such a child to live outside England and Wales (which are governed by paragraph 19 of Schedule 2).

(9)    The power in subsection (3)(b) is subject (in addition to being subject to the provisions of this section) to any right, duty, power, responsibility or authority which a parent or guardian of the child has in relation to the child and his property by virtue of any other enactment.

## 34    Parental contact etc with children in care

(1)    Where a child is in the care of a local authority, the authority shall (subject to the provisions of this section) allow the child reasonable contact with—
    (a)  his parents;
    (b)  any guardian of his;
    (c)  where there was a residence order in force with respect to the child immediately before the care order was made, the person in whose favour the order was made; and
    (d)  where, immediately before the care order was made a person had care of the child by virtue of an order made in the exercise of the High Court's inherent jurisdiction with respect to children, that person.

(2)    On an application made by the authority or the child, the court may make such order as it considers appropriate with respect to the contact which is to be allowed between the child and any named person.

(3)    On an application made by—
    (a)  any person mentioned in paragraphs (a) to (d) of subsection (1); or
    (b)  any person who has obtained the leave of the court to make the application,

the court may make such order as it considers appropriate with respect to the contact which is to be allowed between the child and that person.

(4)    On an application made by the authority or the child, the court may make an order authorising the authority to refuse to allow contact between the child and any person who is mentioned in paragraphs (a) to (d) of subsection (1) and named in the order.

(5)    When making a care order with respect to a child, or in any family proceedings in connection with a child who is in the care of a local authority, the court may make an order under this section, even though no application for such an order has been made with respect to the child, if it considers that the order should be made.

(6)    An authority may refuse to allow the contact that would otherwise be required by virtue of subsection (1) or an order under this section if—
    (a)  they are satisfied that it is necessary to do so in order to safeguard or promote the child's welfare; and
    (b)  the refusal—
        (i)  is decided upon as a matter of urgency; and
        (ii)  does not last for more than seven days.

(7)    An order under this section may impose such conditions as the court considers appropriate.

(8)    The Secretary of State may by regulations make provision as to—
    (a)   the steps to be taken by a local authority who have exercised their powers under subsection (6);
    (b)   the circumstances in which, and conditions subject to which, the terms of any order under this section may be departed from by agreement between the local authority and the person in relation to whom the order is made;
    (c)   notification by a local authority of any variation or suspension of arrangements made (otherwise than under an order under this section) with a view to affording any person contact with a child to whom this section applies.

(9)    The court may vary or discharge any order made under this section on the application of the authority, the child concerned or the person named in the order.

(10)  An order under this section may be made either at the same time as the care order itself or later.

(11)  Before making a care order with respect to any child the court shall—
    (a)   consider the arrangements which the authority have made, or propose to make, for affording any person contact with a child to whom this section applies; and
    (b)   invite the parties to the proceedings to comment on those arrangements.

*Supervision orders*

## 35   Supervision orders

(1)    While a supervision order is in force it shall be the duty of the supervisor—
    (a)   to advise, assist and befriend the supervised child;
    (b)   to take such steps as are reasonably necessary to give effect to the order; and
    (c)   where—
        (i)   the order is not wholly complied with; or
        (ii)  the supervisor considers that the order may no longer be necessary,
        to consider whether or not to apply to the court for its variation or discharge.

(2)    Parts I and II of Schedule 3 make further provision with respect to supervision orders.

## 36   Education supervision orders

(1)    On the application of any local education authority, the court may make an order putting the child with respect to whom the application is made under the supervision of a designated local education authority.

(2)    In this Act "an education supervision order" means an order under subsection   (1).

(3)    A court may only make an education supervision order if it is satisfied that the child concerned is of compulsory school age and is not being properly educated.

(4)    For the purposes of this section, a child is being properly educated only if he is receiving efficient full-time education suitable to his age, ability and aptitude and any special educational needs he may have.

(5)   Where a child is—
  (a)   the subject of a school attendance order which is in force under [section 437 of the Education Act 1996] and which has not been complied with; or
  (b)   a registered pupil at a school which he is not attending regularly within the meaning of [section 444] of that Act,

then, unless it is proved that he is being properly educated, it shall be assumed that he is not.

(6)   An education supervision order may not be made with respect to a child who is in the care of a local authority.

(7)   The local education authority designated in an education supervision order must be—
  (a)   the authority within whose area the child concerned is living or will live; or
  (b)   where—
    (i)   the child is a registered pupil at a school; and
    (ii)   the authority mentioned in paragraph (a) and the authority within whose area the school is situated agree,

the latter authority.

(8)   Where a local education authority propose to make an application for an education supervision order they shall, before making the application, consult the . . . appropriate local authority.

(9)   The appropriate local authority is—
  (a)   in the case of a child who is being provided with accommodation by, or on behalf of, a local authority, that authority; and
  (b)   in any other case, the local authority within whose area the child concerned lives, or will live.

(10)   Part III of Schedule 3 makes further provision with respect to education supervision orders.

---

NOTES

  Sub-s (5): words in square brackets in paras (a), (b) substituted by the Education Act 1996, s 582(1), Sch 37, para 85.
  Sub-s (8): words omitted repealed by the Education Act 1993, s 307(1), (3), Sch 19, para 149, Sch 21, Pt II.

---

*Powers of court*

## 37   Powers of court in certain family proceedings

(1)   Where, in any family proceedings in which a question arises with respect to the welfare of any child, it appears to the court that it may be appropriate for a care or supervision order to be made with respect to him, the court may direct the appropriate authority to undertake an investigation of the child's circumstances.

(2)   Where the court gives a direction under this section the local authority concerned shall, when undertaking the investigation, consider whether they should—
  (a)   apply for a care order or for a supervision order with respect to the child;
  (b)   provide services or assistance for the child or his family; or
  (c)   take any other action with respect to the child.

(3)   Where a local authority undertake an investigation under this section, and decide not to apply for a care order or supervision order with respect to the child concerned, they shall inform the court of—

(a)   their reasons for so deciding;

(b)   any service or assistance which they have provided, or intend to provide, for the child and his family; and

(c)   any other action which they have taken, or propose to take, with respect to the child.

(4)   The information shall be given to the court before the end of the period of eight weeks beginning with the date of the direction, unless the court otherwise directs.

(5)   The local authority named in a direction under subsection (1) must be—

(a)   the authority in whose area the child is ordinarily resident; or

(b)   where the child [is not ordinarily resident] in the area of a local authority, the authority within whose area any circumstances arose in consequence of which the direction is being given.

(6)   If, on the conclusion of any investigation or review under this section, the authority decide not to apply for a care order or supervision order with respect to the child—

(a)   they shall consider whether it would be appropriate to review the case at a later date; and

(b)   if they decide that it would be, they shall determine the date on which that review is to begin.

NOTES

Sub-s (5): words in square brackets in para (b) substituted by the Courts and Legal Services Act 1990, s 116, Sch 16, para 16.

## 38   Interim orders

(1)   Where—

(a)   in any proceedings on an application for a care order or supervision order, the proceedings are adjourned; or

(b)   the court gives a direction under section 37(1),

the court may make an interim care order or an interim supervision order with respect to the child concerned.

(2)   A court shall not make an interim care order or interim supervision order under this section unless it is satisfied that there are reasonable grounds for believing that the circumstances with respect to the child are as mentioned in section 31(2).

(3)   Where, in any proceedings on an application for a care order or supervision order, a court makes a residence order with respect to the child concerned, it shall also make an interim supervision order with respect to him unless satisfied that his welfare will be satisfactorily safeguarded without an interim order being made.

(4)   An interim order made under or by virtue of this section shall have effect for such period as may be specified in the order, but shall in any event cease to have effect on whichever of the following events first occurs—

(a)   the expiry of the period of eight weeks beginning with the date on which the order is made;

(b)   if the order is the second or subsequent such order made with respect to the same child in the same proceedings, the expiry of the relevant period;

   (c)  in a case which falls within subsection (1)(a), the disposal of the application;

   (d)  in a case which falls within subsection (1)(b), the disposal of an application for a care order or supervision order made by the authority with respect to the child;

   (e)  in a case which falls within subsection (1)(b) and in which—

      (i)  the court has given a direction under section 37(4), but

     (ii)  no application for a care order or supervision order has been made with respect to the child,

the expiry of the period fixed by that direction.

(5)    In subsection (4)(b) "the relevant period" means—

   (a)  the period of four weeks beginning with the date on which the order in question is made; or

   (b)  the period of eight weeks beginning with the date on which the first order was made if that period ends later than the period mentioned in paragraph (a).

(6)    Where the court makes an interim care order, or interim supervision order, it may give such directions (if any) as it considers appropriate with regard to the medical or psychiatric examination or other assessment of the child; but if the child is of sufficient understanding to make an informed decision he may refuse to submit to the examination or other assessment.

(7)    A direction under subsection (6) may be to the effect that there is to be—

   (a)  no such examination or assessment; or

   (b)  no such examination or assessment unless the court directs otherwise.

(8)    A direction under subsection (6) may be—

   (a)  given when the interim order is made or at any time while it is in force; and

   (b)  varied at any time on the application of any person falling within any class of person prescribed by rules of court for the purposes of this subsection.

(9)    Paragraphs 4 and 5 of Schedule 3 shall not apply in relation to an interim supervision order.

(10)  Where a court makes an order under or by virtue of this section it shall, in determining the period for which the order is to be in force, consider whether any party who was, or might have been, opposed to the making of the order was in a position to argue his case against the order in full.

## [38A   Power to include exclusion requirement in interim care order

(1)    Where—

   (a)  on being satisfied that there are reasonable grounds for believing that the circumstances with respect to a child are as mentioned in section 31(2)(a) and (b)(i), the court makes an interim care order with respect to a child, and

   (b)  the conditions mentioned in subsection (2) are satisfied,

the court may include an exclusion requirement in the interim care order.

(2)    The conditions are—

   (a)  that there is reasonable cause to believe that, if a person ("the relevant person") is excluded from a dwelling-house in which the child lives, the child will cease to suffer, or cease to be likely to suffer, significant harm, and

(b) that another person living in the dwelling-house (whether a parent of the child or some other person)—

    (i) is able and willing to give to the child the care which it would be reasonable to expect a parent to give him, and

    (ii) consents to the inclusion of the exclusion requirement.

(3) For the purposes of this section an exclusion requirement is any one or more of the following—

(a) a provision requiring the relevant person to leave a dwelling-house in which he is living with the child,

(b) a provision prohibiting the relevant person from entering a dwelling-house in which the child lives, and

(c) a provision excluding the relevant person from a defined area in which a dwelling-house in which the child lives is situated.

(4) The court may provide that the exclusion requirement is to have effect for a shorter period than the other provisions of the interim care order.

(5) Where the court makes an interim care order containing an exclusion requirement, the court may attach a power of arrest to the exclusion requirement.

(6) Where the court attaches a power of arrest to an exclusion requirement of an interim care order, it may provide that the power of arrest is to have effect for a shorter period than the exclusion requirement.

(7) Any period specified for the purposes of subsection (4) or (6) may be extended by the court (on one or more occasions) on an application to vary or discharge the interim care order.

(8) Where a power of arrest is attached to an exclusion requirement of an interim care order by virtue of subsection (5), a constable may arrest without warrant any person whom he has reasonable cause to believe to be in breach of the requirement.

(9) Sections 47(7), (11) and (12) and 48 of, and Schedule 5 to, the Family Law Act 1996 shall have effect in relation to a person arrested under subsection (8) of this section as they have effect in relation to a person arrested under section 47(6) of that Act.

(10) If, while an interim care order containing an exclusion requirement is in force, the local authority have removed the child from the dwelling-house from which the relevant person is excluded to other accommodation for a continuous period of more than 24 hours, the interim care order shall cease to have effect in so far as it imposes the exclusion requirement.]

NOTES

Commencement: to be appointed.

Inserted, together with s 38B, by the Family Law Act 1996, s 52, Sch 6, para 1, as from a day to be appointed.

## [38B   Undertakings relating to interim care orders

(1) In any case where the court has power to include an exclusion requirement in an interim care order, the court may accept an undertaking from the relevant person.

(2) No power of arrest may be attached to any undertaking given under subsection (1).

(3) An undertaking given to a court under subsection (1)—

    (a) shall be enforceable as if it were an order of the court, and

    (b) shall cease to have effect if, while it is in force, the local authority have removed the child from the dwelling house from which the relevant person is excluded to other accommodation for a continuous period of more than 24 hours.

(4) This section has effect without prejudice to the powers of the High Court and county court apart from this section.

(5) In this section "exclusion requirement" and "relevant person" have the same meaning as in section 38A.]

---

NOTES

    Commencement: to be appointed.

    Inserted as noted to s 38A.

---

## 39 Discharge and variation etc of care orders and supervision orders

(1) A care order may be discharged by the court on the application of—

    (a) any person who has parental responsibility for the child;

    (b) the child himself; or

    (c) the local authority designated by the order.

(2) A supervision order may be varied or discharged by the court on the application of—

    (a) any person who has parental responsibility for the child;

    (b) the child himself; or

    (c) the supervisor.

(3) On the application of a person who is not entitled to apply for the order to be discharged, but who is a person with whom the child is living, a supervision order may be varied by the court in so far as it imposes a requirement which affects that person.

[(3A) On the application of a person who is not entitled to apply for the order to be discharged, but who is a person to whom an exclusion requirement contained in the order applies, an interim care order may be varied or discharged by the court in so far as it imposes the exclusion requirement.

(3B) Where a power of arrest has been attached to an exclusion requirement of an interim care order, the court may, on the application of any person entitled to apply for the discharge of the order so far as it imposes the exclusion requirement, vary or discharge the order in so far as it confers a power of arrest (whether or not any application has been made to vary or discharge any other provision of the order).]

(4) Where a care order is in force with respect to a child the court may, on the application of any person entitled to apply for the order to be discharged, substitute a supervision order for the care order.

(5) When a court is considering whether to substitute one order for another under subsection (4) any provision of this Act which would otherwise require section 31(2) to be satisfied at the time when the proposed order is substituted or made shall be disregarded.

NOTES

Commencement: 14 October 1991 (sub-ss (1)–(3), (4), (5)); to be appointed (remainder).

Sub-ss (3A), (3B): inserted by the Family Law Act 1996, s 52, Sch 6, para 2, as from a day to be appointed.

## 40   Orders pending appeals in cases about care or supervision orders

(1)   Where—

(a)   a court dismisses an application for a care order; and

(b)   at the time when the court dismisses the application, the child concerned is the subject of an interim care order,

the court may make a care order with respect to the child to have effect subject to such directions (if any) as the court may see fit to include in the order.

(2)   Where—

(a)   a court dismisses an application for a care order, or an application for a supervision order; and

(b)   at the time when the court dismisses the application, the child concerned is the subject of an interim supervision order,

the court may make a supervision order with respect to the child to have effect subject to such directions (if any) as the court may see fit to include in the order.

(3)   Where a court grants an application to discharge a care order or supervision order, it may order that—

(a)   its decision is not to have effect; or

(b)   the care order, or supervision order, is to continue to have effect but subject to such directions as the court sees fit to include in the order.

(4)   An order made under this section shall only have effect for such period, not exceeding the appeal period, as may be specified in the order.

(5)   Where—

(a)   an appeal is made against any decision of a court under this section; or

(b)   any application is made to the appellate court in connection with a proposed appeal against that decision.

the appellate court may extend the period for which the order in question is to have effect, but not so as to extend it beyond the end of the appeal period.

(6)   In this section "the appeal period" means—

(a)   where an appeal is made against the decision in question, the period between the making of that decision and the determination of the appeal; and

(b)   otherwise, the period during which an appeal may be made against the decision.

*Guardians ad litem*

## 41   Representation of child and of his interests in certain proceedings

(1)   For the purpose of any specified proceedings, the court shall appoint a guardian ad litem for the child concerned unless satisfied that it is not necessary to do so in order to safeguard his interests.

(2)   The guardian ad litem shall—

(a)   be appointed in accordance with the rules of court; and

(b)   be under a duty to safeguard the interests of the child in the manner prescribed by such rules.

(3)   Where—
   (a)   the child concerned is not represented by a solicitor; and
   (b)   any of the conditions mentioned in subsection (4) is satisfied,

the court may appoint a solicitor to represent him.

(4)   The conditions are that—
   (a)   no guardian ad litem has been appointed for the child;
   (b)   the child has sufficient understanding to instruct a solicitor and wishes to do so;
   (c)   it appears to the court that it would be in the child's best interests for him to be represented by a solicitor.

(5)   Any solicitor appointed under or by virtue of this section shall be appointed, and shall represent the child, in accordance with rules of court.

(6)   In this section "specified proceedings" means any proceedings—
   (a)   on an application for a care order or supervision order;
   (b)   in which the court has given a direction under section 37(1) and has made, or is considering whether to make, an interim care order;
   (c)   on an application for the discharge of a care order or the variation or discharge of a supervision order;
   (d)   on an application under section 39(4);
   (e)   in which the court is considering whether to make a residence order with respect to a child who is the subject of a care order;
   (f)   with respect to contact between a child who is the subject of a care order and any other person;
   (g)   under Part V;
   (h)   on an appeal against—
      (i)   the making of, or refusal to make, a care order, supervision order or any order under section 34;
      (ii)   the making of, or refusal to make, a residence order with respect to a child who is the subject of a care order; or
      (iii)   the variation or discharge, or refusal of an application to vary or discharge, an order of a kind mentioned in sub-paragraph (i) or (ii);
      (iv)   the refusal of an application under section 39(4); or
      (v)   the making of, or refusal to make, an order under Part V; or
   (i)   which are specified for the time being, for the purposes of this section, by rules of court.

(7)   The Secretary of State may by regulations provide for the establishment of panels of persons from whom guardians ad litem appointed under this section must be selected.

(8)   Subsection (7) shall not be taken to prejudice the power of the Lord Chancellor to confer or impose duties on the Official Solicitor under section 90(3) of the Supreme Court Act 1981.

(9)   The regulations may, in particular, make provision—
   (a)   as to the constitution, administration and procedures of panels;
   (b)   requiring two or more specified local authorities to make arrangements for the joint management of a panel;
   (c)   for the defrayment by local authorities of expenses incurred by members of panels;
   (d)   for the payment by local authorities of fees and allowances for members of panels;

(e)   as to the qualifications for membership of a panel;

(f)   as to the training to be given to members of panels;

(g)   as to the co-operation required of specified local authorities in the provision of panels in specified areas; and

(h)   for monitoring the work of guardians ad litem.

(10) Rules of court may make provision as to—

(a)   the assistance which any guardian ad litem may be required by the court to give to it;

(b)   the consideration to be given by any guardian ad litem, where an order of a specified kind has been made in the proceedings in question, as to whether to apply for the variation or discharge of the order;

(c)   the participation of guardians ad litem in reviews, of a kind specified in the rules, which are conducted by the court.

(11) Regardless of any enactment or rule of law which would otherwise prevent it from doing so, the court may take account of—

(a)   any statement contained in a report made by a guardian ad litem who is appointed under this section for the purpose of the proceedings in question; and

(b)   any evidence given in respect of the matters referred to in the report,

in so far as the statement or evidence is, in the opinion of the court, relevant to the question which the court is considering.

[(12) The Secretary of State may, with the consent of the Treasury, make such grants with respect to expenditure of any local authority—

(a)   in connection with the establishment and administration of guardian ad litem panels in accordance with this section;

(b)   in paying expenses, fees, allowances and in the provision of training for members of such panels,

as he considers appropriate.]

---

NOTES

Sub-s (12): added by the Courts and Legal Services Act 1990, s 116, Sch 16, para 17.

---

## 42   Right of guardian ad litem to have access to local authority records

(1)   Where a person has been appointed as a guardian ad litem under this Act he shall have the right at all reasonable times to examine and take copies of—

(a)   any records of, or held by, a local authority [or an authorised person] which were compiled in connection with the making, or proposed making, by any person of any application under this Act with respect to the child concerned;. . .

(b)   any. . .records of, or held by, a local authority which were compiled in connection with any functions which stand referred to their social services committee under the Local Authority Social Services Act 1970, so far as those records relate to that child [; or

(c)   any records of, or held by, an authorised person which were compiled in connection with the activities of that person, so far as those records relate to that child].

(2)   Where a guardian ad litem takes a copy of any record which he is entitled to examine under this section, that copy or any part of it shall be admissible as evidence of any matter referred to in any—

(a)  report which he makes to the court in the proceedings in question; or

(b)  evidence which he gives in those proceedings.

(3)  Subsection (2) has effect regardless of any enactment or rule of law which would otherwise prevent the record in question being admissible in evidence.

[(4)  In this section "authorised person" has the same meaning as in section 31.]

NOTES

Sub-s (1): words omitted repealed, and words in square brackets inserted, by the Courts and Legal Services Act 1990, ss 116, 125(7), Sch 16, para 18, Sch 20.

Sub-s (4): added by the Courts and Legal Services Act 1990, s 116, Sch 16, para 18.

# PART V
# PROTECTION OF CHILDREN

## 43  Child assessment orders

(1)  On the application of a local authority or authorised person for an order to be made under this section with respect to a child, the court may make the order if, but only if, it is satisfied that—

(a)  the applicant has reasonable cause to suspect that the child is suffering, or is likely to suffer, significant harm;

(b)  an assessment of the state of the child's health or development, or of the way in which he has been treated, is required to enable the applicant to determine whether or not the child is suffering, or is likely to suffer, significant harm; and

(c)  it is unlikely that such an assessment will be made, or be satisfactory, in the absence of an order under this section.

(2)  In this Act "a child assessment order" means an order under this section.

(3)  A court may treat an application under this section as an application for an emergency protection order.

(4)  No court shall make a child assessment order if it is satisfied—

(a)  that there are grounds for making an emergency protection order with respect to the child; and

(b)  that it ought to make such an order rather than a child assessment order.

(5)  A child assessment order shall—

(a)  specify the date by which the assessment is to begin; and

(b)  have effect for such period, not exceeding 7 days beginning with that date, as may be specified in the order.

(6)  Where a child assessment order is in force with respect to a child it shall be the duty of any person who is in a position to produce the child—

(a)  to produce him to such person as may be named in the order; and

(b)  to comply with such directions relating to the assessment of the child as the court thinks fit to specify in the order.

(7)  A child assessment order authorises any person carrying out the assessment, or any part of the assessment, to do so in accordance with the terms of the order.

(8)  Regardless of subsection (7), if the child is of sufficient understanding to make an informed decision he may refuse to submit to a medical or psychiatric examination or other assessment.

(9)  The child may only be kept away from home—
 (a) in accordance with directions specified in the order;
 (b) if it is necessary for the purposes of the assessment; and
 (c) for such period or periods as may be specified in the order.

(10)  Where the child is to be kept away from home, the order shall contain such directions as the court thinks fit with regard to the contact that he must be allowed to have with other persons while away from home.

(11)  Any person making an application for a child assessment order shall take such steps as are reasonably practicable to ensure that notice of the application is given to—
 (a) the child's parents;
 (b) any person who is not a parent of his but who has parental responsibility for him;
 (c) any other person caring for the child;
 (d) any person in whose favour a contact order is in force with respect to the child;
 (e) any person who is allowed to have contact with the child by virtue of an order under section 34; and
 (f) the child,

before the hearing of the application.

(12)  Rules of court may make provision as to the circumstances in which—
 (a) any of the persons mentioned in subsection (11); or
 (b) such other person as may be specified in the rules,

may apply to the court for a child assessment order to be varied or discharged.

(13)  In this section "authorised person" means a person who is an authorised person for the purposes of section 31.

## 44  Orders for emergency protection of children

(1)  Where any person ("the applicant") applies to the court for an order to be made under this section with respect to a child, the court may make the order if, but only if, it is satisfied that—
 (a) there is reasonable cause to believe that the child is likely to suffer significant harm if—
  (i) he is not removed to accommodation provided by or on behalf of the applicant; or
  (ii) he does not remain in the place in which he is then being accommodated;
 (b) in the case of an application made by a local authority—
  (i) enquiries are being made with respect to the child under section 47(1)(b); and
  (ii) those enquiries are being frustrated by access to the child being unreasonably refused to a person authorised to seek access and that the applicant has reasonable cause to believe that access to the child is required as a matter of urgency; or
 (c) in the case of an application made by an authorised person—
  (i) the applicant has reasonable cause to suspect that a child is suffering, or is likely to suffer, significant harm;
  (ii) the applicant is making enquiries with respect to the child's welfare; and

(iii) those enquiries are being frustrated by access to the child being unreasonably refused to a person authorised to seek access and the applicant has reasonable cause to believe that access to the child is required as a matter of urgency.

(2) In this section—

    (a) "authorised person" means a person who is an authorised person for the purposes of section 31; and

    (b) "a person authorised to seek access" means—

        (i) in the case of an application by a local authority, an officer of the local authority or a person authorised by the authority to act on their behalf in connection with the enquiries; or

        (ii) in the case of an application by an authorised person, that person.

(3) Any person—

    (a) seeking access to a child in connection with enquiries of a kind mentioned in subsection (1); and

    (b) purporting to be a person authorised to do so,

shall, on being asked to do so, produce some duly authenticated document as evidence that he is such a person.

(4) While an order under this section ("an emergency protection order") is in force it—

    (a) operates as a direction to any person who is in a position to do so to comply with any request to produce the child to the applicant;

    (b) authorises—

        (i) the removal of the child at any time to accommodation provided by or on behalf of the applicant and his being kept there; or

        (ii) the prevention of the child's removal from any hospital, or other place, in which he was being accommodated immediately before the making of the order; and

    (c) gives the applicant parental responsibility for the child.

(5) Where an emergency protection order is in force with respect to a child, the applicant—

    (a) shall only exercise the power given by virtue of subsection (4)(b) in order to safeguard the welfare of the child;

    (b) shall take, and shall only take, such action in meeting his parental responsibility for the child as is reasonably required to safeguard or promote the welfare of the child (having regard in particular to the duration of the order); and

    (c) shall comply with the requirements of any regulations made by the Secretary of State for the purposes of this subsection.

(6) Where the court makes an emergency protection order, it may give such directions (if any) as it considers appropriate with respect to—

    (a) the contact which is, or is not, to be allowed between the child and any named person;

    (b) the medical or psychiatric examination or other assessment of the child.

(7) Where any direction is given under subsection (6)(b), the child may, if he is of sufficient understanding to make an informed decision, refuse to submit to the examination or other assessment.

(8) A direction under subsection (6)(a) may impose conditions and one under subsection (6)(b) may be to the effect that there is to be—

> (a) no such examination or assessment; or
>
> (b) no such examination or assessment unless the court directs otherwise.

(9) A direction under subsection (6) may be—

> (a) given when the emergency protection order is made or at any time while it is in force; and
>
> (b) varied at any time on the application of any person falling within any class of person prescribed by rules of court for the purposes of this subsection.

(10) Where an emergency protection order is in force with respect to a child and—

> (a) the applicant has exercised the power given by subsection (4)(b)(i) but it appears to him that it is safe for the child to be returned; or
>
> (b) the applicant has exercised the power given by subsection (4)(b)(ii) but it appears to him that it is safe for the child to be allowed to be removed from the place in question,

he shall return the child or (as the case may be) allow him to be removed.

(11) Where he is required by subsection (10) to return the child the applicant shall—

> (a) return him to the care of the person from whose care he was removed; or
>
> (b) if that is not reasonably practicable, return him to the care of—
>
> > (i) a parent of his;
> >
> > (ii) any person who is not a parent of his but who has parental responsibility for him; or
> >
> > (iii) such other person as the applicant (with the agreement of the court) considers appropriate.

(12) Where the applicant has been required by subsection (10) to return the child, or to allow him to be removed, he may again exercise his powers with respect to the child (at any time while the emergency protection order remains in force) if it appears to him that a change in the circumstances of the case makes it necessary for him to do so.

(13) Where an emergency protection order has been made with respect to a child, the applicant shall, subject to any direction given under subsection (6), allow the child reasonable contact with—

> (a) his parents;
>
> (b) any person who is not a parent of his but who has parental responsibility for him;
>
> (c) any person with whom he was living immediately before the making of the order;
>
> (d) any person in whose favour a contact order is in force with respect to him;
>
> (e) any person who is allowed to have contact with the child by virtue of an order under section 34; and
>
> (f) any person acting on behalf of any of those persons.

(14) Wherever it is reasonably practicable to do so, an emergency protection order shall name the child; and where it does not name him it shall describe him as clearly as possible.

(15) A person shall be guilty of an offence if he intentionally obstructs any person exercising the power under subsection (4)(b) to remove, or prevent the removal of, a child.

(16) A person guilty of an offence under subsection (15) shall be liable on summary conviction to a fine not exceeding level 3 on the standard scale.

**[44A Power to include exclusion requirement in emergency protection order**

(1)  Where—

    (a)  on being satisfied as mentioned in section 44(1)(a), (b) emergency or (c), the court makes an emergency protection order with respect to a child, and

    (b)  the conditions mentioned in subsection (2) are satisfied,

the court may include an exclusion requirement in the emergency protection order.

(2)  The conditions are—

    (a)  that there is reasonable cause to believe that, if a person ("the relevant person") is excluded from a dwelling-house in which the child lives, then—

        (i)  in the case of an order made on the ground mentioned in section 44(1)(a), the child will not be likely to suffer significant harm, even though the child is not removed as mentioned in section 44(1)(a)(i) or does not remain as mentioned in section 44(1)(a)(ii), or

        (ii)  in the case of an order made on the ground mentioned in paragraph (b) or (c) of section 44(1), the enquiries referred to in that paragraph will cease to be frustrated, and

    (b)  that another person living in the dwelling-house (whether a parent of the child or some other person)—

        (i)  is able and willing to give to the child the care which it would be reasonable to expect a parent to give him, and

        (ii)  consents to the inclusion of the exclusion requirement.

(3)  For the purposes of this section an exclusion requirement is any one or more of the following—

    (a)  a provision requiring the relevant person to leave a dwelling-house in which he is living with the child,

    (b)  a provision prohibiting the relevant person from entering a dwelling-house in which the child lives, and

    (c)  a provision excluding the relevant person from a defined area in which a dwelling-house in which the child lives is situated.

(4)  The court may provide that the exclusion requirement is to have effect for a shorter period than the other provisions of the order.

(5)  Where the court makes an emergency protection order containing an exclusion requirement, the court may attach a power of arrest to the exclusion requirement.

(6)  Where the court attaches a power of arrest to an exclusion requirement of an emergency protection order, it may provide that the power of arrest is to have effect for a shorter period than the exclusion requirement.

(7)  Any period specified for the purposes of subsection (4) or (6) may be extended by the court (on one or more occasions) on an application to vary or discharge the emergency protection order.

(8)  Where a power of arrest is attached to an exclusion requirement of an emergency protection order by virtue of subsection (5), a constable may arrest without warrant any person whom he has reasonable cause to believe to be in breach of the requirement.

(9)  Sections 47(7), (11) and (12) and 48 of, and Schedule 5 to, the Family Law Act 1996 shall have effect in relation to a person arrested under subsection (8) of this section as they have effect in relation to a person arrested under section 47(6) of that Act.

(10) If, while an emergency protection order containing an exclusion requirement is in force, the applicant has removed the child from the dwelling-house from which the relevant person is excluded to other accommodation for a continuous period of more than 24 hours, the order shall cease to have effect in so far as it imposes the exclusion requirement.]

NOTES

Commencement: to be appointed.

Inserted, together with s 44B, by the Family Law Act 1996, s 52, Sch 6, para 3, as from a day to be appointed.

## [44B    Undertakings relating to emergency protection orders

(1)    In any case where the court has power to include an exclusion requirement in an emergency protection order, the court may accept an undertaking from the relevant person.

(2)    No power of arrest may be attached to any undertaking given under subsection    (1).

(3)    An undertaking given to a court under subsection (1)—
    (a)    shall be enforceable as if it were an order of the court, and
    (b)    shall cease to have effect if, while it is in force, the applicant has removed the child from the dwelling-house from which the relevant person is excluded to other accommodation for a continuous period of more than 24 hours.

(4)    This section has effect without prejudice to the powers of the High Court and county court apart from this section.

(5)    In this section "exclusion requirement" and "relevant person" have the same meaning as in section 44A.]

NOTES

Commencement: to be appointed.

Inserted as noted to s 44A.

## 45    Duration of emergency protection orders and other supplemental provisions

(1)    An emergency protection order shall have effect for such period, not exceeding eight days, as may be specified in the order.

(2)    Where—
    (a)    the court making an emergency protection order would, but for this subsection, specify a period of eight days as the period for which the order is to have effect; but
    (b)    the last of those eight days is a public holiday (that is to say, Christmas Day, Good Friday, a bank holiday or a Sunday),

the court may specify a period which ends at noon on the first later day which is not such a holiday.

(3)    Where an emergency protection order is made on an application under section    46(7), the period of eight days mentioned in subsection (1) shall begin with the first day on which the child was taken into police protection under section 46.

(4)   Any person who—
   (a)  has parental responsibility for a child as the result of an emergency protection order; and
   (b)  is entitled to apply for a care order with respect to the child,

may apply to the court for the period during which the emergency protection order is to have effect to be extended.

(5)   On an application under subsection (4) the court may extend the period during which the order is to have effect by such period, not exceeding seven days, as it thinks fit, but may do so only if it has reasonable cause to believe that the child concerned is likely to suffer significant harm if the order is not extended.

(6)   An emergency protection order may only be extended once.

(7)   Regardless of any enactment or rule of law which would otherwise prevent it from doing so, a court hearing an application for, or with respect to, an emergency protection order may take account of—
   (a)  any statement contained in any report made to the court in the course of, or in connection with, the hearing; or
   (b)  any evidence given during the hearing,

which is, in the opinion of the court, relevant to the application.

(8)   Any of the following may apply to the court for an emergency protection order to be discharged—
   (a)  the child;
   (b)  a parent of his;
   (c)  any person who is not a parent of his but who has parental responsibility for him; or
   (d)  any person with whom he was living immediately before the making of the order.

[(8A) On the application of a person who is not entitled to apply for the order to be discharged, but who is a person to whom an exclusion requirement contained in the order applies, an emergency protection order may be varied or discharged by the court in so far as it imposes the exclusion requirement.

(8B) Where a power of arrest has been attached to an exclusion requirement of an emergency protection order, the court may, on the application of any person entitled to apply for the discharge of the order so far as it imposes the exclusion requirement, vary or discharge the order in so far as it confers a power of arrest (whether or not any application has been made to vary or discharge any other provision of the order).]

(9)   No application for the discharge of an emergency protection order shall be heard by the court before the expiry of the period of 72 hours beginning with the making of the order.

[(10) No appeal may be made against—
   (a)  the making of, or refusal to make, an emergency protection order;
   (b)  the extension of, or refusal to extend, the period during which such an order is to have effect;
   (c)  the discharge of, or refusal to discharge, such an order; or
   (d)  the giving of, or refusal to give, any direction in connection with such an order.]

(11)  Subsection (8) does not apply—
  (a)  where the person who would otherwise be entitled to apply for the emergency protection order to be discharged—
    (i)  was given notice (in accordance with rules of court) of the hearing at which the order was made; and
    (ii)  was present at that hearing; or
  (b)  to any emergency protection order the effective period of which has been extended under subsection (5).

(12)  A court making an emergency protection order may direct that the applicant may in exercising any powers which he has by virtue of the order, be accompanied by a registered medical practitioner, registered nurse or registered health visitor, if he so chooses.

NOTES
  Commencement: 14 October 1991 (sub-ss (1)–(8), (9)–(12)); to be appointed (remainder).
  Sub-ss (8A), (8B): inserted by the Family Law Act 1996, s 52, Sch 6, para 4, as from a day to be appointed.
  Sub-s (10): substituted by the Courts and Legal Services Act 1990, s 116, Sch 16, para 19.

## 46  Removal and accommodation of children by police in cases of emergency

(1)  Where a constable has reasonable cause to believe that a child would otherwise be likely to suffer significant harm, he may—
  (a)  remove the child to suitable accommodation and keep him there; or
  (b)  take such steps as are reasonable to ensure that the child's removal from any hospital, or other place, in which he is then being accommodated is prevented.

(2)  For the purposes of this Act, a child with respect to whom a constable has exercised his powers under this section is referred to as having been taken into police protection.

(3)  As soon as is reasonably practicable after taking a child into police protection, the constable concerned shall—
  (a)  inform the local authority within whose area the child was found of the steps that have been, and are proposed to be, taken with respect to the child under this section and the reasons for taking them;
  (b)  give details to the authority within whose area the child is ordinarily resident ("the appropriate authority") of the place at which the child is being accommodated;
  (c)  inform the child (if he appears capable of understanding)—
    (i)  of the steps that have been taken with respect to him under this section and of the reasons for taking them; and
    (ii)  of the further steps that may be taken with respect to him under this section;
  (d)  take such steps as are reasonably practicable to discover the wishes and feelings of the child;
  (e)  secure that the case is inquired into by an officer designated for the purposes of this section by the chief officer of the police area concerned; and
  (f)  where the child was taken into police protection by being removed to accommodation which is not provided—

(i) by or on behalf of a local authority; or

(ii) as a refuge, in compliance with the requirements of section 51,

secure that he is moved to accommodation which is so provided.

(4)　As soon as is reasonably practicable after taking a child into police protection, the constable concerned shall take such steps as are reasonably practicable to inform—

    (a) the child's parents;

    (b) every person who is not a parent of his but who has parental responsibility for him; and

    (c) any other person with whom the child was living immediately before being taken into police protection,

of the steps that he has taken under this section with respect to the child, the reasons for taking them and the further steps that may be taken with respect to him under this section.

(5)　On completing any inquiry under subsection (3)(e), the officer conducting it shall release the child from police protection unless he considers that there is still reasonable cause for believing that the child would be likely to suffer significant harm if released.

(6)　No child may be kept in police protection for more than 72 hours.

(7)　While a child is being kept in police protection, the designated officer may apply on behalf of the appropriate authority for an emergency protection order to be made under section 44 with respect to the child.

(8)　An application may be made under subsection (7) whether or not the authority know of it or agree to its being made.

(9)　While a child is being kept in police protection—

    (a) neither the constable concerned nor the designated officer shall have parental responsibility for him; but

    (b) the designated officer shall do what is reasonable in all the circumstances of the case for the purpose of safeguarding or promoting the child's welfare (having regard in particular to the length of the period during which the child will be so protected).

(10)　Where a child has been taken into police protection, the designated officer shall allow—

    (a) the child's parents;

    (b) any person who is not a parent of the child but who has parental responsibility for him;

    (c) any person with whom the child was living immediately before he was taken into police protection;

    (d) any person in whose favour a contact order is in force with respect to the child;

    (e) any person who is allowed to have contact with the child by virtue of an order under section 34; and

    (f) any person acting on behalf of any of those persons,

to have such contact (if any) with the child as, in the opinion of the designated officer, is both reasonable and in the child's best interests.

(11)　Where a child who has been taken into police protection is in accommodation provided by, or on behalf of, the appropriate authority, subsection (10) shall have effect as if it referred to the authority rather than to the designated officer.

### 47 Local authority's duty to investigate

(1)  Where a local authority—
  (a)  are informed that a child who lives, or is found, in their area—
    (i)  is the subject of an emergency protection order; or
    (ii)  is in police protection; or
  (b)  have reasonable cause to suspect that a child who lives, or is found, in their area is suffering, or is likely to suffer, significant harm,

the authority shall make, or cause to be made, such enquiries as they consider necessary to enable them to decide whether they should take any action to safeguard or promote the child's welfare.

(2)  Where a local authority have obtained an emergency protection order with respect to a child, they shall make, or cause to be made, such enquiries as they consider necessary to enable them to decide what action they should take to safeguard or promote the child's welfare.

(3)  The enquiries shall, in particular, be directed towards establishing—
  (a)  whether the authority should make any application to the court, or exercise any of their other powers under this Act, with respect to the child;
  (b)  whether, in the case of a child—
    (i)  with respect to whom an emergency protection order has been made; and
    (ii)  who is not in accommodation provided by or on behalf of the authority,
    it would be in the child's best interests (while an emergency protection order remains in force) for him to be in such accommodation; and
  (c)  whether, in the case of a child who has been taken into police protection, it would be in the child's best interests for the authority to ask for an application to be made under section 46(7).

(4)  Where enquiries are being made under subsection (1) with respect to a child, the local authority concerned shall (with a view to enabling them to determine what action, if any, to take with respect to him) take such steps as are reasonably practicable—
  (a)  to obtain access to him; or
  (b)  to ensure that access to him is obtained, on their behalf, by a person authorised by them for the purpose,

unless they are satisfied that they already have sufficient information with respect to him.

(5)  Where, as a result of any such enquiries, it appears to the authority that there are matters connected with the child's education which should be investigated, they shall consult the relevant local education authority.

(6)  Where, in the course of enquiries made under this section—
  (a)  any officer of the local authority concerned; or
  (b)  any person authorised by the authority to act on their behalf in connection with those enquiries—
    (i)  is refused access to the child concerned; or
    (ii)  is denied information as to his whereabouts,

the authority shall apply for an emergency protection order, a child assessment order, a care order or a supervision order with respect to the child unless they are satisfied that his welfare can be satisfactorily safeguarded without their doing so.

(7)  If, on the conclusion of any enquiries or review made under this section, the authority decide not to apply for an emergency protection order, a child assessment order, a care order or a supervision order they shall—

(a)  consider whether it would be appropriate to review the case at a later date; and

(b)  if they decide that it would be, determine the date on which that review is to begin.

(8)  Where, as a result of complying with this section, a local authority conclude that they should take action to safeguard or promote the child's welfare they shall take that action (so far as it is both within their power and reasonably practicable for them to do so).

(9)  Where a local authority are conducting enquiries under this section, it shall be the duty of any person mentioned in subsection (11) to assist them with those enquiries (in particular by providing relevant information and advice) if called upon by the authority to do so.

(10)  Subsection (9) does not oblige any person to assist a local authority where doing so would be unreasonable in all the circumstances of the case.

(11)  The persons are—

(a)  any local authority;

(b)  any local education authority;

(c)  any local housing authority;

(d)  any [Health Authority, Special Health Authority] [or National Health Service Trust]; and

(e)  any person authorised by the Secretary of State for the purposes of this section.

(12)  Where a local authority are making enquiries under this section with respect to a child who appears to them to be ordinarily resident within the area of another authority, they shall consult that other authority, who may undertake the necessary enquiries in their place.

---

NOTES

Sub-s (11): words in first pair of square brackets in para (d) substituted by the Health Authorities Act 1995, s 2(1), Sch 1, para 118(7), words in second pair of square brackets inserted by the Courts and Legal Services Act 1990, s 116, Sch 16, para 20.

---

## 48  Powers to assist in discovery of children who may be in need of emergency protection

(1)  Where it appears to a court making an emergency protection order that adequate information as to the child's whereabouts—

(a)  is not available to the applicant for the order; but

(b)  is available to another person,

it may include in the order a provision requiring that other person to disclose, if asked to do so by the applicant, any information that he may have as to the child's whereabouts.

(2)  No person shall be excused from complying with such a requirement on the ground that complying might incriminate him or his spouse of an offence; but a statement or admission made in complying shall not be admissible in evidence against either of them in proceedings for any offence other than perjury.

(3)    An emergency protection order may authorise the applicant to enter premises specified by the order and search for the child with respect to whom the order is made.

(4)    Where the court is satisfied that there is reasonable cause to believe that there may be another child on those premises with respect to whom an emergency protection order ought to be made, it may make an order authorising the applicant to search for that other child on those premises.

(5)    Where—
    (a)    an order has been made under subsection (4);
    (b)    the child concerned has been found on the premises; and
    (c)    the applicant is satisfied that the grounds for making an emergency protection order exist with respect to him,

the order shall have effect as if it were an emergency protection order.

(6)    Where an order has been made under subsection (4), the applicant shall notify the court of its effect.

(7)    A person shall be guilty of an offence if he intentionally obstructs any person exercising the power of entry and search under subsection (3) or (4).

(8)    A person guilty of an offence under subsection (7) shall be liable on summary conviction to a fine not exceeding level 3 on the standard scale.

(9)    Where, on an application made by any person for a warrant under this section, it appears to the court—
    (a)    that a person attempting to exercise powers under an emergency protection order has been prevented from doing so by being refused entry to the premises concerned or access to the child concerned; or
    (b)    that any such person is likely to be so prevented from exercising any such powers,

it may issue a warrant authorising any constable to assist the person mentioned in paragraph (a) or (b) in the exercise of those powers, using reasonable force if necessary.

(10)    Every warrant issued under this section shall be addressed to, and executed by, a constable who shall be accompanied by the person applying for the warrant if—
    (a)    that person so desires; and
    (b)    the court by whom the warrant is issued does not direct otherwise.

(11)    A court granting an application for a warrant under this section may direct that the constable concerned may, in executing the warrant, be accompanied by a registered medical practitioner, registered nurse or registered health visitor if he so chooses.

(12)    An application for a warrant under this section shall be made in the manner and form prescribed by rules of court.

(13)    Wherever it is reasonably practicable to do so, an order under subsection (4), an application for a warrant under this section and any such warrant shall name the child; and where it does not name him it shall describe him as clearly as possible.

## 49    Abduction of children in care etc

(1)    A person shall be guilty of an offence if, knowingly and without lawful authority or reasonable excuse, he—

(a) takes a child to whom this section applies away from the responsible person;

(b) keeps such a child away from the responsible person; or

(c) induces, assists or incites such a child to run away or stay away from the responsible person.

(2) This section applies in relation to a child who is—

(a) in care;

(b) the subject of an emergency protection order; or

(c) in police protection,

and in this section "the responsible person" means any person who for the time being has care of him by virtue of the care order, the emergency protection order, or section 46, as the case may be.

(3) A person guilty of an offence under this section shall be liable on summary conviction to imprisonment for a term not exceeding six months, or to a fine not exceeding level 5 on the standard scale, or to both.

## 50 Recovery of abducted children etc

(1) Where it appears to the court that there is reason to believe that a child to whom this section applies—

(a) has been unlawfully taken away or is being unlawfully kept away from the responsible person;

(b) has run away or is staying away from the responsible person; or

(c) is missing,

the court may make an order under this section ("a recovery order").

(2) This section applies to the same children to whom section 49 applies and in this section "the responsible person" has the same meaning as in section 49.

(3) A recovery order—

(a) operates as a direction to any person who is in a position to do so to produce the child on request to any authorised person;

(b) authorises the removal of the child by any authorised person;

(c) requires any person who has information as to the child's whereabouts to disclose that information, if asked to do so, to a constable or an officer of the court;

(d) authorises a constable to enter any premises specified in the order and search for the child, using reasonable force if necessary.

(4) The court may make a recovery order only on the application of—

(a) any person who has parental responsibility for the child by virtue of a care order or emergency protection order; or

(b) where the child is in police protection, the designated officer.

(5) A recovery order shall name the child and—

(a) any person who has parental responsibility for the child by virtue of a care order or emergency protection order; or

(b) where the child is in police protection, the designated officer.

(6) Premises may only be specified under subsection (3)(d) if it appears to the court that there are reasonable grounds for believing the child to be on them.

(7)　In this section—

"an authorised person" means—

    (a)　any person specified by the court;

    (b)　any constable;

    (c)　any person who is authorised—

        (i)　after the recovery order is made; and

        (ii)　by a person who has parental responsibility for the child by virtue of a care order or an emergency protection order,

to exercise any power under a recovery order; and

"the designated officer" means the officer designated for the purposes of section 46.

(8)　Where a person is authorised as mentioned in subsection (7)(c)—

    (a)　the authorisation shall identify the recovery order; and

    (b)　any person claiming to be so authorised shall, if asked to do so, produce some duly authenticated document showing that he is so authorised.

(9)　A person shall be guilty of an offence if he intentionally obstructs an authorised person exercising the power under subsection (3)(b) to remove a child.

(10)　A person guilty of an offence under this section shall be liable on summary conviction to a fine not exceeding level 3 on the standard scale.

(11)　No person shall be excused from complying with any request made under subsection (3)(c) on the ground that complying with it might incriminate him or his spouse of an offence; but a statement or admission made in complying shall not be admissible in evidence against either of them in proceedings for an offence other than perjury.

(12)　Where a child is made the subject of a recovery order whilst being looked after by a local authority, any reasonable expenses incurred by an authorised person in giving effect to the order shall be recoverable from the authority.

(13)　A recovery order shall have effect in Scotland as if it had been made by the Court of Session and as if that court had had jurisdiction to make it.

(14)　In this section "the court", in relation to Northern Ireland, means a magistrates' court within the meaning of the Magistrates' Courts (Northern Ireland) Order 1981.

## 51　Refuges for children at risk

(1)　Where it is proposed to use a voluntary home or registered children's home to provide a refuge for children who appear to be at risk of harm, the Secretary of State may issue a certificate under this section with respect to that home.

(2)　Where a local authority or voluntary organisation arrange for a foster parent to provide such a refuge, the Secretary of State may issue a certificate under this section with respect to that foster parent.

(3)　In subsection (2) "foster parent" means a person who is, or who from time to time is, a local authority foster parent or a foster parent with whom children are placed by a voluntary organisation.

(4)　The Secretary of State may by regulations—

    (a)　make provision as to the manner in which certificates may be issued;

    (b)　impose requirements which must be complied with while any certificate is in force; and

    (c)　provide for the withdrawal of certificates in prescribed circumstances.

(5)   Where a certificate is in force with respect to a home, none of the provisions mentioned in subsection (7) shall apply in relation to any person providing a refuge for any child in that home.

(6)   Where a certificate is in force with respect to a foster parent, none of those provisions shall apply in relation to the provision by him of a refuge for any child in accordance with arrangements made by the local authority or voluntary organisation.

(7)   The provisions are—

    (a)   section 49;

    [(b)   sections 82 (recovery of certain fugitive children) and 83 (harbouring) of the Children (Scotland) Act 1995, so far as they apply in relation to anything done in England and Wales;]

    (c)   section 32(3) of the Children and Young Persons Act 1969 (compelling, persuading, inciting or assisting any person to be absent from detention, etc.), so far as it applies in relation to anything done in England and Wales;

    (d)   section 2 of the Child Abduction Act 1984.

**NOTES**

Sub-s (7): para (b) substituted by the Children (Scotland) Act 1995, s 105(4), Sch 4, para 48(3).

# PART XI
# SECRETARY OF STATE'S SUPERVISORY FUNCTIONS AND RESPONSIBILITIES

## 84   Local authority failure to comply with statutory duty: default power of Secretary of State

(1)   If the Secretary of State is satisfied that any local authority has failed, without reasonable excuse, to comply with any of the duties imposed on them by or under this Act he may make an order declaring that authority to be in default with respect to that duty.

(2)   An order under subsection (1) shall give the Secretary of State's reasons for making it.

(3)   An order under subsection (1) may contain such directions for the purpose of ensuring that the duty is complied with, within such period as may be specified in the order, as appears to the Secretary of State to be necessary.

(4)   Any such direction shall, on the application of the Secretary of State, be enforceable by mandamus.

# PART XII
# MISCELLANEOUS AND GENERAL

*Effect and duration of orders etc*

## 91   Effect and duration of orders etc

(1)   The making of a residence order with respect to a child who is the subject of a care order discharges the care order.

(2)   The making of a care order with respect to a child who is the subject of any section 8 order discharges that order.

(3) The making of a care order with respect to a child who is the subject of a supervision order discharges that other order.

(4) The making of a care order with respect to a child who is a ward of court brings that wardship to an end.

(5) The making of a care order with respect to a child who is the subject of a school attendance order made under [section 437 of the Education Act 1996] discharges the school attendance order.

(6) Where an emergency protection order is made with respect to a child who is in care, the care order shall have effect subject to the emergency protection order.

(7) Any order made under section 4(1) or 5(1) shall continue in force until the child reaches the age of eighteen, unless it is brought to an end earlier.

(8) Any—
    (a) agreement under section 4; or
    (b) appointment under section 5(3) or (4),

shall continue in force until the child reaches the age of eighteen, unless it is brought to an end earlier.

(9) An order under Schedule 1 has effect as specified in that Schedule.

(10) A section 8 order shall, if it would otherwise still be in force, cease to have effect when the child reaches the age of sixteen, unless it is to have effect beyond that age by virtue of section 9(6).

(11) Where a section 8 order has effect with respect to a child who has reached the age of sixteen, it shall, if it would otherwise still be in force, cease to have effect when he reaches the age of eighteen.

(12) Any care order, other than an interim care order, shall continue in force until the child reaches the age of eighteen, unless it is brought to an end earlier.

(13) Any order made under any other provision of this Act in relation to a child shall, if it would otherwise still be in force, cease to have effect when he reaches the age of eighteen.

(14) On disposing of any application for an order under this Act, the court may (whether or not it makes any other order in response to the application) order that no application for an order under this Act of any specified kind may be made with respect to the child concerned by any person named in the order without leave of the court.

(15) Where an application ("the previous application") has been made for—
    (a) the discharge of a care order;
    (b) the discharge of a supervision order;
    (c) the discharge of an education supervision order;
    (d) the substitution of a supervision order for a care order; or
    (e) a child assessment order,

no further application of a kind mentioned in paragraphs (*a*) to (*e*) may be made with respect to the child concerned, without leave of the court, unless the period between the disposal of the previous application and the making of the further application exceeds six months.

(16) Subsection (15) does not apply to applications made in relation to interim orders.

(17)  Where—
- (a)  a person has made an application for an order under section 34;
- (b)  the application has been refused; and
- (c)  a period of less than six months has elapsed since the refusal,

that person may not make a further application for such an order with respect to the same child, unless he has obtained the leave of the court.

NOTES

Sub-s (5): words in square brackets substituted by the Education Act 1996, s 582(1), Sch 37, Pt I, para 90.

*Jurisdiction and procedure etc*

## 96  Evidence given by, or with respect to, children

(1)  Subsection (2) applies where a child who is called as a witness in any civil proceedings does not, in the opinion of the court, understand the nature of an oath.

(2)  The child's evidence may be heard by the court if, in its opinion—
- (a)  he understands that it is his duty to speak the truth; and
- (b)  he has sufficient understanding to justify his evidence being heard.

(3)  The Lord Chancellor may by order make provision for the admissibility of evidence which would otherwise be inadmissible under any rule of law relating to hearsay.

(4)  An order under subsection (3) may only be made with respect to—
- (a)  civil proceedings in general or such civil proceedings, or class of civil proceedings, as may be prescribed; and
- (b)  evidence in connection with the upbringing, maintenance or welfare of a child.

(5)  An order under subsection (3)—
- (a)  may, in particular, provide for the admissibility of statements which are made orally or in a prescribed form or which are recorded by any prescribed method of recording;
- (b)  may make different provision for different purposes and in relation to different descriptions of court; and
- (c)  may make such amendments and repeals in any enactment relating to evidence (other than in this Act) as the Lord Chancellor considers necessary or expedient in consequence of the provision made by the order.

(6)  Subsection (5)(b) is without prejudice to section 104(4).

(7)  In this section—
["civil proceedings" means civil proceedings, before any tribunal, in relation to which the strict rules of evidence apply, whether as a matter of law or by agreement of the parties, and references to "the court" shall be construed accordingly;]
"prescribed" means prescribed by an order under subsection (3).

NOTES

Sub-s (7): definition "civil proceedings" substituted by the Civil Evidence Act 1995, s 15(1), Sch 1, para 16.

## 98   Self-incrimination

(1)   In any proceedings in which a court is hearing an application for an order under Part IV or V, no person shall be excused from—

    (a)   giving evidence on any matter; or

    (b)   answering any question put to him in the course of his giving evidence,

on the ground that doing so might incriminate him or his spouse of an offence.

(2)   A statement or admission made in such proceedings shall not be admissible in evidence against the person making it or his spouse in proceedings for an offence other than perjury.

## 99   Legal aid

(1)–(4). . .

(5)   The Lord Chancellor may by order make such further amendments in the Legal Aid Act 1988 as he considers necessary or expedient in consequence of any provision made by or under this Act.

NOTES

Sub-ss (1)–(4): outside the scope of this work.

## 100   Restrictions on use of wardship jurisdiction

(1)   . . .

(2)   No court shall exercise the High Court's inherent jurisdiction with respect to children—

    (a)   so as to require a child to be placed in the care, or put under the supervision, of a local authority;

    (b)   so as to require a child to be accommodated by or on behalf of a local authority;

    (c)   so as to make a child who is the subject of a care order a ward of court; or

    (d)   for the purpose of conferring on any local authority power to determine any question which has arisen, or which may arise, in connection with any aspect of parental responsibility for a child.

(3)   No application for any exercise of the court's inherent jurisdiction with respect to children may be made by a local authority unless the authority have obtained the leave of the court.

(4)   The court may only grant leave if it is satisfied that—

    (a)   the result which the authority wish to achieve could not be achieved through the making of any order of a kind to which subsection (5) applies; and

    (b)   there is reasonable cause to believe that if the court's inherent jurisdiction is not exercised with respect to the child he is likely to suffer significant harm.

(5)   This subsection applies to any order—

    (a)   made otherwise than in the exercise of the court's inherent jurisdiction; and

    (b)   which the local authority is entitled to apply for (assuming, in the case of any application which may only be made with leave, that leave is granted).

NOTES

Sub-s (1): outside the scope of this work.

*General*

## 105   Interpretation

(1)   In this Act—

"adoption agency" means a body which may be referred to as an adoption agency by virtue of section 1 of the Adoption Act 1976;

. . .

"care order" has the meaning given by section 31(11) and also includes any order which by or under any enactment has the effect of, or is deemed to be, a care order for the purposes of this Act; and any reference to a child who is in the care of an authority is a reference to a child who is in their care by virtue of a care order;

"child" means, subject to paragraph 16 of Schedule 1, a person under the age of eighteen;

"child assessment order" has the meaning given by section 43(2);

"child minder" has the meaning given by section 71;

"child of the family", in relation to the parties to a marriage, means—

(a)   a child of both of those parties;

(b)   any other child, not being a child who is placed with those parties as foster parents by a local authority or voluntary organisation, who has been treated by both of those parties as a child of their family;

"children's home" has the same meaning as in section 63;

"community home" has the meaning given by section 53;

"contact order" has the meaning given by section 8(1);

"day care" has the same meaning as in section 18;

"disabled", in relation to a child, has the same meaning as in section 17(11);

. . . . .

"domestic premises" has the meaning given by section 71(12);

. . . . .

"education supervision order" has the meaning given in section 36;

"emergency protection order" means an order under section 44;

"family assistance order" has the meaning given in section 16(2);

"family proceedings" has the meaning given by section 8(3);

. . . . .

"guardian of a child" means a guardian (other than a guardian of the estate of a child) appointed in accordance with the provisions of section 5;

"harm" has the same meaning as in section 31(9) and the question of whether harm is significant shall be determined in accordance with section 31(10);

. . . . .

"local authority" means, in relation to England . . ., the council of a county, a metropolitan district, a London Borough or the Common Council of the City of London[, in relation to Wales, the council of a county or a county borough] and, in relation to Scotland, a local authority within the meaning of section 1(2) of the Social Work (Scotland) Act 1968;

. . . . .

"parental responsibility" has the meaning given in section 3;

"parental responsibility agreement" has the meaning given in section 4(1);

. . . . .

(2)   References in this Act to a child whose father and mother were, or (as the case may be) were not, married to each other at the time of his birth must be read with section 1 of the Family Law Reform Act 1987 (which extends the meaning of such references).

(3)　References in this Act to—

    (a)　a person with whom a child lives, or is to live, as the result of a residence order; or

    (b)　a person in whose favour a residence order is in force,

shall be construed as references to the person named in the order as the person with whom the child is to live.

(4)　. . .

(5)　References in this Act to accommodation provided by or on behalf of a local authority are references to accommodation so provided in the exercise of functions which stand referred to the social services committee of that or any other local authority under the Local Authority Social Services Act 1970.

(6)　In determining the "ordinary residence" of a child for any purpose of this Act, there shall be disregarded any period in which he lives in any place—

    (a)　which is a school or other institution;

    (b)　in accordance with the requirements of a supervision order under this Act or an order under section 7(7)(b) of the Children and Young Persons Act 1969; or

    (c)　while he is being provided with accommodation by or on behalf of a local authority.

(7)–(10). . .

**NOTES**

Sub-s (1): second definition omitted repealed, and other definitions omitted outside the scope of this work; in definition "local authority" words omitted repealed, and words in square brackets inserted, by the Local Government (Wales) Act 1994, ss 22(4), 66(8), Sch 10, para 13, Sch 18.

Sub-ss (7)–(10): outside the scope of this work.

## 108　Short title, commencement, extent etc

(1)　This Act may be cited as the Children Act 1989.

(2)–(12). . .

**NOTES**

Sub-ss (2)–(12): outside the scope of this work.

# NATIONAL HEALTH SERVICE AND COMMUNITY CARE ACT 1990

## (C 19)

*An Act to make further provision about health authorities and other bodies constituted in accordance with the National Health Service Act 1977; to provide for the establishment of National Health Service trusts; to make further provision about the financing of the practices of medical practitioners; to amend Part VII of the Local Government (Scotland) Act 1973 and Part III of the Local Government Finance Act 1982; to amend the National Health Service Act 1977 and the National Health Service (Scotland) Act 1978; to amend Part VIII of the Mental Health (Scotland) Act 1984; to make further provision concerning the provision of accommodation and other welfare services by local authorities and the powers of the Secretary of State as respects the social services functions of such authorities; to make provision for and in connection with the establishment of a Clinical Standards Advisory Group; to repeal the Health Services Act 1976; and for connected purposes*

[29 June 1990]

## PART III
## COMMUNITY CARE

## ENGLAND AND WALES

*General provisions concerning community care services*

### 46  Local authority plans for community care services

(1)  Each local authority—
  (a)  shall, within such period after the day appointed for the coming into force of this section as the Secretary of State may direct, prepare and publish a plan for the provision of community care services in their area;
  (b)  shall keep the plan prepared by them under paragraph (a) above and any further plans prepared by them under this section under review; and
  (c)  shall, at such intervals as the Secretary of State may direct, prepare and publish modifications to the current plan, or if the case requires, a new plan.

(2)  In carrying out any of their functions under paragraphs (a) to (c) of subsection  (1) above, a local authority shall consult—
  (a)  any [Health Authority the whole or any part of whose area] lies within the area of the local authority;
  (b)  . . .
  (c)  in so far as any proposed plan, review or modifications of a plan may affect or be affected by the provision or availability of housing and the local authority is not itself a local housing authority, within the meaning of the Housing Act 1985, every such local housing authority whose area is within the area of the local authority;
  (d)  such voluntary organisations as appear to the authority to represent the interests of persons who use or are likely to use any community care services within the area of the authority or the interests of private carers who, within that area, provide care to persons for whom, in the exercise of their social services functions, the local authority have a power or a duty to provide a service;
  (e)  such voluntary housing agencies and other bodies as appear to the local authority to provide housing or community care services in their area; and
  (f)  such other persons as the Secretary of State may direct.

(3)  In this section—
  "local authority" means the council of a county, [a county borough,] a metropolitan district or a London borough or the Common Council of the City of London;
  "community care services" means services which a local authority may provide or arrange to be provided under any of the following provisions—
  (a)  Part III of the National Assistance Act 1948;
  (b)  section 45 of the Health Services and Public Health Act 1968;
  (c)  section 21 of and Schedule 8 to the National Health Service Act 1977; and
  (d)  section 117 of the Mental Health Act 1983; and
  "private carer" means a person who is not employed to provide the care in question by any body in the exercise of its functions under any enactment.

NOTES

Sub-s (2): words in square brackets in para (a) substituted, and para (b) repealed, by the Health Authorities Act 1995, ss 2(1), 5(1), Sch 1, Pt II, paras 65, 80, Sch 3.

Sub-s (3): in definition "local authority" words in square brackets inserted by the Local Government (Wales) Act 1994, s 22(4), Sch 10, para 14.

## 47 Assessment of needs for community care services

(1)    Subject to subsections (5) and (6) below, where it appears to a local authority that any person for whom they may provide or arrange for the provision of community care services may be in need of any such services, the authority—

    (a)    shall carry out an assessment of his needs for those services; and

    (b)    having regard to the results of that assessment, shall then decide whether his needs call for the provision by them of any such services.

(2)    If at any time during the assessment of the needs of any person under subsection  (1)(a) above it appears to a local authority that he is a disabled person, the authority—

    (a)    shall proceed to make such a decision as to the services he requires as is mentioned in section 4 of the Disabled Persons (Services, Consultation and Representation) Act 1986 without his requesting them to do so under that section; and

    (b)    shall inform him that they will be doing so and of his rights under that Act.

(3)    If at any time during the assessment of the needs of any person under subsection  (1)(a) above, it appears to a local authority—

    (a)    that there may be a need for the provision to that person by such [Health Authority] as may be determined in accordance with regulations of any services under the National Health Service Act 1977, or

    (b)    that there may be a need for the provision to him of any services which fall within the functions of a local housing authority (within the meaning of the Housing Act 1985) which is not the local authority carrying out the assessment,

the local authority shall notify that [Health Authority] or local housing authority and invite them to assist, to such extent as is reasonable in the circumstances, in the making of the assessment; and, in making their decision as to the provision of the services needed for the person in question, the local authority shall take into account any services which are likely to be made available for him by that [Health Authority] or local housing authority.

(4)    The Secretary of State may give directions as to the manner in which an assessment under this section is to be carried out or the form it is to take but, subject to any such directions and to subsection (7) below, it shall be carried out in such manner and take such form as the local authority consider appropriate.

(5)    Nothing in this section shall prevent a local authority from temporarily providing or arranging for the provision of community care services for any person without carrying out a prior assessment of his needs in accordance with the preceding provisions of this section if, in the opinion of the authority, the condition of that person is such that he requires those services as a matter of urgency.

(6)    If, by virtue of subsection (5) above, community care services have been provided temporarily for any person as a matter of urgency, then, as soon as practicable thereafter, an assessment of his needs shall be made in accordance with the preceding provisions of this section.

(7)    This section is without prejudice to section 3 of the Disabled Persons (Services, Consultation and Representation) Act 1986.

(8)    In this section—

"disabled person" has the same meaning as in that Act; and

"local authority" and "community care services" have the same meanings as in section 46 above.

NOTES

Commencement: 1 April 1993.

Sub-s (3): words in square brackets substituted by the Health Authorities Act 1995, s 2(1), Sch 1, Pt II, paras 65, 81.

## 48    Inspection of premises used for provision of community care services

(1)    Any person authorised by the Secretary of State may at any reasonable time enter and inspect any premises (other than premises in respect of which any person is registered under the Registered Homes Act 1984) in which community care services are or are proposed to be provided by a local authority, whether directly or under arrangements made with another person.

(2)    Any person inspecting any premises under this section may—

(a)    make such examination into the state and management of the premises and the facilities and services provided therein as he thinks fit;

(b)    inspect any records (in whatever form they are held) relating to the premises, or any person for whom community care services have been or are to be provided there; and

(c)    require the owner of, or any person employed in, the premises to furnish him with such information as he may request.

(3)    Any person exercising the power to inspect records conferred by subsection    (2)(b) above—

(a)    shall be entitled at any reasonable time to have access to, and inspect and check the operation of, any computer and any associated apparatus or material which is or has been in use in connection with the records in question; and

(b)    may require—

(i)    the person by whom or on whose behalf the computer is or has been so used; or

(ii)    any person having charge of or otherwise concerned with the operation of the computer, apparatus or material,

to give him such reasonable assistance as he may require.

(4)    Any person inspecting any premises under this section—

(a)    may interview any person residing there in private—

(i)    for the purpose of investigating any complaint as to those premises or the community care services provided there, or

(ii)    if he has reason to believe that the community care services being provided there for that person are not satisfactory; and

(b)    may examine any such person in private.

(5)    No person may—

(a)    exercise the power conferred by subsection (2)(b) above so as to inspect medical records; or

(b)    exercise the power conferred by subsection (4)(b) above,

unless he is a registered medical practitioner and, in the case of the power conferred by subsection (2)(b) above, the records relate to medical treatment given at the premises in question.

(6)　Any person exercising the power of entry under subsection (1) above shall, if so required, produce some duly authenticated document showing his authority to do so.

(7)　Any person who intentionally obstructs another in the exercise of that power shall be guilty of an offence and liable on summary conviction to a fine not exceeding level 3 on the standard scale.

(8)　In this section "local authority" and "community care services" have the same meanings as in section 46 above.

# PART V
# MISCELLANEOUS AND GENERAL

## 67　Short title, commencement and extent

(1)　This Act may be cited as the National Health Service and Community Care Act 1990.

(2)　This Act, other than this section, shall come into force on such day as the Secretary of State may by order made by statutory instrument appoint, and different days may be so appointed for different provisions or for different purposes and for different areas or descriptions of areas.

(3)　An order under subsection (2) above may contain such transitional provisions and savings (whether or not involving the modification of any statutory provision) as appear to the Secretary of State necessary or expedient in connection with the provisions brought into force.

(4)　Part I of this Act, other than section 15(4), does not extend to Scotland; Part II, other than section 34, and Part IV of this Act do not extend to England and Wales; and Part III of this Act, other than subsections (3) and (4) of section 42, subsections (1) and (3) to (6) of section 44 and section 45, does not extend to Scotland.

(5)　This Act, other than sections 59 [, 61 and 62], does not extend to Northern Ireland.

(6)　The Secretary of State may by order made by statutory instrument provide that so much of this Act as extends to England and Wales shall apply to the Isles of Scilly with such modifications, if any, as are specified in the order and, except as provided in pursuance of this subsection, Parts I and III of this Act do not apply to the Isles of Scilly.

---

NOTES

Sub-s (5): words in square brackets substituted by the Health and Personal Social Services (Northern Ireland Consequential Amendments) Order 1991, SI 1991/195, art 7(8).

---

# CHILD SUPPORT ACT 1991

## (C 48)

*An Act to make provision for the assessment, collection and enforcement of periodical maintenance payable by certain parents with respect to children of theirs who are not in their care; for the collection and enforcement of certain other kinds of maintenance; and for connected purposes*

[25 July 1991]

### The basic principles

## 1 The duty to maintain

(1) For the purposes of this Act, each parent of a qualifying child is responsible for maintaining him.

(2) For the purposes of this Act, an absent parent shall be taken to have met his responsibility to maintain any qualifying child of his by making periodical payments of maintenance with respect to the child of such amount, and at such intervals, as may be determined in accordance with the provisions of this Act.

(3) Where a maintenance assessment made under this Act requires the making of periodical payments, it shall be the duty of the absent parent with respect to whom the assessment was made to make those payments.

NOTES

Commencement: 5 April 1993.

## 2 Welfare of children: the general principle

Where, in any case which falls to be dealt with under this Act, the Secretary of State or any child support officer is considering the exercise of any discretionary power conferred by this Act, he shall have regard to the welfare of any child likely to be affected by his decision.

NOTES

Commencement: 5 April 1993.

## 10 Relationship between maintenance assessments and certain court orders and related matters

(1) Where an order of a kind prescribed for the purposes of this subsection is in force with respect to any qualifying child with respect to whom a maintenance assessment is made, the order—

(a) shall, so far as it relates to the making or securing of periodical payments, cease to have effect to such extent as may be determined in accordance with regulations made by the Secretary of State; or

(b) where the regulations so provide, shall, so far as it so relates, have effect subject to such modifications as may be so determined.

(2) Where an agreement of a kind prescribed for the purposes of this subsection is in force with respect to any qualifying child with respect to whom a maintenance assessment is made, the agreement—

(a) shall, so far as it relates to the making or securing of periodical payments, be unenforceable to such extent as may be determined in accordance with regulations made by the Secretary of State; or

(b) where the regulations so provide, shall, so far as it so relates, have effect subject to such modifications as may be so determined.

(3) Any regulations under this section may, in particular, make such provision with respect to—

(a) any case where any person with respect to whom an order or agreement of a kind prescribed for the purposes of subsection (1) or (2) has effect applies to the prescribed court, before the end of the prescribed period, for the order or agreement to be varied in the light of the maintenance assessment and of the provisions of this Act;

(b) the recovery of any arrears under the order or agreement which fell due before the coming into force of the maintenance assessment,

as the Secretary of State considers appropriate and may provide that, in prescribed circumstances, an application to any court which is made with respect to an order of a prescribed kind relating to the making or securing of periodical payments to or for the benefit of a child shall be treated by the court as an application for the order to be revoked.

(4) The Secretary of State may by regulations make provision for—

(a) notification to be given by the child support officer concerned to the prescribed person in any case where that officer considers that the making of a maintenance assessment has affected, or is likely to affect, any order of a kind prescribed for the purposes of this subsection;

(b) notification to be given by the prescribed person to the Secretary of State in any case where a court makes an order which it considers has affected, or is likely to affect, a maintenance assessment.

(5) Rules may be made under section 144 of the Magistrates' Courts Act 1980 (rules of procedure) requiring any person who, in prescribed circumstances, makes an application to a magistrates' court for a maintenance order to furnish the court with a statement in a prescribed form, and signed by a child support officer, as to whether or not, at the time when the statement is made, there is a maintenance assessment in force with respect to that person or the child concerned.

In this subsection—

"maintenance order" means an order of a prescribed kind for the making or securing of periodical payments to or for the benefit of a child; and

"prescribed" means prescribed by the rules.

NOTES
Commencement: 17 June 1992.

*Reviews and appeals*

## 24 Appeal to Child Support Commissioner

(1) Any person who is aggrieved by a decision of a child support appeal tribunal, and any child support officer, may appeal to a Child Support Commissioner on a question of law.

[(1A) The Secretary of State may appeal to a Child Support Commissioner on a question of law in relation to any decision of a child support appeal tribunal made in connection with an application for a departure direction.]

(2) Where, on an appeal under this section, a Child Support Commissioner holds that the decision appealed against was wrong in law he shall set it aside.

(3)    Where a decision is set aside under subsection (2), the Child Support Commissioner may—

(a)    if he can do so without making fresh or further findings of fact, give the decision which he considers should have been given by the child support appeal tribunal;

(b)    if he considers it expedient, make such findings and give such decision as he considers appropriate in the light of those findings; or

[(c)    on an appeal by the Secretary of State, refer the case to a child support appeal tribunal with directions for its determination; or

(d)    on any other appeal, refer the case to a child support officer or, if he considers it appropriate, to a child support appeal tribunal with directions for its determination.]

(4)    Any reference under subsection (3) to a child support officer shall, subject to any direction of the Child Support Commissioner, be to a child support officer who has taken no part in the decision originally appealed against.

(5)    On a reference under subsection (3) to a child support appeal tribunal, the tribunal shall, subject to any direction of the Child Support Commissioner, consist of persons who were not members of the tribunal which gave the decision which has been appealed against.

(6)    No appeal lies under this section without the leave—

(a)    of the person who was the chairman of the child support appeal tribunal when the decision appealed against was given or of such other chairman of a child support appeal tribunal as may be determined in accordance with regulations made by the Lord Chancellor; or

(b)    subject to and in accordance with regulations so made, of a Child Support Commissioner.

(7)    The Lord Chancellor may by regulations make provision as to the manner in which, and the time within which, appeals under this section are to be brought and applications for leave under this section are to be made.

(8)    Where a question which would otherwise fall to be determined by a child support officer first arises in the course of an appeal to a Child Support Commissioner, he may, if he thinks fit, determine it even though it has not been considered by a child support officer.

(9)    Before making any regulations under subsection (6) or (7), the Lord Chancellor shall consult the Lord Advocate.

NOTES

Commencement: 1 September 1992.

Sub-s (1A): inserted by the Child Support Act 1995, s 30(5), Sch 3, para 7(2).

Sub-s (3): paras (c), (d) substituted for para (c) as originally enacted by the Child Support Act 1995, s    30(5), Sch 3, para 7(3).

## 27    Reference to court for declaration of parentage

[(1)    Subsection (1A) applies in any case where—

(a)    an application for a maintenance assessment has been made, or a maintenance assessment is in force, with respect to a person ("the alleged parent") who denies that he is a parent of a child with respect to whom the application or assessment was made; and

(b)    a child support officer to whom the case is referred is not satisfied that the case falls within one of those set out in section 26(2).

(1A) In any case where this subsection applies, the Secretary of State or the person with care may apply to the court for a declaration as to whether or not the alleged parent is one of the child's parents.]

(2)   If, on hearing any application under subsection [(1A)], the court is satisfied that the alleged parent is, or is not, a parent of the child in question it shall make a declaration to that effect.

[(3)   A declaration under this section shall have effect only for the purposes of—
   (a)   this Act; and
   (b)   proceedings in which a court is considering whether to make a maintenance order in the circumstances mentioned in subsection (6), (7) or (8) of section 8.]

(4)   In this section "court" means, subject to any provision made under Schedule 11 to the Children Act 1989 (jurisdiction of courts with respect to certain proceedings relating to children) the High Court, a county court or a magistrates' court.

(5)   . . .

(6)   This section does not apply to Scotland.

NOTES
   Commencement: 4 September 1995 (sub-ss (1), (1A), (3)); 5 April 1993 (remainder).
   Sub-ss (1), (1A): substituted for sub-s (1) as originally enacted by the Child Support Act 1995, s 20(2).
   Sub-s (2): number in square brackets substituted by the Child Support Act 1995, s 20(3).
   Sub-s (3): substituted by the Child Support Act 1995, s 20(4).
   Sub-s (5): amends the Civil Evidence Act 1968, s 12(5).

# CRIMINAL JUSTICE ACT 1991

## (C 53)

*An Act to make further provision with respect to the treatment of offenders and the position of children and young persons and persons having responsibility for them; to make provision with respect to certain services provided or proposed to be provided for purposes connected with the administration of justice or the treatment of offenders; to make financial and other provision with respect to that administration; and for connected purposes*

[25 July 1991]

## PART I
## POWERS OF COURTS TO DEAL WITH OFFENDERS

*Custodial sentences*

### 1   Restrictions on imposing custodial sentences

(1)   This section applies where a person is convicted of an offence punishable with a custodial sentence other than one fixed by law.

(2)   Subject to subsection (3) below, the court shall not pass a custodial sentence on the offender unless it is of the opinion—
   [(a)   that the offence, or the combination of the offence and one or more offences associated with it, was so serious that only such a sentence can be justified for the offence; or]

     (b)  where the offence is a violent or sexual offence, that only such a sentence would be adequate to protect the public from serious harm from him.

(3)    Nothing in subsection (2) above shall prevent the court from passing a custodial sentence on the offender if he refuses to give his consent to a community sentence which is proposed by the court and requires that consent.

(4)    Where a court passes a custodial sentence, it shall be its duty—
     (a)  in a case not falling within subsection (3) above, to state in open court that it is of the opinion that either or both of paragraphs (a) and (b) of subsection (2) above apply and why it is of that opinion; and
     (b)  in any case, to explain to the offender in open court and in ordinary language why it is passing a custodial sentence on him.

(5)    A magistrates' court shall cause a reason stated by it under subsection (4) above to be specified in the warrant of commitment and to be entered in the register.

---

NOTES
  Commencement: 1 October 1992.
  Sub-s (2): para (a) substituted by the Criminal Justice Act 1993, s 66(1), (9).

---

## 3   Procedural requirements for custodial sentences

(1)    Subject to subsection (2) below, a court shall obtain and consider a pre-sentence report before forming any such opinion as is mentioned in subsection (2) of section 1 or 2 above.

(2)    . . . Subsection (1) above does not apply if, in the circumstances of the case, the court is of the opinion that it is unnecessary to obtain a pre-sentence report.

[(2A) In the case of an offender under the age of eighteen years, save where the offence or any other offence associated with it is triable only on indictment, the court shall not form such an opinion as is mentioned in subsection (2) above or subsection   (4A) below unless there exists a previous pre-sentence report obtained in respect of the offender and the court has had regard to the information contained in that report, or, if there is more than one such report, the most recent report.]

(3)    In forming any such opinion as is mentioned in subsection (2) of section 1 or 2 above a court—
     (a)  shall take into account all such information about the circumstances of the offence [or (as the case may be) of the offence and the offence or offences associated with it,] (including any aggravating or mitigating factors) as is available to it; and
     (b)  in the case of any such opinion as is mentioned in paragraph (b) of that subsection, may take into account any information about the offender which is before it.

(4)    No custodial sentence . . . shall be invalidated by the failure of a court to [obtain and consider a pre-sentence report before forming an opinion referred to in subsection (1) above] but any court on an appeal against such a sentence—
     (a)  shall[, subject to subsection (4A) below,] obtain a pre-sentence report if none was obtained by the court below; and
     (b)  shall consider any such report obtained by it or by that court.

[(4A) Subsection (4)(a) above does not apply if the court is of the opinion—
     (a)  that the court below was justified in forming an opinion that it was unnecessary to obtain a pre-sentence report, or

(b) that, although the court below was not justified in forming that opinion, in the circumstances of the case at the time it is before the court, it is unnecessary to obtain a pre-sentence report.]

(5) In this Part "pre-sentence report" means a report in writing which—
- (a) with a view to assisting the court in determining the most suitable method of dealing with an offender, is made or submitted by a probation officer or by a social worker of a local authority social services department; and
- (b) contains information as to such matters, presented in such manner, as may be prescribed by rules made by the Secretary of State.

**NOTES**
Commencement: 3 February 1995 (sub-ss (2A), (4A)); 1 October 1992 (remainder).
Sub-s (2): words omitted repealed by the Criminal Justice and Public Order Act 1994, s 168(1), (3), Sch 9, para 40(1), (2)(a), Sch 11.
Sub-ss (2A), (4A): inserted by the Criminal Justice and Public Order Act 1994, s 168(1), Sch 9, para 40(1), (2)(b), (d).
Sub-s (3): words in square brackets in para (a) inserted by the Criminal Justice Act 1993, s 66(3), (9).
Sub-s (4): words omitted repealed, words in first pair of square brackets substituted, and words in second pair of square brackets inserted, by the Criminal Justice and Public Order Act 1994, s 168(1), (3), Sch 9, para 40(1), (2)(c), Sch 11.

*Probation and community service orders*

## 11 Orders combining probation and community service

(1) Where a court by or before which a person of or over the age of sixteen years is convicted of an offence punishable with imprisonment (not being an offence for which the sentence is fixed by law [or falls to be imposed under section 2(2), 3(2) or 4(2) of the Crime (Sentences) Act 1997]) is of the opinion mentioned in subsection (2) below, the court may make a combination order, that is to say, an order requiring him both—
- (a) to be under the supervision of a probation officer for a period specified in the order, being not less than twelve months nor more than three years; and
- (b) to perform unpaid work for a number of hours so specified, being in the aggregate not less than 40 nor more than 100.

(2) The opinion referred to in subsection (1) above is that the making of a combination order is desirable in the interests of—
- (a) securing the rehabilitation of the offender; or
- (b) protecting the public from harm from him or preventing the commission by him of further offences.

(3) Subject to subsection (1) above, Part I of the 1973 Act shall apply in relation to combination orders—
- (a) in so far as they impose such a requirement as is mentioned in paragraph (a) of that subsection, as if they were probation orders; and
- (b) in so far as they impose such a requirement as is mentioned in paragraph (b) of that subsection, as if they were community service orders.

**NOTES**
Commencement: 1 October 1992.
Sub-s (1): words in square brackets inserted by the Crime (Sentences) Act 1997, s 55, Sch 4, para 15(8), as from a day to be appointed.
1973 Act: Powers of Criminal Courts Act 1973.

*Curfew orders*

## 12   Curfew orders

(1)   Where a person *of or over the age of sixteen years* is convicted of an offence (not being an offence for which the sentence is fixed by law [or falls to be imposed under section 2(2), 3(2) or 4(2) of the Crime (Sentences) Act 1997]), the court by or before which he is convicted may make a curfew order, that is to say, an order requiring him to remain, for periods specified in the order, at a place so specified.

(2)   A curfew order may specify different places or different periods for different days, but shall not specify—
(a)   periods which fall outside the period of six months beginning with the day on which it is made; or
(b)   periods which amount to less than 2 hours or more than 12 hours in any one day.

[(2A) In relation to an offender who is under the age of sixteen years, subsection   (2)(a) above shall have effect as if the reference to six months were a reference to three months.]

(3)   The requirements in a curfew order shall, as far as practicable, be such as to avoid—
(a)   any conflict with the offender's religious beliefs or with the requirements of any other community order to which he may be subject; and
(b)   any interference with the times, if any, at which he normally works or attends school or other educational establishment.

(4)   A curfew order shall include provision for making a person responsible for monitoring the offender's whereabouts during the curfew periods specified in the order; and a person who is made so responsible shall be of a description specified in an order made by the Secretary of State.

[(4A) A court shall not make a curfew order unless the court has been notified by the Secretary of State that arrangements for monitoring the offender's whereabouts are available in the area in which the place proposed to be specified in the order is situated and the notice has not been withdrawn.]

(5)   Before making a curfew order, the court shall explain to the offender in ordinary language—
(a)   the effect of the order (including any additional requirements proposed to be included in the order in accordance with section 13 below);
(b)   the consequences which may follow under Schedule 2 to this Act if he fails to comply with any of the requirements of the order; and
(c)   that the court has under that Schedule power to review the order on the application either of the offender or of the supervising officer,

and the court shall not make the order unless he expresses his willingness to comply with its requirements.

(6)   Before making a curfew order, the court shall obtain and consider information about the place proposed to be specified in the order (including information as to the attitude of persons likely to be affected by the enforced presence there of the offender).

[(6A) Before making a curfew order in respect of an offender who is under the age of sixteen years, the court shall obtain and consider information about his family circumstances and the likely effect of such an order on those circumstances.]

(7)    The Secretary of State may by order direct—

(a)    that subsection (2) above shall have effect with the substitution, for any period there specified, of such period as may be specified in the order; or

(b)    that subsection (3) above shall have effect with such additional restrictions as may be so specified.

NOTES

Commencement: 9 January 1995 (sub-ss (1), (2), (3)–(6), (7)); to be appointed (remainder).

Sub-s (1): words in italics repealed, and words in square brackets inserted, by the Crime (Sentences) Act 1997, ss 43(1), 55, 56(2), Sch 4, para 15(9), Sch 6, as from a day to be appointed.

Sub-ss (2A), (6A): inserted by the Crime (Sentences) Act 1997, s 43(2), (3), as from a day to be appointed.

Sub-s (4A): inserted by the Criminal Justice and Public Order Act 1994, s 168(1), Sch 9, para 41.

Sub-s (5):words in italics repealed by the Crime (Sentences) Act 1997, s 56(2), Sch 6, as from a day to be appointed.

## 13    Electronic monitoring of curfew orders

(1)    Subject to subsection (2) below, a curfew order may in addition include requirements for securing the electronic monitoring of the offender's whereabouts during the curfew periods specified in the order.

(2)    A court shall not make a curfew order which includes such requirements unless the court—

(a)    has been notified by the Secretary of State that electronic monitoring arrangements are available in the area in which the place proposed to be specified in the order is situated; and

(b)    is satisfied that the necessary provision can be made under those arrangements.

(3)    Electronic monitoring arrangements made by the Secretary of State under this section may include entering into contracts with other persons for the electronic monitoring by them of offenders' whereabouts.

NOTES

Commencement: 9 January 1995.

*Orders: supplemental*

## 14    Enforcement etc of community orders

(1)    Schedule 2 to this Act (which makes provision for dealing with failures to comply with the requirements of certain community orders, for amending such orders and for revoking them with or without the substitution of other sentences) shall have effect.

(2)    . . .

NOTES

Commencement: 1 October 1992.

Sub-s (2): outside the scope of this work.

## 15    Regulation of community orders

(1)    The Secretary of State may make rules for regulating—

(a), (b). . .

(c) the monitoring of the whereabouts of persons who are subject to curfew orders (including electronic monitoring in cases where arrangements for such monitoring are available); and

(d) without prejudice to the generality of [paragraph (c)] above, the functions of the responsible officers of such persons as are mentioned in [that paragraph].

(2)  . . .

(3)  In this Part "responsible officer" means—

(a) in relation to an offender who is subject to a probation order, the probation officer responsible for his supervision;

(b) in relation to an offender who is subject to a community service order, the relevant officer within the meaning of section 14(4) of the 1973 Act; and

(c) in relation to an offender who is subject to a curfew order, the person responsible for monitoring his whereabouts during the curfew periods specified in the order.

(4)  . . .

NOTES

Commencement: 1 October 1992.

Sub-s (1): paras (a), (b) repealed, and words in square brackets in para (d) substituted, by the Probation Service Act 1993, s 32, Sch 3, para 10, Sch 4.

Sub-ss (2), (4): repealed by the Probation Service Act 1993, s 32(3), Sch 4.

1973 Act: Powers of Criminal Courts Act 1973.

## 16  Reciprocal enforcement of certain orders

Schedule 3 to this Act shall have effect for making provision for and in connection with—

(a) the making and amendment in England and Wales of community orders relating to persons residing in Scotland or Northern Ireland; and

(b) the making and amendment in Scotland or Northern Ireland of corresponding orders relating to persons residing in England and Wales.

NOTES

Commencement: 1 October 1992.

*Financial penalties*

## [18  Fixing of fines

[(1)  Before fixing the amount of any fine to be imposed on an offender who is an individual, a court shall inquire into his financial circumstances.]

(2)  The amount of any fine fixed by a court shall be such as, in the opinion of the court, reflects the seriousness of the offence.

(3)  In fixing the amount of any fine [to be imposed on an offender (whether an individual or other person)], a court shall take into account the circumstances of the case including, among other things, the financial circumstances of the offender so far as they are known, or appear, to the court.

(4)  Where—

(a) an offender has been convicted in his absence in pursuance of section 11 or 12 of the Magistrates' Courts Act 1980 (non-appearance of accused),

(b) an offender—
  (i) has failed to comply with an order under section 20(1) below; or
  (ii) has otherwise failed to co-operate with the court in its inquiry into his financial circumstances, or
(c) the parent or guardian of an offender who is a child or young person—
  (i) has failed to comply with an order under section 20(1B) below; or
  (ii) has otherwise failed to co-operate with the court in its inquiry into his financial circumstances,

and the court considers that it has insufficient information to make a proper determination of the financial circumstances of the offender, it may make such determination as it thinks fit.

(5) Subsection (3) above applies whether taking into account the financial circumstances of the offender has the effect of increasing or reducing the amount of the fine.]

---

NOTES

Commencement: 3 February 1995 (sub-s (1)); 20 September 1993 (remainder).

Substituted by the Criminal Justice Act 1993, s 65(1), (4).

Sub-s (1): substituted by the Criminal Justice and Public Order Act 1994, s 168(1), Sch 9, para 42(1), (2)(a), (5).

Sub-s (3): words in square brackets inserted by the Criminal Justice and Public Order Act 1994, s   168(1), Sch 9, para 42(1), (2)(b), (5).

## 24   Recovery of fines etc by deductions from income support

(1) The Secretary of State may by regulations provide that where a fine has been imposed on an offender by a magistrates' court, or a sum is required to be paid by a compensation order which has been made against an offender by such a court, and (in either case) the offender is entitled to income support [or a jobseeker's allowance]—
  (a) the court may apply to the Secretary of State asking him to deduct sums from any amounts payable to the offender by way of [that benefit], in order to secure the payment of any sum which is or forms part of the fine or compensation; and
  (b) the Secretary of State may deduct sums from any such amounts and pay them to the court towards satisfaction of any such sum.

(2) The regulations may include—
  (a) provision that, before making an application, the court shall make an enquiry as to the offender's means;
  (b) provision allowing or requiring adjudication as regards an application, and provision as to appeals and reviews;
  (c) provision as to the circumstances and manner in which and the times at which sums are to be deducted and paid;
  (d) provision as to the calculation of such sums (which may include provision to secure that amounts payable to the offender by way of income support [or a jobseeker's allowance] do not fall below prescribed figures);
  (e) provision as to the circumstances in which the Secretary of State is to cease making deductions;
  (f) provision requiring the Secretary of State to notify the offender, in a prescribed manner and at any prescribed time, of the total amount of sums deducted up to the time of notification; and
  (g) provision that, where the whole amount to which the application relates has been paid, the court shall give notice of that fact to the Secretary of State.

(3)  In subsection (1) above—

(a)  the reference to a fine having been imposed by a magistrates' court includes a reference to a fine being treated, by virtue of section 32 of the 1973 Act, as having been so imposed; and

(b)  the reference to a sum being required to be paid by a compensation order which has been made by a magistrates' court includes a reference to a sum which is required to be paid by such an order being treated, by virtue of section 41 of the Administration of Justice Act 1970, as having been adjudged to be paid on conviction by such a court;

[(c)  the reference in paragraph (a) to "the court" includes a reference to a court to which the function in that paragraph has been transferred by virtue of a transfer of fine order under section 89(1) or (3) or 90(1)(a) of the 1980 Act (power of magistrates' court to make transfer of fine order) or under [section 222(1)(a) or (b) of the Criminal Procedure (Scotland) Act 1995] (analogous provision as respects Scotland) and a reference to a court to which that function has been remitted by virtue of section 196(2) of the said Act of 1975 (enforcement of fine imposed by High Court of Justiciary).]

(4)  In this section—
"fine" includes—

(a)  a penalty imposed under [section 29 or 37 of the Vehicle Excise and Registration Act 1994] or section 102(3)(aa) of the Customs and Excise Management Act 1979 (penalties imposed for certain offences in relation to vehicle excise licences);

(b)  an amount ordered to be paid, in addition to any penalty so imposed, under [section 30, 36 or 38 of the Vehicle Excise and Registration Act 1994] (liability to additional duty);

(c)  an amount ordered to be paid by way of costs which is, by virtue of section 41 of the Administration of Justice Act 1970, treated as having been adjudged to be paid on a conviction by a magistrates' court;

"income support" means income support within the meaning of the Social Security Act 1986, either alone or together with any . . . [incapacity] benefit, retirement pension or severe disablement allowance which is paid by means of the same instrument of payment;

"prescribed" means prescribed by regulations made by the Secretary of State.

(5)  In the application of this section to Scotland—

(a)  references in subsections (1) and (2) above to a magistrates' court shall be construed as references to a court; and

(b)  in subsection (3) above, for paragraphs (a) and (b) there shall be substituted the following paragraphs—

"(a)  the reference to a fine having been imposed by a court includes a reference to a fine being treated, by virtue of [section 211(4) of the Criminal Procedure (Scotland) Act 1995], as having been so imposed; and

(b)  the reference to a compensation order having been made by a court includes a reference to such an order being treated, by virtue of [section 252 of the Criminal Procedure (Scotland) Act 1995], as having been so made."

**NOTES**

Commencement: 1 October 1992.

Sub-s (1): words in first pair of square brackets inserted, and words in second pair of square brackets substituted, by the Jobseekers Act 1995, s 41(4), Sch 2, para 21(1)–(3).

Sub-s (2): words in square brackets in para (d) inserted by the Jobseekers Act 1995, s 41(4), Sch 2, para 21(1), (4).

Sub-s (3): para (c) added by the Criminal Justice and Public Order Act 1994, s 47(3), words in square brackets substituted by the Criminal Procedure (Consequential Provisions) (Scotland) Act 1995, ss 4, 5, Sch 3, Sch 4, para 80(1), (2)(c).

Sub-s (4): in definition "fine" words in square brackets substituted by the Vehicle Excise and Registration Act 1994, s 63, Sch 3, para 30; in definition "income support" words omitted repealed by the Jobseekers Act 1995, s 41(5), Sch 3, word in square brackets substituted by the Social Security (Incapacity for Work) Act 1994, s 11(1), Sch 1, Pt II, para 55.

Sub-s (5): words in square brackets substituted by the Criminal Procedure (Consequential Provisions) (Scotland) Act 1995, s 5, Sch 4, para 80(1), (2)(a), (b).

1973 Act: Powers of Criminal Courts Act 1973.

## PART VI
## SUPPLEMENTAL

**102    Short title, commencement and extent**

(1)    This Act may be cited as the Criminal Justice Act 1991.

(2)    This Act shall come into force on such day as the Secretary of State may by order made by statutory instrument appoint, and different days may be appointed for different provisions or for different purposes.

(3)    Without prejudice to the provisions of Schedule 12 to this Act, an order under subsection (2) above may make such transitional provisions and savings as appear to the Secretary of State necessary or expedient in connection with any provision brought into force by the order.

(4)    Subject to subsections (5) to (8) below, this Act extends to England and Wales only.

(5)–(8). . .

**NOTES**

Sub-ss (5)–(8): outside the scope of this work.

# SOCIAL SECURITY CONTRIBUTIONS AND BENEFITS ACT 1992

## (C 4)

*An Act to consolidate certain enactments relating to social security contributions and benefits with amendments to give effect to recommendations of the Law Commission and the Scottish Law Commission*

[13 February 1992]

## PART II
## CONTRIBUTORY BENEFITS

*Preliminary*

*[Incapacity benefit*

**30A    Incapacity benefit: entitlement**

(1)    Subject to the following provisions of this section, a person who satisfies either of the following conditions is entitled to short-term incapacity benefit in respect of any day of incapacity for work which forms part of a period of incapacity for work.

(2)   The conditions are that—

    (a)  he is under pensionable age on the day in question and satisfies the contribution conditions specified for short-term incapacity benefit in Schedule 3, Part I, paragraph 2; or

    (b)  on that day he is over pensionable age but not more than 5 years over that age, the period of incapacity for work began before he attained pensionable age, and—

        (i)  he would be entitled to a Category A retirement pension if his entitlement had not been deferred or if he had not made an election under section 54(1) below, or

        (ii) he would be entitled to a Category B retirement pension by virtue of the contributions of his deceased spouse, but for any such deferment or election.

(3)   A person is not entitled to short-term incapacity benefit for the first 3 days of any period of incapacity for work.

(4)   In any period of incapacity for work a person is not entitled to short-term incapacity benefit for more than 364 days.

(5)   Where a person ceases by virtue of subsection (4) above to be entitled to short-term incapacity benefit, he is entitled to long-term incapacity benefit in respect of any subsequent day of incapacity for work in the same period of incapacity for work on which he is not over pensionable age.]

---

NOTES

    Commencement: 13 April 1995.

    Inserted, together with preceding cross-heading, by the Social Security (Incapacity for Work) Act 1994, s 1(1).

---

## [30B   Incapacity benefit: rate

(1)   The amount payable by way of incapacity benefit in respect of any day is 1/7th of the appropriate weekly rate.

(2)   Subject to the following provisions of this section, the weekly rate of short-term incapacity benefit is the lower or higher rate specified in Schedule 4, Part I, paragraph 2.

    The benefit is payable at the lower rate so specified for the first 196 days of entitlement in any period of incapacity for work and at the higher rate so specified thereafter.

(3)   In the case of a person over pensionable age the weekly rate of short-term incapacity benefit is, subject to subsection (4) below, that at which the relevant retirement pension referred to in section 30A(2)(b) above would have been payable.

    But in determining that rate any increase of the following descriptions shall be disregarded—

    (a)  any increase [(for married people) under section 51A(2)] below or (for deferred retirement) under Schedule 5 to this Act;

    (b)  any increase (for dependants) under section 80, 83 or 85 below; and

    (c)  any increase (for Category A or Category B pensioners) under section 150 of the Administration Act (annual up-rating) of the sums mentioned in subsection (1)(e) of that section.

(4)    In the case of a person who has been entitled to short-term incapacity benefit for 196 days or more in any period of incapacity for work and—

    (a)   is terminally ill, or

    (b)   he is entitled to the highest rate of the care component of disability living allowance,

the weekly rate of short-term incapacity benefit payable, if greater than the rate otherwise payable to him under subsection (2) or (3) above, shall be equal to the rate at which long-term incapacity benefit under section 30A above would be payable to him if he were entitled to it.

For the purposes of this subsection a person is terminally ill if he suffers from a progressive disease and his death in consequence of that disease can reasonably be expected within 6 months.

(5)    References to short-term incapacity benefit at the higher rate shall be construed as including short-term incapacity benefit payable to any person who has been entitled to that benefit for 196 days or more in a period of incapacity for work, notwithstanding that the rate of benefit is determined in accordance with subsection    (3) or (4) above.

(6)    Subject as follows, the weekly rate of long-term incapacity benefit under section 30A above is that specified in Schedule 4, Part I, paragraph 2A.

(7)    Regulations may provide that if a person is, on the qualifying date in relation to a period of incapacity for work, under such age as may be prescribed, the rate of long-term incapacity benefit under section 30A above payable to him in respect of any day in that period shall be increased by such amount as may be prescribed.

For this purpose "the qualifying date" means the first day of the period of incapacity for work or such earlier day as may be prescribed.]

---

NOTES

    Commencement: 13 April 1995 (sub-ss (1)–(6)); 18 November 1994 (remainder).

    Inserted by the Social Security (Incapacity for Work) Act 1994, s 2(1).

    Sub-s (3): words in square brackets in para (a) substituted, and number in italics in para (b) substituted by "83A", as from 6 April 2010, by the Pensions Act 1995, s 126, Sch 4, paras 18(b), 20, 21(3).

    Administration Act: Social Security Administration Act 1992.

---

*Maternity*

## 35    State maternity allowance

(1)    A woman shall be entitled to a maternity allowance at [the appropriate weekly rate determined under subsection (1A) below], if—

    (a)   she has become pregnant and has reached, or been confined before reaching, the commencement of the 11th week before the expected week of confinement; and

    (b)   she has been engaged in employment as an employed or self-employed earner for at least 26 weeks in the [66 weeks immediately preceding] before the expected week of confinement; and

    (c)   she satisfies the contribution condition for a maternity allowance specified in Schedule 3, Part I, paragraph 3; and

    (d)   she is not entitled to statutory maternity pay for the same week in respect of the same pregnancy.

[(1A) For the purposes of subsection (1) above the appropriate weekly rate is—
  (a)  in the case of a woman who is engaged in employment as an employed earner in the week immediately preceding the 14th week before the expected week of confinement, a weekly rate equal to the lower rate of statutory maternity pay for the time being prescribed under section 166(3) below or the weekly rate specified in Schedule 4, Part I, paragraph 4, whichever is the higher; and
  (b)  in any other case, the weekly rate specified in Schedule 4, Part I, paragraph 4.]

(2)  Subject to the following provisions of this section, a maternity allowance shall be payable for the period ("the maternity allowance period") which, if she were entitled to statutory maternity pay, would be the maternity pay period under section 165 below.

(3)  Regulations may provide—
  (a)  for disqualifying a woman for receiving a maternity allowance if—
     (i)  during the maternity allowance period she does any work in employment as an employed or self-employed earner, or fails without good cause to observe any prescribed rules of behaviour; or
     (ii)  at any time before she is confined she fails without good cause to attend for, or submit herself to, any medical examination required in accordance with the regulations;
  (b)  that this section and Schedule 3, Part I, paragraph 3 shall have effect subject to prescribed modifications in relation to cases in which a woman has been confined and—
     (i)  has not made a claim for a maternity allowance in expectation of that confinement (other than a claim which has been disallowed); or
     (ii)  has made a claim for a maternity allowance in expectation of that confinement (other than a claim which has been disallowed), but she was confined more than 11 weeks before the expected week of confinement.
  [(c)  that subsection (2) above shall have effect subject to prescribed modifications in relation to cases in which a woman fails to satisfy the conditions referred to in subsection (1)(b) and (c) above at the commencement of the 11th week before the expected week of confinement, but subsequently satisfies those conditions at any time before she is confined.]

(4)  A woman who has become entitled to a maternity allowance shall cease to be entitled to it if she dies before the beginning of the maternity allowance period; and if she dies after the beginning, but before the end, of that period, the allowance shall not be payable for any week subsequent to that in which she dies.

(5)  Where for any purpose of this Part of this Act or of regulations it is necessary to calculate the daily rate of a maternity allowance—
  (a)  Sunday or such other day in each week as may be prescribed shall be disregarded; and
  (b)  the amount payable by way of that allowance for any other day shall be taken as one sixth of the weekly rate of the allowance.

(6)  In this section "confinement" means—
  (a)  labour resulting in the issue of a living child, or
  (b)  labour after [24 weeks] of pregnancy resulting in the issue of a child whether alive or dead,

and "confined" shall be construed accordingly; and where a woman's labour begun on one day results in the issue of a child on another day she shall be taken to be confined on the day of the issue of the child or, if labour results in the issue of twins or a greater number of children, she shall be taken to be confined on the day of the issue of the last of them.

(7)    The fact that the mother of a child is being paid maternity allowance shall not be taken into consideration by any court in deciding whether to order payment of expenses incidental to the birth of the child.

NOTES

Commencement: 16 October 1994 (sub-s (1A), certain purposes); 1 July 1992 (remainder).

Sub-s (1): words in square brackets substituted by the Maternity Allowance and Statutory Maternity Pay Regulations 1994, SI 1994/1230, regs 1(2), 2(1)(a), (b), in relation to any case where the expected week of confinement begins on or after 16 October 1994.

Sub-s (1A): inserted by SI 1994/1230, regs 1(2), 2(2), in relation to any case where the expected week of confinement begins on or after 16 October 1994.

Sub-s (3): para (c) added by SI 1994/1230, reg 2(3), in relation to any case where the expected week of confinement begins on or after 16 October 1994.

Sub-s (6): words in square brackets substituted by the Still-Birth (Definition) Act 1992, ss 2(1), 4(2).

*Benefits for widows and widowers*

## 36    Widow's payment

(1)    A woman who has been widowed shall be entitled to a widow's payment of the amount specified in Schedule 4, Part II if—

(a)    she was under pensionable age at the time when her late husband died, or he was then not entitled to a Category A retirement pension under section 44 below; and

(b)    her late husband satisfied the contribution condition for a widow's payment specified in Schedule 3, Part I, paragraph 4.

(2)    The payment shall not be payable to a widow if she and a man to whom she is not married are living together as husband and wife at the time of her husband's death.

(3)    A widow's payment is payable only in cases where the husband dies on or after 11th April 1988 (the coming into force of section 36(1) of the 1986 Act, which introduced the widow's payment by making provision corresponding to this section).

NOTES

1986 Act: Social Security Act 1986.

# PART III
# NON-CONTRIBUTORY BENEFITS

*Severe disablement allowance*

## 68    Entitlement and rate

(1)    Subject to the provisions of this section, a person shall be entitled to a severe disablement allowance for any day ("the relevant day") if he satisfies—

(a)    the conditions specified in subsection (2) below; or

(b)    the conditions specified in subsection (3) below.

(2) The conditions mentioned in subsection (1)(a) above are that—
- (a) on the relevant day he is incapable of work; and
- (b) he has been incapable of work for a period of not less than 196 consecutive days—
  - (i) beginning not later than the day on which he attained the age of 20; and
  - (ii) ending immediately before the relevant day.

(3) The conditions mentioned in subsection (1)(b) above are that—
- (a) on the relevant day he is both incapable of work and disabled; and
- (b) he has been both incapable of work and disabled for a period of not less than 196 consecutive days ending immediately before the relevant day.

(4) A person shall not be entitled to a severe disablement allowance if—
- (a) he is under the age of 16; or
- (b) he is receiving full-time education; or
- (c) he does not satisfy the prescribed conditions—
  - (i) as to residence in Great Britain; or
  - (ii) as to presence there; or
- (d) he has attained [the age of 65] and—
  - (i) was not entitled to a severe disablement allowance immediately before he attained that age; and
  - (ii) is not treated by regulations as having been so entitled immediately before he attained that age.

(5) A person shall not be entitled to a severe disablement allowance for any day which as between him and his employer falls within a period of entitlement for the purposes of statutory sick pay.

(6) A person is disabled for the purposes of this section if he suffers from loss of physical or mental faculty such that the extent of the resulting disablement assessed in accordance with Schedule 6 to this Act amounts to not less than 80 per cent.

(7) A severe disablement allowance shall be paid at the weekly rate specified in Schedule 4, Part III, paragraph 2.

(8) The amount of severe disablement allowance payable for any relevant day shall be [1/7th of the weekly rate].

(9) In any case where—
- (a) a severe disablement allowance is payable to a woman in respect of one or more relevant days in a week; and
- (b) an amount of statutory maternity pay becomes payable to her on any day in that week,

the amount of the severe disablement allowance (including any increase for a child or adult dependant under section 90(a) below) so payable shall be reduced by the amount of the statutory maternity pay, and only the balance (if any) shall be payable.

(10) Where—
- (a) a person who is engaged and normally engaged in remunerative work ceases to be so engaged; and
- (b) he is entitled to a disability working allowance for the week in which there falls the last day on which he is so engaged; and
- (c) he qualified for a disability working allowance for that week by virtue of a severe disablement allowance having been payable to him; and

(d) the first day after he ceases to be engaged as mentioned in paragraph (a) above is a day on which he is incapable of work and falls not later than the end of the period of two years beginning with the last day for which he was entitled to a severe disablement allowance,

any day since that day which fell within a week for which he was entitled to a disability working allowance shall be treated for the purposes of any claim for a severe disablement allowance for a period commencing after he ceases to be engaged as mentioned in paragraph (a) above as having been a day on which he was both incapable of work and disabled.

[(10A) Where—

(a) a person becomes engaged in training for work, and

(b) he was entitled to a severe disablement allowance for one or more of the 56 days immediately before he became so engaged, and

(c) the first day after he ceases to be so engaged is for him a day on which he is incapable of work and falls not later than the end of the period of two years beginning with the last day for which he was entitled to a severe disablement allowance,

any day since that day in which he was engaged in training for work shall be treated for the purposes of any claim for a severe disablement allowance as having been a day on which he was both incapable of work and disabled.

In this subsection "training for work" means training for work in pursuance of arrangements made under section 2(1) of the Employment and Training Act 1973 or section 2(3) of the Enterprise and New Towns (Scotland) Act 1990 or training of such other description as may be prescribed.]

(11) Regulations—

(a) may direct that persons who—

(i) have attained [the age of 65]; and

(ii) were entitled to a severe disablement allowance immediately before they attained that age,

shall continue to be so entitled notwithstanding that they do not satisfy the conditions specified in subsection (2) or (3) above;

(b) may direct—

(i) that persons who have previously been entitled to a severe disablement allowance shall be entitled to such an allowance notwithstanding that they do not satisfy the conditions specified in subsection (2)(b) or (3)(b) above;

(ii) that subsections (2)(b) and (3)(b) above shall have effect in relation to such persons subject to such modifications as may be specified in the regulations;

[(ca) may prescribe circumstances in which a person is or is not to be treated as incapable of work;

(cb) may prescribe the circumstances in which a person is or is not to be treated as receiving full-time education;]

[(cc) may prescribe evidence which is to be treated as establishing that a person suffers from loss of physical or mental faculty such that the extent of the resulting disablement amounts to not less than 80 per cent;] [and

(d) may make in relation to severe disablement allowance any such provision as is made in relation to incapacity benefit by section 30E above.] . . .

(e) . . .

(12) ...

[(13) In this section "retiring age" means 70 in the case of a man and 65 in the case of a woman.]

NOTES

Commencement: 13 April 1995 (sub-s (10A) certain purposes, sub-s (13)); 18 November 1994 (sub-s (10A) remaining purposes); 1 July 1992 (remainder).

Sub-s (4): words in square brackets in para (d) substituted by the Social Security (Severe Disablement Allowance and Invalid Care Allowance) Amendment Regulations 1994, SI 1994/2556, reg 2(1), (2)(a).

Sub-s (8): words in square brackets substituted by the Social Security (Incapacity for Work) Act 1994, s 11(1), Sch 1, para 18(2).

Sub-s (10A): inserted by the Social Security (Incapacity for Work) Act 1994, s 9(1), (2).

Sub-s (11): words in square brackets in para (a) substituted by SI 1994/2556, reg 2(1), (2)(b); paras (ca), (cb), (d) substituted for paras (c), (d) as originally enacted, para (cc) inserted, and para (e) and preceding word omitted repealed, by the Social Security (Incapacity for Work) Act 1994, ss 9(1), (3), 11, Sch 1, Pt I, para 18(3)–(5), Sch 2.

Sub-s (12): repealed by the Social Security (Incapacity for Work) Act 1994, s 11, Sch 1, para 18(6), Sch 2.

Sub-s (13): substituted by the Social Security (Incapacity for Work) Act 1994, s 11(1), Sch 1, para 18(6).

Administration Act: Social Security Administration Act 1992.

## 69 Severe disablement allowance: age related addition

(1) If a person was under the age of 60 on the day on which he qualified for severe disablement allowance, the weekly rate of his severe disablement allowance shall be increased by an age related addition at whichever of the weekly rates specified in the second column of paragraph 3 of Part III of Schedule 4 to this Act is applicable in his case, that is to say—

(a) the higher rate, if he was under the age of 40 on the day on which he qualified for severe disablement allowance;

(b) the middle rate, if he was between the ages of 40 and 50 on that day; or

(c) the lower rate, if he was between the ages of 50 and 60 on that day.

(2) Subject to subsection (4) below, for the purposes of this section the day on which a person qualified for severe disablement allowance is his first day of incapacity for work in the period of not less than 196 consecutive days mentioned in section 68(2)(b) or (3)(b) above, as the case may be, which preceded the first day in his current period of entitlement.

(3) For the purposes of this section, a person's "current period of entitlement" is a current period—

(a) which consists of one or more consecutive days on which he is or has been entitled to a severe disablement allowance; and

(b) which begins immediately after the last period of one or more consecutive days for which he was not entitled to such an allowance.

(4) Regulations —

(a) may prescribe cases where a person is to be treated for the purposes of this section as having qualified for severe disablement allowance on a prescribed day earlier than the day ascertained in accordance with subsection (2) above;

(b) may provide for days which are not days of incapacity for work in relation to a person to be treated as days of incapacity for work for the purpose of determining under this section the day on which he qualified for severe disablement allowance; and

(c) may make provision for disregarding prescribed days in computing any period of consecutive days for the purposes of subsection (3) above.

*Invalid care allowance*

## 70 Invalid care allowance

(1) A person shall be entitled to an invalid care allowance for any day on which he is engaged in caring for a severely disabled person if—

    (a) he is regularly and substantially engaged in caring for that person;

    (b) he is not gainfully employed; and

    (c) the severely disabled person is either such relative of his as may be prescribed or a person of any such other description as may be prescribed.

(2) In this section, "severely disabled person" means a person in respect of whom there is payable either an attendance allowance or a disability living allowance by virtue of entitlement to the care component at the highest or middle rate or such other payment out of public funds on account of his need for attendance as may be prescribed.

(3) A person shall not be entitled to an allowance under this section if he is under the age of 16 or receiving full-time education.

(4) A person shall not be entitled to an allowance under this section unless he satisfies prescribed conditions as to residence or presence in Great Britain.

(5) Subject to subsection (6) below, a person who has attained [the age of 65] shall not be entitled to an allowance under this section unless he was so entitled (or is treated by regulations as having been so entitled) immediately before attaining that age.

(6) Regulations may make provision whereby a person who has attained [the age of 65], and was entitled to an allowance under this section immediately before attaining that age, continues to be so entitled notwithstanding that he is not caring for a severely disabled person or no longer satisfies the requirements of subsection (1)(a) or (b) above.

(7) No person shall be entitled for the same day to more than one allowance under this section; and where, apart from this subsection, two or more persons would be entitled for the same day to such an allowance in respect of the same severely disabled person, one of them only shall be entitled and that shall be such one of them—

    (a) as they may jointly elect in the prescribed manner, or

    (b) as may, in default of such an election, be determined by the Secretary of State in his discretion.

(8) Regulations may prescribe the circumstances in which a person is or is not to be treated for the purposes of this section as engaged, or regularly and substantially engaged, in caring for a severely disabled person, as gainfully employed or as receiving full-time education.

(9) An invalid care allowance shall be payable at the weekly rate specified in Schedule 4, Part III, paragraph 4.

(10) . . .

---

NOTES

    Sub-ss (5), (6): words in square brackets substituted by the Social Security (Severe Disablement Allowance and Invalid Care Allowance) Amendment Regulations 1994, SI 1994/2556, reg 2(1), (3)(a), (b).

    Sub-s (10): repealed by SI 1994/2556, reg 2(1), (3)(c).

*Disability living allowance*

## 73 The mobility component

(1)  Subject to the provisions of this Act, a person shall be entitled to the mobility component of a disability living allowance for any period in which he is over the age of 5 and throughout which—

    (a)  he is suffering from physical disablement such that he is either unable to walk or virtually unable to do so; or

    (b)  he falls within subsection (2) below; or

    (c)  he falls within subsection (3) below; or

    (d)  he is able to walk but is so severely disabled physically or mentally that, disregarding any ability he may have to use routes which are familiar to him on his own, he cannot take advantage of the faculty out of doors without guidance or supervision from another person most of the time.

(2)  A person falls within this subsection if—

    (a)  he is both blind and deaf; and

    (b)  he satisfies such other conditions as may be prescribed.

(3)  A person falls within this subsection if—

    (a)  he is severely mentally impaired; and

    (b)  he displays severe behavioural problems; and

    (c)  he satisfies both the conditions mentioned in section 72(1)(b) and (c) above.

(4)  For the purposes of this section in its application to a person for any period in which he is under the age of 16, the condition mentioned in subsection (1)(d) above shall not be taken to be satisfied unless—

    (a)  he requires substantially more guidance or supervision from another person than persons of his age in normal physical and mental health would require; or

    (b)  persons of his age in normal physical and mental health would not require such guidance or supervision.

(5)  Subject to subsection (4) above, circumstances may be prescribed in which a person is to be taken to satisfy or not to satisfy a condition mentioned in subsection   (1)(a) or (d) or subsection (2)(a) above.

(6)  Regulations shall specify the cases which fall within subsection (3)(a) and (b) above.

(7)  A person who is to be taken for the purposes of section 72 above to satisfy or not to satisfy a condition mentioned in subsection (1)(b) or (c) of that section is to be taken to satisfy or not to satisfy it for the purposes of subsection (3)(c) above.

(8)  A person shall not be entitled to the mobility component for a period unless during most of that period his condition will be such as permits him from time to time to benefit from enhanced facilities for locomotion.

(9)  A person shall not be entitled to the mobility component of a disability living allowance unless—

    (a)  throughout—

        (i)  the period of 3 months immediately preceding the date on which the award of that component would begin; or

        (ii)  such other period of 3 months as may be prescribed,

    he has satisfied or is likely to satisfy one or other of the conditions mentioned in subsection (1) above; and

(b) he is likely to continue to satisfy one or other of those conditions throughout—

    (i) the period of 6 months beginning with that date; or

    (ii) (if his death is expected within the period of 6 months beginning with that date) the period so beginning and ending with his death.

(10) Two weekly rates of the mobility component shall be prescribed.

(11) The weekly rate of the mobility component payable to a person for each week in the period for which he is awarded that component shall be—

(a) the higher rate, if he falls within subsection (9) above by virtue of having satisfied or being likely to satisfy one or other of the conditions mentioned in subsection (1)(a), (b) and (c) above throughout both the period mentioned in paragraph (a) of subsection (9) above and that mentioned in paragraph (b) of that subsection; and

(b) the lower rate in any other case.

(12) For the purposes of this section in its application to a person who is terminally ill, as defined in section 66(2) above, and who makes a claim expressly on the ground that he is such a person—

(a) subsection (9)(a) above shall be omitted; and

(b) subsection (11)(a) above shall have effect as if for the words from "both" to "subsection", in the fourth place where it occurs, there were substituted the words "the period mentioned in subsection (9)(b) above".

(13) Regulations may prescribe cases in which a person who has the use—

(a) of an invalid carriage or other vehicle provided by the Secretary of State under section 5(2)(a) of the National Health Service Act 1977 and Schedule 2 to that Act or under section 46 of the National Health Service (Scotland) Act 1978 or provided under Article 30(1) of the Health and Personal Social Services (Northern Ireland) Order 1972; or

(b) of any prescribed description of appliance supplied under the enactments relating to the National Health Service being such an appliance as is primarily designed to afford a means of personal and independent locomotion out of doors,

is not to be paid any amount attributable to entitlement to the mobility component or is to be paid disability living allowance at a reduced rate in so far as it is attributable to that component.

(14) A payment to or in respect of any person which is attributable to his entitlement to the mobility component, and the right to receive such a payment, shall (except in prescribed circumstances and for prescribed purposes) be disregarded in applying any enactment or instrument under which regard is to be had to a person's means.

*Guardian's allowance*

## 77  Guardian's allowance

(1) A person shall be entitled to a guardian's allowance in respect of a child if—

(a) he is entitled to child benefit in respect of that child, and

(b) the circumstances are any of those specified in subsection (2) below;

but this subsection is subject, in particular, to section 81 below.

(2)   The circumstances referred to in subsection (1)(b) above are—

   (a)   that both of the child's parents are dead; or

   (b)   that one of the child's parents is dead and the person claiming a guardian's allowance shows that he was at the date of the death unaware of, and has failed after all reasonable efforts to discover, the whereabouts of the other parent; or

   (c)   that one of the child's parents is dead and the other is in prison.

(3)   There shall be no entitlement to a guardian's allowance in respect of a child unless at least one of the child's parents satisfies, or immediately before his death satisfied, such conditions as may be prescribed as to nationality, residence, place of birth or other matters.

(4)   Where, apart from this subsection, a person is entitled to receive, in respect of a particular child, payment of an amount by way of a guardian's allowance, that amount shall not be payable unless one of the conditions specified in subsection (5) below is satisfied.

(5)   Those conditions are—

   (a)   that the beneficiary would be treated for the purposes of Part IX of this Act as having the child living with him; or

   (b)   that the requisite contributions are being made to the cost of providing for the child.

(6)   The condition specified in subsection (5)(b) above is to be treated as satisfied if, but only if—

   (a)   such contributions are being made at a weekly rate not less than the amount referred to in subsection (4) above—

     (i)   by the beneficiary; or

     (ii)   where the beneficiary is one of two spouses residing together, by them together; and

   (b)   except in prescribed cases, the contributions are over and above those required for the purpose of satisfying section 143(1)(b) below.

(7)   A guardian's allowance in respect of a child shall be payable at the weekly rate specified in Schedule 4, Part III, paragraph 5.

(8)   Regulations —

   (a)   may modify subsection (2) or (3) above in relation to cases in which a child has been adopted or is illegitimate, or the marriage of a child's parents has been terminated by divorce;

   (b)   shall prescribe the circumstances in which a person is to be treated for the purposes of this section as being in prison (by reference to his undergoing a sentence of imprisonment for life or of a prescribed minimum duration, or to his being in legal custody in prescribed circumstances); and

   (c)   may, for cases where entitlement to a guardian's allowance is established by reference to a person being in prison, provide—

     (i)   for requiring him to pay to the National Insurance Fund sums paid by way of a guardian's allowance;

     (ii)   for suspending payment of an allowance where a conviction, sentence or order of a court is subject to appeal, and for matters arising from the decision of an appeal;

     (iii)   for reducing the rate of an allowance in cases where the person in prison contributes to the cost of providing for the child.

(9)   Where a husband and wife are residing together and, apart from this subsection, they would each be entitled to a guardian's allowance in respect of the same child, only the wife shall be entitled, but payment may be made either to her or to him unless she elects in the prescribed manner that payment is not to be made to him.

(10)   Subject to subsection (11) below, no person shall be entitled to a guardian's allowance in respect of a child of which he or she is the parent.

(11)   Where a person—

    (a)   has adopted a child; and

    (b)   was entitled to guardian's allowance in respect of the child immediately before the adoption,

subsection (10) above shall not terminate his entitlement.

## PART IV
## INCREASES FOR DEPENDANTS

*Miscellaneous*

### 93   Dependency increases on termination of employment after period of entitlement to disability working allowance

Where—

    [(a)   a person becomes entitled—

        (i)   to the higher rate of short-term incapacity benefit, or to long-term incapacity benefit, by virtue of section 30C(5) or (6) or section 42 above, or

        (ii)   to severe disablement allowance by virtue of section 68(10) or (10A) above; and]

    (b)   when he was last entitled to that [benefit or] allowance, it was increased in respect of a dependant by virtue of—

        (i)   regulation 8(6) of the Social Security Benefit (Dependency) Regulations 1977;

        (ii)   regulation 2 of the Social Security (Savings for Existing Beneficiaries) Regulations 1984;

        (iii)   regulation 3 of the Social Security Benefit (Dependency) Amendment Regulations 1984; or

        (iv)   regulation 4 of the Social Security Benefit (Dependency and Computation of Earnings) Amendment Regulations 1989,

for the purpose of determining whether his [benefit or] allowance should be increased by virtue of that regulation for any period beginning with the day on which he again becomes entitled to his [benefit or] allowance, the increase in respect of that dependant shall be treated as having been payable to him on each day between the last day on which his [benefit or] allowance was previously payable and the day on which he again becomes entitled to it.

---

NOTES

    Words in square brackets substituted by the Social Security (Incapacity for Work) Act 1994, s 11(1), Sch 1, Pt I, para 28.

---

# PART V
# BENEFIT FOR INDUSTRIAL INJURIES

*General provisions*

## 94  Right to industrial injuries benefit

(1)  Industrial injuries benefit shall be payable where an employed earner suffers personal injury caused after 4th July 1948 by accident arising out of and in the course of his employment, being employed earner's employment.

(2)  Industrial injuries benefit consists of the following benefits—

    (a)  disablement benefit payable in accordance with sections 103 to 105 below, paragraphs 2 and 3 of Schedule 7 below and Parts II and III of that Schedule;

    (b)  reduced earnings allowance payable in accordance with Part IV;

    (c)  retirement allowance payable in accordance with Part V; and

    (d)  industrial death benefit, payable in accordance with Part VI.

(3)  For the purposes of industrial injuries benefit an accident arising in the course of an employed earner's employment shall be taken, in the absence of evidence to the contrary, also to have arisen out of that employment.

(4)  Regulations may make provision as to the day which, in the case of night workers and other special cases, is to be treated for the purposes of industrial injuries benefit as the day of the accident.

(5)  Subject to sections 117, 119 and 120 below, industrial injuries benefit shall not be payable in respect of an accident happening while the earner is outside Great Britain.

(6)  In the following provisions of this Part of this Act "work" in the contexts "incapable of work" and "incapacity for work" means work which the person in question can be reasonably expected to do.

## 95  Relevant employments

(1)  In section 94 above, this section and sections 98 to 109 below "employed earner's employment" shall be taken to include any employment by virtue of which a person is, or is treated by regulations as being for the purposes of industrial injuries benefit, an employed earner.

(2)  Regulations may provide that any prescribed employment shall not be treated for the purposes of industrial injuries benefit as employed earner's employment notwithstanding that it would be so treated apart from the regulations.

(3)  For the purposes of the provisions of this Act mentioned in subsection (1) above an employment shall be an employed earner's employment in relation to an accident if (and only if) it is, or is treated by regulations as being, such an employment when the accident occurs.

(4)  Any reference in the industrial injuries and diseases provisions to an "employed earner" or "employed earner's employment" is to be construed, in relation to any time before 6th April 1975, as a reference respectively to an "insured person" or "insurable employment" within the meaning of the provisions relating to industrial injuries and diseases which were in force at that time.

(5)  In subsection (4) above "the industrial injuries and diseases provisions" means—

    (a)  this section and sections 96 to 110 below;

    (b)  any other provisions of this Act so far as they relate to those sections; and

    (c)  any provisions of the Administration Act so far as they so relate.

NOTES

Administration Act: Social Security Administration Act 1992.

## 96 Persons treated as employers for certain purposes

In relation to—

    (a) a person who is an employed earner for the purposes of this Part of this Act otherwise than by virtue of a contract of service or apprenticeship; or

    (b) any other employed earner—

        (i) who is employed for the purpose of any game or recreation and is engaged or paid through a club; or

        (ii) in whose case it appears to the Secretary of State there is special difficulty in the application of all or any of the provisions of this Part of this Act relating to employers,

regulations may provide for a prescribed person to be treated in respect of industrial injuries benefit and its administration as the earner's employer.

## 97 Accidents in course of illegal employments

(1) Subsection (2) below has effect in any case where—

    (a) a claim is made for industrial injuries benefit in respect of an accident, or of a prescribed disease or injury; or

    (b) an application is made under section 44 of the Administration Act for a declaration that an accident was an industrial accident, or for a corresponding declaration as to a prescribed disease or injury.

(2) The Secretary of State may direct that the relevant employment shall, in relation to that accident, disease or injury, be treated as having been employed earner's employment notwithstanding that by reason of a contravention of, or non-compliance with, some provision contained in or having effect under an enactment passed for the protection of employed persons or any class of employed persons, either—

    (a) the contract purporting to govern the employment was void; or

    (b) the employed person was not lawfully employed in the relevant employment at the time when, or in the place where, the accident happened or the disease or injury was contracted or received.

(3) In subsection (2) above "relevant employment" means—

    (a) in relation to an accident, the employment out of and in the course of which the accident arises; and

    (b) in relation to a prescribed disease or injury, the employment to the nature of which the disease or injury is due.

NOTES

Administration Act: Social Security Administration Act 1992.

## 98 Earner acting in breach of regulations, etc

An accident shall be taken to arise out of and in the course of an employed earner's employment, notwithstanding that he is at the time of the accident acting in contravention of any statutory or other regulations applicable to his employment, or of any orders given by or on behalf of his employer, or that he is acting without instructions from his employer, if—

(a) the accident would have been taken so to have arisen had the act not been done in contravention of any such regulations or orders, or without such instructions, as the case may be; and

(b) the act is done for the purposes of and in connection with the employer's trade or business.

## 99 Earner travelling in employer's transport

(1) An accident happening while an employed earner is, with the express or implied permission of his employer, travelling as a passenger by any vehicle to or from his place of work shall, notwithstanding that he is under no obligation to his employer to travel by that vehicle, be taken to arise out of and in the course of his employment if—

(a) the accident would have been taken so to have arisen had he been under such an obligation; and

(b) at the time of the accident, the vehicle—

(i) is being operated by or on behalf of his employer or some other person by whom it is provided in pursuance of arrangements made with his employer; and

(ii) is not being operated in the ordinary course of a public transport service,

(2) In this section references to a vehicle include a ship, vessel, hovercraft or aircraft.

## 100 Accidents happening while meeting emergency

An accident happening to an employed earner in or about any premises at which he is for the time being employed for the purposes of his employer's trade or business shall be taken to arise out of and in the course of his employment if it happens while he is taking steps, on an actual or supposed emergency at those premises, to rescue, succour or protect persons who are, or are thought to be or possibly to be, injured or imperilled, or to avert or minimise serious damage to property.

## 101 Accident caused by another's misconduct etc

An accident happening after 19th December 1961 shall be treated for the purposes of industrial injuries benefit, where it would not apart from this section be so treated, as arising out of an employed earner's employment if—

(a) the accident arises in the course of the employment; and

(b) the accident either is caused—

(i) by another person's misconduct, skylarking or negligence, or

(ii) by steps taken in consequence of any such misconduct, skylarking or negligence, or

(iii) by the behaviour or presence of an animal (including a bird, fish or insect),

or is caused by or consists in the employed earner being struck by any object or by lightning; and

(c) the employed earner did not directly or indirectly induce or contribute to the happening of the accident by his conduct outside the employment or by any act not incidental to the employment.

*Disablement pension*

## 103 Disablement pension

(1) Subject to the provisions of this section, an employed earner shall be entitled to disablement pension if he suffers as the result of the relevant accident from loss of physical or mental faculty such that the assessed extent of the resulting disablement amounts to not less than 14 per cent. or, on a claim made before 1st October 1986, 20 per cent.

(2)    In the determination of the extent of an employed earner's disablement for the purposes of this section there may be added to the percentage of the disablement resulting from the relevant accident the assessed percentage of any present disablement of his—

   (a)   which resulted from any other accident after 4th July 1948 arising out of and in the course of his employment, being employed earner's employment, and

   (b)   in respect of which a disablement gratuity was not paid to him after a final assessment of his disablement,

(as well as any percentage which may be so added in accordance with regulations under subsection (2) of section 109 below made by virtue of subsection (4)(b) of that section).

(3)    Subject to subsection (4) below, where the assessment of disablement is a percentage between 20 and 100 which is not a multiple of 10, it shall be treated—

   (a)   if it is a multiple of 5, as being the next higher percentage which is a multiple of 10, and

   (b)   if it is not a multiple of 5, as being the nearest percentage which is a multiple of 10,

and where the assessment of disablement on a claim made on or after 1st October 1986 is less than 20 per cent., but not less than 14 per cent.,it shall be treated as 20 per cent.

(4)    Where subsection (2) above applies, subsection (3) above shall have effect in relation to the aggregate percentage and not in relation to any percentage forming part of the aggregate.

(5)    In this Part of this Act "assessed", in relation to the extent of any disablement, means assessed in accordance with Schedule 6 to this Act; and for the purposes of that Schedule there shall be taken to be no relevant loss of faculty when the extent of the resulting disablement, if so assessed, would not amount to 1 per cent.

(6)    A person shall not be entitled to a disablement pension until after the expiry of the period of 90 days (disregarding Sundays) beginning with the day of the relevant accident.

(7)    Subject to subsection (8) below, where disablement pension is payable for a period, it shall be paid at the appropriate weekly rate specified in Schedule 4, Part V, paragraph 1.

(8)    Where the period referred to in subsection (7) above is limited by reference to a definite date, the pension shall cease on the death of the beneficiary before that date.

# PART VII
# INCOME-RELATED BENEFITS

*Income support*

## 124   Income support

(1)    A person in Great Britain is entitled to income support if—

   [(a)   he is of or over the age of 16;]

   (b)   he has no income or his income does not exceed the applicable amount;

   (c)   he is not engaged in remunerative work and, if he is a member of a married or unmarried couple, the other member is not so engaged; . . .

[(d) except in such circumstances as may be prescribed, he is not receiving relevant education;]

[(e) he falls within a prescribed category of person; and

(f) he is not entitled to a jobseeker's allowance and, if he is a member of a married or unmarried couple, the other member of the couple is not entitled to an income-based jobseeker's allowance.]

(2), (3). . .

(4) Subject to subsection (5) below, where a person is entitled to income support, then—

(a) if he has no income, the amount shall be the applicable amount; and

(b) if he has income, the amount shall be the difference between his income and the applicable amount.

(5) Where a person is entitled to income support for a period to which this subsection applies, the amount payable for that period shall be calculated in such manner as may be prescribed.

(6) Subsection (5) above applies—

(a) to a period of less than a week which is the whole period for which income support is payable; and

(b) to any other period of less than a week for which it is payable.

NOTES

Sub-s (1): paras (a), (d) substituted, word omitted from para (c) repealed, and paras (e), (f), added, by the Jobseekers Act 1995, s 41(4), (5), Sch 2, para 30, Sch 3.

Sub-ss (2), (3): repealed by the Jobseekers Act 1995, s 41(5), Sch 3.

## 126 Trade disputes

(1) This section applies to a person, other than a child or a person of a prescribed description—

(a) who [is prevented from being entitled to a jobseeker's allowance by section 14 of the Jobseekers Act 1995 (trade disputes)]; or

(b) who would be so [prevented] if otherwise entitled to that benefit,

except during any period shown by the person to be a period of incapacity for work . . . or to be within the maternity period.

(2) In subsection (1) above "the maternity period" means the period commencing at the beginning of the 6th week before the expected week of confinement and ending at the end of the 7th week after the week in which confinement takes place.

(3) For the purpose of calculating income support—

(a) so long as this section applies to a person who is not a member of a family, the applicable amount shall be disregarded;

(b) so long as it applies to a person who is a member of a family but is not a member of a married or unmarried couple, the portion of the applicable amount which is included in respect of him shall be disregarded;

(c) so long as it applies to one of the members of a married or unmarried couple—

(i) if the applicable amount consists only of an amount in respect of them, it shall be reduced to one half; and

(ii) if it includes other amounts, the portion of it which is included in respect of them shall be reduced to one-half and any further portion of it which is included in respect of the member of the couple to whom this section applies shall be disregarded;

(d) so long as it applies to both the members of a married or unmarried couple—

(i) if neither of them is responsible for a child or person of a prescribed description who is a member of the same household, the applicable amount shall be disregarded; and

(ii) in any other case, the portion of the applicable amount which is included in respect of them and any further portion of it which is included in respect of either of them shall be disregarded.

(4) Where a reduction under subsection (3)(c) above would not produce a sum which is a multiple of 5p, the reduction shall be to the nearest lower sum which is such a multiple.

(5) Where this section applies to a person for any period, then, except so far as regulations provide otherwise—

(a) in calculating the entitlement to income support of that person or a member of his family the following shall be treated as his income and shall not be disregarded—

(i) any payment which he or a member of his family receives or is entitled to obtain by reason of the person to whom this section applies being without employment for that period; and

(ii) without prejudice to the generality of sub-paragraph (i) above, any amount which becomes or would on an application duly made become available to him in that period by way of repayment of income tax deducted from his emoluments in pursuance of section 203 of the Income and Corporation Taxes Act 1988 (PAYE); and

(b) any payment by way of income support for that period or any part of it which apart from this paragraph would be made to him, or to a person whose applicable amount is aggregated with his—

(i) shall not be made if the weekly rate of payment is equal to or less than the relevant sum; or

(ii) if it is more than the relevant sum, shall be at a weekly rate equal to the difference.

(6) In respect of any period less than a week, subsection (5) above shall have effect subject to such modifications as may be prescribed.

(7) Subject to subsection (8) below, "the relevant sum" for the purposes of subsection (5) above shall be [£26.50].

(8) If an order under section 150 of the Administration Act (annual up-rating) has the effect of increasing payments of income support, from the time when the order comes into force there shall be substituted, in subsection (5)(b) above, for the references to the sum for the time being mentioned in it references to a sum arrived at by—

(a) increasing that sum by the percentage by which the personal allowance under paragraph 1(1) of Part I of Schedule 2 to the Income Support (General) Regulations 1987 for a single person aged not less than 25 has been increased by the order; and

(b) if the sum as so increased is not a multiple of 50p, disregarding the remainder if it is 25p and, if it is not, rounding it up or down to the nearest 50p,

and the order shall state the substituted sum.

NOTES
Sub-s (1): words in square brackets substituted by the Jobseekers Act 1995, s 41(4), Sch 2, para 31; words omitted repealed by the Social Security (Incapacity for Work) Act 1994, s 11, Sch 1, Pt I, para 31, Sch 2.
Sub-s (7): sum in square brackets substituted by the Social Security Benefits Up-rating Order 1997, SI 1997/543, art 20.
Administration Act: Social Security Administration Act 1992.

## 127 Effect of return to work

If a person returns to work with the same employer after a period during which section 126 above applies to him, and whether or not his return is before the end of any stoppage of work in relation to which he is or would be [prevented from being entitled to a jobseeker's allowance]—

(a) that section shall cease to apply to him at the commencement of the day on which he returns to work; and

(b) until the end of the period of 15 days beginning with that day, section 124(1) above shall have effect in relation to him as if the following paragraph were substituted for paragraph (c)—

"(c) in the case of a member of a married or unmarried couple, the other member is not engaged in remunerative work; and"; and

(c) any sum paid by way of income support for that period of 15 days to him or, where he is a member of a married or unmarried couple, to the other member of that couple, shall be recoverable in accordance with the regulations from the person to whom it was paid or from any prescribed person or, where the person to whom it was paid is a member of a married or unmarried couple, from the other member of the couple.

NOTES
Words in square brackets substituted by the Jobseekers Act 1995, s 41(4), Sch 2, para 32.

*Family credit*

## 128 Family credit

(1) Subject to regulations under section 5(1)(a) of the Administration Act, a person in Great Britain is entitled to family credit if, when the claim for it is made or is treated as made—

(a) his income—

(i) does not exceed the amount which is the applicable amount at such date as may be prescribed; or

(ii) exceeds it, but only by such an amount that there is an amount remaining if the deduction for which subsection (2)(b) below provides is made;

(b) he or, if he is a member of a married or unmarried couple, he or the other member of the couple, is engaged and normally engaged in remunerative work;

(c) except in such circumstances as may be prescribed, neither he nor any member of his family is entitled to a disability working allowance; and

(d) he or, if he is a member of a married or unmarried couple, he or the other member, is responsible for a member of the same household who is a child or a person of a prescribed description.

(2) Where a person is entitled to family credit, then—

    (a) if his income does not exceed the amount which is the applicable amount at the date prescribed under subsection (1)(a)(i) above, the amount of the family credit shall be the amount which is the appropriate maximum family credit in his case; and

    (b) if his income exceeds the amount which is the applicable amount at that date, the amount of the family credit shall be what remains after the deduction from the appropriate maximum family credit of a prescribed percentage of the excess of his income over the applicable amount.

(3) Family credit shall be payable for a period of 26 weeks or such other period as may be prescribed and, subject to regulations, an award of family credit and the rate at which it is payable shall not be affected by any change of circumstances during that period or by any order under section 150 of the Administration Act.

(4) Regulations may provide that an award of family credit shall terminate—

    (a) if a person who was a member of the family at the date of the claim becomes a member of another family and some member of that family is entitled to family credit; or

    (b) if income support[, an income-based jobseeker's allowance] or a disability working allowance becomes payable in respect of a person who was a member of the family at the date of the claim for family credit.

(5) Regulations shall prescribe the manner in which the appropriate maximum family credit is to be determined in any case.

(6) The provisions of this Act relating to family credit apply in relation to persons employed by or under the Crown as they apply in relation to persons employed otherwise than by or under the Crown.

NOTES

    Sub-s (4): words in square brackets in para (b) inserted by the Jobseekers Act 1995, s 41(4), Sch 2, para 33.

    Administration Act: Social Security Administration Act 1992.

*Disability working allowance*

## 129 Disability working allowance

(1) A person in Great Britain who has attained the age of 16 and [qualifies under subsection (2) or (2A) below] is entitled to a disability working allowance if, when the claim for it is made or is treated as made—

    (a) he is engaged and normally engaged in remunerative work;

    (b) he has a physical or mental disability which puts him at a disadvantage in getting a job;

    (c) his income—

        (i) does not exceed the amount which is the applicable amount at such date as may be prescribed; or

        (ii) exceeds it, but only by such an amount that there is an amount remaining if the deduction for which subsection (5)(b) below provides is made; and

    (d) except in such circumstances as may be prescribed, neither he nor, if he has a family, any member of it, is entitled to family credit.

(2)  Subject to subsection (4) below, a person qualifies under this subsection if—

(a)  for one or more of the 56 days immediately preceding the date when the claim for a disability working allowance is made or is treated as made there was payable to him one or more of the following—

[(i)  the higher rate of short-term incapacity benefit or long-term incapacity benefit;]

(ii)  a severe disablement allowance;

(iii)  income support[, an income-based jobseeker's allowance], housing benefit or [council tax benefit],

or a corresponding benefit under any enactment having effect in Northern Ireland;

(b)  when the claim for a disability working allowance is made or is treated as made, there is payable to him one or more of the following—

(i)  an attendance allowance;

(ii)  a disability living allowance;

(iii)  an increase of disablement pension under section 104 above;

(iv)  an analogous pension increase under a war pension scheme or an industrial injuries scheme,

or a corresponding benefit under any enactment having effect in Northern Ireland; or

(c)  when the claim for a disability working allowance is made or is treated as made, he has an invalid carriage or other vehicle provided by the Secretary of State under section 5(2)(a) of the National Health Service Act 1977 and Schedule 2 to that Act or under section 46 of the National Health Service (Scotland) Act 1978 or provided under Article 30(1) of the Health and Personal Social Services (Northern Ireland) Order 1972.

[(2A) A person qualifies under this subsection if—

(a)  on one or more of the 56 days immediately preceding the date when the claim for a disability working allowance is made or is treated as made he was engaged in training for work and

(b)  a relevant benefit was payable to him for one or more of the 56 days immediately preceding—

(i)  the first day of training for work falling within the 56 days mentioned in paragraph (a) above or

(ii)  an earlier day of training for work which formed part of the same period of training for work as that day.

(2B)  For the purposes of subsection (2A) above—

(a)  the following are relevant benefits—

(i)  the higher rate of short-term incapacity benefit

(ii)  long-term incapacity benefit

(iii)  a severe disablement allowance,

or a corresponding benefit under any enactment having effect in Northern Ireland;

(b)  "training for work" means training for work in pursuance of arrangements made under section 2(1) of the Employment and Training Act 1973 or section 2(3) of the Enterprise and New Towns (Scotland) Act 1990 or training of such other description as may be prescribed; and

(c)  a period of training for work means a series of consecutive days of training for work, there being disregarded for this purpose such days as may be prescribed.]

(3)    For the purposes of subsection (1) above a person has a disability which puts him at a disadvantage in getting a job only if he satisfies prescribed conditions or prescribed circumstances exist in relation to him.

(4)    If the only benefit mentioned in paragraph (a) of subsection (2) above which is payable to a person as there mentioned is—
    (a)    a benefit mentioned in sub-paragraph (iii) of that paragraph; or
    (b)    a corresponding benefit under any enactment having effect in Northern Ireland,

he only qualifies under that subsection in prescribed circumstances.

(5)    Where a person is entitled to a disability working allowance, then—
    (a)    if his income does not exceed the amount which is the applicable amount at the date prescribed under subsection (1)(c)(i) above, the amount of the disability working allowance shall be the amount which is the appropriate maximum disability working allowance in his case; and
    (b)    if his income exceeds that amount, the amount of the disability working allowance shall be what remains after the deduction from the appropriate maximum disability working allowance of a prescribed percentage of the excess of his income over that amount.

(6)    A disability working allowance shall be payable for a period of 26 weeks or such other period as may be prescribed and, subject to regulations, an award of a disability working allowance and the rate at which it is payable shall not be affected by any change of circumstances during that period or by any order under section 150 of the Administration Act.

(7)    Regulations may provide that an award of a disability working allowance to a person shall terminate if—
    (a)    a disability working allowance becomes payable in respect of some other person who was a member of his family at the date of his claim for a disability working allowance; or
    (b)    income support[, an income-based jobseeker's allowance] or family credit becomes payable in respect of a person who was a member of the family at that date.

(8)    Regulations shall prescribe the manner in which the appropriate maximum disability working allowance is to be determined in any case.

(9)    The provisions of this Act relating to disability working allowance apply in relation to persons employed by or under the Crown as they apply in relation to persons employed otherwise than by or under the Crown.

NOTES

    Commencement: 13 April 1995 (sub-s (2A), sub-s (2B) certain purposes); 18 November 1994 (sub-s (2B), remaining purposes); 1 July 1992 (remainder).

    Sub-s (1): words in square brackets substituted by the Social Security (Incapacity for Work) Act 1994, s 10(1), (2).

    Sub-s (2): sub-para (a)(i) substituted by the Social Security (Incapacity for Work) Act 1994, s 11(1), Sch 1, Pt I, para 32; words in first pair of square brackets in sub-para (a)(iii) inserted by the Jobseekers Act 1995, s 41(4), Sch 2, para 34, words in second pair of square brackets substituted by the Local Government Finance Act 1992, s 103, Sch 9, para 2.

    Sub-ss (2A), (2B): inserted by the Social Security (Incapacity for Work) Act 1994, s 10(1), (3).

    Sub-s (7): words in square brackets in para (b) inserted by the Jobseekers Act 1995, s 41(4), Sch 2, para 34.

    Administration Act: Social Security Administration Act 1992.

*Housing benefit*

## 130 Housing benefit

(1) A person is entitled to housing benefit if—

    (a) he is liable to make payments in respect of a dwelling in Great Britain which he occupies as his home;

    (b) there is an appropriate maximum housing benefit in his case; and

    (c) either—

        (i) he has no income or his income does not exceed the applicable amount; or

        (ii) his income exceeds that amount, but only by so much that there is an amount remaining if the deduction for which subsection (3)(b) below provides is made.

(2) In subsection (1) above "payments in respect of a dwelling" means such payments as may be prescribed, but the power to prescribe payments does not include power to prescribe

    [(a) payments to a billing or [local authority in Scotland] in respect of council tax; or

    (b) mortgage payments, or, in relation to Scotland, payments under heritable securities].

(3) Where a person is entitled to housing benefit, then—

    (a) if he has no income or his income does not exceed the applicable amount, the amount of the housing benefit shall be the amount which is the appropriate maximum housing benefit in his case; and

    (b) if his income exceeds the applicable amount, the amount of the housing benefit shall be what remains after the deduction from the appropriate maximum housing benefit of prescribed percentages of the excess of his income over the applicable amount.

(4) Regulations shall prescribe the manner in which the appropriate maximum housing benefit is to be determined in any case.

(5) . . .

---

NOTES

    Sub-s (2): words in outer pair of square brackets substituted by the Local Government Finance Act 1992, s 103, Sch 9, para 3; words in inner pair of square brackets substituted by the Local Government etc (Scotland) Act 1994, s 180(1), Sch 13, para 174(1), (4).

    Sub-s (5): repealed with savings by the Housing Act 1996, s 227, Sch 19, Pt VI.

---

# PART VIII
# THE SOCIAL FUND

## 140 Principles of determination

(1) In determining whether to make an award to the applicant òr the amount or value to be awarded a social fund officer shall have regard, subject to subsection (2) below, to all the circumstances of the case and, in particular—

    (a) the nature, extent and urgency of the need;

    (b) the existence of resources from which the need may be met;

    (c) the possibility that some other person or body may wholly or partly meet it;

(d) where the payment is repayable, the likelihood of repayment and the time within which repayment is likely;

(e) any relevant allocation under section 168(1) to (4) of the Administration Act.

(2) A social fund officer shall determine any question in accordance with any general directions issued by the Secretary of State and in determining any question shall take account of any general guidance issued by him.

(3) Without prejudice to the generality of subsection (2) above, the Secretary of State may issue directions under that subsection for the purpose of securing that a social fund officer or group of social fund officers shall not in any specified period make awards of any specified description which in the aggregate exceed the amount, or a specified portion of the amount, allocated to that officer or group of officers under section 168(1) to (4) of the Administration Act for payments under awards of that description in that period.

(4) Without prejudice to the generality of subsection (2) above, the power to issue general directions conferred on the Secretary of State by that subsection includes power to direct—

(a) that in circumstances specified in the direction a social fund officer shall not determine an application and, without prejudice to the generality of this paragraph, that a social fund officer shall not determine an application which is made before the end of a specified period after the making of an application by the same person for a payment such as is mentioned in section 138(1)(b) above to meet the same need and without there having been any relevant change of circumstances since the previous application;

(b) that for a category of need specified in the direction a social fund officer shall not award less than an amount specified in the direction;

(c) that for a category of need specified in the direction a social fund officer shall not award more than an amount so specified;

(d) that payments to meet a category of need specified in the direction shall in all cases or in no case be made by instalments;

(e) that payments to meet a category of need specified in the direction shall in all cases or in no case be repayable; and

(f) that a payment such as is mentioned in section 138(1)(b) above shall only be awarded to a person if either—

(i) he is in receipt of a benefit which is specified in the direction and the circumstances are such as are so specified; or

(ii) in a case where the conditions specified in sub-paragraph (i) above are not satisfied, the circumstances are such as are specified in the direction,

and the power to issue general guidance conferred on him by that subsection includes power to give social fund officers guidance as to any matter to which directions under that subsection may relate.

(5) In determining a question a social fund officer shall take account (subject to any directions or guidance issued by the Secretary of State under this section) of any guidance issued by the social fund officer nominated for his area under section 64 of the Administration Act.

NOTES

Administration Act: Social Security Administration Act 1992.

# PART IX
# CHILD BENEFIT

### 143 Meaning of "person responsible for child"

(1)   For the purposes of this Part of this Act a person shall be treated as responsible for a child in any week if—

(a)  he has the child living with him in that week; or

(b)  he is contributing to the cost of providing for the child at a weekly rate which is not less than the weekly rate of child benefit payable in respect of the child for that week.

(2)   Where a person has had a child living with him at some time before a particular week he shall be treated for the purposes of this section as having the child living with him in that week notwithstanding their absence from one another unless, in the 16 weeks preceding that week, they were absent from one another for more than 56 days not counting any day which is to be disregarded under subsection (3) below.

(3)   Subject to subsection (4) below, a day of absence shall be disregarded for the purposes of subsection (2) above if it is due solely to the child's—

(a)  receiving full-time education by attendance at a recognised educational establishment;

(b)  undergoing medical or other treatment as an in-patient in a hospital or similar institution; or

(c)  being, in such circumstances as may be prescribed, in residential accommodation pursuant to arrangements made under—

(i)  *section 21 of the National Assistance Act 1948;*

(ii)  *the Children Act 1989; or*

(iii)  *the Social Work (Scotland) Act 1968.*

(4)   The number of days that may be disregarded by virtue of subsection (3)(b) or   (c) above in the case of any child shall not exceed such number as may be prescribed unless the person claiming to be responsible for the child regularly incurs expenditure in respect of the child.

(5)   Regulations may prescribe the circumstances in which a person is or is not to be treated—

(a)  as contributing to the cost of providing for a child as required by subsection (1)(b) above; or

(b)  as regularly incurring expenditure in respect of a child as required by subsection (4) above;

and such regulations may in particular make provision whereby a contribution made or expenditure incurred by two or more persons is to be treated as made or incurred by one of them or whereby a contribution made or expenditure incurred by one of two spouses residing together is to be treated as made or incurred by the other.

---

NOTES

Sub-s (3): words in italics in para (c) temporarily substituted by virtue of the Social Security (Consequential Provisions) Act 1992, s 6, Sch 4, para 5, until a day appointed under Sch 4, para 1(3) thereof, as follows—

"(i)  paragraph 2 of Schedule 8 to the National Health Service Act 1977;

(ii)  the Children Act 1989; or

(iii)  section 37 of the National Health Service (Scotland) Act 1978.".

---

**144  Exclusions and priority**

(1)  Regulations may provide that child benefit shall not be payable by virtue—

    (a)  of paragraph (b) of section 142(1) above and regulations made under that paragraph; or

    (b)  of paragraph (c) of that subsection,

in such cases as may be prescribed.

(2)  Schedule 9 to this Act shall have effect for excluding entitlement to child benefit in other cases.

(3)  Where, apart from this subsection, two or more persons would be entitled to child benefit in respect of the same child for the same week, one of them only shall be entitled; and the question which of them is entitled shall be determined in accordance with Schedule 10 to this Act.

**145  Rate of child benefit**

(1)  Child benefit shall be payable at such weekly rate as may be prescribed.

(2)  Different rates may be prescribed in relation to different cases, whether by reference to the age of the child in respect of whom the benefit is payable or otherwise.

(3)  The power to prescribe different rates under subsection (2) above shall be exercised so as to bring different rates into force on such day as the Secretary of State may by order specify.

(4)  No rate prescribed in place of a rate previously in force shall be lower than the rate that it replaces.

(5)  Regulations under this section shall be made by the Secretary of State in conjunction with the Treasury.

(6)  An order under subsection (3) above may be varied or revoked at any time before the date specified thereby.

(7)  An order under that subsection shall be laid before Parliament after being made.

**146  Persons outside Great Britain**

(1)  Regulations may modify the provisions of this Part of this Act in their application to persons who are or have been outside Great Britain at any prescribed time or in any prescribed circumstances.

(2)  Subject to any regulations under subsection (1) above, no child benefit shall be payable in respect of a child for any week unless—

    (a)  he is in Great Britain in that week; and

    (b)  either he or at least one of his parents has been in Great Britain for more than 182 days in the 52 weeks preceding that week.

(3)  Subject to any regulations under subsection (1) above, no person shall be entitled to child benefit for any week unless—

    (a)  he is in Great Britain in that week; and

    (b)  he has been in Great Britain for more than 182 days in the 52 weeks preceding that week.

**[146A   Persons subject to immigration control**

No person subject to immigration control within the meaning of the Asylum and Immigration Act 1996 shall be entitled to child benefit for any week unless he satisfies prescribed conditions.]

NOTES

Commencement: 19 August 1996 (certain purposes); 7 October 1996 (otherwise).
Inserted by the Asylum and Immigration Act 1996, s 10.

# PART XI
# STATUTORY SICK PAY

*The qualifying conditions*

## 152   Period of incapacity for work

(1)   The first condition is that the day in question forms part of a period of incapacity for work.

(2)   In this Part of this Act "period of incapacity for work" means any period of four or more consecutive days, each of which is a day of incapacity for work in relation to the contract of service in question.

(3)   Any two periods of incapacity for work which are separated by a period of not more than 8 weeks shall be treated as a single period of incapacity for work.

(4)   The Secretary of State may by regulations direct that a larger number of weeks specified in the regulations shall be substituted for the number of weeks for the time being specified in subsection (3) above.

(5)   No day of the week shall be disregarded in calculating any period of consecutive days for the purposes of this section.

(6)   A day may be a day of incapacity for work in relation to a contract of service, and so form part of a period of incapacity for work, notwithstanding that—

(a)   it falls before the making of the contract or after the contract expires or is brought to an end; or

(b)   it is not a day on which the employee concerned would be required by that contract to be available for work.

## 153   Period of entitlement

(1)   The second condition is that the day in question falls within a period which is, as between the employee and his employer, a period of entitlement.

(2)   For the purposes of this Part of this Act a period of entitlement, as between an employee and his employer, is a period beginning with the commencement of a period of incapacity for work and ending with whichever of the following first occurs—

(a)   the termination of that period of incapacity for work;

(b)   the day on which the employee reaches, as against the employer concerned, his maximum entitlement to statutory sick pay (determined in accordance with section 155 below);

(c)   the day on which the employee's contract of service with the employer concerned expires or is brought to an end;

(d)   in the case of an employee who is, or has been, pregnant, the day immediately preceding the beginning of the disqualifying period.

(3)    Schedule 11 to this Act has effect for the purpose of specifying circumstances in which a period of entitlement does not arise in relation to a particular period of incapacity for work.

(4)    A period of entitlement as between an employee and an employer of his may also be, or form part of, a period of entitlement as between him and another employer of his.

(5)    The Secretary of State may by regulations—

(a)   specify circumstances in which, for the purpose of determining whether an employee's maximum entitlement to statutory sick pay has been reached in a period of entitlement as between him and an employer of his, days falling within a previous period of entitlement as between the employee and any person who is or has in the past been an employer of his are to be counted; and

(b)   direct that in prescribed circumstances an employer shall provide a person who is about to leave his employment, or who has been employed by him in the past, with a statement in the prescribed form containing such information as may be prescribed in relation to any entitlement of the employee to statutory sick pay.

(6)    Regulations may provide, in relation to prescribed cases, for a period of entitlement to end otherwise than in accordance with subsection (2) above.

(7)    In a case where the employee's contract of service first takes effect on a day which falls within a period of incapacity for work, the period of entitlement begins with that day.

(8)    In a case where the employee's contract of service first takes effect between two periods of incapacity for work which by virtue of section 152(3) above are treated as one, the period of entitlement begins with the first day of the second of those periods.

(9)    In any case where, otherwise than by virtue of section 6(1)(b) above, an employee's earnings under a contract of service in respect of the day on which the contract takes effect do not attract a liability to pay secondary Class 1 contributions, subsections (7) and (8) above shall have effect as if for any reference to the contract first taking effect there were substituted a reference to the first day in respect of which the employee's earnings attract such a liability.

(10)  Regulations shall make provision as to an employer's liability under this Part of this Act to pay statutory sick pay to an employee in any case where the employer's contract of service with that employee has been brought to an end by the employer solely, or mainly, for the purpose of avoiding liability for statutory sick pay.

(11)  Subsection (2)(d) above does not apply in relation to an employee who has been pregnant if her pregnancy terminated, before the beginning of the disqualifying period, otherwise than by confinement.

(12)  In this section—

"confinement" is to be construed in accordance with section 171(1) below;

"disqualifying period" means—

(a)   in relation to a woman entitled to statutory maternity pay, the maternity pay period; and

(b)   in relation to a woman entitled to maternity allowance, the maternity allowance period;

"maternity allowance period" has the meaning assigned to it by section 35(2) above, and

"maternity pay period" has the meaning assigned to it by section 165(1) below.

**154   Qualifying days**

(1)   The third condition is that the day in question is a qualifying day.

(2)   The days which are for the purposes of this Part of this Act to be qualifying days as between an employee and an employer of his (that is to say, those days of the week on which he is required by his contract of service with that employer to be available for work or which are chosen to reflect the terms of that contract) shall be such day or days as may, subject to regulations, be agreed between the employee and his employer or, failing such agreement, determined in accordance with regulations.

(3)   In any case where qualifying days are determined by agreement between an employee and his employer there shall, in each week (beginning with Sunday), be at least one qualifying day.

(4)   A day which is a qualifying day as between an employee and an employer of his may also be a qualifying day as between him and another employer of his.

*Limitations on entitlement, etc*

**155   Limitations on entitlement**

(1)   Statutory sick pay shall not be payable for the first three qualifying days in any period of entitlement.

(2)   An employee shall not be entitled, as against any one employer, to an aggregate amount of statutory sick pay in respect of any one period of entitlement which exceeds his maximum entitlement.

(3)   The maximum entitlement as against any one employer is reached on the day on which the amount to which the employee has become entitled by way of statutory sick pay during the period of entitlement in question first reaches or passes the entitlement limit.

(4)   The entitlement limit is an amount equal to 28 times [the weekly rate applicable in accordance with] section 157 below.

(5)   Regulations may make provision for calculating the entitlement limit in any case where an employee's entitlement to statutory sick pay is calculated by reference to different weekly rates in the same period of entitlement.

NOTES
   Sub-s (4): words in square brackets substituted by the Social Security (Incapacity for Work) Act 1994, s 8(4).

# PART XIII
# GENERAL

*Short title, commencement and extent*

**177   Short title, commencement and extent**

(1)   This Act may be cited as the Social Security Contributions and Benefits Act 1992.

(2)   This Act is to be read, where appropriate, with the Administration Act and the Consequential Provisions Act.

(3)–(6). . .

NOTES
   Sub-ss (3)–(6): outside the scope of this work.
   Administration Act: Social Security Administration Act 1992.
   Consequential Provisions Act: Social Security (Consequential Provisions) Act 1992.

# SOCIAL SECURITY ADMINISTRATION ACT 1992

## (C 5)

*An Act to consolidate certain enactments relating to the administration of social security and related matters with amendments to give effect to recommendations of the Law Commission and the Scottish Law Commission*

[13 February 1992]

## PART III
## OVERPAYMENTS AND ADJUSTMENTS OF BENEFIT

*Adjustments of benefits*

### 74 Income support and other payments

(1) Where—

    (a) a payment by way of prescribed income is made after the date which is the prescribed date in relation to the payment; and

    (b) it is determined that an amount which has been paid by way of income support [or an income-based jobseeker's allowance] would not have been paid if the payment had been made on the prescribed date,

the Secretary of State shall be entitled to recover that amount from the person to whom it was paid.

(2) Where—

    (a) a prescribed payment which apart from this subsection falls to be made from public funds in the United Kingdom or under the law of any other member State is not made on or before the date which is the prescribed date in relation to the payment; and

    (b) it is determined that an amount ("the relevant amount") has been paid by way of income support [or an income-based jobseeker's allowance] that would not have been paid if the payment mentioned in paragraph (a) above had been made on the prescribed date,

then—

    (i) in the case of a payment from public funds in the United Kingdom, the authority responsible for making it may abate it by the relevant amount; and

    (ii) in the case of any other payment, the Secretary of State shall be entitled to receive the relevant amount out of the payment.

(3) Where—

    (a) a person (in this subsection referred to as A) is entitled to any prescribed benefit for any period in respect of another person (in this subsection referred to as B); and

    (b) either—

      (i) B has received income support [or an income-based jobseeker's allowance] for that period; or

      (ii) B was, during that period, a member of the same family as some person other than A who received income support [or an income-based jobseeker's allowance] for that period; and

(c) the amount of the income support [or an income-based jobseeker's allowance] has been determined on the basis that A has not made payments for the maintenance of B at a rate equal to or exceeding the amount of the prescribed benefit,

the amount of the prescribed benefit may, at the discretion of the authority administering it, be abated by the amount by which the amounts paid by way of income support [or an income-based jobseeker's allowance] exceed what it is determined that they would have been had A, at the time the amount of the income support [or an income-based jobseeker's allowance] was determined, been making payments for the maintenance of B at a rate equal to the amount of the prescribed benefit.

(4) Where an amount could have been recovered by abatement by virtue of subsection (2) or (3) above but has not been so recovered, the Secretary of State may recover it otherwise than by way of abatement—

(a) in the case of an amount which could have been recovered by virtue of subsection (2) above, from the person to whom it was paid; and

(b) in the case of an amount which could have been recovered by virtue of subsection (3) above, from the person to whom the prescribed benefit in question was paid.

(5) Where a payment is made in a currency other than sterling, its value in sterling shall be determined for the purposes of this section in accordance with regulations.

NOTES

Sub-ss (1)–(3): words in square brackets inserted by the Jobseekers Act 1995, s 41(4), Sch 2, para 50.

## [74A Payment of benefit where maintenance payments collected by Secretary of State

(1) This section applies where—

(a) a person ("the claimant") is entitled to a benefit to which this section applies;

(b) the Secretary of State is collecting periodical payments of child or spousal maintenance made in respect of the claimant or a member of the claimant's family; and

(c) the inclusion of any such periodical payment in the claimant's relevant income would, apart from this section, have the effect of reducing the amount of the benefit to which the claimant is entitled.

(2) The Secretary of State may, to such extent as he considers appropriate, treat any such periodical payment as not being relevant income for the purposes of calculating the amount of benefit to which the claimant is entitled.

(3) The Secretary of State may, to the extent that any periodical payment collected by him is treated as not being relevant income for those purposes, retain the whole or any part of that payment.

(4) Any sum retained by the Secretary of State under subsection (3) shall be paid by him into the Consolidated Fund.

(5) In this section—

"child" means a person under the age of 16;

"child maintenance", "spousal maintenance" and "relevant income" have such meaning as may be prescribed;

"family" means—
- (a) a married or unmarried couple;
- (b) a married or unmarried couple and a member of the same household for whom one of them is, or both are, responsible and who is a child or a person of a prescribed description;
- (c) except in prescribed circumstances, a person who is not a member of a married or unmarried couple and a member of the same household for whom that person is responsible and who is a child or a person of a prescribed description;

"married couple" means a man and woman who are married to each other and are members of the same household; and

"unmarried couple" means a man and woman who are not married to each other but are living together as husband and wife otherwise than in prescribed circumstances.

(6) For the purposes of this section, the Secretary of State may by regulations make provision as to the circumstances in which—
- (a) persons are to be treated as being or not being members of the same household;
- (b) one person is to be treated as responsible or not responsible for another.

(7) The benefits to which this section applies are income support, an income-based jobseeker's allowance and such other benefits (if any) as may be prescribed.]

NOTES
Commencement: 1 October 1995.
Inserted by the Child Support Act 1995, s 25.

*Social fund awards*

## 78 Recovery of social fund awards

(1) A social fund award which is repayable shall be recoverable by the Secretary of State.

(2) Without prejudice to any other method of recovery, the Secretary of State may recover an award by deduction from prescribed benefits.

(3) The Secretary of State may recover an award—
- (a) from the person to or for the benefit of whom it was made;
- (b) where that person is a member of a married or unmarried couple, from the other member of the couple;
- (c) from a person who is liable to maintain the person by or on behalf of whom the application for the award was made or any person in relation to whose needs the award was made.

[(3A) Where—
- (a) a jobseeker's allowance is payable to a person from whom an award is recoverable under subsection (3) above; and
- (b) that person is subject to a bankruptcy order,

a sum deducted from that benefit under subsection (2) above shall not be treated as income of his for the purposes of the Insolvency Act 1986.

(3B) Where—
- (a) a jobseeker's allowance is payable to a person from whom an award is recoverable under subsection (3) above; and
- (b) the estate of that person is sequestrated,

a sum deducted from that benefit under subsection (2) above shall not be treated as income of his for the purposes of the Bankruptcy (Scotland) Act 1985.]

(4)    Payments to meet funeral expenses may in all cases be recovered, as if they were funeral expenses, out of the estate of the deceased, and (subject to section 71 above) by no other means.

(5)    In this section—

"married couple" means a man and woman who are married to each other and are members of the same household;

"unmarried couple" means a man and woman who are not married to each other but are living together as husband and wife otherwise than in circumstances prescribed under section 132 of the Contributions and Benefits Act.

(6)    For the purposes of this section—

(a)    a man shall be liable to maintain his wife and any children of whom he is the father;

(b)    a woman shall be liable to maintain her husband and any children of whom she is the mother;

(c)    a person shall be liable to maintain another person throughout any period in respect of which the first-mentioned person has, on or after 23rd May 1980 (the date of the passing of the Social Security Act 1980) and either alone or jointly with a further person, given an undertaking in writing in pursuance of immigration rules within the meaning of the Immigration Act 1971 to be responsible for the maintenance and accommodation of the other person; and

(d)    "child" includes a person who has attained the age of 16 but not the age of 19 and in respect of whom either parent, or some person acting in the place of either parent, is receiving income support [or an income-based jobseeker's allowance].

(7)    Any reference in subsection (6) above to children of whom the man or the woman is the father or the mother shall be construed in accordance with section 1 of the Family Law Reform Act 1987.

(8)    Subsection (7) above does not apply in Scotland, and in the application of subsection (6) above to Scotland any reference to children of whom the man or the woman is the father or the mother shall be construed as a reference to any such children whether or not their parents have ever been married to one another.

(9)    A document bearing a certificate which—

(a)    is signed by a person authorised in that behalf by the Secretary of State; and

(b)    states that the document apart from the certificate is, or is a copy of, such an undertaking as is mentioned in subsection (6)(c) above,

shall be conclusive of the undertaking in question for the purposes of this section; and a certificate purporting to be so signed shall be deemed to be so signed until the contrary is proved.

---

NOTES

Commencement: 7 October 1996 (sub-ss (3A), (3B)); 1 July 1992 (remainder).

Sub-ss (3A), (3B): inserted by the Jobseekers Act 1995, s 32(2).

Sub-s (6): words in square brackets in para (d) added by the Jobseekers Act 1995, s 41(4), Sch 2, para 51.

Contributions and Benefits Act: Social Security Contributions and Benefits Act 1992.

---

# PART V
# INCOME SUPPORT AND THE DUTY TO MAINTAIN

### 105 Failure to maintain—general

(1) If—

(a) any person persistently refuses or neglects to maintain himself or any person whom he is liable to maintain; and

(b) in consequence of his refusal or neglect income support [or an income-based jobseeker's allowance] is paid to or in respect of him or such a person,

he shall be guilty of an offence and liable on summary conviction to imprisonment for a term not exceeding 3 months or to a fine of an amount not exceeding level 4 on the standard scale or to both.

(2) For the purposes of subsection (1) above a person shall not be taken to refuse or neglect to maintain himself or any other person by reason only of anything done or omitted in furtherance of a trade dispute.

(3) [Subject to subsection (4) below,] subsections (6) to (9) of section 78 above shall have effect for the purposes of this Part of this Act as they have effect for the purposes of that section.

[(4) For the purposes of this section, in its application to an income-based jobseeker's allowance, a person is liable to maintain another if that other person is his or her spouse.]

---

NOTES

Commencement: 11 June 1996 (sub-s (4)); 1 July 1992 (remainder).

Sub-ss (1), (3): words in square brackets inserted by the Jobseekers Act 1995, s 41(4), Sch 2, para 53(2), (3).

Sub-s (4): added by the Jobseekers Act 1995, s 41(4), Sch 2, para 53(4).

---

### 106 Recovery of expenditure on benefit from person liable for maintenance

(1) Subject to the following provisions of this section, if income support is claimed by or in respect of a person whom another person is liable to maintain or paid to or in respect of such a person, the Secretary of State may make a complaint against the liable person to a magistrates' court for an order under this section.

(2) On the hearing of a complaint under this section the court shall have regard to all the circumstances and, in particular, to the income of the liable person, and may order him to pay such sum, weekly or otherwise, as it may consider appropriate, except that in a case falling within section 78(6)(c) above that sum shall not include any amount which is not attributable to income support (whether paid before or after the making of the order).

(3) In determining whether to order any payments to be made in respect of income support for any period before the complaint was made, or the amount of any such payments, the court shall disregard any amount by which the liable person's income exceeds the income which was his during that period.

(4) Any payments ordered to be made under this section shall be made—

(a) to the Secretary of State in so far as they are attributable to any income support (whether paid before or after the making of the order);

   (b)  to the person claiming income support or (if different) the dependant; or

   (c)  to such other person as appears to the court expedient in the interests of the dependant.

(5)   An order under this section shall be enforceable as a magistrates' court maintenance order within the meaning of section 150(1) of the Magistrates' Courts Act 1980.

(6)   In the application of this section to Scotland, subsection (5) above shall be omitted and for the references to a complaint and to a magistrates' court there shall be substituted respectively references to an application and to the sheriff.

(7)   On an application under subsection (1) above a court in Scotland may make a finding as to the parentage of a child for the purpose of establishing whether a person is, for the purposes of section 105 above and this section, liable to maintain him.

## 107   Recovery of expenditure on income support: additional amounts and transfer of orders

(1)   In any case where—

   (a)  the claim for income support referred to in section 106(1) above is or was made by the parent of one or more children in respect of both himself and those children; and

   (b)  the other parent is liable to maintain those children but, by virtue of not being the claimant's husband or wife, is not liable to maintain the claimant,

the sum which the court may order that other parent to pay under subsection (2) of that section may include an amount, determined in accordance with regulations, in respect of any income support paid to or for the claimant by virtue of such provisions as may be prescribed.

(2)   Where the sum which a court orders a person to pay under section 106 above includes by virtue of subsection (1) above an amount (in this section referred to as a "personal allowance element") in respect of income support by virtue of paragraph 1(2) of Schedule 2 to the Income Support (General) Regulations 1987 (personal allowance for lone parent) the order shall separately identify the amount of the personal allowance element.

(3)   In any case where—

   (a)  there is in force an order under subsection (2) of section 106 above made against a person ("the liable parent") who is the parent of one or more children, in respect of the other parent or the children; and

   (b)  payments under the order fall to be made to the Secretary of State by virtue of subsection (4)(a) of that section; and

   (c)  that other parent ("the dependent parent") ceases to claim income support,

the Secretary of State may, by giving notice in writing to the court which made the order and to the liable parent and the dependent parent, transfer to the dependent parent the right to receive the payments under the order, exclusive of any personal allowance element, and to exercise the relevant rights in relation to the order, except so far as relating to that element.

(4)   Notice under subsection (3) above shall not be given (and if purportedly given, shall be of no effect) at a time when there is in force a maintenance order made against the liable parent—

   (a)  in favour of the dependent parent or one or more of the children; or

(b)   in favour of some other person for the benefit of the dependent parent or one or more of the children;

and if such a maintenance order is made at any time after notice under that subsection has been given, the order under section 106(2) above shall cease to have effect.

(5)   In any case where—

(a)   notice is given to a magistrates' court under subsection (3) above,

(b)   payments under the order are required to be made by any method of payment falling within section 59(6) of the Magistrates' Courts Act 1980 (standing order, etc), and

(c)   the clerk to the justices for the petty sessions area for which the court is acting decides that payment by that method is no longer possible,

the clerk shall amend the order to provide that payments under the order shall be made by the liable parent to the clerk.

(6)   Except as provided by subsections (8) and (12) below, where the Secretary of State gives notice under subsection (3) above, he shall cease to be entitled—

(a)   to receive any payment under the order in respect of any personal allowance element; or

(b)   to exercise the relevant rights, so far as relating to any such element,

notwithstanding that the dependent parent does not become entitled to receive any payment in respect of that element or to exercise the relevant rights so far as so relating.

(7)   If, in a case where the Secretary of State gives notice under subsection (3) above, a payment under the order is or has been made to him wholly or partly in respect of the whole or any part of the period beginning with the day on which the transfer takes effect and ending with the day on which the notice under subsection   (3) above is given to the liable parent, the Secretary of State shall—

(a)   repay to or for the liable parent so much of the payment as is referable to any personal allowance element in respect of that period or, as the case may be, the part of it in question; and

(b)   pay to or for the dependent parent so much of any remaining balance of the payment as is referable to that period or part;

and a payment under paragraph (b) above shall be taken to discharge, to that extent, the liability of the liable parent to the dependent parent under the order in respect of that period or part.

(8)   If, in a case where the Secretary of State has given notice under subsection (3) above, the dependent parent makes a further claim for income support, then—

(a)   the Secretary of State may, by giving a further notice in writing to the court which made the order and to the liable parent and the dependent parent, transfer back from the dependent parent to himself the right to receive the payments and to exercise the relevant rights; and

(b)   that transfer shall revive the Secretary of State's right to receive payment under the order in respect of any personal allowance element and to exercise the relevant rights so far as relating to any such element.

(9)   Subject to subsections (10) and (11) below, in any case where—

(a)   notice is given to a magistrates' court under subsection (8) above, and

(b)   the method of payment under the order which subsists immediately before the day on which the transfer under subsection (8) above takes effect differs from the method of payment which subsisted immediately before the day on which the transfer under subsection (3) above (or, if there has been more than one such transfer, the last such transfer) took effect, the clerk to the justices for the petty sessions area for which the court is acting shall amend the order by reinstating the method of payment under the order which subsisted immediately before the day on which the transfer under subsection (3) above (or, as the case may be, the last such transfer) took effect.

(10)  The clerk shall not amend the order under subsection (9) above if the Secretary of State gives notice in writing to the clerk, on or before the day on which the notice under subsection (8) above is given, that the method of payment under the order which subsists immediately before the day on which the transfer under subsection (8) above takes effect is to continue.

(11)  In any case where—
    (a)  notice is given to a magistrates' court under subsection (8) above,
    (b)  the method of payment under the order which subsisted immediately before the day on which the transfer under subsection (3) above (or, if there has been more than one such transfer, the last such transfer) took effect was any method of payment falling within section 59(6) of the Magistrates' Courts Act 1980 (standing order, etc), and
    (c)  the clerk decides that payment by that method is no longer possible,

the clerk shall amend the order to provide that payments under the order shall be made by the liable parent to the clerk.

(12)  A transfer under subsection (3) or (8) above does not transfer or otherwise affect the right of any person—
    (a)  to receive a payment which fell due to him at a time before the transfer took effect; or
    (b)  to exercise the relevant rights in relation to any such payment;

and, where notice is given under subsection (3), subsection (6) above does not deprive the Secretary of State of his right to receive such a payment in respect of any personal allowance element or to exercise the relevant rights in relation to such a payment.

(13)  For the purposes of this section—
    (a)  a transfer under subsection (3) above takes effect on the day on which the dependent parent ceases to be in receipt of income support in consequence of the cessation referred to in paragraph (c) of that subsection, and
    (b)  a transfer under subsection (8) above takes effect on—
       (i)  the first day in respect of which the dependent parent receives income support after the transfer under subsection (3) above took effect, or
      (ii)  such later day as may be specified for the purpose in the notice under subsection (8),

irrespective of the day on which notice under the subsection in question is given.

(14)  Any notice required to be given to the liable parent under subsection (3) or (8) above shall be taken to have been given if it has been sent to his last known address.

(15)  In this section—
    "child" means a person under the age of 16, notwithstanding section 78(6)(d) above;
    "court" shall be construed in accordance with section 106 above;
    "maintenance order" —
       (a)  in England and Wales, means—

     (i)   any order for the making of periodical payments or for the payment of a lump sum which is, or has at any time been, a maintenance order within the meaning of the Attachment of Earnings Act 1971;

    (ii)   any order under Part III of the Matrimonial and Family Proceedings Act 1984 (overseas divorce) for the making of periodical payments or for the payment of a lump sum;

  (b)   in Scotland, has the meaning assigned by section 106 of the Debtors (Scotland) Act 1987, but disregarding paragraph (h) (alimentary bond or agreement);

"the relevant rights", in relation to an order under section 106(2) above, means the right to bring any proceedings, take any steps or do any other thing under or in relation to the order which the Secretary of State could have brought, taken or done apart from any transfer under this section.

## PART XVI
## GENERAL

*Supplementary*

### 192   Short title, commencement and extent

(1)   This Act may be cited as the Social Security Administration Act 1992.

(2)   This Act is to be read, where appropriate, with the Contributions and Benefits Act and the Consequential Provisions Act.

(3)   The enactments consolidated by this Act are repealed, in consequence of the consolidation, by the Consequential Provisions Act.

(4)   Except as provided in Schedule 4 to the Consequential Provisions Act, this Act shall come into force on 1st July 1992.

(5), (6). . .

NOTES

   Sub-ss (5), (6): outside the scope of this work.
   Contributions and Benefits Act: Social Security Contributions and Benefits Act 1992.
   Consequential Provisions Act: Social Security (Consequential Provisions) Act 1992.

# CRIMINAL JUSTICE AND PUBLIC ORDER ACT 1994

### (C 33)

*An Act to make further provision in relation to criminal justice (including employment in the prison service); to amend or extend the criminal law and powers for preventing crime and enforcing that law; to amend the Video Recordings Act 1984; and for purposes connected with those purposes*

[3 November 1994]

## PART II
## BAIL

### 25   No bail for defendants charged with or convicted of homicide or rape after previous conviction of such offences

(1)   A person who in any proceedings has been charged with or convicted of an offence to which this section applies in circumstances to which it applies shall not be granted bail in those proceedings.

(2)    This section applies, subject to subsection (3) below, to the following offences, that is to say—

    (a)   murder;

    (b)   attempted murder;

    (c)   manslaughter;

    (d)   rape; or

    (e)   attempted rape.

(3)    This section applies to a person charged with or convicted of any such offence only if he has been previously convicted by or before a court in any part of the United Kingdom of any such offence or of culpable homicide and, in the case of a previous conviction of manslaughter or of culpable homicide, if he was then sentenced to imprisonment or, if he was then a child or young person, to long-term detention under any of the relevant enactments.

(4)    This section applies whether or not an appeal is pending against conviction or sentence.

(5)    In this section—

"conviction" includes—

    (a)   a finding that a person is not guilty by reason of insanity;

    (b)   a finding under section 4A(3) of the Criminal Procedure (Insanity) Act 1964 (cases of unfitness to plead) that a person did the act or made the omission charged against him; and

    (c)   a conviction of an offence for which an order is made placing the offender on probation or discharging him absolutely or conditionally;

and "convicted" shall be construed accordingly; and

"the relevant enactments" means—

    (a)   as respects England and Wales, section 53(2) of the Children and Young Persons Act 1933;

    [(b)   as respects Scotland, sections 205(1) to (3) and 208 of the Criminal Procedure (Scotland) Act 1995;]

    (c)   as respects Northern Ireland, section 73(2) of the Children and Young Persons Act (Northern Ireland) 1968.

(6)    This section does not apply in relation to proceedings instituted before its commencement.

---

NOTES

Commencement: 10 April 1995.

Sub-s (5): in definition "the relevant enactments" para (b) substituted by the Criminal Procedure (Consequential Provisions) (Scotland) Act 1995, s 5, Sch 4, para 93(2).

---

# PART III
## COURSE OF JUSTICE

## EVIDENCE, PROCEDURE, ETC

*Inferences from accused's silence*

### 34    Effect of accused's failure to mention facts when questioned or charged

(1)    Where, in any proceedings against a person for an offence, evidence is given that the accused—

    (a)   at any time before he was charged with the offence, on being questioned under caution by a constable trying to discover whether or by whom the offence had been committed, failed to mention any fact relied on in his defence in those proceedings; or

(b) on being charged with the offence or officially informed that he might be prosecuted for it, failed to mention any such fact,

being a fact which in the circumstances existing at the time the accused could reasonably have been expected to mention when so questioned, charged or informed, as the case may be, subsection (2) below applies.

(2) Where this subsection applies—

[(a) a magistrates' court inquiring into the offence as examining justices;]

(b) a judge, in deciding whether to grant an application made by the accused under—

(i) section 6 of the Criminal Justice Act 1987 (application for dismissal of charge of serious fraud in respect of which notice of transfer has been given under section 4 of that Act); or

(ii) paragraph 5 of Schedule 6 to the Criminal Justice Act 1991 (application for dismissal of charge of violent or sexual offence involving child in respect of which notice of transfer has been given under section 53 of that Act);

(c) the court, in determining whether there is a case to answer; and

(d) the court or jury, in determining whether the accused is guilty of the offence charged,

may draw such inferences from the failure as appear proper.

(3) Subject to any directions by the court, evidence tending to establish the failure may be given before or after evidence tending to establish the fact which the accused is alleged to have failed to mention.

(4) This section applies in relation to questioning by persons (other than constables) charged with the duty of investigating offences or charging offenders as it applies in relation to questioning by constables; and in subsection (1) above "officially informed" means informed by a constable or any such person.

(5) This section does not—

(a) prejudice the admissibility in evidence of the silence or other reaction of the accused in the face of anything said in his presence relating to the conduct in respect of which he is charged, in so far as evidence thereof would be admissible apart from this section; or

(b) preclude the drawing of any inference from any such silence or other reaction of the accused which could properly be drawn apart from this section.

(6) This section does not apply in relation to a failure to mention a fact if the failure occurred before the commencement of this section.

(7) . . .

NOTES

Commencement: 10 April 1995.

Sub-s (2): para (a) substituted by the Criminal Procedure and Investigations 1996, s 44(3), (7), in relation to an inquiry into an offence by a magistrates' court as examining justices begun on or after 5 July 1996.

Sub-s (7): repealed by the Criminal Procedure and Investigations Act 1996, ss 44(4), (7), 80, Sch 5, in relation to an inquiry into an offence by a magistrates' court as examining justices begun on or after 5 July 1996.

*Juries*

## 40 Disqualification for jury service of persons on bail in criminal proceedings

(1)   A person who is on bail in criminal proceedings shall not be qualified to serve as a juror in the Crown Court.

(2)   In this section "bail in criminal proceedings" has the same meaning as in the Bail Act 1976.

---

NOTES

Commencement: 3 February 1995.

---

# PART IV
# POLICE POWERS

*Powers of police to stop and search*

## 60 Powers to stop and search in anticipation of violence

(1)   Where a police officer of or above the rank of superintendent reasonably believes that—

    (a)   incidents involving serious violence may take place in any locality in his area, and

    (b)   it is expedient to do so to prevent their occurrence,

he may give an authorisation that the powers to stop and search persons and vehicles conferred by this section shall be exercisable at any place within that locality for a period not exceeding twenty four hours.

(2)   The power conferred by subsection (1) above may be exercised by a chief inspector or an inspector if he reasonably believes that incidents involving serious violence are imminent and no superintendent is available.

(3)   If it appears to *the officer who gave the authorisation or to a* superintendent that it is expedient to do so, having regard to offences which have, or are reasonably suspected to have, been committed in connection with any *incident* falling within the authorisation, he may direct that the authorisation shall continue in being for a further *six* hours.

[(3A) If an inspector gives an authorisation under subsection (1) he must, as soon as it is practicable to do so, cause an officer of or above the rank of superintendent to be informed.]

(4)   This section confers on any constable in uniform power—

    (a)   to stop any pedestrian and search him or anything carried by him for offensive weapons or dangerous instruments;

    (b)   to stop any vehicle and search the vehicle, its driver and any passenger for offensive weapons or dangerous instruments.

(5)   A constable may, in the exercise of those powers, stop any person or vehicle and make any search he thinks fit whether or not he has any grounds for suspecting that the person or vehicle is carrying weapons or articles of that kind.

(6)   If in the course of a search under this section a constable discovers a dangerous instrument or an article which he has reasonable grounds for suspecting to be an offensive weapon, he may seize it.

(7)   This section applies (with the necessary modifications) to ships, aircraft and hovercraft as it applies to vehicles.

(8)   A person who fails to stop or (as the case may be) to stop the vehicle when required to do so by a constable in the exercise of his powers under this section shall be liable on summary conviction to imprisonment for a term not exceeding one month or to a fine not exceeding level 3 on the standard scale or both.

(9)   Any authorisation under this section shall be in writing signed by the officer giving it and shall specify [the grounds on which it is given and] the locality in which and the period during which the powers conferred by this section are exercisable and a direction under subsection (3) above shall also be given in writing or, where that is not practicable, recorded in writing as soon as it is practicable to do so.

(10)   Where a vehicle is stopped by a constable under this section, the driver shall be entitled to obtain a written statement that the vehicle was stopped under the powers conferred by this section if he applies for such a statement not later than the end of the period of twelve months from the day on which the vehicle was stopped *and similarly as respects a pedestrian who is stopped and searched under this section.*

[(10A)A person who is searched by a constable under this section shall be entitled to obtain a written statement that he was searched under the powers conferred by this section if he applies for such a statement not later than the end of the period of twelve months from the day on which he was searched.]

(11)   In this section—

"dangerous instruments" means instruments which have a blade or are sharply pointed;

"offensive weapon" has the meaning given by section 1(9) of the Police and Criminal Evidence Act 1984 [or, in relation to Scotland, section 47(4) of the Criminal Law (Consolidation) (Scotland) Act 1995]; and

"vehicle" includes a caravan as defined in section 29(1) of the Caravan Sites and Control of Development Act 1960.

[(11A)For the purposes of this section, a person carries a dangerous instrument or an offensive weapon if he has it in his possession.]

(12)   The powers conferred by this section are in addition to and not in derogation of, any power otherwise conferred.

---

NOTES

Commencement: 10 April 1995 (sub-ss (1)–(3), (4)–(10), (11), (12)); to be appointed (sub-ss (3A), (10A), (11A)).

Sub-s (1): substituted by the Knives Act 1997, s 8(2), as from a day to be appointed, as follows—

"(1) If a police officer of or above the rank of inspector reasonably believes—
   (a)   that incidents involving serious violence may take place in any locality in his police area, and that it is expedient to give an authorisation under this section to prevent their occurrence, or
   (b)   that persons are carrying dangerous instruments or offensive weapons in any locality in his police area without good reason,
he may give an authorisation that the powers conferred by this section are to be exercisable at any place within that locality for a specified period not exceeding 24 hours.".

Sub-s (2): repealed by the Knives Act 1997, s 8(3), as from a day to be appointed.

Sub-s (3): first words in italics substituted by the words "an officer of or above the rank of", second word in italics substituted by "activity", and number in italics substituted by "24" by the Knives Act 1997 s 8(4), as from a day to be appointed.

Sub-ss (3A), (10A), (11A): inserted by the Knives Act 1997, s 8(5), (8), (10), as from a day to be appointed.

Sub-ss (9), (11): words in square brackets inserted by the Knives Act 1997, s 8(6), (9), as from a day to be appointed.

Sub-s (10): words in italics repealed by the Knives Act 1997, s 8(7), as from a day to be appointed.

---

# PART V
# PUBLIC ORDER

## COLLECTIVE TRESPASS OR NUISANCE ON LAND

*Powers to remove trespassers on land*

### 61   Power to remove trespassers on land

(1)   If the senior police officer present at the scene reasonably believes that two or more persons are trespassing on land and are present there with the common purpose of residing there for any period, that reasonable steps have been taken by or on behalf of the occupier to ask them to leave and—

(a)   that any of those persons has caused damage to the land or to property on the land or used threatening, abusive or insulting words or behaviour towards the occupier, a member of his family or an employee or agent of his, or

(b)   that those persons have between them six or more vehicles on the land,

he may direct those persons, or any of them, to leave the land and to remove any vehicles or other property they have with them on the land.

(2)   Where the persons in question are reasonably believed by the senior police officer to be persons who were not originally trespassers but have become trespassers on the land, the officer must reasonably believe that the other conditions specified in subsection (1) are satisfied after those persons became trespassers before he can exercise the power conferred by that subsection.

(3)   A direction under subsection (1) above, if not communicated to the persons referred to in subsection (1) by the police officer giving the direction, may be communicated to them by any constable at the scene.

(4)   If a person knowing that a direction under subsection (1) above has been given which applies to him—

(a)   fails to leave the land as soon as reasonably practicable, or

(b)   having left again enters the land as a trespasser within the period of three months beginning with the day on which the direction was given,

he commits an offence and is liable on summary conviction to imprisonment for a term not exceeding three months or a fine not exceeding level 4 on the standard scale, or both.

(5)   A constable in uniform who reasonably suspects that a person is committing an offence under this section may arrest him without a warrant.

(6)   In proceedings for an offence under this section it is a defence for the accused to show—

(a)   that he was not trespassing on the land, or

(b)   that he had a reasonable excuse for failing to leave the land as soon as reasonably practicable or, as the case may be, for again entering the land as a trespasser.

(7)   In its application in England and Wales to common land this section has effect as if in the preceding subsections of it—

(a)   references to trespassing or trespassers were references to acts and persons doing acts which constitute either a trespass as against the occupier or an infringement of the commoners' rights; and

      (b)  references to "the occupier" included the commoners or any of them or, in the case of common land to which the public has access, the local authority as well as any commoner.

(8)    Subsection (7) above does not—

      (a)  require action by more than one occupier; or

      (b)  constitute persons trespassers as against any commoner or the local authority if they are permitted to be there by the other occupier.

(9)    In this section—

"common land" means common land as defined in section 22 of the Commons Registration Act 1965;

"commoner" means a person with rights of common as defined in section 22 of the Commons Registration Act 1965;

"land" does not include—

      (a)  buildings other than—

          (i)  agricultural buildings within the meaning of, in England and Wales, paragraphs 3 to 8 of Schedule 5 to the Local Government Finance Act 1988 or, in Scotland, section 7(2) of the Valuation and Rating (Scotland) Act 1956, or

         (ii)  scheduled monuments within the meaning of the Ancient Monuments and Archaeological Areas Act 1979;

      (b)  land forming part of—

          (i)  a highway unless it falls within the classifications in section 54 of the Wildlife and Countryside Act 1981 (footpath, bridleway or byway open to all traffic or road used as a public path) or is a cycle track under the Highways Act 1980 or the Cycle Tracks Act 1984; or

         (ii)  a road within the meaning of the Roads (Scotland) Act 1984 unless it falls within the definitions in section 151(2)(a)(ii) or (b) (footpaths and cycle tracks) of that Act or is a bridleway within the meaning of section 47 of the Countryside (Scotland) Act 1967;

"the local authority", in relation to common land, means any local authority which has powers in relation to the land under section 9 of the Commons Registration Act 1965;

"occupier" (and in subsection (8) "the other occupier") means—

      (a)  in England and Wales, the person entitled to possession of the land by virtue of an estate or interest held by him; and

      (b)  in Scotland, the person lawfully entitled to natural possession of the land;

"property", in relation to damage to property on land, means—

      (a)  in England and Wales, property within the meaning of section 10(1) of the Criminal Damage Act 1971; and

      (b)  in Scotland, either—

          (i)  heritable property other than land; or

         (ii)  corporeal moveable property,

and "damage" includes the deposit of any substance capable of polluting the land;

"trespass" means, in the application of this section—

      (a)  in England and Wales, subject to the extensions effected by subsection (7) above, trespass as against the occupier of the land;

      (b)  in Scotland, entering, or as the case may be remaining on, land without lawful authority and without the occupier's consent; and "trespassing" and "trespasser" shall be construed accordingly;

"vehicle" includes—

    (a) any vehicle, whether or not it is in a fit state for use on roads, and includes any chassis or body, with or without wheels, appearing to have formed part of such a vehicle, and any load carried by, and anything attached to, such a vehicle; and

    (b) a caravan as defined in section 29(1) of the Caravan Sites and Control of Development Act 1960;

and a person may be regarded for the purposes of this section as having a purpose of residing in a place notwithstanding that he has a home elsewhere.

NOTES

Commencement: 3 November 1994.

## 62 Supplementary powers of seizure

(1) If a direction has been given under section 61 and a constable reasonably suspects that any person to whom the direction applies has, without reasonable excuse—

    (a) failed to remove any vehicle on the land which appears to the constable to belong to him or to be in his possession or under his control; or

    (b) entered the land as a trespasser with a vehicle within the period of three months beginning with the day on which the direction was given,

the constable may seize and remove that vehicle.

(2) In this section, "trespasser" and "vehicle" have the same meaning as in section 61.

NOTES

Commencement: 10 April 1995.

*Powers in relation to raves*

## 63 Powers to remove persons attending or preparing for a rave

(1) This section applies to a gathering on land in the open air of 100 or more persons (whether or not trespassers) at which amplified music is played during the night (with or without intermissions) and is such as, by reason of its loudness and duration and the time at which it is played, is likely to cause serious distress to the inhabitants of the locality; and for this purpose

    (a) such a gathering continues during intermissions in the music and, where the gathering extends over several days, throughout the period during which amplified music is played at night (with or without intermissions); and

    (b) "music" includes sounds wholly or predominantly characterised by the emission of a succession of repetitive beats.

(2) If, as respects any land in the open air, a police officer of at least the rank of superintendent reasonably believes that—

    (a) two or more persons are making preparations for the holding there of a gathering to which this section applies,

    (b) ten or more persons are waiting for such a gathering to begin there, or

    (c) ten or more persons are attending such a gathering which is in progress,

he may give a direction that those persons and any other persons who come to prepare or wait for or to attend the gathering are to leave the land and remove any vehicles or other property which they have with them on the land.

(3) A direction under subsection (2) above, if not communicated to the persons referred to in subsection (2) by the police officer giving the direction, may be communicated to them by any constable at the scene.

(4) Persons shall be treated as having had a direction under subsection (2) above communicated to them if reasonable steps have been taken to bring it to their attention.

(5) A direction under subsection (2) above does not apply to an exempt person.

(6) If a person knowing that a direction has been given which applies to him—
   (a) fails to leave the land as soon as reasonably practicable, or
   (b) having left again enters the land within the period of 7 days beginning with the day on which the direction was given,

he commits an offence and is liable on summary conviction to imprisonment for a term not exceeding three months or a fine not exceeding level 4 on the standard scale, or both.

(7) In proceedings for an offence under this section it is a defence for the accused to show that he had a reasonable excuse for failing to leave the land as soon as reasonably practicable or, as the case may be, for again entering the land.

(8) A constable in uniform who reasonably suspects that a person is committing an offence under this section may arrest him without a warrant.

(9) This section does not apply—
   (a) in England and Wales, to a gathering licensed by an entertainment licence; or
   (b) in Scotland, to a gathering in premises which, by virtue of section 41 of the Civic Government (Scotland) Act 1982, are licensed to be used as a place of public entertainment.

(10) In this section—
   "entertainment licence" means a licence granted by a local authority under—
      (a) Schedule 12 to the London Government Act 1963;
      (b) section 3 of the Private Places of Entertainment (Licensing) Act 1967; or
      (c) Schedule 1 to the Local Government (Miscellaneous Provisions) Act 1982;
   "exempt person", in relation to land (or any gathering on land), means the occupier, any member of his family and any employee or agent of his and any person whose home is situated on the land;
   "land in the open air" includes a place partly open to the air;
   "local authority" means—
      (a) in Greater London, a London borough council or the Common Council of the City of London;
      (b) in England outside Greater London, a district council or the council of the Isles of Scilly;
      (c) in Wales, a county council or county borough council; and
   "occupier", "trespasser" and "vehicle" have the same meaning as in section 61.

(11) Until 1st April 1996, in this section "local authority" means, in Wales, a district council.

NOTES
Commencement: 3 November 1994.

## 64 Supplementary powers of entry and seizure

(1)   If a police officer of at least the rank of superintendent reasonably believes that circumstances exist in relation to any land which would justify the giving of a direction under section 63 in relation to a gathering to which that section applies he may authorise any constable to enter the land for any of the purposes specified in subsection (2) below.

(2)   Those purposes are—
 (a)  to ascertain whether such circumstances exist; and
 (b)  to exercise any power conferred on a constable by section 63 or subsection (4) below.

(3)   A constable who is so authorised to enter land for any purpose may enter the land without a warrant.

(4)   If a direction has been given under section 63 and a constable reasonably suspects that any person to whom the direction applies has, without reasonable excuse—
 (a)  failed to remove any vehicle or sound equipment on the land which appears to the constable to belong to him or to be in his possession or under his control; or
 (b)  entered the land as a trespasser with a vehicle or sound equipment within the period of 7 days beginning with the day on which the direction was given,

the constable may seize and remove that vehicle or sound equipment.

(5)   Subsection (4) above does not authorise the seizure of any vehicle or sound equipment of an exempt person.

(6)   In this section—
 "exempt person" has the same meaning as in section 63;
 "sound equipment" means equipment designed or adapted for amplifying music and any equipment suitable for use in connection with such equipment, and "music" has the same meaning as in section 63; and
 "vehicle" has the same meaning as in section 61.

---

NOTES

Commencement: 10 April 1995 (sub-ss (4)–(6)); 3 February 1995 (sub-ss (1)–(3), certain purposes); to be appointed (sub-ss (1)–(3), remaining purposes).

---

## 65 Raves: power to stop persons from proceeding

(1)   If a constable in uniform reasonably believes that a person is on his way to a gathering to which section 63 applies in relation to which a direction under section   63(2) is in force, he may, subject to subsections (2) and (3) below—
 (a)  stop that person, and
 (b)  direct him not to proceed in the direction of the gathering.

(2)   The power conferred by subsection (1) above may only be exercised at a place within 5 miles of the boundary of the site of the gathering.

(3)   No direction may be given under subsection (1) above to an exempt person.

(4)   If a person knowing that a direction under subsection (1) above has been given to him fails to comply with that direction, he commits an offence and is liable on summary conviction to a fine not exceeding level 3 on the standard scale.

(5)   A constable in uniform who reasonably suspects that a person is committing an offence under this section may arrest him without a warrant.

(6)   In this section, "exempt person" has the same meaning as in section 63.

---

NOTES

Commencement: 3 November 1994.

---

## 66   Power of court to forfeit sound equipment

(1)   Where a person is convicted of an offence under section 63 in relation to a gathering to which that section applies and the court is satisfied that any sound equipment which has been seized from him under section 64(4), or which was in his possession or under his control at the relevant time, has been used at the gathering the court may make an order for forfeiture under this subsection in respect of that property.

(2)   The court may make an order under subsection (1) above whether or not it also deals with the offender in respect of the offence in any other way and without regard to any restrictions on forfeiture in any enactment.

(3)   In considering whether to make an order under subsection (1) above in respect of any property a court shall have regard—
   (a)   to the value of the property; and
   (b)   to the likely financial and other effects on the offender of the making of the order (taken together with any other order that the court contemplates making).

(4)   An order under subsection (1) above shall operate to deprive the offender of his rights, if any, in the property to which it relates, and the property shall (if not already in their possession) be taken into the possession of the police.

(5)   Except in a case to which subsection (6) below applies, where any property has been forfeited under subsection (1) above, a magistrates' court may, on application by a claimant of the property, other than the offender from whom it was forfeited under subsection (1) above, make an order for delivery of the property to the applicant if it appears to the court that he is the owner of the property.

(6)   In a case where forfeiture under subsection (1) above has been by order of a Scottish court, a claimant such as is mentioned in subsection (5) above may, in such manner as may be prescribed by act of adjournal, apply to that court for an order for the return of the property in question.

(7)   No application shall be made under subsection (5), or by virtue of subsection   (6), above by any claimant of the property after the expiration of 6 months from the date on which an order under subsection (1) above was made in respect of the property.

(8)   No such application shall succeed unless the claimant satisfies the court either that he had not consented to the offender having possession of the property or that he did not know, and had no reason to suspect, that the property was likely to be used at a gathering to which section 63 applies.

(9)   An order under subsection (5), or by virtue of subsection (6), above shall not affect the right of any person to take, within the period of 6 months from the date of an order under subsection (5), or as the case may be by virtue of subsection (6), above, proceedings for the recovery of the property from the person in possession of it in pursuance of the order, but on the expiration of that period the right shall cease.

(10) The Secretary of State may make regulations for the disposal of property, and for the application of the proceeds of sale of property, forfeited under subsection (1) above where no application by a claimant of the property under subsection (5), or by virtue of subsection (6), above has been made within the period specified in subsection (7) above or no such application has succeeded.

(11) The regulations may also provide for the investment of money and for the audit of accounts.

(12) The power to make regulations under subsection (10) above shall be exercisable by statutory instrument which shall be subject to annulment in pursuance of a resolution of either House of Parliament.

(13) In this section—
    "relevant time", in relation to a person—
        (a) convicted in England and Wales of an offence under section 63, means the time of his arrest for the offence or of the issue of a summons in respect of it;
        (b) so convicted in Scotland, means the time of his arrest for, or of his being cited as an accused in respect of, the offence;
    "sound equipment" has the same meaning as in section 64.

NOTES
Commencement: 10 April 1995 (sub-ss (1)–(5), (7)–(9)); 3 February 1995 (remainder).

*Disruptive trespassers*

## 68 Offence of aggravated trespass

(1) A person commits the offence of aggravated trespass if he trespasses on land in the open air and, in relation to any lawful activity which persons are engaging in or are about to engage in on that or adjoining land in the open air, does there anything which is intended by him to have the effect—
    (a) of intimidating those persons or any of them so as to deter them or any of them from engaging in that activity,
    (b) of obstructing that activity, or
    (c) of disrupting that activity.

(2) Activity on any occasion on the part of a person or persons on land is "lawful" for the purposes of this section if he or they may engage in the activity on the land on that occasion without committing an offence or trespassing on the land.

(3) A person guilty of an offence under this section is liable on summary conviction to imprisonment for a term not exceeding three months or a fine not exceeding level 4 on the standard scale, or both.

(4) A constable in uniform who reasonably suspects that a person is committing an offence under this section may arrest him without a warrant.

(5) In this section "land" does not include—
    (a) the highways and roads excluded from the application of section 61 by paragraph (b) of the definition of "land" in subsection (9) of that section; or
    (b) a road within the meaning of the Roads (Northern Ireland) Order 1993.

NOTES
Commencement: 3 November 1994.

## PART XII
## MISCELLANEOUS AND GENERAL

*General*

**172    Short title, commencement and extent**

(1)    This Act may be cited as the Criminal Justice and Public Order Act 1994.

(2)    With the exception of section 82 and subject to subsection (4) below, this Act shall come into force on such day as the Secretary of State or, in the case of sections    52 and 53, the Lord Chancellor may appoint by order made by statutory instrument, and different days may be appointed for different provisions or different purposes.

(3)    Any order under subsection (2) above may make such transitional provisions and savings as appear to the authority making the order necessary or expedient in connection with any provision brought into force by the order.

(4)    The following provisions and their related amendments, repeals and revocations shall come into force on the passing of this Act, namely sections 5 to 15 (and Schedules 1 and 2), 61, 63, 65, 68 to 71, 77 to 80, 81, 83, 90, Chapters I and IV of Part VIII, sections 142 to 148, 150, 158(1), (3) and (4), 166, 167, 171, paragraph 46 of Schedule 9 and this section.

(5)    No order shall be made under subsection (6) of section 166 above unless a draft of the order has been laid before, and approved by a resolution of, each House of Parliament.

(6)    For the purposes of subsection (4) above—
    (a)    the following are the amendments related to the provisions specified in that subsection, namely, in Schedule 10, paragraphs 26, 35, 36, 59, 60 and 63(1), (3), (4) and (5);
    (b)    the repeals and revocations related to the provisions specified in that subsection are those specified in the Note at the end of Schedule 11.

(7)    Except as regards any provisions applied under section 39 and subject to the following provisions, this Act extends to England and Wales only.

(8)    Sections 47(3), 49, *61 to 67*, 70, 71, 81, 82, 146(4), 157(1), 163, 169 and 170 also extend to Scotland.

(9)    Section 83(1) extends to England and Wales and Northern Ireland.

(10)    This section, sections 68, 69, 83(3) to (5), 88 to 92, 136 to 141, 156, 157(2), (3), (4), (5) and (9), 158, 159, 161, 162, 164, 165, 168, 171 and Chapter IV of Part VIII extend to the United Kingdom and sections 158 and 159 also extend to the Channel Islands and the Isle of Man.

(11)    Sections 93, 95 and 101(8), so far as relating to the delivery of prisoners to or from premises situated in a part of the British Islands outside England and Wales, extend to that part of those Islands.

(12)    Sections 102(1) to (3), 104, 105 and 117, so far as relating to the transfer of prisoners to or from premises situated in a part of the British Islands outside Scotland, extend to that part of those Islands, but otherwise Chapter II of Part VIII extends to Scotland only.

(13)    Sections 47(4), 83(2), 84(5) to (7), 87, Part IX, sections 145(2), 146(2), 148, 151(2), 152(2), 153, 157(7) and 160(2) extend to Scotland only.

(14)  Sections 118, 120, 121 and 125, so far as relating to the delivery of prisoners to or from premises situated in a part of the British Islands outside Northern Ireland, extend to that part of those islands, but otherwise Chapter III of Part VIII extends to Northern Ireland only.

(15)  Sections 53, 84(8) to (11), 85(4) to (6), 86(2), 145(3), 147 and 157(8) extend to Northern Ireland only.

(16)  Where any enactment is amended, repealed or revoked by Schedule 9, 10 or 11 to this Act the amendment, repeal or revocation has the same extent as that enactment; except that Schedules 9 and 11 do not extend to Scotland in so far as they relate to section 17(1) of the Video Recordings Act 1984.

### NOTES

Commencement: 3 November 1994.

Sub-s (8): words in italics substituted by the words "60 to 67" by the Knives Act 1997, s 8(11), as from a day to be appointed.

# CARERS (RECOGNITION AND SERVICES) ACT 1995

## (C 12)

*An Act to provide for the assessment of the ability of carers to provide care; and for connected purposes*

[28 June 1995]

## 1  Assessment of ability of carers to provide care: England and Wales

(1)  Subject to subsection (3) below, in any case where—

   (a)  a local authority carry out an assessment under section 47(1)(a) of the National Health Service and Community Care Act 1990 of the needs of a person ("the relevant person") for community care services, and

   (b)  an individual ("the carer") provides or intends to provide a substantial amount of care on a regular basis for the relevant person,

the carer may request the local authority, before they make their decision as to whether the needs of the relevant person call for the provision of any services, to carry out an assessment of his ability to provide and to continue to provide care for the relevant person; and if he makes such a request, the local authority shall carry out such an assessment and shall take into account the results of that assessment in making that decision.

(2)  Subject to subsection (3) below, in any case where—

   (a)  a local authority assess the needs of a disabled child for the purposes of Part III of the Children Act 1989 or section 2 of the Chronically Sick and Disabled Persons Act 1970, and

   (b)  an individual ("the carer") provides or intends to provide a substantial amount of care on a regular basis for the disabled child,

the carer may request the local authority, before they make their decision as to whether the needs of the disabled child call for the provision of any services, to carry out an assessment of his ability to provide and to continue to provide care for the disabled child; and if he makes such a request, the local authority shall carry out such an assessment and shall take into account the results of that assessment in making that decision.

(3)    No request may be made under subsection (1) or (2) above by an individual who provides or will provide the care in question—

    (a)    by virtue of a contract of employment or other contract with any person; or

    (b)    as a volunteer for a voluntary organisation.

(4)    The Secretary of State may give directions as to the manner in which an assessment under subsection (1) or (2) above is to be carried out or the form it is to take but, subject to any such directions, it shall be carried out in such manner and take such form as the local authority consider appropriate.

(5)    Section 8 of the Disabled Persons (Services, Consultation and Representation) Act 1986 (duty of local authority to take into account ability of carers) shall not apply in any case where—

    (a)    an assessment is made under subsection (1) above in respect of an individual who provides the care in question for a disabled person; or

    (b)    an assessment is made under subsection (2) above.

(6)    In this section—

    "community care services" has the meaning given by section 46(3) of the National Health Service and Community Care Act 1990;

    "child" means a person under the age of eighteen;

    "disabled child" means a child who is disabled within the meaning of Part III of the Children Act 1989;

    "disabled person" means a person to whom section 29 of the National Assistance Act 1948 applies;

    "local authority" has the meaning given by section 46(3) of the National Health Service and Community Care Act 1990; and

    "voluntary organisation" has the same meaning as in the National Assistance Act 1948.

(7)    . . .

**NOTES**

Commencement: 1 April 1996.

Sub-s (7): outside the scope of this work.

## 5    Short title, commencement and extent

(1)    This Act may be cited as the Carers (Recognition and Services) Act 1995.

(2)    This Act shall come into force on 1st April 1996.

(3)    Sections 1 and 3 do not extend to Scotland.

(4)    Section 2 does not extend to England and Wales.

(5)    This Act does not extend to Northern Ireland.

**NOTES**

Commencement: 1 April 1996.

# DISABILITY DISCRIMINATION ACT 1995

## (C 50)

*An Act to make it unlawful to discriminate against disabled persons in connection with employment, the provision of goods, facilities and services or the disposal or management of premises; to make provision about the employment of disabled persons; and to establish a National Disability Council.*

[8 November 1995]

## PART I
## DISABILITY

### 1 Meaning of "disability" and "disabled person"

(1) Subject to the provisions of Schedule 1, a person has a disability for the purposes of this Act if he has a physical or mental impairment which has a substantial and long-term adverse effect on his ability to carry out normal day-to-day activities.

(2) In this Act "disabled person" means a person who has a disability.

---

NOTES

Commencement: 17 May 1996.

---

### 2 Past disabilities

(1) The provisions of this Part and Parts II and III apply in relation to a person who has had a disability as they apply in relation to a person who has that disability.

(2) Those provisions are subject to the modifications made by Schedule 2.

(3) Any regulations or order made under this Act may include provision with respect to persons who have had a disability.

(4) In any proceedings under Part II or Part III of this Act, the question whether a person had a disability at a particular time ("the relevant time") shall be determined, for the purposes of this section, as if the provisions of, or made under, this Act in force when the act complained of was done had been in force at the relevant time.

(5) The relevant time may be a time before the passing of this Act.

---

NOTES

Commencement: 17 May 1996.

---

### 3 Guidance

(1) The Secretary of State may issue guidance about the matters to be taken into account in determining—
   (a) whether an impairment has a substantial adverse effect on a person's ability to carry out normal day-to-day activities; or
   (b) whether such an impairment has a long-term effect.

(2) The guidance may, among other things, give examples of—
   (a) effects which it would be reasonable, in relation to particular activities, to regard for purposes of this Act as substantial adverse effects;
   (b) effects which it would not be reasonable, in relation to particular activities, to regard for such purposes as substantial adverse effects;

(c) substantial adverse effects which it would be reasonable to regard, for such purposes, as long-term;

(d) substantial adverse effects which it would not be reasonable to regard, for such purposes, as long-term.

(3)   A tribunal or court determining, for any purpose of this Act, whether an impairment has a substantial and long-term adverse effect on a person's ability to carry out normal day-to-day activities, shall take into account any guidance which appears to it to be relevant.

(4)   In preparing a draft of any guidance, the Secretary of State shall consult such persons as he considers appropriate.

(5)   Where the Secretary of State proposes to issue any guidance, he shall publish a draft of it, consider any representations that are made to him about the draft and, if he thinks it appropriate, modify his proposals in the light of any of those representations.

(6)   If the Secretary of State decides to proceed with any proposed guidance, he shall lay a draft of it before each House of Parliament.

(7)   If, within the 40-day period, either House resolves not to approve the draft, the Secretary of State shall take no further steps in relation to the proposed guidance.

(8)   If no such resolution is made within the 40-day period, the Secretary of State shall issue the guidance in the form of his draft.

(9)   The guidance shall come into force on such date as the Secretary of State may appoint by order.

(10)  Subsection (7) does not prevent a new draft of the proposed guidance from being laid before Parliament.

(11)  The Secretary of State may—

(a) from time to time revise the whole or part of any guidance and re-issue it;

(b) by order revoke any guidance.

(12)  In this section—

"40-day period", in relation to the draft of any proposed guidance, means—

(a) if the draft is laid before one House on a day later than the day on which it is laid before the other House, the period of 40 days beginning with the later of the two days, and

(b) in any other case, the period of 40 days beginning with the day on which the draft is laid before each House,

no account being taken of any period during which Parliament is dissolved or prorogued or during which both Houses are adjourned for more than 4 days; and

"guidance" means guidance issued by the Secretary of State under this section and includes guidance which has been revised and re-issued.

NOTES

Commencement: 17 May 1996.

# PART II
# EMPLOYMENT

*Discrimination by employers*

## 4 Discrimination against applicants and employees

(1) It is unlawful for an employer to discriminate against a disabled person—
  (a) in the arrangements which he makes for the purpose of determining to whom he should offer employment;
  (b) in the terms on which he offers that person employment; or
  (c) by refusing to offer, or deliberately not offering, him employment.

(2) It is unlawful for an employer to discriminate against a disabled person whom he employs—
  (a) in the terms of employment which he affords him;
  (b) in the opportunities which he affords him for promotion, a transfer, training or receiving any other benefit;
  (c) by refusing to afford him, or deliberately not affording him, any such opportunity; or
  (d) by dismissing him, or subjecting him to any other detriment.

(3) Subsection (2) does not apply to benefits of any description if the employer is concerned with the provision (whether or not for payment) of benefits of that description to the public, or to a section of the public which includes the employee in question, unless—
  (a) that provision differs in a material respect from the provision of the benefits by the employer to his employees; or
  (b) the provision of the benefits to the employee in question is regulated by his contract of employment; or
  (c) the benefits relate to training.

(4) In this Part "benefits" includes facilities and services.

(5) In the case of an act which constitutes discrimination by virtue of section 55, this section also applies to discrimination against a person who is not disabled.

(6) This section applies only in relation to employment at an establishment in Great Britain.

---

**NOTES**

Commencement: 2 December 1996.

## 5 Meaning of "discrimination"

(1) For the purposes of this Part, an employer discriminates against a disabled person if—
  (a) for a reason which relates to the disabled person's disability, he treats him less favourably than he treats or would treat others to whom that reason does not or would not apply; and
  (b) he cannot show that the treatment in question is justified.

(2) For the purposes of this Part, an employer also discriminates against a disabled person if—
  (a) he fails to comply with a section 6 duty imposed on him in relation to the disabled person; and
  (b) he cannot show that his failure to comply with that duty is justified.

(3)   Subject to subsection (5), for the purposes of subsection (1) treatment is justified if, but only if, the reason for it is both material to the circumstances of the particular case and substantial.

(4)   For the purposes of subsection (2), failure to comply with a section 6 duty is justified if, but only if, the reason for the failure is both material to the circumstances of the particular case and substantial.

(5)   If, in a case falling within subsection (1), the employer is under a section 6 duty in relation to the disabled person but fails without justification to comply with that duty, his treatment of that person cannot be justified under subsection (3) unless it would have been justified even if he had complied with the section 6 duty.

(6)   Regulations may make provision, for purposes of this section, as to circumstances in which—

(a)   treatment is to be taken to be justified;

(b)   failure to comply with a section 6 duty is to be taken to be justified;

(c)   treatment is to be taken not to be justified;

(d)   failure to comply with a section 6 duty is to be taken not to be justified.

(7)   Regulations under subsection (6) may, in particular—

(a)   make provision by reference to the cost of affording any benefit; and

(b)   in relation to benefits under occupational pension schemes, make provision with a view to enabling uniform rates of contributions to be maintained.

NOTES

Commencement: 6 June 1996 (sub-ss (6), (7)); 2 December 1996 (sub-ss (1)–(5)).

## 6   Duty of employer to make adjustments

(1)   Where—

(a)   any arrangements made by or on behalf of an employer, or

(b)   any physical feature of premises occupied by the employer,

place the disabled person concerned at a substantial disadvantage in comparison with persons who are not disabled, it is the duty of the employer to take such steps as it is reasonable, in all the circumstances of the case, for him to have to take in order to prevent the arrangements or feature having that effect.

(2)   Subsection (1)(a) applies only in relation to—

(a)   arrangements for determining to whom employment should be offered;

(b)   any term, condition or arrangements on which employment, promotion, a transfer, training or any other benefit is offered or afforded.

(3)   The following are examples of steps which an employer may have to take in relation to a disabled person in order to comply with subsection (1)—

(a)   making adjustments to premises;

(b)   allocating some of the disabled person's duties to another person;

(c)   transferring him to fill an existing vacancy;

(d)   altering his working hours;

(e)   assigning him to a different place of work;

(f)   allowing him to be absent during working hours for rehabilitation, assessment or treatment;

(g)   giving him, or arranging for him to be given, training;

(h)   acquiring or modifying equipment;

(i)   modifying instructions or reference manuals;

(j)   modifying procedures for testing or assessment;

(k)   providing a reader or interpreter;

(l)   providing supervision.

(4)    In determining whether it is reasonable for an employer to have to take a particular step in order to comply with subsection (1), regard shall be had, in particular, to—

   (a)   the extent to which taking the step would prevent the effect in question;
   (b)   the extent to which it is practicable for the employer to take the step;
   (c)   the financial and other costs which would be incurred by the employer in taking the step and the extent to which taking it would disrupt any of his activities;
   (d)   the extent of the employer's financial and other resources;
   (e)   the availability to the employer of financial or other assistance with respect to taking the step.

   This subsection is subject to any provision of regulations made under subsection    (8).

(5)    In this section, "the disabled person concerned" means—

   (a)   in the case of arrangements for determining to whom employment should be offered, any disabled person who is, or has notified the employer that he may be, an applicant for that employment;
   (b)   in any other case, a disabled person who is—
       (i)   an applicant for the employment concerned; or
       (ii)   an employee of the employer concerned.

(6)    Nothing in this section imposes any duty on an employer in relation to a disabled person if the employer does not know, and could not reasonably be expected to know—

   (a)   in the case of an applicant or potential applicant, that the disabled person concerned is, or may be, an applicant for the employment; or
   (b)   in any case, that that person has a disability and is likely to be affected in the way mentioned in subsection (1).

(7)    Subject to the provisions of this section, nothing in this Part is to be taken to require an employer to treat a disabled person more favourably than he treats or would treat others.

(8)    Regulations may make provision, for the purposes of subsection (1)—

   (a)   as to circumstances in which arrangements are, or a physical feature is, to be taken to have the effect mentioned in that subsection;
   (b)   as to circumstances in which arrangements are not, or a physical feature is not, to be taken to have that effect;
   (c)   as to circumstances in which it is reasonable for an employer to have to take steps of a prescribed description;
   (d)   as to steps which it is always reasonable for an employer to have to take;
   (e)   as to circumstances in which it is not reasonable for an employer to have to take steps of a prescribed description;
   (f)   as to steps which it is never reasonable for an employer to have to take;
   (g)   as to things which are to be treated as physical features;
   (h)   as to things which are not to be treated as such features.

(9)    Regulations made under subsection (8)(c), (d), (e) or (f) may, in particular, make provision by reference to the cost of taking the steps concerned.

(10)    Regulations may make provision adding to the duty imposed on employers by this section, including provision of a kind which may be made under subsection (8).

(11)    This section does not apply in relation to any benefit under an occupational pension scheme or any other benefit payable in money or money's worth under a scheme or arrangement for the benefit of employees in respect of—

(a) termination of service;

(b) retirement, old age or death;

(c) accident, injury, sickness or invalidity; or

(d) any other prescribed matter.

(12) This section imposes duties only for the purpose of determining whether an employer has discriminated against a disabled person; and accordingly a breach of any such duty is not actionable as such.

NOTES

Commencement: 2 December 1996 (sub-ss (1)–(7), (11), (12)); 6 June 1996 (sub-ss (8)–(10)).

## 7 Exemption for small businesses

(1) Nothing in this Part applies in relation to an employer who has fewer than 20 employees.

(2)–(10) . . .

NOTES

Commencement: 2 December 1996.

Sub-ss (2)–(10): outside the scope of this work.

*Enforcement etc*

## 8 Enforcement, remedies and procedure

(1) A complaint by any person that another person—

(a) has discriminated against him in a way which is unlawful under this Part, or

(b) is, by virtue of section 57 or 58, to be treated as having discriminated against him in such a way,

may be presented to an industrial tribunal.

(2) Where an industrial tribunal finds that a complaint presented to it under this section is well-founded, it shall take such of the following steps as it considers just and equitable—

(a) making a declaration as to the rights of the complainant and the respondent in relation to the matters to which the complaint relates;

(b) ordering the respondent to pay compensation to the complainant;

(c) recommending that the respondent take, within a specified period, action appearing to the tribunal to be reasonable, in all the circumstances of the case, for the purpose of obviating or reducing the adverse effect on the complainant of any matter to which the complaint relates.

(3) Where a tribunal orders compensation under subsection (2)(b), the amount of the compensation shall be calculated by applying the principles applicable to the calculation of damages in claims in tort or (in Scotland) in reparation for breach of statutory duty.

(4) For the avoidance of doubt it is hereby declared that compensation in respect of discrimination in a way which is unlawful under this Part may include compensation for injury to feelings whether or not it includes compensation under any other head.

(5) If the respondent to a complaint fails, without reasonable justification, to comply with a recommendation made by an industrial tribunal under subsection (2)(c) the tribunal may, if it thinks it just and equitable to do so—

    (a)   increase the amount of compensation required to be paid to the complainant in respect of the complaint, where an order was made under subsection (2)(b); or

    (b)   make an order under subsection (2)(b).

(6)   Regulations may make provision—

    (a)   for enabling a tribunal, where an amount of compensation falls to be awarded under subsection (2)(b), to include in the award interest on that amount; and

    (b)   specifying, for cases where a tribunal decides that an award is to include an amount in respect of interest, the manner in which and the periods and rate by reference to which the interest is to be determined.

(7)  ...

(8)   Part I of Schedule 3 makes further provision about the enforcement of this Part and about procedure.

---

**NOTES**

    Commencement: 2 December 1996 (sub-ss (1)–(5)); 6 June 1996 (sub-s (6)).

    Sub-s (7): outside the scope of this work.

---

## 9   Validity of certain agreements

(1)   Any term in a contract of employment or other agreement is void so far as it purports to—

    (a)   require a person to do anything which would contravene any provision of, or made under, this Part;

    (b)   exclude or limit the operation of any provision of this Part; or

    (c)   prevent any person from presenting a complaint to an industrial tribunal under this Part.

(2)   Paragraphs (b) and (c) of subsection (1) do not apply to an agreement not to institute proceedings under section 8(1), or to an agreement not to continue such proceedings, if—

    (a)   a conciliation officer has acted under [section 18 of the Industrial Tribunals Act 1996] in relation to the matter; or

    (b)   the conditions set out in subsection (3) are satisfied.

(3)   The conditions are that—

    (a)   the complainant must have received independent legal advice from a qualified lawyer as to the terms and effect of the proposed agreement (and in particular its effect on his ability to pursue his complaint before an industrial tribunal);

    (b)   when the adviser gave the advice there must have been in force a policy of insurance covering the risk of a claim by the complainant in respect of loss arising in consequence of the advice; and

    (c)   the agreement must be in writing, relate to the particular complaint, identify the adviser and state that the conditions are satisfied.

(4)   In this section—

    "independent", in relation to legal advice to the complainant, means that it is given by a lawyer who is not acting for the other party or for a person who is connected with that other party; and

    "qualified lawyer" means—

(a) as respects proceedings in England and Wales, a barrister (whether in practice as such or employed to give legal advice) or a solicitor of the Supreme Court who holds a practising certificate; and

(b) as respects proceedings in Scotland, an advocate, whether in practice as such or employed to give legal advice) or a solicitor who holds a practising certificate.

(5) For the purposes of subsection (4), any two persons are to be treated as connected if—

(a) one is a company of which the other (directly or indirectly) has control, or

(b) both are companies of which a third person (directly or indirectly) has control.

**NOTES**

Commencement: 2 December 1996.

Sub-s (2): words in square brackets in para (a) substituted by the Industrial Tribunals Act 1996, s 43, Sch 1, para 12(1), (3).

## 10 Charities and support for particular groups of persons

(1) Nothing in this Part—

(a) affects any charitable instrument which provides for conferring benefits on one or more categories of person determined by reference to any physical or mental capacity; or

(b) makes unlawful any act done by a charity or recognised body in pursuance of any of its charitable purposes, so far as those purposes are connected with persons so determined.

(2) Nothing in this Part prevents—

(a) a person who provides supported employment from treating members of a particular group of disabled persons more favourably than other persons in providing such employment; or

(b) the Secretary of State from agreeing to arrangements for the provision of supported employment which will, or may, have that effect.

(3) In this section—

"charitable instrument" means an enactment or other instrument (whenever taking effect) so far as it relates to charitable purposes;

"charity" has the same meaning as in the Charities Act 1993;

"recognised body" means a body which is a recognised body for the purposes of Part I of the Law Reform (Miscellaneous Provisions) (Scotland) Act 1990; and

"supported employment" means facilities provided, or in respect of which payments are made, under section 15 of the Disabled Persons (Employment) Act 1944.

(4), (5) . . .

**NOTES**

Commencement: 2 December 1996.

Sub-ss (4), (5): outside the scope of this work.

## 11 Advertisements suggesting that employers will discriminate against disabled persons

(1)    This section applies where—

(a)   a disabled person has applied for employment with an employer;

(b)   the employer has refused to offer, or has deliberately not offered, him the employment;

(c)   the disabled person has presented a complaint under section 8 against the employer;

(d)   the employer has advertised the employment (whether before or after the disabled person applied for it); and

(e)   the advertisement indicated, or might reasonably be understood to have indicated, that any application for the advertised employment would, or might, be determined to any extent by reference to—

(i)   the successful applicant not having any disability or any category of disability which includes the disabled person's disability; or

(ii)   the employer's reluctance to take any action of a kind mentioned in section 6.

(2)    The tribunal hearing the complaint shall assume, unless the contrary is shown, that the employer's reason for refusing to offer, or deliberately not offering, the employment to the complainant was related to the complainant's disability.

(3)    In this section "advertisement" includes every form of advertisement or notice, whether to the public or not.

NOTES
Commencement: 2 December 1996.

*Discrimination by other persons*

## 12 Discrimination against contract workers

(1)    It is unlawful for a principal, in relation to contract work, to discriminate against a disabled person—

(a)   in the terms on which he allows him to do that work;

(b)   by not allowing him to do it or continue to do it;

(c)   in the way he affords him access to any benefits or by refusing or deliberately omitting to afford him access to them; or

(d)   by subjecting him to any other detriment.

(2)    Subsection (1) does not apply to benefits of any description if the principal is concerned with the provision (whether or not for payment) of benefits of that description to the public, or to a section of the public which includes the contract worker in question, unless that provision differs in a material respect from the provision of the benefits by the principal to contract workers.

(3)    The provisions of this Part (other than subsections (1) to (3) of section 4) apply to any principal, in relation to contract work, as if he were, or would be, the employer of the contract worker and as if any contract worker supplied to do work for him were an employee of his.

(4)    In the case of an act which constitutes discrimination by virtue of section 55, this section also applies to discrimination against a person who is not disabled.

(5)    This section applies only in relation to contract work done at an establishment in Great Britain (the provisions of section 68 about the meaning of "employment at an establishment in Great Britain" applying for the purposes of this subsection with the appropriate modifications).

(6)  In this section—

"principal" means a person ("A") who makes work available for doing by individuals who are employed by another person who supplies them under a contract made with A;

"contract work" means work so made available; and

"contract worker" means any individual who is supplied to the principal under such a contract.

NOTES

Commencement: 2 December 1996 (sub-ss (1), (2), (4), (5)); 6 June 1996 (sub-ss (3), (6)).

### 13  Discrimination by trade organisations

(1)  It is unlawful for a trade organisation to discriminate against a disabled person—

(a)  in the terms on which it is prepared to admit him to membership of the organisation; or

(b)  by refusing to accept, or deliberately not accepting, his application for membership.

(2)  It is unlawful for a trade organisation, in the case of a disabled person who is a member of the organisation, to discriminate against him—

(a)  in the way it affords him access to any benefits or by refusing or deliberately omitting to afford him access to them;

(b)  by depriving him of membership, or varying the terms on which he is a member; or

(c)  by subjecting him to any other detriment.

(3)  In the case of an act which constitutes discrimination by virtue of section 55, this section also applies to discrimination against a person who is not disabled.

(4)  In this section "trade organisation" means an organisation of workers, an organisation of employers or any other organisation whose members carry on a particular profession or trade for the purposes of which the organisation exists.

NOTES

Commencement: 2 December 1996.

# PART VII
# SUPPLEMENTAL

### 55  Victimisation

(1)  For the purposes of Part II or Part III, a person ("A") discriminates against another person ("B") if—

(a)  he treats B less favourably than he treats or would treat other persons whose circumstances are the same as B's; and

(b)  he does so for a reason mentioned in subsection (2).

(2)  The reasons are that—

(a)  B has—

(i)  brought proceedings against A or any other person under this Act; or

(ii)  given evidence or information in connection with such proceedings brought by any person; or

(iii)  otherwise done anything under this Act in relation to A or any other person; or

(iv)  alleged that A or any other person has (whether or not the allegation so states) contravened this Act; or

(b) A believes or suspects that B has done or intends to do any of those things.

(3)   Where B is a disabled person, or a person who has had a disability, the disability in question shall be disregarded in comparing his circumstances with those of any other person for the purposes of subsection (1)(a).

(4)   Subsection (1) does not apply to treatment of a person because of an allegation made by him if the allegation was false and not made in good faith.

NOTES
Commencement: 2 December 1996.

## 56   Help for persons suffering discrimination

(1)   For the purposes of this section—
   (a) a person who considers that he may have been discriminated against, in contravention of any provision of Part II, is referred to as "the complainant"; and
   (b) a person against whom the complainant may decide to make, or has made, a complaint under Part II is referred to as "the respondent".

(2)   The Secretary of State shall, with a view to helping the complainant to decide whether to make a complaint against the respondent and, if he does so, to formulate and present his case in the most effective manner, by order prescribe—
   (a) forms by which the complainant may question the respondent on his reasons for doing any relevant act, or on any other matter which is or may be relevant; and
   (b) forms by which the respondent may if he so wishes reply to any questions.

(3)   Where the complainant questions the respondent in accordance with forms prescribed by an order under subsection (2)—
   (a) the question, and any reply by the respondent (whether in accordance with such an order or not), shall be admissible as evidence in any proceedings under Part II;
   (b) if it appears to the tribunal in any such proceedings—
      (i) that the respondent deliberately, and without reasonable excuse, omitted to reply within a reasonable period, or
      (ii) that the respondent's reply is evasive or equivocal,
      it may draw any inference which it considers it just and equitable to draw, including an inference that the respondent has contravened a provision of Part II.

(4)   The Secretary of State may by order prescribe—
   (a) the period within which questions must be duly served in order to be admissible under subsection (3)(a); and
   (b) the manner in which a question, and any reply by the respondent, may be duly served.

(5)   This section is without prejudice to any other enactment or rule of law regulating interlocutory and preliminary matters in proceedings before an industrial tribunal, and has effect subject to any enactment or rule of law regulating the admissibility of evidence in such proceedings.

NOTES
Commencement: 6 June 1996.

# SCHEDULES

## SCHEDULE 1
### PROVISIONS SUPPLEMENTING SECTION 1

Section 1(1)

*Impairment*

1.—(1) "Mental impairment" includes an impairment resulting from or consisting of a mental illness only if the illness is a clinically well-recognised illness.

(2) Regulations may make provision, for the purposes of this Act—
  (a) for conditions of a prescribed description to be treated as amounting to impairments;
  (b) for conditions of a prescribed description to be treated as not amounting to impairments.

(3) Regulations made under sub-paragraph (2) may make provision as to the meaning of "condition" for the purposes of those regulations.

*Long-term effects*

2.—(1) The effect of an impairment is a long-term effect if—
  (a) it has lasted at least 12 months;
  (b) the period for which it lasts is likely to be at least 12 months; or
  (c) it is likely to last for the rest of the life of the person affected.

(2) Where an impairment ceases to have a substantial adverse effect on a person's ability to carry out normal day-to-day activities, it is to be treated as continuing to have that effect if that effect is likely to recur.

(3) For the purposes of sub-paragraph (2), the likelihood of an effect recurring shall be disregarded in prescribed circumstances.

(4) Regulations may prescribe circumstances in which, for the purposes of this Act—
  (a) an effect which would not otherwise be a long-term effect is to be treated as such an effect; or
  (b) an effect which would otherwise be a long-term effect is to be treated as not being such an effect.

*Severe disfigurement*

3.—(1) An impairment which consists of a severe disfigurement is to be treated as having a substantial adverse effect on the ability of the person concerned to carry out normal day-to-day activities.

(2) Regulations may provide that in prescribed circumstances a severe disfigurement is not to be treated as having that effect.

(3) Regulations under sub-paragraph (2) may, in particular, make provision with respect to deliberately acquired disfigurements.

*Normal day-to-day activities*

4.—(1) An impairment is to be taken to affect the ability of the person concerned to carry out normal day-to-day activities only if it affects one of the following—
  (a) mobility;
  (b) manual dexterity;
  (c) physical co-ordination;
  (d) continence;
  (e) ability to lift, carry or otherwise move everyday objects;
  (f) speech, hearing or eyesight;
  (g) memory or ability to concentrate, learn or understand; or
  (h) perception of the risk of physical danger.

(2)  Regulations may prescribe—
- (a)  circumstances in which an impairment which does not have an effect falling within sub-paragraph (1) is to be taken to affect the ability of the person concerned to carry out normal day-to-day activities;
- (b)  circumstances in which an impairment which has an effect falling within sub-paragraph (1) is to be taken not to affect the ability of the person concerned to carry out normal day-to-day activities.

### Substantial adverse effects

5.  Regulations may make provision for the purposes of this Act—
- (a)  for an effect of a prescribed kind on the ability of a person to carry out normal day-to-day activities to be treated as a substantial adverse effect;
- (b)  for an effect of a prescribed kind on the ability of a person to carry out normal day-to-day activities to be treated as not being a substantial adverse effect.

### Effect of medical treatment

6.—(1)  An impairment which would be likely to have a substantial adverse effect on the ability of the person concerned to carry out normal day-to-day activities, but for the fact that measures are being taken to treat or correct it, is to be treated as having that effect.

(2)  In sub-paragraph (1) "measures" includes, in particular, medical treatment and the use of a prosthesis or other aid.

(3)  Sub-paragraph (1) does not apply—
- (a)  in relation to the impairment of a person's sight, to the extent that the impairment is, in his case, correctable by spectacles or contact lenses or in such other ways as may be prescribed; or
- (b)  in relation to such other impairments as may be prescribed, in such circumstances as may be prescribed.

### Persons deemed to be disabled

7.—(1)  Sub-paragraph (2) applies to any person whose name is, both on 12th January 1995 and on the date when this paragraph comes into force, in the register of disabled persons maintained under section 6 of the Disabled Persons (Employment) Act 1944.

(2)  That person is to be deemed—
- (a)  during the initial period, to have a disability, and hence to be a disabled person; and
- (b)  afterwards, to have had a disability and hence to have been a disabled person during that period.

(3)  A certificate of registration shall be conclusive evidence, in relation to the person with respect to whom it was issued, of the matters certified.

(4)  Unless the contrary is shown, any document purporting to be a certificate of registration shall be taken to be such a certificate and to have been validly issued.

(5)  Regulations may provide for prescribed descriptions of person to be deemed to have disabilities, and hence to be disabled persons, for the purposes of this Act.

(6)  Regulations may prescribe circumstances in which a person who has been deemed to be a disabled person by the provisions of sub-paragraph (1) or regulations made under sub-paragraph (5) is to be treated as no longer being deemed to be such a person.

(7)  In this paragraph—
"certificate of registration" means a certificate issued under regulations made under section 6 of the Act of 1944; and
"initial period" means the period of three years beginning with the date on which this paragraph comes into force.

*Progressive conditions*

8.—(1) Where—

    (a) a person has a progressive condition (such as cancer, multiple sclerosis or muscular dystrophy or infection by the human immunodeficiency virus),

    (b) as a result of that condition, he has an impairment which has (or had) an effect on his ability to carry out normal day-to-day activities, but

    (c) that-effect is not (or was not) a substantial adverse effect,

he shall be taken to have an impairment which has such a substantial adverse effect if the condition is likely to result in his having such an impairment.

(2) Regulations may make provision, for the purposes of this paragraph—

    (a) for conditions of a prescribed description to be treated as being progressive;

    (b) for conditions of a prescribed description to be treated as not being progressive.

## NOTES

Commencement: 17 May 1996 (paras 1–6, 8); 2 December 1996 (para 7).

# JOBSEEKERS ACT 1995

## (C 18)

*An Act to provide for a jobseeker's allowance and to make other provision to promote the employment of the unemployed and the assistance of persons without a settled way of life*

[28 June 1995]

## PART I
## THE JOBSEEKER'S ALLOWANCE

*Entitlement*

## 1 The jobseeker's allowance

(1) An allowance, to be known as a jobseeker's allowance, shall be payable in accordance with the provisions of this Act.

(2) Subject to the provisions of this Act, a claimant is entitled to a jobseeker's allowance if he—

    (a) is available for employment;

    (b) has entered into a jobseeker's agreement which remains in force;

    (c) is actively seeking employment;

    (d) satisfies either—

      (i) the conditions set out in section 2; or

      (ii) the conditions set out in section 3;

    (e) is not engaged in remunerative work;

    (f) is capable of work;

    (g) is not receiving relevant education;

    (h) is under pensionable age; and

    (i) is in Great Britain.

(3)  A jobseeker's allowance is payable in respect of a week.

(4)  In this Act—

"a contribution-based jobseeker's allowance" means a jobseeker's allowance entitlement to which is based on the claimant's satisfying conditions which include those set out in section 2; and

"an income-based jobseeker's allowance" means a jobseeker's allowance entitlement to which is based on the claimant's satisfying conditions which include those set out in section 3.

**NOTES**

Commencement: 7 October 1996.

## 2  The contribution-based conditions

(1)  The conditions referred to in section 1(2)(d)(i) are that the claimant—

(a)  has actually paid Class 1 contributions in respect of one ("the base year") of the last two complete years before the beginning of the relevant benefit year and satisfies the additional conditions set out in subsection (2);

(b)  has, in respect of the last two complete years before the beginning of the relevant benefit year, either paid Class 1 contributions or been credited with earnings and satisfies the additional condition set out in subsection (3);

(c)  does not have earnings in excess of the prescribed amount; and

(d)  is not entitled to income support.

(2)  The additional conditions mentioned in subsection (1)(a) are that—

(a)  the contributions have been paid before the week for which the jobseeker's allowance is claimed;

(b)  the earnings factor derived from earnings upon which primary Class 1 contributions have been paid or treated as paid is not less than the base year's lower earnings limit multiplied by 25.

(3)  The additional condition mentioned in subsection (1)(b) is that the earnings factor derived from earnings upon which primary Class 1 contributions have been paid or treated as paid or from earnings credited is not less, in each of the two complete years, than the lower earnings limit for the year multiplied by 50.

(4)  For the purposes of this section—

(a)  "benefit year" means a period which is a benefit year for the purposes of Part II of the Benefits Act or such other period as may be prescribed for the purposes of this section;

(b)  "the relevant benefit year" is the benefit year which includes—

(i)  the beginning of the jobseeking period which includes the week for which a jobseeker's allowance is claimed, or

(ii)  (if earlier) the beginning of any linked period; and

(c)  other expressions which are used in this section and the Benefits Act have the same meaning in this section as they have in that Act.

**NOTES**

Commencement: 7 October 1996 (sub-ss (1)(a), (b), (d), (2), (3), (4)(a), (c), sub-ss (1)(c), (4)(b) certain purposes); 12 December 1995 (sub-ss (1)(c), (4)(b), remaining purposes).

Benefits Act: Social Security Contributions and Benefits Act 1992.

## 4  Amount payable by way of a jobseeker's allowance

(1)   In the case of a contribution-based jobseeker's allowance, the amount payable in respect of a claimant ("his personal rate") shall be calculated by—

  (a)  determining the age-related amount applicable to him; and

  (b)  making prescribed deductions in respect of earnings and pension payments.

(2)   The age-related amount applicable to a claimant, for the purposes of subsection   (1)(a), shall be determined in accordance with regulations.

(3)   In the case of an income-based jobseeker's allowance, the amount payable shall be—

  (a)  if a claimant has no income, the applicable amount;

  (b)  if a claimant has an income, the amount by which the applicable amount exceeds his income.

(4)   Except in prescribed circumstances, a jobseeker's allowance shall not be payable where the amount otherwise payable would be less than a prescribed minimum.

(5)   The applicable amount shall be such amount or the aggregate of such amounts as may be determined in accordance with regulations.

(6)   Where a claimant satisfies both the contribution-based conditions and the income-based conditions but has no income, the amount payable shall be—

  (a)  the applicable amount, if that is greater than his personal rate; and

  (b)  his personal rate, if it is not.

(7)   Where the amount payable to a claimant to whom subsection (6) applies is the applicable amount, the amount payable to him by way of a jobseeker's allowance shall be taken to consist of two elements—

  (a)  one being an amount equal to his personal rate; and

  (b)  the other being an amount equal to the excess of the applicable amount over his personal rate.

(8)   Where a claimant satisfies both the contribution-based conditions and the income-based conditions and has an income, the amount payable shall be—

  (a)  the amount by which the applicable amount exceeds his income, if the amount of that excess is greater than his personal rate; and

  (b)  his personal rate, if it is not.

(9)   Where the amount payable to a claimant to whom subsection (8) applies is the amount by which the applicable amount exceeds his income, the amount payable to him by way of a jobseeker's allowance shall be taken to consist of two elements—

  (a)  one being an amount equal to his personal rate; and

  (b)  the other being an amount equal to the amount by which the difference between the applicable amount and his income exceeds his personal rate.

(10)  The element of a jobseeker's allowance mentioned in subsection (7)(a) and that mentioned in subsection (9)(a) shall be treated, for the purpose of identifying the source of the allowance, as attributable to the claimant's entitlement to a contribution-based jobseeker's allowance.

(11)   The element of a jobseeker's allowance mentioned in subsection (7)(b) and that mentioned in subsection (9)(b) shall be treated, for the purpose of identifying the source of the allowance, as attributable to the claimant's entitlement to an income-based jobseeker's allowance.

(12)   Regulations under subsection (5) may provide that, in prescribed cases, an applicable amount is to be nil.

NOTES

Commencement: 7 October 1996 (sub-ss (1)(a), (3), (6)–(11), sub-ss(1)(b), (2), (4), (5), (12) certain purposes); 12 December 1995 (sub-ss (1)(b), (2), (4), (5), (12), remaining purposes).

## 5   Duration of a contribution-based jobseeker's allowance

(1)   The period for which a person is entitled to a contribution-based jobseeker's allowance shall not exceed, in the aggregate, 182 days in any period for which his entitlement is established by reference (under section 2(1)(b)) to the same two years.

(2)   The fact that a person's entitlement to a contribution-based jobseeker's allowance ("his previous entitlement") has ceased as a result of subsection (1), does not prevent his being entitled to a further contribution-based jobseeker's allowance if—

(a)   he satisfies the contribution-based conditions; and

(b)   the two years by reference to which he satisfies those conditions includes at least one year which is later than the second of the two years by reference to which his previous entitlement was established.

(3)   Regulations may provide that a person who would be entitled to a contribution-based jobseeker's allowance but for the operation of prescribed provisions of, or made under, this Act shall be treated as if entitled to the allowance for the purposes of this section.

NOTES

Commencement: 7 October 1996 (sub-ss (1), (2), sub-s (3) certain purposes); 12 December 1995 (sub-s (3), remaining purposes).

*Jobseeking*

## 6   Availability for employment

(1)   For the purposes of this Act, a person is available for employment if he is willing and able to take up immediately any employed earner's employment.

(2)   Subsection (1) is subject to such provisions as may be made by regulations; and those regulations may, in particular, provide that a person—

(a)   may restrict his availability for employment in any week in such ways as may be prescribed; or

(b)   may restrict his availability for employment in any week in such circumstances as may be prescribed (for example, on grounds of conscience, religious conviction or physical or mental condition or because he is caring for another person) and in such ways as may be prescribed.

(3)   The following are examples of restrictions for which provision may be made by the regulations—

    (a)  restrictions on the nature of the employment for which a person is available;

    (b)  restrictions on the periods for which he is available;

    (c)  restrictions on the terms or conditions of employment for which he is available;

    (d)  restrictions on the locality or localities within which he is available.

(4)    Regulations may prescribe circumstances in which, for the purposes of this Act, a person is or is not to be treated as available for employment.

(5)    Regulations under subsection (4) may, in particular, provide for a person who is available for employment—

    (a)  only in his usual occupation,

    (b)  only at a level of remuneration not lower than that which he is accustomed to receive, or

    (c)  only in his usual occupation and at a level of remuneration not lower than that which he is accustomed to receive,

to be treated, for a permitted period, as available for employment.

(6)    Where it has been determined ("the first determination") that a person is to be treated, for the purposes of this Act, as available for employment in any week, the question whether he is available for employment in that week may be subsequently determined on a review of the first determination.

(7)    In this section "permitted period", in relation to any person, means such period as may be determined in accordance with the regulations made under subsection (4).

(8)    Regulations under subsection (4) may prescribe, in relation to permitted periods—

    (a)  the day on which any such period is to be regarded as having begun in any case;

    (b)  the shortest and longest periods which may be determined in any case;

    (c)  factors which an adjudication officer may take into account in determining the period in any case.

(9)    For the purposes of this section "employed earner's employment" has the same meaning as in the Benefits Act.

---

NOTES

    Commencement: 7 October 1996 (sub-ss (1), (6), (9), sub-ss (2)–(5), (7), (8) certain purposes); 12 December 1995 (sub-ss (2)–(5), (7), (8), remaining purposes).

    Benefits Act: Social Security Contributions and Benefits Act 1992.

---

## 7   Actively seeking employment

(1)    For the purposes of this Act, a person is actively seeking employment in any week if he takes in that week such steps as he can reasonably be expected to have to take in order to have the best prospects of securing employment.

(2)    Regulations may make provision—

    (a)  with respect to steps which it is reasonable, for the purposes of subsection (1), for a person to be expected to have to take in any week;

    (b)  as to circumstances (for example, his skills, qualifications, abilities and physical or mental limitations) which, in particular, are to be taken into account in determining whether, in relation to any steps taken by a person, the requirements of subsection (1) are satisfied in any week.

(3)   Regulations may make provision for acts of a person which would otherwise be relevant for purposes of this section to be disregarded in such circumstances (including circumstances constituted by, or connected with, his behaviour or appearance) as may be prescribed.

(4)   Regulations may prescribe circumstances in which, for the purposes of this Act, a person is to be treated as actively seeking employment.

(5)   Regulations under subsection (4) may, in particular, provide for a person who is actively seeking employment—

(a)   only in his usual occupation,

(b)   only at a level of remuneration not lower than that which he is accustomed to receive, or

(c)   only in his usual occupation and at a level of remuneration not lower than that which he is accustomed to receive,

to be treated, for the permitted period determined in his case for the purposes of section 6(5), as actively seeking employment during that period.

(6)   Regulations may provide for this section, and any regulations made under it, to have effect in relation to a person who has reached the age of 16 but not the age of 18 as if "employment" included "training".

(7)   Where it has been determined ("the first determination") that a person is to be treated, for the purposes of this Act, as actively seeking employment in any week, the question whether he is actively seeking employment in that week may subsequently be determined on a review of the first determination.

(8)   For the purposes of this section—

"employment" means employed earner's employment or, in prescribed circumstances—

(a)   self-employed earner's employment; or

(b)   employed earner's employment and self-employed earner's employment; and

"employed earner's employment" and "self-employed earner's employment" have the same meaning as in the Benefits Act.

---

NOTES

Commencement: 7 October 1996 (sub-ss (1), (7), sub-ss (2)–(6), (8) certain purposes); 12 December 1995 (sub-ss (2)–(6), (8), remaining purposes).

Benefits Act: Social Security Contributions and Benefits Act 1992.

## 8   Attendance, information and evidence

(1)   Regulations may make provision for requiring a claimant—

(a)   to attend at such place and at such time as the Secretary of State may specify; and

(b)   to provide information and such evidence as may be prescribed as to his circumstances, his availability for employment and the extent to which he is actively seeking employment.

(2)   Regulations under subsection (1) may, in particular—

(a)   prescribe circumstances in which entitlement to a jobseeker's allowance is to cease in the case of a claimant who fails to comply with any regulations made under that subsection;

(b)   provide for entitlement to cease at such time (after he last attended in compliance with requirements of the kind mentioned in subsection (1)(a)) as may be determined in accordance with any such regulations;

(c) provide for entitlement not to cease if the claimant shows, within a prescribed period of his failure to comply, that he had good cause for that failure; and

(d) prescribe—

    (i) matters which are, or are not, to be taken into account in determining whether a person has, or does not have, good cause for failing to comply with any such regulations; and

    (ii) circumstances in which a person is, or is not, to be regarded as having, or not having, good cause for failing to comply with any such regulations.

NOTES

Commencement: 7 October 1996 (certain purposes); 12 December 1995 (remaining purposes).

## 9 The jobseeker's agreement

(1) An agreement which is entered into by a claimant and an employment officer and which complies with the prescribed requirements in force at the time when the agreement is made is referred to in this Act as "a jobseeker's agreement".

(2) A jobseeker's agreement shall have effect only for the purposes of section 1.

(3) A jobseeker's agreement shall be in writing and be signed by both parties.

(4) A copy of the agreement shall be given to the claimant.

(5) An employment officer shall not enter into a jobseeker's agreement with a claimant unless, in the officer's opinion, the conditions mentioned in section 1(2)(a) and (c) would be satisfied with respect to the claimant if he were to comply with, or be treated as complying with, the proposed agreement.

(6) The employment officer may, and if asked to do so by the claimant shall forthwith, refer a proposed jobseeker's agreement to an adjudication officer for him to determine—

(a) whether, if the claimant concerned were to comply with the proposed agreement, he would satisfy—

    (i) the condition mentioned in section 1(2)(a), or

    (ii) the condition mentioned in section 1(2)(c); and

(b) whether it is reasonable to expect the claimant to have to comply with the proposed agreement.

(7) An adjudication officer to whom a reference is made under subsection (6)—

(a) shall, so far as practicable, dispose of it in accordance with this section before the end of the period of 14 days from the date of the reference;

(b) may give such directions, with respect to the terms on which the employment officer is to enter into a jobseeker's agreement with the claimant, as the adjudication officer considers appropriate;

(c) may direct that, if such conditions as he considers appropriate are satisfied, the proposed jobseeker's agreement is to be treated (if entered into) as having effect on such date, before it would otherwise have effect, as may be specified in the direction.

(8) Regulations may provide—

(a) for such matters as may be prescribed to be taken into account by an adjudication officer in giving a direction under subsection (7)(c); and

(b) for such persons as may be prescribed to be notified of—

    (i) any determination of an adjudication officer under this section;

    (ii) any direction given by an adjudication officer under this section.

(9)   Any determination of an adjudication officer under this section shall be binding.

(10)   Regulations may provide that, in prescribed circumstances, a claimant is to be treated as having satisfied the condition mentioned in section 1(2)(b).

(11)   Regulations may provide that, in prescribed circumstances, a jobseeker's agreement is to be treated as having effect on a date, to be determined in accordance with the regulations, before it would otherwise have effect.

(12)   Except in such circumstances as may be prescribed, a jobseeker's agreement entered into by a claimant shall cease to have effect on the coming to an end of an award of a jobseeker's allowance made to him.

(13)   In this section and section 10 "employment officer" means an officer of the Secretary of State or such other person as may be designated for the purposes of this section by an order made by the Secretary of State.

---

NOTES

Commencement: 7 October 1996 (sub-ss (1), (8), (10)–(12) certain purposes, sub-ss (2)–(7), (9)); 12 December 1995 (sub-ss (1), (8), (10)–(12) remaining purposes, sub-s (13)).

---

## 10   Variation of jobseeker's agreement

(1)   A jobseeker's agreement may be varied, in the prescribed manner, by agreement between the claimant and any employment officer.

(2)   Any agreement to vary a jobseeker's agreement shall be in writing and be signed by both parties.

(3)   A copy of the agreement, as varied, shall be given to the claimant.

(4)   An employment officer shall not agree to a variation of a jobseeker's agreement, unless, in the officer's opinion, the conditions mentioned in section 1(2)(a) and (c) would continue to be satisfied with respect to the claimant if he were to comply with, or be treated as complying with, the agreement as proposed to be varied.

(5)   The employment officer may, and if asked to do so by the claimant shall forthwith, refer a proposed variation of a jobseeker's agreement to an adjudication officer for him to determine—
   (a)   whether, if the claimant concerned were to comply with the agreement as proposed to be varied, he would satisfy—
      (i)   the condition mentioned in section 1(2)(a), or
      (ii)   the condition mentioned in section 1(2)(c); and
   (b)   whether it is reasonable to expect the claimant to have to comply with the agreement as proposed to be varied.

(6)   An adjudication officer to whom a reference is made under subsection (5)—
   (a)   shall, so far as practicable, dispose of it in accordance with this section before the end of the period of 14 days from the date of the reference;
   (b)   shall give such directions as he considers appropriate as to—
      (i)   whether the jobseeker's agreement should be varied, and
      (ii)   if so, the terms on which the claimant and the employment officer are to enter into an agreement to vary it;
   (c)   may bring the jobseeker's agreement to an end where the claimant fails, within a prescribed period, to comply with a direction given under paragraph (b)(ii);

    (d)  may direct that, if—
        (i)  the jobseeker's agreement is varied, and
        (ii)  such conditions as he considers appropriate are satisfied,
      the agreement as varied is to be treated as having effect on such date, before it would otherwise have effect, as may be specified in the direction.

(7)    Regulations may provide—

    (a)  for such matters as may be prescribed to be taken into account by an adjudication officer in giving a direction under subsection (6)(b) or (d); and

    (b)  for such persons as may be prescribed to be notified of—
        (i)  any determination of an adjudication officer under this section;
        (ii)  any direction given by an adjudication officer under this section.

(8)    Any determination of an adjudication officer under this section shall be binding.

---

**NOTES**

    Commencement: 7 October 1996 (sub-ss (1), (6)(c), (7) certain purposes, sub-ss (2)–(5), (6)(a), (b), (d), (8)); 12 December 1995 (sub-ss (1), (6)(c), (7), remaining purposes).

---

## 11   Jobseeker's agreement: reviews and appeals

(1)    Any determination of, or direction given by, an adjudication officer under section 9 or 10 may be reviewed (by a different adjudication officer) on the application of the claimant or of an employment officer.

(2)    Regulations may make provision with respect to the procedure to be followed on a review under this section.

(3)    The claimant may appeal to a social security appeal tribunal against any determination of, or direction given by, an adjudication officer on a review under this section.

(4)    A social security appeal tribunal determining an appeal under this section may give a direction of a kind which an adjudication officer may give under section   9(7)(b) or (c) or (as the case may be) section 10(6)(b) or (d).

(5)    Where a social security appeal tribunal gives a direction under subsection (4) of a kind which may be given by an adjudication officer under section 10(6)(b)(ii), an adjudication officer may bring the jobseeker's agreement to an end if the claimant fails to comply with the direction within a prescribed period.

(6)    An appropriate person may, on the ground that it was erroneous in point of law, appeal to a Commissioner against the decision of a social security appeal tribunal on an appeal under this section.

(7)    Any of the following is an appropriate person for the purposes of subsection   (6)—

    (a)  the claimant;
    (b)  an adjudication officer;
    (c)  in prescribed circumstances, a trade union;
    (d)  in prescribed circumstances, any other association which exists to promote the interests and welfare of its members.

(8)    Subsections (7) to (10) of section 23 of the Administration Act (appeals to Commissioners) shall apply in relation to appeals under this section as they apply in relation to appeals under that section.

(9)    In this section "Commissioner" has the same meaning as in the Administration Act.

**NOTES**
    Commencement: 7 October 1996 (sub-ss (1), (3), (4), (6), (9), sub-ss (2), (5), (7), (8) certain purposes); 12 December 1995 (sub-ss (2), (5), (7), (8), remaining purposes).
    Administration Act: Social Security Administration Act 1992.

## PART III
## MISCELLANEOUS AND SUPPLEMENTAL

**41    Short title, commencement, extent etc**

(1)    This Act may be cited as the Jobseekers Act 1995.

(2)    Section 39 and this section (apart from subsections (4) and (5)) come into force on the passing of this Act, but otherwise the provisions of this Act come into force on such day as the Secretary of State may by order appoint.

(3)    Different days may be appointed for different purposes.

(4), (5). . .

(6)    Apart from this section, section 39 and paragraphs 11 to 16, 28, 67 and 68 of Schedule 2, this Act does not extend to Northern Ireland.

**NOTES**
    Commencement: 28 June 1995 (sub-ss (1)–(3), (6)).
    Sub-ss (4), (5): outside the scope of this work.

# CHILD SUPPORT ACT 1995

## (C 34)

*An Act to make provision with respect to child support maintenance and other maintenance; and to provide for a child maintenance bonus*

[19 July 1995]

*The child maintenance bonus*

**10    The child maintenance bonus**

(1)    The Secretary of State may by regulations make provision for the payment, in prescribed circumstances, of sums to persons—
    (a)    who are or have been in receipt of child maintenance; and
    (b)    to or in respect of whom income support or a jobseeker's allowance is or has been paid.

(2)    A sum payable under the regulations shall be known as "a child maintenance bonus".

(3)    A child maintenance bonus shall be treated for all purposes as payable by way of income support or (as the case may be) a jobseeker's allowance.

(4)    Subsection (3) is subject to section 617 of the Income and Corporation Taxes Act 1988 (which, as amended by paragraph 1 of Schedule 3, provides for a child maintenance bonus not to be taxable).

(5)   The regulations may, in particular, provide for—

   (a)   a child maintenance bonus to be payable only on the occurrence of a prescribed event;

   (b)   a bonus not to be payable unless a claim is made before the end of the prescribed period;

   (c)   the amount of a bonus (subject to any maximum prescribed by virtue of paragraph (f)) to be determined in accordance with the regulations;

   (d)   enabling amounts to be calculated by reference to periods of entitlement to income support and periods of entitlement to a jobseeker's allowance;

   (e)   treating a bonus as payable wholly by way of a jobseeker's allowance or wholly by way of income support, in a case where amounts have been calculated in accordance with provision made by virtue of paragraph (d);

   (f)   the amount of a bonus not to exceed a prescribed maximum;

   (g)   a bonus not to be payable if the amount of the bonus which would otherwise be payable is less than the prescribed minimum;

   (h)   prescribed periods to be disregarded for prescribed purposes;

   (i)   a bonus which has been paid to a person to be treated, in prescribed circumstances and for prescribed purposes, as income or capital of hers or of any other member of her family;

   (j)   treating the whole or a prescribed part of an amount which has accrued towards a person's bonus—

      (i)   as not having accrued towards her bonus; but

      (ii)   as having accrued towards the bonus of another person.

(6)   The Secretary of State may by regulations provide—

   (a)   for the whole or a prescribed part of a child maintenance bonus to be paid in such circumstances as may be prescribed to such person, other than the person who is or had been in receipt of child maintenance, as may be determined in accordance with the regulations;

   (b)   for any payments of a prescribed kind which have been collected by the Secretary of State, and retained by him, to be treated for the purposes of this section as having been received by the appropriate person as payments of child maintenance.

(7)   In this section—

"appropriate person" has such meaning as may be prescribed;

"child" means a person under the age of 16;

"child maintenance" has such meaning as may be prescribed;

"family" means—

   (a)   a married or unmarried couple;

   (b)   a married or unmarried couple and a member of the same household for whom one of them is, or both are, responsible and who is a child or a person of a prescribed description;

   (c)   except in prescribed circumstances, a person who is not a member of a married or unmarried couple and a member of the same household for whom that person is responsible and who is a child or a person of a prescribed description;

"married couple" means a man and woman who are married to each other and are members of the same household; and

"unmarried couple" means a man and woman who are not married to each other but are living together as husband and wife otherwise than in prescribed circumstances.

(8)   For the purposes of this section, the Secretary of State may by regulations make provision as to the circumstances in which—

   (a)   persons are to be treated as being or not being members of the same household;

   (b)   one person is to be treated as responsible or not responsible for another.

NOTES

  Commencement: 14 October 1996.

*Supplemental*

## 30   Short title, commencement, extent etc

(1)   This Act may be cited as the Child Support Act 1995.

(2)   This Act and the 1991 Act may be cited together as the Child Support Acts 1991 and 1995.

(3)   . . .

(4)   The other provisions of this Act come into force on such day as the Secretary of State may by order appoint and different days may be appointed for different purposes.

(5), (6). . .

NOTES

  Commencement: 19 July 1995 (sub-ss (1), (2), (4)).
  Sub-ss (3), (5), (6): outside the scope of this work.

# ASYLUM AND IMMIGRATION ACT 1996

## (C 49)

*An Act to amend and supplement the Immigration Act 1971 and the Asylum and Immigration Appeals Act 1993; to make further provision with respect to persons subject to immigration control and the employment of such persons; and for connected purposes*

[24 July 1996]

*Asylum claims*

## 2   Removal etc of asylum claimants to safe third countries

(1)   Nothing in section 6 of the 1993 Act (protection of claimants from deportation etc) shall prevent a person who has made a claim for asylum being removed from the United Kingdom if—

   (a)   the Secretary of State has certified that, in his opinion, the conditions mentioned in subsection (2) below are fulfilled;

   (b)   the certificate has not been set aside on an appeal under section 3 below; and

   (c)   except in the case of a person who is to be sent to a country or territory to which subsection (3) below applies, the time for giving notice of such an appeal has expired and no such appeal is pending.

(2)    The conditions are—

(a)    that the person is not a national or citizen of the country or territory to which he is to be sent;

(b)    that his life and liberty would not be threatened in that country or territory by reason of his race, religion, nationality, membership of a particular social group, or political opinion; and

(c)    that the government of that country or territory would not send him to another country or territory otherwise than in accordance with the Convention.

(3)    This subsection applies to any country or territory which is or forms part of a member State, or is designated for the purposes of this subsection in an order made by the Secretary of State by statutory instrument.

(4)    The first order under this section shall not be made unless a draft of the order has been laid before and approved by a resolution of each House of Parliament.

(5)    A statutory instrument containing a subsequent order under this section shall be subject to annulment in pursuance of a resolution of either House of Parliament.

(6)    For the purposes of this section, an appeal under section 3 below is pending during the period beginning when notice of appeal is duly given and ending when the appeal is finally determined or withdrawn.

(7)    In this section "claim for asylum" and "the Convention" have the same meanings as in the 1993 Act.

NOTES

Commencement: 1 September 1996.

## 3    Appeals against certificates under section 2

(1)    Where a certificate has been issued under section 2(1) above in respect of any person—

(a)    that person may appeal against the certificate to a special adjudicator on the ground that any of the conditions mentioned in section 2(2) above was not fulfilled when the certificate was issued, or has since ceased to be fulfilled; but

(b)    unless and until the certificate is set aside on such an appeal, he shall not be entitled to bring or pursue any appeal under—

(i)    Part II of the 1971 Act (appeals: general); or

(ii)    section 8 of the 1993 Act (appeals to special adjudicator on Convention grounds),

as respects matters arising before his removal from the United Kingdom.

(2)    A person who has been, or is to be, sent to a country or territory to which section 2(3) above applies shall not be entitled to bring or pursue an appeal under this section so long as he is in the United Kingdom.

(3)    The Lord Chancellor shall designate such number of the adjudicators appointed for the purposes of Part II of the 1971 Act as he thinks necessary to act as special adjudicators for the purposes of this section and may from time to time vary that number and the persons who are so designated.

(4)    Subject to subsection (5) below, the following provisions of the 1971 Act, namely—

(a) section 18 (notice of decisions appealable under that Part and statement of appeal rights etc);

(b) section 19 (determination of appeals under that Part by adjudicators);

(c) section 21 (references of cases by Secretary of State for further consideration);

(d) section 22(1) to (4), (6) and (7) (rules of procedure for appeals);

(e) section 23 (grants to voluntary organisations helping persons with rights of appeal); and

(f) Schedule 5 (provisions about adjudicators and Immigration Appeal Tribunal),

shall have effect as if this section were contained in Part II of that Act.

(5) Rules of procedure under section 22 of the 1971 Act—

(a) may make special provision in relation to appeals under this section; and

(b) may make different provision in relation to appeals by persons who have been, or are to be, sent to countries or territories of different descriptions;

and so much of paragraph 5 of Schedule 5 to that Act as relates to the allocation of duties among the adjudicators shall have effect subject to subsection (3) above.

(6) Paragraph 29 of Schedule 2 to the 1971 Act (grant of bail pending appeal) shall have effect as if the references to appeals under sections 13(1), 15(1)(a) and 16 of that Act included references to appeals under this section.

---

NOTES

Commencement: 1 September 1996 (sub-ss (1), (2), (4), (6)); 26 July 1996 (remainder).

---

*Immigration offences*

## 7 Power of arrest and search warrants

(1) A constable or immigration officer may arrest without warrant anyone whom he has reasonable grounds for suspecting to have committed an offence to which this section applies.

(2) If—

(a) a justice of the peace is by written information on oath satisfied that there is reasonable ground for suspecting that a person who is liable to be arrested under subsection (1) above is to be found on any premises; or

(b) in Scotland, a sheriff, or a justice of the peace, having jurisdiction in the place where the premises are situated is by evidence on oath so satisfied,

he may grant a warrant authorising any constable to enter, if need be by force, the premises named in the warrant for the purposes of searching for and arresting that person.

(3) The following provisions, namely—

(a) section 8 of the Police and Criminal Evidence Act 1984 (power of justice to authorise entry and search of premises); and

(b) Article 10 of the Police and Criminal Evidence (Northern Ireland) Order 1989 (corresponding provision for Northern Ireland),

shall have effect as if the reference in subsection (1) of that section or, as the case may be, paragraph (1) of that Article to a serious arrestable offence included a reference to an offence to which this section applies.

(4)    This section applies to the following offences under section 24(1) of the 1971 Act, namely—

    (a)   an offence under paragraph (a) (illegal entry);

    (b)   an offence under paragraph (aa) (obtaining leave to enter or remain by deception); and

    (c)   an offence under paragraph (b) (remaining beyond time limited by leave or failing to observe condition of leave).

(5)    In this section "immigration officer" has the same meaning as in the 1971 Act.

**NOTES**

Commencement: 1 October 1996.

*Persons subject to immigration control*

## 8    Restrictions on employment

(1)    Subject to subsection (2) below, if any person ("the employer") employs a person subject to immigration control ("the employee") who has attained the age of 16, the employer shall be guilty of an offence if—

    (a)   the employee has not been granted leave to enter or remain in the United Kingdom; or

    (b)   the employee's leave is not valid and subsisting, or is subject to a condition precluding him from taking up the employment,

and (in either case) the employee does not satisfy such conditions as may be specified in an order made by the Secretary of State.

(2)    Subject to subsection (3) below, in proceedings under this section, it shall be a defence to prove that—

    (a)   before the employment began, there was produced to the employer a document which appeared to him to relate to the employee and to be of a description specified in an order made by the Secretary of State; and

    (b)   either the document was retained by the employer, or a copy or other record of it was made by the employer in a manner specified in the order in relation to documents of that description.

(3)    The defence afforded by subsection (2) above shall not be available in any case where the employer knew that his employment of the employee would constitute an offence under this section.

(4)    A person guilty of an offence under this section shall be liable on summary conviction to a fine not exceeding level 5 on the standard scale.

(5)    Where an offence under this section committed by a body corporate is proved to have been committed with the consent or connivance of, or to be attributable to any neglect on the part of—

    (a)   any director, manager, secretary or other similar officer of the body corporate; or

    (b)   any person who was purporting to act in any such capacity,

he as well as the body corporate shall be guilty of the offence and shall be liable to be proceeded against and punished accordingly.

(6)    Where the affairs of a body corporate are managed by its members, subsection    (5) above shall apply in relation to the acts and defaults of a member in connection with his functions of management as if he were a director of the body corporate.

(7)    An order under this section shall be made by statutory instrument which shall be subject to annulment in pursuance of a resolution of either House of Parliament.

(8)    In this section—

"contract of employment" means a contract of service or apprenticeship, whether express or implied, and (if it is express) whether it is oral or in writing;

"employ" means employ under a contract of employment and "employment" shall be construed accordingly.

NOTES

Commencement: 27 January 1997 (sub-ss (1), (2) certain purposes, sub-ss (3)–(8)); 1 December 1996 (sub-ss (1), (2), remaining purposes).

## 9    Entitlement to housing accommodation and assistance

(1)    Each [local housing authority within the meaning of the Housing Act 1985] shall secure that, so far as practicable, no tenancy of, or licence to occupy, housing accommodation provided under [Part II of that Act] is granted to a person subject to immigration control unless he is of a class specified in an order made by the Secretary of State.

(2)    . . .

(3)    An order under this section—

(a)    may make different provision for different circumstances or for accommodation . . . of different descriptions; and

(b)    shall be made by statutory instrument which shall be subject to annulment in pursuance of a resolution of either House of Parliament.

(4)    In this section—

. . . . .

"tenancy" . . . has the same meaning as it has in the Housing Act 1985.

[(5)    This section does not apply in relation to any allocation of housing accommodation to which Part VI of the Housing Act 1996 (allocation of housing accommodation) applies.]

NOTES

Commencement: 1 April 1997 (sub-s (5)); 19 August 1996 (sub-ss (1), (2) certain purposes, sub-s (4)); 26 July 1996 (sub-ss (1), (2) remaining purposes, sub-s (3)).

Sub-s (1): words in square brackets substituted, in relation to England and Wales, by the Housing Act 1996, s 173, Sch 16, para 3(2).

Sub-s (2): repealed with savings, in relation to England and Wales, by the Housing Act 1996, s 227, Sch 19, Pt VIII; for savings see the Housing Act 1996 (Commencement No 5 and Transitional Provisions) Order 1996, SI 1996/2959, Schedule, para 1.

Sub-s (3): words omitted repealed with savings, in relation to England and Wales, by the Housing Act 1996, s 227, Sch 19, Pt VIII; for savings see SI 1996/2959, Schedule, para 1.

Sub-s (4): definitions omitted repealed with savings, in relation to England and Wales, and in definition "tenancy" words omitted repealed, in relation to England and Wales, by the Housing Act 1996, s 227, Sch 19, Pts VII, VIII, for savings see SI 1996/2959, Schedule, para 1.

Sub-s (5): added, in relation to England and Wales, by the Housing Act 1996, s 173, Sch 16, para 3(2).

## 11    Saving for social security regulations

(1)    Notwithstanding any enactment or rule of law, regulations may exclude any person who has made a claim for asylum from entitlement to any of the following benefits, namely—

(a)    income support, housing benefit and council tax benefit under the Social Security Contributions and Benefits Act 1992;

    (b) income support and housing benefit under the Social Security Contributions and Benefits (Northern Ireland) Act 1992; and

    (c) jobseeker's allowance under the Jobseekers Act 1995 or the Jobseekers (Northern Ireland) Order 1995.

(2) Regulations may provide that, where such a person who is so excluded is subsequently recorded by the Secretary of State as a refugee within the meaning of the Convention—

    (a) that person may, within a prescribed period, claim the whole or any prescribed proportion of any income support, housing benefit or council tax benefit to which he would have been entitled had he been recorded as a refugee immediately after he made the claim for asylum; and

    (b) where he makes such a claim as is mentioned in paragraph (a) above in respect of housing benefit or council tax benefit having resided in the areas of two or more local authorities in Great Britain, the claim shall be investigated and determined, and any benefit awarded shall be paid or allowed, by such one of those authorities as may be prescribed.

(3) Regulations making such provision as is mentioned in subsection (2)(b) above may require the other authorities there mentioned to supply the prescribed authority with such information as it may reasonably require in connection with the exercise of its functions under the regulations.

(4) Schedule 1 to this Act—

    (a) Part I of which modifies the Social Security (Persons from Abroad) Miscellaneous Amendments Regulations 1996; and

    (b) Part II of which modifies the Social Security (Persons from Abroad) (Miscellaneous Amendments) Regulations (Northern Ireland) 1996,

shall have effect.

(5) The Jobseeker's Allowance (Amendment) Regulations 1996 shall have effect as if they had been made on the day on which this Act is passed.

(6) In this section—

"claim for asylum" and "the Convention" have the same meanings as in the 1993 Act;

"prescribed" means prescribed by regulations;

"regulations"—

    (a) in relation to income support, housing benefit or council tax benefit under the Social Security Contributions and Benefits Act 1992, means regulations under that Act or the Social Security Administration Act 1992;

    (b) in relation to income support or housing benefit under the Social Security Contributions and Benefits (Northern Ireland) Act 1992, means regulations under that Act or the Social Security Administration (Northern Ireland) Act 1992;

    (c) in relation to jobseeker's allowance under the Jobseekers Act 1995, means regulations under that Act or the Social Security Administration Act 1992;

    (d) in relation to jobseeker's allowance under the Jobseekers (Northern Ireland) Order 1995, means regulations under that Order or the Social Security Administration (Northern Ireland) Act 1992.

NOTES

Commencement: 24 July 1996.

**13   Short title, interpretation, commencement and extent**

(1)   This Act may be cited as the Asylum and Immigration Act 1996.

(2)   In this Act—
"the 1971 Act" means the Immigration Act 1971;
"the 1993 Act" means the Asylum and Immigration Appeals Act 1993;
"person subject to immigration control" means a person who under the 1971 Act requires leave to enter or remain in the United Kingdom (whether or not such leave has been given).

(3)   This Act, except section 11 and Schedule 1, shall come into force on such day as the Secretary of State may by order made by statutory instrument appoint, and different days may be appointed for different purposes.

(4)   An order under subsection (3) above may make such transitional and supplemental provision as the Secretary of State thinks necessary or expedient.

(5)   Her Majesty may by Order in Council direct that any of the provisions of this Act shall extend, with such modifications as appear to Her Majesty to be appropriate, to any of the Channel Islands or the Isle of Man.

(6)   This Act extends to Northern Ireland.

NOTES
Commencement: 26 July 1996.

# FAMILY LAW ACT 1996
## (C 27)

*An Act to make provision with respect to: divorce and separation; legal aid in connection with mediation in disputes relating to family matters; proceedings in cases where marriages have broken down; rights of occupation of certain domestic premises; prevention of molestation; the inclusion in certain orders under the Children Act 1989 of provisions about the occupation of a dwelling-house; the transfer of tenancies between spouses and persons who have lived together as husband and wife; and for connected purposes*

[4 July 1996]

## PART I
## PRINCIPLES OF PARTS II AND III

**1   The general principles underlying Parts II and III**

The court and any person, in exercising functions under or in consequence of Parts II and III, shall have regard to the following general principles—

(a)   that the institution of marriage is to be supported;

(b)   that the parties to a marriage which may have broken down are to be encouraged to take all practicable steps, whether by marriage counselling or otherwise, to save the marriage;

(c)   that a marriage which has irretrievably broken down and is being brought to an end should be brought to an end—
(i)   with minimum distress to the parties and to the children affected;
(ii)   with questions dealt with in a manner designed to promote as good a continuing relationship between the parties and any children affected as is possible in the circumstances; and
(iii)   without costs being unreasonably incurred in connection with the procedures to be followed in bringing the marriage to an end; and

(d) that any risk to one of the parties to a marriage, and to any children, of violence from the other party should, so far as reasonably practicable, be removed or diminished.

NOTES
Commencement: 21 March 1997.

# PART II
# DIVORCE AND SEPARATION

*Court orders*

## 2   Divorce and separation

(1)   The court may—
   (a)   by making an order (to be known as a divorce order), dissolve a marriage; or
   (b)   by making an order (to be known as a separation order), provide for the separation of the parties to a marriage.

(2)   Any such order comes into force on being made.

(3)   A separation order remains in force—
   (a)   while the marriage continues; or
   (b)   until cancelled by the court on the joint application of the parties.

NOTES
Commencement: to be appointed.

## 3   Circumstances in which orders are made

(1)   If an application for a divorce order or for a separation order is made to the court under this section by one or both of the parties to a marriage, the court shall make the order applied for if (but only if)—
   (a)   the marriage has broken down irretrievably;
   (b)   the requirements of section 8 about information meetings are satisfied;
   (c)   the requirements of section 9 about the parties' arrangements for the future are satisfied; and
   (d)   the application has not been withdrawn.

(2)   A divorce order may not be made if an order preventing divorce is in force under section 10.

(3)   If the court is considering an application for a divorce order and an application for a separation order in respect of the same marriage it shall proceed as if it were considering only the application for a divorce order unless—
   (a)   an order preventing divorce is in force with respect to the marriage;
   (b)   the court makes an order preventing divorce; or
   (c)   section 7(6) or (13) applies.

NOTES
Commencement: to be appointed.

## 4 Conversion of separation order into divorce order

(1)   A separation order which is made before the second anniversary of the marriage may not be converted into a divorce order under this section until after that anniversary.

(2)   A separation order may not be converted into a divorce order under this section at any time while—

(a)   an order preventing divorce is in force under section 10; or

(b)   subsection (4) applies.

(3)   Otherwise, if a separation order is in force and an application for a divorce order—

(a)   is made under this section by either or both of the parties to the marriage, and

(b)   is not withdrawn,

the court shall grant the application once the requirements of section 11 have been satisfied.

(4)   Subject to subsection (5), this subsection applies if—

(a)   there is a child of the family who is under the age of sixteen when the application under this section is made; or

(b)   the application under this section is made by one party and the other party applies to the court, before the end of such period as may be prescribed by rules of court, for time for further reflection.

(5)   Subsection (4)—

(a)   does not apply if, at the time when the application under this section is made, there is an occupation order or a non-molestation order in force in favour of the applicant, or of a child of the family, made against the other party;

(b)   does not apply if the court is satisfied that delaying the making of a divorce order would be significantly detrimental to the welfare of any child of the family;

(c)   ceases to apply—

(i)   at the end of the period of six months beginning with the end of the period for reflection and consideration by reference to which the separation order was made; or

(ii)   if earlier, on there ceasing to be any children of the family to whom subsection (4)(a) applied.

NOTES

Commencement: to be appointed.

*Marital breakdown*

## 5 Marital breakdown

(1)   A marriage is to be taken to have broken down irretrievably if (but only if)—

(a)   a statement has been made by one (or both) of the parties that the maker of the statement (or each of them) believes that the marriage has broken down;

(b)   the statement complies with the requirements of section 6;

(c)   the period for reflection and consideration fixed by section 7 has ended; and

    (d)  the application under section 3 is accompanied by a declaration by the party making the application that—
        (i)  having reflected on the breakdown, and
       (ii)  having considered the requirements of this Part as to the parties' arrangements for the future,
    the applicant believes that the marriage cannot be saved.

(2)    The statement and the application under section 3 do not have to be made by the same party.

(3)    An application may not be made under section 3 by reference to a particular statement if—
    (a)  the parties have jointly given notice (in accordance with rules of court) withdrawing the statement; or
    (b)  a period of one year ("the specified period") has passed since the end of the period for reflection and consideration.

(4)    Any period during which an order preventing divorce is in force is not to count towards the specified period mentioned in subsection (3)(b).

(5)    Subsection (6) applies if, before the end of the specified period, the parties jointly give notice to the court that they are attempting reconciliation but require additional time.

(6)    The specified period—
    (a)  stops running on the day on which the notice is received by the court; but
    (b)  resumes running on the day on which either of the parties gives notice to the court that the attempted reconciliation has been unsuccessful.

(7)    If the specified period is interrupted by a continuous period of more than 18 months, any application by either of the parties for a divorce order or for a separation order must be by reference to a new statement received by the court at any time after the end of the 18 months.

(8)    The Lord Chancellor may by order amend subsection (3)(b) by varying the specified period.

---

NOTES

Commencement: to be appointed.

---

## 6   Statement of marital breakdown

(1)    A statement under section 5(1)(a) is to be known as a statement of marital breakdown; but in this Part it is generally referred to as "a statement".

(2)    If a statement is made by one party it must also state that that party—
    (a)  is aware of the purpose of the period for reflection and consideration as described in section 7; and
    (b)  wishes to make arrangements for the future.

(3)    If a statement is made by both parties it must also state that each of them—
    (a)  is aware of the purpose of the period for reflection and consideration as described in section 7; and
    (b)  wishes to make arrangements for the future.

(4)    A statement must be given to the court in accordance with the requirements of rules made under section 12.

(5)    A statement must also satisfy any other requirements imposed by rules made under that section.

(6)    A statement made at a time when the circumstances of the case include any of those mentioned in subsection (7) is ineffective for the purposes of this Part.

(7)    The circumstances are—
    (a)    that a statement has previously been made with respect to the marriage and it is, or will become, possible—
      (i)    for an application for a divorce order, or
      (ii)   for an application for a separation order,
    to be made by reference to the previous statement;
    (b)    that such an application has been made in relation to the marriage and has not been withdrawn;
    (c)    that a separation order is in force.

NOTES

Commencement: to be appointed.

*Reflection and consideration*

## 7    Period for reflection and consideration

(1)    Where a statement has been made, a period for the parties—
    (a)    to reflect on whether the marriage can be saved and to have an opportunity to effect a reconciliation, and
    (b)    to consider what arrangements should be made for the future,

must pass before an application for a divorce order or for a separation order may be made by reference to that statement.

(2)    That period is to be known as the period for reflection and consideration.

(3)    The period for reflection and consideration is nine months beginning with the fourteenth day after the day on which the statement is received by the court.

(4)    Where—
    (a)    the statement has been made by one party,
    (b)    rules made under section 12 require the court to serve a copy of the statement on the other party, and
    (c)    failure to comply with the rules causes inordinate delay in service,

the court may, on the application of that other party, extend the period for reflection and consideration.

(5)    An extension under subsection (4) may be for any period not exceeding the time between—
    (a)    the beginning of the period for reflection and consideration; and
    (b)    the time when service is effected.

(6)    A statement which is made before the first anniversary of the marriage to which it relates is ineffective for the purposes of any application for a divorce order.

(7)    Subsection (8) applies if, at any time during the period for reflection and consideration, the parties jointly give notice to the court that they are attempting a reconciliation but require additional time.

(8)    The period for reflection and consideration—
    (a)    stops running on the day on which the notice is received by the court; but
    (b)    resumes running on the day on which either of the parties gives notice to the court that the attempted reconciliation has been unsuccessful.

(9)   If the period for reflection and consideration is interrupted under sub-section   (8) by a continuous period of more than 18 months, any application by either of the parties for a divorce order or for a separation order must be by reference to a new statement received by the court at any time after the end of the 18 months.

(10)   Where an application for a divorce order is made by one party, subsection (13) applies if—
    (a)   the other party applies to the court, within the prescribed period, for time for further reflection; and
    (b)   the requirements of section 9 (except any imposed under section 9(3)) are satisfied.

(11)   Where any application for a divorce order is made, subsection (13) also applies if there is a child of the family who is under the age of sixteen when the application is made.

(12)   Subsection (13) does not apply if—
    (a)   at the time when the application for a divorce order is made, there is an occupation order or a non-molestation order in force in favour of the applicant, or of a child of the family, made against the other party; or
    (b)   the court is satisfied that delaying the making of a divorce order would be significantly detrimental to the welfare of any child of the family.

(13)   If this subsection applies, the period for reflection and consideration is extended by a period of six months, but—
    (a)   only in relation to the application for a divorce order in respect of which the application under subsection (10) was made; and
    (b)   without invalidating that application for a divorce order.

(14)   A period for reflection and consideration which is extended under sub-section   (13), and which has not otherwise come to an end, comes to an end on there ceasing to be any children of the family to whom subsection (11) applied.

---

NOTES
Commencement: to be appointed.

---

## 8   Attendance at information meetings

(1)   The requirements about information meetings are as follows.

(2)   A party making a statement must (except in prescribed circumstances) have attended an information meeting not less than three months before making the statement.

(3)   Different information meetings must be arranged with respect to different marriages.

(4)   In the case of a statement made by both parties, the parties may attend separate meetings or the same meeting.

(5)   Where one party has made a statement, the other party must (except in prescribed circumstances) attend an information meeting before—
    (a)   making any application to the court—
       (i)   with respect to a child of the family; or
       (ii)   of a prescribed description relating to property or financial matters; or
    (b)   contesting any such application.

(6)   In this section "information meeting" means a meeting organised, in accordance with prescribed provisions for the purpose—

  (a)   of providing, in accordance with prescribed provisions, relevant information to the party or parties attending about matters which may arise in connection with the provisions of, or made under, this Part or Part III; and

  (b)   of giving the party or parties attending the information meeting the opportunity of having a meeting with a marriage counsellor and of encouraging that party or those parties to attend that meeting.

(7)   An information meeting must be conducted by a person who—

  (a)   is qualified and appointed in accordance with prescribed provisions; and

  (b)   will have no financial or other interest in any marital proceedings between the parties.

(8)   Regulations made under this section may, in particular, make provision—

  (a)   about the places and times at which information meetings are to be held;

  (b)   for written information to be given to persons attending them;

  (c)   for the giving of information to parties (otherwise than at information meetings) in cases in which the requirement to attend such meetings does not apply;

  (d)   for information of a prescribed kind to be given only with the approval of the Lord Chancellor or only by a person or by persons approved by him; and

  (e)   for information to be given, in prescribed circumstances, only with the approval of the Lord Chancellor or only by a person, or by persons, approved by him.

(9)   Regulations made under subsection (6) must, in particular, make provision with respect to the giving of information about—

  (a)   marriage counselling and other marriage support services;

  (b)   the importance to be attached to the welfare, wishes and feelings of children;

  (c)   how the parties may acquire a better understanding of the ways in which children can be helped to cope with the breakdown of a marriage;

  (d)   the nature of the financial questions that may arise on divorce or separation, and services which are available to help the parties;

  (e)   protection available against violence, and how to obtain support and assistance;

  (f)   mediation;

  (g)   the availability to each of the parties of independent legal advice and representation;

  (h)   the principles of legal aid and where the parties can get advice about obtaining legal aid;

  (i)   the divorce and separation process.

(10)   Before making any regulations under subsection (6), the Lord Chancellor must consult such persons concerned with the provision of relevant information as he considers appropriate.

(11)   A meeting with a marriage counsellor arranged under this section—

  (a)   must be held in accordance with prescribed provisions; and

  (b)   must be with a person qualified and appointed in accordance with prescribed provisions.

(12) A person who would not be required to make any contribution towards mediation provided for him under Part IIIA of the Legal Aid Act 1988 shall not be required to make any contribution towards the cost of a meeting with a marriage counsellor arranged for him under this section.

(13) In this section "prescribed" means prescribed by regulations made by the Lord Chancellor.

NOTES

Commencement: to be appointed.

## 9 Arrangements for the future

(1)   The requirements as to the parties' arrangements for the future are as follows.

(2)   One of the following must be produced to the court—

    (a)   a court order (made by consent or otherwise) dealing with their financial arrangements;

    (b)   a negotiated agreement as to their financial arrangements;

    (c)   a declaration by both parties that they have made their financial arrangements;

    (d)   a declaration by one of the parties (to which no objection has been notified to the court by the other party) that—

      (i)   he has no significant assets and does not intend to make an application for financial provision;

      (ii)   he believes that the other party has no significant assets and does not intend to make an application for financial provision; and

      (iii)   there are therefore no financial arrangements to be made.

(3)   If the parties—

    (a)   were married to each other in accordance with usages of a kind mentioned in section 26(1) of the Marriage Act 1949 (marriages which may be solemnized on authority of superintendent registrar's certificate), and

    (b)   are required to co-operate if the marriage is to be dissolved in accordance with those usages,

the court may, on the application of either party, direct that there must also be produced to the court a declaration by both parties that they have taken such steps as are required to dissolve the marriage in accordance with those usages.

(4)   A direction under subsection (3)—

    (a)   may be given only if the court is satisfied that in all the circumstances of the case it is just and reasonable to give it; and

    (b)   may be revoked by the court at any time.

(5)   The requirements of section 11 must have been satisfied.

(6)   Schedule 1 supplements the provisions of this section.

(7)   If the court is satisfied, on an application made by one of the parties after the end of the period for reflection and consideration, that the circumstances of the case are—

    (a)   those set out in paragraph 1 of Schedule 1,

    (b)   those set out in paragraph 2 of that Schedule,

    (c)   those set out in paragraph 3 of that Schedule, or

    (d)   those set out in paragraph 4 of that Schedule,

it may make a divorce order or a separation order even though the requirements of subsection (2) have not been satisfied.

(8)    If the parties' arrangements for the future include a division of pension assets or rights under section 25B of the 1973 Act or section 10 of the Family Law (Scotland) Act 1985, any declaration under subsection (2) must be a statutory declaration.

NOTES
Commencement: to be appointed.

*Orders preventing divorce*

## 10    Hardship: orders preventing divorce

(1)    If an application for a divorce order has been made by one of the parties to a marriage, the court may, on the application of the other party, order that the marriage is not to be dissolved.

(2)    Such an order (an "order preventing divorce") may be made only if the court is satisfied—
(a)    that dissolution of the marriage would result in substantial financial or other hardship to the other party or to a child of the family; and
(b)    that it would be wrong, in all the circumstances (including the conduct of the parties and the interests of any child of the family), for the marriage to be dissolved.

(3)    If an application for the cancellation of an order preventing divorce is made by one or both of the parties, the court shall cancel the order unless it is still satisfied—
(a)    that dissolution of the marriage would result in substantial financial or other hardship to the party in whose favour the order was made or to a child of the family; and
(b)    that it would be wrong, in all the circumstances (including the conduct of the parties and the interests of any child of the family), for the marriage to be dissolved.

(4)    If an order preventing a divorce is cancelled, the court may make a divorce order in respect of the marriage only if an application is made under section 3 or 4(3) after the cancellation.

(5)    An order preventing divorce may include conditions which must be satisfied before an application for cancellation may be made under subsection (3).

(6)    In this section "hardship" includes the loss of a chance to obtain a future benefit (as well as the loss of an existing benefit).

NOTES
Commencement: to be appointed.

*Welfare of children*

## 11    Welfare of children

(1)    In any proceedings for a divorce order or a separation order, the court shall consider—
(a)    whether there are any children of the family to whom this section applies; and
(b)    where there are any such children, whether (in the light of the arrangements which have been, or are proposed to be, made for their upbringing and welfare) it should exercise any of its powers under the Children Act 1989 with respect to any of them.

(2)    Where, in any case to which this section applies, it appears to the court that—

(a)    the circumstances of the case require it, or are likely to require it, to exercise any of its powers under the Children Act 1989 with respect to any such child,

(b)    it is not in a position to exercise the power, or (as the case may be) those powers, without giving further consideration to the case, and

(c)    there are exceptional circumstances which make it desirable in the interests of the child that the court should give a direction under this section,

it may direct that the divorce order or separation order is not to be made until the court orders otherwise.

(3)    In deciding whether the circumstances are as mentioned in subsection (2)(a), the court shall treat the welfare of the child as paramount.

(4)    In making that decision, the court shall also have particular regard, on the evidence before it, to—

(a)    the wishes and feelings of the child considered in the light of his age and understanding and the circumstances in which those wishes were expressed;

(b)    the conduct of the parties in relation to the upbringing of the child;

(c)    the general principle that, in the absence of evidence to the contrary, the welfare of the child will be best served by—

(i)    his having regular contact with those who have parental responsibility for him and with other members of his family; and

(ii)    the maintenance of as good a continuing relationship with his parents as is possible; and

(d)    any risk to the child attributable to—

(i)    where the person with whom the child will reside is living or proposes to live;

(ii)    any person with whom that person is living or with whom he proposes to live; or

(iii)    any other arrangements for his care and upbringing.

(5)    This section applies to—

(a)    any child of the family who has not reached the age of sixteen at the date when the court considers the case in accordance with the requirements of this section; and

(b)    any child of the family who has reached that age at that date and in relation to whom the court directs that this section shall apply.

NOTES

Commencement: to be appointed.

*Resolution of disputes*

## 13    Directions with respect to mediation

(1)    After the court has received a statement, it may give a direction requiring each party to attend a meeting arranged in accordance with the direction for the purpose—

(a)    of enabling an explanation to be given of the facilities available to the parties for mediation in relation to disputes between them; and

(b)    of providing an opportunity for each party to agree to take advantage of those facilities.

(2)    A direction may be given at any time, including in the course of proceedings connected with the breakdown of the marriage (as to which see section 25).

(3)    A direction may be given on the application of either of the parties or on the initiative of the court.

(4)    The parties are to be required to attend the same meeting unless—
    (a)   one of them asks, or both of them ask, for separate meetings; or
    (b)   the court considers separate meetings to be more appropriate.

(5)    A direction shall—
    (a)   specify a person chosen by the court (with that person's agreement) to arrange and conduct the meeting or meetings; and
    (b)   require such person as may be specified in the direction to produce to the court, at such time as the court may direct, a report stating—
        (i)   whether the parties have complied with the direction; and
        (ii)  if they have, whether they have agreed to take part in any mediation.

NOTES
Commencement: to be appointed.

## 14    Adjournments

(1)    The court's power to adjourn any proceedings connected with the breakdown of a marriage includes power to adjourn—
    (a)   for the purpose of allowing the parties to comply with a direction under section 13; or
    (b)   for the purpose of enabling disputes to be resolved amicably.

(2)    In determining whether to adjourn for either purpose, the court shall have regard in particular to the need to protect the interests of any child of the family.

(3)    If the court adjourns any proceedings connected with the breakdown of a marriage for either purpose, the period of the adjournment must not exceed the maximum period prescribed by rules of court.

(4)    Unless the only purpose of the adjournment is to allow the parties to comply with a direction under section 13, the court shall order one or both of them to produce to the court a report as to—
    (a)   whether they have taken part in mediation during the adjournment;
    (b)   whether, as a result, any agreement has been reached between them;
    (c)   the extent to which any dispute between them has been resolved as a result of any such agreement;
    (d)   the need for further mediation; and
    (e)   how likely it is that further mediation will be successful.

NOTES
Commencement: to be appointed.

*Financial provision*

## 15    Financial arrangements

(1)    Schedule 2 amends the 1973 Act.

(2)    The main object of Schedule 2 is—

(a) to provide that, in the case of divorce or separation, an order about financial provision may be made under that Act before a divorce order or separation order is made; but

(b) to retain (with minor changes) the position under that Act where marriages are annulled.

(3) Schedule 2 also makes minor and consequential amendments of the 1973 Act connected with the changes mentioned in subsection (1).

**NOTES**

Commencement: to be appointed.

*Marriage support services*

## 22 Funding for marriage support services

(1) The Lord Chancellor may, with the approval of the Treasury, make grants in connection with—
(a) the provision of marriage support services;
(b) research into the causes of marital breakdown;
(c) research into ways of preventing marital breakdown.

(2) Any grant under this section may be made subject to such conditions as the Lord Chancellor considers appropriate.

(3) In exercising his power to make grants in connection with the provision of marriage support services, the Lord Chancellor is to have regard, in particular, to the desirability of services of that kind being available when they are first needed.

**NOTES**

Commencement: 21 March 1997.

## 23 Provision of marriage counselling

(1) The Lord Chancellor or a person appointed by him may secure the provision, in accordance with regulations made by the Lord Chancellor, of marriage counselling.

(2) Marriage counselling may only be provided under this section at a time when a period for reflection and consideration—
(a) is running in relation to the marriage; or
(b) is interrupted under section 7(8) (but not for a continuous period of more than 18 months).

(3) Marriage counselling may only be provided under this section for persons who would not be required to make any contribution towards the cost of mediation provided for them under Part IIIA of the Legal Aid Act 1988.

(4) Persons for whom marriage counselling is provided under this section are not to be required to make any contribution towards the cost of the counselling.

(5)–(9) . . .

**NOTES**

Commencement: to be appointed.
Sub-ss (5)–(9): outside the scope of this work.

## PART IV
## FAMILY HOMES AND DOMESTIC VIOLENCE

*Rights to occupy matrimonial home*

**30   Rights concerning matrimonial home where one spouse has no estate, etc**

(1)   This section applies if—

    (a)   one spouse is entitled to occupy a dwelling-house by virtue of—

        (i)   a beneficial estate or interest or contract; or

        (ii)   any enactment giving that spouse the right to remain in occupation; and

    (b)   the other spouse is not so entitled.

(2)   Subject to the provisions of this Part, the spouse not so entitled has the following rights ("matrimonial home rights")—

    (a)   if in occupation, a right not to be evicted or excluded from the dwelling-house or any part of it by the other spouse except with the leave of the court given by an order under section 33;

    (b)   if not in occupation, a right with the leave of the court so given to enter into and occupy the dwelling-house.

(3)   If a spouse is entitled under this section to occupy a dwelling-house or any part of a dwelling-house, any payment or tender made or other thing done by that spouse in or towards satisfaction of any liability of the other spouse in respect of rent, mortgage payments or other outgoings affecting the dwelling-house is, whether or not it is made or done in pursuance of an order under section 40, as good as if made or done by the other spouse.

(4)   A spouse's occupation by virtue of this section—

    (a)   is to be treated, for the purposes of the Rent (Agriculture) Act 1976 and the Rent Act 1977 (other than Part V and sections 103 to 106 of that Act), as occupation by the other spouse as the other spouse's residence, and

    (b)   if the spouse occupies the dwelling-house as that spouse's only or principal home, is to be treated, for the purposes of the Housing Act 1985[, Part I of the Housing Act 1988 and Chapter I of Part V of the Housing Act 1996], as occupation by the other spouse as the other spouse's only or principal home.

(5)   If a spouse ("the first spouse")—

    (a)   is entitled under this section to occupy a dwelling-house or any part of a dwelling-house, and

    (b)   makes any payment in or towards satisfaction of any liability of the other spouse ("the second spouse") in respect of mortgage payments affecting the dwelling-house,

the person to whom the payment is made may treat it as having been made by the second spouse, but the fact that that person has treated any such payment as having been so made does not affect any claim of the first spouse against the second spouse to an interest in the dwelling-house by virtue of the payment.

(6)   If a spouse is entitled under this section to occupy a dwelling-house or part of a dwelling-house by reason of an interest of the other spouse under a trust, all the provisions of subsections (3) to (5) apply in relation to the trustees as they apply in relation to the other spouse.

(7)    This section does not apply to a dwelling-house which has at no time been, and which was at no time intended by the spouses to be, a matrimonial home of theirs.

(8)    A spouse's matrimonial home rights continue—
   (a)   only so long as the marriage subsists, except to the extent that an order under section 33(5) otherwise provides; and
   (b)   only so long as the other spouse is entitled as mentioned in subsection (1) to occupy the dwelling-house, except where provision is made by section 31 for those rights to be a charge on an estate or interest in the dwelling-house.

(9)    It is hereby declared that a spouse—
   (a)   who has an equitable interest in a dwelling-house or in its proceeds of sale, but
   (b)   is not a spouse in whom there is vested (whether solely or as joint tenant) a legal estate in fee simple or a legal term of years absolute in the dwelling-house,

is to be treated, only for the purpose of determining whether he has matrimonial home rights, as not being entitled to occupy the dwelling-house by virtue of that interest.

---

NOTES
   Commencement: 1 October 1997.
   Sub-s (4): words in square brackets in para (b) substituted by the Housing Act 1996 (Consequential Amendments) Order 1997, SI 1997/74, art 2, Schedule, para 10(a).

---

### 31    Effect of matrimonial home rights as charge on dwelling-house

(1)    Subsections (2) and (3) apply if, at any time during a marriage, one spouse is entitled to occupy a dwelling-house by virtue of a beneficial estate or interest.

(2)    The other spouse's matrimonial home rights are a charge on the estate or interest.

(3)    The charge created by subsection (2) has the same priority as if it were an equitable interest created at whichever is the latest of the following dates—
   (a)   the date on which the spouse so entitled acquires the estate or interest;
   (b)   the date of the marriage; and
   (c)   1st January 1968 (the commencement date of the Matrimonial Homes Act 1967).

(4)    Subsections (5) and (6) apply if, at any time when a spouse's matrimonial home rights are a charge on an interest of the other spouse under a trust, there are, apart from either of the spouses, no persons, living or unborn, who are or could become beneficiaries under the trust.

(5)    The rights are a charge also on the estate or interest of the trustees for the other spouse.

(6)    The charge created by subsection (5) has the same priority as if it were an equitable interest created (under powers overriding the trusts) on the date when it arises.

(7)    In determining for the purposes of subsection (4) whether there are any persons who are not, but could become, beneficiaries under the trust, there is to be disregarded any potential exercise of a general power of appointment exercisable by either or both of the spouses alone (whether or not the exercise of it requires the consent of another person).

(8)   Even though a spouse's matrimonial home rights are a charge on an estate or interest in the dwelling-house, those rights are brought to an end by—

(a)   the death of the other spouse, or

(b)   the termination (otherwise than by death) of the marriage,

unless the court directs otherwise by an order made under section 33(5).

(9)   If—

(a)   a spouse's matrimonial home rights are a charge on an estate or interest in the dwelling-house, and

(b)   that estate or interest is surrendered to merge in some other estate or interest expectant on it in such circumstances that, but for the merger, the person taking the estate or interest would be bound by the charge,

the surrender has effect subject to the charge and the persons thereafter entitled to the other estate or interest are, for so long as the estate or interest surrendered would have endured if not so surrendered, to be treated for all purposes of this Part as deriving title to the other estate or interest under the other spouse or, as the case may be, under the trustees for the other spouse, by virtue of the surrender.

(10)   If the title to the legal estate by virtue of which a spouse is entitled to occupy a dwelling-house (including any legal estate held by trustees for that spouse) is registered under the Land Registration Act 1925 or any enactment replaced by that Act—

(a)   registration of a land charge affecting the dwelling-house by virtue of this Part is to be effected by registering a notice under that Act; and

(b)   a spouse's matrimonial home rights are not an overriding interest within the meaning of that Act affecting the dwelling-house even though the spouse is in actual occupation of the dwelling-house.

(11)   A spouse's matrimonial home rights (whether or not constituting a charge) do not entitle that spouse to lodge a caution under section 54 of the Land Registration Act 1925.

(12)   If—

(a)   a spouse's matrimonial home rights are a charge on the estate of the other spouse or of trustees of the other spouse, and

(b)   that estate is the subject of a mortgage,

then if, after the date of the creation of the mortgage ("the first mortgage"), the charge is registered under section 2 of the Land Charges Act 1972, the charge is, for the purposes of section 94 of the Law of Property Act 1925 (which regulates the rights of mortgagees to make further advances ranking in priority to subsequent mortgages), to be deemed to be a mortgage subsequent in date to the first mortgage.

(13)   It is hereby declared that a charge under subsection (2) or (5) is not registrable under subsection (10) or under section 2 of the Land Charges Act 1972 unless it is a charge on a legal estate.

---

NOTES

Commencement: 1 October 1997.

---

## 33   Occupation orders where applicant has estate or interest etc or has matrimonial home rights

(1)   If—

    (a)   a person ("the person entitled")—

        (i)   is entitled to occupy a dwelling-house by virtue of a beneficial estate or interest or contract or by virtue of any enactment giving him the right to remain in occupation, or

        (ii)   has matrimonial home rights in relation to a dwelling-house, and

    (b)   the dwelling-house—

        (i)   is or at any time has been the home of the person entitled and of another person with whom he is associated, or

        (ii)   was at any time intended by the person entitled and any such other person to be their home,

the person entitled may apply to the court for an order containing any of the provisions specified in subsections (3), (4) and (5).

(2)   If an agreement to marry is terminated, no application under this section may be made by virtue of section 62(3)(e) by reference to that agreement after the end of the period of three years beginning with the day on which it is terminated.

(3)   An order under this section may—

    (a)   enforce the applicant's entitlement to remain in occupation as against the other person ("the respondent");

    (b)   require the respondent to permit the applicant to enter and remain in the dwelling-house or part of the dwelling-house;

    (c)   regulate the occupation of the dwelling-house by either or both parties;

    (d)   if the respondent is entitled as mentioned in subsection (1)(a)(i), prohibit, suspend or restrict the exercise by him of his right to occupy the dwelling-house;

    (e)   if the respondent has matrimonial home rights in relation to the dwelling-house and the applicant is the other spouse, restrict or terminate those rights;

    (f)   require the respondent to leave the dwelling-house or part of the dwelling-house; or

    (g)   exclude the respondent from a defined area in which the dwelling-house is included.

(4)   An order under this section may declare that the applicant is entitled as mentioned in subsection (1)(a)(i) or has matrimonial home rights.

(5)   If the applicant has matrimonial home rights and the respondent is the other spouse, an order under this section made during the marriage may provide that those rights are not brought to an end by—

    (a)   the death of the other spouse; or

    (b)   the termination (otherwise than by death) of the marriage.

(6)   In deciding whether to exercise its powers under subsection (3) and (if so) in what manner, the court shall have regard to all the circumstances including—

    (a)   the housing needs and housing resources of each of the parties and of any relevant child;

    (b)   the financial resources of each of the parties;

    (c)   the likely effect of any order, or of any decision by the court not to exercise its powers under subsection (3), on the health, safety or well-being of the parties and of any relevant child; and

    (d)   the conduct of the parties in relation to each other and otherwise.

(7)   If it appears to the court that the applicant or any relevant child is likely to suffer significant harm attributable to conduct of the respondent if an order under this section containing one or more of the provisions mentioned in subsection (3) is not made, the court shall make the order unless it appears to it that—

   (a)   the respondent or any relevant child is likely to suffer significant harm if the order is made; and

   (b)   the harm likely to be suffered by the respondent or child in that event is as great as, or greater than, the harm attributable to conduct of the respondent which is likely to be suffered by the applicant or child if the order is not made.

(8)   The court may exercise its powers under subsection (5) in any case where it considers that in all the circumstances it is just and reasonable to do so.

(9)   An order under this section—

   (a)   may not be made after the death of either of the parties mentioned in subsection (1); and

   (b)   except in the case of an order made by virtue of subsection (5)(a), ceases to have effect on the death of either party.

(10)   An order under this section may, in so far as it has continuing effect, be made for a specified period, until the occurrence of a specified event or until further order.

NOTES
Commencement: 1 October 1997.

## 34   Effect of order under s 33 where rights are charge on dwelling-house

(1)   If a spouse's matrimonial home rights are a charge on the estate or interest of the other spouse or of trustees for the other spouse—

   (a)   an order under section 33 against the other spouse has, except so far as a contrary intention appears, the same effect against house. persons deriving title under the other spouse or under the trustees and affected by the charge, and

   (b)   sections 33(1), (3), (4) and (10) and 30(3) to (6) apply in relation to any person deriving title under the other spouse or under the trustees and affected by the charge as they apply in relation to the other spouse.

(2)   The court may make an order under section 33 by virtue of subsection (1)(b) if it considers that in all the circumstances it is just and reasonable to do so.

NOTES
Commencement: 1 October 1997.

## 35   One former spouse with no existing right to occupy

(1)   This section applies if—

   (a)   one former spouse is entitled to occupy a dwelling-house by virtue of a beneficial estate or interest or contract, or by virtue of any enactment giving him the right to remain in occupation;

   (b)   the other former spouse is not so entitled; and

   (c)   the dwelling-house was at any time their matrimonial home or was at any time intended by them to be their matrimonial home.

(2)   The former spouse not so entitled may apply to the court for an order under this section against the other former spouse ("the respondent").

(3)    If the applicant is in occupation, an order under this section must contain provision—

    (a)    giving the applicant the right not to be evicted or excluded from the dwelling-house or any part of it by the respondent for the period specified in the order; and

    (b)    prohibiting the respondent from evicting or excluding the applicant during that period.

(4)    If the applicant is not in occupation, an order under this section must contain provision—

    (a)    giving the applicant the right to enter into and occupy the dwelling-house for the period specified in the order; and

    (b)    requiring the respondent to permit the exercise of that right.

(5)    An order under this section may also—

    (a)    regulate the occupation of the dwelling-house by either or both of the parties;

    (b)    prohibit, suspend or restrict the exercise by the respondent of his right to occupy the dwelling-house;

    (c)    require the respondent to leave the dwelling-house or part of the dwelling-house; or

    (d)    exclude the respondent from a defined area in which the dwelling-house is included.

(6)    In deciding whether to make an order under this section containing provision of the kind mentioned in subsection (3) or (4) and (if so) in what manner, the court shall have regard to all the circumstances including—

    (a)    the housing needs and housing resources of each of the parties and of any relevant child;

    (b)    the financial resources of each of the parties;

    (c)    the likely effect of any order, or of any decision by the court not to exercise its powers under subsection (3) or (4), on the health, safety or well-being of the parties and of any relevant child;

    (d)    the conduct of the parties in relation to each other and otherwise;

    (e)    the length of time that has elapsed since the parties ceased to live together;

    (f)    the length of time that has elapsed since the marriage was dissolved or annulled; and

    (g)    the existence of any pending proceedings between the parties—

        (i)    for an order under section 23A or 24 of the Matrimonial Causes Act 1973 (property adjustment orders in connection with divorce proceedings etc);

        (ii)    for an order under paragraph 1(2)(d) or (e) of Schedule 1 to the Children Act 1989 (orders for financial relief against parents); or

        (iii)    relating to the legal or beneficial ownership of the dwelling-house.

(7)    In deciding whether to exercise its power to include one or more of the provisions referred to in subsection (5) ("a subsection (5) provision") and (if so) in what manner, the court shall have regard to all the circumstances including the matters mentioned in subsection (6)(a) to (e).

(8)    If the court decides to make an order under this section and it appears to it that, if the order does not include a subsection (5) provision, the applicant or any relevant child is likely to suffer significant harm attributable to conduct of the respondent, the court shall include the subsection (5) provision in the order unless it appears to the court that—

(a) the respondent or any relevant child is likely to suffer significant harm if the provision is included in the order; and

(b) the harm likely to be suffered by the respondent or child in that event is as great as or greater than the harm attributable to conduct of the respondent which is likely to be suffered by the applicant or child if the provision is not included.

(9) An order under this section—

(a) may not be made after the death of either of the former spouses; and

(b) ceases to have effect on the death of either of them.

(10) An order under this section must be limited so as to have effect for a specified period not exceeding six months, but may be extended on one or more occasions for a further specified period not exceeding six months.

(11) A former spouse who has an equitable interest in the dwelling-house or in the proceeds of sale of the dwelling-house but in whom there is not vested (whether solely or as joint tenant) a legal estate in fee simple or a legal term of years absolute in the dwelling-house is to be treated (but only for the purpose of determining whether he is eligible to apply under this section) as not being entitled to occupy the dwelling-house by virtue of that interest.

(12) Subsection (11) does not prejudice any right of such a former spouse to apply for an order under section 33.

(13) So long as an order under this section remains in force, subsections (3) to (6) of section 30 apply in relation to the applicant—

(a) as if he were the spouse entitled to occupy the dwelling-house by virtue of that section; and

(b) as if the respondent were the other spouse.

---

NOTES

Commencement: 1 October 1997.

---

## 36 One cohabitant or former cohabitant with no existing right to occupy

(1) This section applies if—

(a) one cohabitant or former cohabitant is entitled to occupy a dwelling-house by virtue of a beneficial estate or interest or contract or by virtue of any enactment giving him the right to remain in occupation;

(b) the other cohabitant or former cohabitant is not so entitled; and

(c) that dwelling-house is the home in which they live together as husband and wife or a home in which they at any time so lived together or intended so to live together.

(2) The cohabitant or former cohabitant not so entitled may apply to the court for an order under this section against the other cohabitant or former cohabitant ("the respondent").

(3) If the applicant is in occupation, an order under this section must contain provision—

(a) giving the applicant the right not to be evicted or excluded from the dwelling-house or any part of it by the respondent for the period specified in the order; and

(b) prohibiting the respondent from evicting or excluding the applicant during that period.

(4)   If the applicant is not in occupation, an order under this section must contain provision—

    (a)   giving the applicant the right to enter into and occupy the dwelling-house for the period specified in the order; and

    (b)   requiring the respondent to permit the exercise of that right.

(5)   An order under this section may also—

    (a)   regulate the occupation of the dwelling-house by either or both of the parties;

    (b)   prohibit, suspend or restrict the exercise by the respondent of his right to occupy the dwelling-house;

    (c)   require the respondent to leave the dwelling-house or part of the dwelling-house; or

    (d)   exclude the respondent from a defined area in which the dwelling-house is included.

(6)   In deciding whether to make an order under this section containing provision of the kind mentioned in subsection (3) or (4) and (if so) in what manner, the court shall have regard to all the circumstances including—

    (a)   the housing needs and housing-resources of each of the parties and of any relevant child;

    (b)   the financial resources of each of the parties;

    (c)   the likely effect of any order, or of any decision by the court not to exercise its powers under subsection (3) or (4), on the health, safety or well-being of the parties and of any relevant child;

    (d)   the conduct of the parties in relation to each other and otherwise;

    (e)   the nature of the parties' relationship;

    (f)   the length of time during which they have lived together as husband and wife;

    (g)   whether there are or have been any children who are children of both parties or for whom both parties have or have had parental responsibility;

    (h)   the length of time that has elapsed since the parties ceased to live together; and

    (i)   the existence of any pending proceedings between the parties—

        (i)   for an order under paragraph 1 (2)(d) or (e) of Schedule to the Children Act 1989 (orders for financial relief against parents); or

        (ii)   relating to the legal or beneficial ownership of the dwelling-house.

(7)   In deciding whether to exercise its powers to include one or more of the provisions referred to in subsection (5) ("a subsection (5) provision") and (if so) in what manner, the court shall have regard to all the circumstances including—

    (a)   the matters mentioned in subsection (6)(a) to (d); and

    (b)   the questions mentioned in subsection (8).

(8)   The questions are—

    (a)   whether the applicant or any relevant child is likely to suffer significant harm attributable to conduct of the respondent if the subsection (5) provision is not included in the order; and

    (b)   whether the harm likely to be suffered by the respondent or child if the provision is included is as great as or greater than the harm attributable to conduct of the respondent which is likely to be suffered by the applicant or child if the provision is not included.

(9)   An order under this section—

    (a)   may not be made after the death of either of the parties; and

    (b)   ceases to have effect on the death of either of them.

(10)   An order under this section must be limited so as to have effect for a specified period not exceeding six months, but may be extended on one occasion for a further specified period not exceeding six months.

(11)   A person who has an equitable interest in the dwelling-house or in the proceeds of sale of the dwelling-house but in whom there is not vested (whether solely or as joint tenant) a legal estate in fee simple or a legal term of years absolute in the dwelling-house is to be treated (but only for the purpose of determining whether he is eligible to apply under this section) as not being entitled to occupy the dwelling-house by virtue of that interest.

(12)   Subsection (11) does not prejudice any right of such a person to apply for an order under section 33.

(13)   So long as the order remains in force, subsections (3) to (6) of section 30 apply in relation to the applicant—

  (a)   as if he were a spouse entitled to occupy the dwelling-house by virtue of that section; and

  (b)   as if the respondent were the other spouse.

NOTES
Commencement: 1 October 1997.

## 37   Neither spouse entitled to occupy

(1)   This section applies if—

  (a)   one spouse or former spouse and the other spouse or former spouse occupy a dwelling-house which is or was the matrimonial home; but

  (b)   neither of them is entitled to remain in occupation—

   (i)   by virtue of a beneficial estate or interest or contract; or

   (ii)   by virtue of any enactment giving him the right to remain in occupation.

(2)   Either of the parties may apply to the court for an order against the other under this section.

(3)   An order under this section may—

  (a)   require the respondent to permit the applicant to enter and remain in the dwelling-house or part of the dwelling-house;

  (b)   regulate the occupation of the dwelling-house by either or both of the spouses;

  (c)   require the respondent to leave the dwelling-house or part of the dwelling-house; or

  (d)   exclude the respondent from a defined area in which the dwelling-house is included.

(4)   Subsections (6) and (7) of section 33 apply to the exercise by the court of its powers under this section as they apply to the exercise by the court of its powers under subsection (3) of that section.

(5)   An order under this section must be limited so as to have effect for a specified period not exceeding six months, but may be extended on one or more occasions for a further specified period not exceeding six months.

NOTES
Commencement: 1 October 1997.

## 38 Neither cohabitant or former cohabitant entitled to occupy

(1) This section applies if—

    (a) one cohabitant or former cohabitant and the other cohabitant or former cohabitant occupy a dwelling-house which is the home in which they live or lived together as husband and wife; but

    (b) neither of them is entitled to remain in occupation—

        (i) by virtue of a beneficial estate or interest or contract; or

        (ii) by virtue of any enactment giving him the right to remain in occupation.

(2) Either of the parties may apply to the court for an order against the other under this section.

(3) An order under this section may—

    (a) require the respondent to permit the applicant to enter and remain in the dwelling-house or part of the dwelling-house;

    (b) regulate the occupation of the dwelling-house by either or both of the parties;

    (c) require the respondent to leave the dwelling-house or part of the dwelling-house; or

    (d) exclude the respondent from a defined area in which the dwelling-house is included.

(4) In deciding whether to exercise its powers to include one or more of the provisions referred to in subsection (3) ("a subsection (3) provision") and (if so) in what manner, the court shall have regard to all the circumstances including—

    (a) the housing needs and housing resources of each of the parties and of any relevant child;

    (b) the financial resources of each of the parties;

    (c) the likely effect of any order, or of any decision by the court not to exercise its powers under subsection (3), on the health, safety or well-being of the parties and of any relevant child;

    (d) the conduct of the parties in relation to each other and otherwise; and

    (e) the questions mentioned in subsection (5).

(5) The questions are—

    (a) whether the applicant or any relevant child is likely to suffer significant harm attributable to conduct of the respondent if the subsection (3) provision is not included in the order; and

    (b) whether the harm likely to be suffered by the respondent or child if the provision is included is as great as or greater than the harm attributable to conduct of the respondent which is likely to be suffered by the applicant or child if the provision is not included.

(6) An order under this section shall be limited so as to have effect for a specified period not exceeding six months, but may be extended on one occasion for a further specified period not exceeding six months.

---

NOTES

Commencement: 1 October 1997.

---

## 39 Supplementary provisions

(1)   In this Part an "occupation order" means an order under section 33, 35, 36, 37 or 38.

(2)   An application for an occupation order may be made in other family proceedings or without any other family proceedings being instituted.

(3)   If—

    (a)   an application for an occupation order is made under section 33, 35, 36, 37 or 38, and

    (b)   the court considers that it has no power to make the order under the section concerned, but that it has power to make an order under one of the other sections,

the court may make an order under that other section.

(4)   The fact that a person has applied for an occupation order under sections 35 to   38, or that an occupation order has been made, does not affect the right of any person to claim a legal or equitable interest in any property in any subsequent proceedings (including subsequent proceedings under this Part).

NOTES

Commencement: 1 October 1997.

## 40 Additional provisions that may be included in certain occupation orders

(1)   The court may on, or at any time after, making an occupation order under section 33, 35 or 36—

    (a)   impose on either party obligations as to—

        (i)   the repair and maintenance of the dwelling-house; or

        (ii)   the discharge of rent, mortgage payments or other outgoings affecting the dwelling-house;

    (b)   order a party occupying the dwelling-house or any part of it (including a party who is entitled to do so by virtue of a beneficial estate or interest or contract or by virtue of any enactment giving him the right to remain in occupation) to make periodical payments to the other party in respect of the accommodation, if the other party would (but for the order) be entitled to occupy the dwelling-house by virtue of a beneficial estate or interest or contract or by virtue of any such enactment;

    (c)   grant either party possession or use of furniture or other contents of the dwelling-house;

    (d)   order either party to take reasonable care of any furniture or other contents of the dwelling-house;

    (e)   order either party to take reasonable steps to keep the dwelling-house and any furniture or other contents secure.

(2)   In deciding whether and, if so, how to exercise its powers under this section, the court shall have regard to all the circumstances of the case including—

    (a)   the financial needs and financial resources of the parties; and

    (b)   the financial obligations which they have, or are likely to have in the foreseeable future, including financial obligations to each other and to any relevant child.

(3)   An order under this section ceases to have effect when the occupation order to which it relates ceases to have effect.

NOTES

Commencement: 1 October 1997.

## 41 Additional considerations if parties are cohabitants or former cohabitants

(1)  This section applies if the parties are cohabitants or former cohabitants.

(2)  Where the court is required to consider the nature of the parties' relationship, it is to have regard to the fact that they have not given each other the commitment involved in marriage.

NOTES
Commencement: 1 October 1997.

*Non-molestation orders*

## 42 Non-molestation orders

(1)  In this Part a "non-molestation order" means an order containing either or both of the following provisions—
  (a)  provision prohibiting a person ("the respondent") from molesting another person who is associated with the respondent;
  (b)  provision prohibiting the respondent from molesting a relevant child.

(2)  The court may make a non-molestation order—
  (a)  if an application for the order has been made (whether in other family proceedings or without any other family proceedings being instituted) by a person who is associated with the respondent; or
  (b)  if in any family proceedings to which the respondent is a party the court considers that the order should be made for the benefit of any other party to the proceedings or any relevant child even though no such application has been made.

(3)  In subsection (2) "family proceedings" includes proceedings in which the court has made an emergency protection order under section 44 of the Children Act 1989 which includes an exclusion requirement (as defined in section 44A(3) of that Act).

(4)  Where an agreement to marry is terminated, no application under subsection  (2)(a) may be made by virtue of section 62(3)(e) by reference to that agreement after the end of the period of three years beginning with the day on which it is terminated.

(5)  In deciding whether to exercise its powers under this section and, if so, in what manner, the court shall have regard to all the circumstances including the need to secure the health, safety and well-being—
  (a)  of the applicant or, in a case falling within subsection (2)(b), the person for whose benefit the order would be made; and
  (b)  of any relevant child.

(6)  A non-molestation order may be expressed so as to refer to molestation in general, to particular acts of molestation, or to both.

(7)  A non-molestation order may be made for a specified period or until further order.

(8)  A non-molestation order which is made in other family proceedings ceases to have effect if those proceedings are withdrawn or dismissed.

NOTES
Commencement: 1 October 1997.

*Enforcement powers of magistrates' courts*

## 50 Power of magistrates' court to suspend execution of committal order

(1) If, under section 63(3) of the Magistrates' Courts Act 1980, a magistrates' court has power to commit a person to custody for breach of a relevant requirement, the court may by order direct that the execution of the order of committal is to be suspended for such period or on such terms and conditions as it may specify.

(2) In subsection (1) "a relevant requirement" means—

    (a) an occupation order or non-molestation order;

    (b) an exclusion requirement included by virtue of section 38A of the Children Act 1989 in an interim care order made under section 38 of that Act; or

    (c) an exclusion requirement included by virtue of section 44A of the Children Act 1989 in an emergency protection order under section 44 of that Act.

NOTES
Commencement: 1 October 1997.

## 51 Power of magistrates' court to order hospital admission or guardianship

(1) A magistrates' court has the same power to make a hospital order or guardianship order under section 37 of the Mental Health Act 1983 or an interim hospital order under section 38 of that Act in the case of a person suffering from mental illness or severe mental impairment who could otherwise be committed to custody for breach of a relevant requirement as a magistrates' court has under those sections in the case of a person convicted of an offence punishable on summary conviction with imprisonment.

(2) In subsection (1) "a relevant requirement" has the meaning given by section 50(2).

NOTES
Commencement: 1 October 1997.

# PART V
# SUPPLEMENTAL

## 64 Provision for separate representation for children

(1) The Lord Chancellor may by regulations provide for the separate representation of children in proceedings in England and Wales for which relate to any matter in respect of which a question has arisen, or may arise, under—

    (a) Part II;

    (b) Part IV;

    (c) the 1973 Act; or

    (d) the Domestic Proceedings and Magistrates' Courts Act 1978.

(2) The regulations may provide for such representation only in specified circumstances.

NOTES
Commencement: 1 October 1997.

**67   Short title, commencement and extent**

(1)   This Act may be cited as the Family Law Act 1996.

(2)   Section 65 and this section come into force on the passing of this Act.

(3)   The other provisions of this Act come into force on such day as the Lord Chancellor may by order appoint; and different days may be appointed for different purposes.

(4)   . . .

NOTES
Commencement: 4 July 1996.
Sub-s (4): outside the scope of this work.

# COMMUNITY CARE (DIRECT PAYMENTS) ACT 1996

## (C 30)

*An Act to enable local authorities responsible for community care services to make payments to persons in respect of their securing the provision of such services; and for connected purposes*
[4 July 1996]

*England and Wales*

**1   Direct payments**

(1)   Where—
   (a)   an authority have decided under section 47 of the National Health Service and Community Care Act 1990 (assessment by local authorities of needs for community care services) that the needs of a person call for the provision of any community care services, and
   (b)   the person is of a description which is specified for the purposes of this subsection by regulations made by the Secretary of State,

the authority may, if the person consents, make to him, in respect of his securing the provision of any of the services for which they have decided his needs call, a payment of such amount as, subject to subsections (2) and (3) below, they think fit.

(2)   If—
   (a)   an authority pay under subsection (1) above at a rate below their estimate of the reasonable cost of securing the provision of the service concerned, and
   (b)   the payee satisfies the authority that his means are insufficient for it to be reasonably practicable for him to make up the difference,

the authority shall so adjust the payment to him under that subsection as to avoid there being a greater difference than that which appears to them to be reasonably practicable for him to make up.

(3)   In the case of a service which, apart from this Act, would be provided under section 117 of the Mental Health Act 1983 (after-care), an authority shall not pay under subsection (1) above at a rate below their estimate of the reasonable cost of securing the provision of the service.

(4)    A payment under subsection (1) above shall be subject to the condition that the person to whom it is made shall not secure the provision of the service to which it relates by a person who is of a description specified for the purposes of this subsection by regulations made by the Secretary of State.

(5)    The Secretary of State may by regulations provide that the power conferred by subsection (1) above shall not be exercisable in relation to the provision of residential accommodation for any person for a period in excess of such period as may be specified in the regulations.

(6)    If the authority by whom a payment under subsection (1) above is made are not satisfied, in relation to the whole or any part of the payment—

(a)    that it has been used to secure the provision of the service to which it relates, or

(b)    that the condition imposed by subsection (4) above, or any condition properly imposed by them, has been met in relation to its use,

they may require the payment or, as the case may be, the part of the payment to be repaid.

(7)    Regulations under this section may—

(a)    make different provision for different cases, and

(b)    include such supplementary, incidental, consequential and transitional provisions and savings as the Secretary of State thinks fit.

(8)    The power to make regulations under this section shall be exercisable by statutory instrument which shall be subject to annulment in pursuance of a resolution of either House of Parliament.

(9)    In this section, "community care services" has the same meaning as in section   46 of the National Health Service and Community Care Act 1990.

---

NOTES

Commencement: to be appointed.

---

## 2    Relationship with other functions

(1)    Except as provided by subsection (2) below, the fact that an authority make a payment under section 1(1) above shall not affect their functions with respect to the provision under the relevant community care enactment of the service to which the payment relates.

(2)    Where an authority make a payment under section 1(1) above, they shall not be under any obligation to the payee with respect to the provision under the relevant community care enactment of the service to which the payment relates as long as they are satisfied that the need which calls for the provision of the service will be met by virtue of the payee's own arrangements.

(3)    In subsections (1) and (2) above, references to the relevant community care enactment, in relation to the provision of a service, are to the enactment under which the service would fall to be provided apart from this Act.

---

NOTES

Commencement: to be appointed.

---

*General*

## 7   Short title, commencement and extent

(1)   This Act may be cited as the Community Care (Direct Payments) Act 1996.

(2)   This Act, except section 6, shall come into force on such day as the Secretary of State may by order made by statutory instrument appoint; and different days may be so appointed for different purposes.

(3)   The Secretary of State may by order made by statutory instrument provide that this Act shall have effect in its application to the Isles of Scilly with such modifications as are specified in the order.

(4)   Sections 1 to 3 above extend to England and Wales only.

(5)   Sections 4 and 5 above extend to Scotland only.

(6)   This Act, except this section and section 6, does not extend to Northern Ireland.

---

NOTES

Commencement: 4 July 1996.

---

# PART II
# STATUTORY INSTRUMENTS

# ADOPTION AGENCIES REGULATIONS 1983

## (SI 1983/1964)

NOTES

Made: 30 December 1983.

Commencement: 27 May 1984.

Authority: Adoption Act 1958, s 32 (repealed); Children Act 1975, s 4(1) (repealed) (see now the Adoption Act 1976, ss 3, 9(1)).

## 1 Citation, commencement, extent and interpretation

(1)    These regulations may be cited as the Adoption Agencies Regulations 1983 and shall come into operation on 27th May 1984.

(2)    These regulations shall not apply to Scotland.

(3)    In these regulations, unless the context otherwise requires—

["the Act" means the Adoption Act 1976;]

["the Children Act" means the Children Act 1989;]

"adoption agency" means an approved adoption society or local authority;

"adoption panel" means a panel established in accordance with regulation 5;

"prospective adopter" means a person who proposes to adopt a child.

(4)    Any reference in these regulations to any provision made by or contained in any enactment or instrument shall, except insofar as the context otherwise requires, be construed as including a reference to any provision which may re-enact or replace it, with or without modification.

(5)    Any reference in these regulations to a numbered regulation or the Schedule is to the regulation bearing that number in or the Schedule to a numbered paragraph is a reference to the paragraph bearing that number in that regulation or the Schedule.

NOTES

Para (3): definitions "the Act" and "the Children Act" substituted by the Adoption Agencies and Children (Arrangements for Placement and Reviews) (Miscellaneous Amendments) Regulations 1997, SI   1997/649, reg 2(2).

## 2 Approval of adoption societies

(1)    An applicant to the Secretary of State under [section 3 of the Act] (approval of adoption societies) shall be made in writing on a form supplied by the Secretary of State.

(2)    An unincorporated body of persons shall not apply for approval under [section 3 of the Act].

NOTES

Sub-ss (1), (2): words in square brackets substituted by SI 1997/649, reg 2(3).

## 3 Annual reports and information to be provided by approved adoption societies

Every approved adoption society shall—

(a) furnish the Secretary of State with two copies of the society's annual report as soon as is reasonably practicable after the issue thereof and with such other information as and when the Secretary of State may from time to time require;

(b) notify the Secretary of State in writing of any change in the society's name or in the address of its registered or head office within one month after such change;

(c) where the society proposes to cease, or expects to cease, to act as an adoption society, so notify the Secretary of State in writing not less than one month, or as soon as is reasonably practicable, before the date when the society will cease, or expects to cease, so to act; and

(d) where the society has ceased to act as an adoption society, notify the Secretary of State in writing that it has ceased so to act as soon thereafter as is reasonably practicable.

## 4    Application of regulations to certain adoption agencies

Where an adoption agency operates only for the purpose of putting persons into contact with other adoption agencies and for the purpose of putting such agencies into contact with each other or for either of such purposes, regulation 5 and, to the extent that it requires consultation with the adoption panel and the making of arrangements for the exercise of the panel's functions, regulation 6, shall not apply to such an agency.

## 5    *Establishment of adoption panel and appointment of members*

*(1)    An adoption agency shall forthwith establish at least one adoption panel and shall appoint the persons referred to in paragraphs (2) and (3) to be members of such a panel, so however that no more than 10 members shall be appointed to a panel and the persons appointed to a panel shall include at least one man and one woman.*

*(2)    The adoption agency shall appoint as chairman of an adoption panel a person who has such experience in adoption work as the agency considers appropriate.*

*(3)    In addition to the chairman the persons to be appointed shall include—*

*(a)    two of the social workers in the employment of the adoption agency,*

*(b)    at least one member of the adoption agency's management committee where the agency is an approved adoption society or, where the agency is a local authority, at least one member of that authority's social services committee,*

*(c)    the person nominated as the medical adviser to the adoption agency under regulation 6(4) (or one of them if more than one are appointed), and*

*(d)    at least two other persons not being members or employees of the adoption agency or elected members where the agency is a local authority.*

*(4)    A person appointed to an adoption panel shall hold office subject to such conditions as to the period of his membership and otherwise as may be determined by the adoption agency.*

*(5)    An adoption panel shall make the recommendations specified in regulation 10 only when at least five of its members meet as a panel and one of those is a social worker in the employment of the adoption agency.*

*(6)    An adoption panel shall keep a written record of any of the recommendations specified in regulation 10 which it makes.*

## NOTES

Substituted partly as from 1 July 1997, and fully as from 1 November 1997, together with regs 5A, 5B, for s 5 as originally enacted, by SI 1997/649, reg 2(4), as follows—

### "5 Establishment of adoption panel and appointment of members

(1) Subject to paragraphs (2), (3) and (6), an adoption agency shall establish at least one adoption panel and shall appoint no more than 10 persons, including at least one man and one woman, to be members of such a panel.

(2) The adoption agency shall appoint as chairman of an adoption panel a person who has such experience in adoption work as the agency considers appropriate and the other members of the panel shall include—

(a) subject to paragraph (6), two social workers in the employment of the adoption agency,

(b) subject to paragraph (6), at least one member of the adoption agency's management committee where the agency is an approved adoption society or, where the adoption agency is a local authority, at least one member of that authority's social services committee,

(c) the person nominated as the medical adviser to the adoption agency under regulation 6(4) (or one of them if more than one are nominated), for so long as that person is so nominated, and

(d) at least three other persons ("independent persons"), not being members or employees of the adoption agency, or elected members, where the agency is a local authority who shall where reasonably practicable include an adoptive parent and an adopted person who must be at least 18 years of age.

(3) The adoption agency shall appoint one of the members of the adoption panel as vice-chairman, who, where the chairman of the panel has died or ceased to hold office, or is unable to perform his duties by reason of illness, absence from England and Wales or any other cause, shall act as the chairman for so long as there is no chairman able to do so.

(4) An adoption panel shall make the recommendations specified in regulation 10 only when, subject to paragraph (6), at least six of its members meet as a panel and those members include the chairman or vice-chairman and a social worker in the employment of the adoption agency.

(5) An adoption panel shall keep a written record of any of the recommendations specified in regulation 10 which it makes and the reasons for them.

(6) Any two but no more than three local authorities may establish a joint adoption panel, and where a joint adoption panel is established—

(a) the maximum number of members who may be appointed to that panel shall be increased to eleven,

(b) the chairman shall be appointed by agreement between the local authorities,

(c) one social worker in the employment of each local authority and one member of each local authority's social services committee shall be appointed to the panel,

(d) three independent persons shall be appointed to the panel by agreement between the local authorities,

(e) the vice-chairman shall be appointed from the members of the panel by agreement between the local authorities, and

(f) the quorum set out in paragraph (4) shall be increased to seven.

### 5A Tenure of office of members

(1) Subject to the provisions of this regulation and regulation 5B a member of the adoption panel shall hold office for a term not exceeding three years, and may not hold office as a member of that panel for more than two consecutive terms without an intervening period of at least three years.

(2) An adoption agency shall so arrange the tenure of office of the members of the panel so that so far as possible the term of office of at least one third of its members shall expire each year.

(3) The medical adviser member of the adoption panel shall hold office only for so long as he is the medical adviser nominated under regulation 6(4).

(4) A member may resign his office at any time after appointment by giving notice in writing to that effect to the adoption agency, or if he is a member of a joint adoption panel, by giving notice to one of the local authorities whose panel it is.

(5) Subject to paragraph (6), if an adoption agency is of the opinion that a member is unfit or unable to hold office, the agency may terminate his office by giving him notice in writing with reasons.

(6) If the member whose appointment is to be terminated under paragraph (5) is a member of a joint adoption panel, his appointment may only be terminated with the agreement of all the local authorities whose panel it is.

(7)   Where a member is appointed to replace a person whose appointment has been terminated for any reason before the expiry of the term for which he has been appointed, that member shall hold office as a member of that panel for the unexpired part of the term of the person whom he replaces, and may not hold office for more than one consecutive term after the expiry of that term without an intervening period of three years.

**5B Establishment of new panels on 1st November 1997**
(1)   All members of an adoption panel established before 1st November 1997, shall cease to hold office on that date.
(2)   With effect from the 1st November 1997, an adoption agency shall establish a new adoption panel in accordance with regulations 5 and 5A.".

## 6   Adoption agency arrangements for adoption work

(1)   An adoption agency shall, in consultation with the adoption panel and to the extent specified in paragraph (5) with the adoption agency's medical adviser, make arrangements which shall be set out in writing to govern the exercise of the agency's and the panel's functions and such arrangements shall be reviewed by the agency not less than once every three years.

(2)   Subject to regulations 14 and 15, the arrangements referred to in paragraph (1) shall include provision—
  (a)   for maintaining the confidentiality and safekeeping of adoption information, case records and the indexes to them,
  (b)   for authorising access to such records and indexes or disclosure of information by virtue of regulation 15, and
  (c)   for ensuring that those for whom access is provided or to whom disclosure is made by virtue of regulation 15(2)(a) agree in writing before such authorisation is given that such records, indexes and information will remain confidential, so however that a child who is placed for adoption or who has been adopted and his prospective adopter or adoptive parent shall not be required to give such agreement in respect of that child's adoption.

(3)   The adoption agency shall satisfy itself that social work staff employed on the agency's work have had such experience and hold such qualifications as the adoption agency considers appropriate to that work.

(4)   The adoption agency shall nominate at least one registered medical practitioner to be the agency's medical adviser.

(5)   The adoption agency's medical adviser shall be consulted in relation to the arrangements for access to and disclosure of health information which is required or permitted by virtue of regulation 15.

## 7   Adoption agency's duties in respect of a child and his parents or guardian

(1)   When an adoption agency is considering adoption for a child it shall either—
  (a)   in respect of the child, having regard to his age and understanding, and as the case may be his parents or guardian, so far as is reasonably practicable—
    (i)    provide a counselling service for them,
    (ii)   explain to them the legal implication of and procedures in relation to adoption and freeing for adoption, and
    (iii)  provide them with written information about the matters referred to in head (ii), or
  (b)   satisfy itself that the requirements of sub-paragraph (a) have been carried out by another adoption agency.

(2)   Where, following the procedure referred to in paragraph (1), an adoption agency is considering adoption for a child, the agency shall—

(a)   set up a case record in respect of the child and place on it any information obtained by virtue of this regulation,

(b)   obtain, so far as is reasonably practicable, such particulars of the parents or guardian and having regard to his age and understanding the child as are referred to in parts I and III to V of the Schedule together with any other relevant information which may be requested by the adoption panel,

(c)   arrange and obtain a written report by a registered medical practitioner on the child's health which shall deal with the matters specified in Part II of the Schedule, unless such a report has been made within six months before the setting up of the case record under subparagraph (a) and is available to the agency,

(d)   arrange such other examinations and screening procedures of and tests on the child and, so far as is reasonably practicable, his parents, as are recommended by the adoption agency's medical adviser, and obtain a copy of the written report of such examinations, screening procedures and tests, and

(e)   prepare a written report containing the agency's observations on the matters referred to in this regulation, which shall be passed together with all information obtained by it by virtue of this regulation to the adoption panel or to another adoption agency.

(3)   [Where the father of a child does not have parental responsibility for the child and his identity] is known to the adoption agency, it shall so far as it considers reasonably  practicable and in the interests of the child—

(a)   carry out in respect of the father the requirements of paragraph (1)(a) as if they applied to him unless the agency is satisfied that another adoption agency has so complied with those requirements,

(b)   obtain the particulars of him referred to in Parts III and IV of the Schedule together with any other relevant information which may be requested by the adoption panel, and arrange and obtain a copy of the written report of such examinations, screening procedures and tests on him as are recommended by the adoption agency's medical adviser, and

(c)   ascertain so far as possible whether he intends to apply for custody of the child.

NOTES

Para (3): words in square brackets substituted by SI 1997/649, reg 2(5).

## 8   Adoption agency's duties in respect of a prospective adopter

(1)   Where an adoption agency is considering whether a person may be suitable to be an adoptive parent, either—

(a)   it shall—

(i)   provide a counselling service for him,

(ii)   explain to him the legal implications of and procedures in relation to adoption, and

(iii)   provide him with written information about the matters referred to in head (ii), or

(b)   it shall satisfy itself that the requirements of sub-paragraph (a) have been carried out in respect of him by another adoption agency.

(2)    Where, following the procedure referred to in paragraph (1), an adoption agency considers that a person may be suitable to be an adoptive parent, it shall—

    (a)    set up a case record in respect of him and place on it any information obtained by virtue of this regulation,

    (b)    obtain such particulars as are referred to in Part VI of the Schedule together with, so far as is reasonably practicable, any other relevant information which may be requested by the adoption panel,

    (c)    obtain a written report by a registered medical practitioner on the prospective adopter's health which shall deal with the matters specified in Part VII of the Schedule, unless such a report has been made within six months before the setting up of the case record under sub-paragraph (a) and is available to the agency,

    (d)    obtain a written report in respect of any premises which that person intends to use as his home if he adopts a child,

    (e)    obtain written reports of the interviews with two persons nominated by the prospective adopter to provide personal references to him,

    (f)    obtain a written report from the prospective adopter's local authority in relation to him, . . .

    [(g)    prepare a written report which shall include the agency's assessment of the prospective adopter's suitability to be an adoptive parent and any other observations of the agency on the matters referred to in this regulation,

    (h)    notify the prospective adopter that his application is to be referred to the adoption panel and at the same time send a copy of the agency's assessment referred to in paragraph (g) to the prospective adopter inviting him to send any observations in writing on that assessment to the agency within 28 days, and

    (i)    at the end of the period of 28 days referred to in sub-paragraph (h), (or earlier if any observations made by the prospective adopter on the assessment are received before the 28 days has expired), pass the written report referred to in sub-paragraph (g) and any written observations made by the prospective adopter together with all information obtained by the agency by virtue of this regulation, to the adoption panel or to another adoption agency.]

NOTES

    Para (2): in sub-para (f) word omitted revoked, and sub-paras (g)–(i) substituted, for sub-para (g) as originally enacted, by SI 1997/649, reg 2(6).

## 9    Adoption agency's duties in respect of proposed placement

(1)    Subject to paragraph (2), an adoption agency shall refer its proposal to a place a particular child for adoption with a prospective adopter, which it considers may be appropriate, together with a written report containing its observations on the proposal and any information relevant to the proposed placement, to its adoption panel.

(2)    An adoption agency shall refer its proposal to place a child for adoption to the adoption panel only if—

    (a)    any other adoption agency which has made a decision in accordance with regulation 11(1) that adoption is in the best interests of the child or that the prospective adopter is suitable to be an adoptive parent, has been consulted concerning the proposal, and

(b) any local authority or voluntary organisation [which has parental responsibility for the child by virtue of section 18 or 21 of the Act (freeing for adoption and variation of order to substitute one adoption agency for another)] or in whose care the child is, has been consulted and agrees with the proposal.

(3) An adoption agency which has a proposal to place a particular child for adoption with a prospective adopter shall set up case records in respect of them to the extent that it has not already set up such records and place on the appropriate record any information, reports and decisions referred to it by another adoption agency together with any information to be passed to the adoption panel by virtue of this regulation in respect of them.

(4) An adoption agency shall obtain, so far as is reasonably practicable, any other relevant information which may be requested by the adoption panel in connection with the proposed placement.

**NOTES**

Para (2): in sub-para (b) words in square brackets substituted by SI 1997/649, reg 2(7).

## 10 Adoption panel functions

(1) Subject to paragraphs (2) and (3), an adoption panel shall consider the case of every child, prospective adopter and proposed placement referred to it by the adoption agency and shall make one or more of the recommendations to the agency, as the case may be, as to—

(a) whether adoption is in the best interests of a child and, if the panel recommends that it is, whether an application under [section 18 of the Act] (freeing child for adoption) shall be made to free the child for adoption,

(b) whether a prospective adopter is suitable to be an adoptive parent, and

(c) whether a prospective adopter would be a suitable adoptive parent for a particular child.

(2) An adoption panel may make the recommendations specified in paragraph (1) at the same time or at different times, so however that it shall make the recommendation specified in paragraph (1)(c) in respect of a particular child and prospective adopter only if—

(a) that recommendation is to be made at the same meeting of the panel at which a recommendation has been made that adoption is in the best interests of the child, or

(b) an adoption agency decision has been made in accordance with regulation 11(1) that adoption is in the best interests of the child, and

(c) in either case—

(i) the recommendation specified in paragraph (1)(c) is to be made at the same meeting of the panel at which a recommendation has been made that the prospective adopter is suitable to be an adoptive parent, or

(ii) an adoption agency decision has been made in accordance with regulation 11(1) that the prospective adopter is suitable to be an adoptive parent.

(3) In considering what recommendations to make the panel shall have regard to the duties imposed upon the adoption agency by [sections 6 and 7 of the Act] (duty to promote welfare of child and religious upbringing of adopted child) and shall, as the case may be—

(a)  consider and take into account all the information and reports passed to it by virtue of regulations 7(2)(e), 8(2)(g) and 9(1),

(b)  request the adoption agency to obtain any other relevant information which the panel considers necessary,

(c)  obtain legal advice in relation to each case together with advice on an application for an adoption order or, as the case may be, an application to free a child for adoption.

NOTES

Paras (1), (3): words in square brackets substituted by SI 1997/649, reg 2(8).

## 11  Adoption agency decisions and notifications

(1)  An adoption agency shall make a decision on a matter referred to in regulation   10(1)(a), . . . or (c) only after taking into account the recommendation of the adoption panel made by virtue of that regulation on such matter.

[(1A) No member of an adoption panel shall take part in any decision made by the adoption agency under paragraph (1).]

(2)  As soon as possible after making such a decision the adoption agency shall, as the case may be, notify in writing—

(a)  the parents of the child, including [his father if he does not have parental responsibility for the child but only] where the agency considers this to be in the child's interests, or the guardian of the child, if their whereabouts are known to the agency, of its decision as to whether it considers adoption to be in the best interests of the child,

(b)  the persons to be notified under sub-paragraph (a), if it considers adoption to be in the best interests of the child, of its decision as to whether an application under [section 18 of the Act] (freeing child for adoption) should be made to free the child for adoption.

(c)   . . .

(d)  the prospective adopter of its decision that he would be suitable as such for a particular child.

NOTES

Para (1): figure omitted revoked by SI 1997/649, reg 2(9)(a).

Para (1A): inserted by SI 1997/649, reg 2(9)(b).

Para (2): in sub-paras (a), (b) words in square brackets substituted, and sub-para (c) revoked, by SI   1997/649, reg 2(9)(c).

## [11A Adoption agency decisions and notifications—prospective adopters

(1)  In relation to a matter referred to in regulation 10(1)(b) (panel recommendations—prospective adopters) the adoption agency shall take into account the recommendation of the adoption panel made by virtue of that regulation on that matter before making its decision.

(2)  No member of an adoption panel shall take part in any decision made by the agency under paragraph (1).

(3)  If the agency decide to approve the prospective adopter as suitable to be an adoptive parent, the agency shall notify the prospective adopter in writing of its decision.

(4)  If the agency consider that the prospective adopter is not suitable to be an adoptive parent, the agency shall—

(a)  notify the prospective adopter in writing that it proposes not to approve him as suitable to be an adoptive parent;

(b)  send with that notification their reasons together with a copy of the recommendation of the adoption panel, if different; and

(c)  invite the prospective adopter to submit any representations he wishes to make within 28 days.

(5)  If within the period of 28 days referred to in paragraph (4), the prospective adopter has not made any representations, the agency may proceed to make its decision and shall notify the prospective adopter in writing of its decision together with the reasons for that decision.

(6)  If within the period of 28 days referred to in paragraph (4) the agency receive further representations from the prospective adopter, it may refer the case together with all the relevant information to its adoption panel for further consideration.

(7)  The adoption panel shall reconsider any case referred to it under paragraph (6) and make a fresh recommendation to the agency as to whether the prospective adopter is suitable to be an adoptive parent.

(8)  The agency shall make a decision on the case but if the case has been referred to the adoption panel under paragraph (6) it shall make the decision only after taking into account any recommendation of the adoption panel made by virtue of paragraph   (7).

(9)  As soon as possible after making the decision under paragraph (8), the agency shall notify the prospective adopter in writing of its decision, stating its reasons for that decision if they do not consider the prospective adopter to be suitable to be an adoptive parent, and of the adoption panel's recommendation, if this is different from the agency's decision.]

NOTES
Inserted by SI 1997/649, reg 2(10).

## 12   Placement for adoption

(1)  Where an adoption agency has decided in accordance with regulation 11(1) that a prospective adopter would be a suitable adoptive parent for a particular child it shall provide the prospective adopter with written information about the child, his personal history and background, including his religious and cultural background, his health history and current state of health, together with the adoption agency's written proposals in respect of the adoption, including proposals as to the date of placement for adoption with the prospective adopter.

(2)  If the prospective adopter accepts the adoption agency's proposals the agency shall—

(a)  inform the child of the proposed placement for adoption with the prospective adopter where the child is capable of understanding the proposal,

[(aa) notify in writing the parent or guardian of the child, if their whereabouts are known to the agency, of the proposed placement for adoption, unless the parent or guardian has made a declaration under section 18(6) or 19(4) of the Act (declaration as to no further involvement with child),

(aaa) where the father of the child does not have parental responsibility for him and his identity is known to the agency, notify the father of the proposed placement provided the agency considers this to be in the best interests of the child,]

(b) send a written report of the child's health history and current state of health to the prospective adopter's registered medical practitioner, if any, before the proposed placement, together with particulars of the proposed placement,

(c) notify the local authority and the district health authority in whose area the prospective adopter resides in writing before the placement with particulars of the proposed placement,

(d) notify the local education authority in whose area the prospective adopter resides in writing before the placement with particulars of the proposed placement if the child is of compulsory school age within the meaning of section 35 of the Education Act 1944 or the adoption agency's medical adviser considers the child to be handicapped,

(e) place the child with the prospective adopter, so however that where the child already has his home with the prospective adopter the agency shall notify the prospective adopter in writing of the date the child is placed with him by the agency for adoption,

(f) . . .

(g) ensure that the child is visited within one week of the placement and on such other occasions as the adoption agency considers necessary in order to supervise the child's well-being,

(h) ensure that written reports are obtained of such visits,

(i) provide such advice and assistance to the prospective adopter as the agency considers necessary,

[(j) make appointments for the child to be examined by a registered medical practitioner and for a written assessment on the state of his health and his need for health care to be made—

 (i) at least once in every period of six months before the child's second birthday, and

 (ii) at least once in every period of twelve months after the child's second birthday, unless the child is of sufficient understanding to make an informed decision and refuses to submit to the examination, and]

[(k) review the placement for adoption of the child within four weeks of placement, not more than three months after that review unless an application for an adoption order has been made, and at least every six months thereafter until an application for an adoption order is made.]

[(3) The agency who carry out the review referred to in paragraph (2)(k) shall—

(a) set out in writing the arrangements governing the manner in which the case of each child shall be reviewed and shall draw the written arrangements to the attention of the child, where reasonably practicable having regard to his age and understanding, to the prospective adopters, and to any other person the agency considers relevant,

(b) have regard so far as reasonably practicable to the considerations specified in Part VIII of the Schedule, and

(c) ensure that—

 (i) the information obtained in respect of a child's case,

 (ii) details of the proceedings at any meeting arranged by the agency to consider any aspect of the review of the case, and

 (iii) details of any decision made in the course of or as a result of the review, are recorded in writing.

(4) The agency who carry out the review shall, so far as reasonably practicable, notify details of the result of the review and of any decision taken by them in consequence of the review to—

(a) the child where he is of sufficient age and understanding;

(b) his parents, except where a freeing order has been made under section 18 of the Act and that order has not been revoked,

(c) his father, if he does not have parental responsibility for him and his identity is known, provided that the agency considers this to be in the child's interests;

(d) the prospective adopters; and

(e) any other person whom they consider ought to be notified.]

NOTES

Para (2): sub-paras (aa), (aaa) inserted, sub-para (f) revoked, and sub-paras (j), (k) substituted, by SI 1997/649, reg 2(11)(a)–(d).

Paras (3), (4): added by SI 1997/649, reg 2(11)(e).

## 13 Review of case where no placement made within six months of freeing for adoption

(1) Where a child has been freed for adoption by virtue of an order under [section 18 of the Act] (freeing child for adoption) and six months have elapsed since the making of that order and the child does not have his home with a prospective adopter, the adoption agency [which has parental responsibility for the child by virtue of section 18 or 21 of the Act (freeing for adoption and variation of order to substitute one agency for another)] shall review that child's case to determine why no placement has been made and what action if any should be taken to safeguard and promote his welfare.

(2) A case to which paragraph (1) applies shall be subject to such a review at intervals of not more than six months.

NOTES

Para (1): words in square brackets substituted by SI 1997/649, reg 2(12).

## [13A Information on adoption

As soon as practicable after the making of an adoption order in respect of a child, the adoption agency shall—

(a) provide the adopters with such information about the child as they consider appropriate; and

(b) at the same time advise the adopters that this information should be made available to the child at a time when they consider it is appropriate but no later than the child's eighteenth birthday.]

NOTES

Inserted by SI 1997/649, reg 2(13).

## 14 Confidentiality and preservation of case records

(1) Subject to regulation 15, any information obtained or recommendations or decisions made by virtue of these regulations shall be treated by the adoption agency as confidential.

(2) Where a case record has been set up by an adoption agency under regulations 7(2)(a), 8(2)(a) or 9(3) in respect of a child or a prospective adopter, any report, recommendation or decision made by that agency by virtue of these regulations in respect of that child or that prospective adopter shall be placed on the case record relating to that child or, as the case may be, that prospective adopter, and any case records set up by the agency together with the indexes to them shall be kept in a place of special security.

(3)   Subject to regulation 16(2), an adoption agency shall preserve the indexes to all its case records and the case records in respect of those cases in which an adoption order is made in a place of special security for at least 75 years and shall preserve other case records in a place of special security for so long as it considers appropriate, so however that any case records and indexes may be so preserved on microfilm or such other system as reproduces the total contents of any such record or index.

[(4)   The adoption agency shall ensure that the place of special security referred to in paragraphs (2) and (3) preserve the records etc, so far as is possible, and in particular minimise the risk of damage from fire or water.]

NOTES
Para (4): added by SI 1997/649, reg 2(14).

## 15   Access to case records and disclosure of information

(1)   Subject to paragraph (3), an adoption agency shall provide such access to its case records and the indexes to them and disclose such information in its possession, as may be required—

(a)   to those holding an inquiry under [section 81 of the Children Act] (inquiries), for the purposes of such an inquiry,

(b)   to the Secretary of State,

(c)   subject to the provisions of sections 29(7) and 32(3) of the Local Government Act 1974 (investigations and disclosure), to a Local Commissioner, appointed under section 23 of that Act (Commissioners for Local Administration), for the purposes of any investigation conducted in accordance with Part III of that Act,

[(cc) to any person appointed by the adoption agency for the purposes of the consideration by the agency of any representations (including complaints),]

(d)   to the persons and authorities referred to in regulations 11 and 12 to the extent specified in those regulations,

(e)   to a guardian ad litem or reporting officer appointed under rules made pursuant to [section 65 of the Act] (guardian ad litem and reporting officer) for the purposes of the discharge of his duties in that behalf, and

(f)   to a court having power to make an order under the Act . . .

(2)   Subject to paragraph (3), an adoption agency may provide such access to its case records and the indexes to them and disclose such information in its possession, as it thinks fit—

(a)   for the purposes of carrying out its functions as an adoption agency, and

(b)   to a person who is authorised in writing by the Secretary of State to obtain information for the purposes of research.

(3)   A written record shall be kept by an adoption agency of any access provided or disclosure made by virtue of this regulation.

NOTES
Para (1): in sub-paras (a), (e) words in square brackets substituted, sub-para (cc) inserted, and in sub-para (f) words omitted revoked, by SI 1997/649, reg 2(15).

## 16   Transfer of case records

(1)   Subject to paragraphs (2) and (3), an adoption agency may transfer a copy of a case record (or part thereof) to another adoption agency when it considers this to be in the interests of a child or prospective adopter to whom the record relates, and a written record shall be kept of any such transfer.

(2)    An approved adoption society which intends to cease to act or exist as such shall forthwith either transfer its case records to another adoption agency having first obtained the Secretary of State's approval for such transfer, or transfer its case records—

(a)  to the local authority in whose area the society's head office is situated, or

(b)  in the case of a society which amalgamates with another approved adoption society to form a new approved adoption society, to the new society.

(3)    An adoption agency to which case records are transferred by virtue of paragraph (2)(a) or (b) shall notify the Secretary of State in writing of such transfer.

[**17**    Where parental responsibility for a child who is in Great Britain has been transferred from one adoption agency ("the existing agency") to another ("the substitute agency") by virtue of an order under section 21 of the Act (variation of section 18 order), the substitute agency shall provide such information to the existing agency as that agency considers necessary for it to comply with its duty under section 19(2) and (3) of the Act.]

---

NOTES

Substituted by SI 1997/649, reg 2(16).

---

# SCHEDULE

Regulations 7(2)(b), (c), 3(b), 8(2)(b), (c)

# PART I
## PARTICULARS RELATING TO THE CHILD

1. Name, sex, date and place of birth and address.

2. Whether legitimate or illegitimate at birth and, if illegitimate whether subsequently legitimated.

3. Nationality.

4. Physical description.

5. Personality and social development.

6. Religion, including details of baptism, confirmation or equivalent ceremonies.

7. Details of any wardship proceedings and of any court orders[, or agreement under section 4 of the Children Act, relating to parental responsibility for the child] or to his custody and maintenance.

8. Details of any brothers and sisters, including dates of birth, arrangements in respect of care and custody and whether any brother or sister is also being considered for adoption.

9. Extent of access to members of the child's natural family and, if the child is illegitimate, his father, and in each case the nature of the relationship enjoyed.

10. If the child has been in the care of a local authority or voluntary organisation, details (including dates) of any placements with foster parents, or other arrangements in respect of the care of the child, including particulars of the persons with whom the child has had his home and observations on the care provided.

11. Names, addresses and types of schools attended, with dates and educational attainments.

[12. Any special needs in relation to the child's health (whether physical or mental) and his emotional and behavioural development, and how those are to be met.

12A. Any educational needs which the child has and how these needs are to be met, the result of any assessment carried out in respect of any special educational needs under the Education Act 1996, and how any needs identified in the statement of special educational needs made under section 324 of that Act are to be met.]

13. What, if any, rights to or interest in property or any claim to damages, under the Fatal Accidents Act 1976 or otherwise, the child stands to retain or lose if adopted.

14. Wishes and feelings in relation to adoption and, as the case may be, an application under [section 18 of the Act (freeing child for adoption),] including any wishes in respect of religious and cultural upbringing.

15. Any other relevant information which the agency considers may assist the panel.

NOTES
Paras 7, 14: words square brackets substituted by SI 1997/649, reg 2(17)(a), (c).
Paras 12, 12A: substituted, for para 12 as originally enacted, by SI 1997/649, reg 2(17)(b).

## PART II
## MATTERS TO BE COVERED IN REPORT ON THE CHILD'S HEALTH

1. Name, date of birth, sex, weight and height.

2. A neo-natal report on the child, including—
   - (a)  details of the birth, and any complications,
   - (b)  results of a physical examination and screening tests,
   - (c)  details of any treatment given,
   - (d)  details of any problem in management and feeding,
   - (e)  any other relevant information which may assist the panel,
   - (f)  the name and address of any doctor who may be able to provide further information about any of the above matters.

3. A full health history and examination of the child, including—
   - (a)  details of any serious illness, disability, accident, hospital admission or attendance at an out-patient department, and in each case any treatment given,
   - (b)  details and dates of immunisations,
   - (c)  a physical and developmental assessment according to age, including an assessment of vision and hearing and of neurological, speech and language development and any evidence of emotional disorder,
   - (d)  for a child over five years of age, the school health history (if available),
   - [(dd) how his health and medical history has affected his physical, intellectual, emotional, social or behavioural development;]
   - (e)  any other relevant information which may assist the panel.

4. The signature, name, address and qualifications of the registered medical practitioner who prepared the report, the date of the report and of the examinations carried out together with the name and address of any doctor (if different) who may be able to provide further information about any of the above matters.

NOTES
Para 3: sub-para (dd) inserted by SI 1997/649, reg 2(18).

## PART III
## PARTICULARS RELATING TO EACH NATURAL PARENT, INCLUDING WHERE APPROPRIATE THE FATHER OF AN ILLEGITIMATE CHILD

1. Name, date and place of birth and address.

2. Marital status and date and place of marriage (if any).

3. Past and present relationship (if any) with the other natural parent, including comments on its stability.

4. Physical description.

5. Personality.

6. Religion.

7. Educational attainments.

8. Past and present occupations and interests.

9. Names and brief details of the person circumstances of the parents and any brothers and sisters of the natural parent, with their ages or ages at death.

10. Wishes and feelings in relation to adoption and, as the case may be, an application under [section 18 of the Act (freeing child for adoption),] including any wishes in respect of the child's religious and cultural upbringing.

11. Any other relevant information which the agency considers may assist the panel.

NOTES
Para 10: words in square brackets substituted by SI 1997/649, reg 2(19).

# PART IV
## PARTICULARS RELATING TO THE HEALTH OF EACH NATURAL PARENT INCLUDING WHERE APPROPRIATE THE FATHER OF AN ILLEGITIMATE CHILD

1. Name, date of birth, sex, weight and height.

2. A family health history, covering the parents, the brothers and sisters (if any) and the other children (if any) of the natural parent with details of any serious physical or mental illness and inherited and congenital disease.

3. Past health history, including details of any serious physical or mental illness, disability, accident, hospital admission or attendance at an out-patient department, and in each case any treatment given.

4. A full obstetric history of the mother, including any problems in the ante-natal, labour and post-natal periods, with the results of any tests carried out during or immediately after pregnancy.

5. Details of any present illness, including treatment and prognosis.

6. Any other relevant information which the agency considers may assist the panel.

7. The signature, name, address and qualifications of any registered medical practitioner who supplied any of the information in this Part together with the name and address of any doctor (if different) who may be able to provide further information about any of the above matters.

# PART V
## PARTICULARS RELATING TO A GUARDIAN

1. Particulars referred to in paragraph 1, 6, 10 and 11 of Part III.

# PART VI
## PARTICULARS RELATING TO THE PROSPECTIVE ADOPTER

1. Name, date and place of birth and address.

2. Domicile.

3. Marital status, date and place of marriage (if any) and comments on stability of relationship.

4. Details of any previous marriage.

5. If a married person proposes to adopt a child alone, the reasons for this.

6. Physical description.

7. Personality.

8. Religion, and whether willing to follow any wishes of a child or his natural parents of guardian in respect of the child's religious and cultural upbringing.

9. Educational attainments.

10. Past and present occupations and interests.

11. Details of income and comments on the living standards of the household.

12. Details of income and comments on the living standards of the household.

12. Details of other members of the prospective adopter's household (including any children of the prospective adopter even if not resident in the household).

13. Details of the parents and any brothers or sisters of the prospective adopter, with their ages or ages at death.

14. Attitudes to adoption of such other members of the prospective adopter's household and family as the agency considers appropriate.

15. Previous experience of caring for children as step-parent, foster parent, child-minder or prospective adopter and assessment of ability in this respect, together where appropriate with assessment of ability in bringing up the prospective adopter's own children.

16. Reasons for wishing to adopt a child and extent of understanding of the nature and effect of adoption.

17. Assessment of ability to bring up an adopted child throughout his childhood.

18. Details of any adoption allowance payable.

19.Names and addresses of two referees who will give personal references on the prospective adopter.

20. Name and address of the prospective adopter's registered medical practitioner, if any.

21. Any other relevant information which the agency considers may assist the panel.

# PART VII
## MATTERS TO BE COVERED IN REPORT ON HEALTH OF THE PROSPECTIVE ADOPTER

1. Name, date of birth, sex, weight and height.

2. A family health history, covering the parents, the brothers and sisters (if any) and the children (if any) of the prospective adopter, with details of any serious physical or mental illness and inherited and congenital disease.

3. Marital history, including (if applicable) reasons for inability to have children.

4. Past health history, including details of any serious physical or mental illness, disability, accident, hospital admission or attendance at an out-patient department, and in each case any treatment given.

5. Obstetric history (if applicable).

6. Details of any present illness, including treatment and prognosis.

7. A full medical examination.

8. Details of any daily consumption of alcohol, tobacco and habit-forming drugs.

9. Any other relevant information which the agency considers may assist the panel.

10. The signature, name, address and qualifications of the registered medical practitioner who prepared the report, the date of the report and of the examinations carried out together with the name and address of any doctor (if different) who may be able to provide further information about any of the above matters.

## [PART VIII
## CONSIDERATIONS TO BE INCLUDED IN REVIEW

1. The child's needs (including his educational needs), progress and development, and whether any changes are needed to help to meet those needs or to assist his progress or development.

2. Any arrangements for contact, and whether there is need for any change in such arrangements.

3. Existing arrangements for the child's medical and dental care and treatment, and health and dental surveillance.

4. The possible need for an appropriate course of action to assist any necessary change of such care, treatment or surveillance.

5. The possible need for preventive measures, such as vaccination and immunisation, and screening for vision and hearing.]

NOTES

Added by SI 1997/649, reg 2(20).

# ADOPTION RULES 1984

## (SI 1984/265)

Made: 17 February 1984.
Commencement: 27 May 1984.
Authority: Adoption Act 1958, s 9(3) (repealed), Adoption Act 1968, s 12(1) (repealed) (see now Adoption Act 1976, ss 17(7), 54(1), 61(1), (2), 65(1), 66(1), Sch 1, paras 1(5), 4(2), 6).

## PART I
## INTRODUCTORY

### 1 Citation and commencement

These rules may be cited as the Adoption Rules 1984 and shall come into operation on 27th May 1984.

### 2 Interpretation

(1) In these rules, unless the context otherwise requires—
["the Act" means the Adoption Act 1976];
"adoption agency" means a local authority or approved adoption society;
"the child" means the person whom the applicant for an adoption order or an order authorising a proposed foreign adoption proposes to adopt, or, as the case may be, the person the adoption agency proposes should be freed for adoption;

"Convention proceedings" means proceedings in the High Court on an application for a Convention adoption order and proceedings in the High Court under [the Act];

"the court" means the High Court and any county court [falling within the class specified for the commencement of proceedings under the Act by an Order under Part I of Schedule 11 to the Children Act 1989];

"interim order" means an order under [section 25 of the Act];

"order authorising a proposed foreign adoption" means an order under [section 55 of the Act];

"process" means, in the High Court, a summons and, in a county court, an application;

"proper officer" means, in the High Court, [a district judge] of the Principal Registry of the Family Division and, in a county court, the person defined as "proper officer" by Order 1(3) of the County Court Rules 1981; and

"regular armed forces of the Crown" means the Royal Navy, the Regular Armed Forces as defined by section 225 of the Army Act 1955, the Regular Air Force as defined by section 223 of the Air Force Act 1955, the Queen Alexandra's Royal Naval Nursing Service and the Women's Royal Naval Service.

[(2) Except where a contrary intention appears, a word or phrase used in these rules shall have the same meaning as in the Children Act 1989 or, where the word or phrase does not appear in that Act, as in the Act.]

(3) In these rules . . . a form referred to by number means the form so numbered in Schedule 1 to these rules, or a form substantially to the like effect, with such variations as the circumstances may require.

NOTES
Para (1): definition "the Act", and words in square brackets in definitions "Convention proceedings", "the court", "interim order", "order authorising a proposed foreign adoption" and "proper officer" substituted by the Adoption (Amendment) Rules 1991, SI 1991/1880, r 3(1).
Para (2): substituted by SI 1991/1880, r 3(2).
Para (3): words omitted revoked by SI 1991/1880, r 3(3).

## 3 Extent and application of other rules

(1) These rules shall apply to proceedings in the High Court and in a county court under [the Act], and Part IV of these rules shall apply to Convention proceedings, commenced on or after 27th May 1984.

(2) Subject to the provisions of these rules and any enactment, the Rules of the Supreme Court . . . 1965 and the County Court Rules 1981 shall apply with the necessary modifications to proceedings in the High Court [or a county court under the Act].

(3) For the purposes of paragraph (2) any provision of these rules authorising or requiring anything to be done shall be treated as if it were a provision of the Rules of the Supreme Court 1965 or the County Court Rules 1981 as the case may be.

(4) Unless the contrary intention appears, any power which by these rules may be exercised by the court may be exercised by the proper officer.

NOTES
Para (1): words in square brackets substituted by SI 1991/1880, r 4(1).
Para (2): word omitted revoked, and words in square brackets substituted, by SI 1991/1880, r 4(2).

# PART II
# FREEING FOR ADOPTION

## 4 Commencement of proceedings

(1) Proceedings to free a child for adoption shall be commenced—
  (a) by originating summons in Form 1 issued out of the Principal Registry of the Family Division; or
  (b) by filing in the office of [a] county court an originating application in Form 1.

(2) The applicant shall be the adoption agency and the respondents shall be—
  (a) each parent or guardian of the child;
  [(b) any local authority or voluntary organisation which has parental responsibility for, is looking after, or is caring for, the child;]
  (f) any person liable by virtue of any order or agreement to contribute to the maintenance of the child; and
  (g) in the High Court, the child.

(3) The court may at any time direct that any other person or body, save in a county court the child, be made a respondent to the process.

(4) On filing the originating process the applicant shall pay the appropriate fee and supply three copies of:—
  (a) Form 1, together with any other documents required to be supplied, and
  (b) a report in writing covering all the relevant matters specified in Schedule 2 to these rules.

NOTES

Para (1): in sub-para (b) word in square brackets substituted by SI 1991/1880, r 5(1).
Para (2): sub-para (b) substituted for the original sub-paras (b)–(e) by SI 1991/1880, r 5(2).

## 5 Appointment and duties of reporting officer

(1) As soon as practicable after the originating process has been filed or at any stage thereafter, if it appears that a parent or guardian of the child is willing to agree to the making of an adoption order and is in England or Wales, the proper officer shall appoint a reporting officer in respect of that parent or guardian, and shall send to him a copy of the originating process and any documents attached thereto and of the report supplied by the applicant.

(2) The same person may be appointed as reporting officer in respect of two or more parents or guardians of the child.

(3) The reporting officer shall be appointed from a panel established by [regulations under section 41(7) of the Children Act 1989, if any,] but shall not be a member or employee of the applicant or any respondent body nor have been involved in the making of any arrangements for the adoption of the child.

(4) The reporting officer shall—
  (a) ensure so far as is reasonably practicable that any agreement to the making of an adoption order is given freely and unconditionally and with full understanding of what is involved;
  (b) confirm that the parent or guardian has been given an opportunity of making a declaration under [section 18(6) of the Act] that he prefers not to be involved in future questions concerning the adoption of the child;
  (c) witness the signature by the parent or guardian of the written agreement to the making of an adoption order;

(d)  investigate all the circumstances relevant to that agreement and any such declaration;

(e)  where it is proposed to free [for adoption a child whose parents were not married to each other at the time of his birth and whose father is not his guardian], interview any person claiming to be the father in order to be able to advise the court on the matters listed in [section 18(7) of the Act]; but if more than one reporting officer has been appointed, the proper officer shall nominate one of them to conduct the interview; and

(f)  on completing his investigations make a report in writing to the court, drawing attention to any matters which, in his opinion, may be of assistance to the court in considering the application.

(5)  With a view to obtaining the directions of the court on any matter, the reporting officer may at any time make such interim report to the court as appears to him to be necessary and, in particular, the reporting officer shall make a report if a parent or guardian of the child is unwilling to agree to the making of an adoption order, and in such a case the proper officer shall notify the applicant.

(6)  The court may, at any time before the final determination of the application, require the reporting officer to perform such further duties as the court considers necessary.

(7)  The reporting officer shall attend any hearing of the application if so required by the court.

(8)  Any report made to the court under this rule shall be confidential.

---

NOTES

Paras (3), (4): words in square brackets substituted by SI 1991/1880, r 6.

---

## 6 Appointment and duties of guardian ad litem

(1)  As soon as practicable after the originating process has been filed, or after receipt of the statement of facts supplied under rule 7, if it appears that a parent or guardian of the child is unwilling to agree to the making of an adoption order, the proper officer shall appoint a guardian ad litem of the child and shall send to him a copy of the originating process, together with any documents attached thereto, the statement of facts and the report supplied by the applicant.

(2)  Where there are special circumstances and it appears to the court that the welfare of the child requires it, the court may at any time appoint a guardian ad litem of the child, and where such an appointment is made the court shall indicate any particular matters which it requires the guardian ad litem to investigate, and the proper officer shall send the guardian ad litem a copy of the originating process together with any documents attached thereto and the report supplied by the applicant.

(3)  The same person may be appointed as reporting officer under rule 5(1) in respect of a parent or guardian who appears to be willing to agree to the making of an adoption order, and as guardian ad litem of the child under this rule, and, whether or not so appointed as reporting officer in respect of a parent or guardian of the child who originally was unwilling to agree to the making of an adoption order but who later signifies his or her agreement.

(4)  In the High Court, unless the applicant desires some other person to act as guardian ad litem, the Official Solicitor shall, if he consents, be appointed as the guardian ad litem of the child.

(5) In a county court and where, in the High Court, the Official Solicitor does not consent to act as guardian ad litem, or the applicant desires some other person so to act, the guardian ad litem shall be appointed from a panel established by [regulations under section 41(7) of the Children Act 1989, if any,] but shall not be a member or employee of the applicant or any respondent body nor have been involved in the making of any arrangements for the adoption of the child.

(6) With a view to safeguarding the interests of the child before the court, the guardian ad litem shall, so far as is reasonably practicable—

    (a) investigate—

        (i) so far as he considers necessary, the matters alleged in the originating process, the report supplied by the applicant and, where appropriate, the statement of facts supplied under rule 7, and

        (ii) any other matters which appear to be relevant to the making of an order freeing the child for adoption;

    (b) advise whether, in his opinion, the child should be present at the hearing of the process; and

    (c) perform such other duties as appear to him to be necessary or as the court may direct.

(7) On completing his investigations the guardian ad litem shall make a report in writing to the court, drawing attention to any matters which, in his opinion, may be of assistance to the court in considering the application.

(8) With a view to obtaining the directions of the court on any matter, the guardian ad litem may at any time make such interim report to the court as appears to him to be necessary.

(9) The court may, at any time before the final determination of the application, require the guardian ad litem to perform such further duties as the court considers necessary.

(10) The guardian ad litem shall attend any hearing of the application unless the court otherwise orders.

(11) Any report made to the court under this rule shall be confidential.

---

NOTES

Para (5): words in square brackets substituted by SI 1991/1880, r 7.

---

## 7 Statement of facts in dispensation cases

(1) Where the adoption agency applying for an order freeing a child for adoption intends to request the court to dispense with the agreement of a parent or guardian of the child on any of the grounds specified in [section 16(2) of the Act], the request shall, unless otherwise directed, be made in the originating process, or, if made subsequently, by notice to the proper officer and there shall be attached to the originating process or notice three copies of the statement of facts on which the applicant intends to rely.

(2) Where the applicant has been informed by a person with whom the child has been placed for adoption that he wishes his identity to remain confidential, the statement of facts supplied under paragraph (1) shall be framed in such a way as not to disclose the identify of that person.

(3) Where a statement of facts has been supplied under paragraph (1), the proper officer shall, where and as soon as practicable, inform the parent or guardian of the request to dispense with his agreement and shall send to him a copy of the statement supplied under paragraph (1).

(4) The proper officer shall also send a copy of the statement supplied under paragraph (1) to the guardian ad litem and to the reporting officer if a different person.

NOTES

Para (1): words in square brackets substituted by SI 1991/1880, r 8.

## 8 Agreement

(1) Any document signifying the agreement of a person to the making of an adoption order may be in Form 2, and, if executed by a person outside England and Wales before the commencement of the proceedings, shall be filed with the originating process.

(2) If the document is executed in Scotland it shall be witnessed by a Justice of the Peace or a Sheriff.

(3) If the document is executed in Northern Ireland it shall be witnessed by a Justice of the Peace.

(4) If the document is executed outside the United Kingdom it shall be witnessed by one of the following persons—

    (a) any person for the time being authorised by law in the place where the document is executed to administer an oath for any judicial or other legal purpose;

    (b) a British consular officer;

    (c) a notary public; or

    (d) if the person executing the document is serving in any of the regular armed forces of the Crown, an officer holding a commission in any of those forces.

## 9 Notice of hearing

(1) As soon as practicable after receipt of the originating process, the proper officer shall list the case for hearing by a judge, and shall serve notice of the hearing on all the parties, the reporting officer and the guardian ad litem (if appointed) in Form 3.

(2) The reporting officer and the guardian ad litem (if appointed), but no other person, shall be served with a copy of the originating process and the report supplied by the applicant, and that report shall be confidential.

(3) If, at any stage before the hearing of the process, it appears to the court that directions for the hearing are required, the court may give such directions as it considers necessary and, in any event, the court shall, not less than four weeks before the date fixed for the hearing under paragraph (1), consider the documents relating to the process with a view to giving such further directions for the hearing as appear to the court to be necessary.

## 10 The hearing

(1) On the hearing of the process, any person upon whom notice is required to be served under rule 9 may attend and be heard on the question whether an order freeing the child for adoption should be made.

(2) Any member or employee of a party which is a local authority, adoption agency or other body may address the court if he is duly authorised in that behalf.

(3) Where the court has been informed by the applicant that the child has been placed with a person (whether alone or jointly with another) for adoption and that person wishes his identity to remain confidential, the proceedings shall be conducted with a view to securing that any such person is not seen by or made known to any respondent who is not already aware of his identity except with his consent.

(4) Subject to paragraph (5), the judge shall not make an order freeing the child for adoption except after the personal attendance before him of a representative of the applicant duly authorised in that behalf and of the child.

(5) If there are special circumstances which, having regard to the report of the guardian ad litem (if any), appear to the court to make the attendance of the child unnecessary, the court may direct that the child need not attend.

(6) If there are special circumstances which appear to the court to make the attendance of any other party necessary, the court may direct that that party shall attend.

## 11 Proof of identity of child, etc

(1) Where the child who is the subject of the proceedings is identified in the originating process by reference to a birth certificate which is the same, or relates to the same entry in the Registers of Births, as a birth certificate exhibited to a form of agreement, the child so identified shall be deemed, unless the contrary appears, to be the child to whom the form of agreement refers.

(2) Where the child has previously been adopted, paragraph (1) shall have effect as if for the references to a birth certificate and to the Registers of Births there were substituted respectively references to a certified copy of an entry in the Adopted Children Register and to that Register.

(3) Where the precise date of the child's birth is not proved to the satisfaction of the court, the court shall determine the probable date of his birth and the date so determined may be specified in the order freeing the child for adoption as the date of his birth.

(4) Where the place of birth of the child cannot be proved to the satisfaction of the court but it appears probable that the child was born in the United Kingdom, the Channel Islands or the Isle of Man, he may be treated as having been born in the registration district and sub-district in which the court sits, and in any other case (where the country of birth is not proved) the particulars of the country of birth may be omitted from the order freeing the child for adoption.

## 12 Application for revocation of order freeing a child for adoption

(1) An application by a former parent for an order revoking an order freeing the child for adoption shall be made in Form 4 in the proceedings commenced under rule 4.

(2) Notice of the proceedings shall be served on all parties and on any adoption agency [which has parental responsibility for the child by virtue of section 21 of the Act], save that notice shall not be served on a party to the proceedings who was joined as a party by virtue of [rule 4(2)(b)].

(3) As soon as practicable after receipt of the application, the proper officer shall list the case for hearing by a judge and shall appoint a guardian ad litem of the child in accordance with rule 6(4) or (5) and shall send to him a copy of the application and any documents attached thereto.

(4) The guardian ad litem shall have the same duties as if he had been appointed under rule 6 but as if in that rule:—

    (a)   the reference to an order freeing the child for adoption was a reference to the revocation of an order freeing the child for adoption; and

    (b)   each reference to the report supplied by the applicant was omitted.

NOTES

Para (2): words in square brackets substituted by SI 1991/1880, r 9.

**[13 Substitution of one adoption agency for another]**

(1)  An application [under section 21(1) of the Act] to transfer the parental rights and duties relating to the child between themselves under section 23 of the 1975 Act shall be made in Form 5 in the proceedings commenced under rule 4.

(2)  Notice of any order made under [section 21 of the Act] shall be sent by. the court to the court which made the order under [section 18 of the Act] (if a different court) and to any former parent (as defined in [section 19(1) of the Act]) of the child.

NOTES
> Rule heading: substituted by SI 1991/1880, r 10(1).
> Paras (1), (2): words in square brackets substituted by SI 1991/1880, r 10(2), (3).

# PART III
# ADOPTION ORDERS

## 14 Application for a serial number

If any person proposing to apply to the court for an adoption order wishes his identity to be kept confidential, he may, before commencing proceedings, apply to the proper officer for a serial number to be assigned to him for the purposes of identifying him in the proposed process and a number shall be assigned to him accordingly.

## 15 Commencement of proceedings

(1)  Proceedings for an adoption order shall be commenced—
  (a)  by originating summons in Form 6 issued out of the Principal Registry of the Family Division; or
  (b)  by filing in the office of [a] county court an originating application in Form 6.

(2)  The applicant shall be the proposed adopter and the respondents shall be—
  (a)  each parent or guardian (not being an applicant) of the child, unless the child is free for adoption;
  [(b)  any adoption agency having parental responsibility for the child by virtue of sections 18 or 21 of the Act;]
  (c)  any adoption agency named in the application or in any form of agreement to the making of the adoption order as having taken part in the arrangements for the adoption of the child;
  (d)  any local authority to whom the applicant has given notice under [section 22 of the Act] of his intention to apply for an adoption order;
  [(e)  any local authority or voluntary organisation which has parental responsibility for, is looking after, or is caring for, the child;]
  (h)  any person liable by virtue of any order or agreement to contribute to the maintenance of the child;
  (i)  . . .
  (j)  where the applicant proposes to rely on [section 15(1)(b)(ii) of the Act], the spouse of the applicant; and
  (k)  in the High Court, the child.

(3)  The court may at any time direct that any other person or body, save in a county court the child, be made a respondent to the process.

(4)  On filing the originating process the applicant shall pay the appropriate fee and supply three copies of—

(a) Form 6, together with any other documents required to be supplied, and

(b) were the child was not placed for adoption with the applicant by an adoption agency, save where the applicant or one of the applicants is a parent of the child, reports by a registered medical practitioner made not more than three months earlier on the health of the child and of each applicant, covering the matters specified in Schedule 3 to these rules.

NOTES

Para (1): word in square brackets substituted by SI 1991/1880, r 11(1).

Para (2): sub-para (b) and the words in square brackets in sub-paras (d), (j) substituted, sub-para (e) substituted for the original sub-paras (e)–(g), and sub-para (i) revoked, by SI 1991/1880, r 11(2)–(6).

## 16 Preliminary examination of application

If it appears to the proper officer on receipt of the originating process for an adoption order that the court—

(a) may be precluded, by virtue of [section 24(1) of the Act], from proceeding to hear the application, or

(b) may for any other reason appearing in the process have no jurisdiction to make an adoption order,

he shall refer the process to the [judge or district judge] for directions.

NOTES

Words in square brackets substituted by SI 1991/1880, r 12.

## 17 Appointment and duties of reporting officer

(1) As soon as practicable after the originating process has been filed or at any stage thereafter, if the child is not free for adoption and if it appears that a parent or guardian of the child is willing to agree to the making of an adoption order and is in England and Wales, the proper officer shall appoint a reporting officer in respect of that parent or guardian, and shall send to him a copy of the originating process and any documents attached thereto.

(2) The same person may be appointed as reporting officer in respect of two or more parents or guardians of the child.

(3) The reporting officer shall be appointed from a panel established by [regulations under section 41(7) of the Children Act 1989, if any,] but shall not be a member or employee of any respondent body (except where a local authority is made a respondent only under rule 15(2)(d)) nor have been involved in the making of any arrangements for the adoption of the child.

(4) The reporting officer shall—

(a) ensure so far as is reasonably practicable that any agreement to the making of the adoption order is given freely and unconditionally and with full understanding of what is involved;

(b) witness the signature by the parent or guardian of the written agreement to the making of the adoption order;

(c) investigate all the circumstances relevant to that agreement; and

(d) on completing his investigations make a report in writing to the court, drawing attention to any matters which, in his opinion, may be of assistance to the court in considering the application.

(5) Paragraphs (5) to (8) of rule 5 shall apply to a reporting officer appointed under this rule as they apply to a reporting officer appointed under that rule.

Para (3): words in square brackets substituted by SI 1991/1880, r 13.

## 18 Appointment and duties of guardian ad litem

(1) As soon as practicable after the originating process has been filed, or after receipt of the statement of facts supplied under rule 19, if the child is not free for adoption and if it appears that a parent or guardian of the child is unwilling to agree to the making of the adoption order, the proper officer shall appoint a guardian ad litem of the child and shall send to him a copy of the originating process together with any documents attached thereto.

(2) Where there are special circumstances and it appears to the court that the welfare of the child requires it, the court may at any time appoint a guardian ad litem of the child and where such an appointment is made the court shall indicate any particular matters which it requires the guardian ad litem to investigate, and the proper officer shall send the guardian ad litem a copy of the originating process together with any documents attached thereto.

(3) The same person may be appointed as reporting officer under rule 17(1) in respect of a parent or guardian who appears to be willing to agree to the making of the adoption order, and as guardian ad litem of the child under this rule, and, whether or not so appointed as reporting officer, the guardian ad litem may be appointed as reporting officer in respect of a parent or guardian of the child who originally was unwilling to agree to the making of an adoption order but who later signifies his or her agreement.

(4) In the High Court, unless the applicant desires some other person to act as guardian ad litem, the Official Solicitor shall, if he consents, be appointed as the guardian ad litem of the child.

(5) In a county court and where, in the High Court, the Official Solicitor does not consent to act as guardian ad litem, or the applicant desires some other person so to act, the guardian ad litem shall be appointed from a panel established by [regulations under section 41(7) of the Children Act 1989, if any,] but shall not be a member or employee of any respondent body (except where a local authority is made a respondent only under rule 15(2)(d)) nor have been involved in the making of any arrangements for the adoption of the child.

(6) With a view to safeguarding the interests of the child before the court the guardian ad litem shall, so far as is reasonably practicable—

    (a) investigate—
        (i) so far as he considers necessary, the matters alleged in the originating process, any report supplied under rule 22(1) or (2) and, where appropriate, the statement of facts supplied under rule 19;
        (ii) any other matters which appear to him to be relevant to the making of an adoption order;
    (b) advise whether, in his opinion, the child should be present at the hearing of the process; and
    (c) perform such other duties as appear to him to be necessary or as the court may direct.

(7) Paragraphs (7) to (11) of rule 6 shall apply to a guardian ad litem appointed under this rule as they apply to a guardian ad litem appointed under that rule.

NOTES
Para (5): words in square brackets substituted by SI 1991/1880, r 14.

## 19 Statement of facts in dispensation cases

(1)  Where the child is not free for adoption and the applicant for the adoption order intends to request the court to dispense with the agreement of a parent or guardian of the child on any of the grounds specified in [section 16(2) of the Act], the request shall, unless otherwise directed, be made in the originating process or, if made subsequently, by notice to the proper officer and there shall be attached to the originating process or notice three copies of the statement of facts on which the applicant intends to rely.

(2)  Where a serial number has been assigned to the applicant under rule 14, the statement of facts supplied under paragraph (1) shall be framed in such a way as not to disclose the identity of the applicant.

(3)  Where a statement of facts has been supplied under paragraph (1), the proper officer shall, where and as soon as practicable, inform the parent or guardian of the request to dispense with his agreement and shall send to him a copy of the statement supplied under paragraph (1).

(4)  The proper officer shall also send a copy of the statement supplied under paragraph (1) to the guardian ad litem and to the reporting officer if a different person.

---

NOTES

Para (1): words in square brackets substituted by SI 1991/1880, r 15.

---

## 20 Agreement

(1)  Any document signifying the agreement of a person to the making of the adoption order may be in Form 7, and, if executed by a person outside England and Wales before the commencement of the proceedings, shall be filed with the originating process.

(2)  If the document is executed outside England and Wales it shall be witnessed by one of the persons specified in rule 8(2), (3) or (4), according to the country in which it is executed.

## 21 Notice of hearing

(1)  Subject to paragraph (4), the proper officer shall list the case for hearing by a judge as soon as practicable after the originating process has been filed, and shall serve notice of the hearing on all the parties, the reporting officer and the guardian ad litem (if appointed) in Form 8.

(2)  In a case where [section 22 of the Act] applies, the proper officer shall send a copy of the originating process and, where appropriate, of the report supplied under rule 15(4), to the local authority to whom notice under that section was given.

(3)  No person other than the reporting officer, the guardian ad litem (if appointed) and, in cases where [section 22 of the Act] applies, the local authority to whom notice under that section was given, shall be served with a copy of the originating process.

(4)  Where [section 22 of the Act] applies, the proper officer shall list the case for hearing on a date not less than three months from the date of the notice given to the local authority under that section.

(5)  If, at any stage before the hearing of the process, it appears to the court that directions for the hearing are required, the court may give such directions as it considers necessary and, in any event, the court shall, not less than four weeks before the date fixed for the hearing under paragraph (1), consider the documents relating to the process with a view to giving such further directions for the hearing as appear to the court to be necessary.

NOTES

Paras (2)–(4): words in square brackets substituted by SI 1991/1880, r 16.

## 22 Reports by adoption agency or local authority

(1) Where the child was placed for adoption with the applicant by an adoption agency, that agency shall supply, within six weeks of receipt of the notice of hearing under rule 21, three copies of a report in writing covering the matters specified in Schedule 2 to these rules.

(2) Where the child was not placed for adoption with the applicant by an adoption agency, the local authority to whom the notice under [section 22 of the Act] was given shall supply, within six weeks of receipt of the notice of hearing under rule 21, three copies of a report in writing covering the matters specified in Schedule 2 to these rules.

(3) The court may request a further report under paragraph (1) or (2) and may indicate any particular matters it requires such a further report to cover.

(4) The proper officer shall send a copy of any report supplied under paragraph (1) or (2) to the reporting officer and to the guardian ad litem (if appointed).

(5) No other person shall be supplied with a copy of any report supplied under paragraph (1) or (2) and any such report shall be confidential.

NOTES

Para (2): words in square brackets substituted by SI 1991/1880, r 17.

## 23 The hearing

(1) On the hearing of the process, any person upon whom notice is required to be served under rule 21 may attend and be heard on the question whether an adoption order should be made.

(2) Any member or employee of a party which is a local authority, adoption agency or other body may address the court if he is duly authorised in that behalf.

(3) If a serial number has been assigned to the applicant under rule 14, the proceedings shall be conducted with a view to securing that he is not seen by or made known to any respondent who is not already aware of the applicant's identity except with his consent.

(4) Subject to paragraphs (5) and (7), the judge shall not make an adoption order or an interim order except after the personal attendance before him of the applicant and the child.

(5) If there are special circumstances which, having regard to the report of the guardian ad litem (if any), appear to the court to make the attendance of the child unnecessary, the court may direct that the child need not attend.

(6) If there are special circumstances which appear to the court to make the attendance of any other party necessary, the court may direct that that party shall attend.

(7) In the case of an application under [section 14(1A) or (1B) of the Act], the judge may in special circumstances make an adoption order or an interim order after the personal attendance of one only of the applicants, if the originating process is verified by an affidavit sworn by the other applicant or, if he is outside the United Kingdom, by a declaration made by him and witnessed by any of the persons specified in rule 8(4).

NOTES

Para (7): words in square brackets substituted by SI 1991/1880, r 18.

## 24 Proof of identity of child, etc

(1) Where the child who is the subject of the proceedings is identified in the originating process by reference to a birth certificate which is the same, or relates to the same entry in the Registers of Births, as a birth certificate exhibited to a form of agreement, the child so identified shall be deemed, unless the contrary appears, to be the child to whom the form of agreement refers.

(2) Where the child has previously been adopted, paragraph (1) shall have effect as if for the references to a birth certificate and to the Registers of Births there were substituted respectively references to a certified copy of an entry in the Adopted Children Register and to that Register.

(3) Subject to paragraph (5), where the precise date of the child's birth is not proved to the satisfaction of the court, the court shall determine the probable date of his birth and the date so determined may be specified in the adoption order as the date of his birth.

(4) Subject to paragraph (5), where the place of birth of the child cannot be proved to the satisfaction of the court but it appears probable that the child was born in the United Kingdom, the Channel Islands or the Isle of Man, he may be treated as having been born in the registration district and sub-district in which the court sits, and in any other case (where the country of birth is not proved) the particulars of the country of birth may be omitted from the adoption order.

(5) Where the child is free for adoption, any order made identifying the probable date and place of birth of the child in the proceedings under [section 18 of the Act] shall be sufficient proof of the date and place of birth of the child in proceedings to which this rule applies.

NOTES

Para (5): words in square brackets substituted by SI 1991/1880, r 19.

## 25 Further proceedings after interim order

Where the court has made an interim order, the proper officer shall list the case for further hearing by a judge on a date before the order expires and shall send notice in Form 8 of the date of the hearing to all the parties and to the guardian ad litem (if appointed) not less than one month before that date.

# PART IV
# CONVENTION PROCEEDINGS

## 27 Introductory

(1) This Part of these rules shall apply to Convention proceedings and, subject to the provisions of this Part of these rules, Parts I, III and V of these rules shall apply, with the necessary modifications, to Convention proceedings as they apply to proceedings in the High Court under the . . . Act.

(2) Any reference in this Part of these rules to the nationality of a person who is not solely a United Kingdom national means that person's nationality as determined in accordance with [section 70 of the Act].

NOTES

Para (1): words omitted revoked by SI 1991/1880, r 21(1).
Para (2): words in square brackets substituted by SI 1991/1880, r 21(2).

## 28 Originating process

(1) An applicant for a Convention adoption order shall state in his originating process that he is applying for a Convention adoption order.

(2) The originating process—

   (a) need not contain paragraphs corresponding to paragraphs 2, 24 or 25 of Form 6 but

   (b) shall contain the additional information required by Schedule 4 to these rules.

## 29 Evidence as to nationality

(1) Any document (or copy of a document) which is to be used for the purposes of satisfying the court as to the nationality of the applicant or of the child shall be attached to the originating process.

(2) Where the applicant claims that for the purposes of [section 17(2)(a), (4)(a) or (5)(a) of the Act] he or the child is a national of a Convention country, he shall attach to the originating process a statement by an expert as to the law of that country relating to nationality applicable to that person.

NOTES

Para (2): words in square brackets substituted by SI 1991/1880, r 22.

## 30 Statement at hearing

The requirement that the conditions in [section 17(2), (3) and (4) or (5) of the Act] are satisfied immediately before the order is made may be established by—

   (a) oral evidence at the hearing of an application for a Convention adoption order, or

   (b) a document executed by the applicant containing a statement to that effect attested in accordance with rule 44 and such a statement shall be admissible in evidence without further proof of the signature of the applicant.

NOTES

Words in square brackets substituted by SI 1991/1880, r 23.

## 31 Orders

Within 7 days after a Convention adoption order has been drawn up, the proper officer shall by notice to the Registrar General request him to send the information to the designated authorities of any Convention country—

   (a) of which the child is a national;

   (b) in which the child was born;

   (c) in which the applicant habitually resides; or

   (d) of which the applicant is a national.

*Additional provisions for cases where child is not a United Kingdom national*

## 32 Scope of Rules 33 to 36

Rules 33 to 36 shall apply to any case where the child is not a United Kingdom national, and in such a case—

   (a) the provisions in Part III of these rules, other than rules 17 and 20 (agreement to adoption), and

   (b) paragraphs 9 to 14 of Form 6,

shall apply with the necessary modifications to take account of [section 17(6)(a) of the Act].

NOTES
Words in square brackets substituted by SI 1991/1880, r 24.

## 33 Evidence as to foreign law relating to consents and consultations

The applicant shall file, with his originating process, a statement by an expert as to the provisions relating to consents and consultations of the internal law relating to adoption of the Convention country of which the child is a national.

## 34 Form of consent etc

(1) Any document signifying the consent of a person to, or otherwise containing the opinion of a person on the making of, the Convention adoption order shall be in a form which complies with the internal law relating to adoption of the Convention country of which the child is a national: provided that where the court is not satisfied that a person consents with full understanding of what is involved, it may call for further evidence.

(2) A document referred to in paragraph (1) shall, if sufficiently witnessed, be admissible as evidence of the consent or opinion contained therein without further proof of the signature of the person by whom it is executed.

(3) A document referred to in paragraph (1) shall, if executed before the date of the applicant's originating process referred to in rule 28(2), be attached to that process.

## 35 Notice of hearing

(1) When serving notice of the hearing on the persons specified in rule 21, the proper officer shall also serve notice on any person:—
    (a) whose consent to the making of the order is required, not being an applicant, or
    (b) who, in accordance with the internal law relating to adoption of the Convention country of which the child is a national, has to be consulted about, but does not have to consent to, the adoption.

(2) Any person served or required to be served with notice under this rule shall be treated as if he had been served or was required to be served with notice under rule 21.

## 36 Proper officer to receive opinions on adoption

For the purposes of this rule and of [section 17(7)(a) of the Act], the Senior [District Judge] of the Principal Registry of the Family Division is the proper officer of the court to whom any person whose consent is required under or who is consulted in pursuance of the internal law relating to adoption of the Convention country of which the child is a national may communicate his consent or other opinion on the adoption.

NOTES
Words in square brackets substituted by SI 1991/1880, r 25.

*[Proceedings under sections 52 or 53 of the Act]*

## 37 Application to annul or revoke adoption

(1) An application for an order under [section 52(1) or 53(1) of the Act] shall be made by originating process issued out of the Principal Registry of the Family Division in Form 9; and the person filing the process shall be described as the applicant and the adopted person and any adopter, not being the applicant, shall be described as a respondent.

(2)  An application under [section 53(1) of the Act] shall not, except with the leave of the court, be made later than 2 years after the date of the adoption to which it relates.

NOTES

Cross heading substituted by SI 1991/1880, r 26(1).

Paras (1), (2): words in square brackets substituted by SI 1991/1880, r 26(2), (3).

## 38 Application to declare adoption invalid or determination invalid or affected

An application for an order or decision under [section 53(2) of the Act] shall be made by originating process issued out of the Principal Registry of the Family Division in Form 10; and the person filing the process shall be described as the applicant and the adopted person and any adopter, not being the applicant, shall be described as a respondent.

NOTES

Words in square brackets substituted by SI 1991/1880, r 27.

## 39 Evidence in support of application affected

(1)  Evidence in support of an application under [section 52 or 53 of the Act] shall be given by means of an affidavit in Form 11 which shall be filed within 14 days after the issue of the originating process.

(2)  Where the application is made under [section 53 of the Act] there shall be exhibited to the affidavit a statement of the facts and, subject to rule 42, there shall be filed with the affidavit expert evidence of any provision of foreign law relating to adoption on which the applicant intends to rely.

(3)  The court may order any deponent to give oral evidence concerning the facts stated in, or exhibited to, his affidavit.

NOTES

Paras (1), (2): words in square brackets substituted by SI 1991/1880, r 28(1), (2).

## 40 Guardian ad litem

Where the adopted person is under the age of 18 on the date on which an application under [section 52 or 53 of the Act] is made, rule 18(2) and (4) to (7) shall apply to the application as it applies to an application for an adoption order as if the references in rule 18 to the making of an adoption order were references to the granting of an application under [section 52 or 53 of the Act].

NOTES

Words in square brackets substituted by SI 1991/1880, r 28(1).

## 41 Notice of order made under section 6 etc

(1)  Where under [section 52 or 53 of the Act] the court has ordered that an adoption be annulled or revoked or that an adoption or a determination shall cease to be valid in Great Britain, the proper officer shall serve notice of the order on the Registrar General, and shall state in the notice—

    (a)  the date of the adoption;

    (b)  the name and address of the authority which granted the adoption; and

    (c)  the names of the adopter or adopters and of the adopted person as given in the affidavit referred to in rule 39.

(2) A notice under paragraph (1) in respect of the annulment or revocation of an adoption shall request the Registrar General to send the information to the designated authorities of any Convention country—

    (a) in which the adoption was granted;

    (b) of which the adopted person is a national; or

    (c) in which the adopted person was born;

(3) . . .

**NOTES**

Para (1): words in square brackets substituted by SI 1991/1880, r 28(1).

Para (3): revoked by SI 1991/1880, r 28(3).

The heading to this rule is now inappropriate, and should be read as referring to orders made under the Adoption Act 1976, s 52 or 53.

*Supplementary*

## 42 Evidence as to specified or notified provisions

(1) Where the applicant seeks to satisfy the court as to any question which has arisen or is likely to arise concerning a provision:—

    (a) of the internal law of the Convention country of which the applicant of any other person is or was a national,

    (b) which has been specified in an order—

        (i) under [section 17(8) of the Act] (a "specified provision"), or

        (ii) under [section 54(4) of the Act] (a "notified provision"),

expert evidence of the specified or notified provision shall, where practicable, be attached to the originating process.

(2) Paragraph (1) shall apply, in the case of a person who is or was a United Kingdom national, for the purposes of a notified provision in respect of a Convention country of which a person is or was a national.

**NOTES**

Para (1): words in square brackets substituted by SI 1991/1880, r 29.

## 43 Interim order

Where the applicant is a national or both applicants are nationals of a Convention country, the court shall take account of any specified provision (as defined in [section 17(8) of the Act]) of the internal law of that country before any decision is made to postpone the determination of the application and to make an interim order.

**NOTES**

Words in square brackets substituted by SI 1991/1880, r 30.

## 44 Witnessing of documents

A document shall be sufficiently attested for the purposes of this Part of these rules if it is witnessed by one of the following persons—

    (a) if it is executed in England and Wales, the reporting officer, a Justice of the Peace, an officer of a county court appointed for the purposes of [section 58(1)(c) of the County Courts Act 1984] or a justices' clerk within the meaning of section 70 of the Justices of Peace Act 1979; or

    (b) if it is executed elsewhere, any person specified in rule 8(2), (3) or (4), according to the country in which it is executed.

**NOTES**

Words in square brackets substituted by SI 1991/1880, r 31.

## 45 Service of documents

(1) Any document to be served for the purposes of this Part of these rules may be served out of the jurisdiction without the leave of the court.

(2) Any document served out of the jurisdiction in a country in which English is not an official language shall be accompanied by a translation of the document in the official language of the country in which service is to be effected or, if there is more than one official language of the country, in any one of those languages which is appropriate to the place in that country where service is to be effected.

## 46 Translation of documents

Where a translation of any document is required for the purposes of Convention proceedings, the translation shall, unless otherwise directed, be provided by the applicant.

# PART V
# MISCELLANEOUS

### 47 Application for removal, return etc, of child

[(1)  An application—
    (a)  for leave under section 27 or 28 of the Act to remove a child from the home of a person with whom the child lives,
    (b)  under section 29(2) of the Act for an order directing a person not to remove a child from the home of a person with whom the child lives,
    (c)  under section 29(1) of the Act for an order for the return of a child who has been removed from the home of a person with whom the child lives,
    (d)  under section 30(2) of the Act for leave to give notice of an intention not to give a home to a child or not to allow a child to remain in a person's home, or
    (e)  under section 20(2) of the Act for leave to place a child for adoption,

shall be made in accordance with paragraph (2).]

(2)  The application under paragraph (1) shall be made—
    (a)  if an application for an adoption order or an order under [sections 18 or 20 of the Act] is pending, by process on notice in those proceedings; or
    (b)  if no such application is pending, by filing an originating process in the . . . court.

(3)  . . .

(4)  Any respondent to the originating process made under paragraph (2)(b) who wishes to claim relief shall do so by means of an answer to the process which shall be made within 7 days of the service of the copy of the process on the respondent.

(5)  Subject to paragraph (6), the proper officer shall serve a copy of the process, and of any answer thereto, and a notice of the date of the hearing—
    (a)  in a case where proceedings for an adoption order or an order under [sections 18 or 20 of the Act] are pending (or where such proceedings have subsequently been commenced), on all the parties to those proceedings and on the reporting officer and guardian ad litem, if any,

(b)  in any other case, on any person against whom an order is sought in the application and on the local authority to whom the prospective adopter has given notice under [section 22 of the Act]; and

(c)  in any case, on such other person or body, not being the child, as the court thinks fit.

(6)  If in any application under this rule a serial number has been assigned to a person who has applied or who proposes to apply for an adoption order, or such a person applies to the proper officer in that behalf before filing the originating process and a serial number is assigned accordingly—

(a)  the proper officer shall ensure that the documents served under paragraph (5) do not disclose the identity of that person to any other party to the application under this rule who is not already aware of that person's identity, and

(b)  the proceedings on the application under this rule shall be conducted with a view to securing that he is not seen by or made known to any party who is not already aware of his identity except with his consent.

(7)  Unless otherwise directed, any prospective adopter who is served with a copy of an application under this rule and who wishes to oppose the application shall file his process for an adoption order within 14 days or before or at the time of the hearing of the application under this rule, whichever is the sooner.

(8)  The court may at any time give directions, and if giving directions under paragraph (7) shall give further directions, as to the conduct of any application under this rule and in particular as to the appointment of a guardian ad litem of the child.

(9)  Where an application under paragraph (1)(a) or (d) is granted or an application under paragraph (1)(b) is refused, the judge may thereupon, if process for an adoption order has been filed, treat the hearing of the application as the hearing of the process for an adoption order and refuse an adoption order accordingly.

(10)  Where an application under this rule is determined the proper officer shall serve notice of the effect of the determination on all the parties.

(11)  Paragraphs (6) to (10) shall apply to an answer made under this rule as they apply to an originating process made under this rule as if the answer were the originating process.

---

NOTES

Para (1): substituted by SI 1991/1880, r 32(1).

Para (2): words in square brackets substituted, and words omitted revoked, by SI 1991/1880, r 32(2).

Para (3): revoked by SI 1991/1880, r 32(3).

Para (5): words in square brackets substituted by SI 1991/1880, r 32(4).

---

## 48 Proposed foreign adoption proceedings

(1)  Proceedings for an order authorising a proposed foreign adoption shall be commenced—

(a)  by originating summons in Form 6 issued out of the Principal Registry of the Family Division; or

(b)  by filing in the office of the county court within whose district the child is an originating application in Form 6.

(2)  Subject to paragraph (3), Part III of these rules except rule 15(1) and Part V except rule 52(1)(d) shall apply to an application for an order authorising a proposed foreign adoption as if such an order were an adoption order.

(3) An applicant for an order authorising a proposed foreign adoption shall provide expert evidence of the law of adoption in the country in which he is domiciled and an affidavit as to that law sworn by such a person as is mentioned in section 4(1) of the Civil Evidence Act 1972 (that is to say a person who is suitably qualified on account of his knowledge or experience to give evidence as to that law) shall be admissible in evidence without notice.

## 49 Amendment and revocation of orders

(1) An application under [paragraph 4 of Schedule 1 to the Act] for the amendment of an adoption order or the revocation of a direction to the Registrar General, or [under section 52 of the Act] for the revocation of an adoption order, may be made ex parte in the first instance, but the court may require notice of the application to be served on such persons as it thinks fit.

(2) Where the application is granted, the proper officer shall send to the Registrar General a notice specifying the amendments or informing him of the revocation and shall give sufficient particulars of the order to enable the Registrar General to identify the case.

NOTES

Para (1): words in square brackets substituted by SI 1991/1880, r 33.

## 50 Service of documents

(1) Subject to rule 45 and unless otherwise directed, any document under these rules may be served—

  (a) on a corporation or body of persons, by delivering it at, or sending it by post to, the registered or principal office of the corporation or body;

  (b) on any other person, by delivering it to him, or by sending it by post to him at his usual or last known address.

(2) The person effecting service of any document under these rules shall make, sign and file a certificate showing the date, place and mode of service. If he has failed to effect service of any document, he shall make, sign and file a certificate of non-service showing the reason why service has not been effected.

## 51 Costs

On the determination of proceedings to which the rules apply or on the making of an interim order, the judge may make such order as to the costs as he thinks just and, in particular, may order the applicant to pay—

  (a) the expenses incurred by the reporting officer and the guardian ad litem (if appointed),

  (b) the expenses incurred by any respondent in attending the hearing,

or such part of those expenses as the judge thinks proper.

## 52 Notice and copies of orders etc

(1) In proceedings to which these rules apply orders shall be made in the form indicated in this paragraph—

| Description of order | Form |
| --- | --- |
| (a) Order under [section 18 of the Act] | 12 |
| (b) Order under [section 20 of the Act] | 13 |
| (c) Interim order | 14 |
| (d) Adoption order | 15 |

| *Description of order* | *Form* |
|---|---|
| (e) Convention adoption order | 15 (with the word "Convention" inserted where appropriate) |
| (f) Order authorising a proposed foreign adoption | 15 (with the words "order authorising a proposed foreign adoption" substituted for the words "adoption order" wherever they appear). |

(2) Where an adoption order is made by a court sitting in Wales in respect of a child who was born in Wales (or is treated under rule 24(4) as having been born in the registration district and sub-district in which that court sits) and the adopter so requests before the order is drawn up, the proper officer shall obtain a translation into Welsh of the particulars set out in the order.

(3) Within 7 days of the making of an order in proceedings to which these rules apply, the proper officer shall send a copy of the order (and of any translation into Welsh obtained under paragraph (2)) to the applicant.

(4) Within 7 days of the making of an order to which paragraph (1)(d), (e) or (f) applies, the proper officer shall send a copy of the order (and of any translation into Welsh obtained under paragraph (2)) to the Registrar General and, in the case of a Convention adoption order, shall comply with rule 31; where a translation into Welsh under paragraph (2) has been obtained, the English text shall prevail.

(5) Where an order to which paragraph (1)(a), (b), (d), (e) or (f) applies is made or refused or an order to which paragraph (1)(c) applies is made, the proper officer shall serve notice to that effect on ever respondent.

(6) . . .

(7) The proper officer shall serve notice of the making of an order to which paragraph (1)(a), (b), (d), (e) or (f) applies on any court in Great Britain which appears to him to have made any such order as is referred to in [section 12(8) of the Act (orders relating to parental responsibility for, and maintenance of, the child)].

(8) A copy of any order may be supplied to the Registrar General at his request.

(9) A copy of any order may be supplied to the applicant.

(10) A copy of any order may be supplied to any other person with the leave of the court.

---

NOTES

Para (1): words in square brackets substituted by SI 1991/1880, r 34(1).
Para (6): revoked by SI 1991/1880, r 34(2).
Para (7): words in square brackets substituted by SI 1991/1880, r 34(3).

---

## 53 Custody, inspection and disclosure of documents and information

(1) All documents relating to proceedings under [the Act] (or under any previous enactment relating to adoption) shall, while they are in the custody of the court, be kept in a place of special security.

(2) A party who is an individual and is referred to in a confidential report supplied to the court by an adoption agency, a local authority, a reporting officer or a guardian ad litem may inspect, for the purposes of the hearing, that part of any such report which refers to him, subject to any direction given by the court that—

    (a) no part of one or any of the reports shall be revealed to that party, or

    (b) the part of one or any of the reports referring to that party shall be revealed only to that party's legal advisers, or

(c) the whole or any other part of one or any of the reports shall be revealed to that party.

(3) Any person who obtains any information in the course of, or relating to, any proceedings mentioned in paragraph (1) shall treat that information as confidential and shall only disclose it if—

(a) the disclosure is necessary for the proper exercise of his duties, or

(b) the information is requested—

(i) by a court or public authority (whether in Great Britain or not) having power to determine adoptions and related matters, for the purpose of the discharge of its duties in that behalf, or

(ii) by the Registrar General, or a person authorised in writing by him, where the information requested relates only to the identity of any adoption agency which made the arrangements for placing the child for adoption in the actual custody of the applicants, and of any local authority which was notified of the applicant's intention to apply for an adoption order in respect of the child, or

(iii) by a person who is authorised in writing by the Secretary of State to obtain the information for the purposes of research.

(4) Save as required or authorised by a provision of any enactment or of these rules or with the leave of the court, no document or order held by or lodged with the court in proceedings under [the Act] (or under any previous enactment relating to adoption) shall be open to inspection by any person, and no copy of any such document or order, or of an extract from any such document or order, shall be taken by or issued to any person.

NOTES

Paras (1), (4): words in square brackets substituted by SI 1991/1880, r 35.

# SCHEDULE 1
# GENERAL FORMS

Rule 2(3)

*(The forms (all of which have been amended by SI 1991/1880) are not reproduced in this book, but their titles are listed below.)*

Form

No 1    Originating Process for an Order Freeing a Child for Adoption

No 2    Form 2 Agreement to an Adoption Order (Freeing Cases)

No 3    Notice of Hearing of an Application for an Order Freeing a Child for Adoption

No 4    Application for Revocation of an Order Freeing a Child for Adoption

No 5    [Application for Substitution of One Adoption Agency for Another]

No 6    Originating Process for an Adoption Order/Order Authorising a Proposed Foreign Adoption

No 7    Agreement to an Adoption Order/Proposed Foreign Adoption

No 8    Notice of Hearing of an Application for an Adoption Order/an Order Authorising a Proposed Foreign Adoption

No 9    Originating Process for the Annulment or Revocation of an Adoption

No 10   Originating Process for an Order that an Overseas Adoption or a Determination Cease to be Valid or that a Determination has been Affected by a Subsequent Determination

No 11   Affidavit in Support of Application under [sections 52 and 53 of the Adoption Act 1976]

No 12   Order Freeing a Child for Adoption

No 13   Order Revoking an Order Freeing a Child for Adoption/Dismissing an Application to Revoke an Order Freeing a Child for Adoption

No 14   Interim Order

No 15   (Convention) Adoption Order/Order Authorising a Proposed Foreign Adoption (amended by SI 1991/1880)

# SCHEDULE 2
# MATTERS TO BE COVERED IN REPORTS SUPPLIED UNDER RULES 4(4), 22(1) OR 22(2)

Rule 4(4)

So far as is practicable, the report supplied by the adoption agency or, in the case of a report supplied under rule 22(2), the local authority shall include all the following particulars:—

## 1 The Child

(a)   Name, sex, date and place of birth and address;

[(b)   whether the child's parents were married to each other at the time of his birth and, if not, whether he was subsequently legitimated];

(c)   nationality;

(d)   physical description;

(e)   personality and social development;

(f)   religion, including details of baptism, confirmation or equivalent ceremonies;

(g)   details of any wardship proceedings and of any court orders [relating to parental responsibility for the child or to maintenance and residence].

(h)   details of any brothers and sisters, including dates of birth, arrangements [concerning with whom they are to live] and whether any brother or sister is the subject of a parallel application;

(i)   extent of [contact with] members of the child's natural family and, [if the child's parents were not married to each other at the time of his birth], his father, and in each case the nature of the relationship enjoyed;

(j)   if the child has been in the care of a local authority or voluntary organisation [or is in such care, or is being, or has been, looked after by such an authority or organisation,] details (including dates) of any placements with foster parents, or other arrangements in respect of the care of the child, including particulars of the persons with whom the child has had his home and observations on the care provided;

(k)   date and circumstances of placement with prospective adopter;

(l)   names, addresses and types of schools attended, with dates, and educational attainments;

(m)   any special needs in relation to the child's health (whether physical or mental) and his emotional and behavioural development and whether he is subject to a statement under the Education Act 1981;

(n)   what, if any, rights to or interest in property or any claim to damages, under the Fatal Accidents Act 1976 or otherwise, the child stands to retain or lose if adopted;

(o)   wishes and feelings in relation to adoption and the application, including any wishes in respect of religious and cultural upbringing; and

(p)   any other relevant information which might assist the court.

## 2 Each Natural Parent, . . .

(a)   Name, date and place of birth and address;

(b)   marital status and date and place of marriage (if any);

(c)   past and present relationship (if any) with the other natural parent, including comments on its stability;

(d)   physical description;

(e)   personality;

    (f)   religion;

    (g)   educational attainments;

    (h)   past and present occupations and interests;

    (i)   so far as available, names and brief details of the personal circumstances of the parents and any brothers and sisters of the natural parent, with their ages or ages at death;

    (j)   wishes and feelings in relation to adoption and the application, including any wishes in respect of the child's religious and cultural upbringing;

    (k)   reasons why any of the above information is unavailable; and

    (l)   any other relevant information which might assist the court.

## 3 Guardian(s)

Give the details required under paragraph 2(a), (f) and (l).

## 4 Prospective Adopter(s)

    (a)   Name, date and place of birth and address;

    (b)   relationship (if any) to the child;

    (c)   marital status, date and place of marriage (if any) and comments on stability of relationship;

    (d)   details of any previous marriage;

    (e)   if a parent and step-parent are applying, the reasons why they prefer adoption to [a residence order];

    (f)   if a natural parent is applying alone, the reasons for the exclusion of the other parent;

    (g)   if a married person is applying alone, the reasons for this;

    (h)   physical description;

    (i)   personality;

    (j)   religion, and whether willing to follow any wishes of the child or his parents or guardian in respect of the child's religious and cultural upbringing;

    (k)   educational attainments;

    (l)   past and present occupations and interests;

    (m)   particulars of the home and living conditions (and particulars of any home where the prospective adopter proposes to live with the child, if different);

    (n)   details of income and comments on the living standards of the household;

    (o)   details of other members of the household (including any children of the prospective adopter even if not resident in the household);

    (p)   details of the parents and any brothers or sisters of the prospective adopter, with their ages or ages at death;

    (q)   attitudes to the proposed adoption of such other members of the prospective adopter's household and family as the adoption agency or, as the case may be, the local authority considers appropriate;

    (r)   previous experience of caring for children as step-parent, foster parent, child-minder or prospective adopter and assessment of ability in this respect, together where appropriate with assessment of ability in bringing up the prospective adopter's own children;

    (s)   reasons for wishing to adopt the child and extent of understanding of the nature and effect of adoption;

    (t)   any hopes and expectations for the child's future;

    (u)   assessment of ability to bring up the child throughout his childhood;

    (v)   details of any adoption allowance payable;

    (w)   confirmation that any referees have been interviewed, with a report of their views and opinion of the weight to be placed thereon; and

    (x)   any other relevant information which might assist the court.

## 5 Actions of the adoption agency or local authority supplying the report

    (a)   Reports under rules 4(4) or 22(1):—

  (i) brief account of the agency's actions in the case, with particulars and dates of all written information and notices given to the child, his natural parents and the prospective adopter;

  (ii) details of alternatives to adoption considered;

  (iii) reasons for considering that adoption would be in the child's best interests (with date of relevant decision); and

  (iv) reasons for considering that the prospective adopter would be suitable to be an adoptive parent and that he would be suitable for this child (with dates of relevant decisions) or, if the child has not yet been placed for adoption, reasons for considering that he is likely to be so placed.

 OR

(b) Reports under rule 22(2):—

  (i) confirmation that notice was given under [section 22 of the Act], with the date of that notice;

  (ii) brief account of the local authority's actions in the case; and

  (iii) account of investigations whether child was placed in contravention of [section 11 of the Act].

## 6 Generally

(a) Whether any respondent appears to be under the age of majority or under a mental disability; and

(b) whether, in the opinion of the body supplying the report, any other person should be made a respondent (for example, a person claiming to be the father of [a child whose parents were not married to each other at the time of his birth], a spouse or ex-spouse of a natural parent, a relative of a deceased parent, or a person with [parental responsibility]).

## 7 Conclusions

(This part of the report should contain more than a simple synopsis of the information above. As far as possible, the court should be given a fuller picture of the child, his natural parents and, where appropriate, the prospective adopter).

(a) Except where the applicant or one of them is a parent of the child, a summary by the medical adviser to the body supplying the report, of the health history and state of health of the child, his natural parents and, if appropriate, the prospective adopter, with comments on the implications for the order sought and on how any special health needs of the child might be met;

(b) opinion on whether making the order sought would be in the child's best long-term interests, and on how any special emotional, behavioural and educational needs of the child might be met;

(c) opinion of the effect on the child's natural parents of making the order sought;

(d) if the child has been placed for adoption, opinion on the likelihood of full integration of the child into the household, family and community of the prospective adopter, and on whether the proposed adoption would be in the best long-term interests of the prospective adopter;

(e) opinion, if appropriate, on the relative merits of adoption and [a residence order] and;

(f) final conclusions and recommendations whether the order sought should be made (and, if not, alternative proposals).

---

NOTES

 Para 1: sub-para (b), and words in square brackets in sub-paras (g)–(j), substituted by SI 1991/1880, r 51(a)–(e).

 Para 2: words omitted revoked by SI 1991/1880, r 51(f).

 Para 4: words in square brackets in sub-para (e) substituted by SI 1991/1880, r 51(g).

 Para 5: words in square brackets in sub-para (b) substituted by SI 1991/1880, r 51(h).

 Para 6: words in square brackets in sub-para (b) substituted by SI 1991/1880, r 51(i).

 Para 7: words in square brackets in sub-para (e) substituted by SI 1991/1880, r 51(j).

---

# SCHEDULE 3
# REPORTS ON THE HEALTH OF THE CHILD AND OF THE APPLICANTS

Rule 15(4)

This information is required for reports on the health of a child and of his prospective adopter(s). Its purpose is to build up a full picture of their health history and current state of health, including strengths and weaknesses. This will enable the local authority's medical adviser to base his advice to the court on the fullest possible information, when commenting on the health implications of the proposed adoption. The reports made by the examining doctor should cover, as far as practicable, the following matters.

## 1 The Child
Name, date of birth, sex, weight and height.

    A.   A health history of each natural parent, so far as is possible, including:—

        (i)   name, date of birth, sex, weight and height;

       (ii)   a family health history, covering the parents, the brothers and sisters and the other children of the natural parent, with details of any serious physical or mental illness and inherited and congenital disease;

      (iii)   past health history, including details of any serious physical or mental illness, disability, accident, hospital admission or attendance at an out-patient department, and in each case any treatment given;

      (iv)   a full obstetric history of the mother, including any problems in the ante-natal, labour and post-natal periods, with the results of any tests carried out during or immediately after pregnancy;

       (v)   details of any present illness including treatment and prognosis;

      (vi)   any other relevant information which might assist the medical adviser; and

     (vii)   the name and address of any doctor(s) who might be able to provide further information about any of the above matters.

    B.   A neo-natal report on the child, including:—

        (i)   details of the birth, and any complications;

       (ii)   results of a physical examination and screening tests;

      (iii)   details of any treatment given;

      (iv)   details of any problem in management and feeding;

       (v)   any other relevant information which might assist the medical adviser; and

      (vi)   the name and address of any doctor(s) who might be able to provide further information about any of the above matters.

    C.   A full health history and examination of the child, including:—

        (i)   details of any serious illness, disability, accident, hospital admission or attendance at an out-patient department, and in each case any treatment given;

       (ii)   details and dates of immunisations;

      (iii)   a physical and developmental assessment according to age, including an assessment of vision and hearing and of neurological, speech and language development and any evidence of emotional disorder;

      (iv)   for a child over five years of age, the school health history (if available);

       (v)   any other relevant information which might assist the medical adviser; and

      (vi)   the name and address of any doctor(s) who might be able to provide further information about any of the above matters.

    D.   The signature, name, address and qualifications of the registered medical practitioner who prepared the report, and the date of the report and of the examinations carried out.

## 2 The Applicant
(If there is more than one applicant, a report on each applicant should be supplied covering all the matters listed below.)

    A.   (i)   name, date of birth, sex, weight and height;

    (ii)  a family health history, covering the parents, the brothers and sisters and the children of the applicant, with details of any serious physical or mental illness and inherited and congenital disease;

    (iii)  marital history, including (if applicable) reasons for inability to have children;

    (iv)  past health history, including details of any serious physical or mental illness, disability, accident, hospital admission or attendance at an out-patient department, and in each case any treatment given;

    (v)  obstetric history (if applicable);

    (vi)  details of any present illness, including treatment and prognosis;

    (vii)  a full medical examination;

    (viii)  details of any daily consumption of alcohol, tobacco and habit-forming drugs;

    (ix)  any other relevant information which might assist the medical adviser; and

    (x)  the name and address of any doctor(s) who might be able to provide further information about any of the above matters.

B.    The signature, name, address and qualifications of the registered medical practitioner who prepared the report, and the date of the report and of the examinations carried out.

## SCHEDULE 4

Rule 28(2)(b)

*(The form (as amended by SI 1991/1880) is not reproduced in this book, but its title is listed below.)*

Modification to Form 6 for the Purposes of Convention Proceedings

# RESIDENTIAL CARE HOMES REGULATIONS 1984

## (SI 1984/1345)

NOTES

    Made: 22 August 1984.

    Commencement: 1 January 1985.

    Authority: Registered Homes Act 1984, ss 5(1), 8, 16, 17(4), 57(2), Sch 2, para 4(1)(a)(i).

## 1  Citation, commencement and interpretation

(1)    These regulations may be cited as the Residential Care Homes Regulations 1984 and shall come into operation on 1st January 1985.

(2)    In these regulations, unless the context otherwise requires—

    "the Act" means the Registered Homes Act 1984;

    "the 1980 Act" means the Residential Homes Act 1980;

    ["care authority" in relation to a child, means the local authority who is looking after the child within the meaning of section 22(1) of the Children Act 1989]

    ["care order" has the meaning assigned to it in section 105 of the Children Act 1989];

    "child" means a resident under the age of 18 years and any resident who has attained that age and is the subject of a care order;

    "fire authority", in relation to any home, means the authority discharging in the area in which the home is situated, the function of fire authority under the Fire Services Act 1947;

    "home" means a residential care home;

    ["independent visitor" means a person appointed as a visitor pursuant to paragraph 17 of Schedule 2 to the Children Act 1989];

    "local social services authority" means a council which is a local authority for the purposes of the Local Authority Social Services Act 1970;

"mental handicap" means a state of arrested or incomplete development of mind which includes impairment of intelligence and social functioning;

"person registered" means any person registered in respect of the home;

"relevant date" means the date on which the Act and the repeal of the 1980 Act by Schedule 10 to the Health and Social Services and Social Security Adjudications Act 1983 came into force;

"resident" means any person in the home who is in need of personal care by reason of old age, disablement, past or present dependence on alcohol or drugs, or past or present mental disorder.

**NOTES**

Para (2): definitions "care authority", "care order" and "independent visitor" substituted by the Residential Care Homes (Amendment) Regulations 1991, SI 1991/2502, reg 2.

## 2  Particulars to be supplied on application for registration

On any application for registration made under section 5 of the Act, the applicant shall supply in writing to the registration authority information in regard to the matters mentioned in Schedule 1 to these regulations, and such other information as the registration authority may reasonably require[, except that an applicant for registration in respect of a small home need not supply information in regard to the matters mentioned in paragraphs 3(c), (e), (l), (m) or (n) of that Schedule.]

**NOTES**

Words in square brackets added by the Residential Care Homes (Amendment) (No 2) Regulations 1992, SI 1992/2241, reg 2.

## [2A  Documentary evidence to be supplied on application for registration

An applicant for registration under Part I of the Act shall, if the registration authority so requires, supply to that authority such birth certificate and such other documentary evidence as is specified by that authority as being necessary to substantiate the information supplied in accordance with paragraphs 1(a) or 2(a)(i) of Schedule 1 to these Regulations.]

**NOTES**

Inserted by SI 1991/2502, reg 3.

## 3  Registration fees

(1)  . . . [Subject to paragraph (2) of this regulation,] the registration fee to accompany an application for registration made under section 5 of the Act shall be—

    (a)  in the case of an application in respect of the manager or intended manager of the home who is not the person in control of it (whether as owner or otherwise), [£230];

    (b)  in the case of an application in respect of the person in control of the home, [£840].

[(2)  The registration fee to accompany an application for registration under Part I of the Act of a person in respect of a small home shall be £230.]

**NOTES**

Para (1): words omitted revoked, and sums in square brackets substituted, by the Residential Care Homes (Amendment) Regulations 1992, SI 1992/2007, reg 2(a)–(c); words in square brackets inserted by SI 1992/2241, reg 3(1).

Para (2): para (2) as originally enacted revoked by SI 1992/2007, reg 2(d); new para (2) subsequently added by SI 1992/2241, reg 3(2).

**4   Time limit for registration**

(1)   Where—

    (a)   immediately before the relevant date a person was not required to be registered under the 1980 Act in respect of an establishment; and

    (b)   on that date he is required to be registered under Part I of the Act in respect of that establishment,

he shall within six months of that date apply to the registration authority for registration under that Part and until that application is determined he shall for the purposes of the Act be deemed to be registered under that Part in respect of that establishment.

(2)   A person who immediately before the relevant date was registered under the 1980 Act in respect of an establishment and who on that date is required to be registered in respect of that establishment under Part I of the Act shall for the purposes of the Act and of these regulations be deemed to be registered under that Part in respect of that establishment.

**[5   Annual fee**

(1)   A person registered in respect of a residential care home as being the person in control of it shall pay an annual fee, of an amount determined in accordance with paragraphs (2) to (4) of this regulation, within one month of the date on which the certificate of registration was issued and thereafter in each year no later than the day before the anniversary of that date.

(2)   Where the home is not a small home, the annual fee shall, subject to paragraph   (4) of this regulation, be of an amount equal to £41 multiplied by the maximum number of persons specified (in accordance with section 5(3) of the Act) in the certificate of registration in respect of the home.

(3)   Where the home is a small home, the annual fee shall be £30.

(4)   Where the home is not a small home, but an annual fee was payable in respect of the immediately preceding year and was that payable in accordance with paragraph   (3) of this regulation because the home was then a small home and no application for re-registration under section 5(1) of the Act has been made and accompanied by the registration fee, the amount of the annual fee determined in accordance with paragraph (2) of this regulation shall be increased by £610.]

NOTES

    Substituted by SI 1992/2241, reg 4.

**6   Records**

(1)   [Subject to paragraph (1A) of this regulation,] the person registered shall compile the records specified in Schedule 2 to these regulations and shall keep them in the home at all times available for inspection by any person authorised in that behalf by the registration authority or, as the case may be, the Secretary of State.

[(1A) A person registered in respect of a small home need not compile the records specified in—

    (a)   paragraphs 8 to 16 of Schedule 2 to these Regulations;

    (b)   paragraph 4 of that Schedule, except to the extent that it relates to any medicines administered to a resident; or

    (c)   in paragraph 7 of that Schedule to the extent that it relates to any visits by persons authorised to inspect the home.]

(2)   The person registered shall keep in a safe place in the home the case record of each resident compiled in accordance with paragraph 4 or 5 of the said Schedule 2.

(3)   Any person who is deemed by virtue of regulation 4(2) of these regulations to be registered under Part I of the Act in respect of a home shall within three months of the relevant date compile the records specified in the said Schedule 2.

(4)   Every record compiled in accordance with this regulation shall be retained for a minimum of three years from the date of the last entry in it.

NOTES
   Para (1): words in square brackets inserted by SI 1992/2241, reg 5.
   Para (1A): inserted by SI 1992/2241, reg 5.

## 7   Registers

The registers kept by a registration authority for the purposes of Part I of the Act shall contain the particulars specified in Schedule 3 to these regulations.

## 8   Consultation with fire authority

The person registered shall, [except in respect of a small home,] at such times as may be agreed with the fire authority, consult that authority on fire precautions in the home.

NOTES
   Words in square brackets inserted SI 1992/2241, reg 6.

## 9   Conduct of homes

(1)   The person registered shall arrange for the home to be conducted so as to make proper provision for the welfare, care and, where appropriate, treatment and supervision of all residents.

(2)   In reaching any decision relating to a resident the person registered shall give first consideration to the need to safeguard and promote the welfare of the resident and shall, so far as practicable, ascertain the wishes and feelings of the resident and give due consideration to them as is reasonable having regard to the resident's age and understanding.

(3)   Every home shall be maintained on the basis of good personal and professional relationships between the person registered and persons employed at the home and the residents.

[(4)   The person registered shall ensure that corporal punishment is not used as a sanction in relation to any child in the home.]

NOTES
   Para (4): added by the Residential Care Homes (Amendment) Regulations 1988, SI 1988/1192, reg 4.

## 10   Provision of facilities and services

(1)   [Subject to paragraphs (1A) and (1B) of this regulation,] the person registered shall having regard to the size of the home and the number, age, sex and condition of residents—

    (a)   employ by day and, where necessary, by night suitably qualified and competent staff in numbers which are adequate for the well being of residents;

(b) provide for each resident such accommodation and space by day and by night as is reasonable;

(c) provide adequate and suitable furniture, bedding, curtains, floor covering and, where necessary, equipment and screens in rooms occupied or used by residents;

(d) provide for the use of residents a sufficient number of water closets, and of wash-basins, baths and showers fitted with a hot and cold water supply, and any necessary sluicing facilities;

(e) make such adaptations and provide such facilities as are necessary for residents who are physically handicapped;

(f) provide adequate light, heating and ventilation in all parts of the home occupied or used by residents;

(g) keep all parts of the home occupied or used by residents in good structural repair, clean and reasonably decorated;

(h) take adequate precautions against the risk of fire, including the provision of adequate means of escape in the event of fire, and make adequate arrangements for detecting, containing and extinguishing fires, for the giving of warnings and for the evacuation of all persons in the home in the event of fire and for the maintenance of fire precautions and fire fighting equipment;

(i) make arrangements to secure by means of fire drills and practices that the staff in the home and, so far as practicable, residents know the procedure to be followed in the case of fire including the procedure for saving life;

(j) take adequate precautions against the risk of accidents including the training of staff in first aid;

(k) provide sufficient and suitable kitchen equipment, crockery and cutlery together with adequate facilities for the preparation and storage of food and, so far as may be reasonable and practicable in the circumstances, adequate facilities for residents to prepare their own food and refreshments;

(l) supply suitable, varied and properly prepared wholesome and nutritious food in adequate quantities for residents;

(m) make, after consultation with the local environmental health officer, suitable arrangements for maintaining satisfactory conditions of hygiene in the home;

(n) arrange for regular laundering of linen and clothing and, so far as may be reasonable and practicable in the circumstances, provide adequate facilities for residents to do their own laundering;

(o) make arrangements for any person authorised by the registration authority or, as the case may be, by the Secretary of State, to interview in private any resident;

(p) make arrangements, where necessary, for residents to receive medical and dental services, whether under Part II of the National Health Service Act 1977, or otherwise;

(q) make suitable arrangements for the recording, safekeeping, handling and disposal of drugs;

(r) make suitable arrangements for the training, occupation and recreation of residents including the provision of play and educational facilities for children;

(s) provide a place where the valuables of residents may be deposited for safekeeping.

[(1A) Sub-paragraph (i) of paragraph (1) of this regulation shall not apply in respect of a small home.

(1B) Sub-paragraphs (h), (j) and (m) of paragraph (1) of this regulation shall apply in respect of a small home with the following modifications—

    (a) in sub-paragraph (h) as if the words after the words "risk of fire" were omitted;

    (b) in sub-paragraph (j) as if the words after the word "accidents" were omitted;

    (c) in sub-paragraph (m) as if the words ", after consultation with the local environmental health officer," were omitted.]

(2) The person registered shall arrange for the home to be connected to a public telephone service and shall, so far as may be reasonable and practicable in the circumstances, make arrangements for residents to communicate with others in private by post or telephone.

NOTES

    Para (1): words in square brackets inserted by SI 1992/2241, reg 7.

    Paras (1A), (1B): inserted by SI 1992/2241, reg 7.

## 11   Visits by parents, guardians, etc

(1) The person registered shall provide suitable facilities for visits to the home by parents, guardians, friends or other visitors of any resident and by any officer of a local authority whose duty it is to supervise the welfare of that resident, but the use of such facilities, times of visiting and other arrangements connected with the visits shall be as the person registered may, after consultation with the registration authority, decide[, except that no such consultation is required in respect of a small home.]

(2) The person registered shall ensure that there are facilities in the home whereby residents may, if they so desire, communicate in private with their visitors.

(3) [Except in respect of a small home,] the person registered shall keep affixed in a conspicuous place in the home a notice stating the times during which visits may be made and he shall, at the request of any person wishing to visit a resident, make available to that person details of such times.

NOTES

    Paras (1), (3): words in square brackets inserted or added by SI 1992/2241, reg 8.

## 12   Religious observance

The person registered shall ensure that every resident under the age of 18 years has so far as practicable in the circumstances the opportunity to attend such religious services and to receive such instruction as may be appropriate to the religious persuasion to which the resident belongs.

## 13   Notification of arrival of children

The person registered shall as soon as practicable notify the registration authority and the District Health Authority in whose district the home is situated of the date of arrival of each child in the home and the expected duration of his stay.

## 14   Notification of death, illness, or accident

(1) The person registered shall notify the registration authority not later than 24 hours from the time of its occurrence—

    (a) of the death of any resident under the age of 70 and of the circumstances of his death;

    (b) of the outbreak in the home of any infectious disease which in the opinion of any registered medical practitioner attending persons in the home is sufficiently serious to be so notified, or of any serious injury to or serious illness of any person residing in the home;

    (c)  of any unexplained absence of a child from the home;

    (d)  of any event in the home which affects the well-being of any resident; and

    (e)  of any theft, burglary, fire or accident in the home.

(2)    Where a child is in the home, the person registered shall not later than 24 hours from the time of the occurrence of any of the events specified in paragraph (1)(a) to (d) of this regulation also notify the occurrence of that event to the following persons—

    (a)  his parent or guardian;

    (b)  if the child is in the care of a care authority not being the registration authority, that authority;

    (c)  if the child is the subject of a care order, his independent visitor (if any); and

    (d)  any person or organisation who or which has accepted responsibility wholly or partly for the cost of that child's maintenance in the home.

(3)    The person registered shall notify the Secretary of State not later than 24 hours from the time of its occurrence of the death of any child in the home and of the circumstances of his death.

## 15   Notice of absence

(1)    Subject to paragraph (5) of this regulation, where the person in control of the home or, as the case may be, the manager of it proposes to be absent from the home for a period of four weeks or more the person in control of the home shall give notice in writing to the registration authority of the proposed absence.

(2)    Except in the case of an emergency, the notice referred to in paragraph (1) above shall be given no later than one month before the proposed absence or within such shorter period as may be agreed with the registration authority and the notice shall specify—

    (a)  the length or expected length of the proposed absence;

    (b)  the reason for that absence;

    (c)  the arrangements which have been made for the running of the home during that absence; and

    (d)  the name, address and qualifications of the person who will be responsible for the home during that absence.

(3)    Where the absence arises as a result of an emergency, the person in control of the home shall give notice of the absence within one week of its occurrence and the notice shall specify the matters referred to in sub-paragraphs (a) to (d) of paragraph   (2) of this regulation.

(4)    The person in control of the home shall notify the registration authority in writing of his return or, as the case may be, the return of the manager of the home within one week of that return.

(5)    The provisions of this regulation shall not apply where it is not proposed to accommodate any resident in the home during the absence of the person in control or, as the case may be, the manager of the home.

## 16   Notice of termination of accommodation

(1)    The person registered shall, before terminating any arrangements for the accommodation of a child, give his parent or guardian or, as the case may be, his care authority reasonable notice of his intention to terminate those arrangements.

(2)    Where arrangements for the accommodation of a resident are terminated the person registered shall notify the person who appears to him to be the resident's next of kin and, where the resident is under the supervision of an officer of a local social services authority, the person registered shall also notify that officer.

## 17 Information for residents as to method of making complaints

(1)   The person registered shall inform every resident in writing of the person to whom and the manner in which any request or complaint relating to the home may be made and the person registered shall ensure that any complaint so made by a resident or a person acting on his behalf is fully investigated.

(2)   The person registered shall also inform every resident in writing of the name and address of the registration authority to which complaints in respect of the home may be made by a resident or a person acting on his behalf.

## [18   Inspection of homes

The registration authority shall ensure that any home other than a small home is inspected pursuant to section 17 of the Act not less than twice in every period of 12 months.]

NOTES

Substituted by SI 1992/2241, reg 9.

## 19   Visits by person in control of the home

(1)   Where the person in control of the home is not also the manager of the home he shall at least once in every month visit the home or arrange for another person to visit the home on his behalf and to report in writing to him on the conduct of the home.

(2)   Where the person in control of the home is a company, society, association or other body or firm, the directors or other persons responsible for the management of the body or the partners of the firm shall arrange for one or more of their number to visit the home at least once in every month and to report in writing to them on the conduct of the home.

## 20   Offences

(1)   Subject to paragraph (3) of this regulation, where the registration authority consider that the person registered has contravened or failed to comply with regulation 6, 10, 11, 13, 14, 15, 16 or 19 of these regulations, the authority may serve a notice on the person registered specifying—

   (a)   in what respect in their opinion the person registered has failed or is failing to comply with the requirements of that regulation;

   (b)   what action, in the opinion of the registration authority, the person registered should take so as to comply with that regulation; and

   (c)   the period, not [exceeding] three months, within which the person registered should take action.

(2)   Where notice has been given in accordance with paragraph (1) of this regulation and the period specified in the notice, beginning with the date of the notice, has expired, the person registered who contravenes or fails to comply with any provision of these regulations mentioned in the notice shall be guilty of an offence against these regulations.

(3)   The provisions of this regulation shall not apply where the registration authority has applied to a justice of the peace for an order under section 11 of the Act or while such an order is in force.

NOTES

Para (1): in sub-para (c) word in square brackets substituted by the Residential Care Homes (Amendment) Regulations 1986, SI 1986/457, reg 4.

## 21 Form and service of notices

(1)    Any notice which is required under these regulations to be given to any person shall be in writing and may be served on him by being delivered personally to him or by being sent by post to him in a registered letter or by the recorded delivery service.

(2)    For the purposes of section 7 of the Interpretation Act 1978 (which defines "service by post") a letter to a person registered enclosing a notice under regulation 20 of these regulations shall be deemed to be properly addressed if it is addressed to him at the home.

## 22 Compliance with regulations

Where there is more than one person registered in respect of a home, anything which is required under the foregoing provisions of these regulations to be done by the person registered in respect of the home shall, if done by one of the persons so registered, not be required to be done by any other person registered in respect of the home.

## 23 Appeals

Where a person aggrieved by an order made under section 3 of the 1980 Act before the relevant date—

(a)    had appealed before that date to a magistrates' court under section 4 thereof and that appeal has not been determined by that date the provisions of the 1980 Act shall, notwithstanding the repeal thereof, continue to have effect for the purposes of the determination of that appeal;

(b)    desires to appeal against the order after that date but within the period of 21 days from the date on which the copy of that order was served upon him,   the appeal shall lie to a Registered Homes Tribunal and the provisions of Part III of the Act shall apply for the purposes of the determination of that appeal as if the appeal were an appeal under Part I of that Act.

## [24 Exemption from registration in respect of certain small homes

(1)    Registration under Part I of the Act is not required in respect of a small home if the only person or persons for whom it provides residential accommodation with both board and personal care are—

(a)    a child or children in need of personal care by reason of disablement, past or present dependence on alcohol or drugs, or past or present mental disorder, who are accommodated pursuant to any of the provisions specified in paragraph (2) of this regulation;

(b)    a child or children to whom paragraph (1)(a) of this regulation applies and a person or persons falling within section 1(4)(a) of the Act.

(2)    The provisions referred to in paragraph (1)(a) of this regulation are—

(a)    section 23(2)(a) of the Children Act 1989 (foster placement by a local authority);

(b)    section 59(1)(a) of the Children Act 1989 (foster placement by a voluntary organisation);

(c)    part IX of the Children Act 1989 (private arrangements for fostering children).]

NOTES

Added, together with reg 25, by SI 1992/2241, reg 10.

**[25   Annual returns**

(1)   The person registered in respect of a small home shall make to the registration authority an annual return containing the information referred to in Schedule 4.

(2)   The annual return in respect of a home shall be made each year on or before the anniversary of the date on which the certificate of registration relating to the home was issued, and shall be—

(a)   in the case of the first return, for the period beginning with the date on which the application was made and ending with the date on which the return is made; and

(b)   in the case of subsequent returns, for the period since the last return was made until the date on which the subsequent return is made.]

NOTES

Added as noted to reg 24.

# SCHEDULE 1
# INFORMATION TO BE SUPPLIED ON AN APPLICATION FOR REGISTRATION

Regulation 2

1. Where the application for registration is made by the manager or intended manager of the home and he is not the person in control of it (whether as owner or otherwise) he shall supply in writing to the registration authority the following information—

(a)   his full name, date of birth, address and telephone number (if any);

(b)   details of his professional or technical qualifications and experience (if any) of running a home;

(c)   the names and addresses of his previous employers and of two referees;

(d)   the name, address and telephone number of the home in respect of which registration is required; and

(e)   if the registration authority so requests, a report by a registered medical practitioner on the state of the state of the applicant's health.

2 . Where the application for registration is made by the person in control of the home—

(a)   that person shall, in a case other than one specified in sub-paragraph (b) of this paragraph, supply to the registration authority the following information—

(i)   his full name, date of birth, address and telephone number (if any),

(ii)   details of his professional or technical qualifications and experience (if any) of running a home,

(iii)   the names and addresses of his previous employers and of two referees,

(iv)   the name, address and telephone number of the home in respect of which registration is required [and in the case of a small home if different the name, address and telephone number of the person to whom enquiries are to be made,] and

(v)   if the registration authority so requests, a report by a registered medical practitioner on the state of the applicant's health;

(b)   that person shall, in the case of a company, society, association or other body or firm supply to the registration authority the following information—

(i)   the address of the registered office or principal office of the body or firm and the full names, dates of birth and addresses of the chairman and secretary of the company, or other persons responsible for the management of the body or the partners of the firm, and

(ii)   if the registration authority so requests, details of their professional or technical qualifications and experience (if any) of running a home.

[2A. An applicant for registration who is the intended manager of the home (whether or not he is in control of it) shall—

    (a)    supply in writing to the registration authority details with respect to his criminal convictions (if any);

    (b)    where the registration authority ask him for details of any criminal convictions which are spent convictions within the meaning of section 1 of the Rehabilitation of Offenders Act 1974 and inform him at the time the question is asked that, by virtue of the Rehabilitation of Offenders Act 1974 (Exceptions) Order 1975 spent convictions are to be disclosed, supply in writing to the registration authority details of those convictions.]

3. An applicant to whom paragraph 2 of this Schedule applies shall also supply to the registration authority the following information—

    (a)    the name, address and telephone number of the home in respect of which registration is required;

    (b)    the address of any other home or of any nursing home or mental nursing home within the meaning of Part II of the Act or any voluntary home within the meaning of the Child Care Act 1980, or any children's home within the meaning of the Children's Homes Act 1982 in which the applicant has or had a business interest, and the nature and extent of his interest;

    (c)    the situation of the home and its form of construction and, where requested by the registration authority, details of any comments made by the local fire authority or local environmental health authority;

    (d)    the accommodation available for residents and for persons employed at the home;

    (e)    the date on which the home was established or is to be established;

    (f)    whether any other business is or will be carried out in the same premises as the home and whether the home is also required to be registered under Part II of the Act;

    (g)    the number, sex and categories of residents for whom the home is proposed to be used indicating the various categories by reference to the following code—

| | |
|---|---|
| [old age [(not falling within any other category)] | I |
| mental disorder, other than mental handicap, past or present | MP |
| mental handicap | MH |
| alcohol dependence, past or present | A |
| drug dependence, past or present | D |
| physical disablement | PH |

*add* if the resident is—

    (i)    over 65 years of age [(but not within the category of old age)]    E

    (ii)    a child    C;

    (h)    the full names, dates of birth, qualifications and experience (if any) of persons employed, or proposed to be employed, in the management of the home (apart from a person to whom paragraph 1 of this Schedule applies) and whether they reside or are to reside in the home;

    (i)    the number, sex, position and relevant qualifications of staff, excluding any teaching staff and those referred to in sub-paragraph (h) of this paragraph, employed or proposed to be employed at the home distinguishing between resident staff and non-resident staff and those employed on a full-time and part-time basis and indicating the number of hours per week for which it is intended to employ part-time staff;

    (j)    a statement of the aims and objectives of the home, of the care and attention to be provided in the home and of any arrangements for the supervision of residents;

[(k) details of any special arrangements made or other services available for any particular category of resident and, except in the case of a small home, details of equipment and facilities and services to be provided in the home;]

(l) the arrangements made or proposed to be made for medical and dental supervision and treatment and for nursing care in cases of minor ailments;

(m) the arrangements for the handling and administration of medicines;

(n) details of the scale of charges payable by residents;

[(o) in the case of a small home the number of persons who are participating in the management or running of the home or providing personal care in the home on an informal basis (including any such person who is a relative of the person registered) and their sex, relevant qualifications and position in the home.]

NOTES

Para 2: words in square brackets inserted by SI 1992/2241, reg 11(1).

Para 2A: inserted by SI 1991/2502, reg 4.

Para 3: words in square brackets in sub-para (g) inserted by SI 1986/457, reg 5; sub-para (k) substituted, and sub-para (o) added, by SI 1992/2241, reg 11(2), (3).

# SCHEDULE 2
# REPORTS TO BE KEPT IN A HOME

Regulation 6(1)

The records to be kept under the provisions of paragraph (1) of regulation 6 of these regulations shall be—

1. A copy of the statement of the aims and objectives of the home, of the care and attention to be provided in the home and of any arrangements for the supervision of residents, which statement has in accordance with paragraph 3(j) of Schedule 1 to these regulations been supplied to the registration authority and has been agreed with that authority.

2. A daily register of all residents (excluding persons registered or persons employed at the home and their relatives) which register shall, where applicable, include in respect of each resident, the following particulars—

(a) the name, address, date of birth and marital status of the resident and whether he is the subject of any court order or other process;

(b) the name, address and telephone number of the resident's next of kin or of any person authorised to act on his behalf;

(c) the name, address and telephone number of the resident's registered medical practitioner and of any officer of a local social services authority whose duty it is to supervise the welfare of that person;

(d) the date on which the resident entered the home;

(e) the date on which the resident left the home;

(f) if the resident is transferred to a hospital or nursing home, the date of, and reasons for, the transfer and the name of the hospital or nursing home to which the resident is transferred;

(g) if the resident died in the home, the date, time and cause of death;

(h) if the resident is a child in the care of a care authority, the name, address and telephone number of the care authority, of any officer of the authority whose duty it is to supervise the welfare of the child and of the child's independent visitor (if any);

(i) if the resident is an adult who is subject to the guardianship of a local social services authority, the name, address and telephone number of that authority and of any officer of the authority whose duty it is to supervise the welfare of that resident;

(j) the name, and address of any authority, organisation or other body which arranged the resident's admission to the home;

(k) if the resident is a child, the name of any school which he is attending or any other place where he may be receiving education or vocational training.

3. In homes accommodating children—

    (a)   a statement of the sanctions used in the home to control bad behaviour and a book in which shall be entered a record of any sanction administered to a child and the name of that child;

    (b)   a register in which shall be entered the date on which each child's arrival was notified to the district health authority in whose district the home is situated and, except where the home is an independent school within the meaning of the Education Act 1944, to the local education authority for that district.

4. A case record in respect of each resident which shall include details of any special needs of that resident, any medical treatment required by him including details of any medicines administered to him, and any other information in relation to him as may be appropriate including details of any periodic review of his welfare, health, conduct and progress; and, in the case of a child who is the subject of a care order, such details of any review by the care authority as may have been notified by that authority to the person registered.

5. A record in respect of each child who has special educational needs within the meaning of section 1 of the Education Act 1981 and of the special educational provision within the meaning of that section which is being made in relation to him.

6. A record of all medicines kept in the home for a resident and of their disposal when no longer required.

7. A record book in which shall be recorded the dates of any visits by persons authorised to inspect the home and the occurrence of any event to which regulation 14(1) of these regulations refers.

8. Records of the food provided for residents in sufficient detail to enable any person inspecting the record to judge whether the diet is satisfactory and of any special diets prepared for particular residents.

9. A record of every fire practice, drill or fire alarm test conducted in the home and of any action taken to remedy defects in fire alarm equipment.

10. A statement of the procedure to be followed in the event of fire.

11. A statement of the procedure to be followed in the event of accidents or in the event of a resident becoming missing.

12. A record of each person employed at the home to provide personal care for residents, which record shall include that person's full name, date of birth, qualifications, experience and details of his position and dates of employment at the home and the number of hours for which that person is employed each week.

13. A record of any relatives of the registered person or of persons employed at the home who are residents.

14. A statement of facilities provided in the home for residents and of the arrangements made for visits by their parents, guardians, friends and other visitors.

15. A copy of any report made in accordance with the provisions of regulation 19(2) of these regulations.

16. A record of the scale of charges from time to time applicable including any extras for additional services not covered by that scale and of the amounts paid by or in respect of each resident.

17. A record of all money or other valuables deposited by a resident for safekeeping [or received on the resident's behalf] specifying the date on which such money or valuables were deposited [or received] and the date on which any sum or other valuable was returned to a resident or used, at the request of the resident, on his behalf and the purpose for which it was used.

[18. In the case of a small home a record of each person, whether employed or not, at the home who is providing personal care for residents which record shall include that person's full name, date of birth, qualifications, experience and position in the home.]

NOTES

    Para 17: words in square brackets inserted by SI 1988/1192, reg 6.
    Para 18: added by SI 1992/2241, reg 12.

# SCHEDULE 3
## PARTICULARS TO BE RECORDED IN THE REGISTER KEPT BY REGISTRATION AUTHORITIES

Regulation 7

1. The full name and address of the person registered in respect of the home and, where both the manager and person in control of the home are registered in respect of it, their full names and addresses.

2. Where the person registered is a company, society, association or other body or firm the address of its registered office or principal office and the full names and addresses of the directors, or other persons responsible for the management of that body or the partners of the firm.

3. The name, address and telephone number of the home [and in the case of a small home if different the name, address, and telephone number of the person to whom enquiries are to be made.]

4. The number, sex and categories of residents (excluding persons registered or persons employed at the home and their relatives) indicating the various categories by reference to the following code:—

| | |
|---|---|
| old age [(not falling within any other category)] | I |
| mental disorder, other than mental handicap, past or present | MP |
| mental handicap | MH |
| alcohol dependence, past or present | A |
| drug dependence, past or present | D |
| physical disablement | PH |

*add* if the resident is—

    (i)   over 65 years of age [(but not within the category of old age)]     E

    (ii)  a child     C.

5. The date of registration and of the issue of the certificate of registration and, where applicable, the date of any cancellation of registration.

6. The details of any conditions imposed on registration and of any addition to those conditions or variation thereof.

[7. Whether the certificate of registration issued relates to a small home.]

NOTES
    Para 3: words in square brackets added by SI 1992/2241, reg 13(1).
    Para 4: words in square brackets inserted by SI 1986/457, reg 5.
    Para 7: added by SI 1992/2241, reg 13(2).

# [SCHEDULE 4
## INFORMATION TO BE SUPPLIED IN THE ANNUAL RETURN

Regulation 25

[1.—(a)  The name, address and telephone number of the home, and the name and address of the person registered, indicating which if any of these items of information is different from that previously supplied;

    (b)  the number, sex and category of residents cared for in the home, indicating which if any of these items of information is different from that previously supplied;

    (c)  the number of residents who have left the home since the later of the date of registration or the date when information was previously supplied;

(d) the date and cause of death of any resident who has died in the home since the later of the date of registration or the date when information was previously supplied;

(e) the number of residents who are permanently confined to bed indicating any change since the later of the date of registration or the date when information was previously supplied;

(f) the full names and dates of birth of the persons other than residents who are living in the home, whether or not employed in the management or running of the home or in the provision of care in the home, indicating which if any of these items of information is different from that previously supplied;

(g) the full names and dates of birth, qualifications and experience of the persons employed in the management or running of the home or in the provision of care in the home, whether living in the home or not, and of the persons assisting informally in the management or running of the home or in the provision of care in the home but not living in the home, indicating which if any of these items of information is different from that previously supplied;

(h) any criminal convictions details of which have not been previously supplied, including, where the registration authority ask for details of any criminal convictions which are spent convictions as mentioned in paragraph 2A(b) of Schedule 1 to these Regulations, and inform the person registered as mentioned in that paragraph, details of those spent convictions.

2. In this Schedule "previously supplied" means—

(a) where no annual return has previously been made, supplied in the application for registration;

(b) in relation to any other return supplied in the last annual return made.]

**NOTES**

Added by SI 1992/2241, reg 14.

# REPRESENTATIONS PROCEDURE (CHILDREN) REGULATIONS 1991

## (SI 1991/894)

**NOTES**

Made: 2 April 1991.

Commencement: 14 October 1991.

Authority: Children Act 1989, ss 24(15), 26(5), (6), 59(4), (5), 104(4), Sch 6, para 10(2)(l), Sch 7, para 6.

## PART I
## INTRODUCTORY

### 1 Citation and commencement

These Regulations may be cited as the Representations Procedure (Children) Regulations 1991, and shall come into force on 14th October 1991.

### 2 Interpretation

(1) In these Regulations, unless the context otherwise requires—

"the Act" means the Children Act 1989;

> "complainant" means a person qualifying for advice and assistance about the discharge of their functions by a local authority under Part III of the Act in relation to him, or a person specified in section 26(3)(a) to (e) of the Act making any representations;
>
> "independent person" means in relation to representations made to, or treated as being made to, a local authority, a person who is neither a member nor an officer of that authority;
>
> "panel" means a panel of 3 persons;
>
> "representations" means representations referred to in sections 24(14) or 26(3) of the Act.

(2)    Any notice required under these Regulations is to be given in writing and may be sent by post.

(3)    In these Regulations unless the context requires otherwise—

    (a)    any reference to a numbered section is to the section in the Act bearing that number;

    (b)    any reference to a numbered regulation is to the regulation in these Regulations bearing that number, and any reference in a regulation to a numbered paragraph is to the paragraph of that regulation bearing that number.

# PART II
## REPRESENTATIONS AND THEIR CONSIDERATION

### 3    Local authority action

(1)    The local authority shall appoint one of their officers to assist the authority in the co-ordination of all aspects of their consideration of the representations.

(2)    The local authority shall take all reasonable steps to ensure that everyone involved in the handling of the representations, including independent persons, is familiar with the procedure set out in these Regulations.

### 4    Preliminaries

(1)    Where a local authority receive representations from any complainant, except from a person to whom section 26(3)(e) may apply, they shall send to the complainant an explanation of the procedure set out in these Regulations, and offer assistance and guidance on the use of the procedure, or give advice on where he may obtain it.

(2)    Where oral representations are made, the authority shall forthwith cause them to be recorded in writing, and sent to the complainant, who shall be given the opportunity to [comment on the accuracy of the record.]

[(2A) The authority shall consider any comments made by the complainant under paragraph (2) and shall make any amendments to the record which they consider to be necessary.]

[(3)   For the purposes of the following provisions of these Regulations, the written record referred to in paragraph (2), as amended where appropriate in accordance with paragraph (2A), shall be deemed to be the representations.]

(4)    Where a local authority receive representations from a person to whom they consider section 26(3)(e) may apply they shall—

    (a)    forthwith consider whether the person has a sufficient interest in the child's welfare to warrant his representations being considered by them;

    (b)    if they consider that he has a sufficient interest, cause the representations to be dealt with in accordance with the provisions of these Regulations, and send to the complainant an explanation of the procedure set out in the Regulations, and offer assistance and guidance on the use of the procedure, or give advice on where he may obtain it;

(c) if they consider that he has not got a sufficient interest they shall notify him accordingly in writing, and inform him that no further action will be taken;

(d) if they consider it appropriate to do so having regard to his understanding, they shall notify the child of the result of their consideration.

(5) Where paragraph (4)(b) applies, the date at which the authority conclude that the person has a sufficient interest shall be treated for the purpose of these Regulations as the date of receipt of the representations.

---

**NOTES**

Para (2): words in square brackets substituted by the Children (Representations, Placements and Reviews) (Miscellaneous Amendments) Regulations 1991, SI 1991/2033, reg 2(a).

Para (2A): inserted by SI 1991/2033, reg 2(b).

Para (3): substituted by SI 1991/2033, reg 2(c).

---

## 5 Appointment of independent person

Where the local authority receive representations under regulation 4 they shall appoint an independent person to take part in the consideration of them, unless regulation 4(4)(c) applies.

## 6 Consideration by local authority with independent person

(1) The local authority shall consider the representations with the independent person and formulate a response within 28 days of their receipt.

(2) The independent person shall take part in any discussions which are held by the local authority about the action (if any) to be taken in relation to the child in the light of the consideration of the representations.

## 7 Withdrawal of representations

The representations may be withdrawn at any stage by the person making them.

## 8 Notification to complainant and reference to panel

(1) The local authority shall give notice within the period specified in regulation 6 to—

(a) the complainant;

(b) if different, the person on whose behalf the representations were made, unless the local authority consider that he is not of sufficient understanding or it would be likely to cause serious harm to his health or emotional condition;

(c) the independent person;

(d) any other person whom the local authority consider has sufficient interest in the case

of the proposed result of their consideration of the representations and the complainant's right to have the matter referred to a panel under paragraph (2).

(2) If the complainant informs the authority in writing within 28 days of the date on which notice is given under paragraph (1) that he is dissatisfied with the proposed result and wishes the matter to be referred to a panel for consideration of the representations, a panel shall be appointed by the local authority for that purpose.

(3) The panel shall include at least one independent person.

(4)    The panel shall meet within 28 days of the receipt by the local authority of the complainant's request that the matter be referred to a panel.

(5)    At that meeting the panel shall consider—
    (a)    any oral or written submissions that the complainant or the local authority wish to make; and
    (b)    if the independent person appointed under regulation 5 is different from the independent person on the panel, any oral or written subsmissions which the independent person appointed under regulation 5 wishes to make.

(6)    If the complainant wishes to attend the meeting of the panel he may be accompanied throughout the meeting by another person of his choice, and may nominate that other person to speak on his behalf.

## 9    Recommendations

(1)    When a panel meets under regulation 8, they shall decide on their recommendations and record them with their reasons in writing within 24 hours of the end of the meeting referred to in regulation 8.

(2)    The panel shall give notice of their recommendations to—
    (a)    the local authority;
    (b)    the complainant;
    (c)    the independent person appointed under regulation 5 if different from the independent person on the panel;
    (d)    any other person whom the local authority considers has sufficient interest in the case.

(3)    The local authority shall, together with the independent person appointed to the panel under regulation 8(3) consider what action if any should be taken in relation to the child in the light of the representation, and that independent person shall take part in any [discussions] about any such action.

NOTES

Para (3): word in square brackets substituted by SI 1991/2033, reg 2(d).

## PART III
## REVIEW

## 10    Monitoring of operation of procedure

(1)    Each local authority shall monitor the arrangements that they have made with a view to ensuring that they comply with the Regulations by keeping a record of each representation received, the outcome of each representation, and whether there was compliance with the time limits specified in regulations 6(1), 8(4) and 9(1).

(2)    For the purposes of such monitoring, each local authority shall, at least once in every period of twelve months, compile a report on the operation in that period of the procedure set out in these Regulations.

(3)    The first report referred to in paragraph (2) shall be compiled within twelve months of the date of coming into force of these Regulations.

## PART IV
# APPLICATION OF REGULATIONS TO VOLUNTARY ORGANISATIONS AND REGISTERED CHILDREN'S HOMES AND IN SPECIAL CASES

**11    Application to voluntary organisations and registered children's homes**

(1)    The provisions of Parts I to III of these Regulations shall apply where accommodation is provided for a child by a voluntary organisation, and he is not looked after by a local authority, as if—

(a)    for references to "local authority" there were substituted references to "voluntary organisation";

(b)    for the definition in regulation 2(1) of "complainant" there were substituted—

""complainant" means

(a)    any child who is being provided with accommodation by a voluntary organisation;

(b)    any parent of his;

(c)    any person who is not a parent of his but who has parental responsibility for him;

(d)    such other person as the voluntary organisation consider has a sufficient interest in the child's welfare to warrant his representations being considered by them.";

(c)    for the definition in regulation 2(1) of "independent person" there were substituted—

""independent person" means in relation to representations made to, or treated as being made to a voluntary organisation, a person who is not an officer of that voluntary organisation nor a person engaged in any way in furthering its objects, nor the spouse of any such person;" and

(d)    for the definition in regulation 2(1) of "representations" there were substituted—

""representations" means representations referred to in section 59(4) about the discharge by the voluntary organisation of any of their functions relating to section 61 and any regulations made under it in relation to the child.";

(e)    for the reference in regulation 4(1) and (4) to a person to whom section 26(3)(e) may apply or to whom the local authority consider section 26(3)(e) may apply there was substituted a reference to a person who may fall within sub-paragraph (d) in the definition of "complainant" in these Regulations.

(2)    The provisions of Parts I to III of these Regulations shall apply where accommodation is provided for a child in a registered children's home, but where a child is neither looked after by a local authority nor accommodated on behalf of a voluntary organisation, as if—

(a)    for references to "local authority" there were substituted references to "the person carrying on the home";

(b)    for the definition in regulation 2(1) of "complainant" there were substituted—

465

""complainant" means

> > (i)any child who is being provided with accommodation in a registered children's home;
> >
> > (ii)a parent of his;
> >
> > (iii)any person who is not a parent of his but who has parental responsibility for him;
> >
> > (iv)such other person as the person carrying on the home considers has a sufficient interest in the child's welfare to warrant his representations being considered by them;"

> (c) for the definition in regulation 2(1) of "independent person" there were substituted—

> > ""independent person" means in relation to representations made to a person carrying on a registered children's home, a person who is neither involved in the management or operation of that home nor financially interested in its operation, nor the spouse of any such person;"

> (d) for the definition in regulation 2(1) of "representations" there were substituted—

> > "representations" means any representations (including any complaint) made in relation to the person carrying on the registered children's home by a complainant about the discharge of his functions relating to section 64.";

> (e) for the reference in regulation 4(1) and (4) to a person to whom section 26(3)(e) may apply or to whom the local authority consider section 26(3)(e) may apply there was substituted a reference to a person who may fall within sub-paragraph (d) in the definition of "complainant" in these Regulations.

## [11A   Exceptions to application of Regulations

These Regulations shall not apply to representations made by a child or a person in respect of a child who is being provided with accommodation, otherwise than by a local authority or voluntary organisation—

> (a) in an independent school which is a children's home within the meaning of section 63(6) of the Act; or
>
> (b) in a special school (as defined in section 182 of the Education Act 1993) which is not maintained by a local education authority, or otherwise out of public funds.]

NOTES

Inserted by the Children (Homes, Arrangements for Placement, Reviews and Representations) (Miscellaneous Amendments) Regulations 1993, SI 1993/3069, reg 5.

# PART IV
# APPLICATION OF REGULATIONS TO VOLUNTARY ORGANISATIONS AND REGISTERED CHILDREN'S HOMES AND IN SPECIAL CASES

## 12   Special cases including application to representations by foster parents

(1)   Where representations would fall to be considered by more than one local authority, they shall be considered by the authority which is looking after the child or by the authority within whose area the child is ordinarily resident where no authority has that responsibility.

(2) The provisions of [Parts I to III] of, and of regulation 12(1) of, these Regulations, shall apply to the consideration by a local authority of any representations (including any complaint) made to them by any person exempted or seeking to be exempted under paragraph 4 of Schedule 7 to the Act (foster parents: limits on numbers of foster children) about the discharge of their functions under that paragraph as if—

    (a) for the definition in regulation 2(1) of "complainant" there were substituted: "a person exempted or seeking to be exempted under paragraph 4 of Schedule 7 to the Act making any representations;"

    (b) for the definition in regulation 2(1) of "representations" there were substituted: "representations referred to in paragraph 6 of Schedule 7 to the Act.";

    (c) in regulation 4(1) the words "except from a person to whom section 26(3)(e) may apply" were omitted;

    (d) regulation 4(4) and (5) were omitted.

**NOTES**

Para (2): words in square brackets substituted by SI 1991/2033, reg 2(e).

# GUARDIANS AD LITEM AND REPORTING OFFICERS (PANELS) REGULATIONS 1991

## (SI 1991/2051)

**NOTES**

Made: 10 September 1991.
Commencement: 14 October 1991.
Authority: Adoption Act 1976, ss 41(7), (9), 104(4); Children Act 1989, s 65A(1), (2).

## 1 Citation, commencement and interpretation

(1) These Regulations may be cited as the Guardians Ad Litem and Reporting Officers (Panels) Regulations 1991 and shall come into force on 14th October 1991.

(2) In these Regulations, unless the context otherwise requires—

    "complaints board" means a board established under regulation 3(a) of these Regulations;

    ["joint complaints board" has the meaning given to it in regulation 5(7);

    "justices' clerk" has the same meaning as it has in the Justices of the Peace Act 1997;]

    "panel" means a panel established under regulation 2(1) of these Regulations;

    "panel committee" means a committee established under regulation 3(b) of these Regulations;

    "relevant proceedings" means specified proceedings as defined in section 41(6) of the Children Act 1989 or proceedings on an application for any order referred to in section 65 of the Adoption Act 1976.

**NOTES**

Para (2): definitions "joint complaints board" and "justices' clerk" inserted by the Guardians Ad Litem and Reporting Officers (Panels) (Amendment) Regulations 1997, SI 1997/1662, reg 2(2).

## 2    Panels of guardians ad litem and reporting officers

(1)    Each local authority shall establish a panel of persons in accordance with regulation 4 of these Regulations in respect of their area.

(2)    Guardians ad litem and reporting officers appointed under section 41 of the Children Act 1989 for the purposes of relevant proceedings or under rules made under Section 65 of the Adoption Act 1976 must be selected from the panel established in respect of the local authority's area in which the court is situated (unless selected from another local authority's panel established under these Regulations).

(3)    Each local authority shall ensure that so far as possible the number of persons appointed to the panel established in respect of their area is sufficient to provide guardians ad litem and reporting officers for all relevant proceedings in which guardians ad litem and reporting officers may be appointed and which may be heard in their area.

## 3    Complaints boards and panel committees

For the purpose of assisting them with matters concerning the membership of panels, the administration and procedures of panels and the monitoring of the work of guardians ad litem and reporting officers in relevant proceedings, each local authority shall establish—

   (a)    a board ("complaints board") in accordance with Schedule 1 to these Regulations, which shall have the functions conferred on them by regulations [4A,] 5 and 6 of these Regulations;
   (b)    a committee ("panel committee") in accordance with Schedule 2 to these Regulations, which shall have the functions conferred on it by regulations 8 and 10(1)(a) of these Regulations.

NOTES
   Number in square brackets inserted by SI 1997/1662, reg 2(3).

## 4    Appointments to panels

(1)    The local authority in respect of whose area the panel is established shall appoint persons to be members of the panel.

(2)    The local authority shall decide whether the qualifications and experience of any person who they propose to appoint to the panel are suitable for the purposes of that person's appointment as a guardian ad litem or a reporting officer . . .

(3)    The local authority shall in respect of any person whom they propose to appoint to the panel—

   (a)    interview each such person,
   (b)    consult the panel committee, and
   (c)    obtain the names of at least two persons who can provide a reference in writing for the persons whom they propose to appoint and take up those references.

(4)    The local authority shall notify in writing any person who is appointed to a panel of the appointment which shall, [subject to regulations 4A(5) and 5] of these Regulations, be for such period not exceeding three years at any one time as the local authority shall specify on making the appointment.

(5)    Each local authority shall maintain a record of those persons whom they have appointed to be members of the panel established in respect of their area.

(6)    Every local authority shall have regard to the number of children in their area who may become the subject of specified proceedings and the different racial groups to which they belong, in making appointments under this regulation.

NOTES
Para (2): words omitted revoked by SI 1997/1662, reg 2(4)(a).
Para (4): words in square brackets substituted by SI 1997/1662, reg 2(4)(b).

## [4A Non reappointment to panel

(1)    Where a local authority propose not to reappoint a person to be a panel member, they shall, before the expiry of that person's existing appointment—

(a)    notify him in writing of the reasons why it is proposed that he should not be reappointed to the panel; and

(b)    give him an opportunity of making representations to the local authority.

(2)    Where the local authority, having considered any representations made under paragraph (1)(b), still propose not to reappoint the person, they shall, before the expiry of his existing appointment, advise him in writing that he may refer the matter to a complaints board under this regulation.

(3)    If the person refers the matter to a complaints board, the complaints board shall make a recommendation to the local authority after taking account of any representations of the person whom the local authority propose not to reappoint.

(4)    The local authority shall consider the recommendation of the complaints board as to reappointment, decide whether or not to reappoint the person to be a panel member and give notice to that person in writing of their decision, together with their reasons for the decision.

(5)    Notwithstanding regulation 4(4), the existing appointment of a person who is not reappointed to be a panel member may be extended for the purpose of enabling him to continue to act in any relevant proceedings for which he was appointed before the date on which his appointment would otherwise have expired.]

NOTES
Inserted by SI 1997/1662, reg 2(5), in relation to any member of a panel whose appointment is due to expire after 29 October 1997.

## 5    Termination of panel membership

(1)    The local authority may terminate a person's membership of the panel at any time where they consider that he is unable or unfit to carry out the functions of a guardian ad litem or a reporting officer.

(2)    Before terminating a person's membership of the panel the local authority shall—

(a)    notify him in writing of the reasons why it is proposed that his membership of the panel should be terminated;

(b)    give him an opportunity of making representations to the local authority.

(3)    Where the local authority, having considered any representations made under paragraph (2)(b) of this regulation, still propose to terminate a person's membership, they shall refer the matter to a complaints board.

(4)    The complaints board shall make a recommendation to the authority after taking account of any representations of the person whose membership the local authority proposed to terminate.

(5)    The local authority shall consider the recommendation of the complaints board, as to termination of a person's membership and decide whether or not to terminate membership and give notice to that person in writing of their decision together with their reasons for the decision.

[(6) Notwithstanding the preceding provisions of this regulation and the provisions of regulation 3(a) and Schedule 1, where—

    (a) more than one local authority proposes to terminate the membership of a person who is a member of the panel established by each of those authorities;

    (b) the authorities' reasons for proposing to terminate that person's membership are similar or related; and

    (c) each of the authorities has considered any representations made under paragraph 2(b) of this regulation,

the authorities may agree that they will refer the matter to a joint complaints board.

(7) Membership of a joint complaints board shall be determined by agreement between the authorities concerned and shall consist of a minimum of 3 and a maximum of 6 persons—

    (a) one of whom is neither an officer nor a member of a local authority;

    (b) one or more of whom are involved in the functions in respect of services for children and their families of a local authority other than an authority convening the joint complaints board; and

    (c) one or more of whom are justices' clerks or officers appointed by a magistrates' courts committee to be the deputy to a justices' clerk.]

NOTES

    Paras (6), (7): added by SI 1997/1662, reg 2(6), in relation to any proposal to terminate a person's membership of a panel which is made by a local authority after 29 July 1997.

## 6   Complaints about the operation of panels and members of the panels

(1) For the purpose of monitoring the administration and procedures of the panel and the work of guardians ad litem and reporting officers in relevant proceedings each local authority shall establish a procedure for considering complaints about the operation of the panel in respect of their area, and about any member of that panel  . . .

(2) The local authority shall investigate any such complaint and if they cannot resolve it to the satisfaction of the person making it they shall refer it to the complaints board to make a recommendation to the authority about it in writing.

(3) Any person in respect of whom a complaint is made shall be notified by the local authority in writing of the complaint and they shall give him an opportunity of making representations to them and if the matter is referred to the complaints board they shall provide him with an opportunity to make representations to the complaints board.

(4) The local authority shall only make a decision on a complaint referred to the complaints board having taken into account the recommendation of the complaints board and they shall notify the person who made the complaint and any person in respect of whom the complaint was made in writing of their decision.

[(5) Notwithstanding the preceding provisions of this regulation and the provisions of regulation 3(a) and Schedule 1, where similar or related complaints are made to more than one local authority in respect of a person who is a member of the panel established by each of those authorities, the authorities may agree that they will investigate the complaints jointly, refer the complaints to a joint complaints board and make a joint decision about the complaints.]

NOTES

Para (1): words omitted revoked by SI 1997/1662, reg 2(7)(a).

Para (5): added by SI 1997/1662, reg 2(7)(b), in relation to any complaint made to a local authority after 29 July 1997.

## [6A Determination of non-availability for appointment pending investigation of a complaint about a member of a panel

If a complaint is made about a member of a panel and, before it has made a decision about that complaint in accordance with regulation 6, the local authority considers that the nature of the complaint and the evidence in support of it may indicate that the panel member is unfit to carry out the functions of a guardian ad litem or reporting officer, the local authority—

(a) shall, in respect of all relevant proceedings for which the panel member has been appointed give notice of the complaint to the court before which those proceedings are to be heard; and

(b) without prejudice to the decision of the court whether the panel member should continue to act in relevant proceedings for which he has already been appointed, may determine that the panel member should not be made available for further appointments in relevant proceedings until a decision has been made on the complaint and on any related proposal to terminate the person's panel membership.]

NOTES

Inserted by SI 1997/1662, reg 2(8).

## 7 Administration of the panel

(1) Each local authority shall appoint a person with such qualifications and experience as they consider appropriate to assist them with the administration of the panel in respect of their area and that person shall not participate in the local authority social services functions in respect of services for children and their families (other than the administration of the panel or an inspection unit established under the Secretary of State's directions under section 7A of the Local Authority Social Services Act 1970).

(2) Each local authority shall ensure that records are kept in relation to the operation of the panel which shall include—

(a) the name of each child in respect of whom a guardian ad litem or reporting officer is selected from the panel;

(b) a description of the relevant proceedings in respect of which the selection is made;

(c) the name and level of the court (whether High Court, county court or family proceedings court);

(d) the name of any person selected from the panel and whether he has been appointed in specified proceedings or in proceedings under the Adoption Act 1976 as a guardian ad litem, or in proceedings under the Adoption Act 1976 as a reporting officer;

(e) the date of each appointment, the date on which work started in respect of that appointment and the date on which it finished;

(f) details of fees, expenses and allowances in each case in which there has been such an appointment;

(g) the result of the proceedings in each case in which there has been such an appointment.

## 8   Panel committee functions

The local authority shall make arrangements for the panel committee to assist with liaison between the local authority in their administration of the panel and the courts in the local authority's area and to advise on—

    (a)  the standards of practice of guardians ad litem and reporting officers in relevant proceedings in their area;

    (b)  the appointment and reappointment of guardians ad litem and reporting officers to the panel, termination of their appointment and review of their work;

    (c)  the training of guardians ad litem and reporting officers; and

    [(d)  the handling of complaints concerning guardians ad litem, reporting officers and the administration of the panel, and matters arising from those complaints (but not the investigation of particular complaints).]

**NOTES**

Para (d): substituted by SI 1997/1662, reg 2(9).

## 9   Expenses, fees and allowances of members of panels

(1)    Each local authority shall defray the reasonable expenses incurred in respect of relevant proceedings by members of the panel established in respect of their area and pay fees and allowances for members of such panels in respect of relevant proceedings.

[(2)    No fees shall be paid by local authorities by virtue of paragraph (1) of this regulation in respect of a member of a panel who is employed under a contract of service by a local authority or probation committee for thirty hours or more a week.]

**NOTES**

Para (2): substituted by SI 1997/1662, reg 2(10).

## 10   Monitoring the work of guardians ad litem and reporting officers

(1)    For the purposes of monitoring the work of guardians ad litem and reporting officers each local authority which has established a panel in respect of their area shall—

    (a)  obtain the views of the panel committee on the work of each member of the panel who has been appointed a guardian ad litem or reporting officer, and

    (b)  review the work of each such member of the panel

at least once during the first year of an appointment to the panel.

(2)    The results of each review shall be recorded by the local authority in writing and they shall send a copy of the results to the member of the panel to whom they relate.

## 11   Training

The local authority shall, having regard to the cases in which members of the panel have been or may be appointed as a guardian ad litem or reporting officer, identify any training needs which members of the panel may have and make reasonable provision for such training.

**[13 Contracting out of functions in relation to the provision of panels of guardians ad litem and reporting officers**

Where any function of a local authority under these Regulations is exercised by a person other than the authority in accordance with an Order made under section 70 of the Deregulation and Contracting Out Act 1994, regulation 5(7) (joint complaints board) and Schedule 1 (complaints board) shall have effect in relation to that authority as if, in each case, in paragraph (a) at the end there were inserted the words—

> "nor a person who is authorised to exercise any function of the local authority which is conferred by these Regulations in accordance with an Order made under section 70 of the Deregulation and Contracting Out Act 1994, nor an employee of such a person".]

NOTES

Added by SI 1997/1662, reg 2(11).

# SCHEDULE 1
## COMPLAINTS BOARD

Regulation 3(a)

The complaints board shall consist of three persons,—
- (a) one of whom shall be a person who is neither an officer nor a member of a local authority;
- (b) another of whom shall be a person who is involved in the functions in respect of services for children and their families of a local authority which has not established the panel;
- (c) another of whom shall be a justices' clerk [or an officer appointed by a magistrates' court committee to be the deputy to a justices' clerk].

NOTES

Words in square brackets substituted by SI 1997/1662, reg 2(12).

Modified by the Contracting Out (Functions in relation to the provision of Guardians Ad Litem and Reporting Officers Panels) Order 1996, SI 1996/858, reg 2.

# SCHEDULE 2
## PANEL COMMITTEE

Regulation 3(b)

1. The panel committee shall consist of at least one of [each of] the following—
   - (a) a representative of the local authority;
   - (b) a justices' clerk [or an officer appointed by a magistrates' court committee to be the deputy to a justices' clerk];
   - (c) a person who has relevant experience of child care who is neither an officer nor a member of a local authority;
   - (d) a representative of the panel established under regulation 2(1) of these Regulations.

2. The panel committee shall not be chaired by a representative of the local authority.

3. The membership of the panel committee shall not consist of a majority of representatives of the local authority.

4. Appointments to the panel committee shall be for such period not exceeding three years at any one time as the authority shall specify on making the appointment.

NOTES

Para 1: first words in square brackets inserted, and final words in square brackets substituted, by SI 1997/1662, reg 2(13).

# CHILDREN (ADMISSIBILITY OF HEARSAY EVIDENCE) ORDER 1993

## (SI 1993/621)

NOTES
Made: 3 March 1993.
Commencement: 5 April 1993.
Authority: Children Act 1989, s 96(3).

## 1 Citation and Commencement

This order may be cited as the Children (Admissibility of Hearsay Evidence) Order 1993 and shall come into force on 5th April 1993.

## 2 Admissibility of hearsay evidence

In—

    (a) civil proceedings before the High Court or a county court; and

    (b)

        (i) family proceedings, and

        (ii) civil proceedings under the Child Support Act 1991 in a magistrates' court,

evidence given in connection with the upbringing, maintenance or welfare of a child shall be admissible notwithstanding any rule of law relating to hearsay.

# PART III
## CODE OF PRACTICE
## (MENTAL HEALTH ACT 1983)

# CODE OF PRACTICE
# (MENTAL HEALTH ACT 1983)

NOTES
Selected extracts only are reproduced

## 1 Introduction

1.1   This revised Code of Practice has been prepared in accordance with section 118 of the Mental Health Act 1983 (the Act) by the Secretary of State for Health and the Secretary of State for Wales, after consulting such bodies as appeared to them to be concerned, and laid before Parliament. The Code will come into force on 1 — November 1993. The Act does not impose a legal duty to comply with the Code but failure to follow the Code could be referred to in evidence in legal proceedings.

1.2   The Code imposes no additional duties on statutory authorities. Rather it provides guidance to statutory authorities, Managers (who have defined responsibilities under the provisions of the Act) and professional staff working in health (including mental nursing homes) and social services on how they should proceed when undertaking duties under the Act.

1.3   The Code provides much detailed guidance, but this needs to be read in the light of the following broad principles, that people being assessed for possible admission under the Act or to whom the Act applies should—

—   receive respect for and consideration of their individual qualities and diverse backgrounds - social, cultural, ethnic and religious;

—   have their needs taken fully into account though it is recognised that, within available resources, it may not always be practicable to meet them;

—   be delivered any necessary treatment or care in the least controlled and segregated facilities practicable;

—   be treated or cared for in such a way that promotes to the greatest practicable degree, their self determination and personal responsibility consistent with their needs and wishes;

—   be discharged from any order under the Act to which they are subject immediately it is no longer necessary.

1.4   This means, in particular, that individuals should be as fully involved as practicable, consistent with their needs and wishes, in the formulation and delivery of their care and treatment, and that, where linguistic and sensory difficulties impede such involvement reasonable steps should be taken to attempt to overcome them. It means that patients should have their legal rights drawn to their attention, consistent with their capacity to understand them. Finally, it means that, when treatment or care is provided in conditions of security, patients should be subject only to the level of security appropriate to their individual needs and only for so long as it is required.

1.5   The Code has been made as comprehensive as possible, but inevitably gaps will emerge and amendments and additions to the Code will need to be made as appropriate in the light of experience. The Secretaries of State are required to keep the Code under review.

1.6    Finally a note on presentation. An attempt has been made to draft the Code in such a way as to make it acceptable not only to those for whom the Act requires it to be written but also many patients, their families, friends and supporters. Throughout the Code, the Mental Health Act 1983 is referred to as the Act. Where there is reference to sections of other Acts, the relevant Act is clearly indicated. The glossary [not reproduced] either defines some of the words in the Code or refers to relevant sections of the Act where definitions can be found. Following the style of the Act, the Code uses the terms 'he' and 'his' to encompass both male and female.

## 2    Assessment

### General

2.1    This chapter is about the assessment by Approved Social Workers (ASWs) and doctors of the needs of a person with mental health problems, where it may lead to an application for admission to hospital under the Mental Health Act 1983 (the Act).

2.2    Doctors and ASWs must recognise that both have specific roles to play in assessment and should arrive at their own independent decisions. Such recognition should be underpinned by good working relationships based on knowledge and responsibilities; assessment should be carried out jointly unless good reasons prevent it (although it may be advantageous for each professional to interview the patient alone). An agreement should be reached between the professionals involved in the assessment process as to how their responsibilities can best be discharged.

2.3    A decision *not* to apply for admission under the Act should be clearly thought through, and supported, where necessary, by an alternative framework of care and/or treatment.

2.4    Everyone involved in assessment should be aware of the need to provide mutual support, especially where there is a risk of the patient causing serious physical harm (including, where necessary, the need to call for police assistance and how to use that assistance to minimise the risk of violence).

*Assessment for possible admission under the Mental Health Act*

### 2.5    The objectives of assessment under the Mental Health Act

All those assessing for possible admission under the Act should ensure that—
  (a)   they take all relevant factors into account;
  (b)   they consider and where possible implement appropriate alternatives to compulsory admission;
  (c)   they comply with the legal requirements of the Act.

### The factors to be taken into account at assessment

2.6    A patient may be compulsorily admitted under the Act where this is necessary—
  —   in the interests of his own health, *or*
  —   in the interests of his own safety, *or*
  —   for the protection of other people.

Only one of the above grounds needs to be satisfied *(in addition to those relating to the patient's mental disorder)*. However, a patient may only be admitted for treatment under section 3 if the treatment cannot be provided unless he is detained under the section. In judging whether compulsory admission is appropriate, those concerned should consider not only the statutory criteria but also—

— the patient's wishes and view of his own needs;
— his social and family circumstances;
— the risk of making assumptions based on a person's sex, social and cultural background or ethnic origin;
— the possibility of misunderstandings which may be caused by other medical/health conditions including deafness;
— the nature of the illness/behaviour disorder;
— what may be known about the patient by his nearest relative, any other relatives or friends and professionals involved, assessing in particular how reliable this information is;
— other forms of care or treatment including, where relevant, consideration of whether the patient would be willing to accept medical treatment in hospital informally or as an out—patient;
— the needs of the patient's family or others with whom the patient lives;
— the need for others to be protected from the patient;
— the impact that compulsory admission would have on the patient's life after discharge from detention;
— the burden on those close to the patient of a decision not to admit under the Act;
— the appropriateness of guardianship. (See Chapter 13).

Ordinarily only then should the applicant (in consultation with other professionals) judge whether the criteria stipulated in any of the admission sections are satisfied, and take the decision accordingly. In certain circumstances the urgency of the situation may curtail detailed consideration of all these factors.

## Informal admission

2.7 Where admission to hospital is considered necessary and the patient is willing to be admitted informally this should in general be arranged. Compulsory admission should, however, be considered where the patient's current medical state, together with reliable evidence of past experience, indicates a strong likelihood that he will change his mind about informal admission prior to his actual admission to hospital with a resulting risk to his health *or* safety *or* to the safety of others.

## Protection of others

2.8 In considering 'the protection of other persons' (see sections 2(2)(b) and 3(2)(c)) it is essential to assess both the nature and likelihood of risk and the level of risk others are entitled to be protected from, taking into account—
— reliable evidence of risk to others;
— any relevant details of the patient's medical history and past behaviour;
— the degree of risk and its nature. Too high a risk of physical harm, or serious persistent psychological harm to others, are indicators of the need for compulsory admission;
— the willingness and ability to cope with the risk, by those with whom the patient lives;
— the possibility of misunderstandings resulting from assumptions based on a person's sex, social and cultural background or ethnic origin and from other medical/health conditions including deafness.

## The health of the patient

2.9 A patient may be admitted under sections 2 and 3 solely in the interests of his own health even if there is no risk to his own or other people's safety. Those assessing the patient must consider—

— any evidence suggesting that the patient's mental health will deteriorate if he does not receive treatment;

— the reliability of such evidence which may include the known history of the individual's mental disorder;

— the views of the patient and of any relatives or close friends, especially those living with the patient, about the likely course of his illness and the possibility of its improving;

— the impact that any future deterioration or lack of improvement would have on relatives or close friends, especially those living with the patient, including an assessment of his ability and willingness to cope;

— whether there are other methods of coping with the expected deterioration or lack of improvement.

## Individual professional responsibility – the Approved Social Worker

2.10 It is important to emphasise that where an ASW is assessing a person for possible admission under the Act he has overall responsibility for co-ordinating the process of assessment and, where he decides to make an application, for implementing that decision. The ASW must, at the start of his assessment of the patient, identify himself to the patient, members of the family or friends present with the patient, and the other professionals involved in the assessment, explain in clear terms his role and the purpose of his visit, and ensure that the other professionals have explained their roles. ASWs should carry with them at all times documents identifying them as ASWs.

2.11 The ASW must interview the patient in a 'suitable manner'.

(a) Where the patient and ASW cannot understand each other's language sufficiently, wherever practicable recourse should be had to a trained interpreter who understands the terminology and conduct of a psychiatric interview (and if possible the patient's cultural background).

(b) Where another ASW with an understanding of the patient's language is available, consideration should be given to requesting him to carry out the assessment or assist the ASW assigned to the assessment.

(c) Where the patient has difficulty either in hearing or speaking, wherever practicable an ASW with appropriate communication skills should carry out the assessment or assist the ASW initially assigned to the case. Alternatively the ASW should seek the assistance of a trained interpreter. Social services departments should issue guidance to their ASWs as to where such assistance can be obtained.

(d) The ASW should bear in mind the potential disadvantages of a patient's relative being asked to interpret. Where possible, a trained interpreter should be used in preference to a relative, neighbour or friend.

(e) Where the patient is still unwilling or unable to speak to the ASW (despite assistance from interpreters) the assessment will have to be based on whatever information the ASW can obtain from all reliable sources, making allowance for the risk of false assumptions based on a person's sex or ethnic origin, or other forms of prejudice.

(f) It is not desirable for a patient to be interviewed through a closed door or window except where there is serious risk to other people. Where there is no immediate risk of physical danger to the patient or to others, powers in the Act to secure access (section 135) should be used.

(g)  Where the patient is subject to the effects of sedative medication, or the short-term effects of drugs or alcohol, the ASW should consult with the doctor/s and, unless it is not possible because of the patient's disturbed behaviour and the urgency of the case, either wait until, or arrange to return when, the effects have abated before interviewing the patient. If it is not realistic to wait, the assessment will have to be based on whatever information the ASW can obtain from all reliable sources.

2.12  The patient should ordinarily be given the opportunity of speaking to the ASW alone but if the ASW has reason to fear physical harm he should insist that another professional sees the patient with him. If the patient would like another person (for example a friend) to be with him during the assessment and any subsequent action that may be taken, then ordinarily the ASW should assist in securing that person's attendance unless the urgency of the case or some other proper reason makes it inappropriate to do so.

2.13  The ASW must attempt to identify the patient's nearest relative (see section 26 of the Act and paras 67-8 of the Memorandum), and ensure that his statutory obligations (section 11) to the nearest relative are fulfilled. In addition, the ASW should where possible—

(a)  ascertain the nearest relative's views about the patient's needs and his (the relative's) own needs in relation to the patient;

(b)  inform the nearest relative of the reasons for considering an application for admission under the Mental Health Act and the effects of making such an application.

It is a statutory requirement to take such steps as are practicable to inform the nearest relative about an application for admission under section 2 and of his power of discharge (section 11(3)). Consultation by the ASW with the nearest relative about possible application for admission under section 3 or reception into guardianship is a statutory requirement unless it is not reasonably practicable or would involve unreasonable delay (section 11(4)). Circumstances in which the nearest relative need not be informed or consulted include those where the ASW cannot obtain sufficient information to identify the nearest relative or his location or where to do so would require an excessive amount of investigation. Practicability refers to the availability of the nearest relative and not to the appropriateness of informing or consulting the person concerned.

2.14  If the nearest relative objects to an application being made, for admission for treatment or reception into guardianship, it cannot proceed at that time. The ASW may then need to consider applying to the county court for the nearest relative's 'displacement' (section 29), and local authorities must provide proper assistance, especially legal assistance, in such cases. It is desirable for clear practical guidance on the procedures to be available, and this should be discussed with the relevant county courts.

2.15  Where the ASW is the applicant for the admission of a patient to hospital, he must discuss, in so far as the urgency of the case allows, with other relevant relatives and friends their views of the patient's needs, and should take them into account.

2.16  The ASW should consult wherever possible with other professionals who have been involved with the patient's care, for example home care staff or community psychiatric nurses (CPNs).

2.17  When the ASW has decided whether or not he will make an application for admission he should tell (with reasons)—

— the patient;
— the patient's nearest relative (whenever possible);
— the doctor/s involved in the assessment.

When an application for admission is to be made the ASW should start planning how the patient is to be conveyed to hospital (see Chapter 11).

## Individual professional responsibility – the doctor

2.18 The doctor should—

(a) decide whether the patient is suffering from mental disorder within the meaning of the Act (section 1) and assess its seriousness and the need for further assessment and/or medical treatment in hospital;

(b) consider the factors set out above at para 2.6, discussing his views with the applicant and the other doctor involved;

(c) specifically address the legal criteria for admission under the Mental Health Act and if he is satisfied provide a recommendation setting out those aspects of the patient's symptoms and behaviour which satisfy the legal criteria for admission;

(d) ensure that, where there is to be an application for admission, a hospital bed will be available.

## Medical examination

2.19 A proper medical examination requires—

— direct personal examination of the patient's mental state, excluding any possible preconceptions based on the patient's sex, social and cultural background or ethnic origin;

— consideration of all available relevant medical information including that in the possession of others, professional or non-professional.

Where the patient and doctor cannot understand each other's language the doctor should, wherever practicable, have recourse to a trained interpreter, who understands the terminology and conduct of a psychiatric interview (and if possible the patient's cultural background).

2.20 If direct access to the patient is not immediately possible, and it is not desirable to postpone the examination in order to negotiate access, the relevant powers in the Act must be invoked (section 135) or consideration given to calling the police in order to see if they would exercise any relevant lawful power of entry.

2.21 It may not always be practicable for the patient to be examined by both doctors at the same time; but they should always discuss the patient with each other.

2.22 It is desirable for both doctors to discuss the patient with the applicant. It is essential for at least one of them to do so.

## Joint medical recommendations

2.23 Joint medical recommendation forms (forms 3 and 10) should only be used where the patient has been jointly examined by two doctors. It is desirable that they are completed and signed by both doctors at the same time.

2.24 In all other circumstances separate recommendation forms should be used (forms 4 and 11).

## The second medical recommendation

2.25  Other than in exceptional circumstances, the second medical recommendation should be provided by a doctor with previous acquaintance of the patient. This should be the case even when the 'approved' doctor (who is, for example, a hospital based consultant) already knows the patient. Where this is not possible (for example the patient is not registered with a GP) it is desirable for the second medical recommendation to be provided by an 'approved' doctor (see paras 2.37 and 2.38).

## A decision not to apply for admission

2.26  Most compulsory admissions require prompt action to be taken but it should be remembered that the ASW has up to 14 days from the date of first seeing the patient to make an application for admission for assessment or treatment. Where a decision not to apply for a patient's compulsory admission is taken the professional concerned must decide how to implement those actions (if any) which his assessment indicates are necessary to meet the needs of the patient including, for example, the referral to other social workers or services within the social services department. It is particularly important that any CPCPNN concerned with the patient's care be fully involved in the taking of such decisions. The professionals must ensure that they, the patient and (with the patient's consent except where section 13(4) applies) the patient's nearest relative and any other closely connected relatives have a clear understanding of any alternative arrangements. It is good practice for such arrangements to be recorded in writing and copies made available to all those who need them (subject to the patient's right to confidentiality).

2.27  The ASW must discuss with the patient's nearest relative the reasons for not making an application. The ASW should advise the nearest relative of his right to apply and suggest that he consult with the doctors if he wishes to consider this alternative. Where, moreover, the ASW is carrying out an assessment at the request of the nearest relative (section 13(4)) the reasons for not applying for the patient's admission must be given to the nearest relative in writing. Such a letter should contain sufficient details to enable the nearest relative to understand the decision whilst at the same time preserving the patient's right to confidentiality.

## Particular practice issues

### Disagreements

2.28  Sometimes there will be differences of opinion between assessing professionals. There is nothing wrong with disagreements: handled properly these offer an opportunity to safeguard the interests of the patient by widening the discussion on the best way of meeting the patient's needs. Doctors and ASWs should be ready to consult colleagues (especially CPNs and other community care staff involved with the patient's care), while retaining for themselves the final responsibility. Where disagreements do occur, professionals should ensure that they have set out to each other in discussion their views of the salient features of the case and their conclusions.

2.29  Where there is an unresolved dispute about an application for admission, it is essential that the professionals do not abandon the patient and the family. Rather, they should explore and agree an alternative plan, if necessary on a temporary basis, and ensure that the family is kept informed. It is desirable for such a plan to be recorded in writing and copies made available to all those who need it (subject to the patient's right to confidentiality).

**The choice of applicant**

2.30  The ASW is usually the right applicant, bearing in mind professional training, knowledge of the legislation and of local resources, together with the potential adverse effect that a nearest relative application might have on the relationship with the patient. The doctor should therefore advise the nearest relative that it is preferable for an ASW to make an assessment of the need for a patient to be admitted under the Act, and for the ASW to make the application. When reasonably practicable the doctor should, however, advise the nearest relative of his section 13(4) rights (see para 2.33) and of his right to make an application.

2.31  The doctor should never advise the nearest relative to make an application in order to avoid involving an ASW in an assessment.

# 3
# PART III OF THE MENTAL HEALTH ACT—PATIENTS CONCERNED WITH CRIMINAL PROCEEDINGS

*Assessment*

## General

### Responsibility to patients

3.1  Those subject to criminal proceedings have the same right to psychiatric assessment and treatment as other citizens. The aim should be to ensure that everyone in prison or police custody in need of medical treatment for mental disorder which can only satisfactorily be given in a hospital as defined by the Act is admitted to such a hospital.

3.2  All professionals involved in the operation of Part III of the Act should remember—
  (a) the vulnerability of people, especially those who are mentally disordered, when in police or prison custody. The risk of suicide or other self destructive behaviour should be of special concern;
  (b) that a prison hospital is not a hospital within the meaning of the Act. Treatment facilities are limited, and the provisions of Part IV of the Act do not apply.

### Individual professional responsibilities

3.3  All professionals concerned with the operation of Part III of the Act should be familiar with—
  — the relevant provisions of the Act and paragraphs of the Memorandum (paras 115 to 188);
  — any relevant guidance issued by or under the auspices of the Home Office including that in Home Office Circular 66/90 and E L(90)168, on Provision for Mentally Disordered Offenders;
  — the responsibilities of their own and other disciplines and authorities and agencies;
  — available facilities and services.

### Agency responsibility

3.4  Regional health authorities in England and district health authorities in Wales should—

(a) be able to provide to any requesting court in compliance with section 39 of the Act, and also in response to any other proper request, up-to-date and full information on the range of facilities for a potential patient in hospitals, including secure facilities. Facilities to which the patient might be admitted outside their district or region may need to be specified and the arrangements for their funding clarified;

(b) appoint a named person to respond to these requests.

3.5    Section 27 of the Criminal Justice Act 1991 added a new section 39A to the Act which requires a local social services authority to inform the court if it or any other person is willing to receive the offender into guardianship and, if so, to provide such information as it reasonably can about how the guardian's powers can be expected to be exercised.

3.6    Local authorities should appoint a named person to respond to requests from the courts for them to consider the making of guardianship orders.

## Assessment by a doctor

3.7    Where a doctor is asked to provide an opinion in relation to a possible admission under Part III of the Act—

(a) he should identify himself to the person being assessed, and explain at whose request he is preparing his report, discussing any implications this may have for confidentiality;

(b) he should have access to relevant social enquiry reports, the inmate's medical record (where the defendant is remanded in prison custody) and previous psychiatric treatment records as well as relevant documentation regarding the alleged offence. If he is not given any of this information he should say so clearly in his report (see paras 2.6 and 2.35).

Where a doctor had previously treated the person it may be desirable for him to prepare the report. It would also be desirable for the doctor (or one of them if two doctors are preparing reports) to have appropriate beds at his disposal or where necessary to take responsibility for referring the case to another doctor with access to such facilities.

3.8    The doctor should where possible make contact with independent information about the person's previous history, previous psychiatric treatment and patterns of behaviour.

3.9    Any assessment of the person is a medical responsibility. Appropriate members of the clinical team who would be involved with the individual's care and treatment may also be involved. It is often desirable for a nurse (who will be able to undertake a nursing assessment of the person's needs for nursing care and treatment and advise on whether he can be managed in the hospital) to accompany the assessing doctor where admission to hospital is likely to be recommended. The doctor should make contact with the social worker or probation officer who is preparing a social enquiry report, especially when psychiatric treatment is suggested as a condition of a probation order.

3.10    The doctor should not in his report anticipate the outcome of proceedings to establish guilt or innocence. It is sometimes appropriate to advise that a further report should be submitted to court after conviction and before sentencing. In any report prepared before a verdict is reached, the doctor may give advice on the appropriate disposal of the person in the event that he is convicted.

3.11    When the doctor has concluded that the person needs treatment in hospital, but there is no facility available, the task is not completed until—

    (a) details of the type of provision required have been forwarded in writing to the district health authority, who will need detailed advice in order to discharge their responsibilities;

    (b) in suitable cases contact has been made with the local NHS forensic psychiatrist.

## Role of ASW

3.12 If an ASW has to be called to the prison or to a court to see a prisoner about to be released, with a view to making an application for admission as a detained patient under sections 2 or 3, as much advance warning as possible should be given, and the ASW must be given ample time and facilities for interviewing the prisoner. The ASW should be given access to the social inquiry report as it is difficult within the confines of a prison/court to assess how a prisoner (convicted or on remand) might be able to benefit from alternative treatment in the community.

## Transfer of prisoners to hospital

3.13 The need for in-patient treatment for a prisoner must be identified and acted on swiftly, and contact made urgently between the prison doctor and the hospital doctor. The Home Office must be advised on the urgency of the need for transfer.

3.14 The transfer of a prisoner to hospital under the Act should not be delayed until close to his release date. A transfer in such circumstances may well be seen by the prisoner as being primarily intended to extend his detention and result in an unco-operative attitude towards treatment.

# 5
# SECTION 2 OR SECTION 3

## The choice

5.1 Which admission section should be used? Professional judgment must be applied to the criteria in each section and only when this has been done can a decision be reached as to which, if either, section applies. It must be borne in mind that detention under section 3 need not last any longer than under section 2.

5.2 **Section 2 pointers—**
    (a) where the diagnosis and prognosis of a patient's condition is unclear;
    (b) there is a need to carry out an in-patient assessment in order to formulate a treatment plan;
    (c) where a judgment is needed as to whether the patient will accept treatment on a voluntary basis following admission;
    (d) where a judgment has to be made as to whether a particular treatment proposal, which can only be administered to the patient under Part IV of the Act, is likely to be effective;
    (e) where a patient who has already been assessed, and who has been previously admitted compulsorily under the Act, is judged to have changed since the previous admission and needs further assessment;
    (f) where the patient has not previously been admitted to hospital either compulsorily or informally

5.3 **Section 3 pointers—**
    (a) where a patient has been admitted in the past, is considered to need compulsory admission for the treatment of a mental disorder which is already known to his clinical team, and has been assessed in the recent past by that team;

(b) where a patient already admitted under section 2 and who is assessed as needing further medical treatment for mental disorder under the Act at the conclusion of his detention under section 2 is unwilling to remain in hospital informally and to consent to the medical treatment;

(c) where a patient is detained under section 2 and assessment points to a need for treatment under the Act for a period beyond the 28 day detention under section 2. In such circumstances an application for detention under section 3 should be made at the earliest opportunity and should not be delayed until the end of section 2 detention. Changing a patient's detention status from section 2 to section 3 will not deprive him of a Mental Health Review Tribunal hearing if the change takes place after a valid application has been made to the Tribunal but before it has been heard. The patient's rights to apply for a Tribunal under section 66(1)(b) in the first period of detention after his change of status are unaffected.

5.4 Decisions should **not** be influenced by—

(a) wanting to avoid consulting the nearest relative;

(b) the fact that a proposed treatment to be administered under the Act will last less than 28 days;

(c) the fact that a patient detained under section 2 will get quicker access to a Mental Health Review Tribunal than one detained under section 3.

# 6
# ADMISSION FOR ASSESSMENT IN AN EMERGENCY (SECTION 4)

*(Paras 28 and 29 of the Memorandum)*

## General

6.1 An applicant cannot seek admission for assessment under section 4 unless—

(a) the criteria for admission for assessment are met, and

(b) the matter is of urgent necessity and there is not enough time to get a second medical recommendation.

6.2 Section 4 is for use in a genuine emergency and should never be used for administrative convenience. Those involved in the process of admission are entitled to expect 'second doctors' to be available so that they do not have to consider using section 4 in circumstances other than genuine emergencies.

## Admission

6.3 An emergency arises where those involved cannot cope with the mental state or behaviour of the patient. To be satisfied that an emergency has arisen, there must be evidence of—

— the existence of a significant risk of mental or physical harm to the patient or to others; and/or

— the danger of serious harm to property; and/or

— the need for physical restraint of the patient.

6.4 It is wrong for patients to be admitted under section 4 rather than section 2 because it is more convenient for the second doctor to examine the patient in, rather than outside, hospital. Those assessing an individual's need must be able to secure the attendance within a reasonable time of a second doctor and in particular an approved doctor.

6.5    If a 'second doctor' is not available to support an application under section 2, an application under section 4 cannot be made unless it is of urgent necessity.

6.6    If the ASW has no option but to consider an application for admission under section 4 and is not satisfied with the reasons for the non-availability of the second doctor he must—

(a)    discuss the case with the doctor providing the recommendation and seek to resolve the problem;

(b)    if this is not possible, and the ASW has to make an application for admission under section 4, have access to an officer in his local social services authority sufficiently senior to take up the matter with the health authority. The ASW's local authority should make it clear that the ASW in these circumstances is under an obligation to report the matter in this way.

6.7    The Managers should monitor the use of section 4 and seek to ensure the second doctors are available to visit a patient within a reasonable time after being so requested.

6.8    If a patient is admitted under section 4 an appropriate second doctor should examine him as soon as possible after admission, to decide whether the patient should be detained under section 2.

# 13
# GUARDIANSHIP (SECTION 7)

*(Paras 43–48 of the Memorandum)*

## Purpose of guardianship

13.1 The purpose of guardianship is to enable patients to receive community care where it cannot be provided without the use of compulsory powers. It enables the establishment of an authoritative framework for working with a patient with a minimum of constraint to achieve as independent as life as possible within the community. Where it is used it must be part of the patient's overall care and treatment plan.

## Assessment for guardianship

13.2 ASW's and registered medical practitioners should consider guardianship as a positive alternative when making decisions about a patient's treatment and welfare. In particular it should be actively considered as an alternative both to admission to hospital and to continuing hospital care.

13.3 Any application for guardianship should be based on discussions among most professionals who are or who could be involved in the patient's care, and the ASW assessing the needs and appropriateness of guardianship. This should be by way of a multidisciplinary case discussion, but if guardianship is to be considered as an alternative to admission it may not be possible to arrange such a meeting in the time available. It is important that any procedures instituted by social services departments are no more than the minimum necessary to ensure the proper use of guardianship and that guardianship can be used in a positive and flexible manner. Any application for guardianship should be accompanied by a comprehensive care plan established on the basis of multi-disciplinary discussions.

## Components of effective guardianship

13.4  A comprehensive care plan is required which identifies the services needed by the patient, including as necessary his care arrangements, appropriate accommodation, his treatment and personal support requirements and those who have responsibilities under the care plan. The care plan should indicate which of the powers given by the guardianship order are necessary to achieve the plan. If no power is considered necessary for achieving any part of the care plan guardianship is inappropriate.

13.5 There will need to be the following components—

(a) a recognition by the patient of the 'authority' of the guardian. There must be a willingness on the part of both parties to work together within the terms of the authority which is vested in the guardian by the Act;

(b) the guardian should be willing to 'advocate' on behalf of the patient in relation to those agencies whose services are needed to carry out the care plan;

(c) readily available support from the local authority for the guardian;

(d) an appropriate place of residence taking into account the patient's needs for support, care, treatment and protection;

(e) access to necessary day care, education and training facilities;

(f) effective cooperation and communication between all persons concerned in implementing the care plan;

(g) commitment on the part of all concerned that care should take place in the community.

## Duty of social services department

13.6 Each local authority should prepare and publish a policy setting out the arrangements for—

(a) receiving, considering and scrutinising applications for guardianship. Such arrangements should ensure that applications are adequately, but *speedily*, considered;

(b) monitoring the progress of the guardianship including steps to be taken to fulfil the authority's statutory obligations in relation to private guardians and to arrange visits to the patient;

(c) ensuring the suitability of any proposed private guardian and that the private guardian understand and carry out his statutory duties, including the appointment of a nominated medical attendant;

(d) ensuring that the patients under guardianship receive, both orally and in writing, relevant aspects of the same information that health authorities are required to give to detained patients under section 132;

(e) ensuring, in particular, that the patient is aware of his right to apply to a Mental Health Review Tribunal and that a named officer of the local authority will give any necessary assistance to the patient in making such an application;

(f) maintaining detailed records relating to the person under guardianship;

(g) ensuring the review of the patient's detention under guardianship towards the end of each period of detention;

(h) discharging the guardianship order rather than allowing it to lapse.

## The powers of the guardian

13.7 Section 8 of the Act sets out the three powers of the guardian as follows—

(a) to require the patient to live at a place specified by the guardian. This does not provide the legal authority to detain a patient physically in such a place, nor does it authorise the removal of a patient against his wish. If the patient is absent without leave from the specified place he may be returned within 28 days by those authorised to do so under the Act;

(b) to require the patient to attend at specified places for medical treatment, occupation, education or training. If the patient refuses to attend the guardian is not authorised to use force to secure such attendance, nor does the Act enable medical treatment to be administered in the absence of the patient's consent;

(c) to require access to the patient to be given at the place where he is living to persons detailed in the Act. A refusal without reasonable cause to permit an authorised person to have access to the patient is an offence under section 129. Neither the guardian nor any authorised person can use force to secure entry. If the patient consistently resists the exercise of the guardian's powers it can be concluded that guardianship is not the most appropriate form of care for that person and the guardianship order should be discharged.

### 13.8 Points to remember—

(a) guardianship does not restrict the patient's access to hospital services on a voluntary basis. If the patient should require treatment and there is no need to detain for treatment, he may be admitted informally and may remain under guardianship unless discharged or transferred;

(b) the guardianship order can also remain in force if the patient is admitted to hospital under sections 2 or 4. It does not remain in force if the patient is admitted for treatment under section 3;

(c) it is possible in certain circumstances for a patient liable to be detained in hospital by virtue of an application under Part II of the Act to be transferred into guardianship and for a person subject under Part II of the Act to be transferred into the guardianship of another local social services authority or person approved by such authority or to be transferred to hospital. (See section 19 and rules 7–9 of the Mental Health (Hospital, Guardianship and Consent to Treatment) Regulations 1983.)

### 13.9 Particular practice issues—

(a) guardianship must not be used to require a patient to reside in hospital save in very exceptional circumstances where it is necessary for a very short time in order to provide shelter whilst a place of residence in the community is being obtained;

(b) where an adult is assessed as requiring residential care but owing to mental incapacity is unable to make a decision as to whether he wishes to be placed in residential care, those who are responsible for his care should consider the applicability and appropriateness of guardianship for providing a framework within which decisions about his current and future care can be planned. Guardianship should never be used solely for the purpose of transferring any unwilling person into residential care.

## Guardianship under section 37

13.10 As a potentially useful alternative to hospital orders, courts are empowered to make guardianship orders where the prescribed criteria, which are similar to those of a hospital order, are met and the court having regard to all the circumstances considers reception into the guardianship of the local services authority, or of any other person, appropriate. Guardianship orders may be particularly suitable in helping to meet the needs of mentally impaired offenders who could benefit from occupation, training and education in the community. Before making such an order the court has to be satisfied that the local authority or person is willing to act as guardian. The local authority will need to be satisfied with the arrangements and in considering the appropriateness of guardianship they will be guided by the same principles as apply under Part II of the Act. Similarly the powers and duties conferred on the local authority or private guardian and the provisions as to duration, renewal and discharge are those which apply to guardianship applications except that the power to discharge is not available to the nearest relative.

# 26
# VISITING PATIENTS DETAINED IN HOSPITAL OR REGISTERED MENTAL NURSING HOMES

## The right to be visited

26.1 All detained patients are entitled to maintain contact with and be visited by whomsoever they wish, subject only to some carefully limited exceptions. The prohibition of a visit by a person whom the patient has requested to visit or agreed to see should be regarded as a serious interference with the rights of the patient and to be taken only in exceptional circumstances (see below). A decision to exclude a visitor should only be taken after other means to deal with the problem have been fully explored. Any decision to exclude a visitor should be fully documented and available for independent scrutiny by the Mental Health Act Commission.

## Grounds for excluding a visitor

26.2 There are two principal grounds which may justify the exclusion of a visitor—

    (a) Restriction on clinical grounds

It will sometimes be the case that a patient's relationship with a relative, friend or supporter is anti-therapeutic (in the short or long term) to an extent that discernible arrest of progress or even deterioration in the patient's mental state is evident and can reasonably be anticipated if contact were not to be restricted. Very occasionally, concern may centre primarily on the potential safety of a particular visitor to a disturbed patient. The grounds for any decision by the rmo (which should only be taken after full discussion with the patient's multi-disciplinary care team) should be clearly documented and explained to the patient and the person concerned.

    (b) *Restriction on security grounds*

The behaviour or propensities of a particular visitor may be, or have been in the past, disruptive or subversive to a degree that exclusion from the hospital or mental nursing home is necessary as a last resort. Examples of such behaviour or propensities are: incitement to abscond, smuggling of illicit drugs/alcohol into the hospital, mental nursing home or unit, transfer of potential weapons, or unacceptable aggression or unauthorised media access. A decision to exclude a visitor on the grounds of his behaviour or propensities should be fully documented and explained to the patient and, where possible and appropriate, the person concerned.

## Facilitation of visiting

26.3 Inflexibility on the part of the hospital or mental nursing home should not be allowed to be an unnecessary deterrent to regular visiting as deemed to be desirable or reasonable by the patient, his visitors and those responsible for his treatment, albeit within the legitimate time constraints of his therapeutic programme. Ordinarily, inadequate staff numbers should not be a deterrent to regular visiting. Failure to provide appropriate and congenial facilities should not be a deterrent to regular visiting. Particular consideration needs to be given to the problems associated with the distance visitors may have to travel, which is often encountered with regional and supra-regional facilities.

## Other forms of communication

26.4 Every effort must be made to assist the patient, where appropriate, to make contact with relatives, friends and supporters. In particular patients should have readily accessible and appropriate daytime telephone facilities and no restrictions should be placed upon dispatch and receipt of their mail over and above those referred to in section 134 of the Act.

**Managers**

26.5 Managers should regularly monitor the exclusion from the hospital or mental nursing home of visitors to detained patients.

# 28
# PART III OF THE MENTAL HEALTH ACT – PATIENTS CONCERNED WITH CRIMINAL PROCEEDINGS

*Leaving hospital*

### Discharge/return to court

### 28.1 Conditionally discharged restricted patients – supervision

Those involved in the supervision of a conditionally discharged restricted patient should have copies of and be familiar with Supervision and After-Care of Conditionally Discharged Restricted Patients' (HO/DoH notes of guidance (1987)) and Recall of mentally disordered patients subject to Home Office restrictions on discharge (HSG(93)20/LAC(93)9).

### Recall

28.2 If a conditionally discharged restricted patient requires hospital admission, it will not always be necessary for the Home Secretary to recall the patient to hospital. For example—

(a) The patient may be willing to accept treatment informally. In these circumstances, however, care should be taken to ensure that the possibility of the patient being recalled does not render the patient's consent to informal admission invalid by reason of duress.

(b) In some cases it may be appropriate to consider admitting the patient under Part II of the Act as an alternative.

(c) It may not always be necessary to recall the patient to the same hospital from which he was conditionally discharged. In some cases recall to a hospital with a lesser (or greater) degree of security will be appropriate.

28.3 When a recall is being considered this should be discussed between the doctor and the social supervisor.

28.4 If a patient is recalled, the person taking him into custody should explain that he is being recalled to hospital by the Home Secretary and that a fuller explanation will be given to him later. As soon as possible after admission to hospital, and in any event within 72 hours of admission, the rmo or his deputy and ASW or a representative of the hospital management should explain to the patient the reason for his recall and ensure, in so far as the patient's mental state allows, that he understands. The patient should also be informed that his case will be referred to a Mental Health Review Tribunal within one month.

28.5 The patient's rmo should ensure that—

— the patient is given assistance to inform his legal adviser (if any);

— subject to the patient's consent, his nearest relative and/or other appropriate relative or friend is told.

## 28.6 **Patients on remand/subject to interim hospital orders**

All professionals concerned with ensuring the return to court of a patient on remand or under an interim hospital order should be familiar with the contents of paras 31-33 of Home Office circular number 71/1984. When a patient has been admitted on remand or subject to an interim hospital order, it is the responsibility of the hospital to return the patient to court as required. The court should give adequate notice of the hearing. The hospital should liaise with the courts in plenty of time to affirm the arrangements for escorting the patient to/from hospital. The hospital will be responsible for providing a suitable escort for the patient when he is taken from the hospital to the court and should plan for the provision of necessary staff to do this. The assistance of the police may be requested if necessary. Once on the court premises, the patient will come under the supervision of the police or prison officers there.

# 29
# PEOPLE WITH LEARNING DISABILITIES (MENTAL HANDICAP)

## General

29.1 The guidance given elsewhere in the Code applies to patients with learning disabilities (or mental handicap). This chapter gives guidance on a number of particular issues of importance to this group of patients.

29.2 Very few people with learning disabilities are detained under the Act. Some admission sections can only be considered where the person with a learning disability falls within the legal definition of 'mental impairment' or 'severe mental impairment'. People with learning disabilities can be considered for admission under the Act when they are suffering from another form of mental disorder (for example mental illness).

## Communication

29.3 The assessment of a person with learning disabilities requires special consideration to be given to communication with a person being assessed. Where possible the ASW should have had experience of working with people with learning disabilities or be able to call upon someone who has. It is important that someone who knows the patient, and can communicate with him, is present at the assessment. Someone with a knowledge of Makaton or other communication system may be of assistance.

## Assessment

29.4 It is desirable that no patient should be classified under the Act as mentally impaired or severely mentally impaired without an assessment by a consultant psychiatrist in learning disabilities and without a formal psychological assessment. This assessment should be part of a complete appraisal by medical, nursing, social work and psychology professionals and, wherever appropriate, by those with experience in learning disabilities in consultation with a relevant relative, friend or supporter of the patient. This procedure is also desirable where it is proposed that a patient is to be detained under section 2 on the grounds of mental disorder in the form of arrested or incomplete development of mind, although the urgency of the case may preclude this.

### Mental impairment/severe mental impairment (legally defined in section 1)

29.5 The identification of an individual who falls within these legal categories is a matter for clinical judgement, guided by current professional practice and subject to the relevant legal requirements. Those assessing the patient must be satisfied that the person concerned displays a number of characteristics difficult to define in practice. This section of the chapter sets out guidance in relation to the key factors or components of these legal categories.

*Incomplete or arrested development of mind.* This implies that the features that determine the learning disability were present at some stage which permanently prevented the usual maturation of intellectual and social development. It excludes persons whose learning disability derives from accident, injury or illness occurring after that point usually accepted as complete development.

*Severe or significant impairment of intelligence.* The judgement as to the presence of this particular characteristic must be made on the basis of reliable and careful assessment.

*Severe or significant impairment of social functioning.* The evidence of the degree and nature of social competence should be based on reliable and recent observations, preferably from a number of sources such as social workers, nurses and psychologists. Such evidence should include the results of one or more social functioning assessment tests.

*Abnormally aggressive behaviour.* Any assessment of this category should be based on observations of behaviour which lead to a conclusion that the actions are outside the usual range of aggressive behaviour, and which cause actual damage and/or real distress occurring recently or persistently or with excessive severity.

*Irresponsible conduct.* The assessment of this characteristic should be based on an observation of behaviour which shows a lack of responsibility, a disregard of the consequences of action taken, and where the results cause actual damage or real distress, either recently or persistently or with excessive severity.

# 30
# CHILDREN AND YOUNG PEOPLE UNDER THE AGE OF 18

## General

30.1 The Code of Practice applies to all patients including those under 18. This chapter gives guidance on a number of issues of particular importance to those under the age of 18. There is no minimum age limit for admission to hospital under the Act.

30.2 Practice for this age group should be guided by the following principles—

    (a) young people should be kept as fully informed as possible about their care and treatment; their views and wishes must always be taken into account;

    (b) unless statute specifically overrides, young people should generally be regarded as having the right to make their own decisions (and in particular treatment decisions) when they have sufficient 'understanding and intelligence';

    (c) any intervention in the life of a young person considered necessary by reason of their mental disorder should be the least restrictive possible and result in the least possible segregation from family, friends, community and school;

    (d) all children and young people in hospital should receive appropriate education.

30.3 The legal framework governing the admission to hospital and treatment of young people under the age of 18 (and in particular those under the age of 16) is complex and it is the responsibility of all professionals and the relevant local health authorities and N H S trusts to ensure that there is sufficient guidance available to those responsible for the care of children and young people.

30.4 Whenever the care and treatment of somebody under the age of 16 is being considered, the following questions (amongst many others) need to be asked—

(a) which persons or bodies have parental responsibility for the child (to make decisions for the child)? It is essential that those responsible for the child or young person's care always request copies of any court orders (wardship, care order, residence order (stating with whom the child should live), evidence of appointment as a guardian, contact order, etc) for reference on the hospital ward in relation to examination, assessment or treatment.

(b) if the child is living with either of the parents who are separated, whether there is a residence order and if so in whose favour;

(c) what is the capacity of the child to make his own decisions in terms of emotional maturity, intellectual capacity and psychological state? (see Chapter 15);

(d) where a parent refuses consent to treatment, how sound are the reasons and on what grounds are they made?;

(e) could the needs of the young person be met in a social services or educational placement? To what extent have these authorities exhausted all possible alternative placements?;

(f) how viable would be treatment of an under 16 year old living at home if there was no parental consent and no statutory orders?

## Informal admission to hospital by parents or guardians

30.5 *Children under 16.* Parents or guardians may arrange for the admission of children under the age of 16 to hospitals as informal patients. Where a doctor includes, however, that a child under the age of 16 has the capacity to make such a decision for himself, there is no right to admit him to hospital informally or to keep mim there on an informal basis against his will (but see Re R *(A Minor) (Wardship Consent to Treatment)* 119911 3 W L R 592).

Where a child is willing to be so admitted, but the parents/guardian object, their views should be accorded serious consideration and given due weight. It should be remembered that recourse to law to stop such an admission could be sought.

30.6 *Young people aged 16–17.* Anyone in this age group who is 'capable of expressing his own wishes' can admit or discharge himself as an informal patient to or from hospital, irrespective of the wishes of his parents or guardian (but see Re W (A Minor) (Medical Treatment: Court's Jurisdiction) 1199213W L R 758).

## Consent to medical treatment

30.7 The following guidance applies to young people who are not detained under the Act—

(a) Under 16. If a child has 'sufficient understanding and intelligence' he can take decisions about his own medical treatment in the same way as an adult (but see Re *R and Re W* above). Otherwise the permission of parents/guardians must be sought (save in emergencies where only the treatment necessary to end the emergency should be given). If parents/guardians do not consent to treatment, consideration should be given to both the use of the child care legislation and the Mental Health Act before coming to a final conclusion as to what action should be taken. Under section 100 of the Children Act 1989 a local authority may also seek leave to ask the High Court to exercise its inherent jurisdiction to make orders with respect to children, if the conditions set out in section 100(4) are met.

(b) The same principles concerning consent apply where the under 16 year old is in the care of a local authority. Where such a child does not have sufficient 'understanding and intelligence' to take his own treatment decisions, treatment can be authorised by any person or body with parental responsibility. A local authority has parental responsibility for a child in its care, i e under a care order. Wherever possible, parents should be consulted. However local authorities can in the exercise of their powers under section 33(3)(b) of the Children Act 1989 limit the extent to which parents exercise their parental responsibility. In certain pre-Children Act wardships, although the children are deemed to be in care within the meaning of section 31 of the Children Act 1989, court directions may still require treatment decisions to be agreed by the court. Where children are wards of court (and also not deemed to be subject to a care order under section 31 of the Children Act 1989) the consent of the High Court must be sought. In an emergency consent may be obtained retrospectively (but this should be regarded as wholly exceptional).

(c) *Young people aged 16 and 17.* Young people in this age group who have the capacity to make their own treatment decisions can do so in the same way as adults (section 8 Family Law Reform Act 1969). Where such a young person does not have this capacity the authorisation of either parent, guardian or care authority (whichever has the lawful authority in relation to the particular young person) must be obtained. The consent of teh High Court must be obtained in the case of wards of court.

(d) *Refusal of a minor to consent to treatment.* No minor of whatever age has power by refusing consent to treatment to override a consent to treatment by anyone who has parental responsibility for the minor including a local authority with the benefit of a care order or consent by the court. Nevertheless such a refusal is a very important consideration in making clinical judgements and for parents and the court in deciding whether themselves to give consent. The importance increases with the age and maturity of the minor. (See Re *W (A Minor) (Medical Treatment: Court's Jurisdiction)* [1992] 3 W L R 758 at page 772–also known as Re *J*).

(e) In cases involving emergency protection orders, child assessment orders, interim care orders and full supervision orders under the Children Act 1989, a competent child has a statutory right to refuse to consent to examination, assessment and in certain circumstances treatment. Such refusal is not capable of being overridden.

## Parent/guardians consent

30.8 The fact that a child or young person has been informally admitted by parents/guardians should not lead professionals to assume that they have consented to any treatment regarded as 'necessary'. Consent should be sought for each aspect of the child's care and treatment as it arises. 'Blanket' consent forms must not be used.

## Children placed in secure accommodation

30.9 Where a child is looked after by a local authority and placed in accommodation where liberty is restricted (for example N H S secure units or a registered mental nursing home) application must be made to the family proceedings court within 72 hours if the restriction is to last beyond that period (section 25 of the Children Act 1989 and the Children (Secure Accommodation) Regulations 1991 (SI 1991/1505) and the Children (Secure Accommodation) (No 2) Regulations 1991 (SI 1991/2034). Applications are to be made by local authorities if children are looked after by them and by health authorities, N H S trusts, local education authorities or persons running residential care, nursing or mental nursing homes in other cases involving such establishments. These provisions do not apply to such children who are detained under the Mental Health Act 1983. Where the child is a ward of court, the permission of the High Court must be obtained prior to any restriction of liberty. In cases where the Mental Health Act does not apply the criteria to be applied by the wardship court are those contained in section 25 of the 1989 Act and the accompanying Regulations.

## Information

30.10 The advice concerning the giving of information (see Chapter 14)applies with equal force to patients under the age of 18. In particular where such patients are detained under the Act, it is important that assistance is given to enable their legal representation at any Mental Health Review Tribunal.

## Confidentiality

30.11 Young people's legal rights to confidentiality should be strictly observed. It is important that all professionals have a clear understanding of their obligations and confidentiality to young people and that any limits to such an obligation are made clear to a young person who has the capacity to understand them.

## Placement

30.12 It is always preferable for children and young people admitted to hospital to be accommodated with others of their own age group in children's wards or adolescent units, separate from adults. If, exceptionally, this is not practicable, discrete accommodation in an adult ward, with facilities and staffing appropriate to the needs of children and young people, offers the most satisfactory solution.

## Complaints

30.13 Children and young people in hospital (both as informal and detained patients) and their parents or guardians should have ready access to existing complaints procedures, which should be drawn to their attention on their admission to hospital. The Managers should appoint an officer whose responsibility it is to ensure that this is done and to assist any complainant. Where a child is being looked after by a local authority, accommodation on behalf of a voluntary organisation or otherwise accommodated in a registered children's home, he will be entitled to use the Children Act complaints procedure established in accordance with the Representations Procedure (Children) Regulations 1991 (SI 1991/894).

## Welfare of certain hospital patients

30.14 Local authorities should ensure that they arrange for visits to be made to certain patients (including children and young persons looked after by them whether or not under a care order and those accommodated or intended to be accommodated for three months or more by health authorities, N H S trusts, local education authorities or in residential care, nursing or mental nursing homes–see Review of Children's Cases Regulations 1991 (SI 1991/895) and sections 85 and 86 of the Children Act 1989) quite apart from their duty in respect to children in their care in hospitals or nursing homes in England and Wales as required by section 116. Local authorities should take such other steps in relation to the patient while in hospital or nursing home as would be expected to be taken by his parents. Local authorities are under a duty to promote contact between children who are in need and their families if they live away from home and to help them get back together (paragraphs 10 and 15 of Schedule 2 to the Children Act 1989) and to arrange for persons (independent visitors) to visit and befriend children looked after by the authority wherever they are if they have not been regularly visited by their parents (paragraph 17 of Schedule 2 to the Act).